Barney Google® and Snuffy Smith

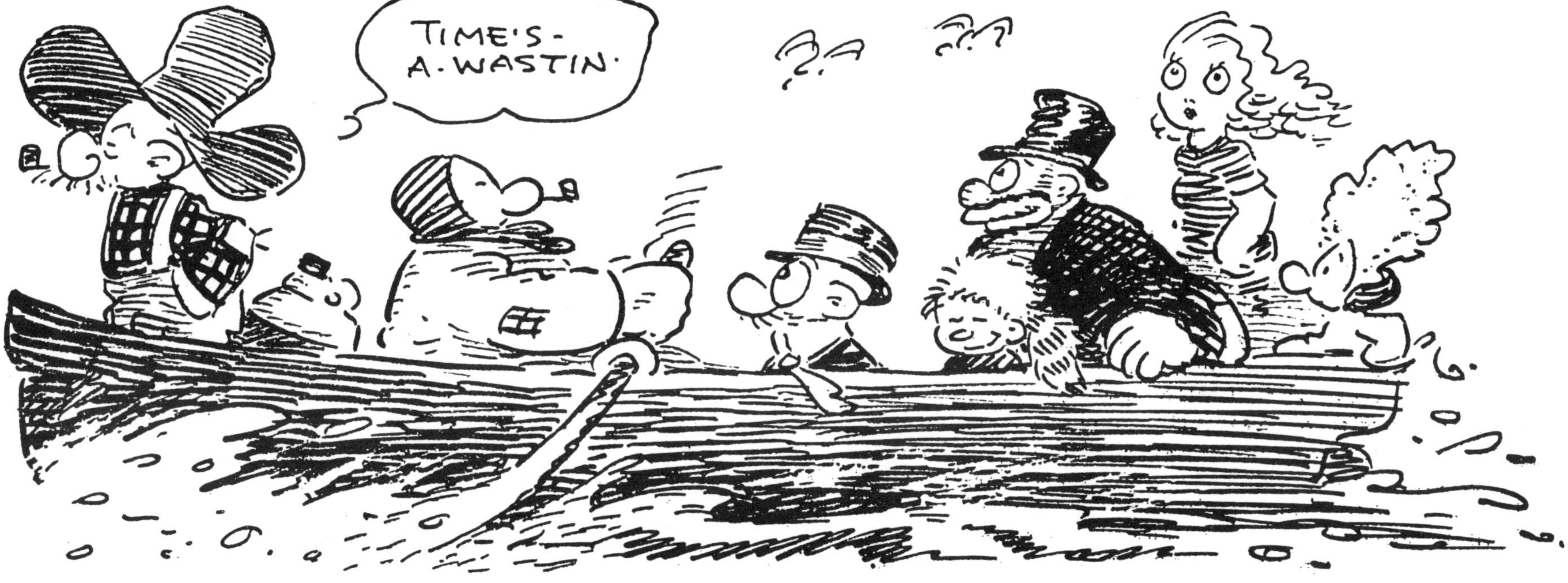
TIME'S - A-WASTIN'

75 Years of An American Legend - by Brian Walker

Published by Comicana Books and Ohio State University Libraries

Front cover artwork: Portrait of Barney Google by Billy DeBeck, 1930's. From the Collection of Ed Black. Portrait of Snuffy Smith by Fred Lasswell, 1980's. Courtesy of Fred Lasswell.
Back cover artwork: "Our First Family Reunion" by Billy DeBeck, late 1930's. (This is the same artwork which was engraved on the "Billy DeBeck Award" and given to the "outstanding cartoonist of the year" by the National Cartoonists Society from 1946 to 1953. Courtesy of Fred Lasswell. "Snuffy and Company Go to the Fair" by Fred Lasswell, 1985. Courtesy of Fred Lasswell.
Title page artwork: Drawing by Billy DeBeck for the 80th anniversary of the *Honolulu Advertiser*, July 2, 1936. Courtesy of the San Francisco Academy of Comic Art.
Back page artwork: Snuffy, Lowizie and Barney walking off into the sunset, from a 1938 Sunday page by Billy DeBeck. Courtesy of King Features Syndicate.

Published by Comicana Books, 34 Old Forge Road, Wilton, CT 06897
and Ohio State University Libraries

Distributed by Kitchen Sink Press, Inc., 320 Riverside Drive,
Northampton, MA 01060

ISBN 0-87816-283-6

First Edition

1 3 5 7 9 10 8 6 4 2

Printed in Canada by Ronalds, 8000, Blaise-Pascal, Montreal, Quebec H1E 2S7

Written, designed and edited by Brian Walker
Cover by Ray Fehrenbach
Editorial Assistance by Bill Janocha
Layout by Carolyn Mayo

The cartoons in this book have appeared in newspapers throughout the United States and abroad under the auspices of King Features Syndicate, Inc.

Library of Congress Cataloging-in-Publication Data

DeBeck, Billy, 1890-1942
[Barney Google and Snuffy Smith]
Barney Google & Snuffy Smith : 75 years of an American legend
[edited] by Brian Walker
p. cm.
Includes bibliographical references.
ISBN 0-87816-283-6 (pbk.) : $16.95
1. Barney Google (Comic strip) — Collectibles. I. Walker, Brian
II. Lasswell, Fred. III. Title. IV. Title: Barney Google and
Snuffy Smith.
PN6728.B33D42 1994 94-9310
741.5'973—dc20 CIP

Contents

Dedicated to my own little Snuffy
David Murphy Walker

Foreward

By Brian Walker

This project began for me in the summer of 1993, when Lucy Caswell asked me to write an essay on Billy DeBeck for the catalogue which would accompany an exhibition at Ohio State University commemorating the seventy-fifth anniversary of "Barney Google and Snuffy Smith." During the eighteen years that I designed and produced exhibitions for the Museum of Cartoon Art, I had always wanted to do a retrospective of what I consider to be one of the great American comic strips. When the Museum closed in June 1992, we still had not done a tribute to "Barney Google and Snuffy Smith." The offer to help with the Ohio State University exhibition was a welcome opportunity to continue my interests in cartoon art history and deepen my appreciation for the work of Billy DeBeck.

When I started the research for my article on DeBeck, I made two discoveries immediately. First, I found that, beyond a few brief entries in cartoon histories and a handful of magazine articles, almost nothing had been written about the career of one of the most successful cartoonists of his time. Secondly, all the collectors and scholars I talked to urged me to expand my efforts and produce a book on "Barney Google and Snuffy Smith." They admitted that such a volume would have limited commercial potential beyond the audience of dedicated comic strip fans, but that it needed to be done. So, I discussed the idea with Lucy Caswell, and we decided to co-publish a book,

combining the resources of Ohio State University Libraries and my company, Comicana Books. King Features Syndicate gave us licensing permission and Denis Kitchen agreed to distribute the book.

In the beginning, we envisioned an expanded exhibition catalogue, which would contain the essays commissioned for the original catalogue, and a generous sampling of artwork by Billy DeBeck and Fred Lasswell. In addition to my biographical piece on DeBeck, M. Thomas Inge would contribute the article, "Sut Lovingood and Snuffy Smith," which had previously appeared in his *Comics as Culture* book, Fred Lasswell would write a personal memoir and Bill Janocha would compile a list of resource material relating to the strip. It wasn't long before I realized that we had a much more ambitious project on our hands.

At first I was frustrated by how little information there was available about the history of "Barney Google and Snuffy Smith." The proofs of the strip in King Features' archives only went back to the late 1930's and biographical files on DeBeck at the syndicate were nonexistent. I started making phone calls to the network of collectors and scholars I had worked with during my years at the Museum of Cartoon Art. I visited Sy Schechter, who met DeBeck during the 1930's and has collected his books and artwork ever since. Ron Goulart, loaned me his near-complete run of "Barney Google" strips from the 1920's and early 1930's and showed me some articles he had written on DeBeck. Bill Blackbeard sent me a huge package of material, containing hundreds of copies of newspaper pages from the San Francisco Academy of Comic Art, spanning the years from DeBeck's early career in Chicago to Lasswell's Sunday pages from the 1950's. Mark Johnson contributed a collection of original newspaper pages containing "Married Life," and early "Barney Google" strips, as well as important dates and facts. Murray Harris sent rare photographs and letters. Tom Horvitz, Bruce Bergstrom, Howard Lowery, Peter Tolan and Morris Weiss made copies of original artwork from their collections. Ed Black filled in many of the details of DeBeck's life with his research and interviews. Richard Marschall came up with song sheets, artwork and more articles about DeBeck. I flew down to Tampa, Florida, and spent four days talking with Fred Lasswell and rummaging through his files.

A trickle of information had turned into a torrent. We discovered that, not only had DeBeck been married more than once, he had married the same woman twice. I was intrigued by the parallels between continuites in the strip and events in DeBeck's life, such as his years in Paris and Barney's European adventures. The pieces of the puzzle were falling into place as the untold story of this great comic strip was coming into focus.

I also became increasingly concerned about how I was going to fit all of this material into a 160-page book. "Barney Google and Snuffy Smith" has survived a lot of changes in seventy-five years, reflecting the life experiences and personalities of its two creators. It would not do justice to the story to leave out any important details of this evolution. As time went on, the book became more of a biography of DeBeck and Lasswell than a reprint collection of their work. Plans to do an extended continuity of strips was abandoned. Reproductions of Sunday pages had to be limited. Chapters on "Bughouse Fables" and "Bunky" had to be cut back. Unable to eliminate any more material, I finally decided to add another sixteen pages to the book.

Undoubtedly, fans of the strip who buy this book may wish there were more material included from their favorite period. What I have tried to do is provide a sampling of artwork representing significant milestones in "Barney Google and Snuffy Smith" and the careers of its creators. Hopefully, this historical overview will give a glimpse of the wealth of material that should be reprinted. A series of books collecting complete stories from the 1920's and 1930's, a color volume of DeBeck's most memorable Sunday pages and a retrospective of Fred Lasswell's sixty-year output, are all projects that should be considered for the future.

Although "Barney Google and Snuffy Smith" is well respected by comic strip experts and fans, it is taken for granted by the general public and rarely given serious attention by academic scholars and art critics. If this book convinces a few of these non-believers that "Barney Google and Snuffy Smith" should stand beside "Little Nemo in Slumberland," "Krazy Kat" and "Pogo" as one of the outstanding creations in comic strip history and that Billy DeBeck and Fred Lasswell are among the most talented cartoonists to work in the medium, then I will be satisfied that I have done my job. I know it will provide a lot of laughs and nostalgic memories. Billy did his job and Fred is still doing his. The proof is in your hands.

I wish to thank all of the collectors and scholars who encouraged me to pursue this project and I hope that they enjoy what should be the first in a series of books reprinting more of the great American legend of "Barney Google and Snuffy Smith."

In addition to the individuals that I have already mentioned I would also like to thank the following who made important contributions: Frank Pauer, for his suggestions about the design of the book; Laura Hough, for her recommendations about the typography of the book; Elaine Wolf, for proof-reading the manuscript; Jerry Beck, for information about film history; Bill Janocha, for meticulously restoring most of the strips; Mort Walker, for his backing and enthusiasm; Larry Olsen, Jay Kennedy, Ted Hannah and Mark Johnson at King Features Syndicate for their co-operation; Denis Kitchen for his advice and input; the Ohio State University Friends of the Libraries, for their support; Lucy Caswell, for her guidance, expertise and encouragement and most of all Fred Lasswell, for his hospitality, his constructive criticism, his creative genius and his lovable bodaciousness.

Right: This little raccoon was Billy DeBeck's mascot when he worked at the *Pittsburgh Gazette-Times* from 1912 to 1914. From the Collection of Richard Marschall.

Introduction

By Lucy Shelton Caswell

Legend has been defined as "an unverifiable popular story handed down from the past." This is an appropriate description of the seventy-five-year-old comic strip "Barney Google and Snuffy Smith." Billy DeBeck began the feature in 1919, and he drew it until his untimely death in 1942. Fate was kind to DeBeck's creation, since his assistant Fred Lasswell, who had worked on the comic strip since 1934, was asked by King Features Syndicate to take it over. Under Lasswell's guidance, "Barney Google and Snuffy Smith" began to change from the time-bound adventures of Barney Google to the timeless tale of rural folklife involving Snuffy Smith, his family and friends.

Elsewhere in this volume, Brian Walker describes Barney Google as the "Everyman of the Jazz Age." DeBeck skillfully exploited the milieu of the 1920's with Barney's outrageous exploits. He incorporated then-current fads such as flag-pole sitting into his comic strip, and he also contributed to the popular culture of the time through his inventive language and the antics of his characters. DeBeck's frenetic stories were well-suited to the time of flappers and prohibition. By the late-thirties, however, comic strip readers were looking for something different.

Under the hand of Fred Lasswell, "Barney Google and Snuffy Smith" was transformed into a tale of Appalachian folklife unaffected by fads. His repertoire of gentle humor is the type which brings a chuckle around the supper table. Lasswell may be best understood as a yarn-spinner, someone who tells and re-tells fables with the understanding that those who read them enjoy their familiarity. One might argue that it is this durable quality which has enabled the comic strip to last for seventy-five years and to be in syndication in twenty-one countries.

Lasswell is also a master of the sight gag. He employs the visual-verbal interplay of his medium to its maximum extent. He is able to make the words and pictures of his comic strip interdependent so that readers must interpret both to understand his message. According to R.C. Harvey, one measure of a comic strip's excellence is "... the extent to which the sense of the words is dependent on the pictures and vice versa." Fred Lasswell accomplishes this with distinction in "Barney Google and Snuffy Smith."

The Ohio State University Cartoon, Graphic, and Photographic Arts Research Library is honored to host the exhibition which celebrates the remarkable excellence and longevity of "Barney Google and Snuffy Smith." The publication of this companion volume provides a permanent record of the commemoration and may serve to introduce a new generation to the delightful history of "Barney Google and Snuffy Smith." We are grateful to the many who have made this possible.

Below: The earliest known photograph of Billy DeBeck, reproduced from the back cover of "DeBeck's Cartoon Hints" published in 1915. From the Collection of Sy & Sandy Schechter.

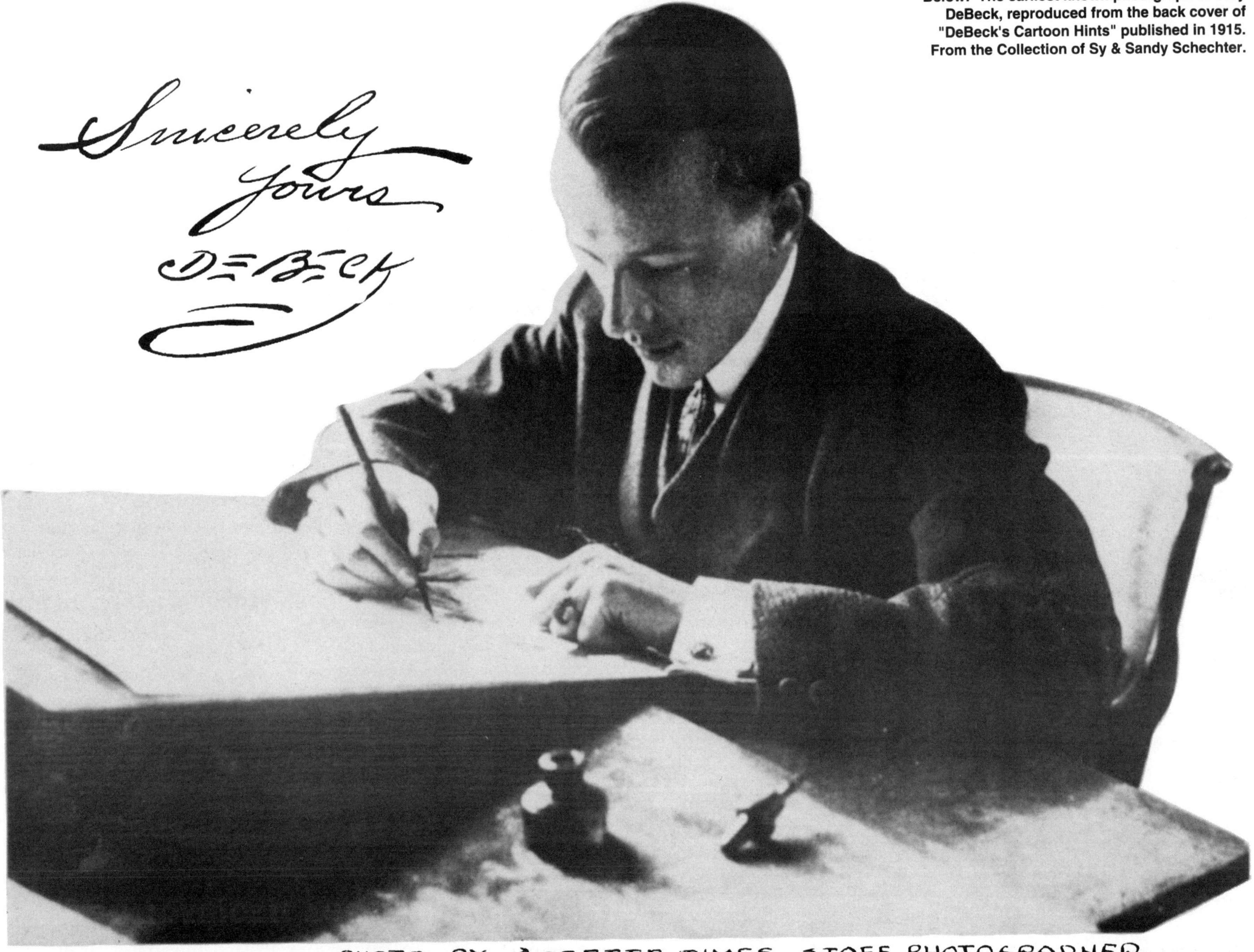
Sincerely Yours
DeBeck

PHOTO BY GAZETTE TIMES STAFF PHOTOGRAPHER.

Before Barney

DeBeck's Early Years

William Morgan DeBeck was born on the South Side of Chicago on April 16, 1890. His father, Louis, was of French stock (their name was originally spelled "De Becque") and his mother, Jessie Lee Morgan, came from Irish and Welsh ancestry. Louis DeBeck, a former newspaperman, had a white-collar job at the Swift and Co. meat-packing plant and Jessie, who grew up on a farm, once worked as a school teacher.

Billy's first artistic influences were John McCutcheon, the Pulitzer Prize-winning political cartoonist for the *Chicago Tribune*, and Clare Briggs, a pioneer in the comic strip field and creator of "When A Feller Needs a Friend." By the time young DeBeck attended Hyde Park High School, he had become proficient at copying the style of the famous illustrator, Charles Dana Gibson, and earned pocket money by selling "gen-u-wine Gibson originals" on the streets of Chicago.

After graduating from high school in 1908, Billy attended the Chicago Academy of Fine Arts, where he had dreams of becoming a painter in the tradition of Rembrandt and the Dutch Masters. During his two year stay at the Academy however, he began selling cartoons to finance his art career, and in 1910 he took his first job on the staff of *Show World*, a Chicago theatrical weekly. He never seriously pursued his fine art aspirations again.

Later that year, he was hired by the *Youngstown* (Ohio) *Telegram* at a salary of $18 a week. His first drawing for the *Telegram*, an editorial cartoon, appeared on the front page on September 21, 1910. During his two-year stint there, he did political cartoons and spot illustrations for news stories, columns, social events and vaudeville shows six days a week (the *Telegram* did not have a Sunday edition). An article accompanying a self-portrait of DeBeck in the *Telegram* on January 20, 1912 claimed, "There is a directness in the DeBeck cartoons that is appealing and some of his efforts tell as much as a column of reading matter. They are almost invariably in a humorous vein and in his ideas Mr. DeBeck is abreast with the latest news happenings."

DeBeck's last cartoon for the *Telegram* appeared on August 31, 1912, after which he began work for the *Pittsburgh Gazette-Times* at a salary of $200 a month. In Pittsburgh, he drew daily political cartoons and introduced a little raccoon character as his mascot. DeBeck returned to Youngstown to marry Marian Shields on March 29, 1914. Seven months later, he decided to leave the *Gazette-Times*, and his last cartoon appeared on November 14, 1914.

DeBeck remembered later that he tried to sell cartoons to *Life* and *Judge* magazines in New York City for a brief time after he left the *Gazette-Times* but was unsuccessful. In May, 1915, *Cartoons Magazine* reported that DeBeck had started a feature service business with a Mr. Carter from Pittsburgh. In addition to selling syndicated cartoons, the two men published a mail order cartoon instruction course which they sold for $1 a copy. An advertisement for "DeBeck's Cartoon Hints" claimed the sale of "two thousand more copies in June! [1915]". In the introductory notes to the course, DeBeck wrote, "It takes an undying effort, perseverance in study and practice, high ideals and ambitions and many other things to become a professional cartoonist, so if this book will place you but one step nearer to the accomplishment of your ambition we shall feel amply repaid."

Struggling to get his own professional career going again, DeBeck returned to his hometown of Chicago and by January, 1916, was drawing a new comic strip entitled "Finn an' Haddie" for the Adams Syndicate. "Mr. DeBeck is looking forward to a life of luxury," claimed an article in Cartoons Magazine. "During his spare time he intends to study at the Chicago Art Institute. He has furnished an apartment on the lake on the North Side."

Although "Finn an' Haddie" never caught on, DeBeck eventually landed a job with the Chicago Herald for $35 a week. His first cartoon for the Herald appeared on December 7, 1915, and two days later on December 9, his first successful comic strip, "Married Life," debuted. The bickering stars of "Married Life," who were anonymous in the beginning, were later named "Aleck" and "Pauline" by DeBeck. On April 2, 1916, a weekly full-page color version of Aleck and Pauline's domestic squabbles was added to the line-up of the Chicago Sunday Herald. "Married Life," as well as two DeBeck one-panel creations, "Victim No...." and "He's Talking to a Stranger," was also distributed to papers around the country by the J. Keeley Syndicate (owned by Herald publisher Jim Keeley).

DeBeck's work in Chicago eventually attracted the attention of the legendary newspaper mogul, William Randolph Hearst, owner of the Chicago Examiner, who telegraphed the editor of the Examiner to hire the young cartoonist. Billy's boss on the Herald raised his salary to $200 a week in response. Never one to be outbid, Hearst bought the Herald in May 1918 and merged it with the Examiner, thereby securing the cartooning services of Billy DeBeck.

"Married Life" continued in the new Chicago Herald and Examiner as a daily and Sunday feature and, beginning on May 15, 1918, DeBeck added a daily sports page cartoon starring a regular cast of characters including Buddy Bacon, Kitty Cop, Addison Sheffield and Polo Pete. Always experimenting, DeBeck occasionally drew a political cartoon instead of his regular sports feature and, on December 11, 1918, temporarily replaced it with a new humor panel entitled "Olie Moses and O'Mara, Inc." Set in the office of a clothing emporium for the first month, Olie, the proprietor, shut down in early January 1919, and moved his whole staff to Hollywood and went into the motion picture business. Famous actors like Fatty Arbuckle, Charlie Chaplin and Mary Pickford made cameo appearances in the short-lived feature.

During this period, Billy also taught night classes at his old alma mater, the Chicago Academy of Fine Arts, and became something of a local celebrity. Legend has it that on Armistice Day, November 11, 1918, DeBeck rode a white horse through the saloons of Chicago and after his night of revelry fell asleep on the desk of Arthur Brisbane, editor-in-chief of the Herald and Examiner. The next morning Brisbane chased Billy out of his private office, but Billy returned shortly after, interrupting an important meeting to retrieve his socks, which were neatly tucked away in Brisbane's dictating machine. Another story claimed that an angry DeBeck disappeared from town after one of his cartoons was yanked from the paper and that he was eventually found in Havana, Cuba, being wined and dined by the local dignitaries, who were convinced he was writing an important story for the American press. Later in his life, Billy summed up his wild Chicago days by saying, "Success, when it comes to a young kid, is unhealthy."

DeBeck took a working vacation to Palm Beach and Miami, Florida, between January 28 and February 14, 1919, sending cartoons back to the Herald and Examiner on a daily basis. Upon returning to Chicago, he resumed "Olie Moses and O'Mara, Inc." with Olie and the cast now going into newspaper publishing. By the opening of the baseball season in April, the mercurial DeBeck had returned again to sports themes.

On June 3, 1919, the Herald and Examiner sent Billy to Toledo, Ohio, to cover the Jess Willard - Jack Dempsey heavyweight championship fight. Dempsey, the challenger, had come out of the West in 1918 and electrified the boxing world with a string of one-round knockouts. In anticipation of the bout, DeBeck sent "Training Camp Sketches" back to Chicago.

He also launched another comic strip, similar to "Married Life," about a henpecked husband who was desperately trying to get a behind-the-scenes look at the preparations for the great fight. DeBeck's newest creation would eclipse all of his previous accomplishments.

The following pages feature a gallery of artwork from Billy DeBeck's early career. Important historical and biographical research for this chapter was provided by Bill Blackbeard, Ed Black, Mark Johnson and Richard Marschall.

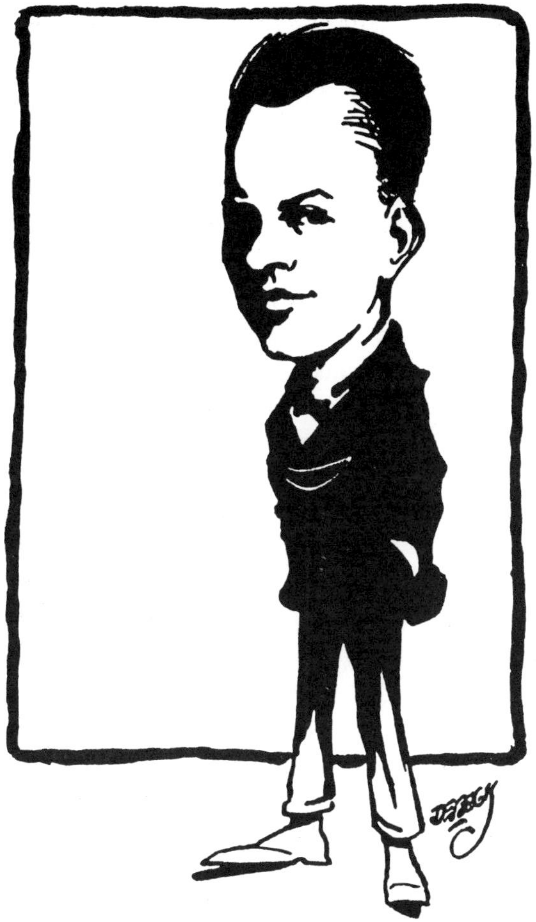
DEBECK

Above: A DeBeck self-portrait which appeared in the *Youngstown Telegram* on January 20, 1912. The headline read: "Artist DeBeck draws his own picture. It is a likeness not a caricature." From the Collection of Ed Black.

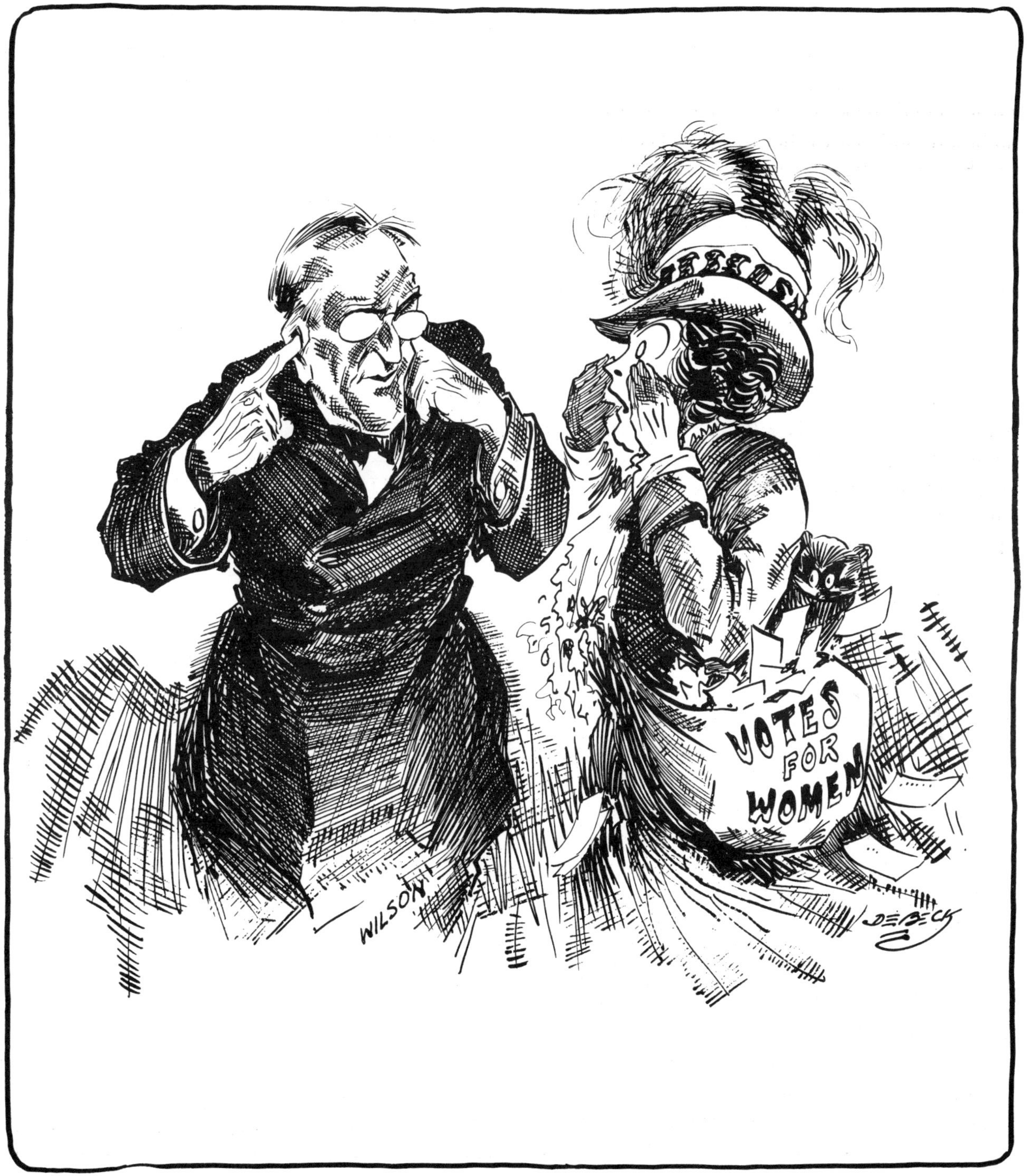
WILSON
VOTES FOR WOMEN
DEBECK

Right: The caption for this DeBeck cartoon of Woodrow Wilson and a suffragette read: "Don't Hear A Word" and appeared in the *Pittsburgh Gazette-Times* in 1913
From the Collection of Sy and Sandy Schechter.

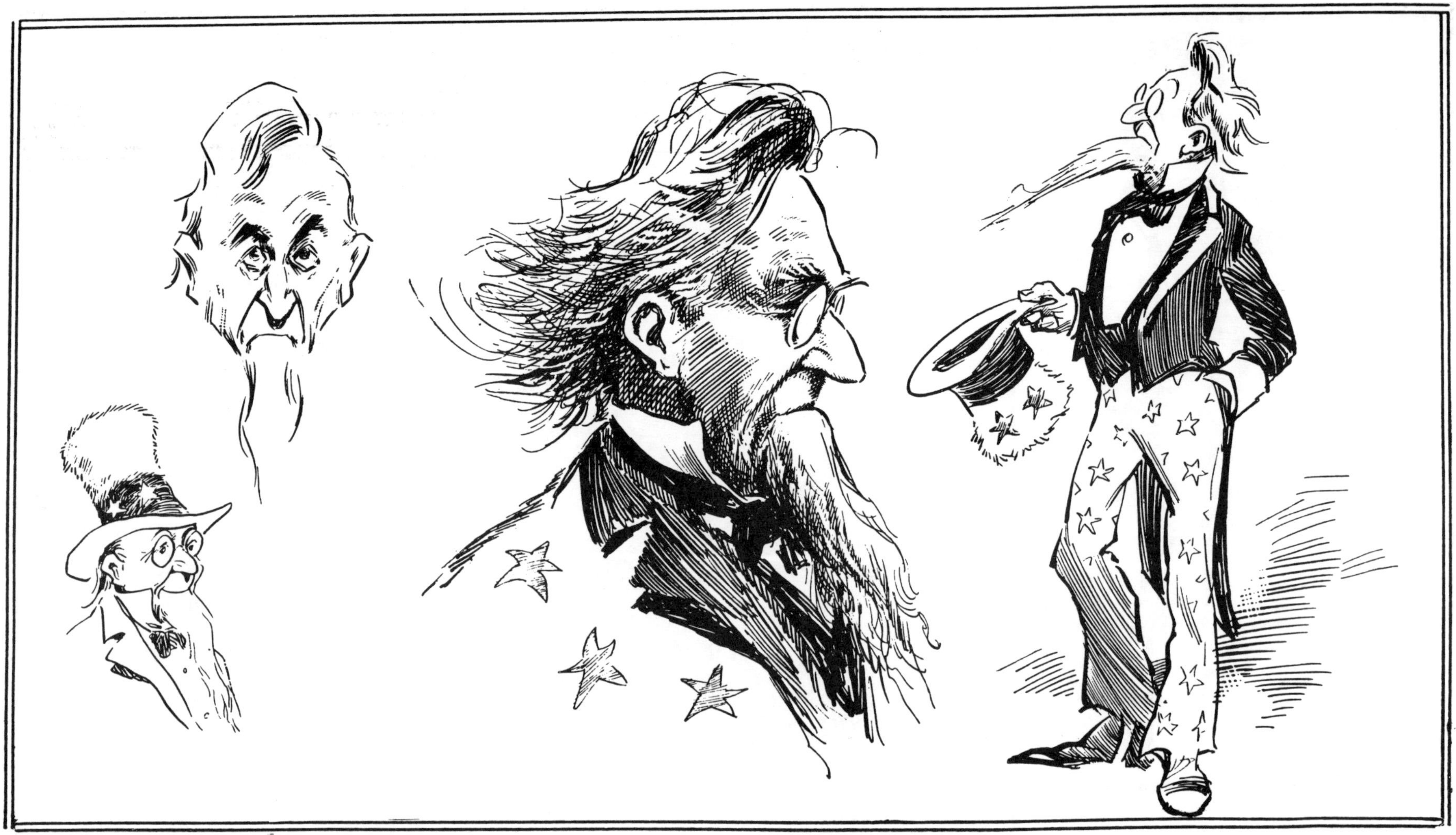

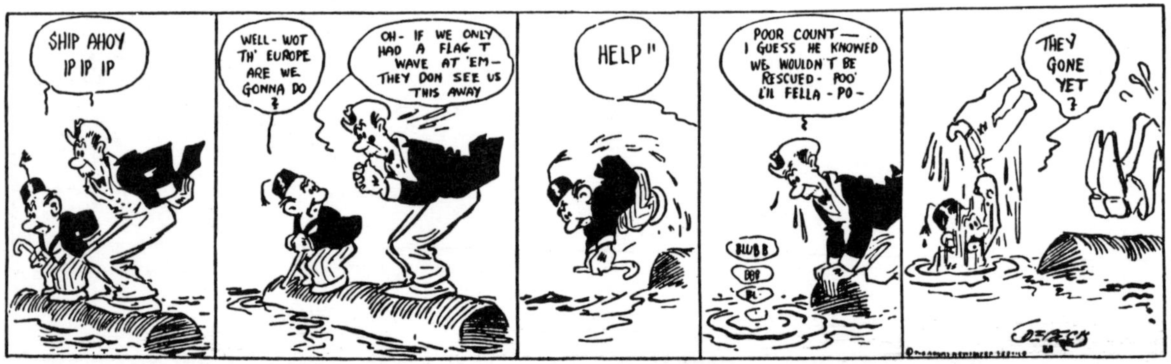
SHIP AHOY IP IP IP
WELL- WOT TH' EUROPE ARE WE GONNA DO ?
OH- IF WE ONLY HAD A FLAG T WAVE AT 'EM- THEY DON SEE US THIS AWAY
HELP"
POOR COUNT— I GUESS HE KNOWED WE WOULDN'T BE RESCUED- POO' L'IL FELLA -PO-
BLUBB
THEY GONE YET ?
DEBECK

Above: Page #3 from "DeBeck's Cartoon Hints" Book One, published in 1915. Uncle Sam drawings by DeBeck. From the Collection of Sy & Sandy Schechter.

Left: "Finn an' Haddie" - A comic strip DeBeck created for the Adams Syndicate in 1916. Reproduced from *Cartoons Magazine*, January, 1916. From the Collection of Richard Marschall.

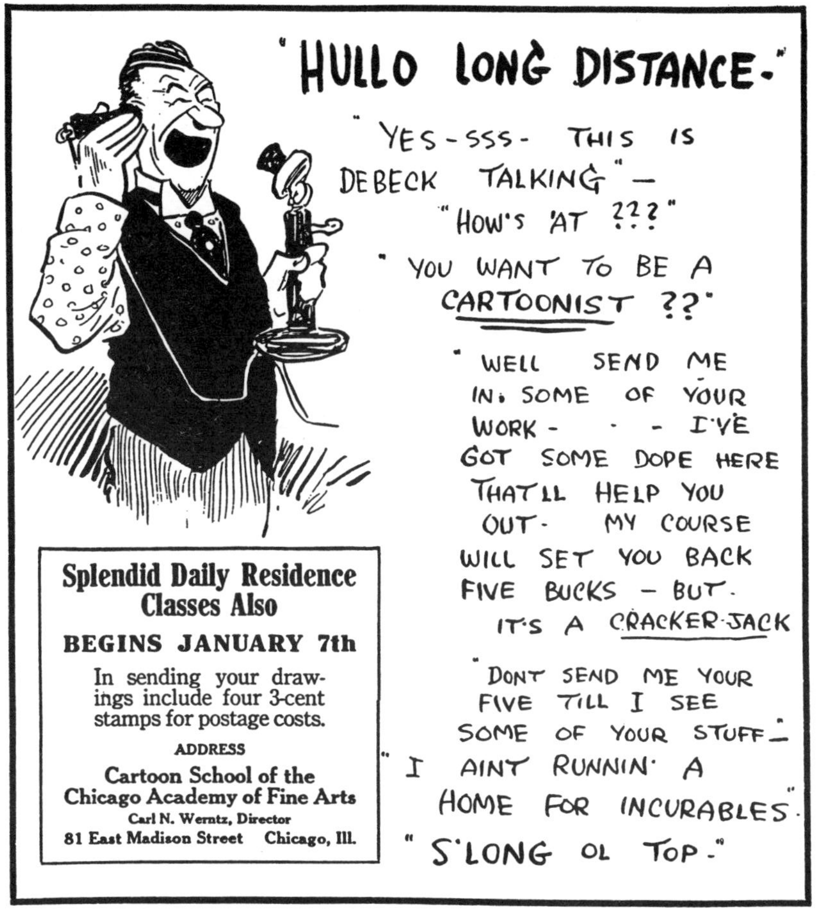
"HULLO LONG DISTANCE-"
"YES-SSS- THIS IS DEBECK TALKING" —
"HOW'S 'AT ???"
"YOU WANT TO BE A CARTOONIST ??"
"WELL SEND ME IN, SOME OF YOUR WORK - - - I'VE GOT SOME DOPE HERE THAT'LL HELP YOU OUT- MY COURSE WILL SET YOU BACK FIVE BUCKS — BUT- IT'S A CRACKER-JACK
"DONT SEND ME YOUR FIVE TILL I SEE SOME OF YOUR STUFF"—
"I AINT RUNNIN' A HOME FOR INCURABLES"
"S'LONG OL TOP-"
Splendid Daily Residence Classes Also
BEGINS JANUARY 7th
In sending your drawings include four 3-cent stamps for postage costs.
ADDRESS
Cartoon School of the Chicago Academy of Fine Arts
Carl N. Werntz, Director
81 East Madison Street Chicago, Ill.

Above: An advertisement for DeBeck's cartoon course at the Chicago Academy of Fine Arts. Reproduced from *Cartoons Magazine*, January 1917. From the Collection of Sy & Sandy Schechter.

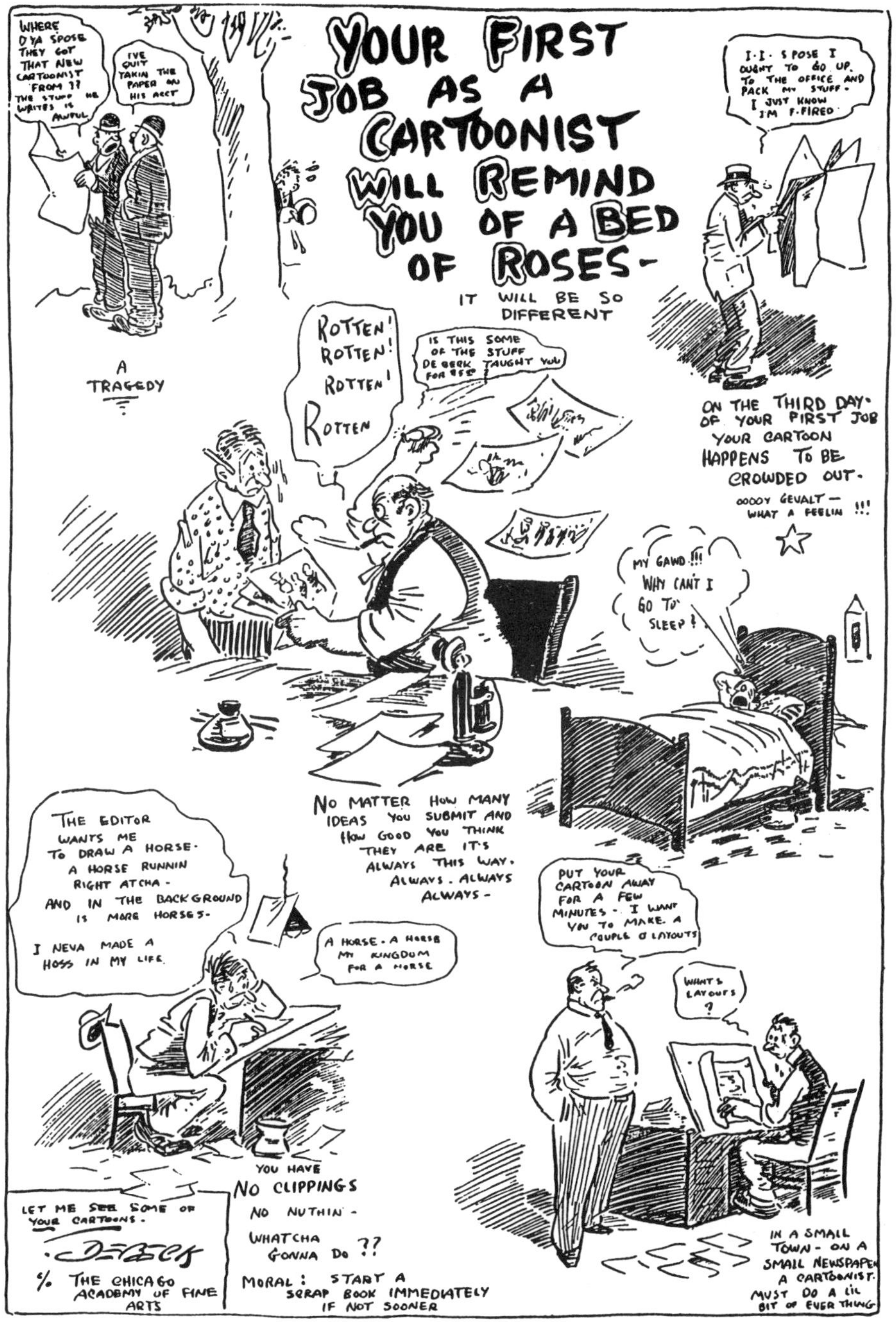
YOUR FIRST JOB AS A CARTOONIST WILL REMIND YOU OF A BED OF ROSES-
IT WILL BE SO DIFFERENT
WHERE D'YA SPOSE THEY GOT THAT NEW CARTOONIST FROM ?? THE STUFF HE WRITES IS AWFUL
I'VE QUIT TAKIN THE PAPER ON HIS ACCT
A TRAGEDY
I-I- S'POSE I OUGHT TO GO UP. TO THE OFFICE AND PACK MY STUFF- I JUST KNOW I'M F-FIRED
ROTTEN! ROTTEN! ROTTEN! ROTTEN
IS THIS SOME OF THE STUFF DE BECK TAUGHT YOU FOR $5??
ON THE THIRD DAY- OF YOUR FIRST JOB YOUR CARTOON HAPPENS TO BE CROWDED OUT-
OOOOY GEVALT — WHAT A FEELIN !!!
MY GAWD!!! WHY CAN'T I GO TO SLEEP!
NO MATTER HOW MANY IDEAS YOU SUBMIT AND HOW GOOD YOU THINK THEY ARE IT'S ALWAYS THIS WAY. ALWAYS. ALWAYS ALWAYS-
THE EDITOR WANTS ME TO DRAW A HORSE- A HORSE RUNNIN RIGHT ATCHA- AND IN THE BACKGROUND IS MORE HORSES-
I NEVA MADE A HOSS IN MY LIFE
A HORSE- A HORSE MY KINGDOM FOR A HORSE
PUT YOUR CARTOON AWAY FOR A FEW MINUTES- I WANT YOU TO MAKE A COUPLE O LAYOUTS
WHAT'S LAYOUTS ?
IN A SMALL TOWN- ON A SMALL NEWSPAPER A CARTOONIST- MUST DO A LIL BIT OF EVER THING
LET ME SEE SOME OF YOUR CARTOONS-
DEBECK
% THE CHICAGO ACADEMY OF FINE ARTS
YOU HAVE NO CLIPPINGS NO NUTHIN'- WHATCHA GONNA DO ??
MORAL: START A SCRAP BOOK IMMEDIATELY IF NOT SOONER

YOUR FIRST WEEK AS A CARTOONIST

It Is Not So Easy as It Looks, According to DeBeck

Right: This DeBeck cartoon appeared in a regular series entitled "What the Cartoonists are Doing." Reproduced from *Cartoons Magazine*, November 1917. From the Collection of Sy & Sandy Schechter.

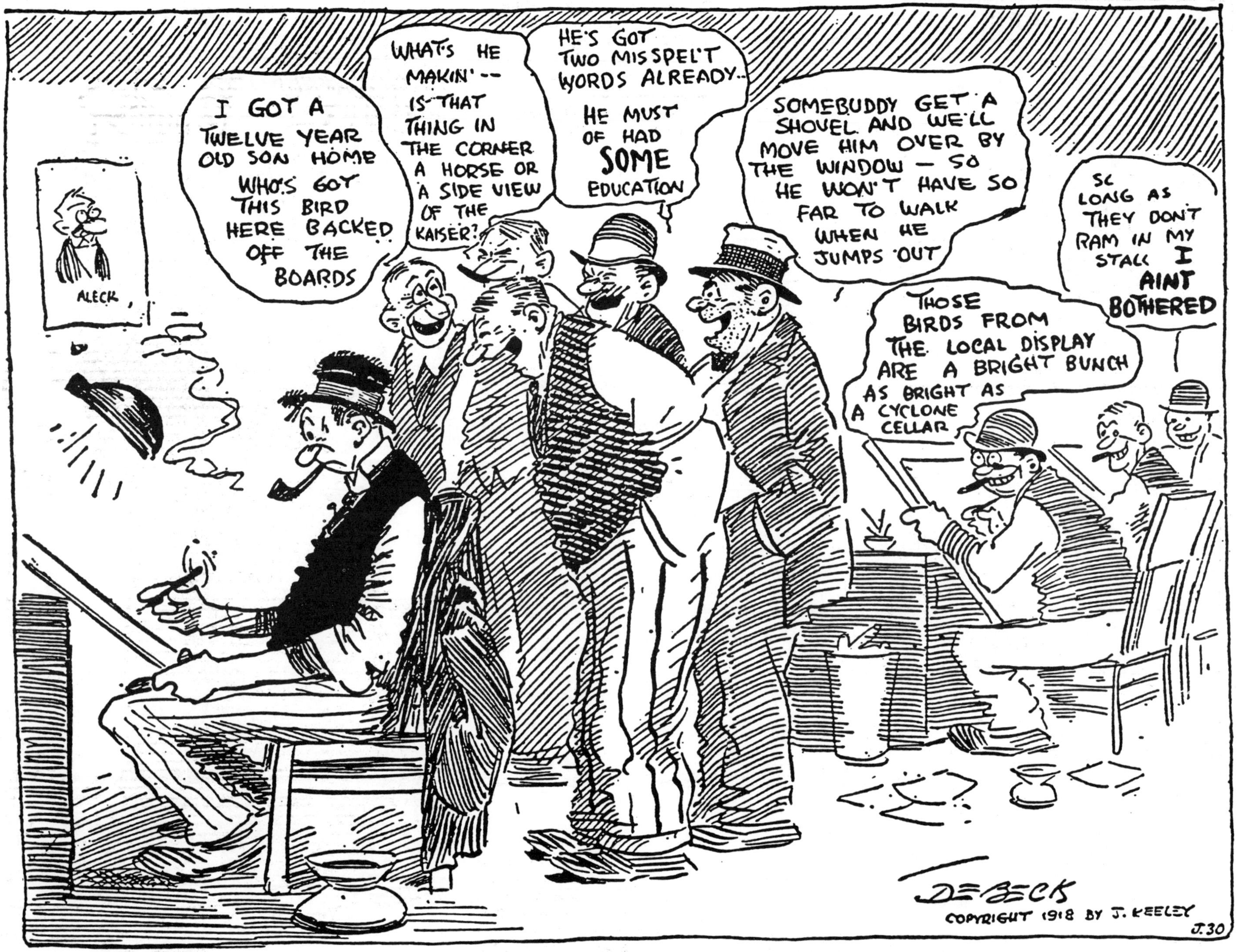
ALECK
I GOT A TWELVE YEAR OLD SON HOME WHO'S GOT THIS BIRD HERE BACKED OFF THE BOARDS
WHAT'S HE MAKIN' -- IS THAT THING IN THE CORNER A HORSE OR A SIDE VIEW OF THE KAISER?
HE'S GOT TWO MISSPELT WORDS ALREADY.. HE MUST OF HAD SOME EDUCATION
SOMEBUDDY GET A SHOVEL AND WE'LL MOVE HIM OVER BY THE WINDOW — SO HE WON'T HAVE SO FAR TO WALK WHEN HE JUMPS OUT
SC LONG AS THEY DON'T RAM IN MY STALL I AINT BOTHERED
THOSE BIRDS FROM THE LOCAL DISPLAY ARE A BRIGHT BUNCH
AS BRIGHT AS A CYCLONE CELLAR
DE BECK
COPYRIGHT 1918 BY J. KEELEY
J.30

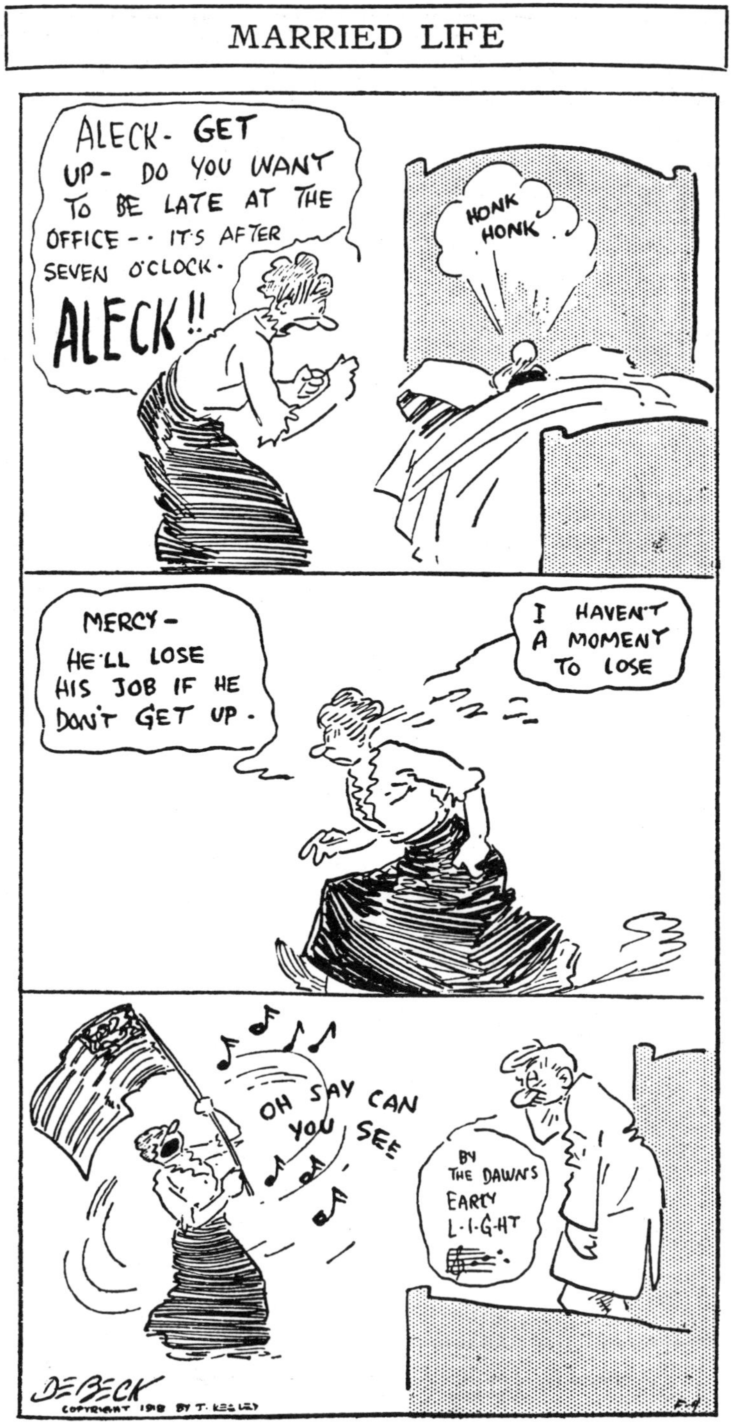
MARRIED LIFE
ALECK- GET UP- DO YOU WANT TO BE LATE AT THE OFFICE - - IT'S AFTER SEVEN O'CLOCK- ALECK!!
HONK HONK
MERCY - HE'LL LOSE HIS JOB IF HE DON'T GET UP.
I HAVEN'T A MOMENT TO LOSE
OH SAY CAN YOU SEE
BY THE DAWN'S EARLY L-I-G-HT
DE BECK

Opposite page: A self-caricature of DeBeck at his drawing board, from "Victim No. 728," a panel DeBeck did for the *Chicago Herald*/Keeley Syndicate, January 30, 1918. Courtesy of the San Francisco Academy of Comic Art.

Left: A typical "Married Life" daily strip, from the *Chicago Herald*, February 4, 1918. From the Collection of Mark Johnson.

Right: Pauline and Aleck, the bickering stars of "Married Life," from the *Chicago Herald and Examiner*, June 27, 1918. Courtesy of the San Francisco Academy of Comic Art.

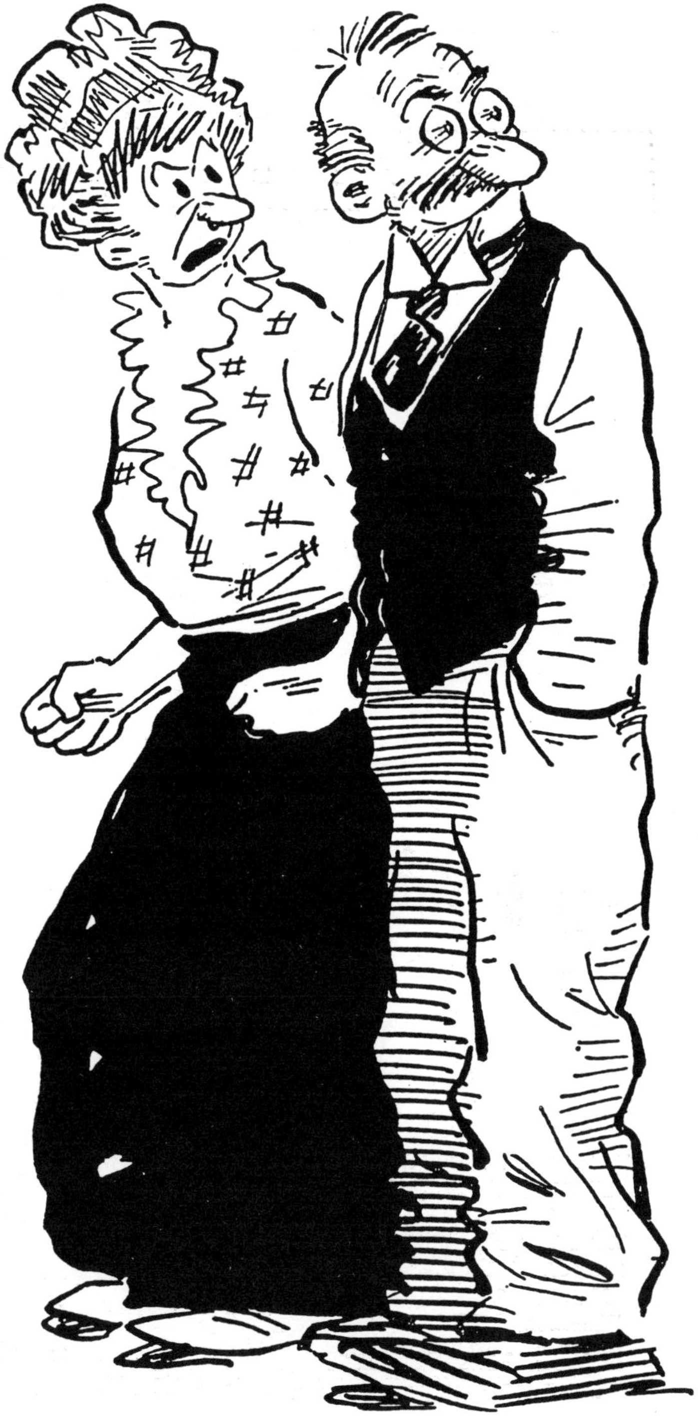

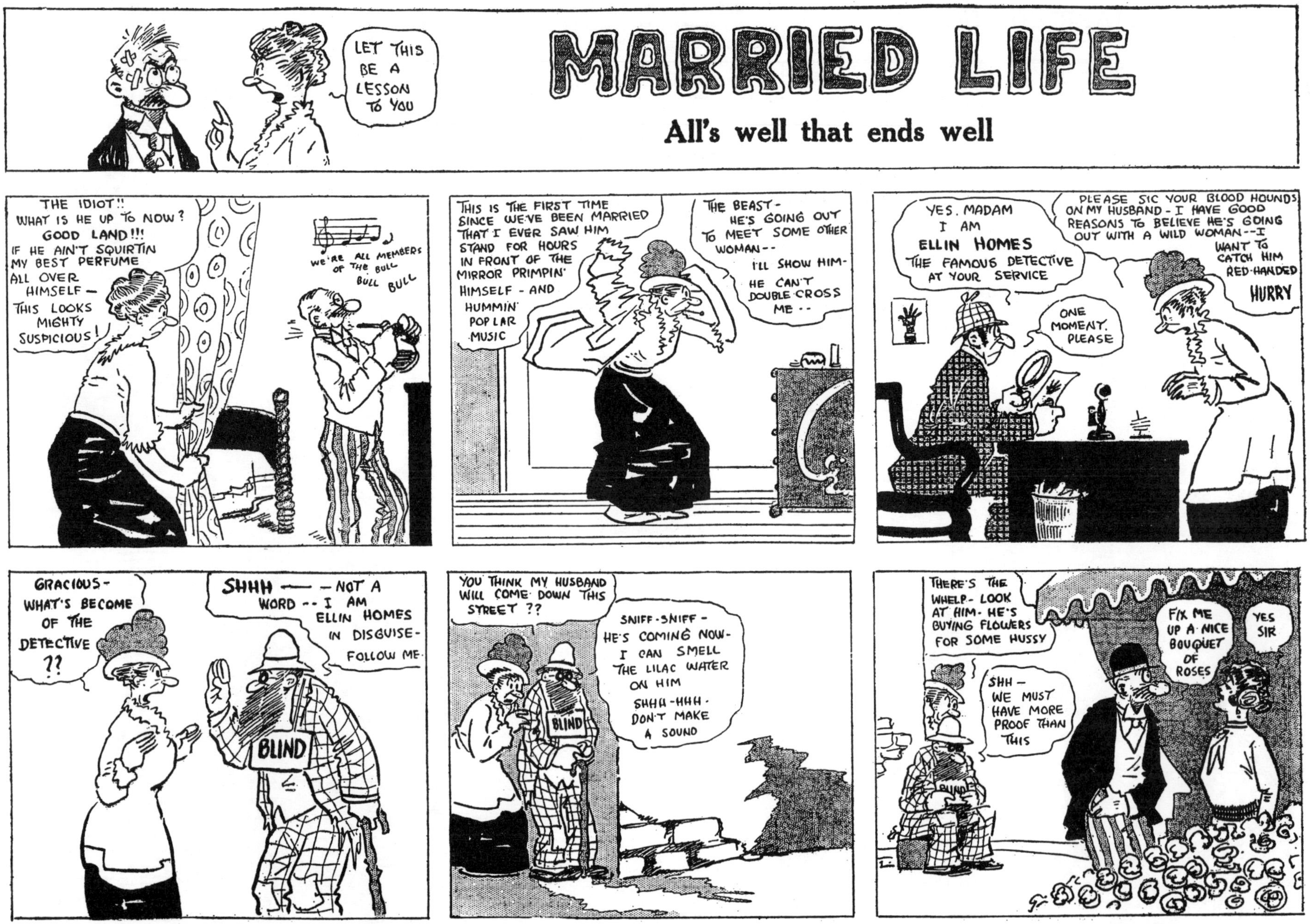

MARRIED LIFE
All's well that ends well
LET THIS BE A LESSON TO YOU
THE IDIOT!! WHAT IS HE UP TO NOW? GOOD LAND!!! IF HE AIN'T SQUIRTIN MY BEST PERFUME ALL OVER HIMSELF — THIS LOOKS MIGHTY SUSPICIOUS!
WE'RE ALL MEMBERS OF THE BULL BULL BULL
THIS IS THE FIRST TIME SINCE WE'VE BEEN MARRIED THAT I EVER SAW HIM STAND FOR HOURS IN FRONT OF THE MIRROR PRIMPIN' HIMSELF - AND HUMMIN' POP'LAR MUSIC
THE BEAST - HE'S GOING OUT TO MEET SOME OTHER WOMAN -- I'LL SHOW HIM - HE CAN'T DOUBLE CROSS ME --
YES, MADAM I AM ELLIN HOMES THE FAMOUS DETECTIVE AT YOUR SERVICE
PLEASE SIC YOUR BLOOD HOUNDS ON MY HUSBAND - I HAVE GOOD REASONS TO BELIEVE HE'S GOING OUT WITH A WILD WOMAN -- I WANT TO CATCH HIM RED-HANDED HURRY
ONE MOMENT, PLEASE
GRACIOUS - WHAT'S BECOME OF THE DETECTIVE ??
SHHH — — NOT A WORD -- I AM ELLIN HOMES IN DISGUISE - FOLLOW ME
BLIND
YOU THINK MY HUSBAND WILL COME DOWN THIS STREET ??
SNIFF - SNIFF - HE'S COMING NOW - I CAN SMELL THE LILAC WATER ON HIM SHHH - HHH - DON'T MAKE A SOUND
BLIND
THERE'S THE WHELP - LOOK AT HIM - HE'S BUYING FLOWERS FOR SOME HUSSY
FIX ME UP A NICE BOUQUET OF ROSES
YES SIR
SHH — WE MUST HAVE MORE PROOF THAN THIS

Above and next page: A classic "Married Life" Sunday page by DeBeck from the *Chicago Herald*/ Keeley Syndicate, 1918. Courtesy of the San Francisco Academy of Comic Art.

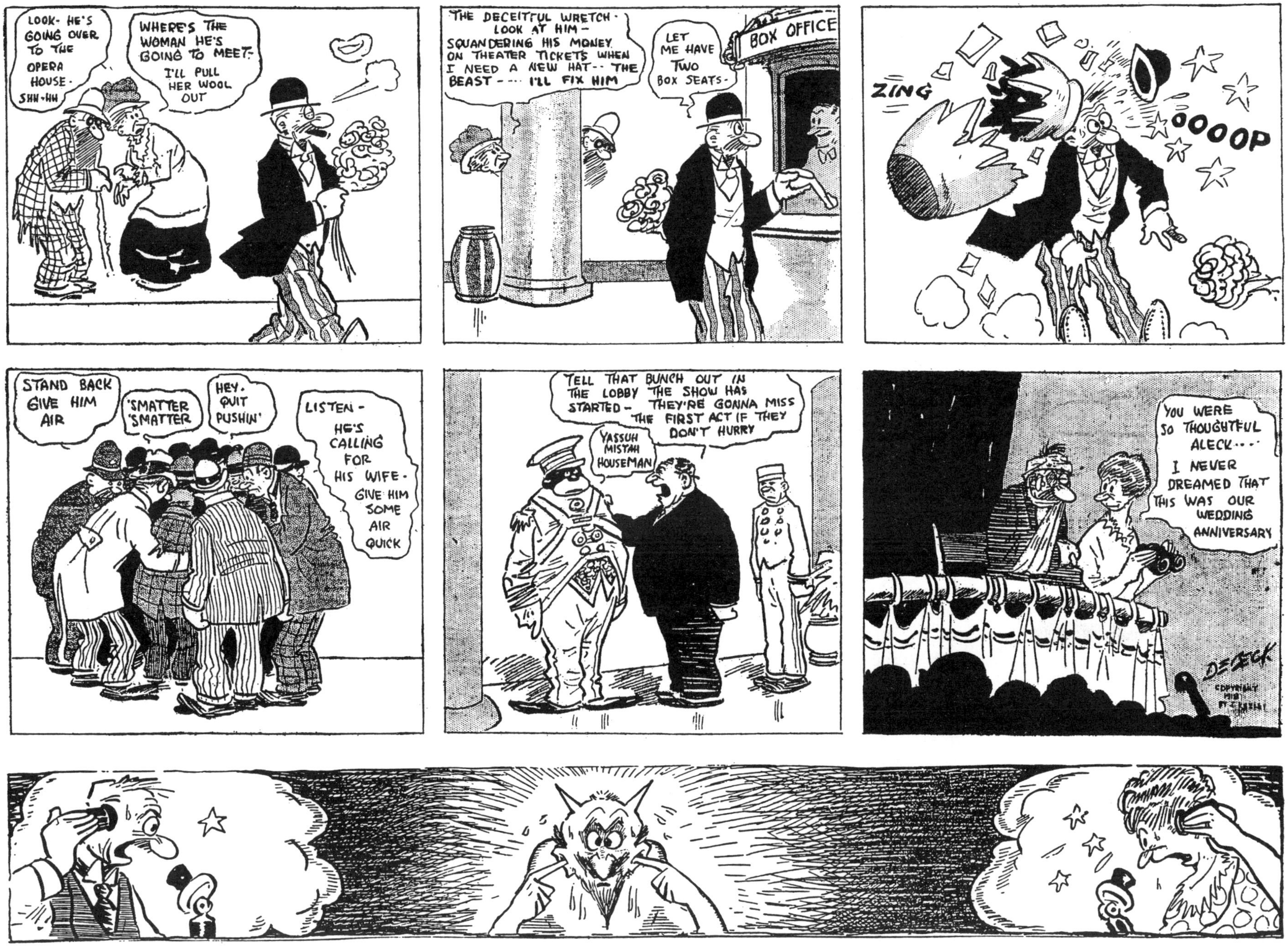
LOOK- HE'S GOING OVER TO THE OPERA HOUSE. SHH-HH
WHERE'S THE WOMAN HE'S GOING TO MEET- I'LL PULL HER WOOL OUT
THE DECEITFUL WRETCH. LOOK AT HIM- SQUANDERING HIS MONEY ON THEATER TICKETS WHEN I NEED A NEW HAT-- THE BEAST--- I'LL FIX HIM
LET ME HAVE TWO BOX SEATS-
BOX OFFICE
ZING
OOOOP
STAND BACK GIVE HIM AIR
'SMATTER 'SMATTER
HEY. QUIT PUSHIN'
LISTEN- HE'S CALLING FOR HIS WIFE- GIVE HIM SOME AIR QUICK
TELL THAT BUNCH OUT IN THE LOBBY THE SHOW HAS STARTED- THEY'RE GONNA MISS THE FIRST ACT IF THEY DON'T HURRY
YASSUH MISTAH HOUSEMAN
YOU WERE SO THOUGHTFUL ALECK--- I NEVER DREAMED THAT THIS WAS OUR WEDDING ANNIVERSARY
DE BECK

Act 1—Keep Your Eye on Kitty Cop   By DeBeck

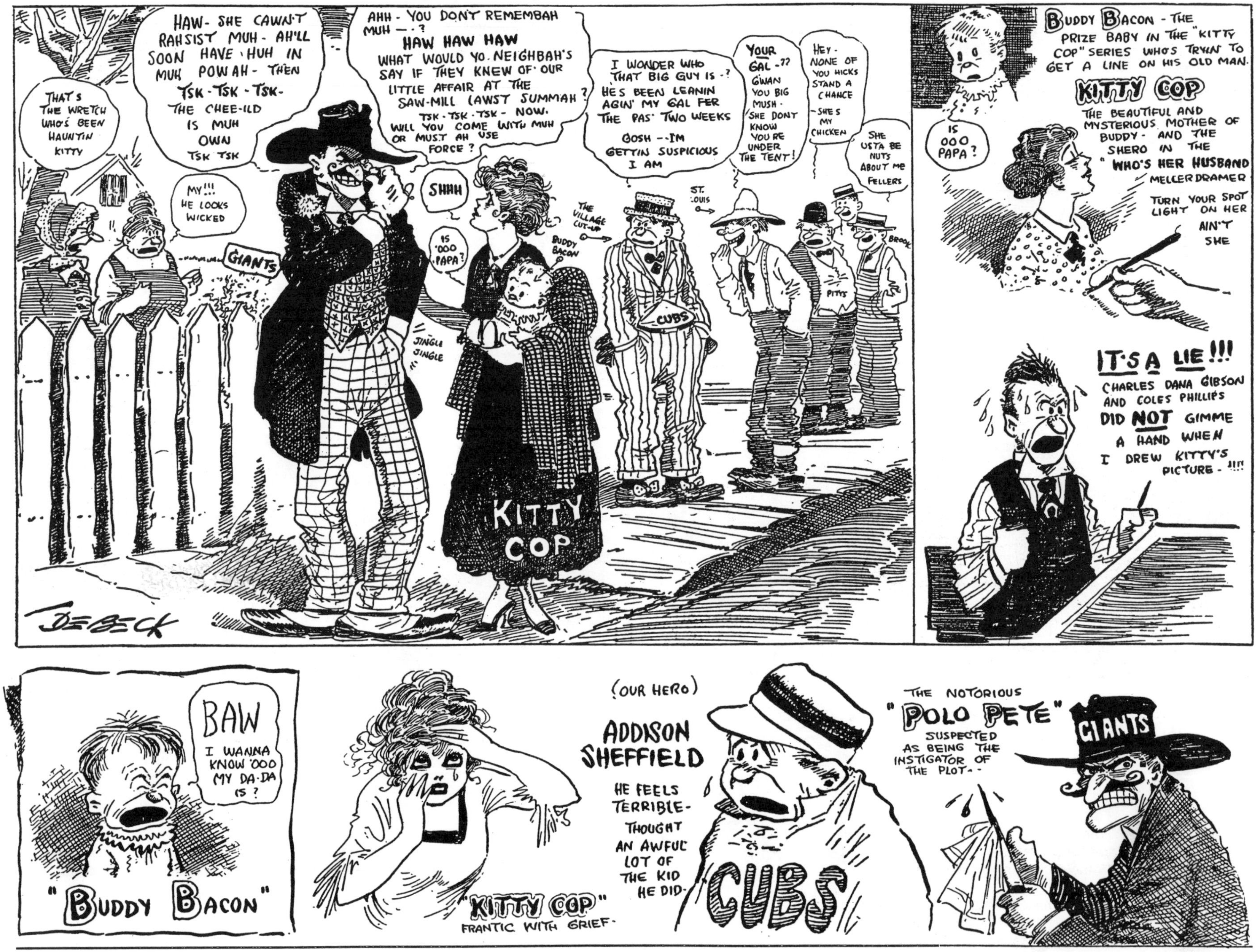
THAT'S THE WRETCH WHO'S BEEN HAUNTIN KITTY
HAW- SHE CAWN'T RAHSIST MUH- AH'LL SOON HAVE HUH IN MUH POWAH- THEN TSK-TSK-TSK- THE CHEE-ILD IS MUH OWN TSK TSK
AHH- YOU DON'T REMEMBAH MUH -- ? HAW HAW HAW WHAT WOULD YO NEIGHBAH'S SAY IF THEY KNEW OF OUR LITTLE AFFAIR AT THE SAW-MILL LAWST SUMMAH ? TSK-TSK-TSK- NOW. WILL YOU COME WITH MUH OR MUST AH USE FORCE ?
MY!!! HE LOOKS WICKED
GIANTS
SHHH
IS 'OOO PAPA?
JINGLE JINGLE
KITTY COP
BUDDY BACON
THE VILLAGE CUT-UP
CUBS
I WONDER WHO THAT BIG GUY IS -? HE'S BEEN LEANIN AGIN' MY GAL FER THE PAS' TWO WEEKS GOSH --I'M GETTIN SUSPICIOUS I AM
ST. LOUIS
YOUR GAL -?? G'WAN YOU BIG MUSH - SHE DONT KNOW YOU'RE UNDER THE TENT!
HEY - NONE OF YOU HICKS STAND A CHANCE - SHE'S MY CHICKEN
SHE USTA BE NUTS ABOUT ME FELLERS
PITTS
BROOK
DEBECK
BUDDY BACON - THE PRIZE BABY IN THE "KITTY COP" SERIES WHO'S TRYIN TO GET A LINE ON HIS OLD MAN.
IS OOO PAPA?
KITTY COP
THE BEAUTIFUL AND MYSTERIOUS MOTHER OF BUDDY - AND THE SHERO IN THE "WHO'S HER HUSBAND" MELLERDRAMER
TURN YOUR SPOT LIGHT ON HER AIN'T SHE
IT'S A LIE!!! CHARLES DANA GIBSON AND COLES PHILLIPS DID NOT GIMME A HAND WHEN I DREW KITTY'S PICTURE - !!!
BAW I WANNA KNOW 'OOO MY DA-DA IS ?
"BUDDY BACON"
"KITTY COP" FRANTIC WITH GRIEF-
(OUR HERO)
ADDISON SHEFFIELD
HE FEELS TERRIBLE- THOUGHT AN AWFUL LOT OF THE KID HE DID-
CUBS
THE NOTORIOUS "POLO PETE" SUSPECTED AS BEING THE INSTIGATOR OF THE PLOT--
GIANTS

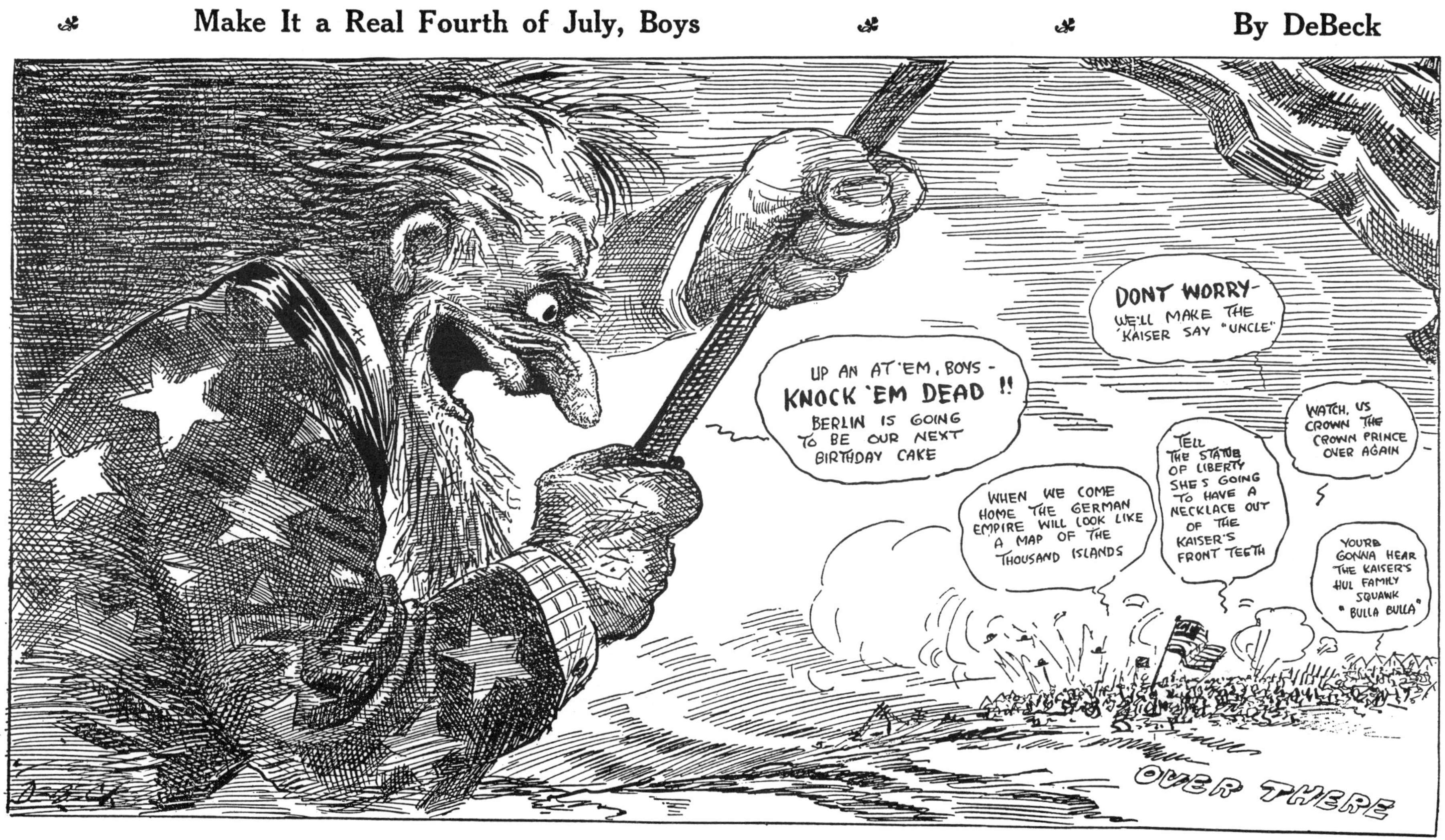
Make It a Real Fourth of July, Boys
By DeBeck
UP AN AT 'EM, BOYS - KNOCK 'EM DEAD !! BERLIN IS GOING TO BE OUR NEXT BIRTHDAY CAKE
DONT WORRY - WE'LL MAKE THE KAISER SAY "UNCLE"
WHEN WE COME HOME THE GERMAN EMPIRE WILL LOOK LIKE A MAP OF THE THOUSAND ISLANDS
TELL THE STATUE OF LIBERTY SHE'S GOING TO HAVE A NECKLACE OUT OF THE KAISER'S FRONT TEETH
WATCH, US CROWN THE CROWN PRINCE OVER AGAIN
YOURE GONNA HEAR THE KAISER'S HUL FAMILY SQUAWK "BULLA BULLA"
OVER THERE

Above: A World War I political cartoon by DeBeck, from the *Chicago Herald and Examiner*, July 4, 1918. Courtesy of the San Francisco Academy of Comic Art.

Opposite page, top: The first of DeBeck's daily sports cartoons, from the *Chicago Herald and Examiner*, May 15, 1918. Courtesy of the San Francisco Academy of Comic Art.

Opposite page, bottom: The cast of DeBeck's daily sports cartoons, from the *Chicago Herald Examiner*, June 17, 1918. Courtesy of the San Francisco Academy of Comic Art.

Olie Moses and O'Mara, Inc. — By DeBeck

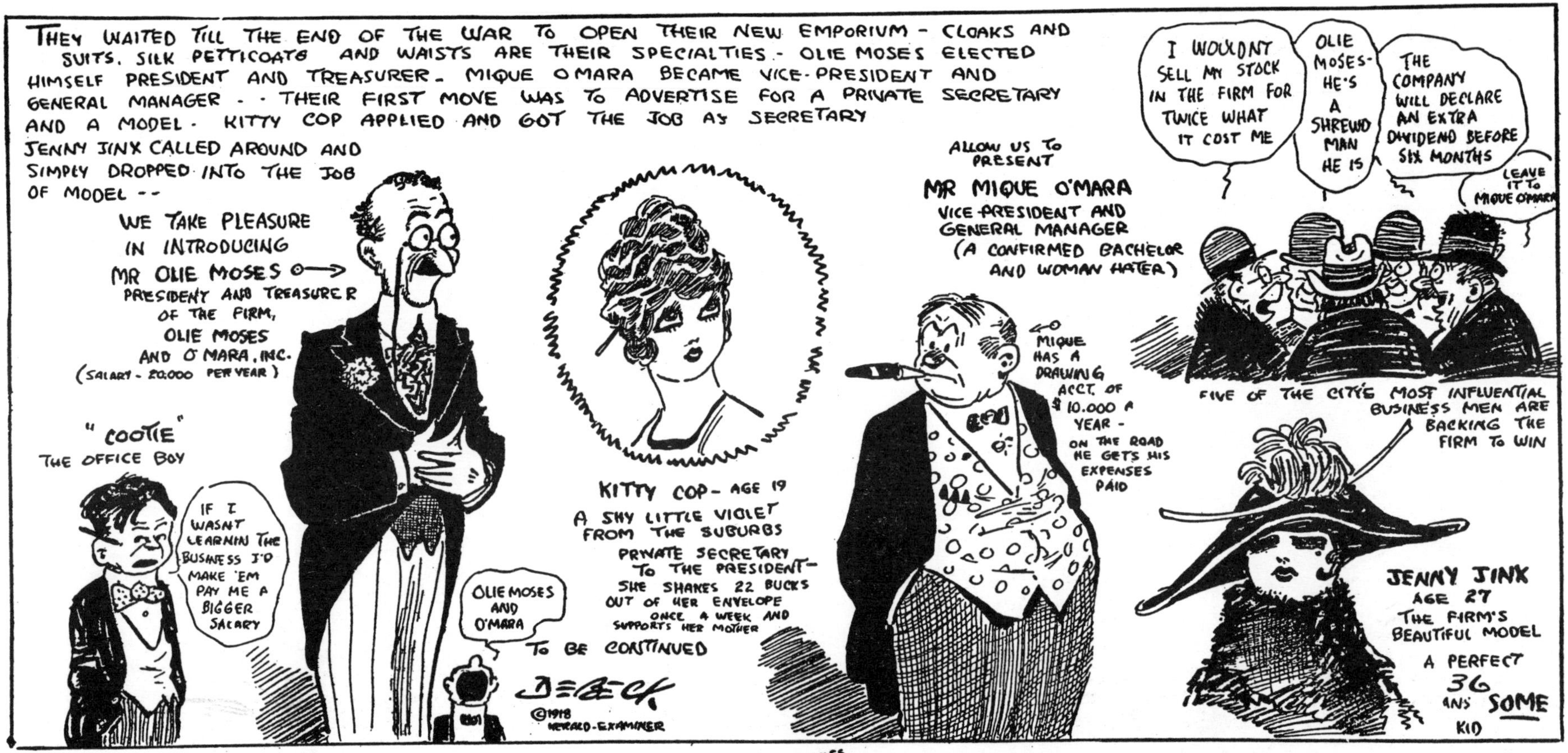

THEY WAITED TILL THE END OF THE WAR TO OPEN THEIR NEW EMPORIUM - CLOAKS AND SUITS, SILK PETTICOATS AND WAISTS ARE THEIR SPECIALTIES - OLIE MOSES ELECTED HIMSELF PRESIDENT AND TREASURER - MIQUE O MARA BECAME VICE-PRESIDENT AND GENERAL MANAGER - - THEIR FIRST MOVE WAS TO ADVERTISE FOR A PRIVATE SECRETARY AND A MODEL - KITTY COP APPLIED AND GOT THE JOB AS SECRETARY
JENNY JINX CALLED AROUND AND SIMPLY DROPPED INTO THE JOB OF MODEL --
WE TAKE PLEASURE IN INTRODUCING MR OLIE MOSES
PRESIDENT AND TREASURER OF THE FIRM, OLIE MOSES AND O MARA, INC.
(SALARY - 20.000 PER YEAR)
"COOTIE" THE OFFICE BOY
IF I WASN'T LEARNIN THE BUSINESS I'D MAKE 'EM PAY ME A BIGGER SALARY
OLIE MOSES AND O'MARA
TO BE CONTINUED
KITTY COP - AGE 19
A SHY LITTLE VIOLET FROM THE SUBURBS
PRIVATE SECRETARY TO THE PRESIDENT - SHE SHAKES 22 BUCKS OUT OF HER ENVELOPE ONCE A WEEK AND SUPPORTS HER MOTHER
DEBECK
©1918 HERALD-EXAMINER
ALLOW US TO PRESENT
MR MIQUE O'MARA
VICE-PRESIDENT AND GENERAL MANAGER
(A CONFIRMED BACHELOR AND WOMAN HATER)
MIQUE HAS A DRAWING ACCT. OF $10.000 A YEAR - ON THE ROAD HE GETS HIS EXPENSES PAID
I WOULDNT SELL MY STOCK IN THE FIRM FOR TWICE WHAT IT COST ME
OLIE MOSES - HE'S A SHREWD MAN HE IS
THE COMPANY WILL DECLARE AN EXTRA DIVIDEND BEFORE SIX MONTHS
LEAVE IT TO MIQUE O'MARA
FIVE OF THE CITY'S MOST INFLUENTIAL BUSINESS MEN ARE BACKING THE FIRM TO WIN
JENNY JINX
AGE 27
THE FIRM'S BEAUTIFUL MODEL
A PERFECT 36
SOME KID

Above: The first "Olie Moses and O'Mara, Inc." panel, from the *Chicago Herald and Examiner*, Dec. 11, 1918. Courtesy of the San Francisco Academy of Comic Art.

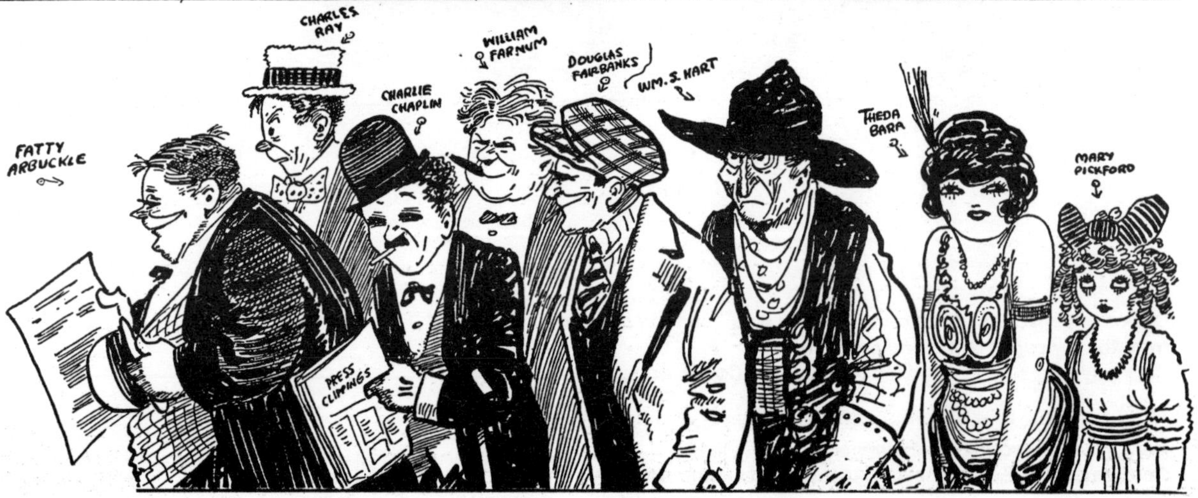

CHARLES RAY
WILLIAM FARNUM
DOUGLAS FAIRBANKS
WM. S. HART
CHARLIE CHAPLIN
FATTY ARBUCKLE
THEDA BARA
MARY PICKFORD
PRESS CLIPPINGS

Right: Movie stars in "Olie Moses and O'Mara, Inc." from the *Chicago Herald and Examiner*, Jan. 12, 1919. Courtesy of the San Francisco Academy of Comic Art.

Opposite page: DeBeck's Christmas greetings, from the *Chicago Herald and Examiner*, Dec. 25, 1918. Courtesy of the San Francisco Academy of Comic Art.

The Whole Family Greets You

By DeBeck

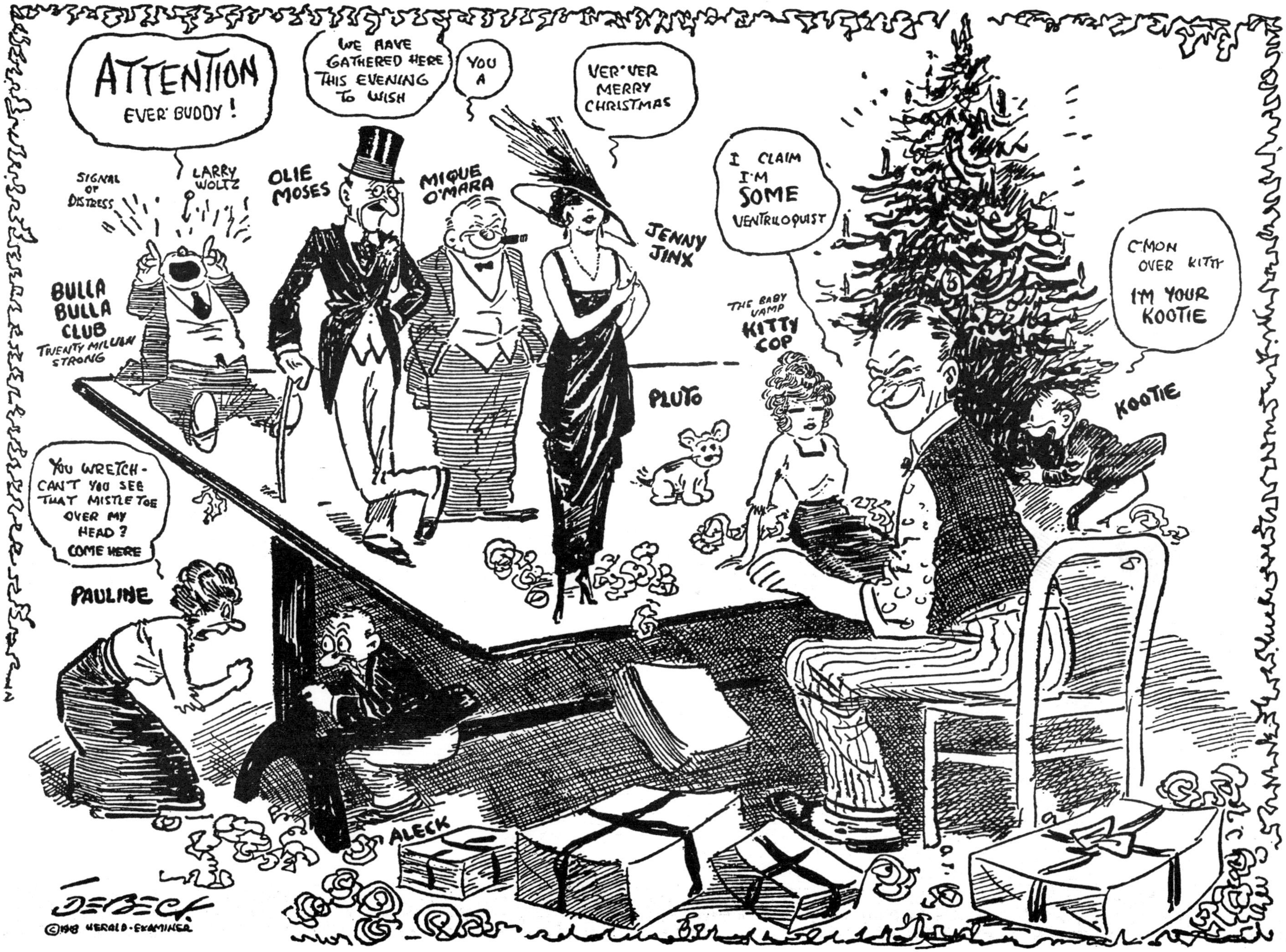
ATTENTION EVER' BUDDY!
WE HAVE GATHERED HERE THIS EVENING TO WISH
YOU A
VER' VER MERRY CHRISTMAS
I CLAIM I'M SOME VENTRILOQUIST
C'MON OVER KITTY I'M YOUR KOOTIE
SIGNAL OF DISTRESS
LARRY WOLTZ
OLIE MOSES
MIQUE O'MARA
JENNY JINX
BULLA BULLA CLUB TWENTY MILLION STRONG
THE BABY VAMP KITTY COP
PLUTO
KOOTIE
YOU WRETCH - CAN'T YOU SEE THAT MISTLETOE OVER MY HEAD? COME HERE
PAULINE
ALECK
DEBECK
©1918 HERALD-EXAMINER

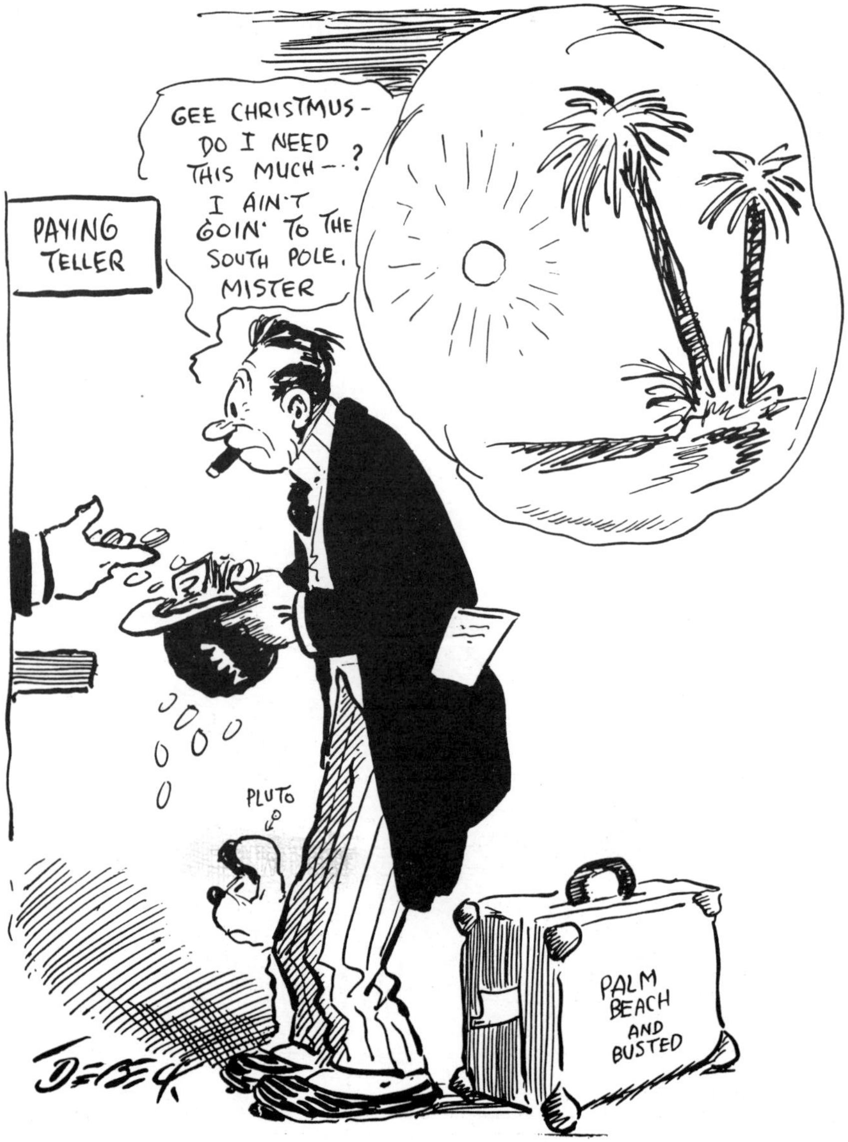
GEE CHRISTMUS - DO I NEED THIS MUCH - - ? I AIN'T GOIN' TO THE SOUTH POLE, MISTER
PAYING TELLER
PLUTO
PALM BEACH AND BUSTED
DEBECK

DeBeck Is on His Way

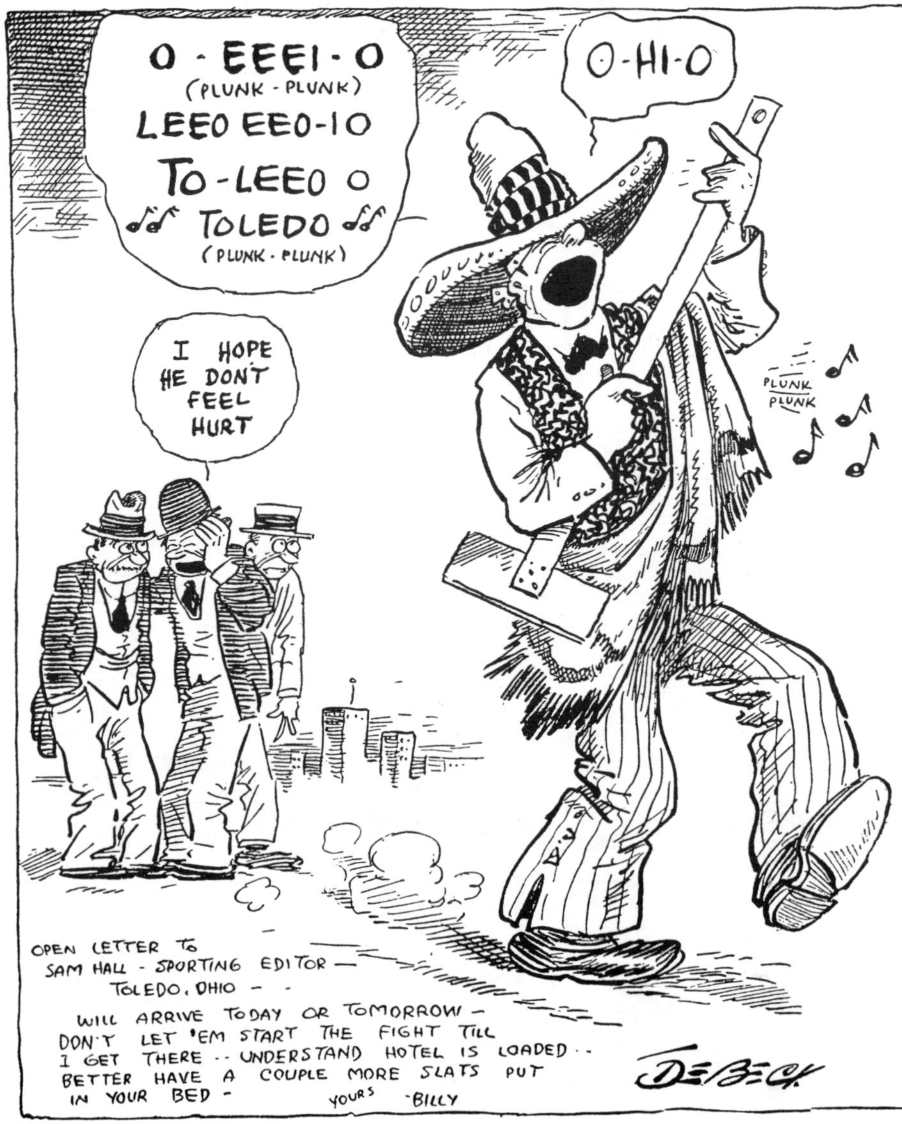
O - EEEI - O (PLUNK - PLUNK) LEEO EEO-IO TO - LEEO O TOLEDO (PLUNK - PLUNK)
O-HI-O
I HOPE HE DON'T FEEL HURT
PLUNK PLUNK
OPEN LETTER TO SAM HALL - SPORTING EDITOR — TOLEDO, OHIO - - WILL ARRIVE TODAY OR TOMORROW - DON'T LET 'EM START THE FIGHT TILL I GET THERE - - UNDERSTAND HOTEL IS LOADED - - BETTER HAVE A COUPLE MORE SLATS PUT IN YOUR BED - YOURS -BILLY
DEBECK

Above left: DeBeck leaves Chicago for Palm Beach, Florida, to take a working vacation, from the *Chicago Herald and Examiner*, January 28, 1919. From the Collection of Sy & Sandy Schechter.

Above right: DeBeck marches off to Toledo, Ohio, to cover the Jess Willard - Jack Dempsey fight, from the *Chicago Herald and Examiner*, June 3, 1919. From the Collection of Mark Johnson.

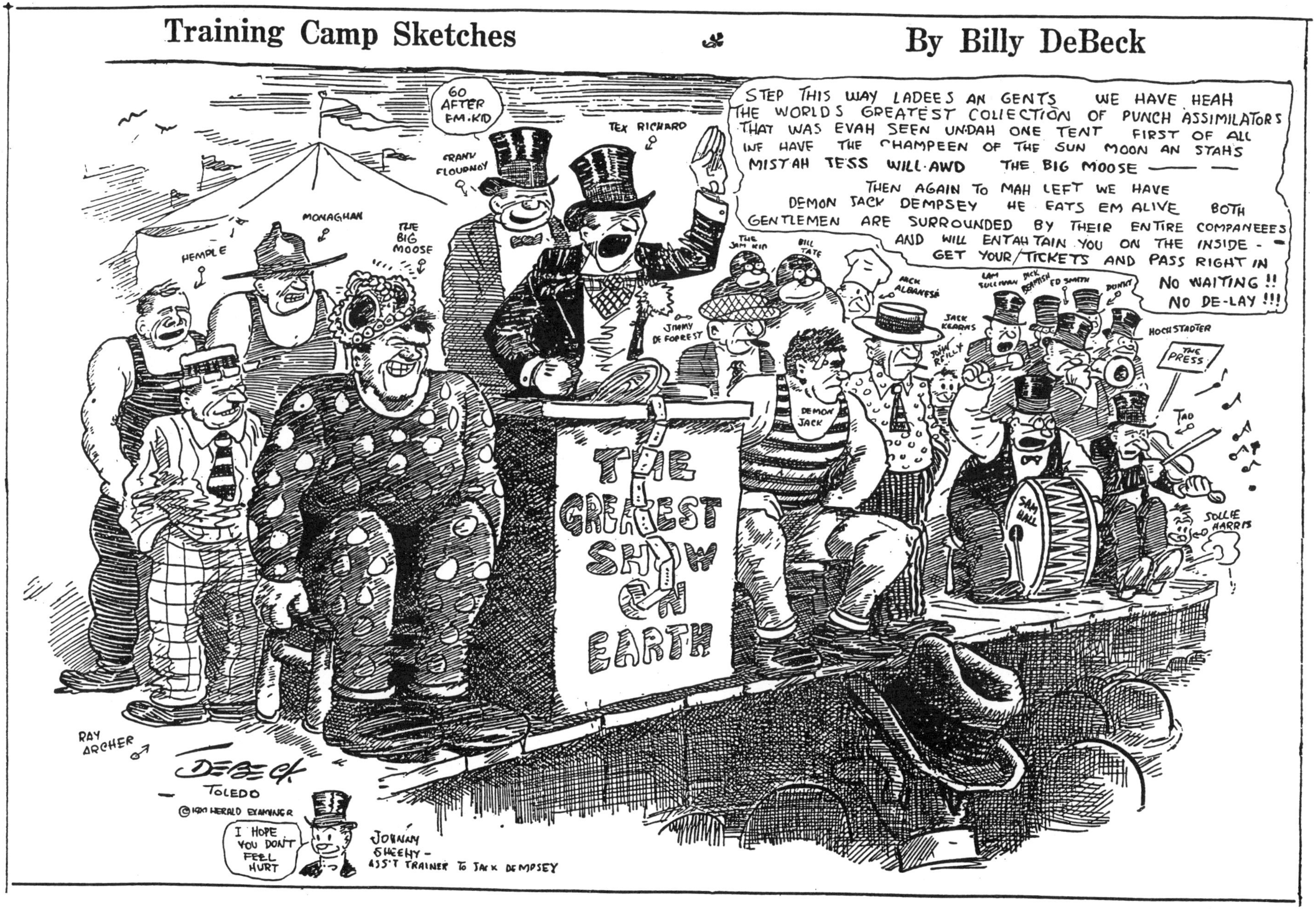
Training Camp Sketches
By Billy DeBeck
STEP THIS WAY LADEES AN GENTS WE HAVE HEAH THE WORLDS GREATEST COLLECTION OF PUNCH ASSIMILATORS THAT WAS EVAH SEEN UNDAH ONE TENT FIRST OF ALL WE HAVE THE CHAMPEEN OF THE SUN MOON AN STAHS MISTAH JESS WILL·AWD THE BIG MOOSE —— —
THEN AGAIN TO MAH LEFT WE HAVE DEMON JACK DEMPSEY HE EATS EM ALIVE BOTH GENTLEMEN ARE SURROUNDED BY THEIR ENTIRE COMPANEEES AND WILL ENTAHTAIN YOU ON THE INSIDE - GET YOUR TICKETS AND PASS RIGHT IN
NO WAITING !!
NO DE-LAY !!!
GO AFTER EM·KID
FRANK FLOURNOY
TEX RICHARD
HEMPLE
MONAGHAN
THE BIG MOOSE
JIMMY DE FORREST
THE JAM KID
BILL TATE
JACK ALBANESE
JACK KEARNS
JOHN REILLY
ED SMITH
DUNNY
HOCHSTADTER
THE PRESS
DEMON JACK
TAD
SAM HALL
SOLLIE HARRIS
THE GREATEST SHOW ON EARTH
RAY ARCHER
DEBECK
TOLEDO
© HERALD EXAMINER
I HOPE YOU DON'T FEEL HURT
JOHNNY SHEEHY - ASS'T TRAINER TO JACK DEMPSEY

Above: One of the series of "Training Camp Sketches" DeBeck sent back to Chicago from the Jess Willard - Jack Dempsey fight, from the *Chicago Herald and Examiner*, June 14, 1919. Courtesy of the San Francisco Academy of Comic Art.

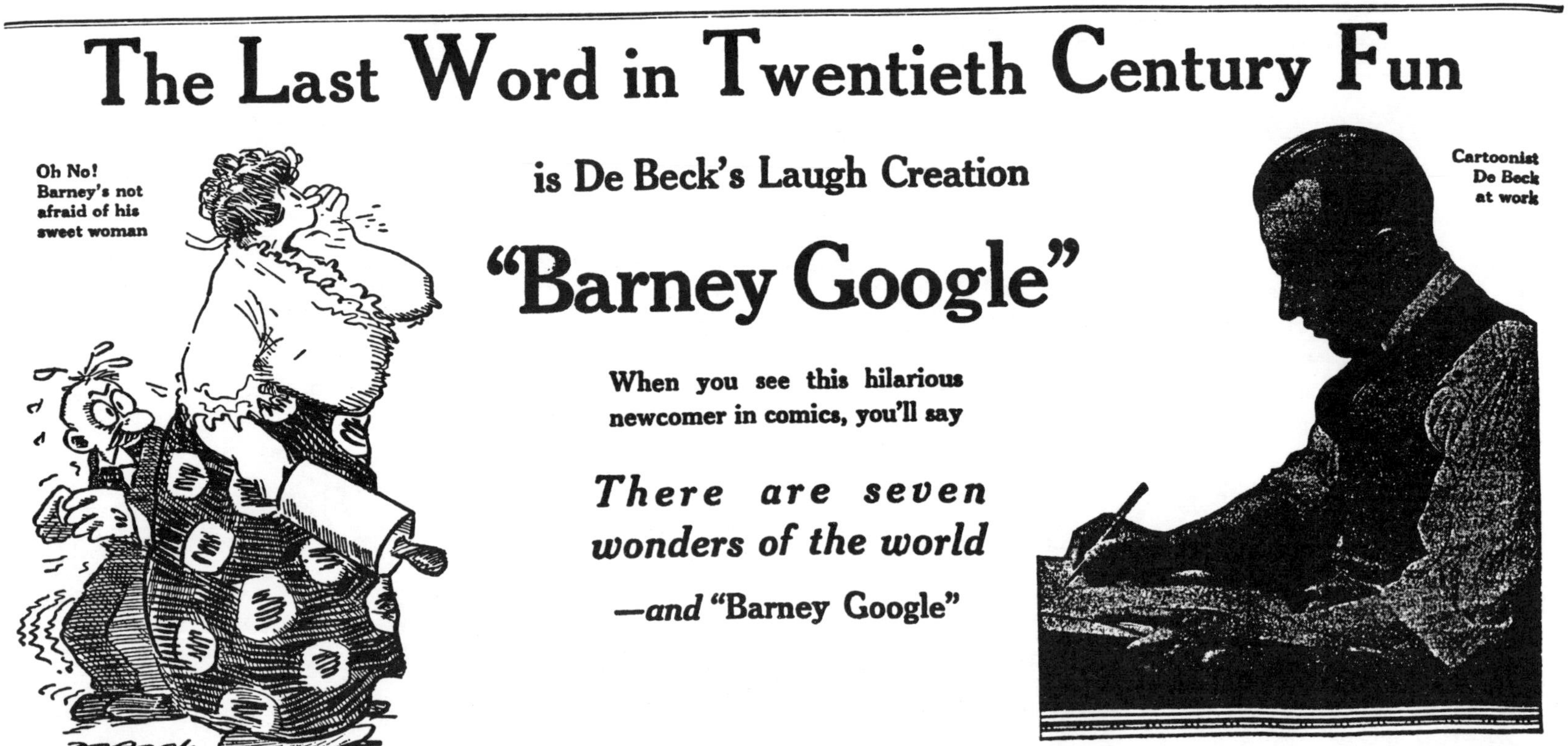
The Last Word in Twentieth Century Fun
is De Beck's Laugh Creation
"Barney Google"
When you see this hilarious newcomer in comics, you'll say
There are seven wonders of the world
—and "Barney Google"
Oh No! Barney's not afraid of his sweet woman
Cartoonist De Beck at work
DEBECK

Above: A newspaper ad for "Barney Google," August 17, 1920, *St. Louis Globe-Democrat.* Courtesy of the San Francisco Academy of Comic Art.

Below: The first "Take Barney Google, F'rinstance" from the *Chicago Herald and Examiner*, June 17, 1919. Collection of Mark Johnson.

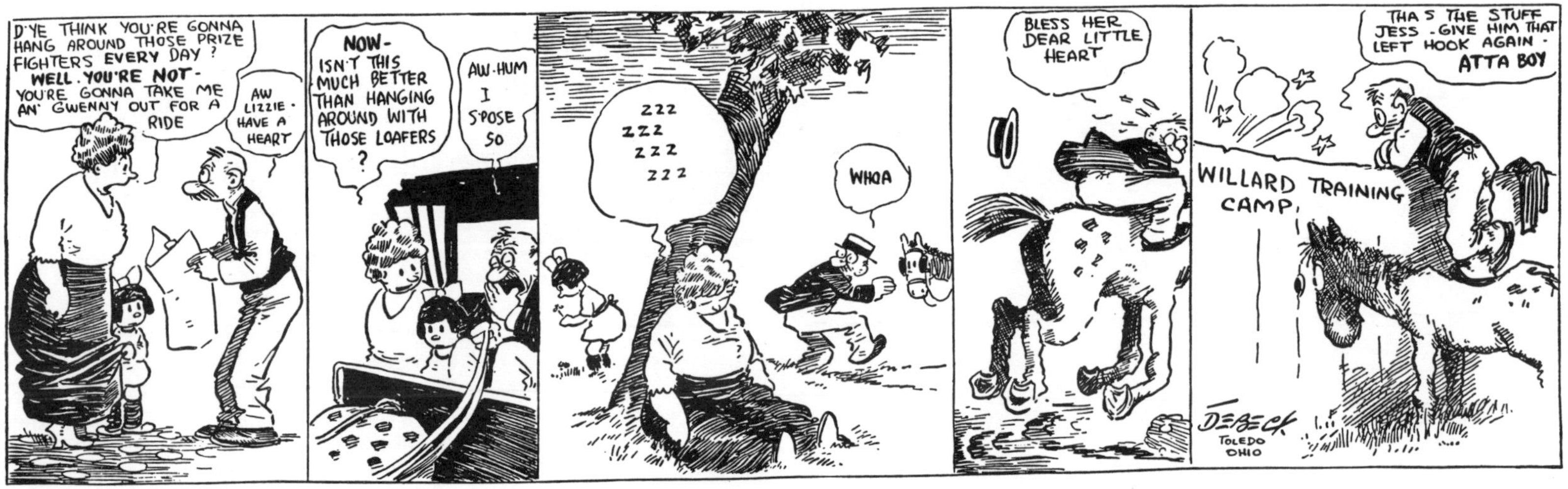
D'YE THINK YOU'RE GONNA HANG AROUND THOSE PRIZE FIGHTERS EVERY DAY? WELL. YOU'RE NOT - YOU'RE GONNA TAKE ME AN' GWENNY OUT FOR A RIDE
AW LIZZIE - HAVE A HEART
NOW - ISN'T THIS MUCH BETTER THAN HANGING AROUND WITH THOSE LOAFERS ?
AW-HUM I S'POSE SO
ZZZ ZZZ ZZZ ZZZ
WHOA
BLESS HER DEAR LITTLE HEART
THA'S THE STUFF JESS - GIVE HIM THAT LEFT HOOK AGAIN - ATTA BOY
WILLARD TRAINING CAMP
DEBECK TOLEDO OHIO

Take
Barney Google
F'rinstance

The Tuesday, June 17, 1919, edition of the *Chicago Herald and Examiner* featured Billy DeBeck's new comic strip, "Take Barney Google, F'rinstance," displayed across the full width of the sports page. (This first strip is reproduced on the opposite page.) Barney, a dead ringer for Aleck, the long-suffering star of DeBeck's now defunct "Married Life" strip, was begging his wife Lizzie, who would soon became known as his "sweet woman," for permission to go to the Willard - Dempsey training camps in spite of his promise to take his daughter Gweeny out for a ride. DeBeck had established his new character as a sports-loving ne'er-do-well, who would rather hang out with his buddies than honor his family responsibilities. The cigar-smoking afternoon commuters back in Chicago identified with Barney Google immediately, and DeBeck finally had fame and fortune within his grasp.

The first few weeks of "Take Barney Google, F'rinstance" revolved around the upcoming heavyweight championship fight. On July 4, 1919, Jack Dempsey, the 190-pound, square-jawed challenger, knocked champion Jess Willard to the canvas seven times in the first round. By the third round, Willard, his cheek bone split, his nose smashed, his body a mass of red welts, told his seconds to throw in the towel. It was one of the most stunning defeats in the history of professional boxing. Barney Google missed all of the excitement because a pickpocket stole his ticket on the trolley car ride to the fight. He was so upset that he tried to hang himself.

After the championship, Barney unsuccessfully pursued an assortment of odd jobs as a song-plugger, a booking agent and an office worker, as DeBeck's new strip became a fixture on the *Herald and Examiner*'s sports page. By October, 1919, when Barney visited the World Series, the strip was appearing in newspapers nationwide, distributed by King Features Syndicate, an arm of the Hearst publishing empire. This was the year of the infamous "Black Sox" scandal, but it was not discovered until much later that the Chicago White Sox players had accepted money to throw the World Series.

Throughout the next few months, Barney continued his shiftless ways, losing all his money playing poker, chasing Ziegfeld showgirls and never learning his lesson. Although Barney's personality was unwavering, another change was taking place. Perhaps in a conscious effort to emphasize his henpecked status or, more likely, as the inevitable result of drawing a figure in the tight confines of a comic strip panel, DeBeck's leading man gradually became more diminutive in size. By mid-1920, Barney Google had evolved into the pop-nosed, bug-eyed runt that millions of readers would come to love during the care-free years of the Jazz Age, a full-page color Sunday page began running in many of the Hearst newspapers and Billy DeBeck had moved to New York City, a rising star in the comic strip business.

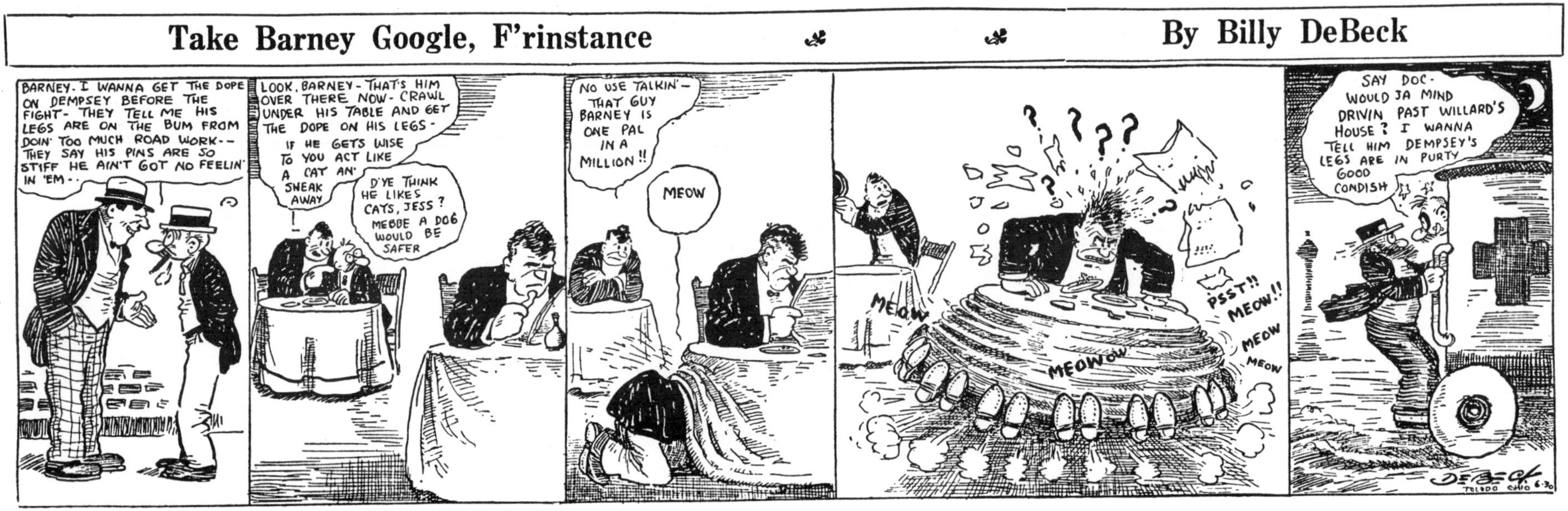
Take Barney Google, F'rinstance
By Billy DeBeck
BARNEY - I WANNA GET THE DOPE ON DEMPSEY BEFORE THE FIGHT - THEY TELL ME HIS LEGS ARE ON THE BUM FROM DOIN' TOO MUCH ROAD WORK -- THEY SAY HIS PINS ARE SO STIFF HE AIN'T GOT NO FEELIN' IN 'EM --
LOOK, BARNEY - THAT'S HIM OVER THERE NOW - CRAWL UNDER HIS TABLE AND GET THE DOPE ON HIS LEGS -
IF HE GETS WISE TO YOU ACT LIKE A CAT AN' SNEAK AWAY
D'YE THINK HE LIKES CATS, JESS? MEBBE A DOG WOULD BE SAFER
NO USE TALKIN' - THAT GUY BARNEY IS ONE PAL IN A MILLION!!
MEOW
MEOW
MEOWOW
PSST!! MEOW!!
MEOW
MEOW
SAY DOC - WOULD JA MIND DRIVIN PAST WILLARD'S HOUSE? I WANNA TELL HIM DEMPSEY'S LEGS ARE IN PURTY GOOD CONDISH
DEBECK TOLEDO OHIO 6-30

Above: Barney tries to get the dope on Dempsey for Willard, from the *Chicago Herald and Examiner*, June 30, 1919. Courtesy of the San Francisco Academy of Comic Art.

Below: A visitor from Youngstown wants to see Barney's den of sin, from the *Chicago Herald and Examiner*, August 11, 1919. Courtesy of the San Francisco Academy of Comic Art.

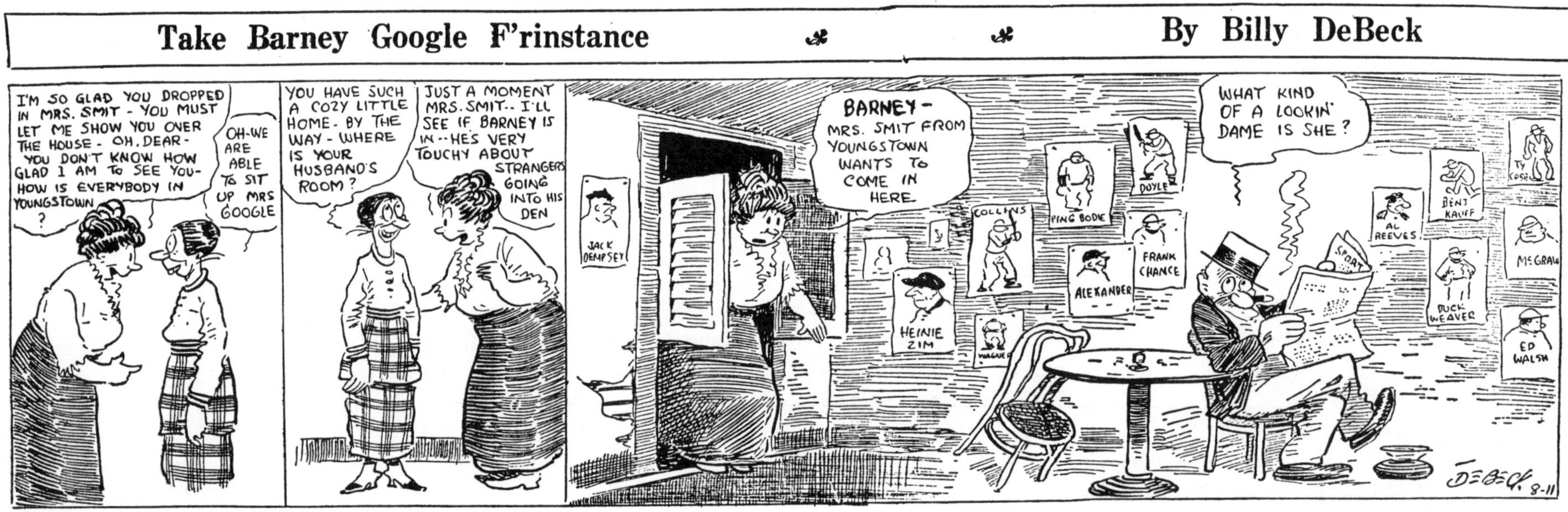
Take Barney Google F'rinstance
By Billy DeBeck
I'M SO GLAD YOU DROPPED IN MRS. SMIT - YOU MUST LET ME SHOW YOU OVER THE HOUSE - OH, DEAR - YOU DON'T KNOW HOW GLAD I AM TO SEE YOU - HOW IS EVERYBODY IN YOUNGSTOWN?
OH - WE ARE ABLE TO SIT UP MRS GOOGLE
YOU HAVE SUCH A COZY LITTLE HOME - BY THE WAY - WHERE IS YOUR HUSBAND'S ROOM?
JUST A MOMENT MRS. SMIT -- I'LL SEE IF BARNEY IS IN -- HE'S VERY TOUCHY ABOUT STRANGERS GOING INTO HIS DEN
BARNEY - MRS. SMIT FROM YOUNGSTOWN WANTS TO COME IN HERE
WHAT KIND OF A LOOKIN' DAME IS SHE?
JACK DEMPSEY
COLLINS
PING BODIE
DOYLE
FRANK CHANCE
ALEXANDER
HEINIE ZIM
WAGNER
AL REEVES
BENJ KAUFF
TY COBB
McGRAW
BUCK WEAVER
ED WALSH
SPORT
DEBECK 8-11

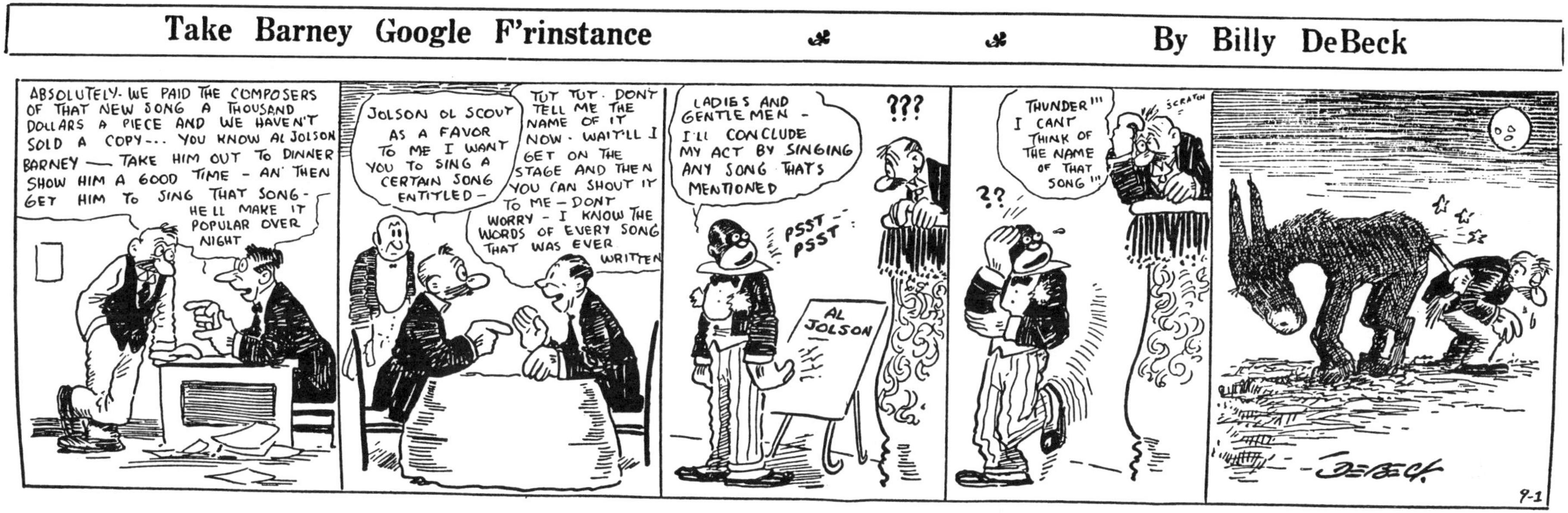
Take Barney Google F'rinstance
By Billy DeBeck
ABSOLUTELY. WE PAID THE COMPOSERS OF THAT NEW SONG A THOUSAND DOLLARS A PIECE AND WE HAVEN'T SOLD A COPY-- YOU KNOW AL JOLSON BARNEY — TAKE HIM OUT TO DINNER SHOW HIM A GOOD TIME - AN' THEN GET HIM TO SING THAT SONG - HE'LL MAKE IT POPULAR OVER NIGHT
JOLSON OL SCOUT AS A FAVOR TO ME I WANT YOU TO SING A CERTAIN SONG ENTITLED -
TUT TUT. DON'T TELL ME THE NAME OF IT NOW. WAIT'LL I GET ON THE STAGE AND THEN YOU CAN SHOUT IT TO ME - DON'T WORRY - I KNOW THE WORDS OF EVERY SONG THAT WAS EVER WRITTEN
LADIES AND GENTLEMEN - I'LL CONCLUDE MY ACT BY SINGING ANY SONG THAT'S MENTIONED
???
PSST - PSST
AL JOLSON
THUNDER!!! I CAN'T THINK OF THE NAME OF THAT SONG!!!
SCRATCH
??
DEBECK.
9-1

Above: Barney, working for a music publisher, tries to get Al Jolson to sing a song, from the *Chicago Herald and Examiner*, September 1, 1919.
Courtesy of the San Francisco Academy of Comic Art.

Below: Mrs. Google puts on Jack Dempsey's boxing gloves, from the *Chicago Herald and Examiner*, October 3, 1919.
Courtesy of the San Francisco Academy of Comic Art.

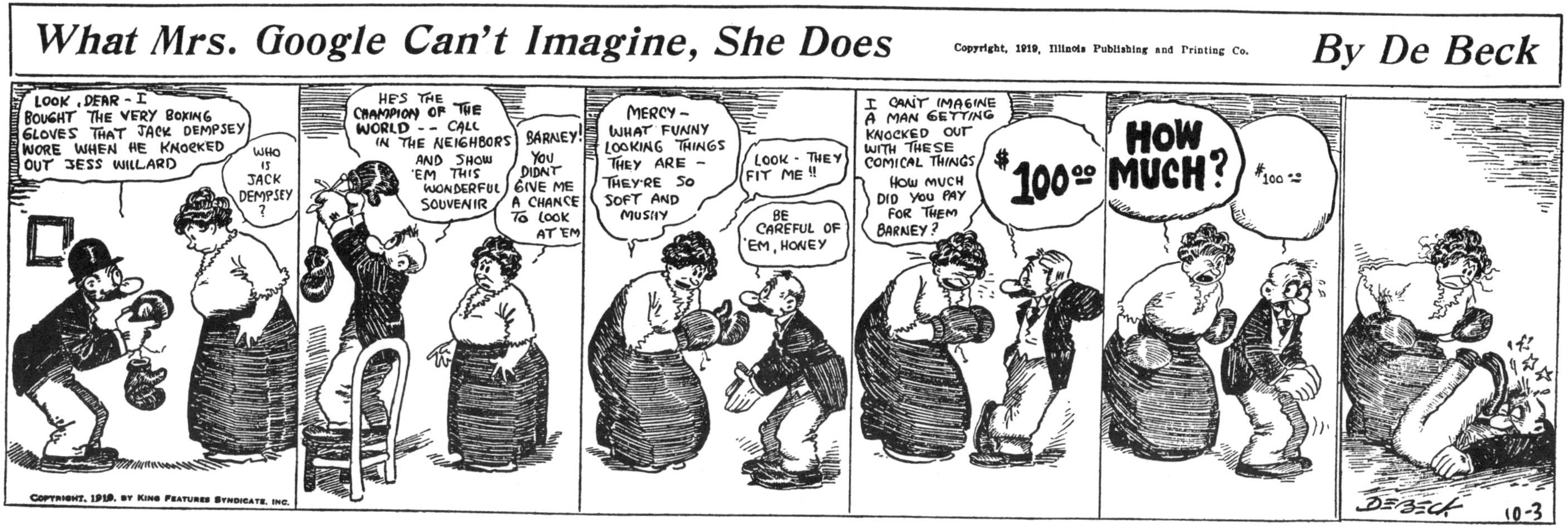
What Mrs. Google Can't Imagine, She Does
Copyright, 1919, Illinois Publishing and Printing Co.
By De Beck
LOOK, DEAR - I BOUGHT THE VERY BOXING GLOVES THAT JACK DEMPSEY WORE WHEN HE KNOCKED OUT JESS WILLARD
WHO IS JACK DEMPSEY ?
HE'S THE CHAMPION OF THE WORLD -- CALL IN THE NEIGHBORS AND SHOW 'EM THIS WONDERFUL SOUVENIR
BARNEY! YOU DIDN'T GIVE ME A CHANCE TO LOOK AT 'EM
MERCY - WHAT FUNNY LOOKING THINGS THEY ARE - THEY'RE SO SOFT AND MUSHY
LOOK - THEY FIT ME !!
BE CAREFUL OF 'EM, HONEY
I CAN'T IMAGINE A MAN GETTING KNOCKED OUT WITH THESE COMICAL THINGS HOW MUCH DID YOU PAY FOR THEM BARNEY ?
$100.00
HOW MUCH?
$100.00
COPYRIGHT, 1919, BY KING FEATURES SYNDICATE, INC.
DEBECK
10-3

Barney Google at the World's Series—By De Beck

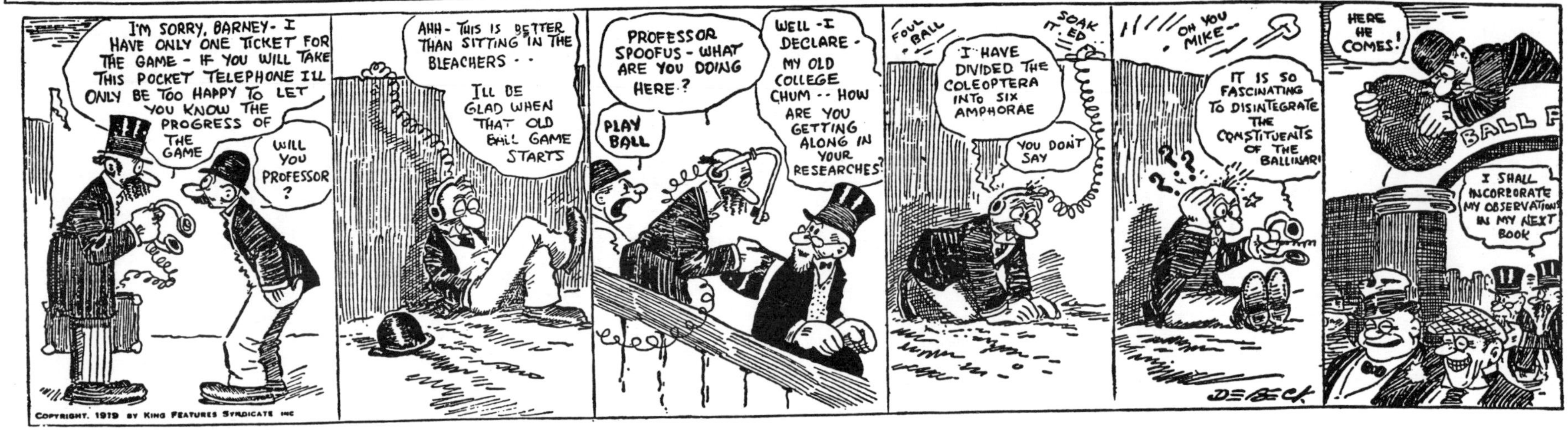

I'M SORRY, BARNEY - I HAVE ONLY ONE TICKET FOR THE GAME - IF YOU WILL TAKE THIS POCKET TELEPHONE I'LL ONLY BE TOO HAPPY TO LET YOU KNOW THE PROGRESS OF THE GAME
WILL YOU PROFESSOR ?
AHH - THIS IS BETTER THAN SITTING IN THE BLEACHERS - -
I'LL BE GLAD WHEN THAT OLD BALL GAME STARTS
PROFESSOR SPOOFUS - WHAT ARE YOU DOING HERE ?
WELL - I DECLARE - MY OLD COLLEGE CHUM - - HOW ARE YOU GETTING ALONG IN YOUR RESEARCHES ?
PLAY BALL
FOUL BALL
SOAK IT, ED
I HAVE DIVIDED THE COLEOPTERA INTO SIX AMPHORAE
YOU DON'T SAY
OH YOU MIKE - -
IT IS SO FASCINATING TO DISINTEGRATE THE CONSTITUENTS OF THE BALLINARI
HERE HE COMES !
BALL P
I SHALL INCORPORATE MY OBSERVATIONS IN MY NEXT BOOK
DE BECK
COPYRIGHT. 1919 BY KING FEATURES SYNDICATE INC

Above: Professor Spoofus offers to give Barney a play-by-play account of the game, from the *Chicago Herald and Examiner*, October 4, 1919. From the Collection of Mark Johnson.

Below: Barney tries to sneak into the World Series in a trunk, from the *Chicago Herald and Examiner*, October 6, 1919. From the Collection of Mark Johnson.

Barney Google at the World's Series—By De Beck

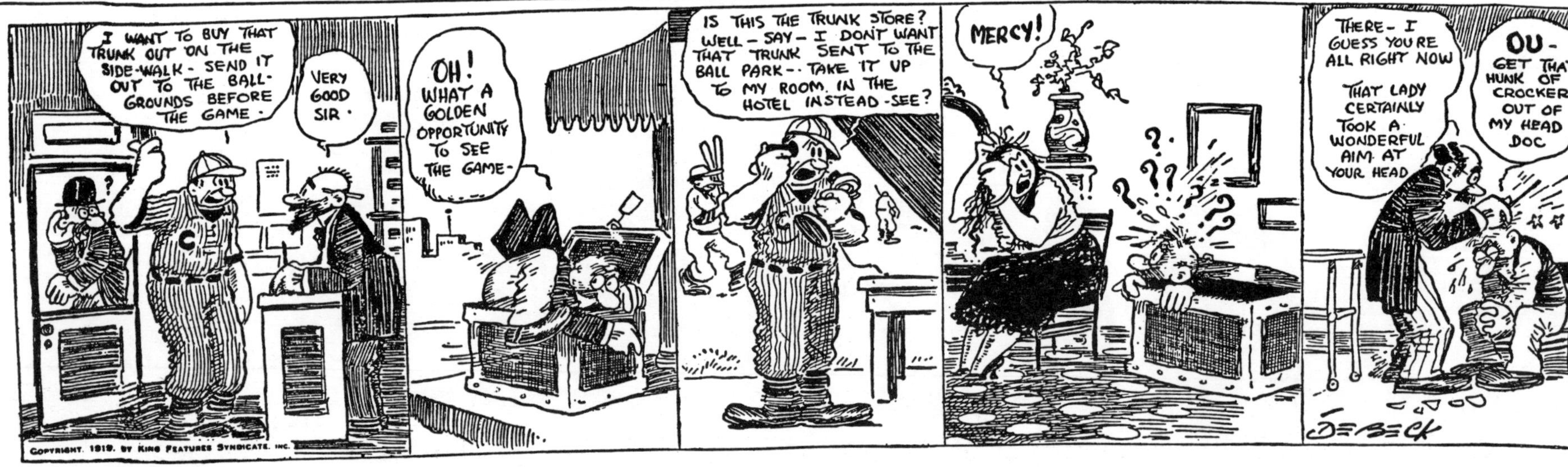

I WANT TO BUY THAT TRUNK OUT ON THE SIDE-WALK - SEND IT OUT TO THE BALL-GROUNDS BEFORE THE GAME .
VERY GOOD SIR .
OH! WHAT A GOLDEN OPPORTUNITY TO SEE THE GAME -
IS THIS THE TRUNK STORE? WELL - SAY - I DON'T WANT THAT TRUNK SENT TO THE BALL PARK - - TAKE IT UP TO MY ROOM. IN THE HOTEL INSTEAD - SEE?
MERCY!
THERE - I GUESS YOU'RE ALL RIGHT NOW
THAT LADY CERTAINLY TOOK A WONDERFUL AIM AT YOUR HEAD
OU - GET THAT HUNK OF CROCKERY OUT OF MY HEAD DOC
DE BECK
COPYRIGHT. 1919. BY KING FEATURES SYNDICATE. INC.

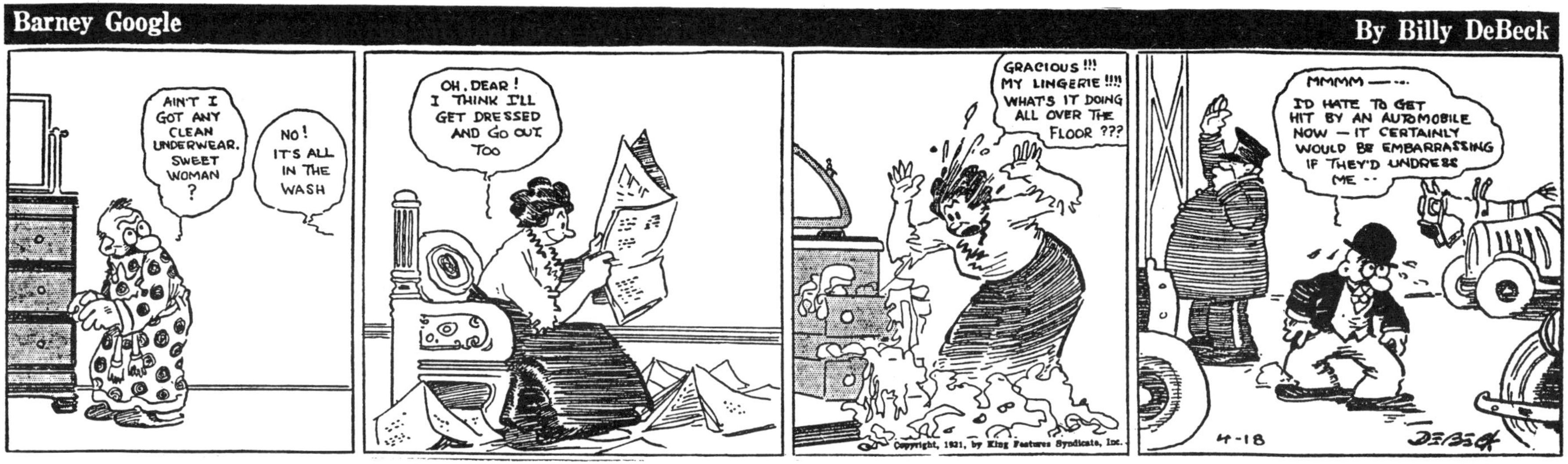
Barney Google
By Billy DeBeck
AIN'T I GOT ANY CLEAN UNDERWEAR, SWEET WOMAN ?
NO! IT'S ALL IN THE WASH
OH, DEAR! I THINK I'LL GET DRESSED AND GO OUT TOO
GRACIOUS!!! MY LINGERIE!!!! WHAT'S IT DOING ALL OVER THE FLOOR ???
MMMM —..
I'D HATE TO GET HIT BY AN AUTOMOBILE NOW — IT CERTAINLY WOULD BE EMBARRASSING IF THEY'D UNDRESS ME --
Copyright, 1921, by King Features Syndicate, Inc.
4-18
DEBECK

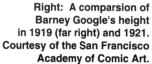

Above: Barney runs out of clean underwear, from the *Chicago Herald and Examiner*, April 18, 1921. From the Collection of Mark Johnson.

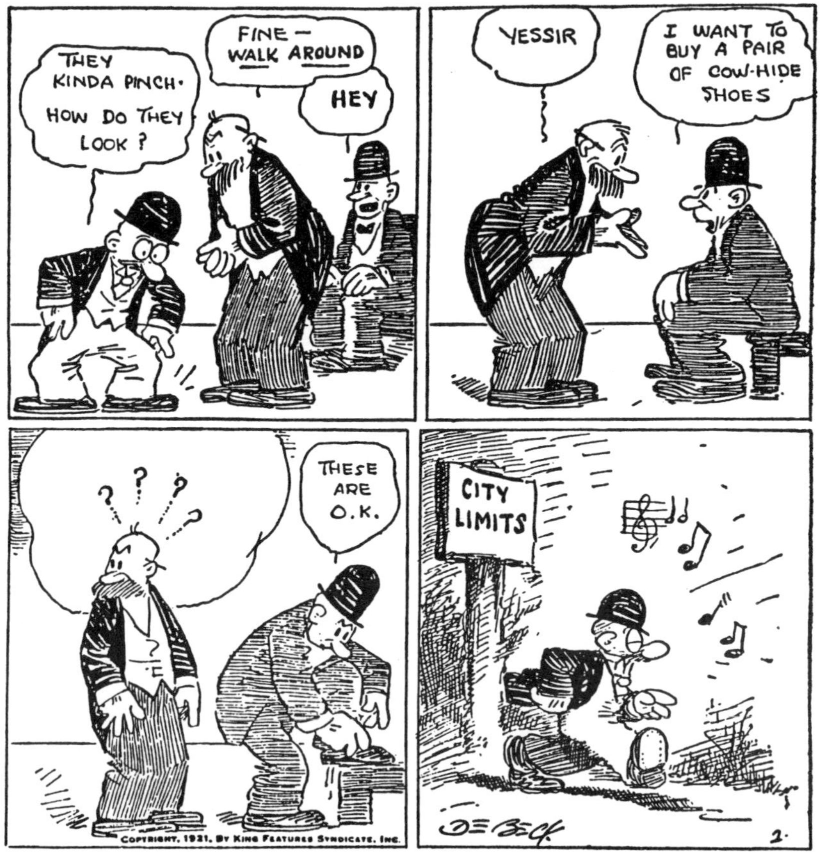
THEY KINDA PINCH. HOW DO THEY LOOK ?
FINE — WALK AROUND
HEY
YESSIR
I WANT TO BUY A PAIR OF COW-HIDE SHOES
? ? ? ?
THESE ARE O.K.
COPYRIGHT, 1921, BY KING FEATURES SYNDICATE, INC.
CITY LIMITS
DEBECK
2.

Left: Barney tries on a new pair of shoes, from the *Chicago Herald and Examiner*, May 9, 1921. From the Collection of Mark Johnson.

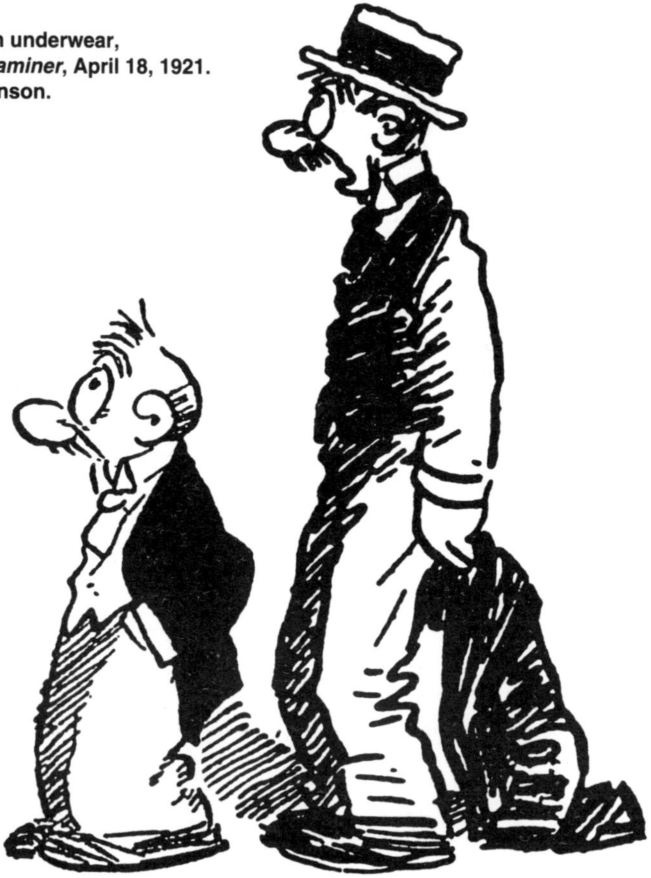

Right: A comparsion of Barney Google's height in 1919 (far right) and 1921. Courtesy of the San Francisco Academy of Comic Art.

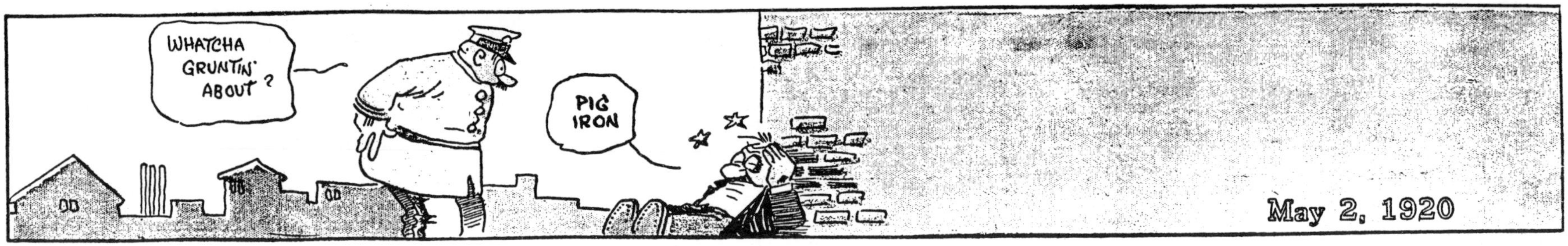
WHATCHA GRUNTIN' ABOUT ?
PIG IRON
May 2, 1920

Barney Google

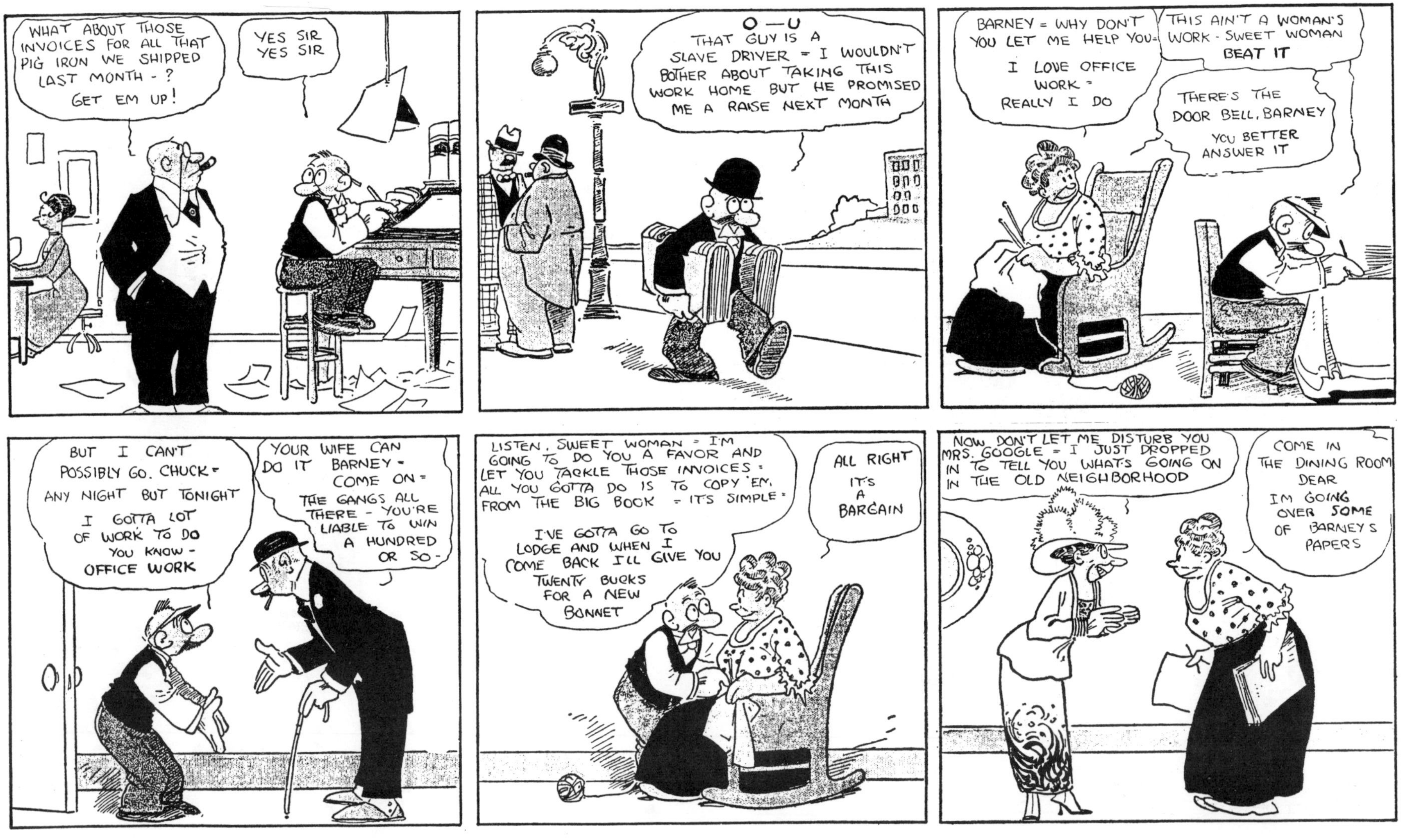
WHAT ABOUT THOSE INVOICES FOR ALL THAT PIG IRON WE SHIPPED LAST MONTH - ? GET EM UP!
YES SIR YES SIR
O — U THAT GUY IS A SLAVE DRIVER = I WOULDN'T BOTHER ABOUT TAKING THIS WORK HOME BUT HE PROMISED ME A RAISE NEXT MONTH
BARNEY = WHY DON'T YOU LET ME HELP YOU = I LOVE OFFICE WORK = REALLY I DO
THIS AIN'T A WOMAN'S WORK - SWEET WOMAN BEAT IT
THERE'S THE DOOR BELL, BARNEY YOU BETTER ANSWER IT
BUT I CAN'T POSSIBLY GO, CHUCK = ANY NIGHT BUT TONIGHT I GOTTA LOT OF WORK TO DO YOU KNOW - OFFICE WORK
YOUR WIFE CAN DO IT BARNEY = COME ON = THE GANGS ALL THERE - YOU'RE LIABLE TO WIN A HUNDRED OR SO -
LISTEN, SWEET WOMAN = I'M GOING TO DO YOU A FAVOR AND LET YOU TACKLE THOSE INVOICES = ALL YOU GOTTA DO IS TO COPY 'EM FROM THE BIG BOOK = IT'S SIMPLE =
I'VE GOTTA GO TO LODGE AND WHEN I COME BACK I'LL GIVE YOU TWENTY BUCKS FOR A NEW BONNET
ALL RIGHT IT'S A BARGAIN
NOW, DON'T LET ME DISTURB YOU MRS. GOOGLE = I JUST DROPPED IN TO TELL YOU WHAT'S GOING ON IN THE OLD NEIGHBORHOOD
COME IN THE DINING ROOM DEAR I'M GOING OVER SOME OF BARNEY'S PAPERS

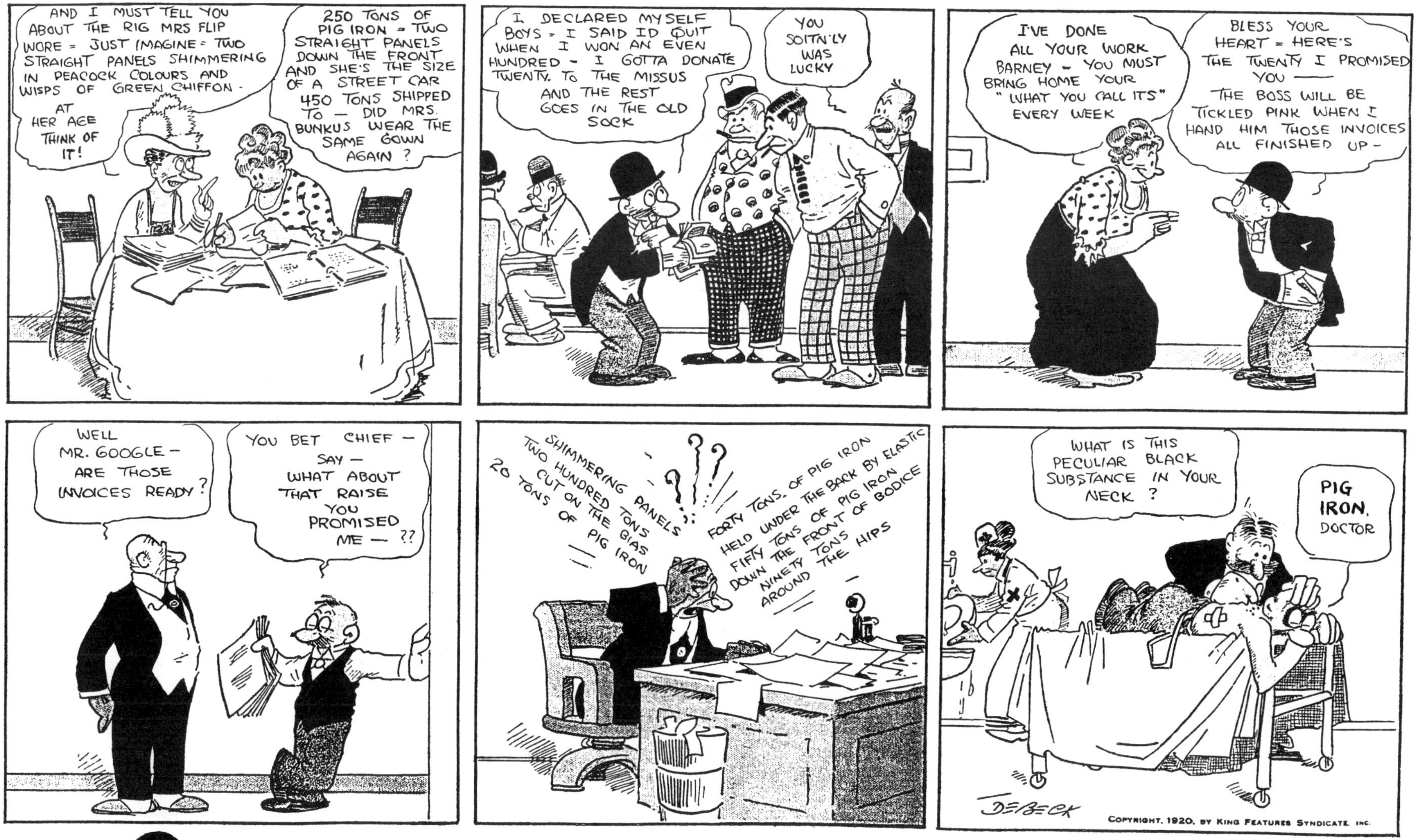
AND I MUST TELL YOU ABOUT THE RIG MRS FLIP WORE = JUST IMAGINE = TWO STRAIGHT PANELS SHIMMERING IN PEACOCK COLOURS AND WISPS OF GREEN CHIFFON -
AT HER AGE THINK OF IT!
250 TONS OF PIG IRON = TWO STRAIGHT PANELS DOWN THE FRONT AND SHE'S THE SIZE OF A STREET CAR 450 TONS SHIPPED TO — DID MRS. BUNKUS WEAR THE SAME GOWN AGAIN ?
I DECLARED MYSELF BOYS = I SAID ID QUIT WHEN I WON AN EVEN HUNDRED - I GOTTA DONATE TWENTY. TO THE MISSUS AND THE REST GOES IN THE OLD SOCK
YOU SOITN'LY WAS LUCKY
I'VE DONE ALL YOUR WORK BARNEY - YOU MUST BRING HOME YOUR "WHAT YOU CALL ITS" EVERY WEEK
BLESS YOUR HEART = HERE'S THE TWENTY I PROMISED YOU — THE BOSS WILL BE TICKLED PINK WHEN I HAND HIM THOSE INVOICES ALL FINISHED UP -
WELL MR. GOOGLE - ARE THOSE INVOICES READY?
YOU BET CHIEF - SAY - WHAT ABOUT THAT RAISE YOU PROMISED ME — ??
SHIMMERING PANELS TWO HUNDRED TONS CUT ON THE BIAS 20 TONS OF PIG IRON
FORTY TONS OF PIG IRON HELD UNDER THE BACK BY ELASTIC FIFTY TONS OF PIG IRON DOWN THE FRONT OF BODICE NINETY TONS AROUND THE HIPS
WHAT IS THIS PECULIAR BLACK SUBSTANCE IN YOUR NECK ?
PIG IRON, DOCTOR
DE BECK
COPYRIGHT, 1920, BY KING FEATURES SYNDICATE, INC.

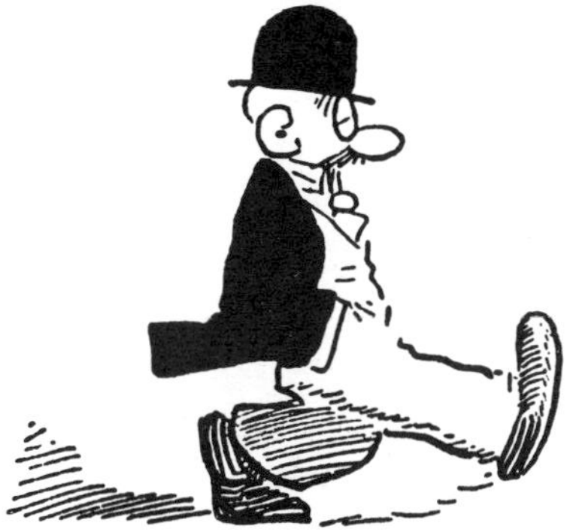

Opposite page and above: One of the earliest "Barney Google" Sunday pages, from the *Indianapolis Star*, May 2, 1920. Courtesy of the San Francisco Academy of Comic Art.

Bughouse Fables

King Features Syndicate launched a one-panel cartoon entitled "Bughouse Fables" on December 24, 1920, which was produced by Billy DeBeck from 1920 to 1926. A "bughouse" was a term commonly used to refer to a mental institution. Therefore "Bughouse Fables" meant the kind of preposterous fiction only a crazy person would believe. In DeBeck's panel, kids asked for castor oil, husbands loved their mother-in-laws and cartoonists demanded a cut in salary. In 1923, a novelty song written by Clarence Gaskill and inspired by DeBeck's creation included the refrain: "My landlord is a kind old gent, never thinks about the rent, last month it was overdue, he said I'll take care of you."

"Bughouse Fables" was unsigned in the beginning, but by the summer of 1921, the signature "Barney Google" began appearing in the panels. It wasn't until 1924 that DeBeck started signing his own name regularly.

Similar to TAD Dorgan's "Indoor/Outdoor Sports," "Bughouse Fables" featured observations of everday people doing foolish things and contained references to current fashions and trends. DeBeck used this feature to popularize words and phrases such as "heebie jeebies," "so I took the $50,000" and "the guy with the green gloves."

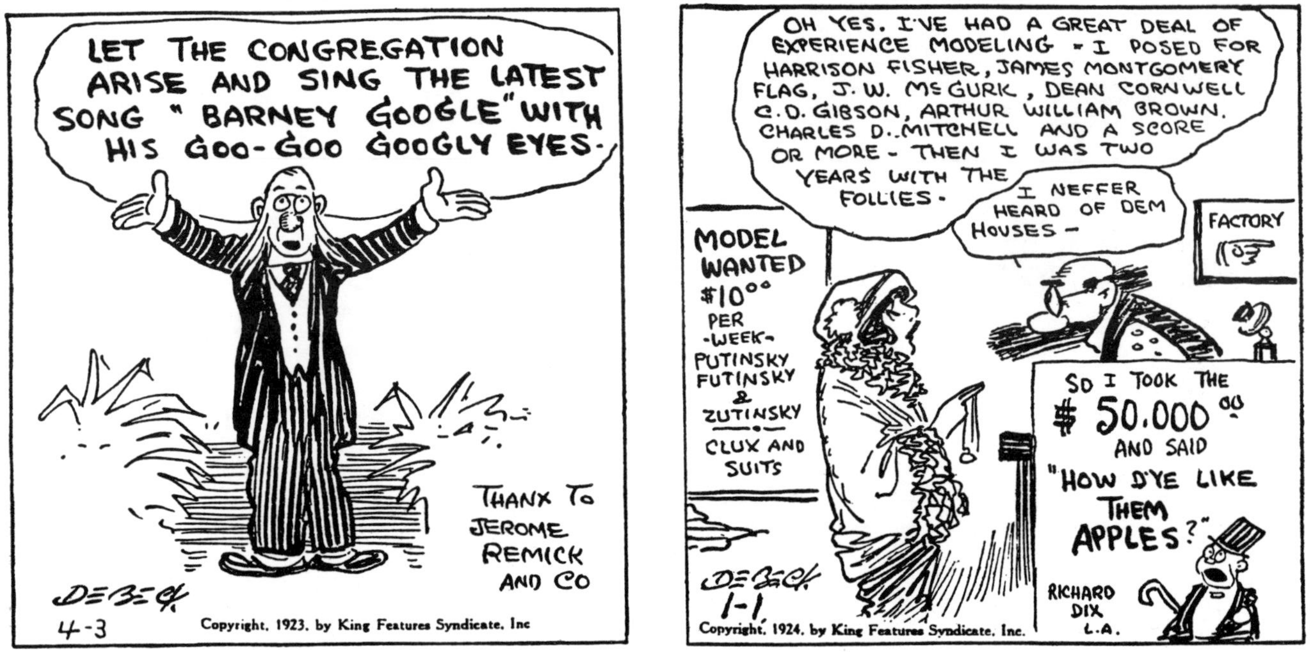

LET THE CONGREGATION ARISE AND SING THE LATEST SONG " BARNEY GOOGLE" WITH HIS GOO-GOO GOOGLY EYES.
THANX TO JEROME REMICK AND CO
DEBECK
4-3
Copyright, 1923, by King Features Syndicate, Inc.
OH YES. I'VE HAD A GREAT DEAL OF EXPERIENCE MODELING - I POSED FOR HARRISON FISHER, JAMES MONTGOMERY FLAG, J. W. MCGURK, DEAN CORNWELL C. D. GIBSON, ARTHUR WILLIAM BROWN, CHARLES D. MITCHELL AND A SCORE OR MORE - THEN I WAS TWO YEARS WITH THE FOLLIES.
I NEFFER HEARD OF DEM HOUSES -
FACTORY
MODEL WANTED $10.00 PER -WEEK- PUTINSKY FUTINSKY & ZUTINSKY CLUX AND SUITS
SO I TOOK THE $ 50,000.00 AND SAID "HOW D'YE LIKE THEM APPLES?"
DEBECK
1-1
RICHARD DIX L.A.
Copyright, 1924, by King Features Syndicate, Inc.

"Bughouse Fables" panels by Billy DeBeck, 1923, 1924 and 1925. From the Collection of Ron Goulart.

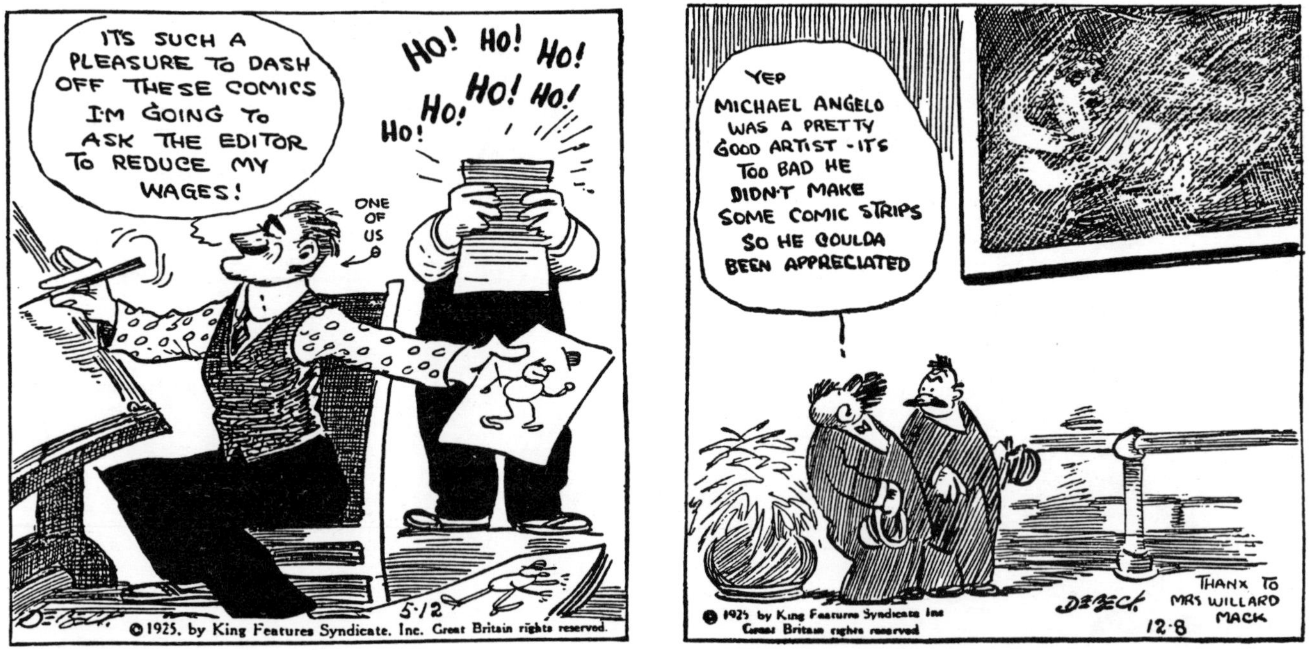

IT'S SUCH A PLEASURE TO DASH OFF THESE COMICS I'M GOING TO ASK THE EDITOR TO REDUCE MY WAGES!
HO! HO! HO! HO! HO! HO! HO!
ONE OF US
5-12
©1925, by King Features Syndicate, Inc. Great Britain rights reserved.
YEP MICHAEL ANGELO WAS A PRETTY GOOD ARTIST - ITS TOO BAD HE DIDN'T MAKE SOME COMIC STRIPS SO HE COULDA BEEN APPRECIATED
DEBECK
THANX TO MRS WILLARD MACK
12-8

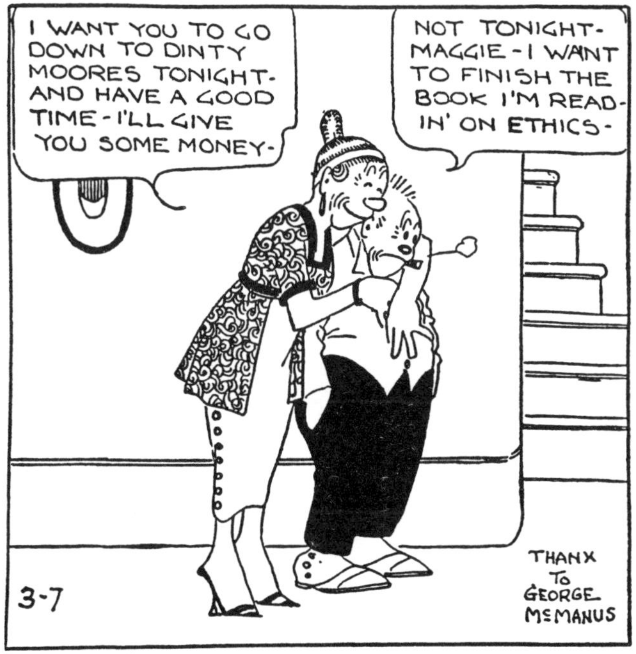
I WANT YOU TO GO DOWN TO DINTY MOORES TONIGHT- AND HAVE A GOOD TIME-I'LL GIVE YOU SOME MONEY-
NOT TONIGHT- MAGGIE-I WANT TO FINISH THE BOOK I'M READ-IN' ON ETHICS-
3-7
THANX TO GEORGE McMANUS

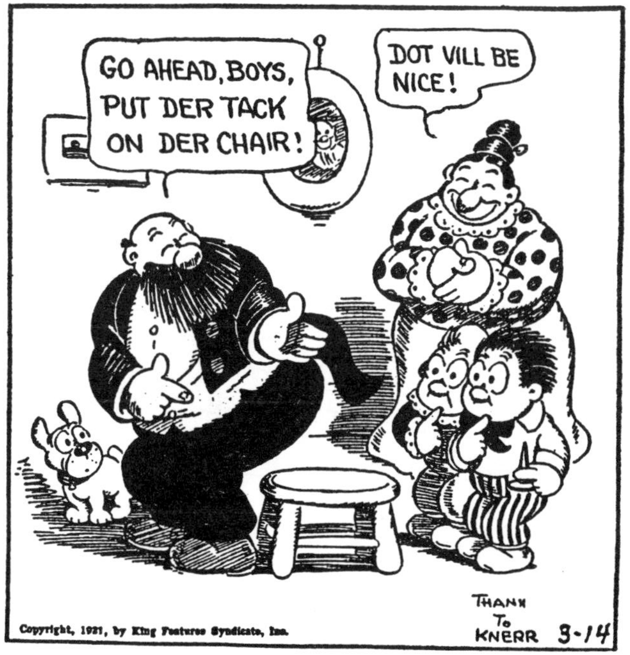
GO AHEAD, BOYS, PUT DER TACK ON DER CHAIR!
DOT VILL BE NICE!
THANX TO KNERR 3-14

"Bughouse Fables" panels by guest artists, 1921. From the Collection of Ron Goulart.

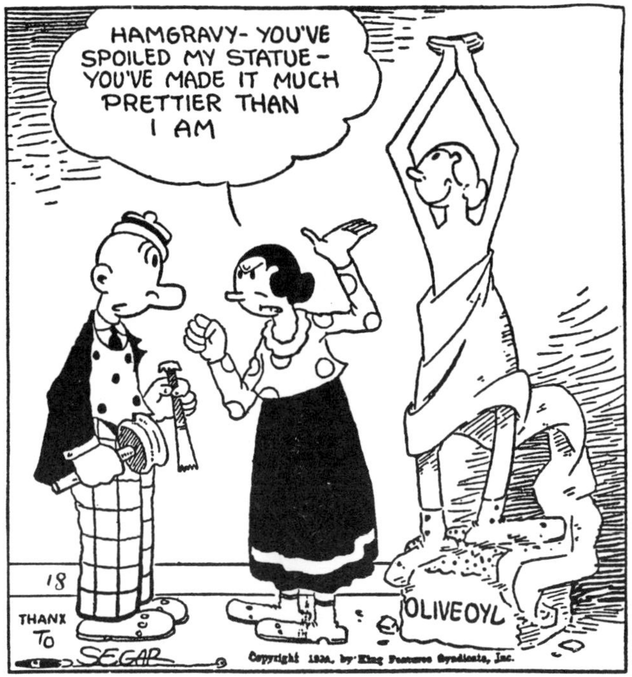
HAMGRAVY- YOU'VE SPOILED MY STATUE- YOU'VE MADE IT MUCH PRETTIER THAN I AM
OLIVE OYL
18
THANX TO SEGAR

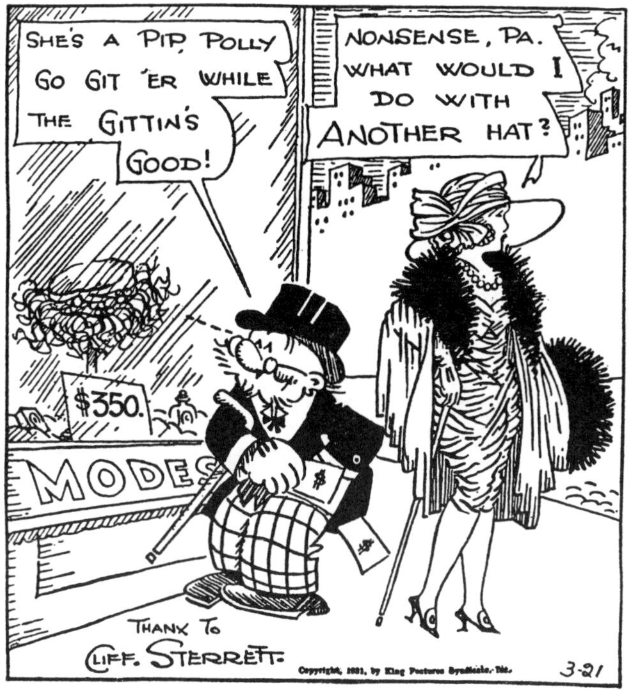
SHE'S A PIP POLLY GO GIT 'ER WHILE THE GITTIN'S GOOD!
NONSENSE, PA. WHAT WOULD I DO WITH ANOTHER HAT?
$350.
MODES
THANX TO CLIFF. STERRETT.
3-21

In the spring of 1921, "Bughouse Fables" ran at the top of the comics page in the *Chicago Herald and Examiner* between "Bringing Up Father" by George McManus and "Barney Google" by Billy DeBeck. The panel was still unsigned at this point, although the drawing style looks like DeBeck's. In March and April 1921, many of the King Features Syndicate cartoonists took turns doing "Bughouse Fables" for a day. Reproduced here are panels by George McManus ("Bringing Up Father"), Harold Knerr ("The Katzenjammer Kids"), E.C. Segar ("Thimble Theater", which later introduced Popeye) and Cliff Sterrett ("Polly and Her Pals"). Other King artists, including Walter Hoban ("Jerry on the Job") and Harry Hershfield ("Abie the Agent") also did guest spots.

The "Barney Google" Sunday page, which began in 1920, ran as a full page in most newspapers. In the early episodes, DeBeck did horizontal "lead-in" or "thow-away" panels featuring Barney at the top of his Sunday pages. On January 17, 1926, he replaced the usual "topper" strip with a "Bughouse Fables" sequence in a horizontal format. This experiment did no last long however, for on May 16, 1926, DeBeck launched the long-running "Parlor, Bedroom & Sink" feature which introduced one of his most memorable characters, Bunky. Paul Fung, who had assisted DeBeck on "Bughouse Fables" since 1923, took over the panel in 1926, and it was continued by a number of artists until November 13, 1937.

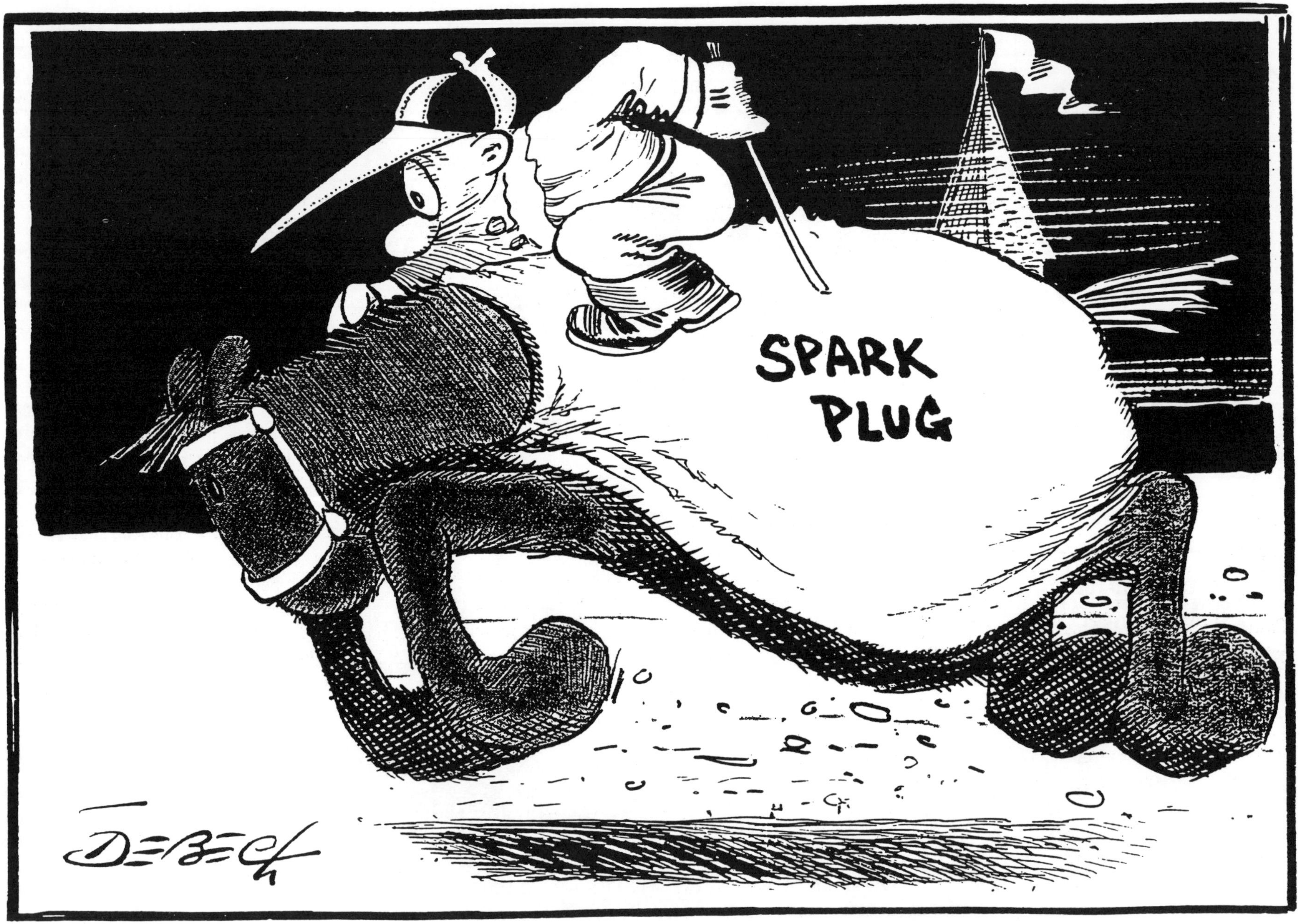
SPARK PLUG
DEBECK

Above: Cover artwork by Billy DeBeck, from *Comic Monthly*, November, 1922. From the Collection of Sy & Sandy Schechter.

Spark Plug
Barney's Brown-Eyed Baby

Barney Google, a perennial loser, had a change of fortune on July 17, 1922. In that day's episode of Billy DeBeck's comic strip, a wealthy-looking gentleman gave Barney a sad-faced race horse named "Spark Plug" to repay Barney for breaking his fall when he was thrown out of the Pastime Jockey Club. (This historic strip is reprinted at the top of the following page). Over the course of the next month, Barney managed to scrape together the $300 required to enter his new nag in the Abadaba Handicap, and became $50,000 richer when Spark Plug miraculously won the race!

Who was this strange, bow-legged animal wearing a seedy horse-blanket with his name written on the side? In the introduction to a book collection of the Abadaba Handicap strips published in November, 1922, DeBeck wrote: "For the benefit of those who don't know it, I wish to say that 'Spark Plug's' pedigree dates back to the wooden horse used by the Ancient Greeks as a ruse to enter the city of Troy. His ancestors carried Alexander, Caesar and Napoleon into the battles of history, and in recent centuries the 'Spark Plug' strain carried the destinies of nations on their broad backs, even up to the day of Paul Revere in the American Revolution."

Spark Plug also changed the destiny of both Barney Google and Billy DeBeck. Barney started wearing silk top hats and smoking fancy Havana cigars, and Billy DeBeck rapidly became one of the most famous and highly-paid cartoonists in America. In 1923, Billy Rose's song about Barney and Sparky with the unforgettable hook "Barney Google with his goo-goo googly eyes," was a smash hit and earned Rose $60,000 that year alone.

Like the Yellow Kid before him and Snoopy and Garfield today, Spark Plug became a merchandising bonanza. "Spark Plug, I am happy to say, has caught on," wrote DeBeck in 1924. "All over the United States you find stuffed Spark Plugs and Spark Plug games and Spark Plug drums and Spark Plug balloons and Spark Plug tin pails. And there is a Spark Plug play on the road. The only thing that is lacking is a Spark Plug grand opera."

The secret to DeBeck's newfound success was in the relationship between Barney and his horse. It was a classic love-hate affair. Although Barney hated to lose a race, which he did more often than not, he always forgave Spark Plug and cherished his companionship. He cared more for him than any man, woman or child. Sparky brought out the human side of Barney.

On the following pages, the Abadaba Handicap story, which ran from July 17 to August 19, 1922, is reproduced from *Comic Monthly*, published by Embee Distributing Inc., New York, N.Y., November, 1922. From the Collection of Sy & Sandy Schechter.

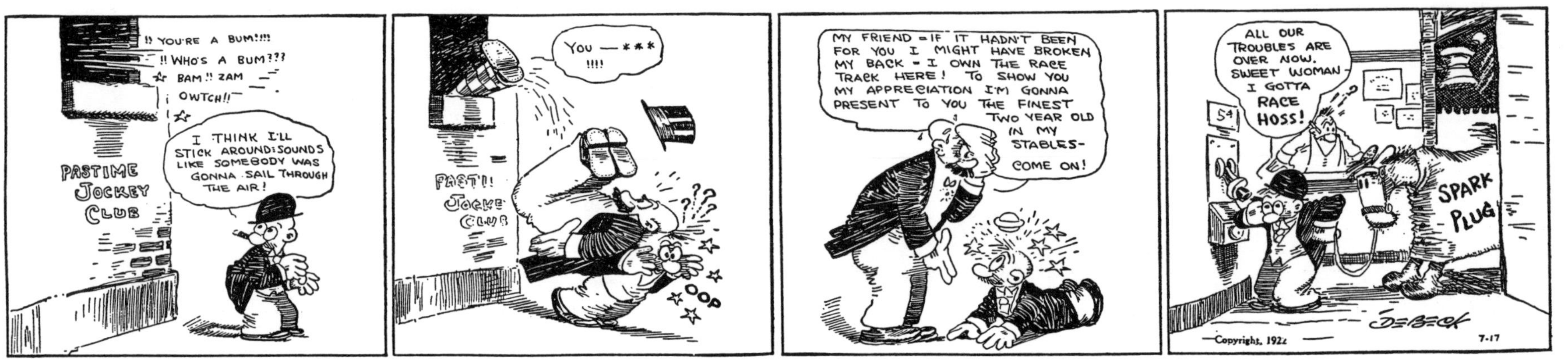
!! YOU'RE A BUM!!!!
!! WHO'S A BUM???
BAM!! ZAM
OWTCH!!
I THINK I'LL STICK AROUND: SOUNDS LIKE SOMEBODY WAS GONNA SAIL THROUGH THE AIR!
PASTIME JOCKEY CLUB
YOU — * * * !!!!
OOP
MY FRIEND = IF IT HADN'T BEEN FOR YOU I MIGHT HAVE BROKEN MY BACK = I OWN THE RACE TRACK HERE! TO SHOW YOU MY APPRECIATION I'M GONNA PRESENT TO YOU THE FINEST TWO YEAR OLD IN MY STABLES — COME ON!
ALL OUR TROUBLES ARE OVER NOW. SWEET WOMAN I GOTTA RACE HOSS!
5¢
SPARK PLUG
DEBECK
—Copyright, 1922
7-17

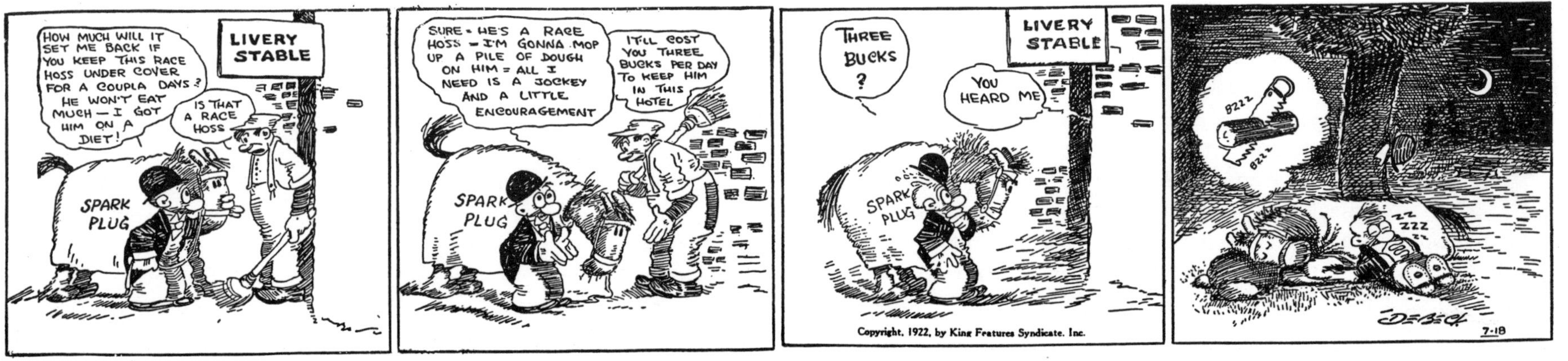
HOW MUCH WILL IT SET ME BACK IF YOU KEEP THIS RACE HOSS UNDER COVER FOR A COUPLA DAYS? HE WON'T EAT MUCH — I GOT HIM ON A DIET!
LIVERY STABLE
IS THAT A RACE HOSS
SPARK PLUG
SURE = HE'S A RACE HOSS = I'M GONNA MOP UP A PILE OF DOUGH ON HIM = ALL I NEED IS A JOCKEY AND A LITTLE ENCOURAGEMENT
IT'LL COST YOU THREE BUCKS PER DAY TO KEEP HIM IN THIS HOTEL
SPARK PLUG
THREE BUCKS ?
LIVERY STABLE
YOU HEARD ME
SPARK PLUG
Copyright, 1922, by King Features Syndicate. Inc.
BZZZ
ZZZ
DEBECK
7-18

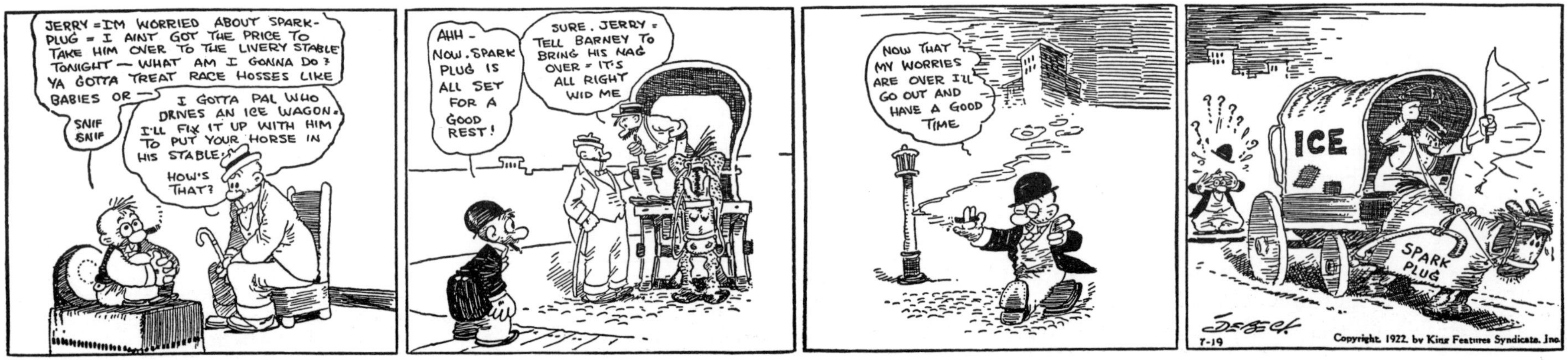
JERRY = I'M WORRIED ABOUT SPARK-PLUG = I AINT GOT THE PRICE TO TAKE HIM OVER TO THE LIVERY STABLE TONIGHT — WHAT AM I GONNA DO? YA GOTTA TREAT RACE HOSSES LIKE BABIES OR —
SNIF SNIF
I GOTTA PAL WHO DRIVES AN ICE WAGON. I'LL FIX IT UP WITH HIM TO PUT YOUR HORSE IN HIS STABLE. HOW'S THAT?
AHH — NOW, SPARK PLUG IS ALL SET FOR A GOOD REST!
SURE, JERRY = TELL BARNEY TO BRING HIS NAG OVER = IT'S ALL RIGHT WID ME
NOW THAT MY WORRIES ARE OVER I'LL GO OUT AND HAVE A GOOD TIME
ICE
SPARK PLUG
DEBECK
7-19
Copyright, 1922, by King Features Syndicate. Inc.

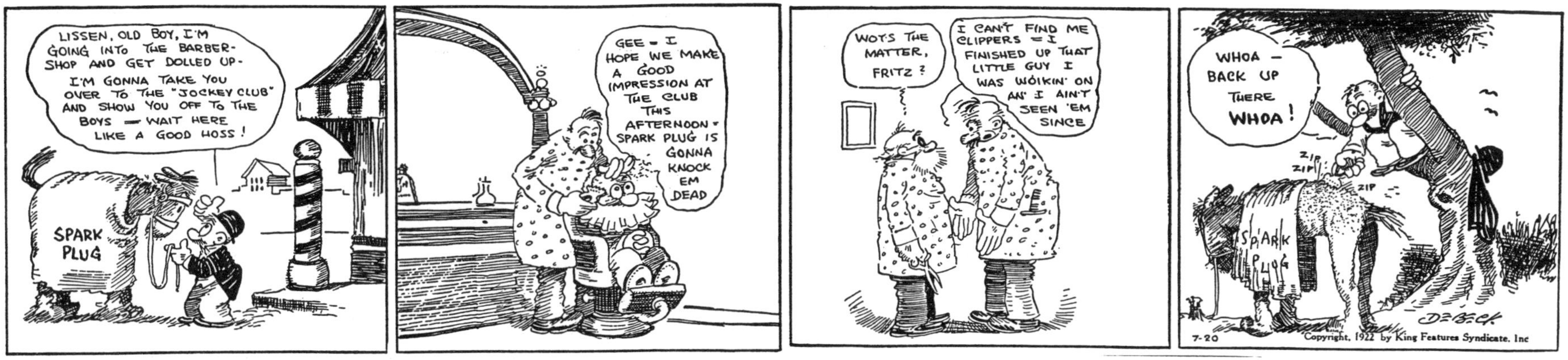
LISSEN, OLD BOY, I'M GOING INTO THE BARBER-SHOP AND GET DOLLED UP- I'M GONNA TAKE YOU OVER TO THE "JOCKEY CLUB" AND SHOW YOU OFF TO THE BOYS — WAIT HERE LIKE A GOOD HOSS!
SPARK PLUG
GEE — I HOPE WE MAKE A GOOD IMPRESSION AT THE CLUB THIS AFTERNOON — SPARK PLUG IS GONNA KNOCK EM DEAD
WOT'S THE MATTER, FRITZ?
I CAN'T FIND ME CLIPPERS — I FINISHED UP THAT LITTLE GUY I WAS WOIKIN' ON AN' I AIN'T SEEN 'EM SINCE
WHOA — BACK UP THERE WHOA!
ZIP ZIP
ZIP
SPARK PLUG
DEBECK
7-20
Copyright, 1922 by King Features Syndicate, Inc

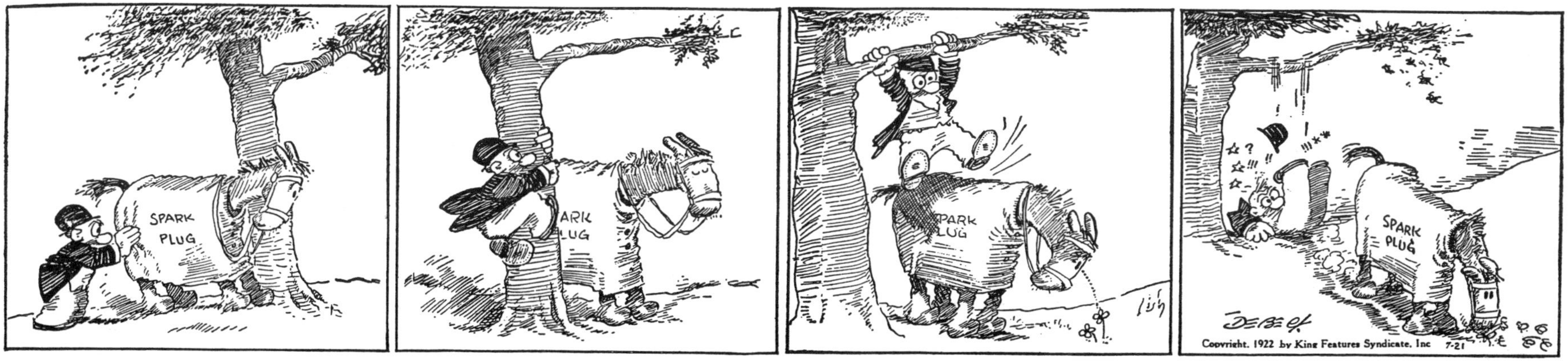
SPARK PLUG
ARK LUG
SPARK PLUG
SPARK PLUG
DEBECK
Copyright, 1922 by King Features Syndicate, Inc
7-21

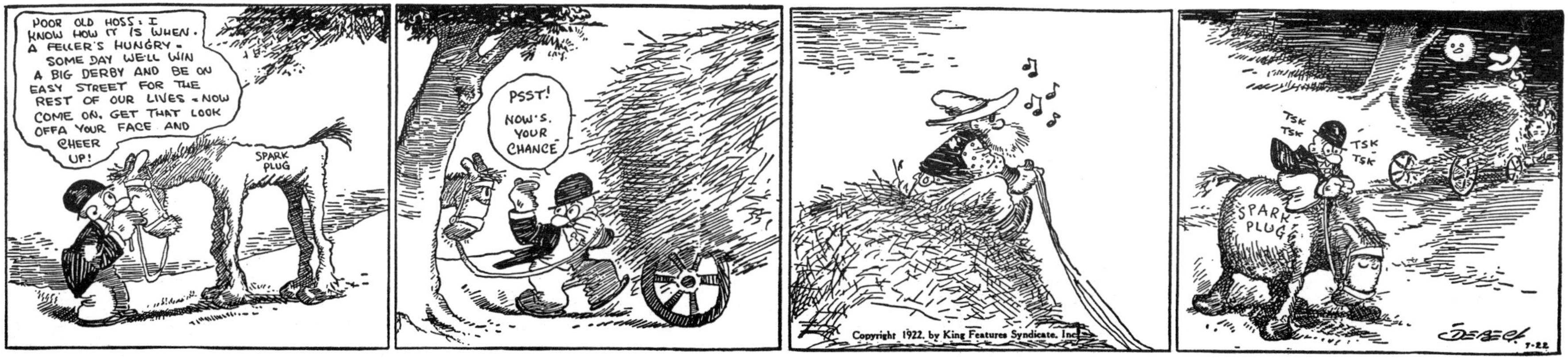
POOR OLD HOSS: I KNOW HOW IT IS WHEN A FELLER'S HUNGRY — SOME DAY WE'LL WIN A BIG DERBY AND BE ON EASY STREET FOR THE REST OF OUR LIVES — NOW COME ON, GET THAT LOOK OFFA YOUR FACE AND CHEER UP!
SPARK PLUG
PSST! NOW'S YOUR CHANCE
Copyright 1922, by King Features Syndicate, Inc
TSK TSK
TSK TSK
SPARK PLUG
DEBECK
7-22

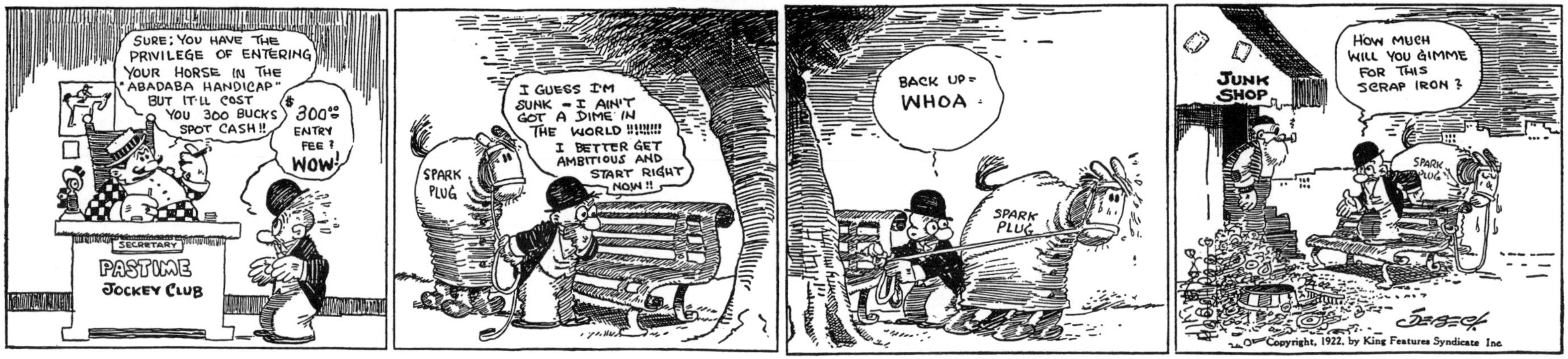
SURE; YOU HAVE THE PRIVILEGE OF ENTERING YOUR HORSE IN THE "ABADABA HANDICAP" BUT IT·LL COST YOU 300 BUCKS SPOT CASH!!
SECRETARY
PASTIME JOCKEY CLUB
$300.00 ENTRY FEE? WOW!
I GUESS I'M SUNK = I AIN'T GOT A DIME IN THE WORLD!!!!!!!! I BETTER GET AMBITIOUS AND START RIGHT NOW!!
SPARK PLUG
BACK UP= WHOA =
SPARK PLUG
JUNK SHOP
HOW MUCH WILL YOU GIMME FOR THIS SCRAP IRON?
SPARK PLUG
DE BECK
Copyright, 1922, by King Features Syndicate Inc.

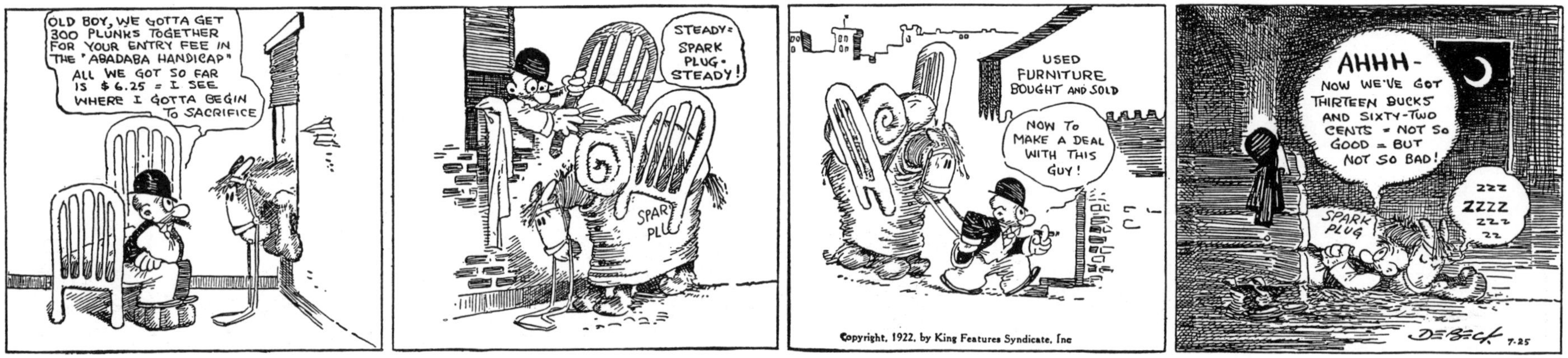
OLD BOY, WE GOTTA GET 300 PLUNKS TOGETHER FOR YOUR ENTRY FEE IN THE "ABADABA HANDICAP" ALL WE GOT SO FAR IS $6.25 = I SEE WHERE I GOTTA BEGIN TO SACRIFICE
STEADY= SPARK PLUG. STEADY!
USED FURNITURE BOUGHT AND SOLD
NOW TO MAKE A DEAL WITH THIS GUY!
Copyright, 1922, by King Features Syndicate, Inc
AHHH- NOW WE'VE GOT THIRTEEN BUCKS AND SIXTY-TWO CENTS = NOT SO GOOD = BUT NOT SO BAD!
ZZZ ZZZZ ZZZ ZZ
SPARK PLUG
DE BECK 7-25

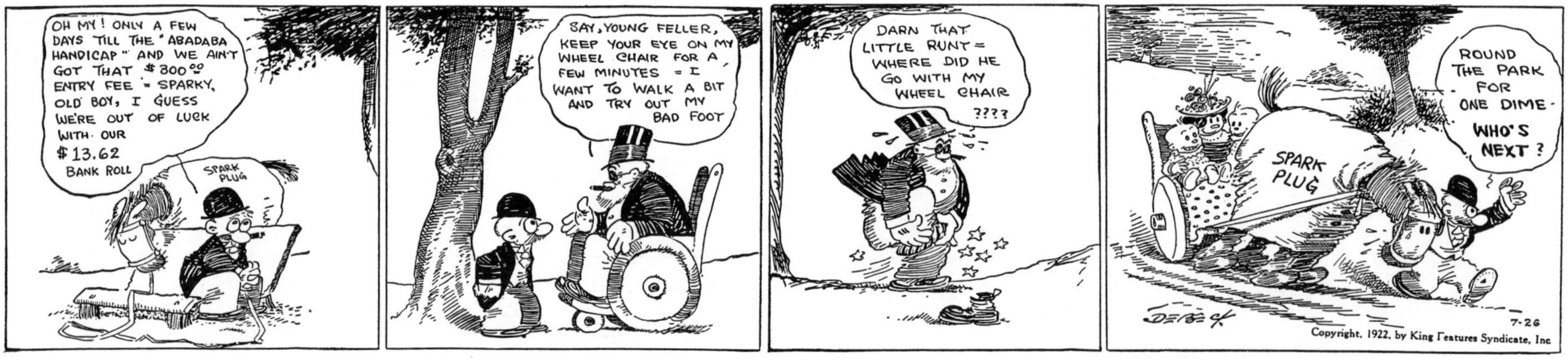
OH MY! ONLY A FEW DAYS TILL THE "ABADABA HANDICAP" AND WE AIN'T GOT THAT $300.00 ENTRY FEE = SPARKY, OLD BOY, I GUESS WE'RE OUT OF LUCK WITH OUR $13.62 BANK ROLL
SPARK PLUG
SAY, YOUNG FELLER, KEEP YOUR EYE ON MY WHEEL CHAIR FOR A FEW MINUTES = I WANT TO WALK A BIT AND TRY OUT MY BAD FOOT
DARN THAT LITTLE RUNT = WHERE DID HE GO WITH MY WHEEL CHAIR ????
ROUND THE PARK FOR ONE DIME- WHO'S NEXT?
SPARK PLUG
DE BECK 7-26
Copyright, 1922, by King Features Syndicate, Inc

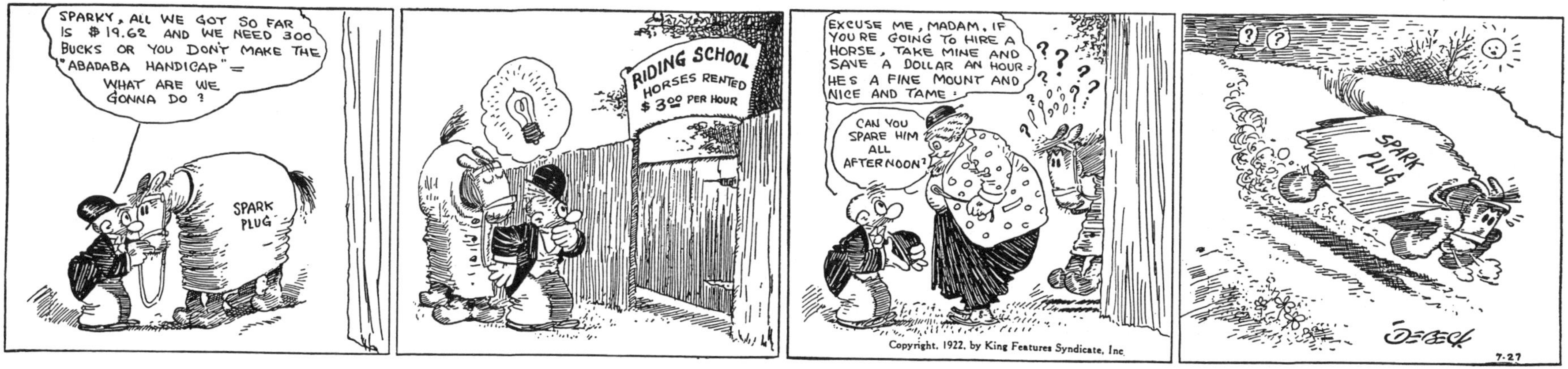
SPARKY, ALL WE GOT SO FAR IS $19.62 AND WE NEED 300 BUCKS OR YOU DON'T MAKE THE "ABADABA HANDICAP" = WHAT ARE WE GONNA DO ?
SPARK PLUG
RIDING SCHOOL
HORSES RENTED $3.00 PER HOUR
EXCUSE ME, MADAM, IF YOU'RE GOING TO HIRE A HORSE, TAKE MINE AND SAVE A DOLLAR AN HOUR = HE'S A FINE MOUNT AND NICE AND TAME =
CAN YOU SPARE HIM ALL AFTERNOON?
Copyright, 1922, by King Features Syndicate, Inc.
SPARK PLUG
DE BECK
7-27

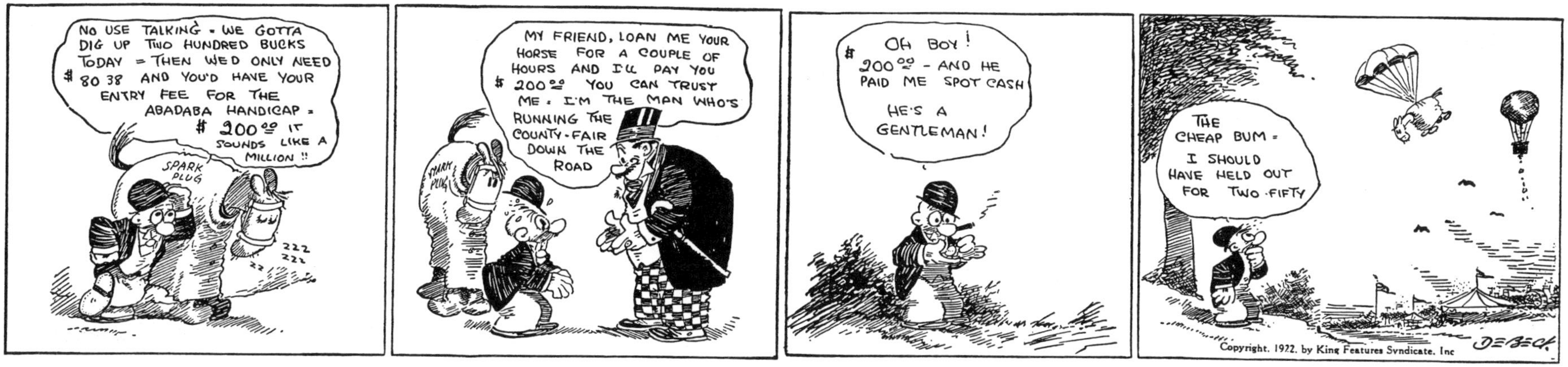
NO USE TALKING = WE GOTTA DIG UP TWO HUNDRED BUCKS TODAY = THEN WE'D ONLY NEED $80.38 AND YOU'D HAVE YOUR ENTRY FEE FOR THE ABADABA HANDICAP = $200.00 IT SOUNDS LIKE A MILLION !!
SPARK PLUG
ZZZ ZZZ ZZ
MY FRIEND, LOAN ME YOUR HORSE FOR A COUPLE OF HOURS AND I'LL PAY YOU $200.00 YOU CAN TRUST ME = I'M THE MAN WHO'S RUNNING THE COUNTY-FAIR DOWN THE ROAD
SPARK PLUG
OH BOY! $200.00 - AND HE PAID ME SPOT CASH
HE'S A GENTLEMAN!
THE CHEAP BUM = I SHOULD HAVE HELD OUT FOR TWO-FIFTY
Copyright, 1922, by King Features Syndicate, Inc
DE BECK

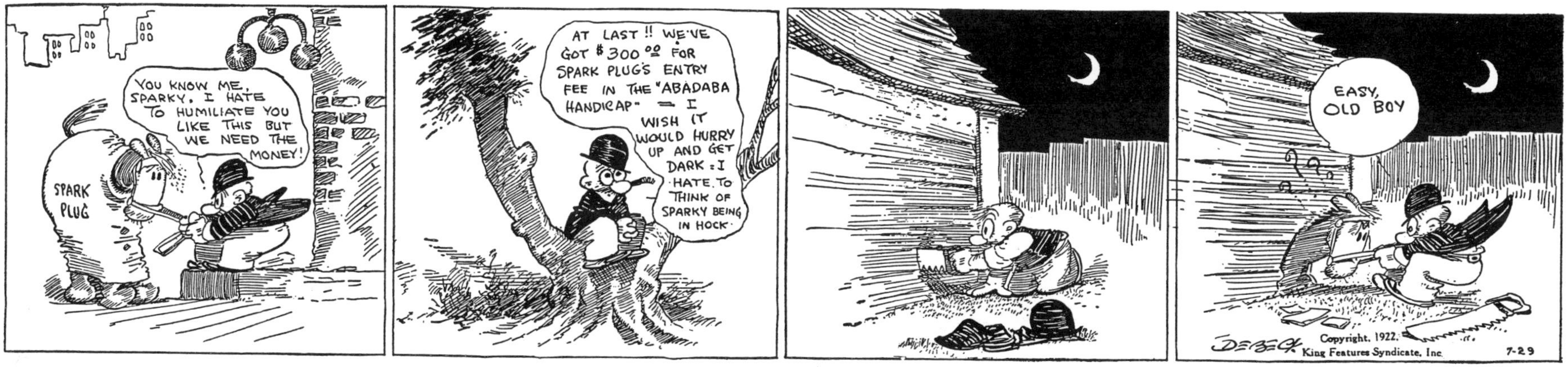
YOU KNOW ME, SPARKY, I HATE TO HUMILIATE YOU LIKE THIS BUT WE NEED THE MONEY!
SPARK PLUG
AT LAST!! WE'VE GOT $300.00 FOR SPARK PLUG'S ENTRY FEE IN THE "ABADABA HANDICAP" = I WISH IT WOULD HURRY UP AND GET DARK = I HATE TO THINK OF SPARKY BEING IN HOCK.
EASY, OLD BOY
DE BECK
Copyright, 1922, King Features Syndicate, Inc.
7-29

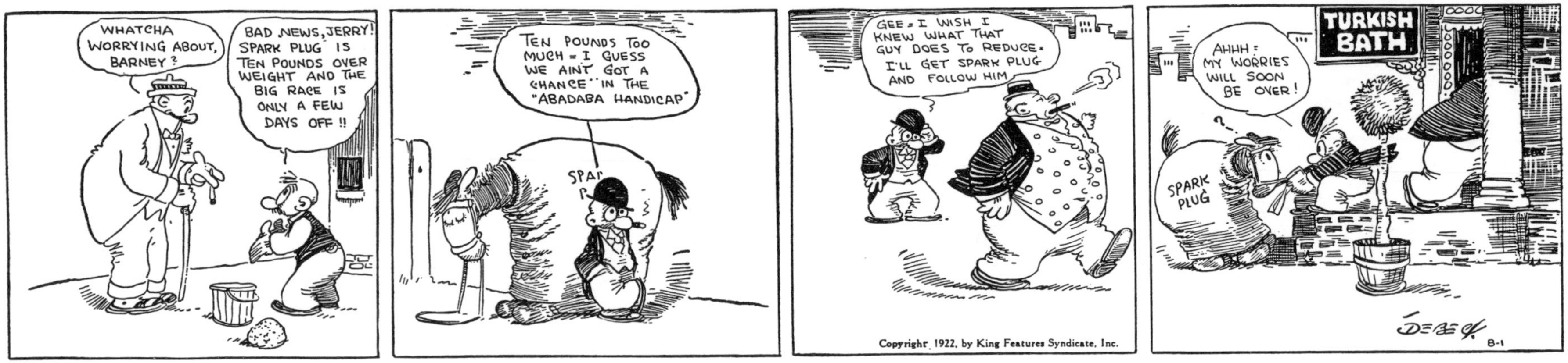
WHATCHA WORRYING ABOUT, BARNEY?
BAD NEWS, JERRY! SPARK PLUG IS TEN POUNDS OVER WEIGHT AND THE BIG RACE IS ONLY A FEW DAYS OFF !!
TEN POUNDS TOO MUCH = I GUESS WE AIN'T GOT A CHANCE IN THE "ABADABA HANDICAP"
GEE = I WISH I KNEW WHAT THAT GUY DOES TO REDUCE - I'LL GET SPARK PLUG AND FOLLOW HIM
TURKISH BATH
AHHH = MY WORRIES WILL SOON BE OVER!
SPARK PLUG
Copyright 1922, by King Features Syndicate, Inc.
DE BECK 8-1

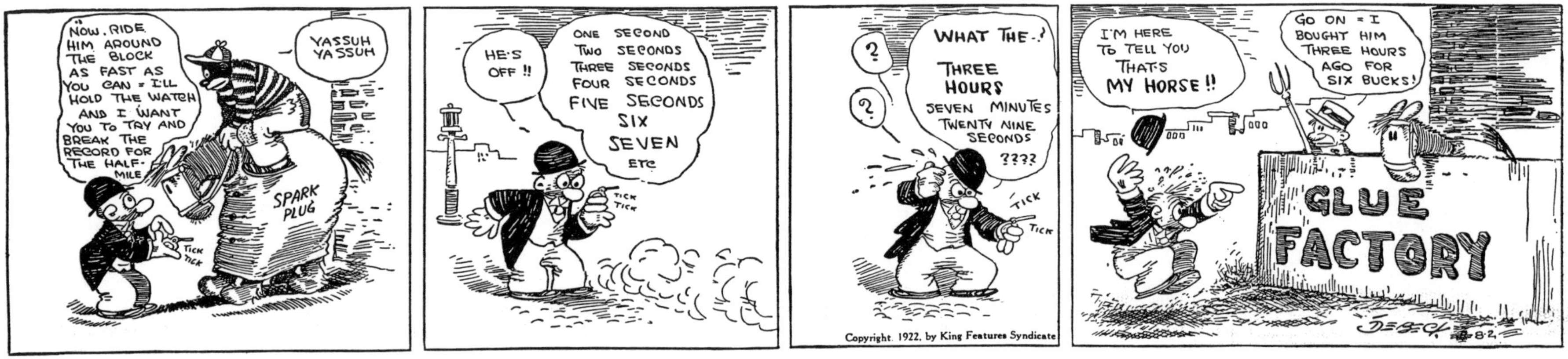
NOW, RIDE HIM AROUND THE BLOCK AS FAST AS YOU CAN = I'LL HOLD THE WATCH AND I WANT YOU TO TRY AND BREAK THE RECORD FOR THE HALF-MILE
YASSUH YASSUH
SPARK PLUG
TICK TICK
HE'S OFF !!
ONE SECOND TWO SECONDS THREE SECONDS FOUR SECONDS FIVE SECONDS SIX SEVEN ETC
?
?
WHAT THE -?
THREE HOURS SEVEN MINUTES TWENTY NINE SECONDS ????
TICK TICK
I'M HERE TO TELL YOU THAT'S MY HORSE !!
GO ON = I BOUGHT HIM THREE HOURS AGO FOR SIX BUCKS!
GLUE FACTORY
Copyright 1922, by King Features Syndicate
DE BECK 8-2

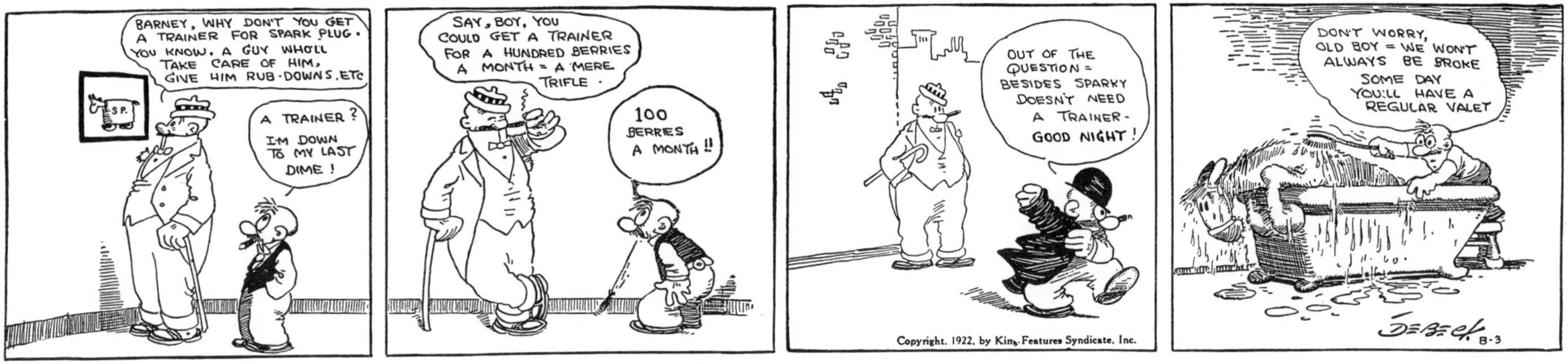
BARNEY, WHY DON'T YOU GET A TRAINER FOR SPARK PLUG - YOU KNOW, A GUY WHO'LL TAKE CARE OF HIM, GIVE HIM RUB-DOWNS, ETC
S.P.
A TRAINER? I'M DOWN TO MY LAST DIME!
SAY, BOY, YOU COULD GET A TRAINER FOR A HUNDRED BERRIES A MONTH = A MERE TRIFLE.
100 BERRIES A MONTH !!
OUT OF THE QUESTION = BESIDES SPARKY DOESN'T NEED A TRAINER - GOOD NIGHT!
DON'T WORRY, OLD BOY = WE WON'T ALWAYS BE BROKE SOME DAY YOU'LL HAVE A REGULAR VALET
Copyright 1922, by King Features Syndicate, Inc.
DE BECK 8-3

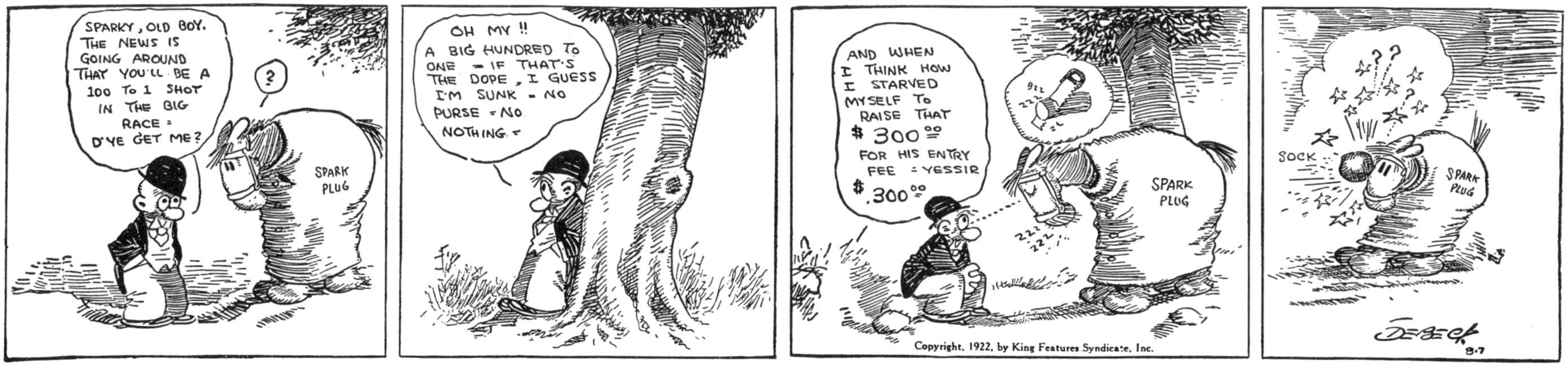
SPARKY, OLD BOY. THE NEWS IS GOING AROUND THAT YOU'LL BE A 100 TO 1 SHOT IN THE BIG RACE = D'YE GET ME?
?
SPARK PLUG
OH MY !! A BIG HUNDRED TO ONE = IF THAT'S THE DOPE, I GUESS I'M SUNK - NO PURSE = NO NOTHING =
AND WHEN I THINK HOW I STARVED MYSELF TO RAISE THAT $300.00 FOR HIS ENTRY FEE = YESSIR $.300.00
SPARK PLUG
Copyright, 1922, by King Features Syndicate, Inc.
SOCK
SPARK PLUG
DEBECK 8-7

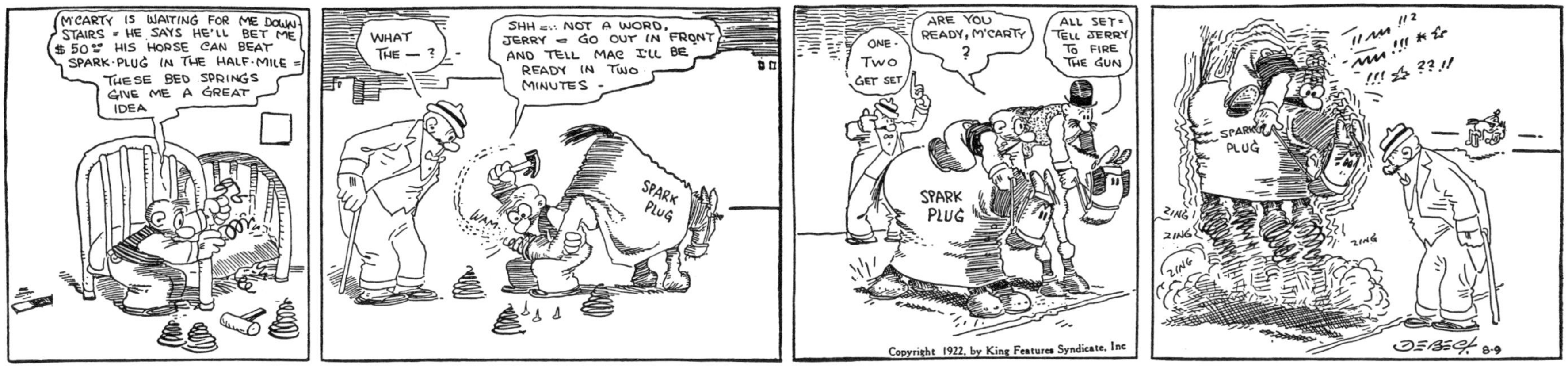
M'CARTY IS WAITING FOR ME DOWN-STAIRS = HE SAYS HE'LL BET ME $50.00 HIS HORSE CAN BEAT SPARK-PLUG IN THE HALF-MILE = THESE BED SPRINGS GIVE ME A GREAT IDEA
WHAT THE — ?
SHH =.. NOT A WORD, JERRY = GO OUT IN FRONT AND TELL MAC I'LL BE READY IN TWO MINUTES -
SPARK PLUG
ONE - TWO GET SET
ARE YOU READY, M'CARTY ?
ALL SET = TELL JERRY TO FIRE THE GUN
SPARK PLUG
Copyright 1922, by King Features Syndicate, Inc
SPARK PLUG
ZING
ZING
ZING
ZING
DEBECK 8-9

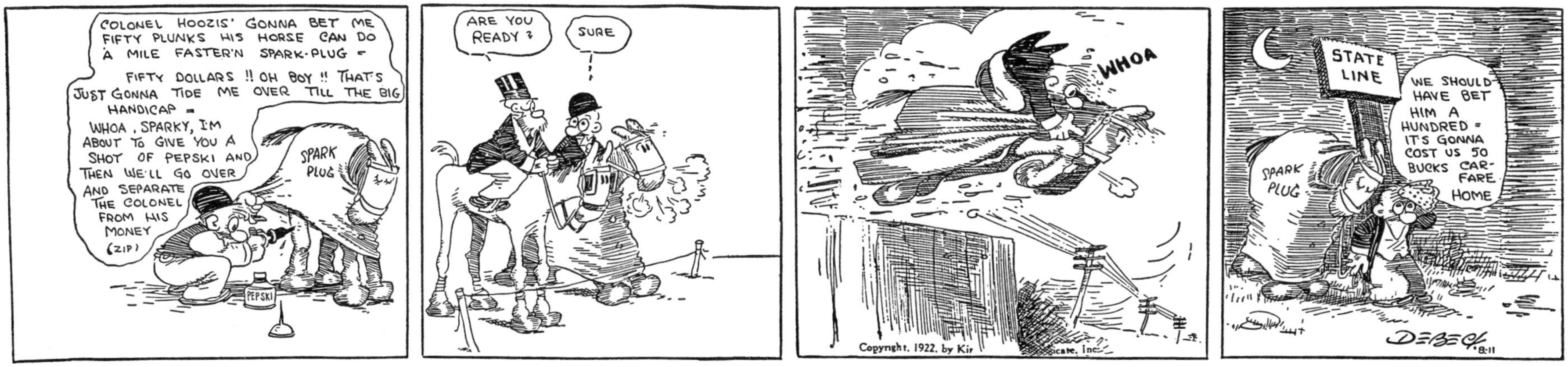
COLONEL HOOZIS' GONNA BET ME FIFTY PLUNKS HIS HORSE CAN DO A MILE FASTER'N SPARK-PLUG = FIFTY DOLLARS !! OH BOY !! THAT'S JUST GONNA TIDE ME OVER TILL THE BIG HANDICAP =
WHOA, SPARKY, I'M ABOUT TO GIVE YOU A SHOT OF PEPSKI AND THEN WE'LL GO OVER AND SEPARATE THE COLONEL FROM HIS MONEY (ZIP)
SPARK PLUG
PEPSKI
ARE YOU READY ?
SURE
WHOA
Copyright, 1922, by Kir icate, Inc.
STATE LINE
WE SHOULD HAVE BET HIM A HUNDRED = IT'S GONNA COST US 50 BUCKS CAR-FARE HOME
SPARK PLUG
DEBECK 8-11

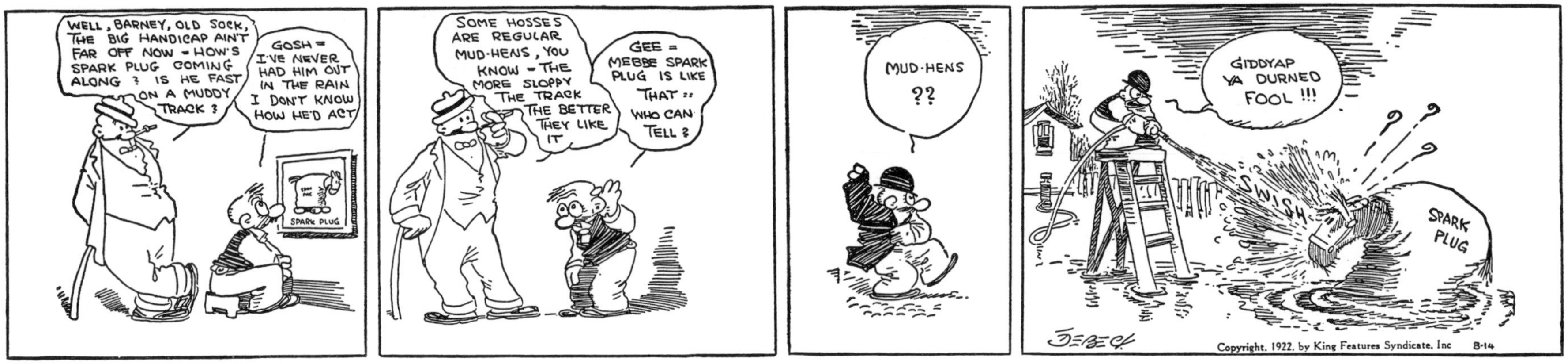
WELL, BARNEY, OLD SOCK, THE BIG HANDICAP AIN'T FAR OFF NOW - HOW'S SPARK PLUG COMING ALONG ? IS HE FAST ON A MUDDY TRACK ?
GOSH = I'VE NEVER HAD HIM OUT IN THE RAIN I DON'T KNOW HOW HE'D ACT
SPARK PLUG
SOME HOSSES ARE REGULAR MUD-HENS, YOU KNOW - THE MORE SLOPPY THE TRACK THE BETTER THEY LIKE IT
GEE = MEBBE SPARK PLUG IS LIKE THAT :: WHO CAN TELL ?
MUD-HENS ??
GIDDYAP YA DURNED FOOL !!!
SWISH
SPARK PLUG
DEBECK
Copyright, 1922, by King Features Syndicate, Inc
8-14

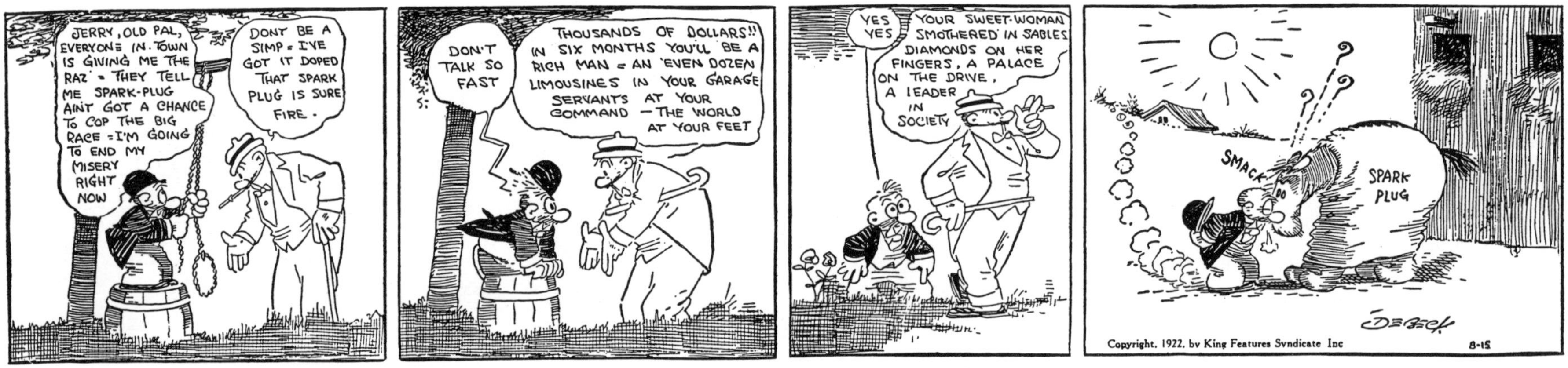
JERRY, OLD PAL, EVERYONE IN TOWN IS GIVING ME THE RAZ - THEY TELL ME SPARK-PLUG AIN'T GOT A CHANCE TO COP THE BIG RACE = I'M GOING TO END MY MISERY RIGHT NOW
DONT BE A SIMP = I'VE GOT IT DOPED THAT SPARK PLUG IS SURE FIRE.
DON'T TALK SO FAST
THOUSANDS OF DOLLARS!! IN SIX MONTHS YOU'LL BE A RICH MAN = AN EVEN DOZEN LIMOUSINES IN YOUR GARAGE SERVANTS AT YOUR COMMAND - THE WORLD AT YOUR FEET
YES YES
YOUR SWEET WOMAN SMOTHERED IN SABLES DIAMONDS ON HER FINGERS, A PALACE ON THE DRIVE, A LEADER IN SOCIETY
SMACK
SPARK PLUG
DEBECK
Copyright, 1922, by King Features Syndicate Inc
8-15

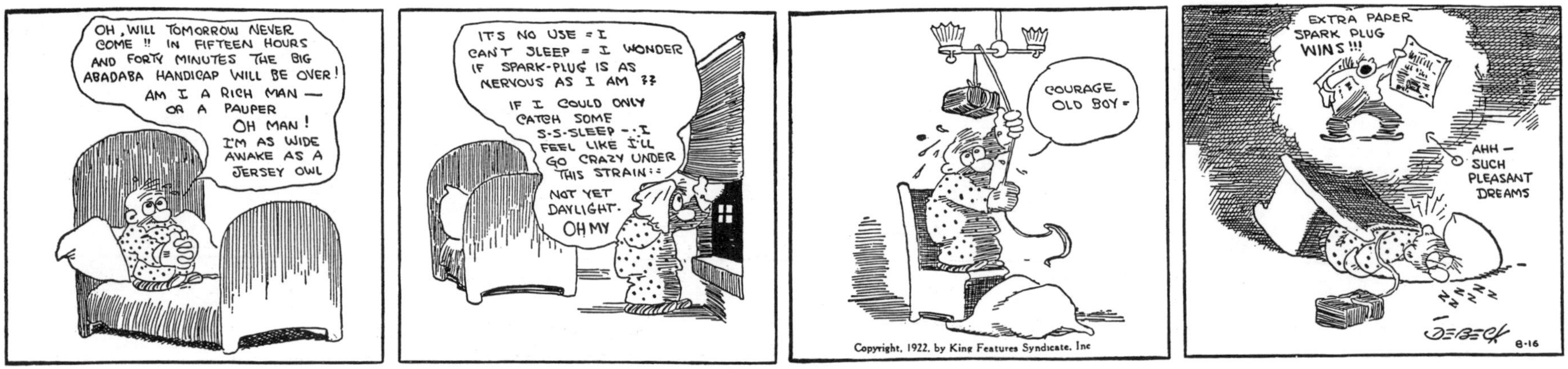
OH, WILL TOMORROW NEVER COME !! IN FIFTEEN HOURS AND FORTY MINUTES THE BIG ABADABA HANDICAP WILL BE OVER! AM I A RICH MAN — OR A PAUPER OH MAN! I'M AS WIDE AWAKE AS A JERSEY OWL
IT'S NO USE = I CAN'T SLEEP = I WONDER IF SPARK-PLUG IS AS NERVOUS AS I AM ?? IF I COULD ONLY CATCH SOME S-S-SLEEP - I FEEL LIKE I'LL GO CRAZY UNDER THIS STRAIN ::
NOT YET DAYLIGHT. OH MY
COURAGE OLD BOY =
Copyright, 1922, by King Features Syndicate, Inc
EXTRA PAPER SPARK PLUG WINS !!!
AHH - SUCH PLEASANT DREAMS
DEBECK
8-16

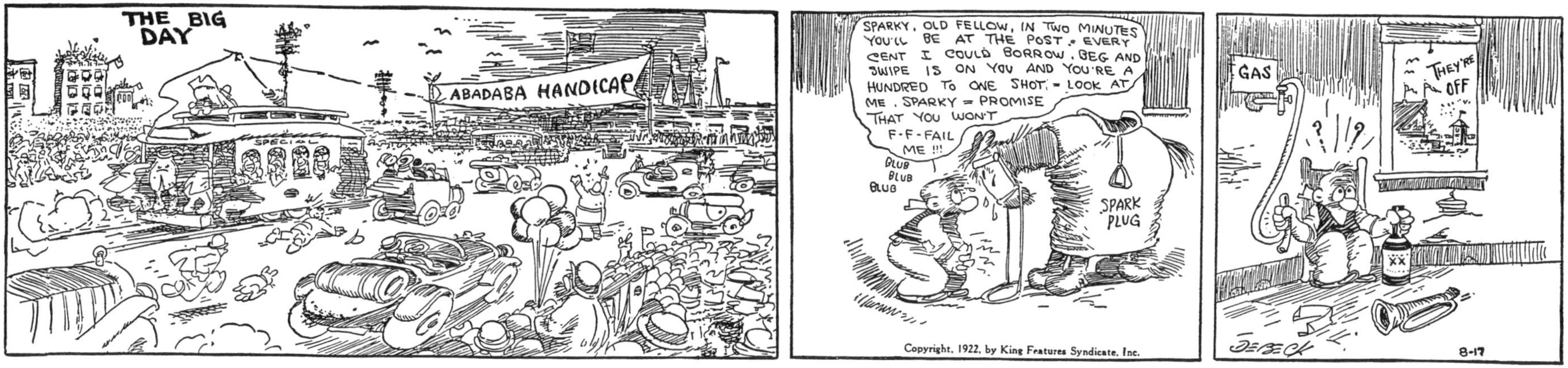
THE BIG DAY
ABADABA HANDICAP
SPECIAL
SPARKY, OLD FELLOW, IN TWO MINUTES YOU'LL BE AT THE POST = EVERY CENT I COULD BORROW, BEG AND SWIPE IS ON YOU AND YOU'RE A HUNDRED TO ONE SHOT. = LOOK AT ME. SPARKY = PROMISE THAT YOU WON'T F-F-FAIL ME !!!
BLUB BLUB BLUB
SPARK PLUG
Copyright, 1922, by King Features Syndicate, Inc.
GAS
THEY'RE OFF
? ? !?
XX
DEBECK
8-17

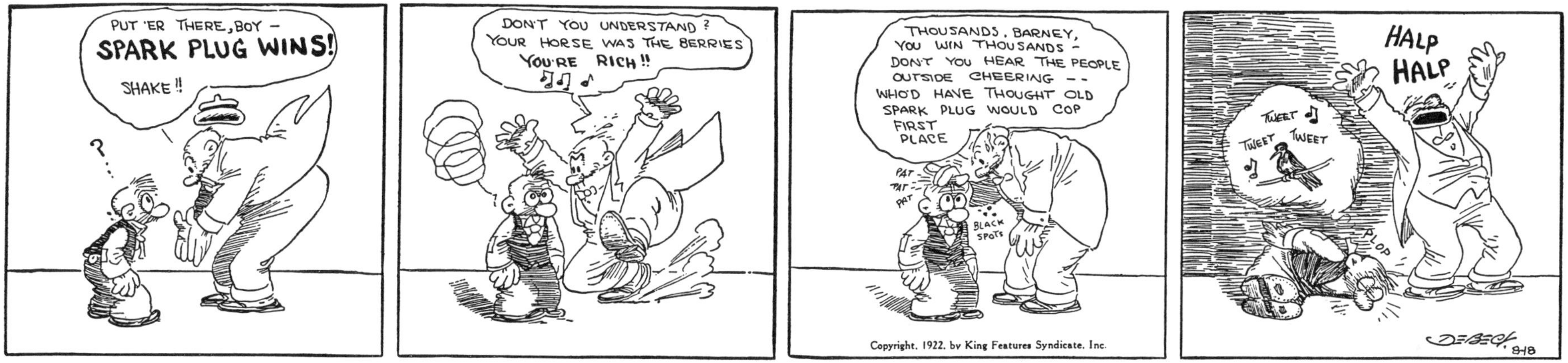
PUT 'ER THERE, BOY - SPARK PLUG WINS!
SHAKE !!
?
DON'T YOU UNDERSTAND ? YOUR HORSE WAS THE BERRIES YOU'RE RICH !!
THOUSANDS, BARNEY, YOU WIN THOUSANDS - DON'T YOU HEAR THE PEOPLE OUTSIDE CHEERING -- WHO'D HAVE THOUGHT OLD SPARK PLUG WOULD COP FIRST PLACE
PAT PAT PAT
BLACK SPOTS
Copyright, 1922, by King Features Syndicate, Inc.
HALP HALP
TWEET TWEET TWEET
PLOP
DEBECK
8-18

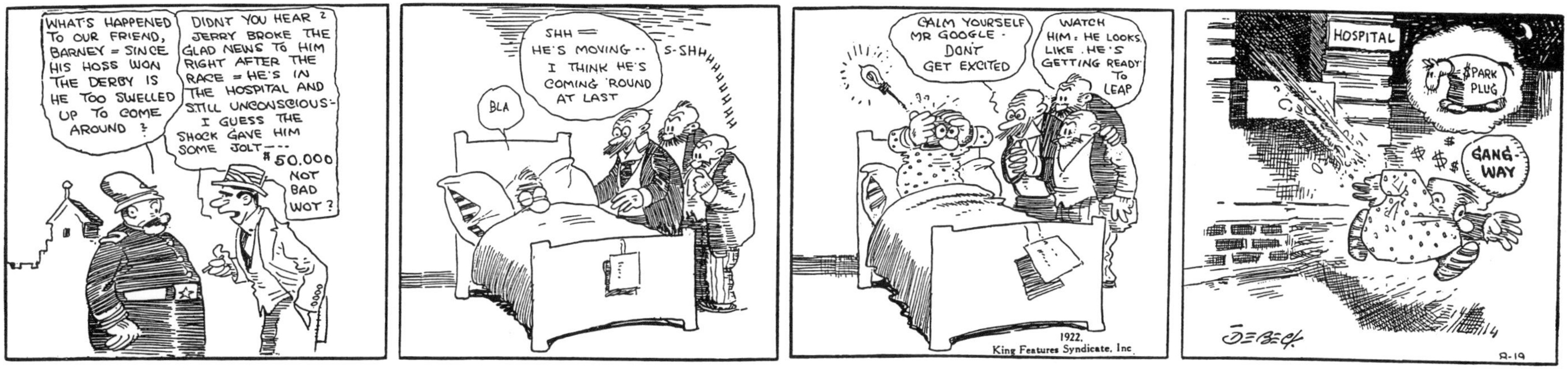
WHAT'S HAPPENED TO OUR FRIEND, BARNEY = SINCE HIS HOSS WON THE DERBY IS HE TOO SWELLED UP TO COME AROUND ?
DIDNT YOU HEAR ? JERRY BROKE THE GLAD NEWS TO HIM RIGHT AFTER THE RACE = HE'S IN THE HOSPITAL AND STILL UNCONSCIOUS - I GUESS THE SHOCK GAVE HIM SOME JOLT --- $50,000 NOT BAD WOT ?
BLA
SHH = HE'S MOVING -- I THINK HE'S COMING 'ROUND AT LAST
S-SHHHHHHHH
CALM YOURSELF MR GOOGLE - DON'T GET EXCITED
WATCH HIM: HE LOOKS LIKE HE'S GETTING READY TO LEAP
1922, King Features Syndicate, Inc.
HOSPITAL
$PARK PLUG
GANG WAY
DEBECK
8-19

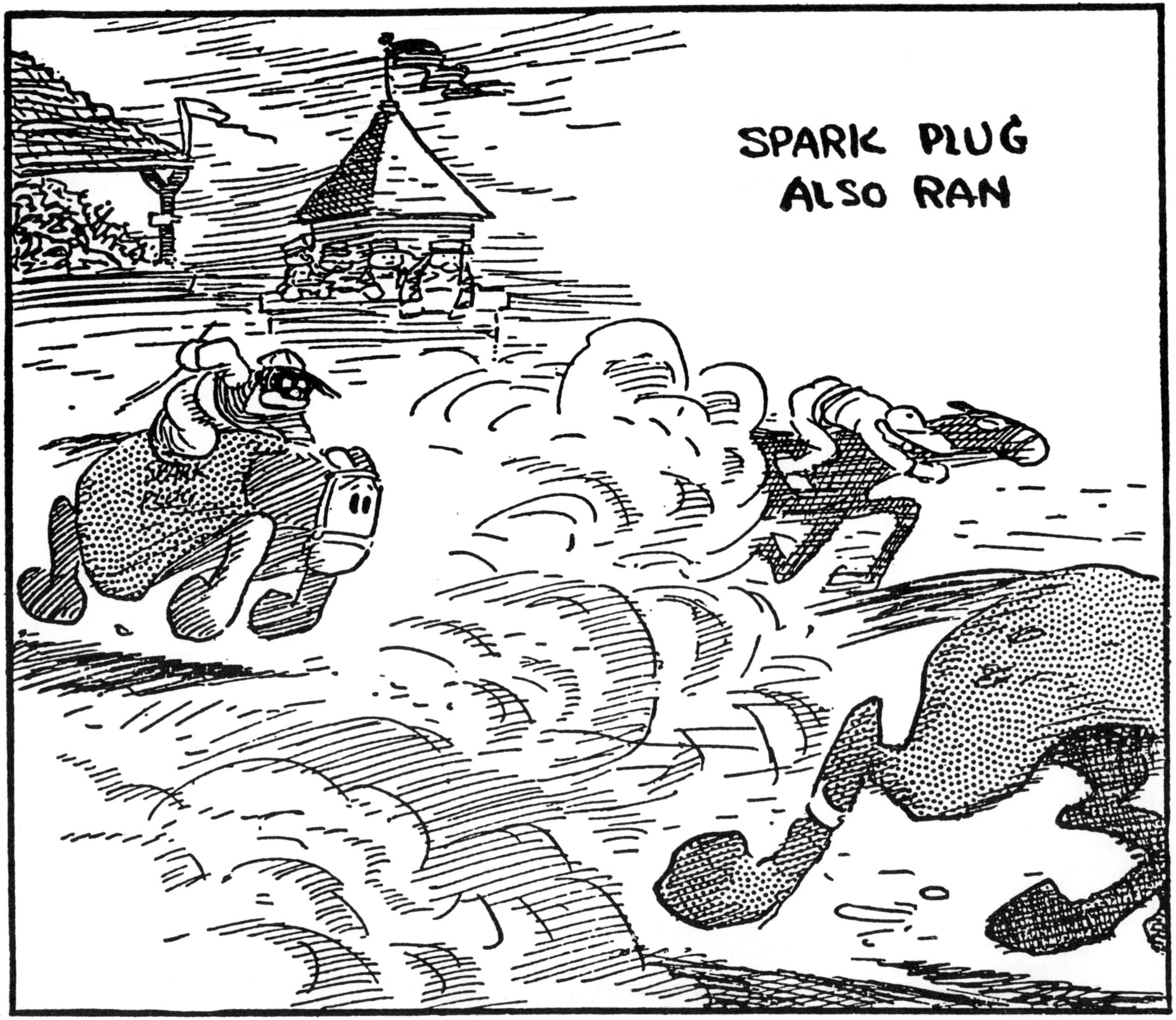
SPARK PLUG
ALSO RAN

Spark Plug loses a race, August 4, 1924. Collection of Bill Janocha.

Off to the Races

1923 — 1926

Billy DeBeck was not the first cartoonist to feature humorous continuity in the comics. Bud Fisher, creator of the first successful daily comic strip, "A. Mutt" (later renamed "Mutt and Jeff"), which debuted on November 15, 1907, introduced a six-week-long story in February 1908. C.W. Kahles ("Hairbreadth Harry"), Harry Hershfield ("Desperate Desmond") and Sydney Smith ("The Gumps") also experimented with continuity in the decade before Spark Plug arrived on the scene. Although DeBeck had stayed with certain themes for weeks at a time in the early "Barney Google" strips, it was not until Sparky arrived that he abandoned the gag-a-day format for more ambitious plot-lines.

Beginning with the Abadaba Handicap, the early Spark Plug stories typically involved races like the Brown Derby, the Horseshoe Handicap and the T-Bone Stakes. Debeck would often build suspense throughout the week, culminating in a "teaser strip" on Saturday, making readers wait until the following Monday to learn the outcome of a race. Barney was endlessly occupied with scraping together enough money for the entry fee, dodging his creditors if he lost, or celebrating in high style if he won.

Between 1923 and 1925, Barney and Sparky traveled the roads and railways of America from Louisville to Baltimore to Saratoga to Detroit to Boston to Palm Beach. In the Sunday page episodes, which were separate from the daily continuities, the two wanderers found themselves in a different town almost every week.

In his spare time, Barney chased beautiful women, caught hell from his own "sweet woman" and rode herd on his faithful black jockey, Sunshine, who, along with Rudy the Ostrich, became a regular member of the cast by mid-1923. Other subplots involved a reunion with his long-lost father and the birth of a baby race horse.

In the latter half of 1926, DeBeck wrote two of his most memorable Spark Plug adventures. Between June 7 and October 1, Barney and Sparky raced the breadth of the United States from New York to San Francisco. To capture his readers' attention, DeBeck conveniently had his characters visit the towns of subscribing newspapers along the way. Right on the heels of this four-month marathon, Barney announced that Sparky was going to swim the English Channel. They sailed for Europe in mid-October.

By December 1926, DeBeck had successfully exhausted both his characters and the possibilities for long distance horse races and dramatic stunts. He had reached another turning point on the road to comic strip immortality.

The "Barney Google" strips on the following pages were reproduced from book collections published by the Cupples & Leon Company from 1923 to 1926 (Courtesy of Bill Janocha), as well as from actual strips clipped from the newspapers (Courtesy of Ron Goulart).

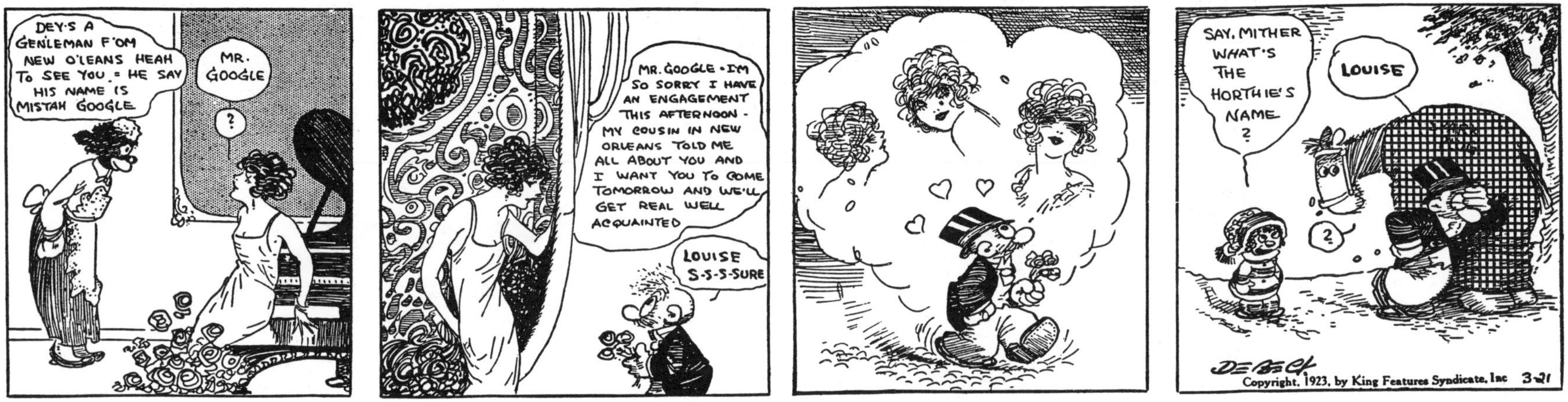
DEY'S A GENILEMAN F'OM NEW O'LEANS HEAH TO SEE YOU = HE SAY HIS NAME IS MISTAH GOOGLE
MR. GOOGLE
?
MR. GOOGLE - I'M SO SORRY I HAVE AN ENGAGEMENT THIS AFTERNOON - MY COUSIN IN NEW ORLEANS TOLD ME ALL ABOUT YOU AND I WANT YOU TO COME TOMORROW AND WE'LL GET REAL WELL ACQUAINTED
LOUISE S-S-S-SURE
SAY, MITHER WHAT'S THE HORTHIE'S NAME ?
LOUISE
?
DE BECK
Copyright, 1923, by King Features Syndicate, Inc 3-21

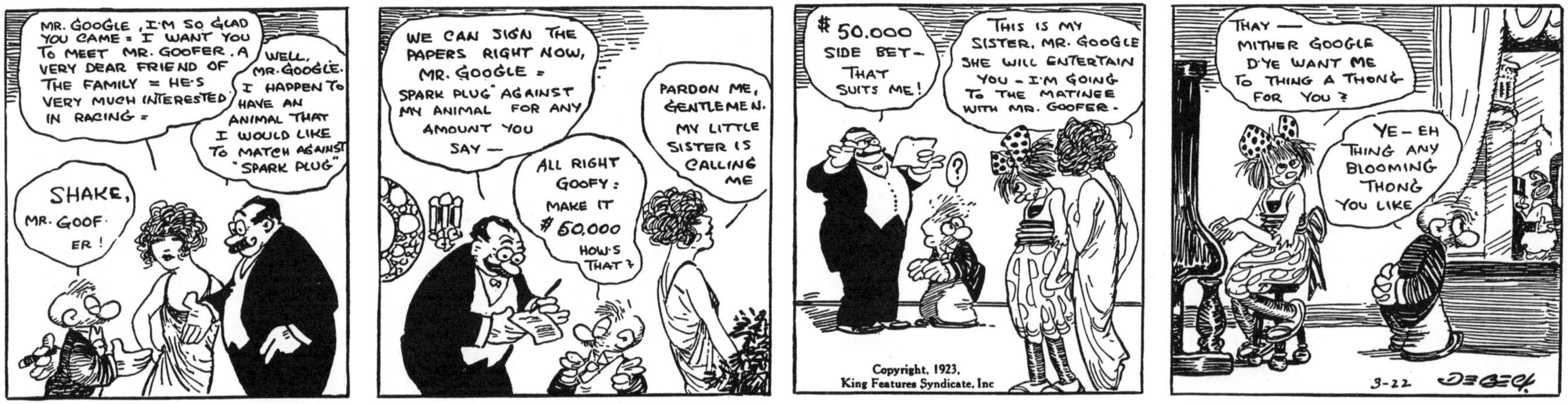
MR. GOOGLE, I'M SO GLAD YOU CAME = I WANT YOU TO MEET MR. GOOFER. A VERY DEAR FRIEND OF THE FAMILY = HE'S VERY MUCH INTERESTED IN RACING =
WELL, MR. GOOGLE. I HAPPEN TO HAVE AN ANIMAL THAT I WOULD LIKE TO MATCH AGAINST "SPARK PLUG"
SHAKE, MR. GOOF ER!
WE CAN SIGN THE PAPERS RIGHT NOW, MR. GOOGLE = "SPARK PLUG" AGAINST MY ANIMAL FOR ANY AMOUNT YOU SAY —
ALL RIGHT GOOFY: MAKE IT $50,000 HOW'S THAT?
PARDON ME, GENTLEMEN. MY LITTLE SISTER IS CALLING ME
$50,000 SIDE BET - THAT SUITS ME!
THIS IS MY SISTER, MR. GOOGLE SHE WILL ENTERTAIN YOU - I'M GOING TO THE MATINEE WITH MR. GOOFER -
?
Copyright, 1923, King Features Syndicate, Inc
THAY — MITHER GOOGLE D'YE WANT ME TO THING A THONG FOR YOU?
YE - EH THING ANY BLOOMING THONG YOU LIKE
3-22 DE BECK

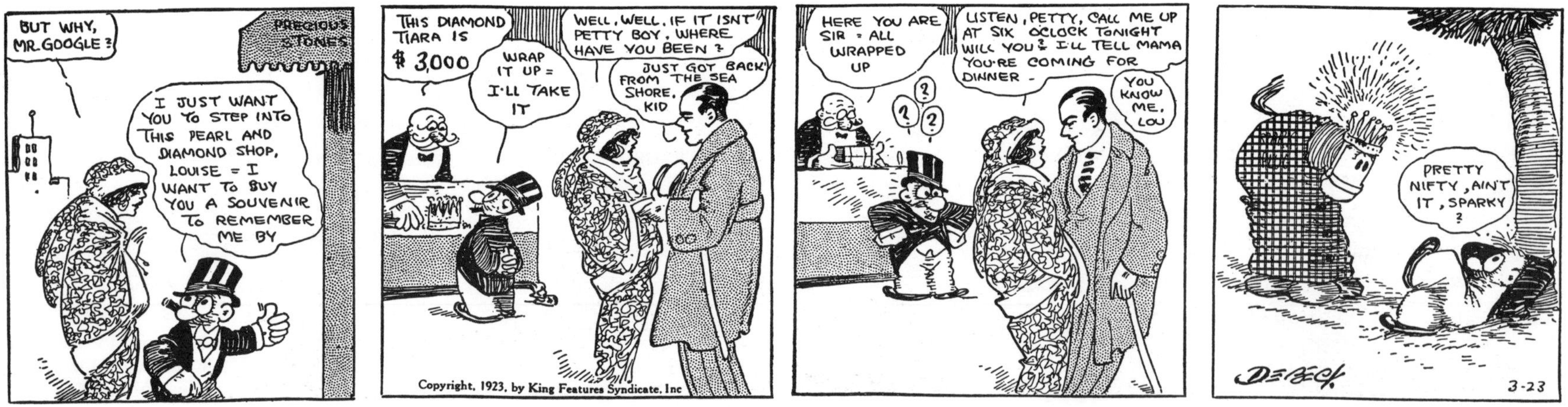
BUT WHY, MR. GOOGLE?
PRECIOUS STONES
I JUST WANT YOU TO STEP INTO THIS PEARL AND DIAMOND SHOP, LOUISE = I WANT TO BUY YOU A SOUVENIR TO REMEMBER ME BY
THIS DIAMOND TIARA IS $3,000
WRAP IT UP = I'LL TAKE IT
WELL, WELL. IF IT ISN'T PETTY BOY. WHERE HAVE YOU BEEN?
JUST GOT BACK FROM THE SEA SHORE, KID
Copyright, 1923, by King Features Syndicate, Inc
HERE YOU ARE SIR = ALL WRAPPED UP
? ? ?
LISTEN, PETTY, CALL ME UP AT SIX O'CLOCK TONIGHT WILL YOU? I'LL TELL MAMA YOU'RE COMING FOR DINNER -
YOU KNOW ME, LOU
PRETTY NIFTY, AIN'T IT, SPARKY ?
DE BECK
3-23

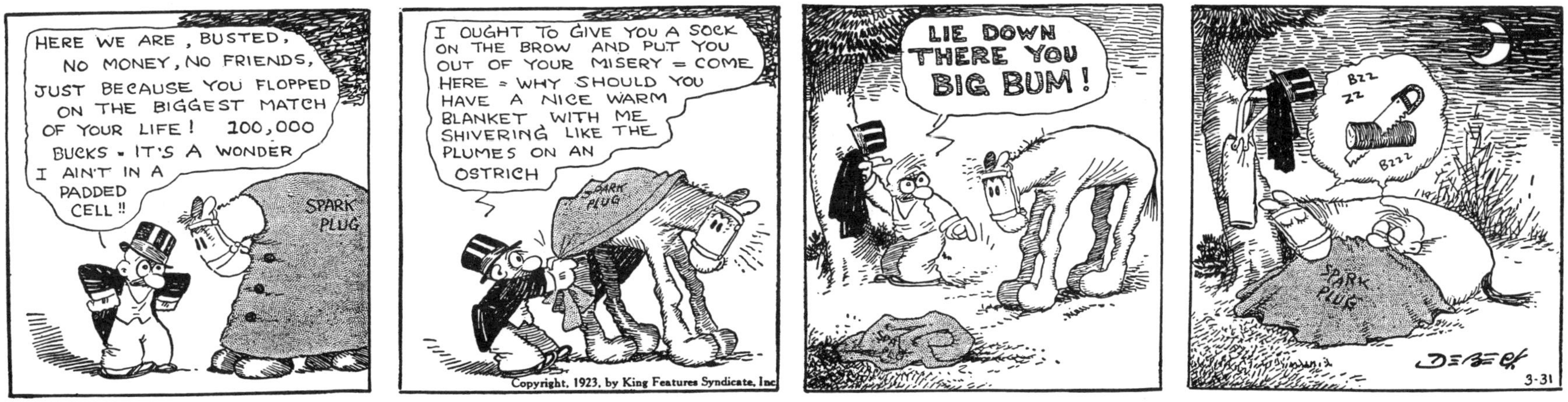
HERE WE ARE, BUSTED, NO MONEY, NO FRIENDS, JUST BECAUSE YOU FLOPPED ON THE BIGGEST MATCH OF YOUR LIFE! 100,000 BUCKS = IT'S A WONDER I AIN'T IN A PADDED CELL!!
SPARK PLUG
I OUGHT TO GIVE YOU A SOCK ON THE BROW AND PUT YOU OUT OF YOUR MISERY = COME HERE = WHY SHOULD YOU HAVE A NICE WARM BLANKET WITH ME SHIVERING LIKE THE PLUMES ON AN OSTRICH
SPARK PLUG
Copyright, 1923, by King Features Syndicate, Inc
LIE DOWN THERE YOU BIG BUM!
BZZ ZZ
BZZZ
SPARK PLUG
DEBECK
3-31

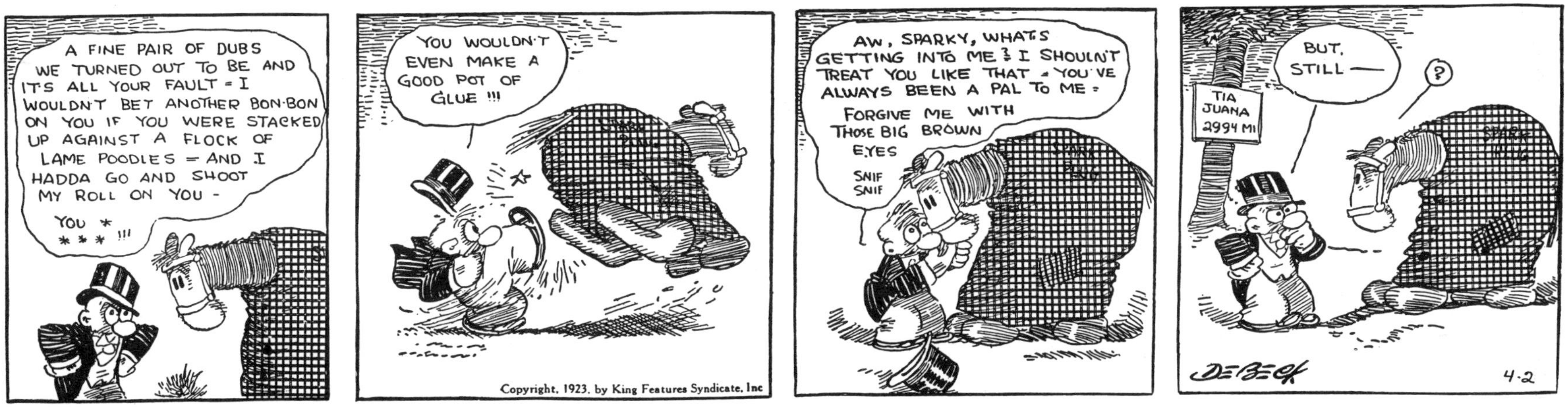
A FINE PAIR OF DUBS WE TURNED OUT TO BE AND IT'S ALL YOUR FAULT = I WOULDN'T BET ANOTHER BON-BON ON YOU IF YOU WERE STACKED UP AGAINST A FLOCK OF LAME POODLES = AND I HADDA GO AND SHOOT MY ROLL ON YOU -
YOU * *** !!!
YOU WOULDN'T EVEN MAKE A GOOD POT OF GLUE !!!
Copyright, 1923, by King Features Syndicate, Inc
AW, SPARKY, WHAT'S GETTING INTO ME? I SHOULN'T TREAT YOU LIKE THAT = YOU'VE ALWAYS BEEN A PAL TO ME =
FORGIVE ME WITH THOSE BIG BROWN EYES
SNIF SNIF
BUT, STILL —
?
TIA JUANA 2994 MI
DEBECK
4-2

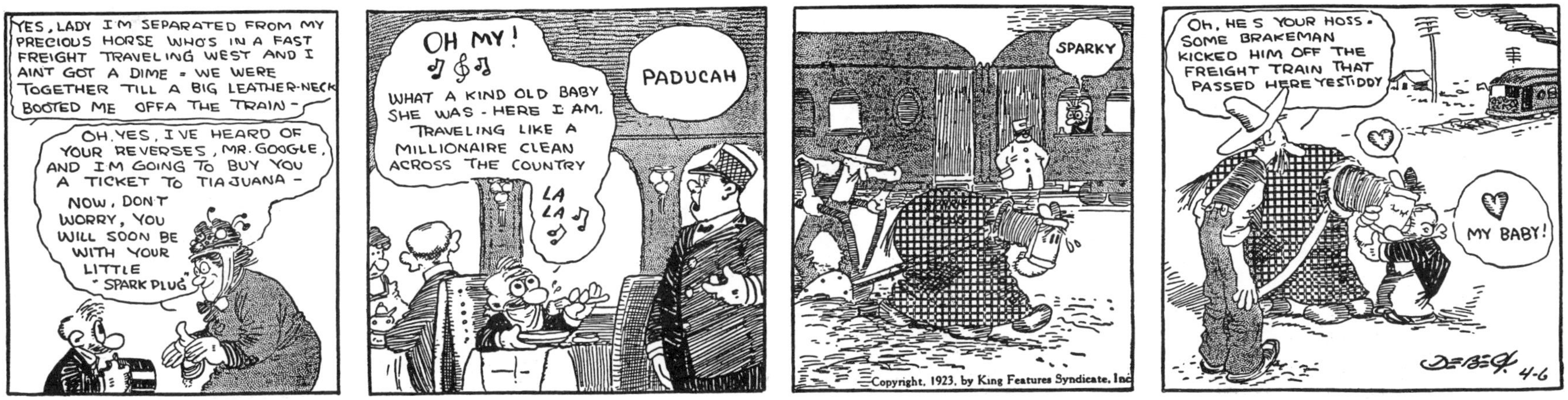
YES, LADY I'M SEPARATED FROM MY PRECIOUS HORSE WHO'S IN A FAST FREIGHT TRAVELING WEST AND I AINT GOT A DIME = WE WERE TOGETHER TILL A BIG LEATHER-NECK BOOTED ME OFFA THE TRAIN -
OH, YES, I'VE HEARD OF YOUR REVERSES, MR. GOOGLE, AND I'M GOING TO BUY YOU A TICKET TO TIAJUANA -
NOW, DON'T WORRY, YOU WILL SOON BE WITH YOUR LITTLE "SPARK PLUG"
OH MY!
WHAT A KIND OLD BABY SHE WAS - HERE I AM. TRAVELING LIKE A MILLIONAIRE CLEAN ACROSS THE COUNTRY
LA LA
PADUCAH
SPARKY
Copyright, 1923, by King Features Syndicate, Inc
OH, HE'S YOUR HOSS. SOME BRAKEMAN KICKED HIM OFF THE FREIGHT TRAIN THAT PASSED HERE YESTIDDY
MY BABY!
DEBECK 4-6

The Brown Derby

1923

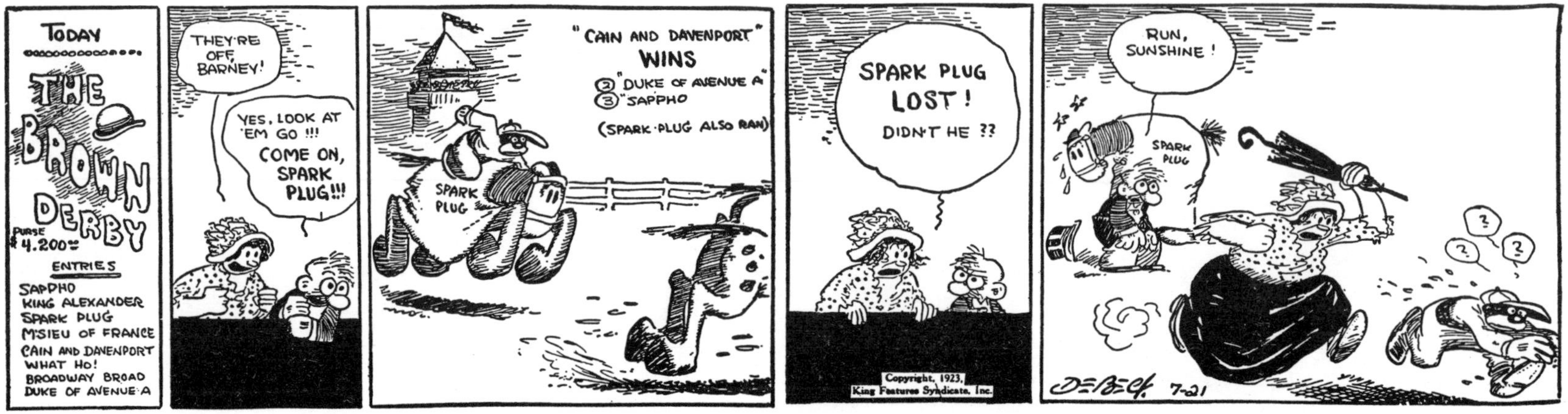

TODAY
THE BROWN DERBY
PURSE $4,200.00
ENTRIES
SAPPHO
KING ALEXANDER
SPARK PLUG
M'SIEU OF FRANCE
CAIN AND DAVENPORT
WHAT HO!
BROADWAY BROAD
DUKE OF AVENUE A
THEY'RE OFF, BARNEY!
YES, LOOK AT 'EM GO !!! COME ON, SPARK PLUG!!!
SPARK PLUG
"CAIN AND DAVENPORT" WINS
② "DUKE OF AVENUE A"
③ "SAPPHO"
(SPARK PLUG ALSO RAN)
SPARK PLUG LOST! DIDN'T HE ??
Copyright, 1923, King Features Syndicate, Inc.
RUN, SUNSHINE!
SPARK PLUG
DE BECK 7-21

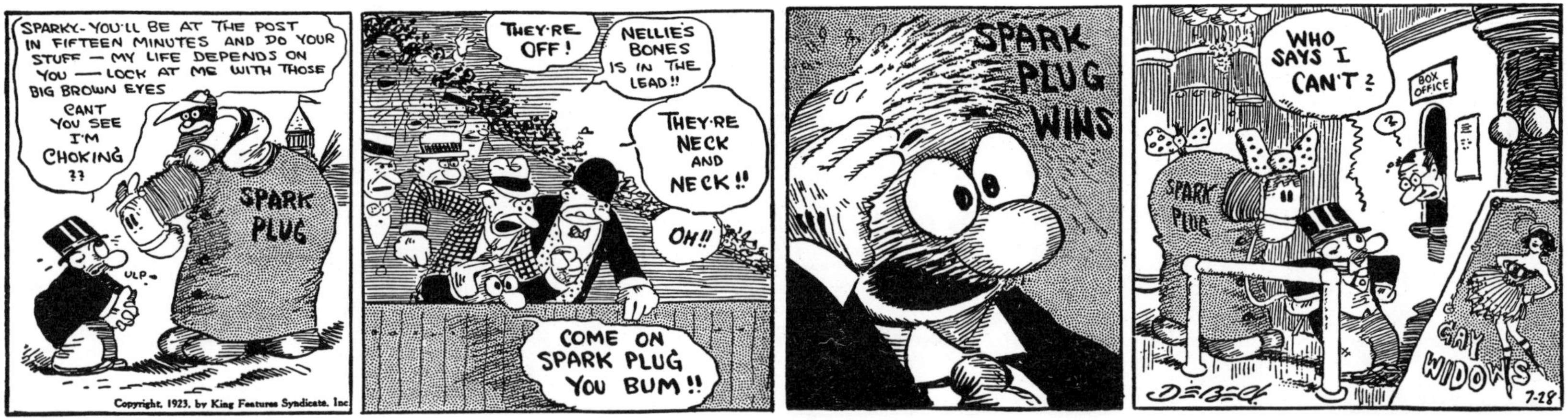

SPARKY- YOU'LL BE AT THE POST IN FIFTEEN MINUTES AND DO YOUR STUFF — MY LIFE DEPENDS ON YOU — LOOK AT ME WITH THOSE BIG BROWN EYES
CANT YOU SEE I'M CHOKING ??
SPARK PLUG
ULP
Copyright, 1923, by King Features Syndicate, Inc
THEY'RE OFF!
NELLIE'S BONES IS IN THE LEAD!!
THEY'RE NECK AND NECK!!
OH!!
COME ON SPARK PLUG YOU BUM!!
SPARK PLUG WINS
WHO SAYS I CAN'T?
BOX OFFICE
SPARK PLUG
GAY WIDOWS
DE BECK 7-28

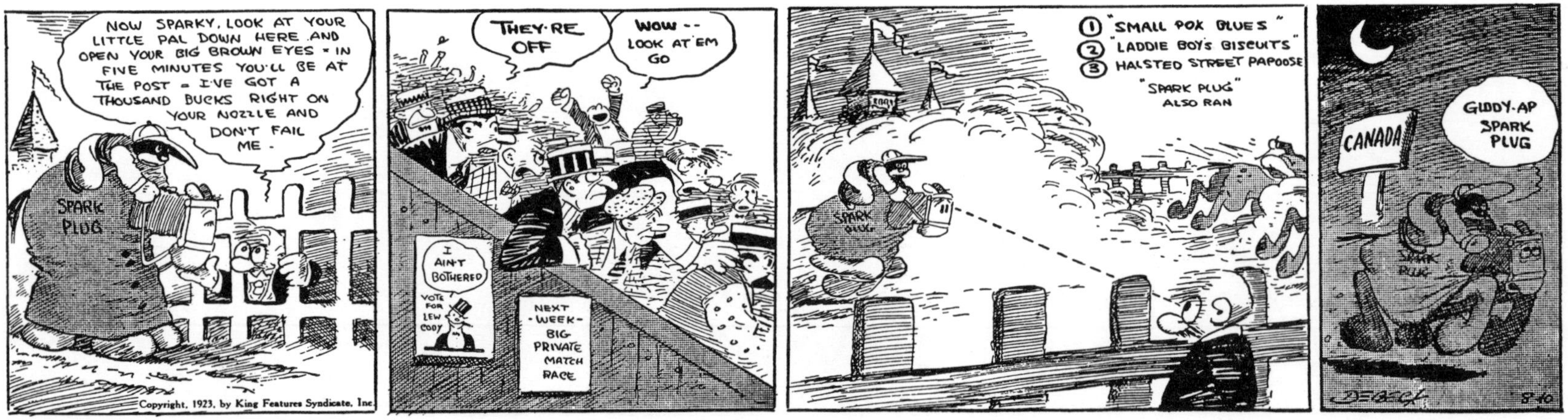

NOW SPARKY, LOOK AT YOUR LITTLE PAL DOWN HERE AND OPEN YOUR BIG BROWN EYES - IN FIVE MINUTES YOU'LL BE AT THE POST - I'VE GOT A THOUSAND BUCKS RIGHT ON YOUR NOZZLE AND DON'T FAIL ME -
SPARK PLUG
Copyright, 1923, by King Features Syndicate, Inc.
THEY'RE OFF
WOW -- LOOK AT 'EM GO
I AIN'T BOTHERED
VOTE FOR LEW CODY
NEXT WEEK BIG PRIVATE MATCH RACE
① "SMALL POX BLUES"
② "LADDIE BOY'S BISCUITS"
③ HALSTED STREET PAPOOSE
"SPARK PLUG" ALSO RAN
SPARK PLUG
CANADA
GIDDY-AP SPARK PLUG
SPARK PLUG
DE BECK 8-10

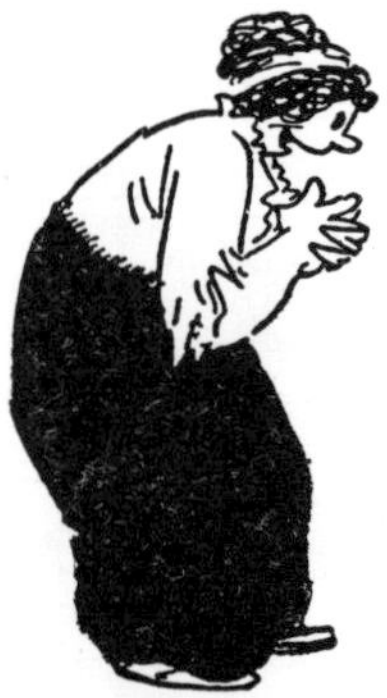

The Horse-shoe Handicap

1923

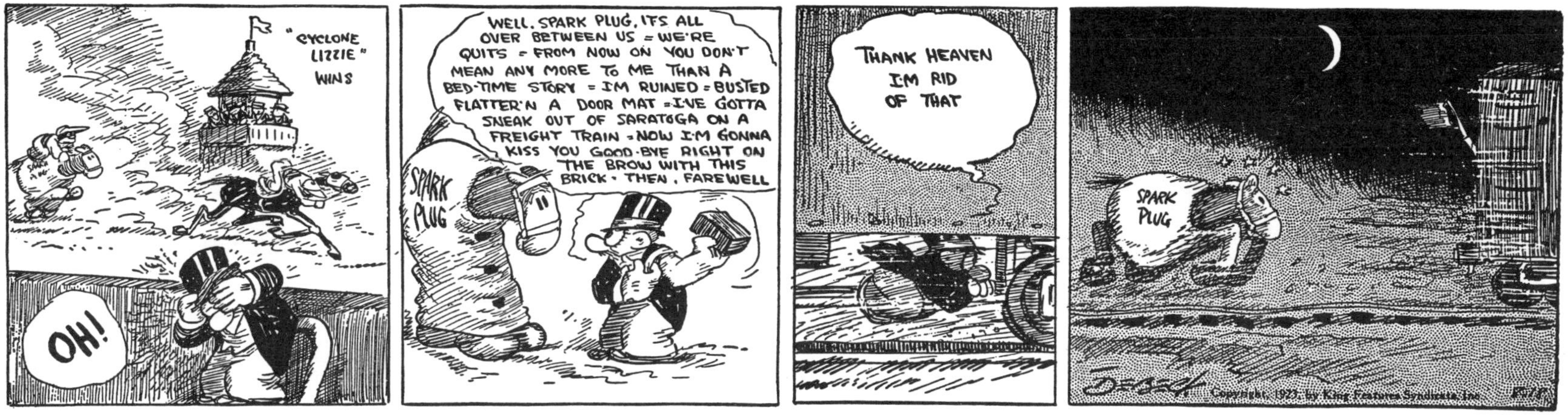
"CYCLONE LIZZIE" WINS
OH!
WELL, SPARK PLUG, IT'S ALL OVER BETWEEN US = WE'RE QUITS = FROM NOW ON YOU DON'T MEAN ANY MORE TO ME THAN A BED-TIME STORY = I'M RUINED = BUSTED FLATTER'N A DOOR MAT = I'VE GOTTA SNEAK OUT OF SARATOGA ON A FREIGHT TRAIN = NOW I'M GONNA KISS YOU GOOD-BYE RIGHT ON THE BROW WITH THIS BRICK - THEN, FAREWELL
SPARK PLUG
THANK HEAVEN I'M RID OF THAT
SPARK PLUG
DE BECK
Copyright, 1923, by King Features Syndicate, Inc.

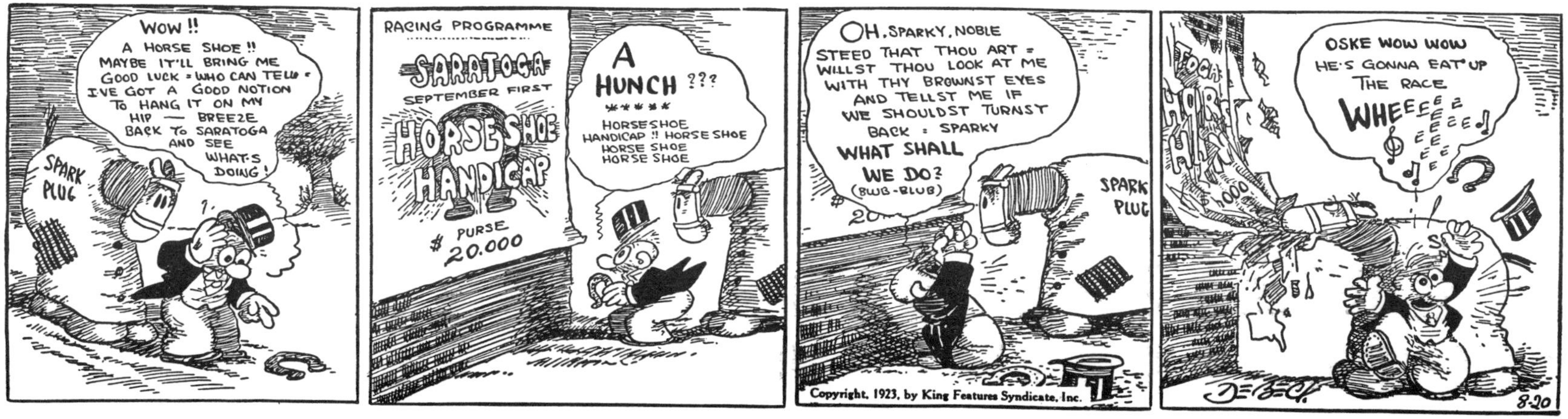
WOW!! A HORSE SHOE!! MAYBE IT'LL BRING ME GOOD LUCK = WHO CAN TELL = I'VE GOT A GOOD NOTION TO HANG IT ON MY HIP — BREEZE BACK TO SARATOGA AND SEE WHAT'S DOING!
SPARK PLUG
RACING PROGRAMME
SARATOGA
SEPTEMBER FIRST
HORSE SHOE HANDICAP
PURSE $ 20.000
A HUNCH ???
*****
HORSESHOE HANDICAP!! HORSE SHOE HORSE SHOE HORSE SHOE
OH, SPARKY, NOBLE STEED THAT THOU ART = WILLST THOU LOOK AT ME WITH THY BROWNST EYES AND TELLST ME IF WE SHOULDST TURNST BACK = SPARKY WHAT SHALL WE DO? (BWB-BLUB)
SPARK PLUG
Copyright, 1923, by King Features Syndicate, Inc.
OSKE WOW WOW HE'S GONNA EAT UP THE RACE WHEEEEEE
DE BECK
8-20

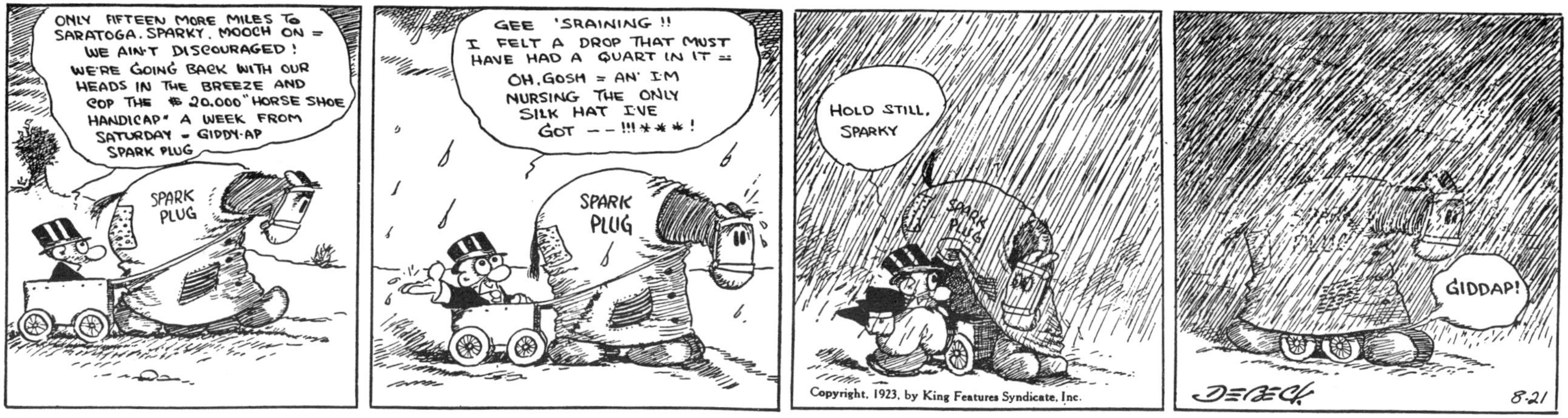
ONLY FIFTEEN MORE MILES TO SARATOGA. SPARKY. MOOCH ON = WE AIN'T DISCOURAGED! WE'RE GOING BACK WITH OUR HEADS IN THE BREEZE AND COP THE $20.000 "HORSE SHOE HANDICAP" A WEEK FROM SATURDAY = GIDDY-AP SPARK PLUG
SPARK PLUG
GEE 'SRAINING!! I FELT A DROP THAT MUST HAVE HAD A QUART IN IT = OH, GOSH = AN' I'M NURSING THE ONLY SILK HAT I'VE GOT --!!!***!
SPARK PLUG
HOLD STILL, SPARKY
SPARK PLUG
Copyright, 1923, by King Features Syndicate, Inc.
GIDDAP!
DE BECK
8-21

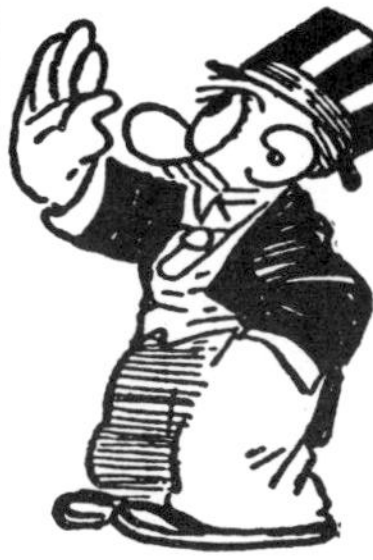

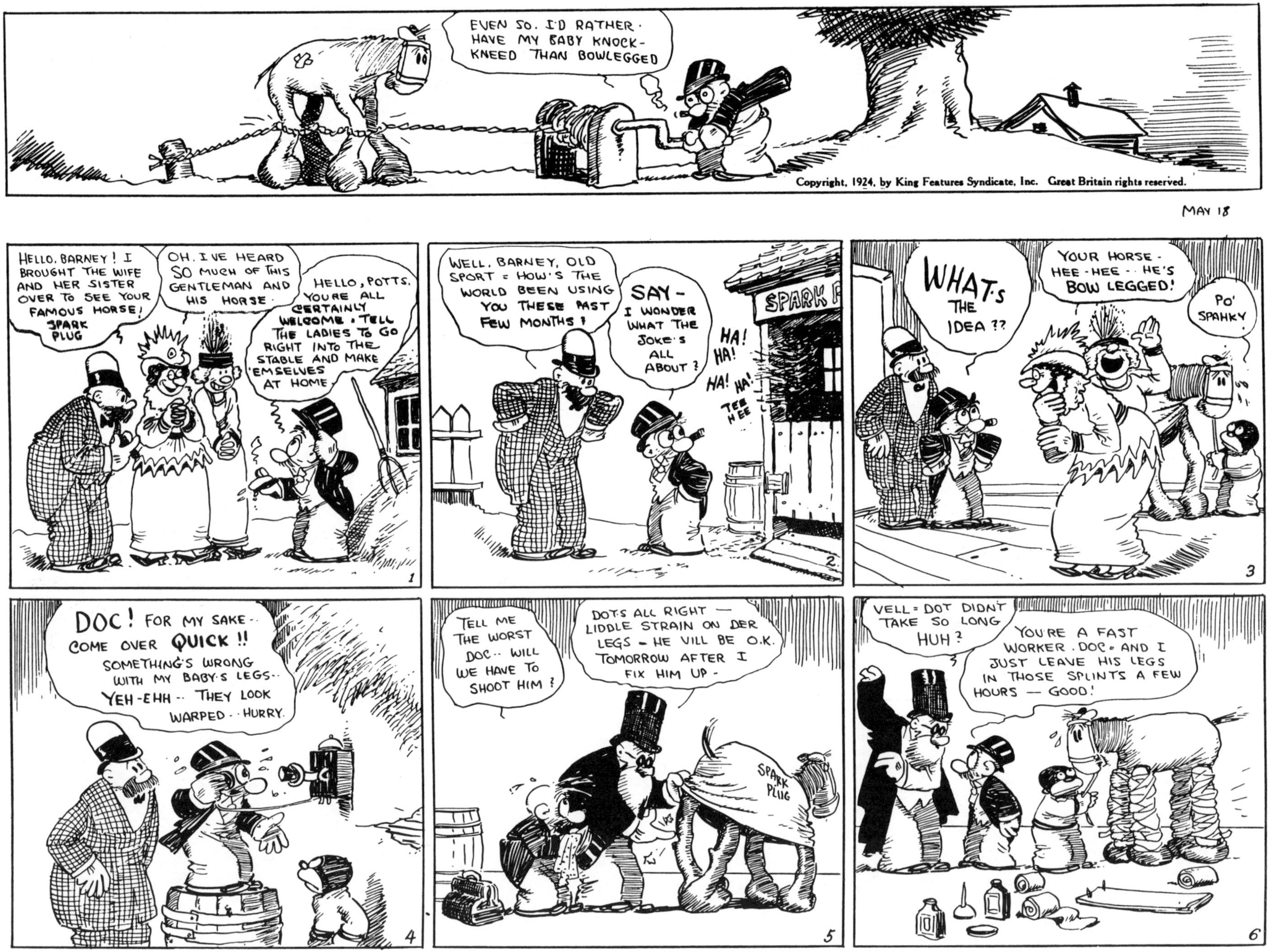
EVEN SO. I'D RATHER. HAVE MY BABY KNOCK-KNEED THAN BOWLEGGED
Copyright, 1924, by King Features Syndicate, Inc. Great Britain rights reserved.
MAY 18
HELLO. BARNEY! I BROUGHT THE WIFE AND HER SISTER OVER TO SEE YOUR FAMOUS HORSE! SPARK PLUG
OH. I'VE HEARD SO MUCH OF THIS GENTLEMAN AND HIS HORSE
HELLO, POTTS. YOU'RE ALL CERTAINLY WELCOME. TELL THE LADIES TO GO RIGHT INTO THE STABLE AND MAKE 'EMSELVES AT HOME
WELL. BARNEY, OLD SPORT = HOW'S THE WORLD BEEN USING YOU THESE PAST FEW MONTHS?
SAY - I WONDER WHAT THE JOKE'S ALL ABOUT?
HA! HA! HA! HA!
TEE HEE
SPARK P
WHAT'S THE IDEA??
YOUR HORSE - HEE-HEE -- HE'S BOW LEGGED!
PO' SPAHKY.
DOC! FOR MY SAKE -- COME OVER QUICK!! SOMETHING'S WRONG WITH MY BABY'S LEGS -- YEH-EHH -- THEY LOOK WARPED -- HURRY.
TELL ME THE WORST DOC -- WILL WE HAVE TO SHOOT HIM?
DOT'S ALL RIGHT — LIDDLE STRAIN ON DER LEGS - HE VILL BE O.K. TOMORROW AFTER I FIX HIM UP -
SPARK PLUG
VELL = DOT DIDN'T TAKE SO LONG HUH?
YOU'RE A FAST WORKER. DOC - AND I JUST LEAVE HIS LEGS IN THOSE SPLINTS A FEW HOURS — GOOD!

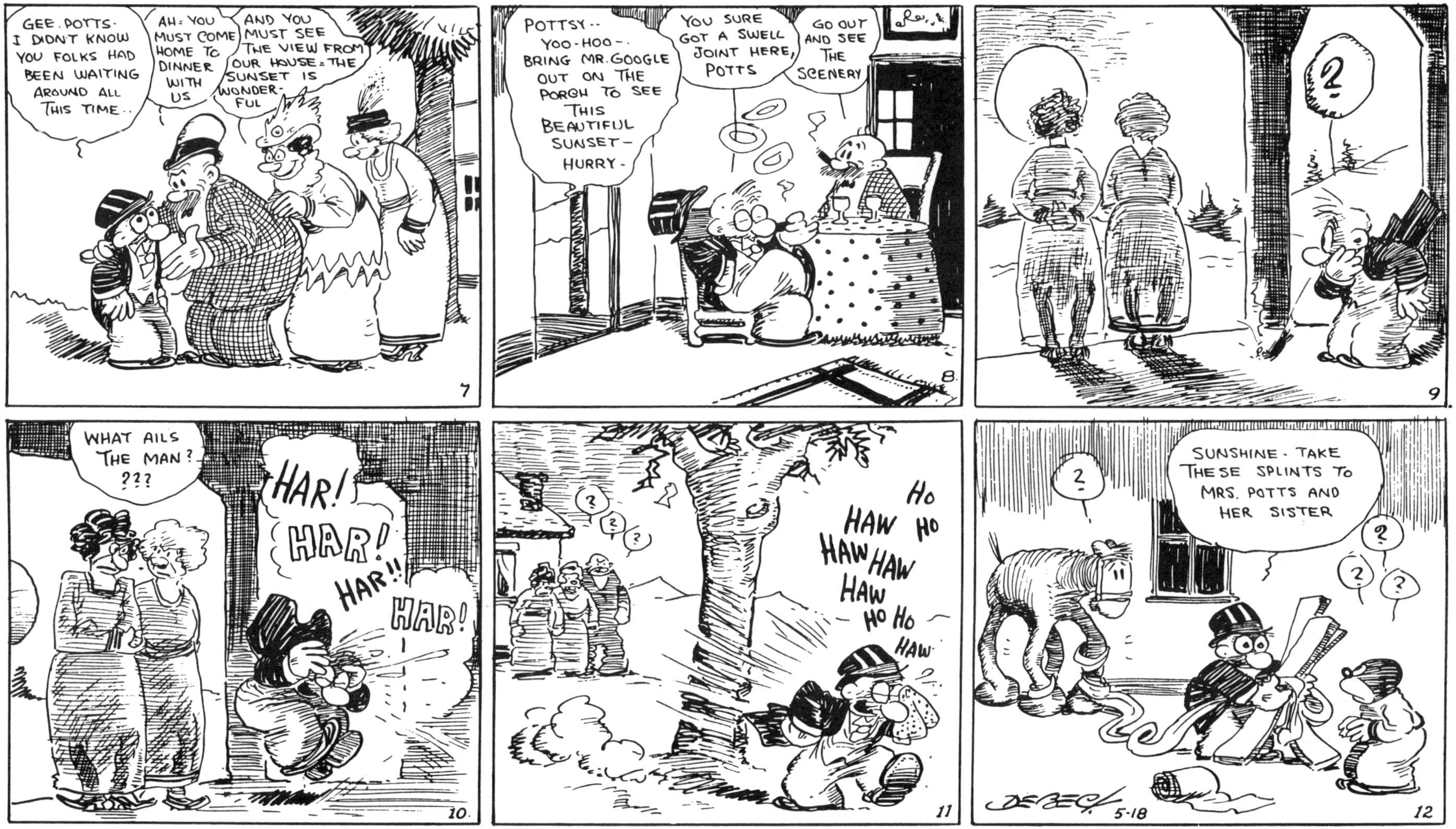

GEE. POTTS. I DIDN'T KNOW YOU FOLKS HAD BEEN WAITING AROUND ALL THIS TIME..
AH: YOU MUST COME HOME TO DINNER WITH US
AND YOU MUST SEE THE VIEW FROM OUR HOUSE: THE SUNSET IS WONDERFUL
POTTSY-- YOO-HOO-- BRING MR. GOOGLE OUT ON THE PORCH TO SEE THIS BEAUTIFUL SUNSET- HURRY-
YOU SURE GOT A SWELL JOINT HERE, POTTS
GO OUT AND SEE THE SCENERY
?
WHAT AILS THE MAN? ???
HAR!
HAR!
HAR!!
HAR!
? ? ?
HO HAW HO HAW HAW HAW HO HO HAW
?
SUNSHINE - TAKE THESE SPLINTS TO MRS. POTTS AND HER SISTER
? ? ?
5-18

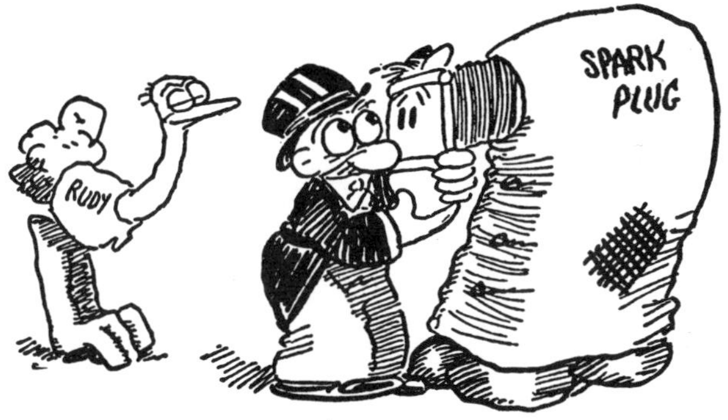

RUDY
SPARK PLUG

Opposite page and above: A classic "Barney Google" Sunday page featuring Barney, Spark Plug and Sunshine, May 18, 1924. From the Collection of Richard Marschall.

Rudy the Ostrich

1924

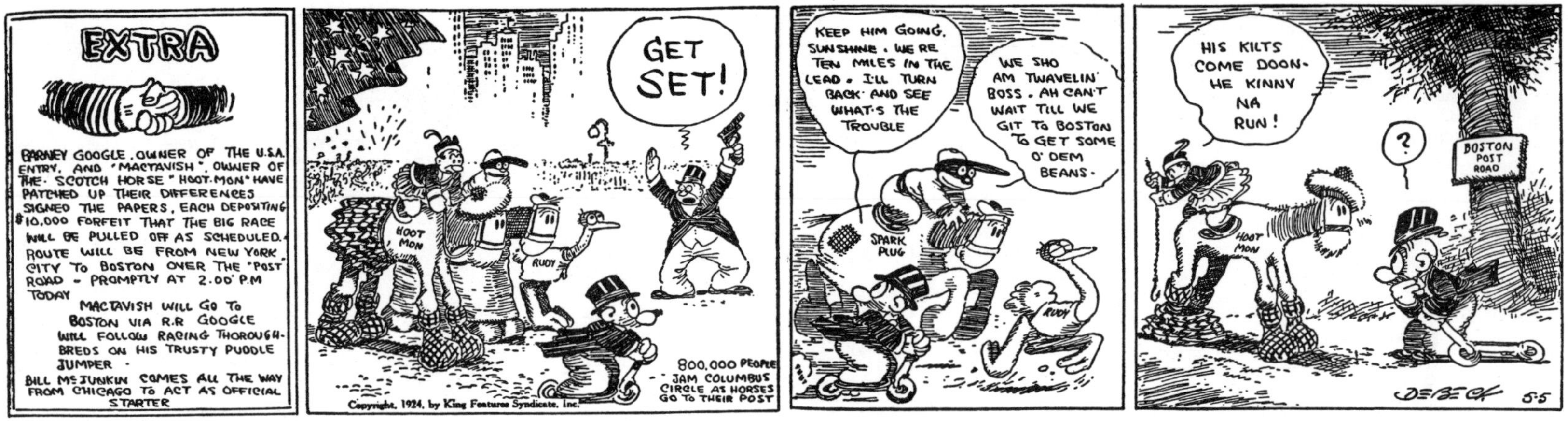
EXTRA
BARNEY GOOGLE, OWNER OF THE U.S.A. ENTRY, AND "MACTAVISH", OWNER OF THE SCOTCH HORSE "HOOT-MON" HAVE PATCHED UP THEIR DIFFERENCES SIGNED THE PAPERS, EACH DEPOSITING $10,000 FORFEIT THAT THE BIG RACE WILL BE PULLED OFF AS SCHEDULED. ROUTE WILL BE FROM NEW YORK CITY TO BOSTON OVER THE "POST ROAD" - PROMPTLY AT 2.00 P.M TODAY
MACTAVISH WILL GO TO BOSTON VIA R.R GOOGLE WILL FOLLOW RACING THOROUGHBREDS ON HIS TRUSTY PUDDLE JUMPER -
BILL McJUNKIN COMES ALL THE WAY FROM CHICAGO TO ACT AS OFFICIAL STARTER
GET SET!
HOOT MON
RUDY
800,000 PEOPLE JAM COLUMBUS CIRCLE AS HORSES GO TO THEIR POST
Copyright, 1924, by King Features Syndicate, Inc.
KEEP HIM GOING, SUNSHINE - WE'RE TEN MILES IN THE LEAD - I'LL TURN BACK AND SEE WHAT'S THE TROUBLE
WE SHO AM TWAVELIN' BOSS - AH CAN'T WAIT TILL WE GIT TO BOSTON TO GET SOME O' DEM BEANS -
SPARK PLUG
RUDY
HIS KILTS COME DOON- HE KINNY NA RUN!
?
BOSTON POST ROAD
HOOT MON
DE BECK 5-5

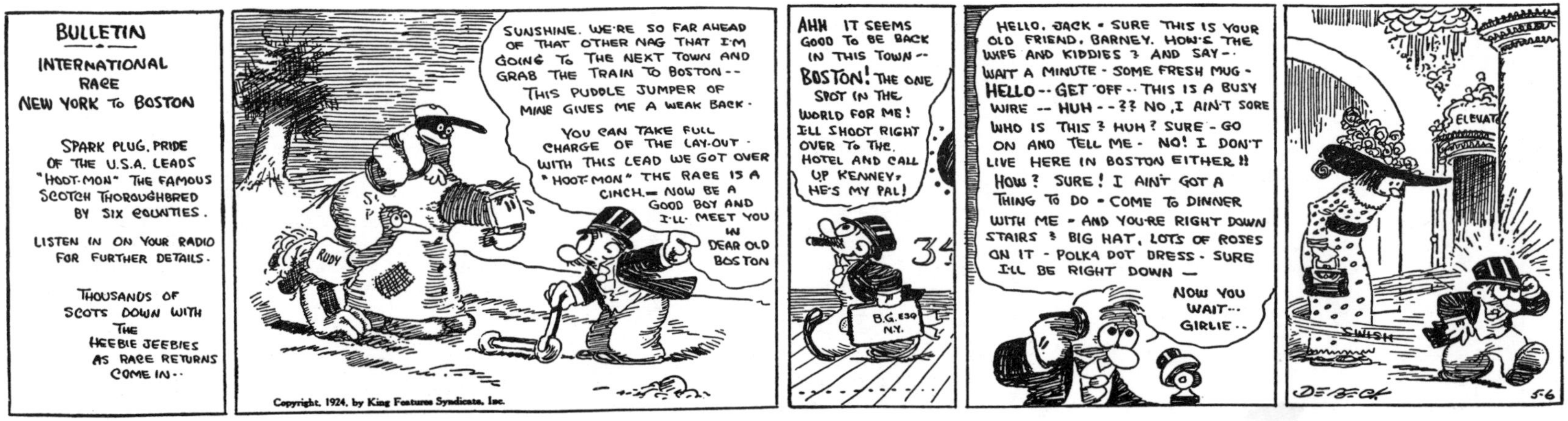
BULLETIN
INTERNATIONAL RACE NEW YORK TO BOSTON
SPARK PLUG, PRIDE OF THE U.S.A. LEADS "HOOT-MON" THE FAMOUS SCOTCH THOROUGHBRED BY SIX COUNTIES.
LISTEN IN ON YOUR RADIO FOR FURTHER DETAILS.
THOUSANDS OF SCOTS DOWN WITH THE HEEBIE JEEBIES AS RACE RETURNS COME IN--
SUNSHINE, WE'RE SO FAR AHEAD OF THAT OTHER NAG THAT I'M GOING TO THE NEXT TOWN AND GRAB THE TRAIN TO BOSTON -- THIS PUDDLE JUMPER OF MINE GIVES ME A WEAK BACK -
YOU CAN TAKE FULL CHARGE OF THE LAY-OUT - WITH THIS LEAD WE GOT OVER "HOOT-MON" THE RACE IS A CINCH. - NOW BE A GOOD BOY AND I'LL MEET YOU IN DEAR OLD BOSTON
RUDY
Copyright, 1924, by King Features Syndicate, Inc.
AHH IT SEEMS GOOD TO BE BACK IN THIS TOWN -- BOSTON! THE ONE SPOT IN THE WORLD FOR ME! I'LL SHOOT RIGHT OVER TO THE HOTEL AND CALL UP KEANNEY, HE'S MY PAL!
B.G. ESQ N.Y.
HELLO, JACK - SURE THIS IS YOUR OLD FRIEND, BARNEY. HOW'S THE WIFE AND KIDDIES ? AND SAY - WAIT A MINUTE - SOME FRESH MUG - HELLO -- GET OFF -- THIS IS A BUSY WIRE -- HUH -- ?? NO, I AIN'T SORE WHO IS THIS ? HUH ? SURE - GO ON AND TELL ME - NO! I DON'T LIVE HERE IN BOSTON EITHER !! HOW ? SURE! I AIN'T GOT A THING TO DO - COME TO DINNER WITH ME - AND YOU'RE RIGHT DOWN STAIRS ? BIG HAT, LOTS OF ROSES ON IT - POLKA DOT DRESS - SURE I'LL BE RIGHT DOWN --
NOW YOU WAIT -- GIRLIE --
SWISH
DE BECK 5-6

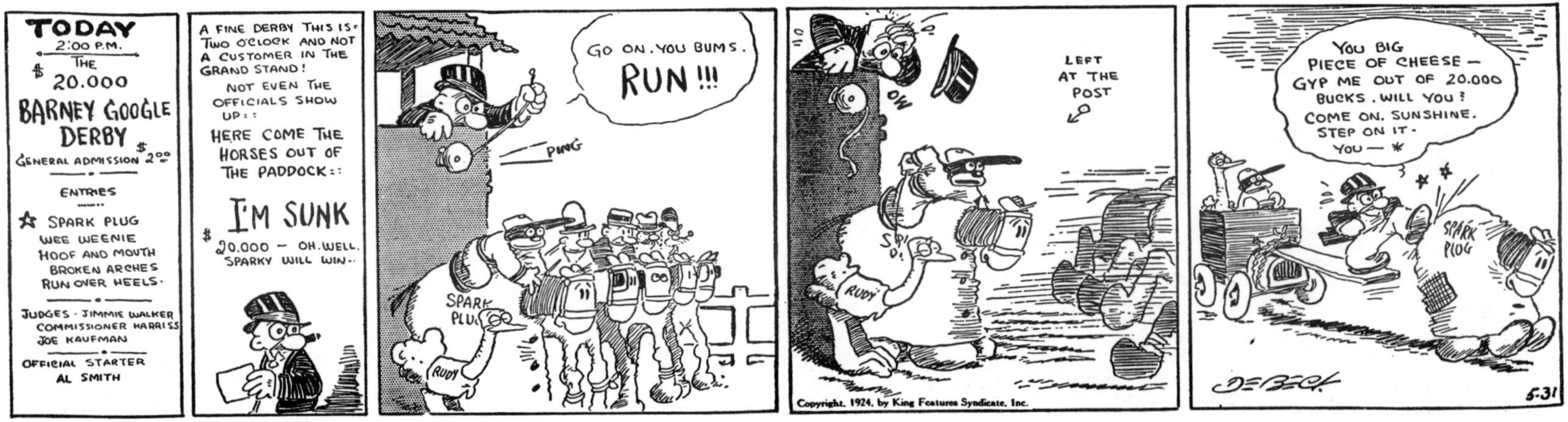
TODAY 2:00 P.M. THE $20.000 BARNEY GOOGLE DERBY
GENERAL ADMISSION $2.00
ENTRIES
SPARK PLUG
WEE WEENIE
HOOF AND MOUTH
BROKEN ARCHES
RUN OVER HEELS -
JUDGES - JIMMIE WALKER COMMISSIONER HARRISS JOE KAUFMAN
OFFICIAL STARTER AL SMITH
A FINE DERBY THIS IS - TWO O'CLOCK AND NOT A CUSTOMER IN THE GRAND STAND! NOT EVEN THE OFFICIALS SHOW UP::
HERE COME THE HORSES OUT OF THE PADDOCK::
I'M SUNK
$20.000 - OH, WELL, SPARKY WILL WIN --
GO ON, YOU BUMS. RUN!!!
PING
SPARK PLUG
RUDY
LEFT AT THE POST
OW
RUDY
Copyright, 1924, by King Features Syndicate, Inc.
YOU BIG PIECE OF CHEESE -- GYP ME OUT OF 20,000 BUCKS, WILL YOU ? COME ON, SUNSHINE, STEP ON IT - YOU -- *
SPARK PLUG
DE BECK 5-31

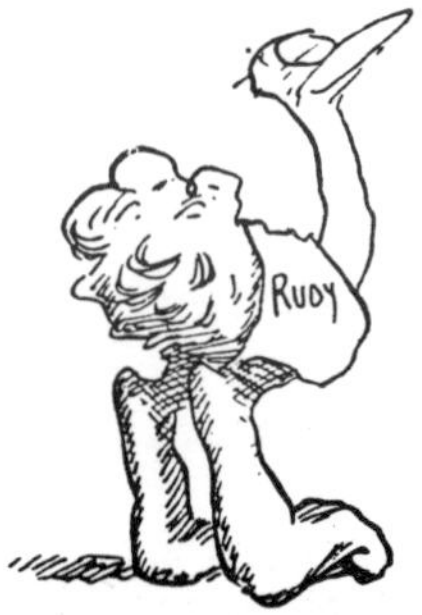
RUDY

The Florida Classic

1925-1926

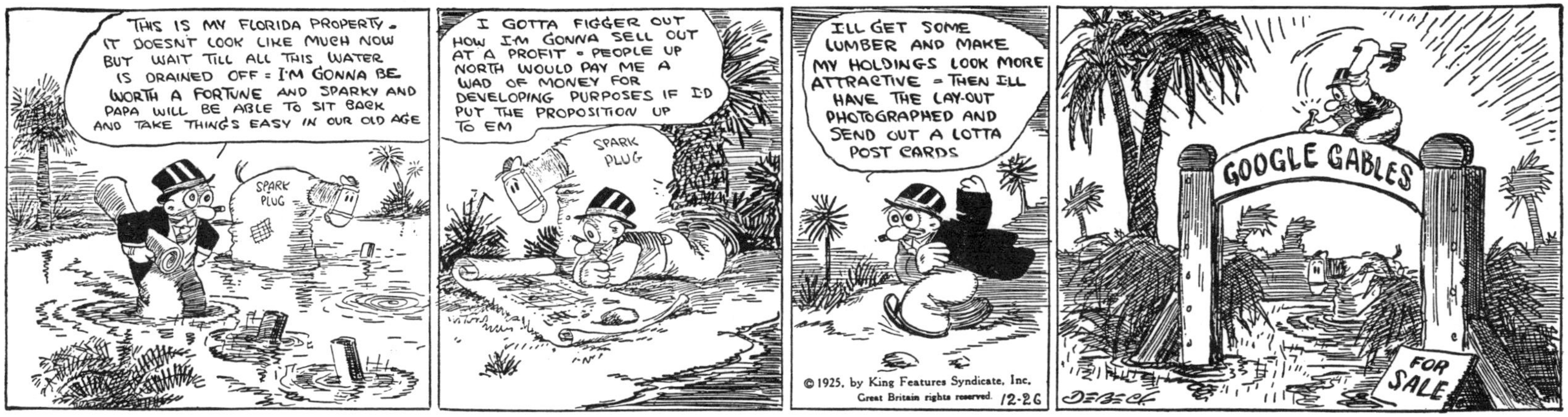

THIS IS MY FLORIDA PROPERTY. IT DOESN'T LOOK LIKE MUCH NOW BUT WAIT TILL ALL THIS WATER IS DRAINED OFF = I'M GONNA BE WORTH A FORTUNE AND SPARKY AND PAPA WILL BE ABLE TO SIT BACK AND TAKE THINGS EASY IN OUR OLD AGE
SPARK PLUG
I GOTTA FIGGER OUT HOW I'M GONNA SELL OUT AT A PROFIT = PEOPLE UP NORTH WOULD PAY ME A WAD OF MONEY FOR DEVELOPING PURPOSES IF I'D PUT THE PROPOSITION UP TO EM
SPARK PLUG
I'LL GET SOME LUMBER AND MAKE MY HOLDINGS LOOK MORE ATTRACTIVE = THEN I'LL HAVE THE LAY-OUT PHOTOGRAPHED AND SEND OUT A LOTTA POST CARDS
© 1925, by King Features Syndicate, Inc. Great Britain rights reserved. 12-26
GOOGLE GABLES
FOR SALE
DE BECK

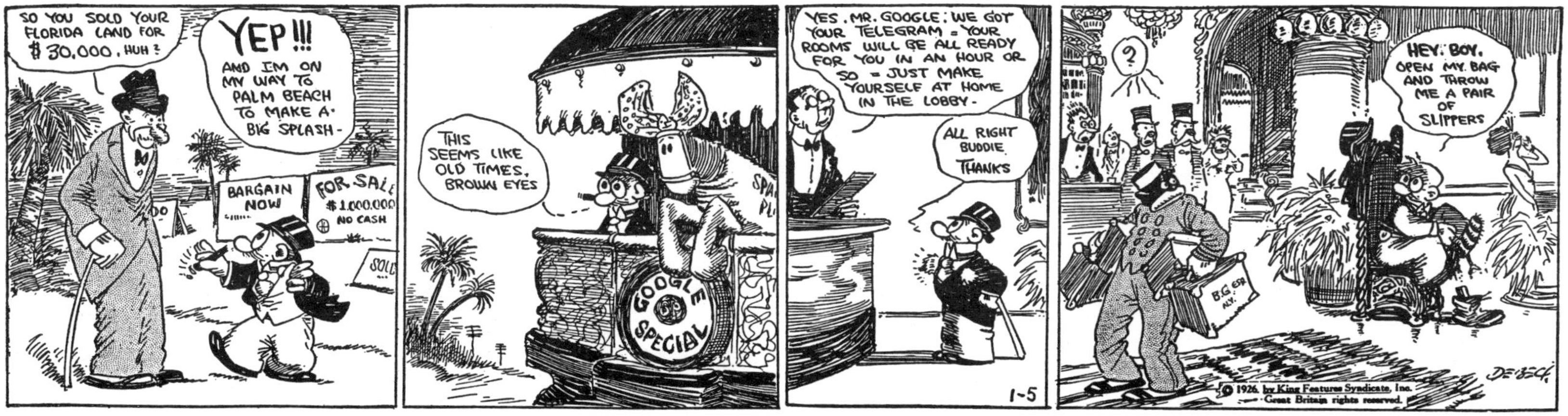

SO YOU SOLD YOUR FLORIDA LAND FOR $30,000, HUH?
YEP!!! AND I'M ON MY WAY TO PALM BEACH TO MAKE A BIG SPLASH -
BARGAIN NOW
FOR SALE $1,000,000 NO CASH
SOLD
THIS SEEMS LIKE OLD TIMES, BROWN EYES
GOOGLE SPECIAL
YES, MR. GOOGLE: WE GOT YOUR TELEGRAM = YOUR ROOMS WILL BE ALL READY FOR YOU IN AN HOUR OR SO = JUST MAKE YOURSELF AT HOME IN THE LOBBY -
ALL RIGHT BUDDIE THANKS
1-5
?
HEY, BOY, OPEN MY BAG AND THROW ME A PAIR OF SLIPPERS
DE BECK
© 1926, by King Features Syndicate, Inc. Great Britain rights reserved.

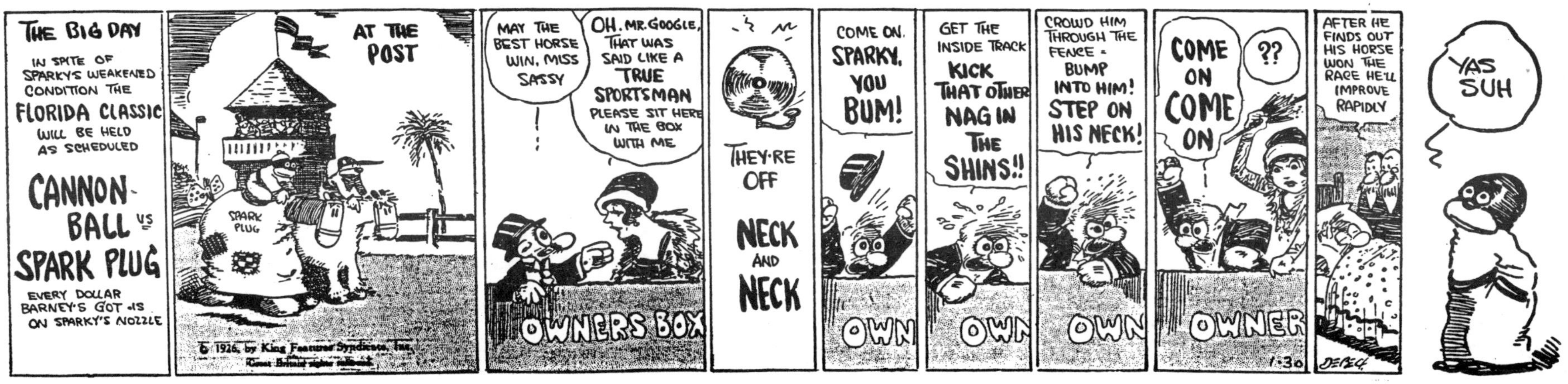

THE BIG DAY
IN SPITE OF SPARKY'S WEAKENED CONDITION THE FLORIDA CLASSIC WILL BE HELD AS SCHEDULED
CANNON-BALL VS SPARK PLUG
EVERY DOLLAR BARNEY'S GOT IS ON SPARKY'S NOZZLE
AT THE POST
SPARK PLUG
© 1926, by King Features Syndicate, Inc. Great Britain rights reserved.
MAY THE BEST HORSE WIN, MISS SASSY
OH, MR. GOOGLE, THAT WAS SAID LIKE A TRUE SPORTSMAN PLEASE SIT HERE IN THE BOX WITH ME
OWNERS BOX
THEY'RE OFF
NECK AND NECK
COME ON, SPARKY, YOU BUM!
OWN
GET THE INSIDE TRACK KICK THAT OTHER NAG IN THE SHINS!!
OWN
CROWD HIM THROUGH THE FENCE = BUMP INTO HIM! STEP ON HIS NECK!
OWN
COME ON COME ON
??
OWNER
1-30
AFTER HE FINDS OUT HIS HORSE WON THE RACE HE'LL IMPROVE RAPIDLY
DE BECK
YAS SUH

The International Championship

1926

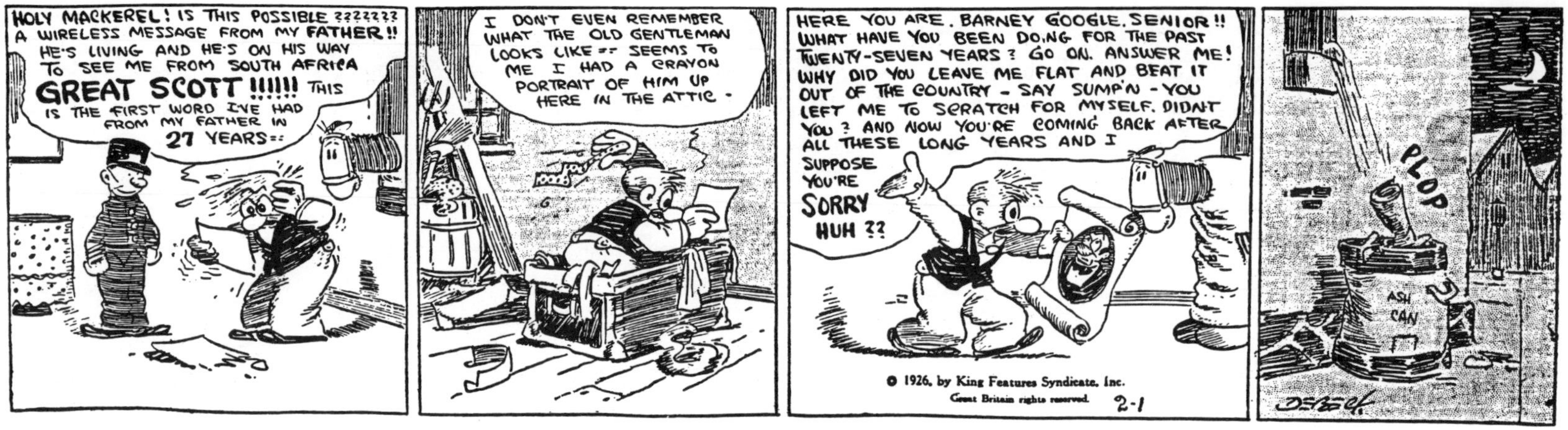

HOLY MACKEREL! IS THIS POSSIBLE ??????? A WIRELESS MESSAGE FROM MY FATHER!! HE'S LIVING AND HE'S ON HIS WAY TO SEE ME FROM SOUTH AFRICA GREAT SCOTT!!!!!! THIS IS THE FIRST WORD I'VE HAD FROM MY FATHER IN 27 YEARS--
I DON'T EVEN REMEMBER WHAT THE OLD GENTLEMAN LOOKS LIKE-- SEEMS TO ME I HAD A CRAYON PORTRAIT OF HIM UP HERE IN THE ATTIC -
HERE YOU ARE. BARNEY GOOGLE. SENIOR!! WHAT HAVE YOU BEEN DOING FOR THE PAST TWENTY-SEVEN YEARS? GO ON. ANSWER ME! WHY DID YOU LEAVE ME FLAT AND BEAT IT OUT OF THE COUNTRY - SAY SUMP'N - YOU LEFT ME TO SCRATCH FOR MYSELF. DIDN'T YOU? AND NOW YOU'RE COMING BACK AFTER ALL THESE LONG YEARS AND I SUPPOSE YOU'RE SORRY HUH??
© 1926, by King Features Syndicate, Inc.
Great Britain rights reserved.
2-1
PLOP
ASH CAN
DE BECK

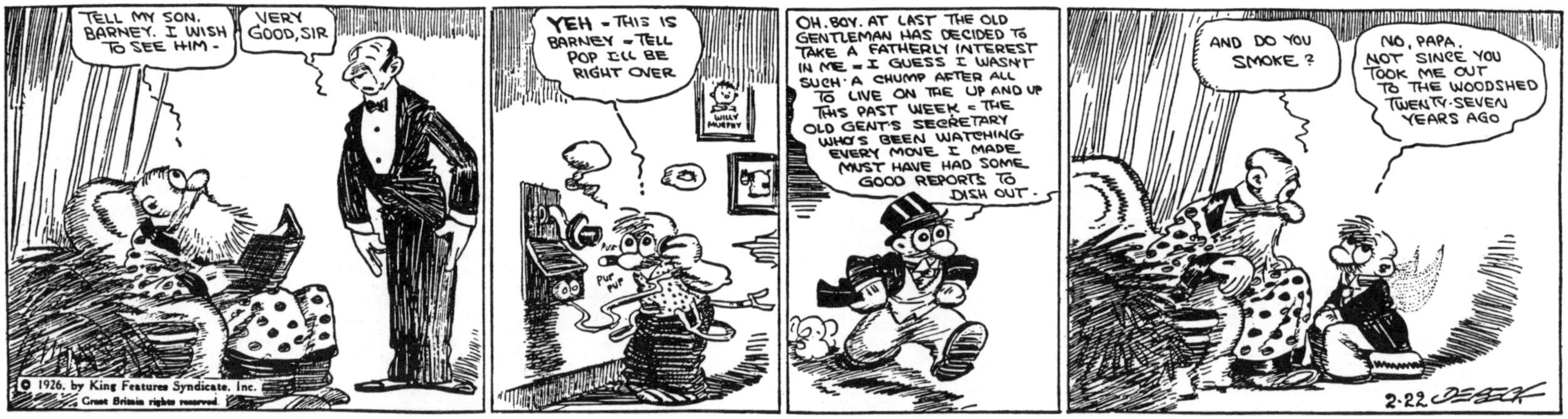

TELL MY SON. BARNEY. I WISH TO SEE HIM -
VERY GOOD, SIR
© 1926, by King Features Syndicate, Inc.
Great Britain rights reserved.
YEH - THIS IS BARNEY - TELL POP I'LL BE RIGHT OVER
WILLY MURPHY
PUF PUF PUF
OH. BOY. AT LAST THE OLD GENTLEMAN HAS DECIDED TO TAKE A FATHERLY INTEREST IN ME - I GUESS I WASN'T SUCH A CHUMP AFTER ALL TO LIVE ON THE UP AND UP THIS PAST WEEK - THE OLD GENT'S SECRETARY WHO'S BEEN WATCHING EVERY MOVE I MADE MUST HAVE HAD SOME GOOD REPORTS TO DISH OUT -
AND DO YOU SMOKE?
NO, PAPA. NOT SINCE YOU TOOK ME OUT TO THE WOODSHED TWENTY-SEVEN YEARS AGO
2-22 DE BECK

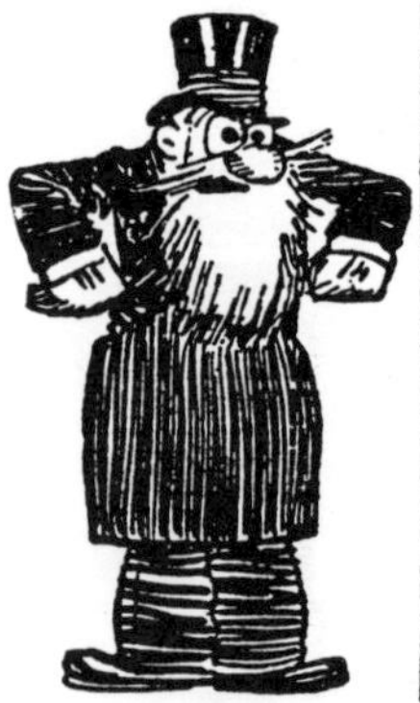

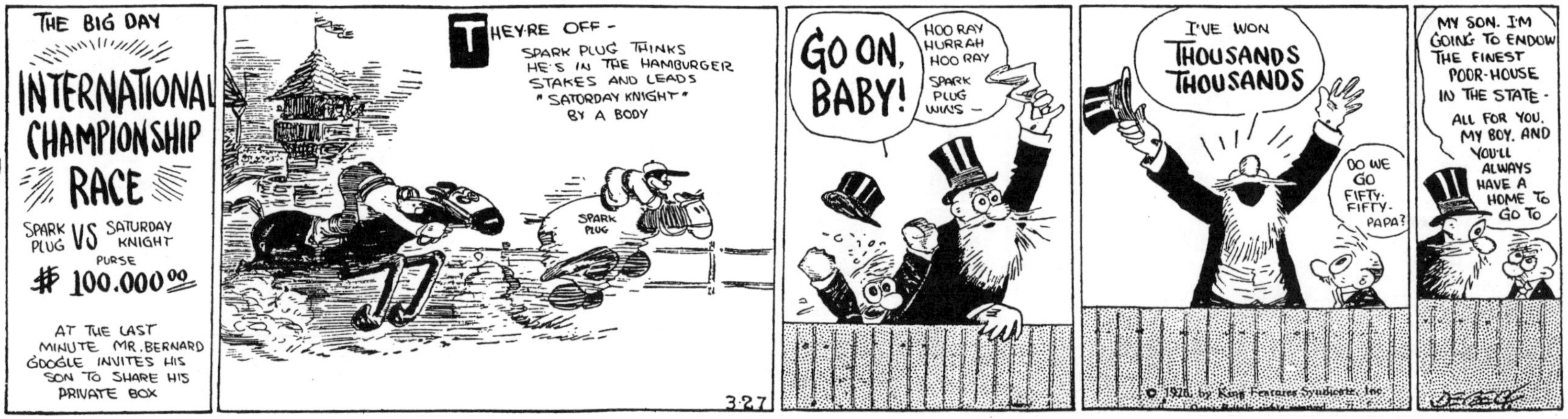

THE BIG DAY
INTERNATIONAL CHAMPIONSHIP RACE
SPARK PLUG VS SATURDAY KNIGHT
PURSE
$ 100.000.00
AT THE LAST MINUTE MR. BERNARD GOOGLE INVITES HIS SON TO SHARE HIS PRIVATE BOX
THEY'RE OFF -
SPARK PLUG THINKS HE'S IN THE HAMBURGER STAKES AND LEADS "SATURDAY KNIGHT" BY A BODY
SPARK PLUG
3-27
GO ON, BABY!
HOO RAY HURRAH HOO RAY SPARK PLUG WINS -
I'VE WON THOUSANDS THOUSANDS
DO WE GO FIFTY-FIFTY-PAPA?
© 1926, by King Features Syndicate, Inc.
MY SON. I'M GOING TO ENDOW THE FINEST POOR-HOUSE IN THE STATE - ALL FOR YOU. MY BOY. AND YOU'LL ALWAYS HAVE A HOME TO GO TO

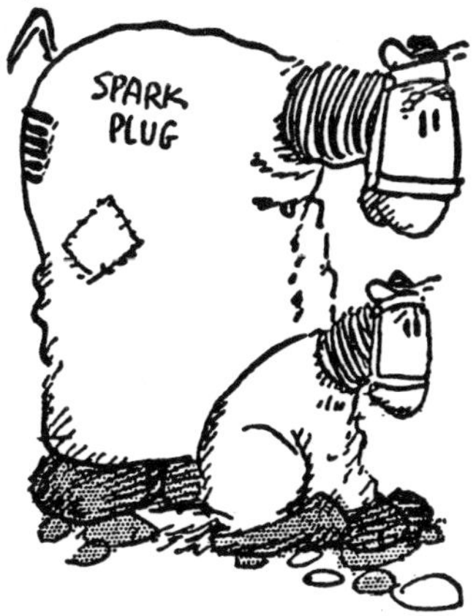
SPARK PLUG

After Barney and his father won the International Championship race on Saturday, March 27, 1926, Billy DeBeck introduced a story about Spark Plug's newborn baby son the following Monday. According to Bill Blackbeard, Director of the San Francisco Academy of Comic Art, the next two weeks of "Barney Google" daily strips, from March 30 to April 11, can not be found in any of the newspapers he has records of in his extensive archives. Sy Schechter, an avid collector of DeBeck's work, did find original artwork for two strips from this sequence, which are reprinted below. It is not known why this story was never printed.

A year later, DeBeck revived the same theme in a series of Sunday pages. On April 10, 1927, Barney, Sunshine and Spark Plug are summoned to Springfield to see Sparky's newborn baby. The last panel of this episode promised, "Barney Google will pay $2.00 (that's all he can dig up right now) to the man, woman, or child who sends in the best name for Sparky's baby! P.S. It's a boy!" One newspaper reported that it had received hundreds of suggestions within days of this solicitation. Some of the names submitted were, "Ignition," "Backfire," "Lightning" and "Skyrocket." The final choice was announced on June 19, 1927, when Barney christened the baby pony, "Ooky."

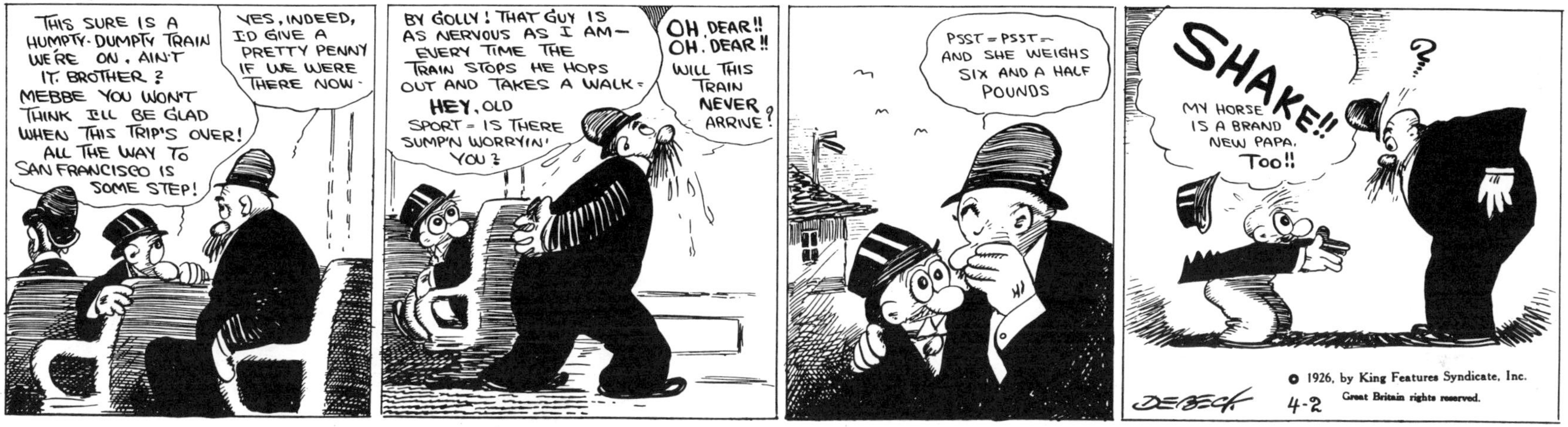
THIS SURE IS A HUMPTY-DUMPTY TRAIN WE'RE ON. AIN'T IT, BROTHER? MEBBE YOU WON'T THINK I'LL BE GLAD WHEN THIS TRIP'S OVER! ALL THE WAY TO SAN FRANCISCO IS SOME STEP!
YES, INDEED, I'D GIVE A PRETTY PENNY IF WE WERE THERE NOW-
BY GOLLY! THAT GUY IS AS NERVOUS AS I AM— EVERY TIME THE TRAIN STOPS HE HOPS OUT AND TAKES A WALK- HEY, OLD SPORT- IS THERE SUMP'N WORRYIN' YOU?
OH, DEAR!! OH, DEAR!! WILL THIS TRAIN NEVER ARRIVE?
PSST-PSST- AND SHE WEIGHS SIX AND A HALF POUNDS
SHAKE!!
?
MY HORSE IS A BRAND NEW PAPA, TOO!!
© 1926, by King Features Syndicate, Inc. Great Britain rights reserved.
DEBECK 4-2

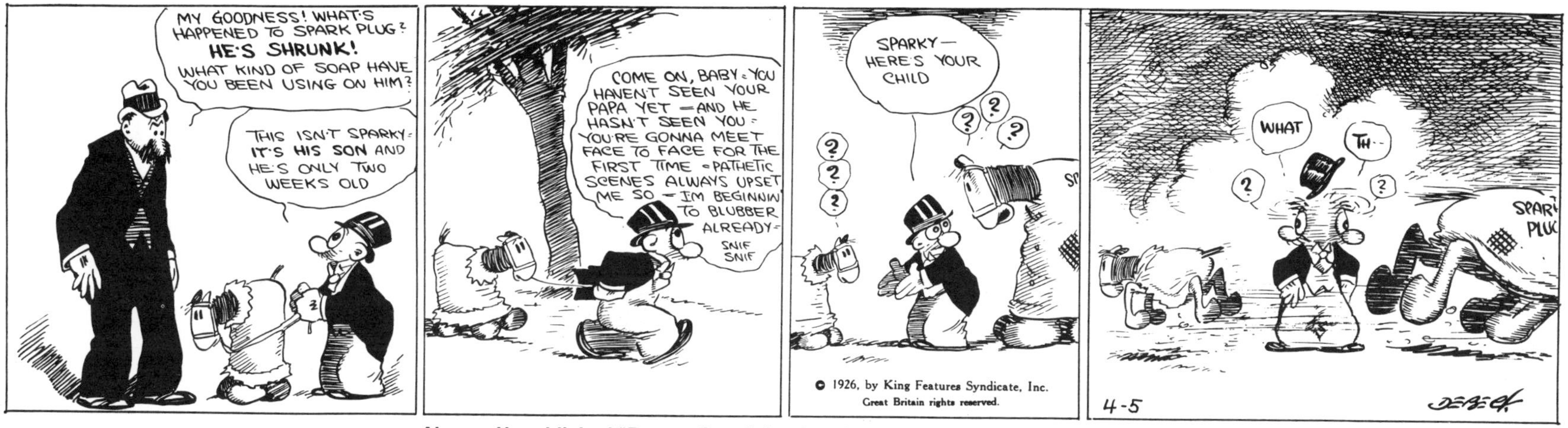
MY GOODNESS! WHAT'S HAPPENED TO SPARK PLUG? HE'S SHRUNK! WHAT KIND OF SOAP HAVE YOU BEEN USING ON HIM?
THIS ISN'T SPARKY- IT'S HIS SON AND HE'S ONLY TWO WEEKS OLD
COME ON, BABY- YOU HAVEN'T SEEN YOUR PAPA YET —AND HE HASN'T SEEN YOU- YOU'RE GONNA MEET FACE TO FACE FOR THE FIRST TIME - PATHETIC SCENES ALWAYS UPSET ME SO — I'M BEGINNIN' TO BLUBBER ALREADY- SNIF SNIF
SPARKY— HERE'S YOUR CHILD
WHAT
TH--
© 1926, by King Features Syndicate, Inc. Great Britain rights reserved.
4-5 DEBECK

Above: Unpublished "Barney Google" strips, dated April 2 and April 5, 1926. From the Collection of Sy and Sandy Schechter.

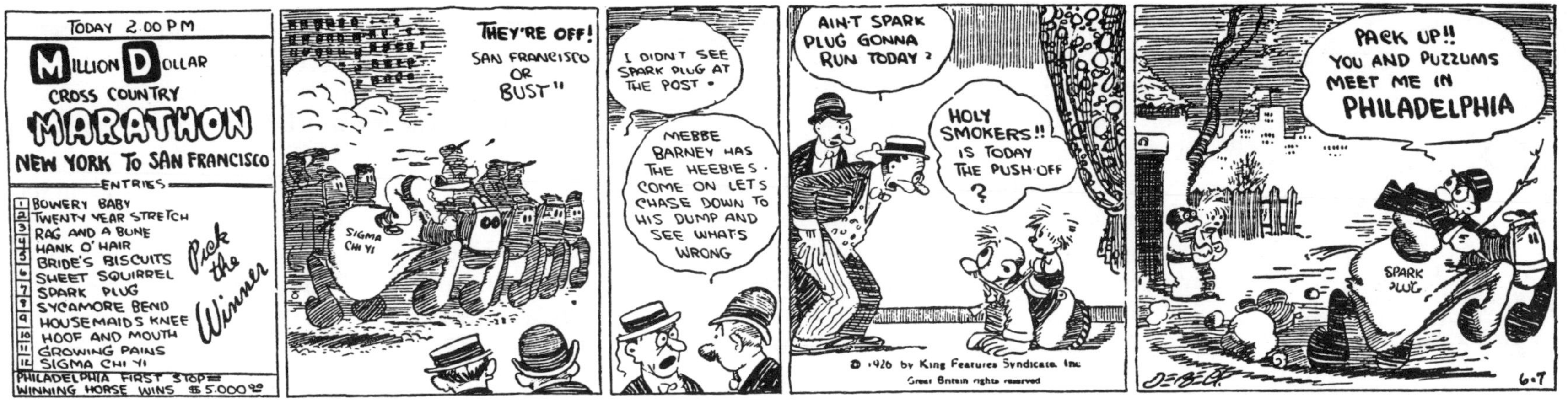
TODAY 2.00 PM
MILLION DOLLAR CROSS COUNTRY MARATHON
NEW YORK TO SAN FRANCISCO
ENTRIES
1 BOWERY BABY
2 TWENTY YEAR STRETCH
3 RAG AND A BONE
4 HANK O' HAIR
5 BRIDE'S BISCUITS
6 SHEET SQUIRREL
7 SPARK PLUG
8 SYCAMORE BEND
9 HOUSEMAID'S KNEE
10 HOOF AND MOUTH
11 GROWING PAINS
12 SIGMA CHI YI
Pick the Winner
PHILADELPHIA FIRST STOP
WINNING HORSE WINS $5.000.00
THEY'RE OFF!
SAN FRANCISCO OR BUST"
SIGMA CHI YI
I DIDN'T SEE SPARK PLUG AT THE POST.
MEBBE BARNEY HAS THE HEEBIES. COME ON LETS CHASE DOWN TO HIS DUMP AND SEE WHATS WRONG
AIN'T SPARK PLUG GONNA RUN TODAY?
HOLY SMOKERS!! IS TODAY THE PUSH-OFF
?
© 1926 by King Features Syndicate, Inc
Great Britain rights reserved
PACK UP!! YOU AND PUZZUMS MEET ME IN PHILADELPHIA
SPARK PLUG
DE BECK
6-7

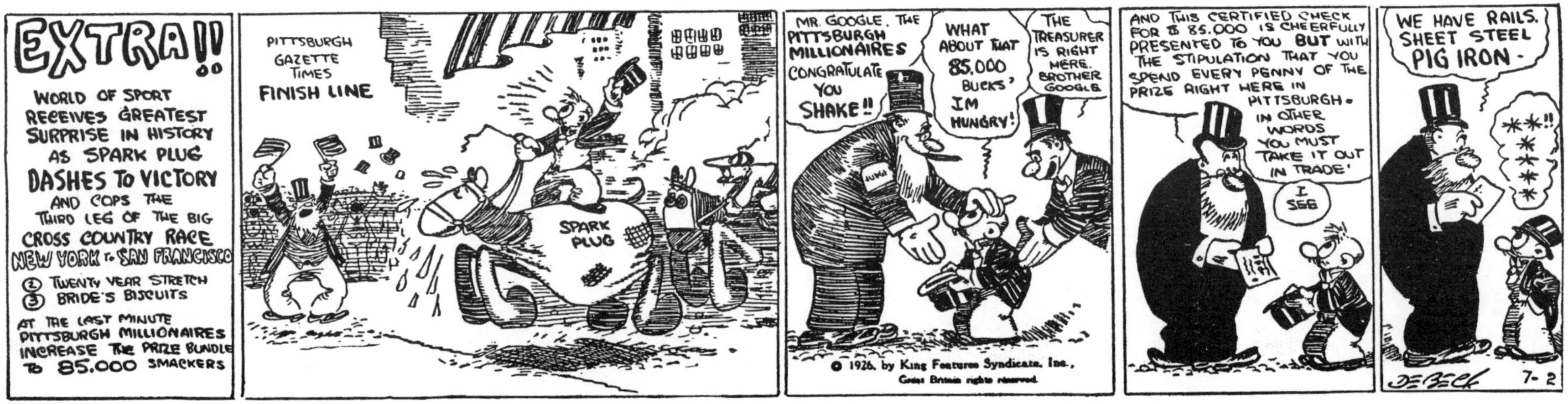
EXTRA!!
WORLD OF SPORT RECEIVES GREATEST SURPRISE IN HISTORY AS SPARK PLUG DASHES TO VICTORY AND COPS THE THIRD LEG OF THE BIG CROSS COUNTRY RACE NEW YORK TO SAN FRANCISCO
2 TWENTY YEAR STRETCH
3 BRIDE'S BISCUITS
AT THE LAST MINUTE PITTSBURGH MILLIONAIRES INCREASE THE PRIZE BUNDLE TO 85.000 SMACKERS
PITTSBURGH GAZETTE TIMES FINISH LINE
SPARK PLUG
MR. GOOGLE. THE PITTSBURGH MILLIONAIRES CONGRATULATE YOU SHAKE!!
WHAT ABOUT THAT 85,000 BUCKS' I'M HUNGRY!
THE TREASURER IS RIGHT HERE. BROTHER GOOGLE
© 1926, by King Features Syndicate, Inc.,
Great Britain rights reserved.
AND THIS CERTIFIED CHECK FOR $85.000 IS CHEERFULLY PRESENTED TO YOU BUT WITH THE STIPULATION THAT YOU SPEND EVERY PENNY OF THE PRIZE RIGHT HERE IN PITTSBURGH. IN OTHER WORDS YOU MUST TAKE IT OUT IN TRADE'
I SEE
WE HAVE RAILS, SHEET STEEL PIG IRON.
*!!
DE BECK
7-2

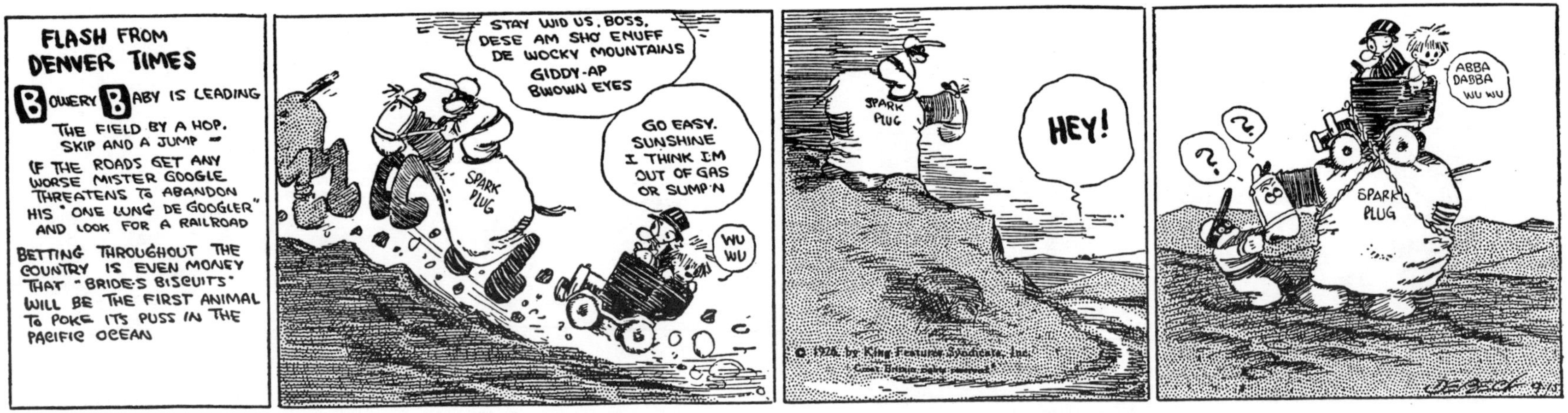
FLASH FROM DENVER TIMES
BOWERY BABY IS LEADING THE FIELD BY A HOP. SKIP AND A JUMP -
IF THE ROADS GET ANY WORSE MISTER GOOGLE THREATENS TO ABANDON HIS "ONE LUNG DE GOOGLER" AND LOOK FOR A RAILROAD
BETTING THROUGHOUT THE COUNTRY IS EVEN MONEY THAT "BRIDE'S BISCUITS" WILL BE THE FIRST ANIMAL TO POKE ITS PUSS IN THE PACIFIC OCEAN
STAY WID US, BOSS, DESE AM SHO' ENUFF DE WOCKY MOUNTAINS GIDDY-AP BWOWN EYES
SPARK PLUG
GO EASY. SUNSHINE I THINK I'M OUT OF GAS OR SUMP'N
WU WU
SPARK PLUG
HEY!
© 1926 by King Features Syndicate, Inc.
? ?
ABBA DABBA WU WU
SPARK PLUG
DE BECK

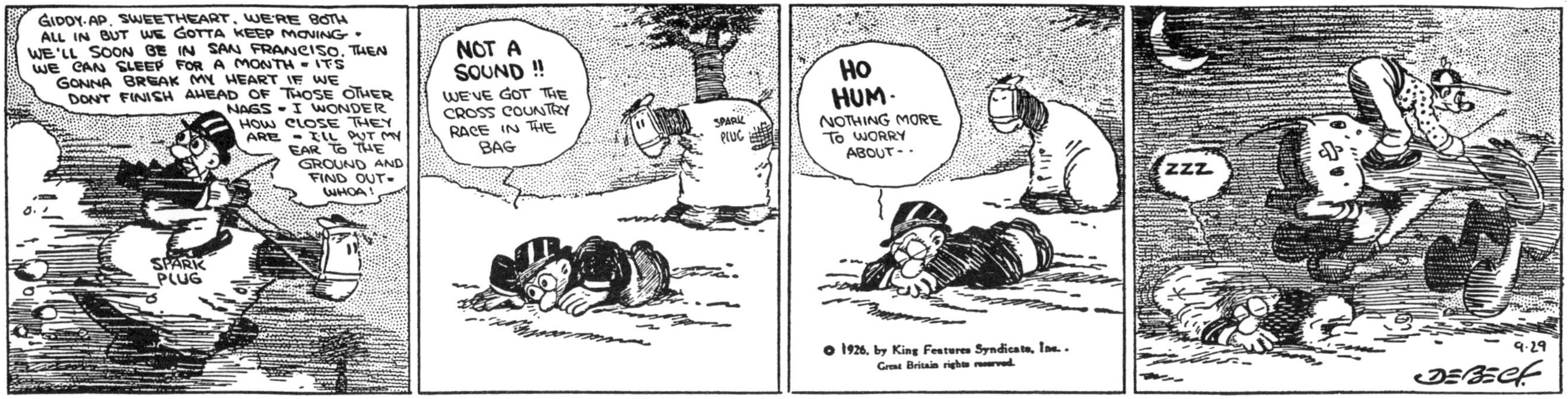
GIDDY-AP, SWEETHEART, WE'RE BOTH ALL IN BUT WE GOTTA KEEP MOVING - WE'LL SOON BE IN SAN FRANCISCO, THEN WE CAN SLEEP FOR A MONTH - IT'S GONNA BREAK MY HEART IF WE DON'T FINISH AHEAD OF THOSE OTHER NAGS - I WONDER HOW CLOSE THEY ARE - I'LL PUT MY EAR TO THE GROUND AND FIND OUT - WHOA!
SPARK PLUG
NOT A SOUND !! WE'VE GOT THE CROSS COUNTRY RACE IN THE BAG
SPARK PLUG
HO HUM - NOTHING MORE TO WORRY ABOUT - -
© 1926, by King Features Syndicate, Inc. Great Britain rights reserved.
ZZZ
9-29
DE BECK

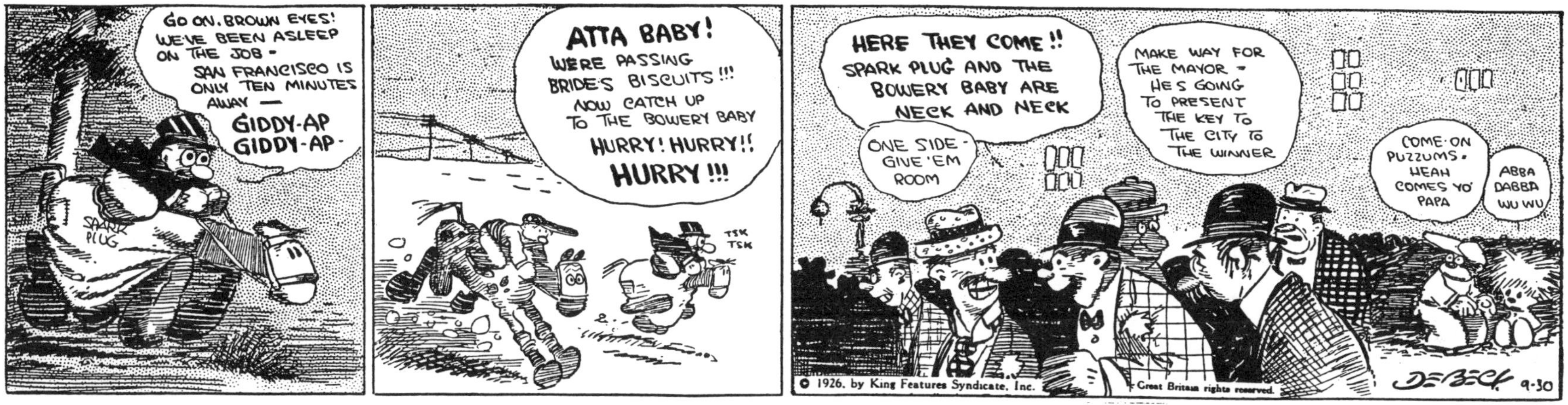
GO ON, BROWN EYES! WE'VE BEEN ASLEEP ON THE JOB - SAN FRANCISCO IS ONLY TEN MINUTES AWAY — GIDDY-AP GIDDY-AP -
SPARK PLUG
ATTA BABY! WERE PASSING BRIDE'S BISCUITS !!! NOW CATCH UP TO THE BOWERY BABY HURRY! HURRY!! HURRY !!!
TSK TSK
HERE THEY COME !! SPARK PLUG AND THE BOWERY BABY ARE NECK AND NECK
ONE SIDE - GIVE 'EM ROOM
MAKE WAY FOR THE MAYOR - HE'S GOING TO PRESENT THE KEY TO THE CITY TO THE WINNER
COME ON PUZZUMS - HEAH COMES YO' PAPA
ABBA DABBA WU WU
© 1926, by King Features Syndicate, Inc. Great Britain rights reserved.
DE BECK 9-30

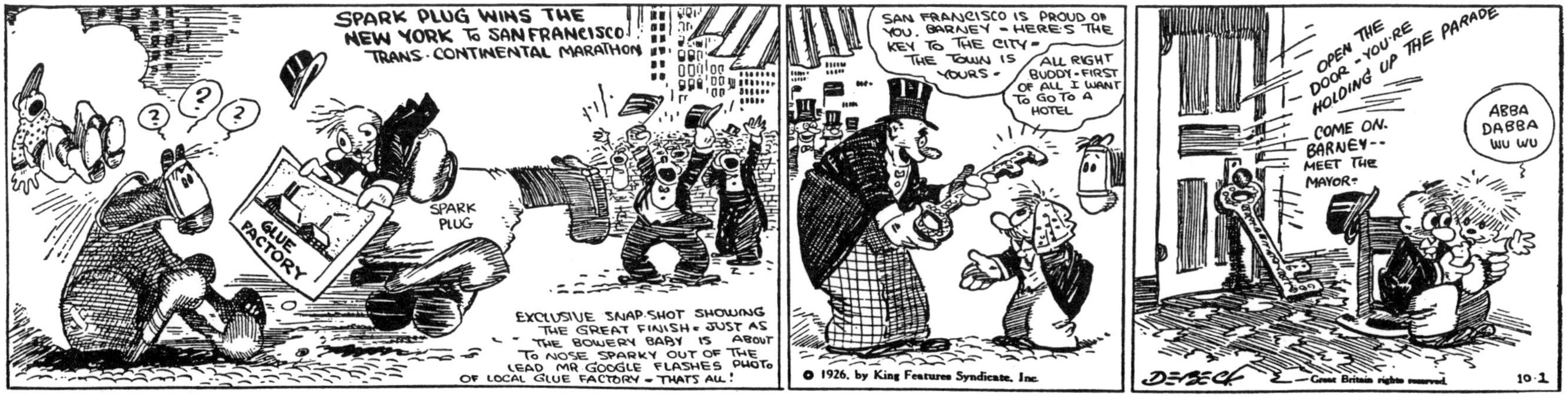
SPARK PLUG WINS THE NEW YORK TO SAN FRANCISCO TRANS-CONTINENTAL MARATHON
? ? ?
GLUE FACTORY
SPARK PLUG
EXCLUSIVE SNAP-SHOT SHOWING THE GREAT FINISH - JUST AS THE BOWERY BABY IS ABOUT TO NOSE SPARKY OUT OF THE LEAD MR GOOGLE FLASHES PHOTO OF LOCAL GLUE FACTORY - THAT'S ALL!
SAN FRANCISCO IS PROUD OF YOU, BARNEY - HERE'S THE KEY TO THE CITY - THE TOWN IS YOURS -
ALL RIGHT BUDDY - FIRST OF ALL I WANT TO GO TO A HOTEL
© 1926, by King Features Syndicate, Inc.
OPEN THE DOOR - YOU'RE HOLDING UP THE PARADE
COME ON, BARNEY - - MEET THE MAYOR -
ABBA DABBA WU WU
DE BECK
Great Britain rights reserved.
10-1

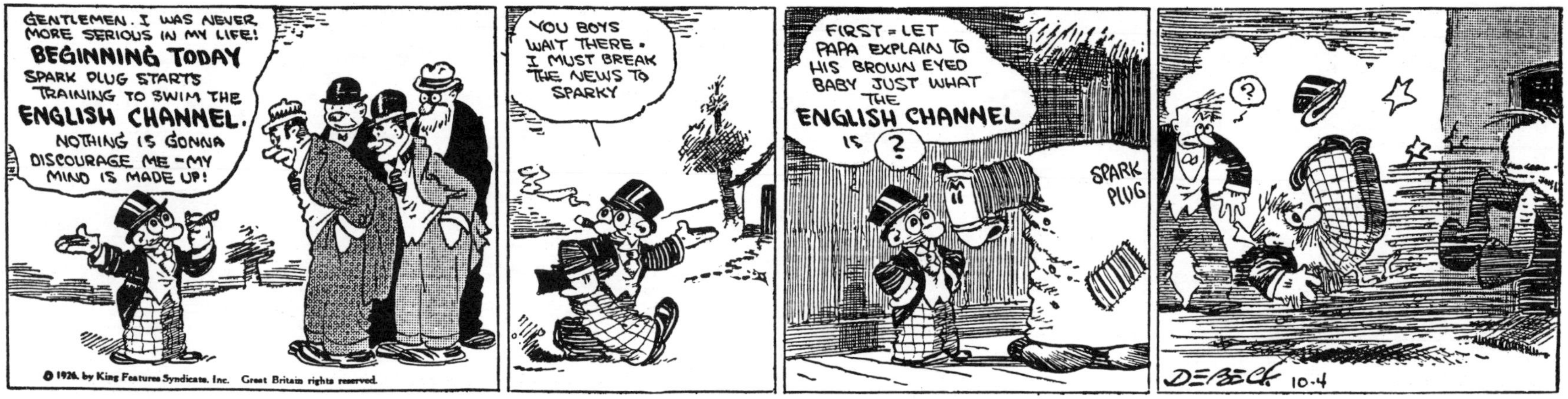
GENTLEMEN. I WAS NEVER MORE SERIOUS IN MY LIFE! BEGINNING TODAY SPARK PLUG STARTS TRAINING TO SWIM THE ENGLISH CHANNEL. NOTHING IS GONNA DISCOURAGE ME - MY MIND IS MADE UP!
© 1926, by King Features Syndicate, Inc. Great Britain rights reserved.
YOU BOYS WAIT THERE. I MUST BREAK THE NEWS TO SPARKY
FIRST = LET PAPA EXPLAIN TO HIS BROWN EYED BABY JUST WHAT THE ENGLISH CHANNEL IS ?
SPARK PLUG
?
DEBECK 10-4

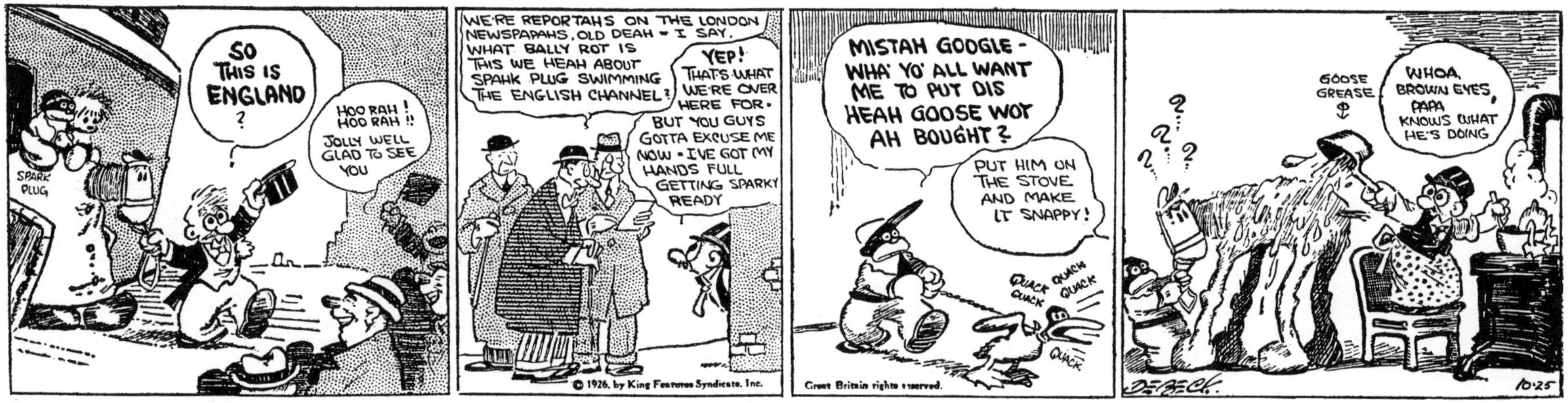
SO THIS IS ENGLAND ?
HOO RAH! HOO RAH!! JOLLY WELL GLAD TO SEE YOU
SPARK PLUG
WE'RE REPORTAHS ON THE LONDON NEWSPAPAHS, OLD DEAH - I SAY. WHAT BALLY ROT IS THIS WE HEAH ABOUT SPAHK PLUG SWIMMING THE ENGLISH CHANNEL?
YEP! THAT'S WHAT WE'RE OVER HERE FOR. BUT YOU GUYS GOTTA EXCUSE ME NOW - I'VE GOT MY HANDS FULL GETTING SPARKY READY
© 1926, by King Features Syndicate, Inc.
MISTAH GOOGLE - WHA' YO' ALL WANT ME TO PUT DIS HEAH GOOSE WOT AH BOUGHT?
PUT HIM ON THE STOVE AND MAKE IT SNAPPY!
QUACK QUACK QUACK QUACK
QUACK
Great Britain rights reserved.
GOOSE GREASE
WHOA, BROWN EYES, PAPA KNOWS WHAT HE'S DOING
? ? ? ?
DEBECK 10-25

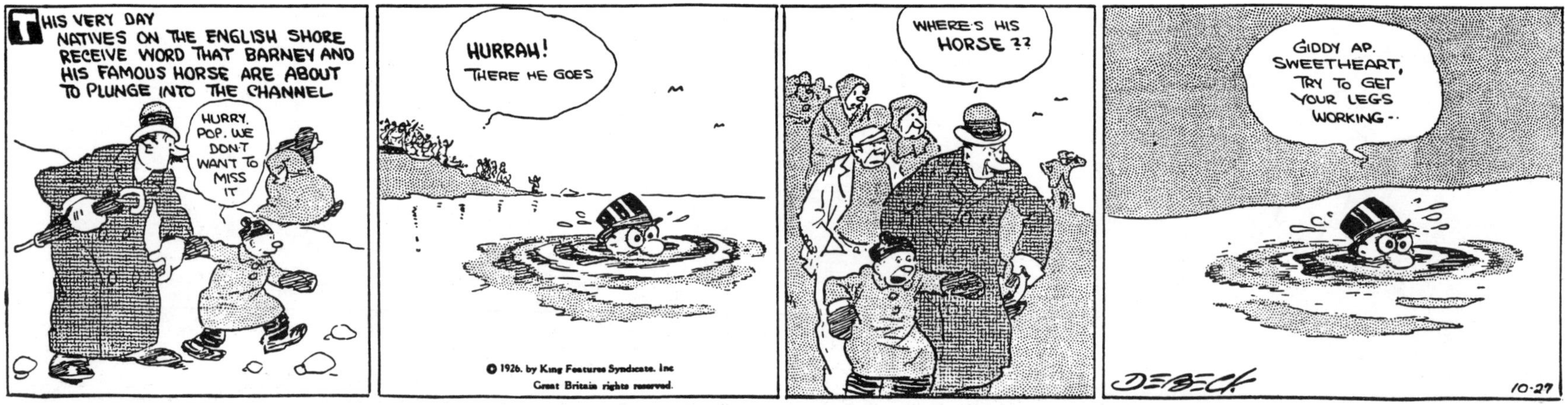
THIS VERY DAY NATIVES ON THE ENGLISH SHORE RECEIVE WORD THAT BARNEY AND HIS FAMOUS HORSE ARE ABOUT TO PLUNGE INTO THE CHANNEL
HURRY. POP. WE DON'T WANT TO MISS IT
HURRAH! THERE HE GOES
© 1926, by King Features Syndicate, Inc Great Britain rights reserved.
WHERE'S HIS HORSE ??
GIDDY AP. SWEETHEART, TRY TO GET YOUR LEGS WORKING..
DEBECK 10-27

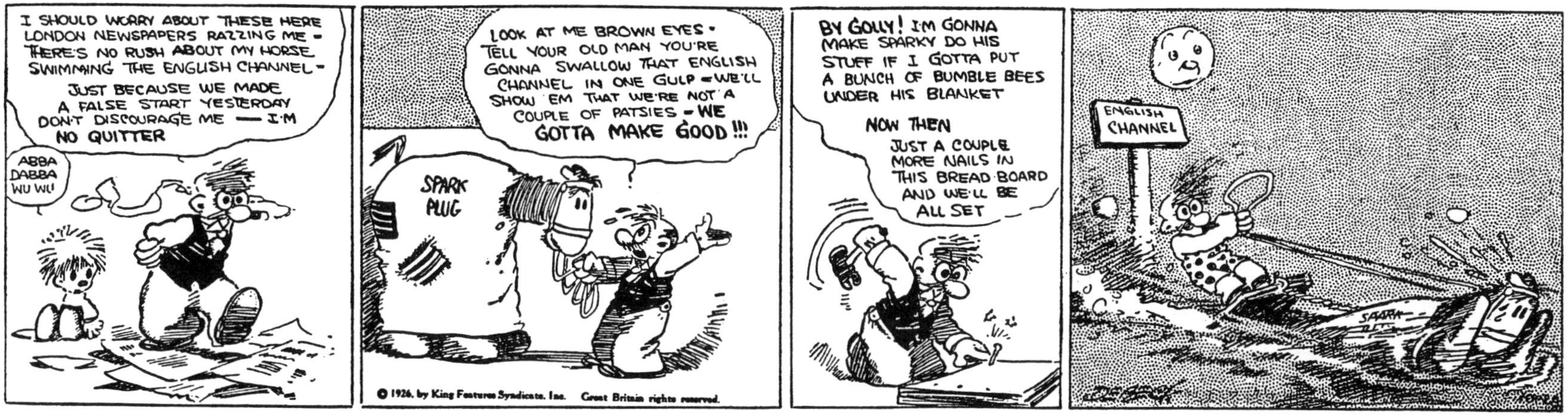
I SHOULD WORRY ABOUT THESE HERE LONDON NEWSPAPERS RAZZING ME = THERE'S NO RUSH ABOUT MY HORSE SWIMMING THE ENGLISH CHANNEL =
JUST BECAUSE WE MADE A FALSE START YESTERDAY DON'T DISCOURAGE ME — I'M NO QUITTER
ABBA DABBA WU WU
LOOK AT ME BROWN EYES = TELL YOUR OLD MAN YOU'RE GONNA SWALLOW THAT ENGLISH CHANNEL IN ONE GULP = WE'LL SHOW 'EM THAT WE'RE NOT A COUPLE OF PATSIES = WE GOTTA MAKE GOOD !!!
SPARK PLUG
© 1926, by King Features Syndicate, Inc. Great Britain rights reserved.
BY GOLLY! I'M GONNA MAKE SPARKY DO HIS STUFF IF I GOTTA PUT A BUNCH OF BUMBLE BEES UNDER HIS BLANKET
NOW THEN
JUST A COUPLE MORE NAILS IN THIS BREAD BOARD AND WE'LL BE ALL SET
ENGLISH CHANNEL
SPARK

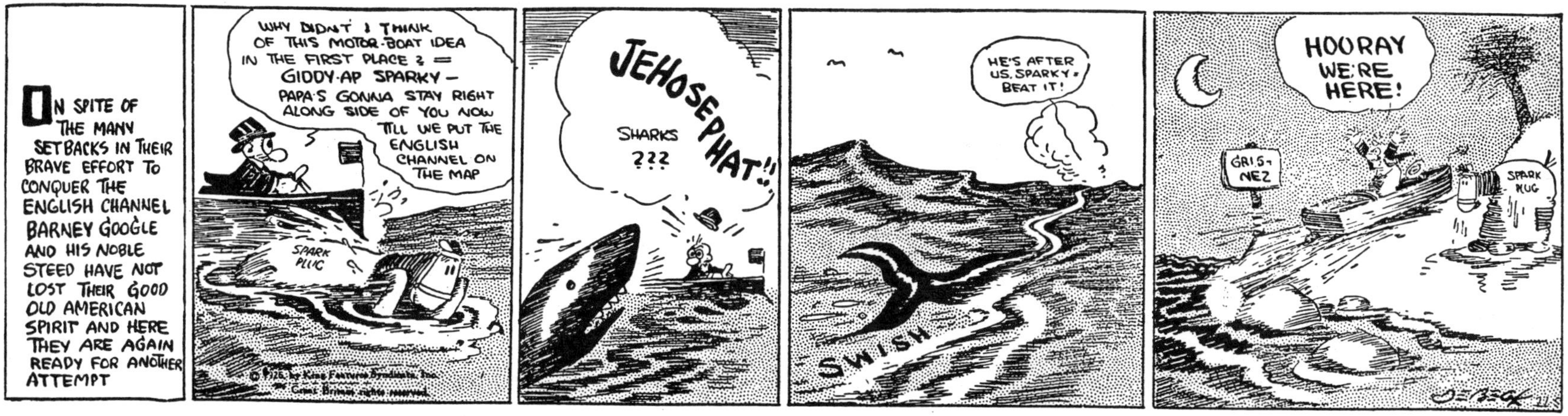
IN SPITE OF THE MANY SETBACKS IN THEIR BRAVE EFFORT TO CONQUER THE ENGLISH CHANNEL BARNEY GOOGLE AND HIS NOBLE STEED HAVE NOT LOST THEIR GOOD OLD AMERICAN SPIRIT AND HERE THEY ARE AGAIN READY FOR ANOTHER ATTEMPT
WHY DIDN'T I THINK OF THIS MOTOR-BOAT IDEA IN THE FIRST PLACE ? = GIDDY-AP SPARKY — PAPA'S GONNA STAY RIGHT ALONG SIDE OF YOU NOW TILL WE PUT THE ENGLISH CHANNEL ON THE MAP
SPARK PLUG
JEHOSEPHAT!!
SHARKS ???
HE'S AFTER US, SPARKY = BEAT IT!
SWISH
HOORAY WE'RE HERE!
GRIS-NEZ
SPARK PLUG

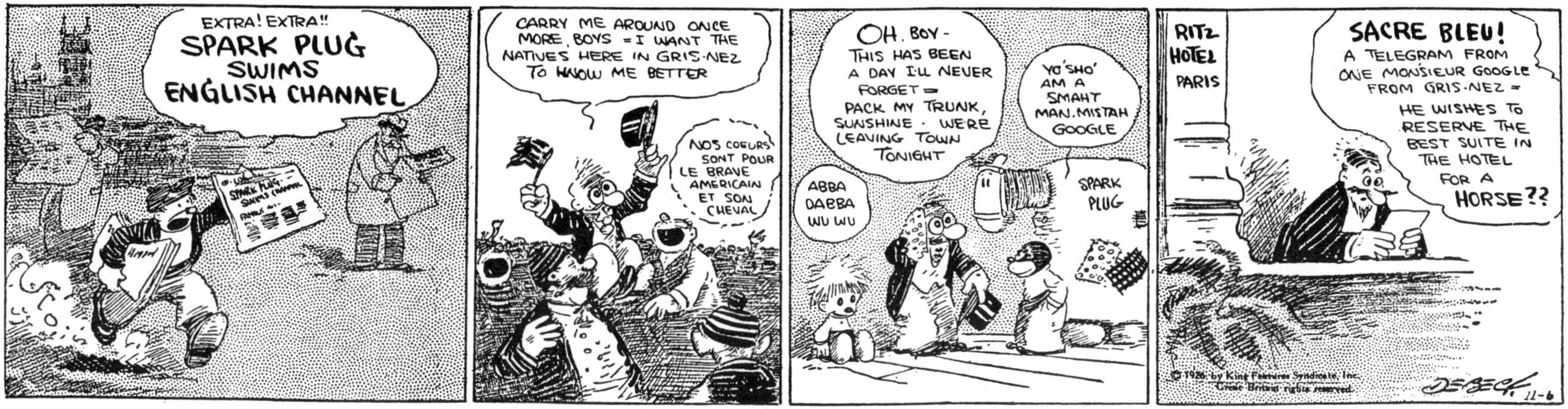
EXTRA! EXTRA!!
SPARK PLUG SWIMS ENGLISH CHANNEL
CARRY ME AROUND ONCE MORE, BOYS = I WANT THE NATIVES HERE IN GRIS-NEZ TO KNOW ME BETTER
NOS COEURS SONT POUR LE BRAVE AMERICAIN ET SON CHEVAL
OH, BOY - THIS HAS BEEN A DAY I'LL NEVER FORGET = PACK MY TRUNK, SUNSHINE - WE'RE LEAVING TOWN TONIGHT
YO'SHO' AM A SMAHT MAN, MISTAH GOOGLE
ABBA DABBA WU WU
SPARK PLUG
RITZ HOTEL PARIS
SACRE BLEU! A TELEGRAM FROM ONE MONSIEUR GOOGLE FROM GRIS-NEZ = HE WISHES TO RESERVE THE BEST SUITE IN THE HOTEL FOR A HORSE??
© 1926, by King Features Syndicate, Inc. Great Britain rights reserved.
DEBECK 11-6

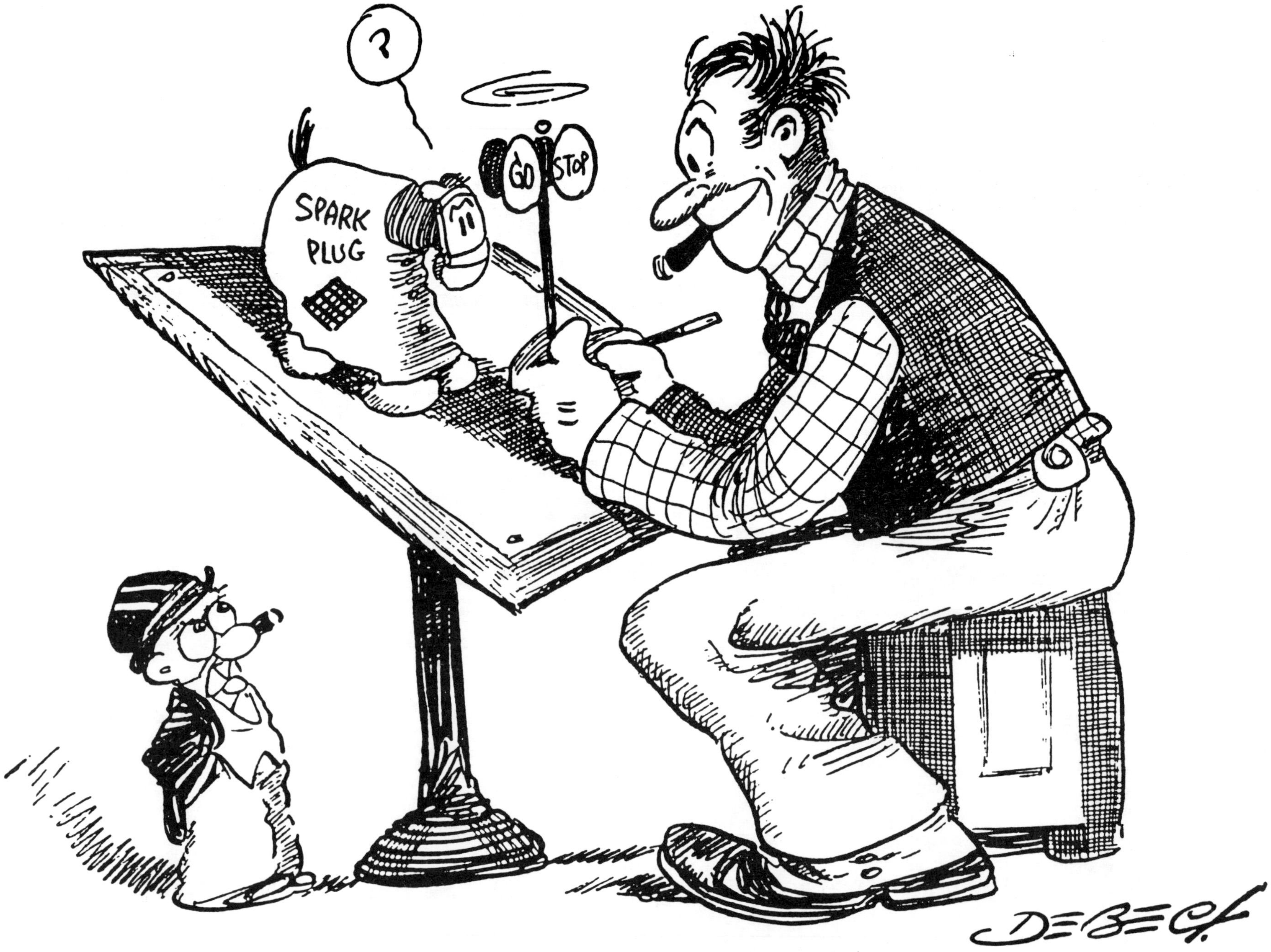
?
SPARK
PLUG
GO
STOP
DEBECK

Above: A self-caricature of DeBeck from "Barney Google and Spark Plug," published by Cupples & Leon, 1924. From the Collection of Bill Janocha.

Melodrama & Mayhem

1927 — 1934

When Billy DeBeck first moved to New York City from Chicago in the early 1920's, fame and fortune followed close behind. The young cartoonist lived in a lavish apartment on Riverside Drive, rubbed elbows with the Broadway crowd and partied nightly into the wee hours. Prohibition never put a damper on his thirst for the good life.

All that changed when he married his second wife, Mary Louise Dunne, in 1927. The newlyweds left for Europe and stayed there for two years. When they returned in 1929, Mary encouraged Billy to steer clear of the fast track. Their new domestic life revolved around homes in New York and Florida.

The strip changed as well. Faced with the challenge of sustaining his success, DeBeck launched into a period of restless experimentation. The years between 1927 and 1934 may be regarded as either the high-water mark in DeBeck's creative evolution or as a period of sloppy story-telling, artistic self-indulgence and forgettable characters. In either case, he displayed a comic versatility that was matched by very few cartoonists of his time.

It started with the Eric Von Horn episode, a role-reversal tale in the tradition of "The Prince and the Pauper," that lasted for more than six months in 1927. Then, after a brief stint as a flagpole sitter, Barney became involved with a secret society, The Brotherhood of Billy Goats, and by the close of 1927, had managed to increase their membership to "twenty million strong."

In 1928, Barney ran for President of the United States and befriended Horseface Klotz, a precursor of Snuffy Smith. Hello Swifty - The Pride of Scotland Yard saved Barney from a murder plot in 1929, and Spark Plug returned to run in the Hamburger Stakes in the spring of 1930. DeBeck encouraged readers to "send in the name of your own hoss and watch him hop in the Comic Strip Derby" later that same year.

Beginning on September 16, 1930, and continuing until April 10, 1931, the Madame La Mousse mystery was DeBeck's most ambitious continuity, featuring a cast of characters worthy of an Agatha Christie whodunit. Sparky reappeared in mid-1931 to race against a pint-sized look-alike named Pony Boy in the International Derby. Sully, the former Sultan of Sulu, arrived on the scene in 1932, and his wrestling and boxing exploits occupied the spotlight until late in 1933. The pivotal year of 1934 began with Barney as the dictator of the Caribbean island of Santiago.

Courtroom drama, murder mysteries, political intrigue, secret societies, wrestling matches, and, of course, horse races - Billy DeBeck was all over the map during this period. By the summer of 1934, after seven-and-a-half years of searching for another magical formula, he probably decided it was time to settle down. Or perhaps he finally found that magic when fate beckoned Barney Google off into the hills of North Carolina.

Eric Van Horn

1927

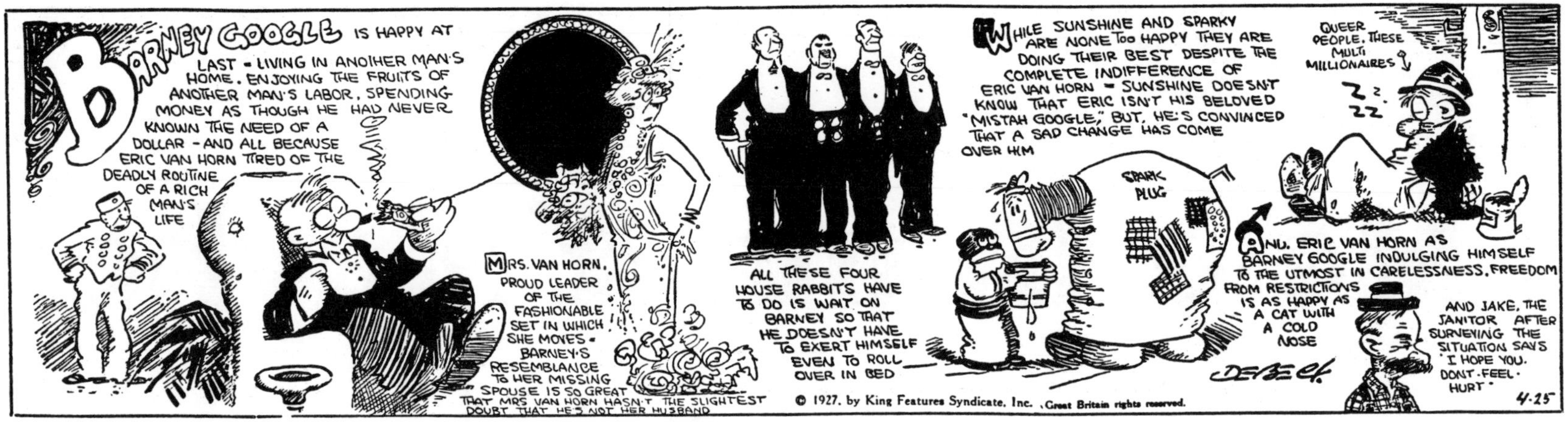

BARNEY GOOGLE IS HAPPY AT LAST - LIVING IN ANOTHER MAN'S HOME. ENJOYING THE FRUITS OF ANOTHER MAN'S LABOR. SPENDING MONEY AS THOUGH HE HAD NEVER KNOWN THE NEED OF A DOLLAR - AND ALL BECAUSE ERIC VAN HORN TIRED OF THE DEADLY ROUTINE OF A RICH MAN'S LIFE
MRS. VAN HORN, PROUD LEADER OF THE FASHIONABLE SET IN WHICH SHE MOVES - BARNEY'S RESEMBLANCE TO HER MISSING SPOUSE IS SO GREAT THAT MRS VAN HORN HASN'T THE SLIGHTEST DOUBT THAT HE'S NOT HER HUSBAND
ALL THESE FOUR HOUSE RABBITS HAVE TO DO IS WAIT ON BARNEY SO THAT HE DOESN'T HAVE TO EXERT HIMSELF EVEN TO ROLL OVER IN BED
WHILE SUNSHINE AND SPARKY ARE NONE TOO HAPPY THEY ARE DOING THEIR BEST DESPITE THE COMPLETE INDIFFERENCE OF ERIC VAN HORN - SUNSHINE DOESN'T KNOW THAT ERIC ISN'T HIS BELOVED "MISTAH GOOGLE," BUT, HE'S CONVINCED THAT A SAD CHANGE HAS COME OVER HIM
SPARK PLUG
QUEER PEOPLE, THESE MULTI MILLIONAIRES
Z Z Z Z
AND, ERIC VAN HORN AS BARNEY GOOGLE INDULGING HIMSELF TO THE UTMOST IN CARELESSNESS, FREEDOM FROM RESTRICTIONS IS AS HAPPY AS A CAT WITH A COLD NOSE
AND JAKE, THE JANITOR AFTER SURVEYING THE SITUATION SAYS "I HOPE YOU. DON'T. FEEL. HURT"
DE BECK
© 1927, by King Features Syndicate, Inc. Great Britain rights reserved.
4-25

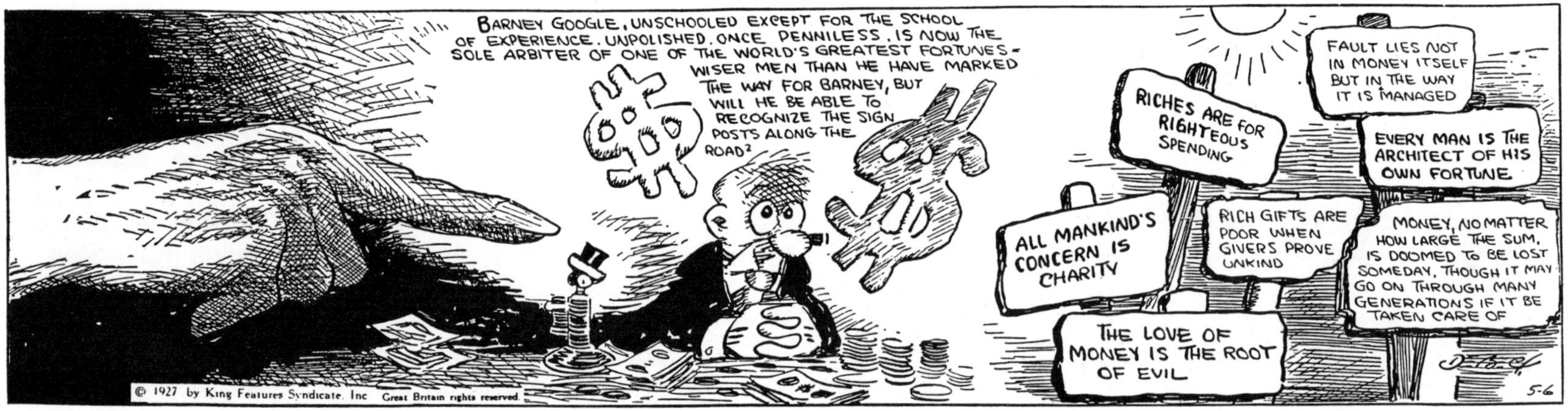

BARNEY GOOGLE, UNSCHOOLED EXCEPT FOR THE SCHOOL OF EXPERIENCE, UNPOLISHED, ONCE PENNILESS, IS NOW THE SOLE ARBITER OF ONE OF THE WORLD'S GREATEST FORTUNES - WISER MEN THAN HE HAVE MARKED THE WAY FOR BARNEY, BUT WILL HE BE ABLE TO RECOGNIZE THE SIGN POSTS ALONG THE ROAD?
RICHES ARE FOR RIGHTEOUS SPENDING
FAULT LIES NOT IN MONEY ITSELF BUT IN THE WAY IT IS MANAGED
EVERY MAN IS THE ARCHITECT OF HIS OWN FORTUNE
ALL MANKIND'S CONCERN IS CHARITY
RICH GIFTS ARE POOR WHEN GIVERS PROVE UNKIND
MONEY, NO MATTER HOW LARGE THE SUM, IS DOOMED TO BE LOST SOMEDAY, THOUGH IT MAY GO ON THROUGH MANY GENERATIONS IF IT BE TAKEN CARE OF
THE LOVE OF MONEY IS THE ROOT OF EVIL
DE BECK
© 1927 by King Features Syndicate, Inc Great Britain rights reserved.
5-6

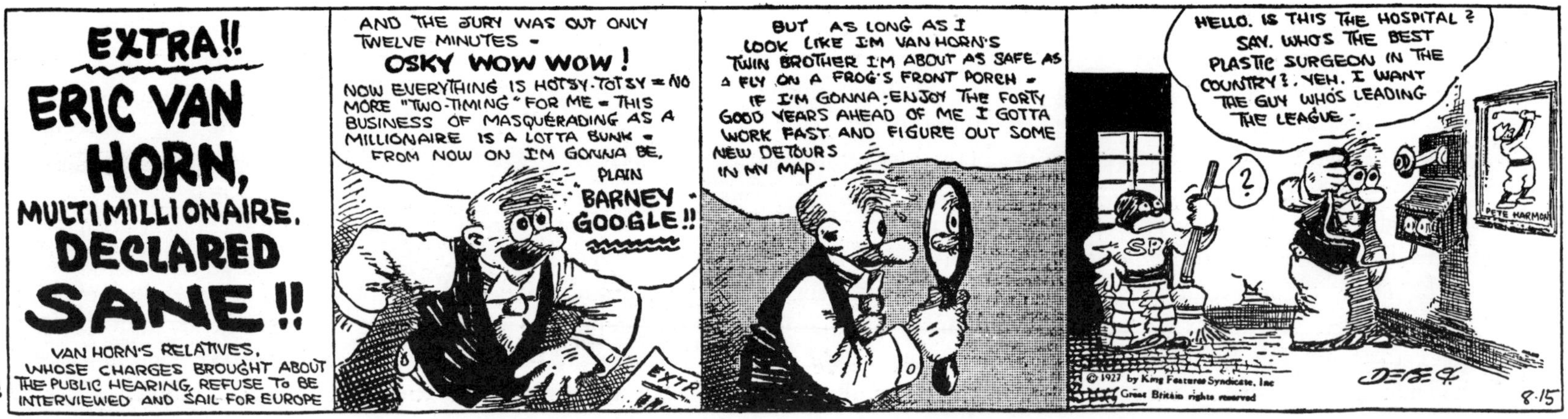

EXTRA!!
ERIC VAN HORN, MULTIMILLIONAIRE, DECLARED SANE!!
VAN HORN'S RELATIVES, WHOSE CHARGES BROUGHT ABOUT THE PUBLIC HEARING, REFUSE TO BE INTERVIEWED AND SAIL FOR EUROPE
AND THE JURY WAS OUT ONLY TWELVE MINUTES - OSKY WOW WOW! NOW EVERYTHING IS HOTSY-TOTSY = NO MORE "TWO-TIMING" FOR ME = THIS BUSINESS OF MASQUERADING AS A MILLIONAIRE IS A LOTTA BUNK - FROM NOW ON I'M GONNA BE, PLAIN "BARNEY GOOGLE!!"
EXTR
BUT AS LONG AS I LOOK LIKE I'M VAN HORN'S TWIN BROTHER I'M ABOUT AS SAFE AS A FLY ON A FROG'S FRONT PORCH - IF I'M GONNA ENJOY THE FORTY GOOD YEARS AHEAD OF ME I GOTTA WORK FAST AND FIGURE OUT SOME NEW DETOURS IN MY MAP -
HELLO. IS THIS THE HOSPITAL? SAY. WHO'S THE BEST PLASTIC SURGEON IN THE COUNTRY?. YEH. I WANT THE GUY WHO'S LEADING THE LEAGUE -
?
SP
PETE HARMON
DE BECK
© 1927 by King Features Syndicate, Inc Great Britain rights reserved
8-15

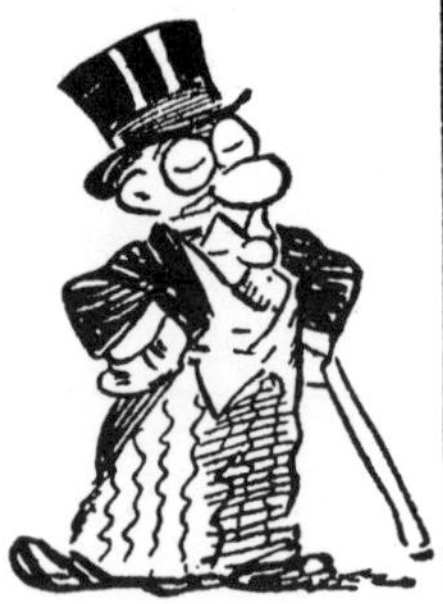

The "Barney Google" daily comic strips in this chapter are reproduced from newspaper strips. From the Collection of Ron Goulart.

The Brother-Hood Of Billy Goats

1927

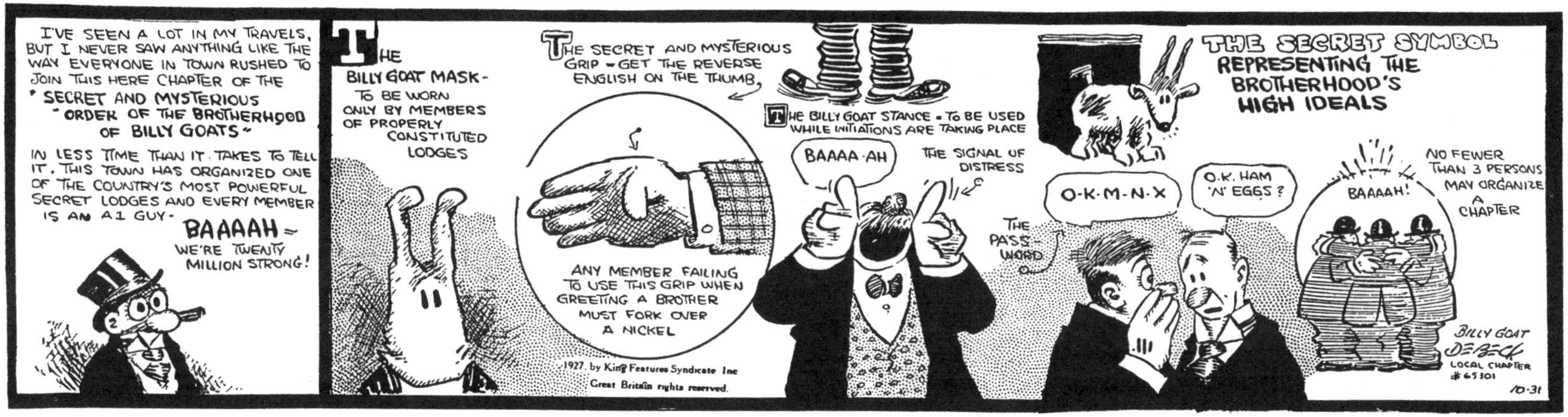

I'VE SEEN A LOT IN MY TRAVELS, BUT I NEVER SAW ANYTHING LIKE THE WAY EVERYONE IN TOWN RUSHED TO JOIN THIS HERE CHAPTER OF THE "SECRET AND MYSTERIOUS "ORDER OF THE BROTHERHOOD OF BILLY GOATS" IN LESS TIME THAN IT TAKES TO TELL IT. THIS TOWN HAS ORGANIZED ONE OF THE COUNTRY'S MOST POWERFUL SECRET LODGES AND EVERY MEMBER IS AN A1 GUY-
BAAAAH = WE'RE TWENTY MILLION STRONG!
THE BILLY GOAT MASK - TO BE WORN ONLY BY MEMBERS OF PROPERLY CONSTITUTED LODGES
THE SECRET AND MYSTERIOUS GRIP = GET THE REVERSE ENGLISH ON THE THUMB,
ANY MEMBER FAILING TO USE THIS GRIP WHEN GREETING A BROTHER MUST FORK OVER A NICKEL
1927, by King Features Syndicate Inc Great Britain rights reserved.
THE BILLY GOAT STANCE = TO BE USED WHILE INITIATIONS ARE TAKING PLACE
BAAAA-AH
THE SIGNAL OF DISTRESS
THE SECRET SYMBOL REPRESENTING THE BROTHERHOOD'S HIGH IDEALS
O-K-M-N-X
O.K. HAM 'N' EGGS?
THE PASS WORD
BAAAAH!
NO FEWER THAN 3 PERSONS MAY ORGANIZE A CHAPTER
BILLY GOAT DE BECK LOCAL CHAPTER #65301
10-31

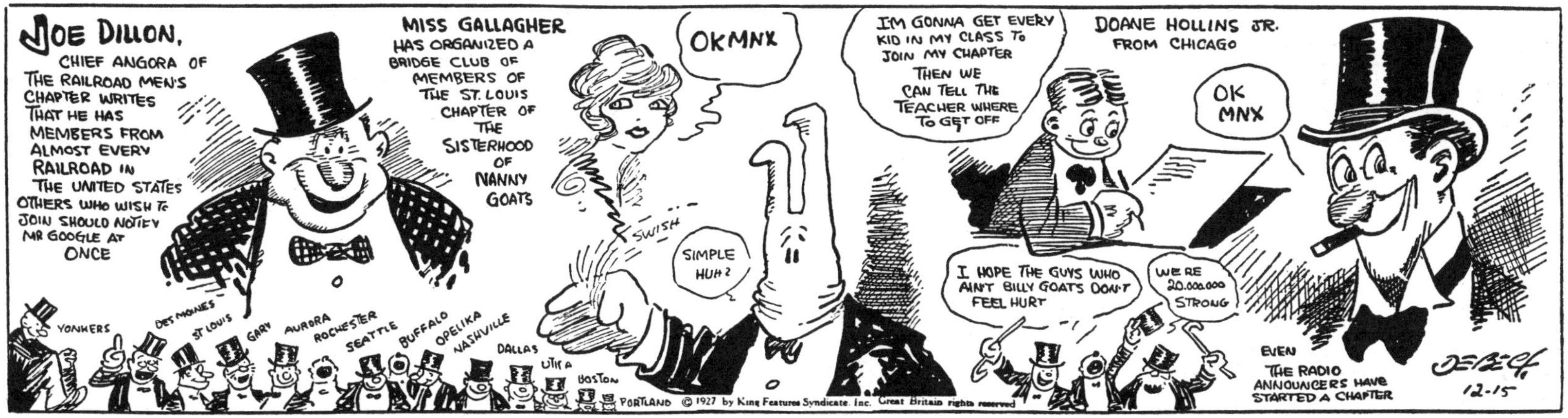

JOE DILLON, CHIEF ANGORA OF THE RAILROAD MEN'S CHAPTER WRITES THAT HE HAS MEMBERS FROM ALMOST EVERY RAILROAD IN THE UNITED STATES OTHERS WHO WISH TO JOIN SHOULD NOTIFY MR GOOGLE AT ONCE
MISS GALLAGHER HAS ORGANIZED A BRIDGE CLUB OF MEMBERS OF THE ST. LOUIS CHAPTER OF THE SISTERHOOD OF NANNY GOATS
OKMNX
SWISH
SIMPLE HUH?
I'M GONNA GET EVERY KID IN MY CLASS TO JOIN MY CHAPTER THEN WE CAN TELL THE TEACHER WHERE TO GET OFF
DOANE HOLLINS JR. FROM CHICAGO
OK MNX
I HOPE THE GUYS WHO AIN'T BILLY GOATS DON'T FEEL HURT
WE'RE 20,000,000 STRONG
YONKERS DES MOINES ST LOUIS GARY AURORA ROCHESTER SEATTLE BUFFALO OPELIKA NASHVILLE DALLAS UTICA BOSTON PORTLAND
© 1927 by King Features Syndicate, Inc. Great Britain rights reserved
EVEN THE RADIO ANNOUNCERS HAVE STARTED A CHAPTER
DE BECK 12-15

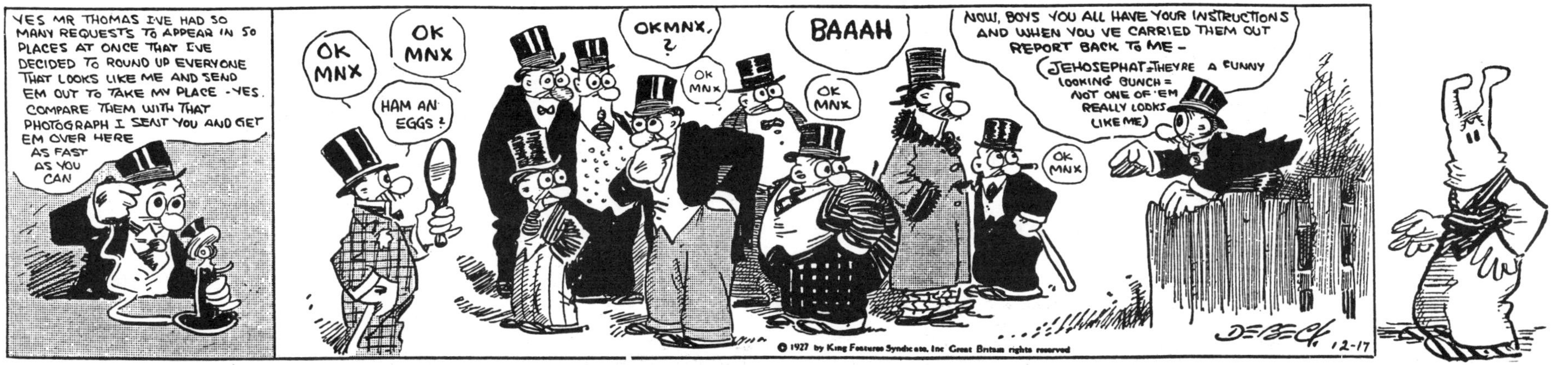

YES MR THOMAS I'VE HAD SO MANY REQUESTS TO APPEAR IN 50 PLACES AT ONCE THAT I'VE DECIDED TO ROUND UP EVERYONE THAT LOOKS LIKE ME AND SEND EM OUT TO TAKE MY PLACE -YES. COMPARE THEM WITH THAT PHOTOGRAPH I SENT YOU AND GET EM OVER HERE AS FAST AS YOU CAN
OK MNX
OK MNX
HAM AN EGGS?
OKMNX, ?
OK MNX
BAAAH
OK MNX
OK MNX
NOW, BOYS YOU ALL HAVE YOUR INSTRUCTIONS AND WHEN YOU'VE CARRIED THEM OUT REPORT BACK TO ME -
(JEHOSEPHAT=THEY'RE A FUNNY LOOKING BUNCH = NOT ONE OF 'EM REALLY LOOKS LIKE ME)
© 1927 by King Features Syndicate, Inc Great Britain rights reserved
DE BECK 12-17

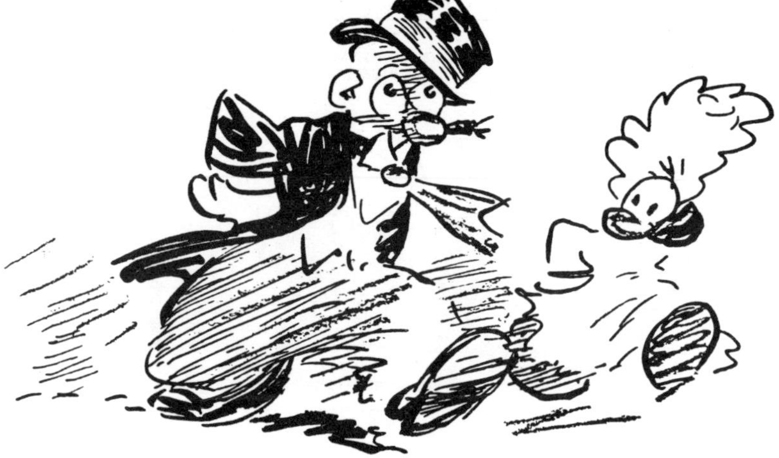

Left: A sketch of Barney and Bunky by DeBeck which was used as a Christmas greeting, date unknown. From the Collection of Richard Marschall.

Opposite page: A "Bunky" Sunday page "topper" strip from the John Thomas story, January 9, 1938. From the Collection of Peter Tolan.

Below: A typical "Parlor, Bedroom & Sink" Sunday page "topper" strip, featuring the perils of Bunky, July 19, 1931. From the Collection of Peter Tolan.

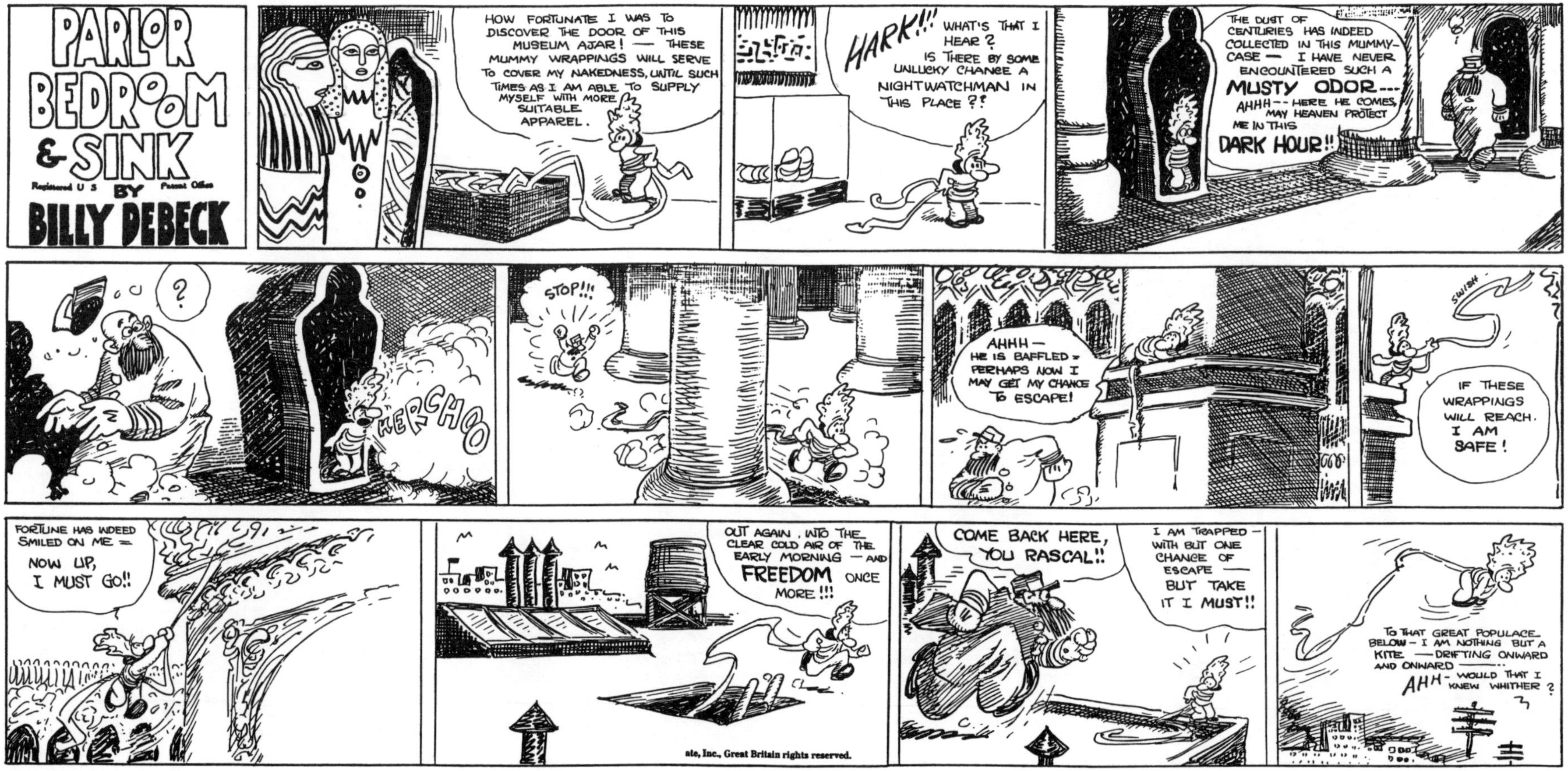
PARLOR BEDROOM & SINK
Registered U S Patent Office
BY BILLY DEBECK
HOW FORTUNATE I WAS TO DISCOVER THE DOOR OF THIS MUSEUM AJAR! — THESE MUMMY WRAPPINGS WILL SERVE TO COVER MY NAKEDNESS, UNTIL SUCH TIMES AS I AM ABLE TO SUPPLY MYSELF WITH MORE SUITABLE APPAREL.
HARK!!!
WHAT'S THAT I HEAR? IS THERE BY SOME UNLUCKY CHANCE A NIGHTWATCHMAN IN THIS PLACE?!
THE DUST OF CENTURIES HAS INDEED COLLECTED IN THIS MUMMY-CASE — I HAVE NEVER ENCOUNTERED SUCH A MUSTY ODOR--- AHHH-- HERE HE COMES, MAY HEAVEN PROTECT ME IN THIS DARK HOUR!!
?
KERCHOO
STOP!!!
AHHH— HE IS BAFFLED— PERHAPS NOW I MAY GET MY CHANCE TO ESCAPE!
SWISH
IF THESE WRAPPINGS WILL REACH. I AM SAFE!
FORTUNE HAS INDEED SMILED ON ME — NOW UP, I MUST GO!!
OUT AGAIN, INTO THE CLEAR COLD AIR OF THE EARLY MORNING — AND FREEDOM ONCE MORE!!!
COME BACK HERE, YOU RASCAL!!
I AM TRAPPED — WITH BUT ONE CHANCE OF ESCAPE — BUT TAKE IT I MUST!!
TO THAT GREAT POPULACE BELOW — I AM NOTHING BUT A KITE —DRIFTING ONWARD AND ONWARD ——— AHH- WOULD THAT I KNEW WHITHER?
ate, Inc., Great Britain rights reserved.

During the 1920's, many cartoonists experimented with creating "topper" strips for their Sunday pages. These were separate features, or spin-offs from the main feature, and occupied the top third or quarter of the newspaper page. DeBeck first tried adapting "Bughouse Fables" as a "topper" in early 1926, but replaced it with "Parlor, Bedroom & Sink" on May 16, 1926.

The debut episode of this new comic strip dealt with the wedding of Bunker Hill Sr. and Bibsy, his bride. After the ceremony, the newlyweds were checking into a hotel when the desk clerk inquired, "The bridal suite, sir?" "No! Just a parlor, bedroom and sink," the skinflint Bunker replied. After a few months of domestic married life, Bibsy pursued a short-lived film career and Bunker Hill, after being sent to prison for robbing his wife, escaped and reunited with her. On November 13, 1927, Bibsy presented Bunker with their new baby, Bunker Hill Jr, or Bunky for short. Within weeks, this bulb-nosed upstart had taken over.

Comics historian Ron Goulart described Billy DeBeck's forgotten brainchild in the October 1983 issue of *Nemo Magazine*, "Bunky, who sprang out of a literary tradition that includes Candide, Oliver Twist and Little Orphan Annie, was a precocious tyke who roamed the world in the baby clothes and bonnet he'd been christened in. He possessed a nose that rivaled that of Jimmy Durante and a vocabulary that many a pundit would envy."

On February 5, 1928, Bunky, who had lost his parents, met the unsavory Fagan, a Dickens-like character who soon became a regular in the strip. Bunky, influenced by Fagan's rough language, would scream at his captor, "Youse is a viper!" which developed into another of DeBeck's famous catch-phrases.

During the 1930's, Bunky was a movie actor, a baseball mascot, a boxer, and a circus performer. He found his parents, lost them and found them again. He even teamed up with Spark Plug in a story from 1933.

In 1932 the name of the strip was changed to "Parlor, Bedroom & Sink starring Bunky" and the title was shortened to "Bunky" in 1935. DeBeck's feature, which began in a two-tiered format and occupied the top third of his Sunday pages, expanded to three-tiers, eventually taking up half of the page.

One of DeBeck's most memorable "Bunky" stories began in 1937 and lasted over a year. In this extended continuity, Bunky met a talking dog named John Thomas who took him to the land of Poochadina where all dogs walked and talked. John Thomas also smoked cigars and bet on horses, much like Barney Google, and in one sequence, worked as a comic artist, much like his creator Billy DeBeck.

When Billy died in 1942, Joe Musial did "Bunky" for a brief time until Fred Lasswell took over the Sunday page in 1945. Lasswell did an admirable job continuing "Bunky" until the last episode in 1948.

BUNKY
by BILLY DE BECK
Registered U. S. Patent Office
WHO'S MAKIN' ALL THAT RACKET OUTSIDE ?? I'M GITTIN' SICK OF THESE GUYS ALWAYS PESTERIN' ME TO GIVE 'EM A HORSE - FROM NOW ON I'M GONNA START LOOKING OUT FOR MYSELF---
I'LL TELL THE GENTLEMAN TO GO AWAY QUIETLY---
SORRY, SIR--- BUT JOHN THOMAS IS IN A STATE TODAY-- HE WON'T SEE ANYBODY---
DID YOU TELL HIM I WANNA HORSE ??
YES SIREEE, BUNKY-- I'M GONNA START BETTIN' MYSELF-- GRAB THAT 'PHONE AN' TELL 'EM I'M BETTIN' $500 ACROSS TH' BOARD ON "LAZY BONES"
AHH
WHEEE--- I GOTTA HORSE--- I GOTTA HORSE!!!
I'M SHOOTIN' MY BANK-ROLL---
"LAZY BONES" ALSO RAN
PLEASE DON'T FEEL SO BAD, JOHN THOMAS-- IT'S JUST ONE OF THOSE THINGS-- YOU CAN PICK 'EM FOR OTHERS, BUT NOT FOR YOURSELF---
BOO HOO
1-9-
THIS MUG BROKE INTO MY ROOM AND FOR NO REASON STARTED MUSSIN' ME UP---
Copr. 1938, King Features Syndicate, Inc., World rights reserved.

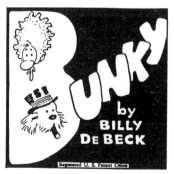

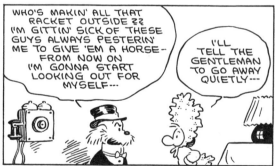

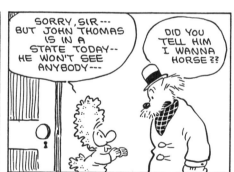

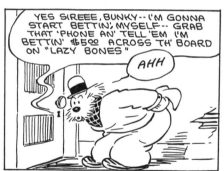

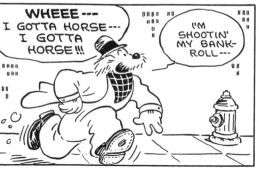

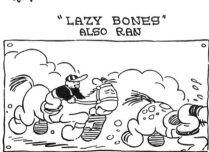

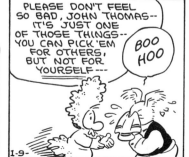

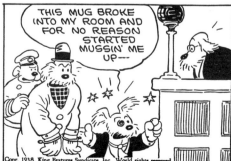

Barney For President

1928

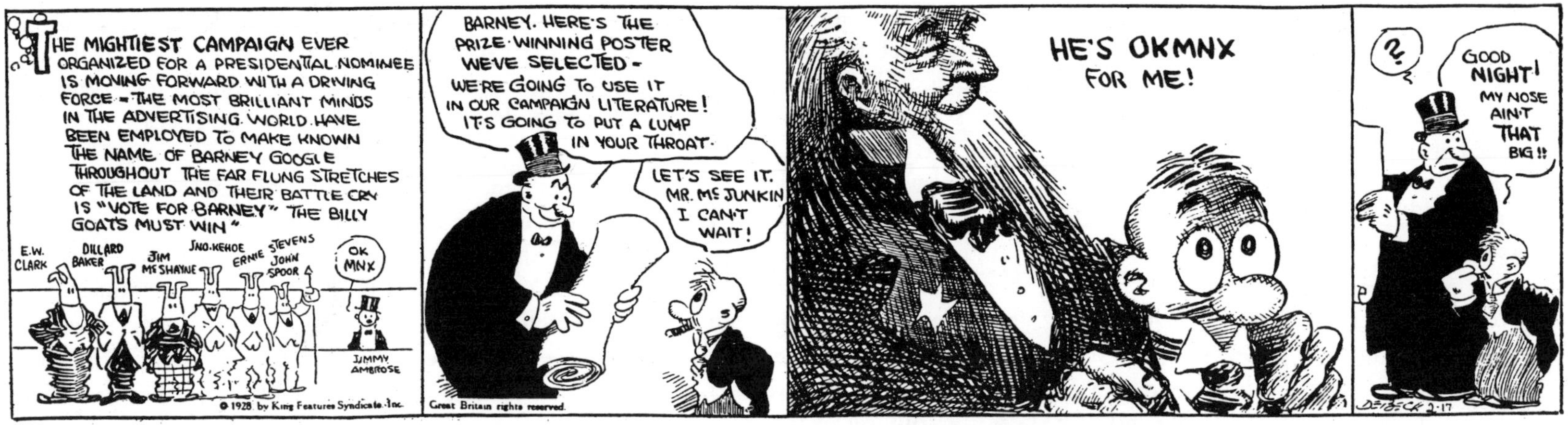
THE MIGHTIEST CAMPAIGN EVER ORGANIZED FOR A PRESIDENTIAL NOMINEE IS MOVING FORWARD WITH A DRIVING FORCE = THE MOST BRILLIANT MINDS IN THE ADVERTISING WORLD HAVE BEEN EMPLOYED TO MAKE KNOWN THE NAME OF BARNEY GOOGLE THROUGHOUT THE FAR FLUNG STRETCHES OF THE LAND AND THEIR BATTLE CRY IS "VOTE FOR BARNEY" THE BILLY GOATS MUST WIN"
E.W. CLARK
DILLARD BAKER
JIM McSHAYNE
JNO. KEHOE
ERNIE STEVENS
JOHN SPOOR
OK MNX
JIMMY AMBROSE
© 1928 by King Features Syndicate Inc.
BARNEY. HERE'S THE PRIZE WINNING POSTER WE'VE SELECTED - WE'RE GOING TO USE IT IN OUR CAMPAIGN LITERATURE! IT'S GOING TO PUT A LUMP IN YOUR THROAT.
LET'S SEE IT. MR. McJUNKIN I CAN'T WAIT!
Great Britain rights reserved.
HE'S OKMNX FOR ME!
?
GOOD NIGHT! MY NOSE AIN'T THAT BIG!!
DEBECK 2-17

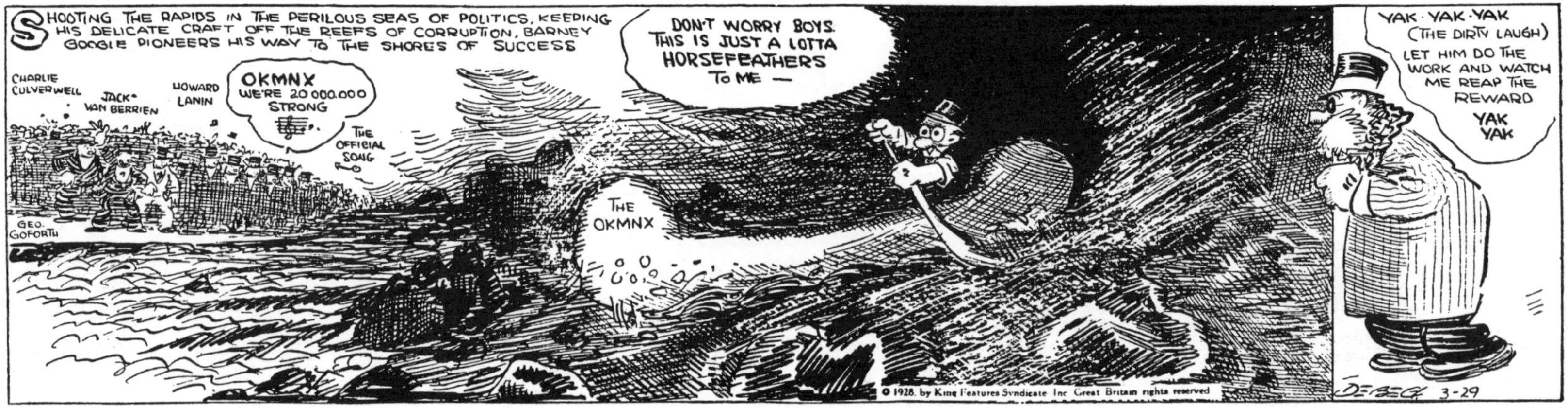
SHOOTING THE RAPIDS IN THE PERILOUS SEAS OF POLITICS, KEEPING HIS DELICATE CRAFT OFF THE REEFS OF CORRUPTION, BARNEY GOOGLE PIONEERS HIS WAY TO THE SHORES OF SUCCESS
CHARLIE CULVERWELL
JACK VAN BERRIEN
HOWARD LANIN
OKMNX WE'RE 20.000.000 STRONG
THE OFFICIAL SONG
GEO. GOFORTH
THE OKMNX
DON'T WORRY BOYS. THIS IS JUST A LOTTA HORSEFEATHERS TO ME —
YAK YAK YAK (THE DIRTY LAUGH) LET HIM DO THE WORK AND WATCH ME REAP THE REWARD YAK YAK
© 1928. by King Features Syndicate Inc Great Britain rights reserved
DEBECK 3-29

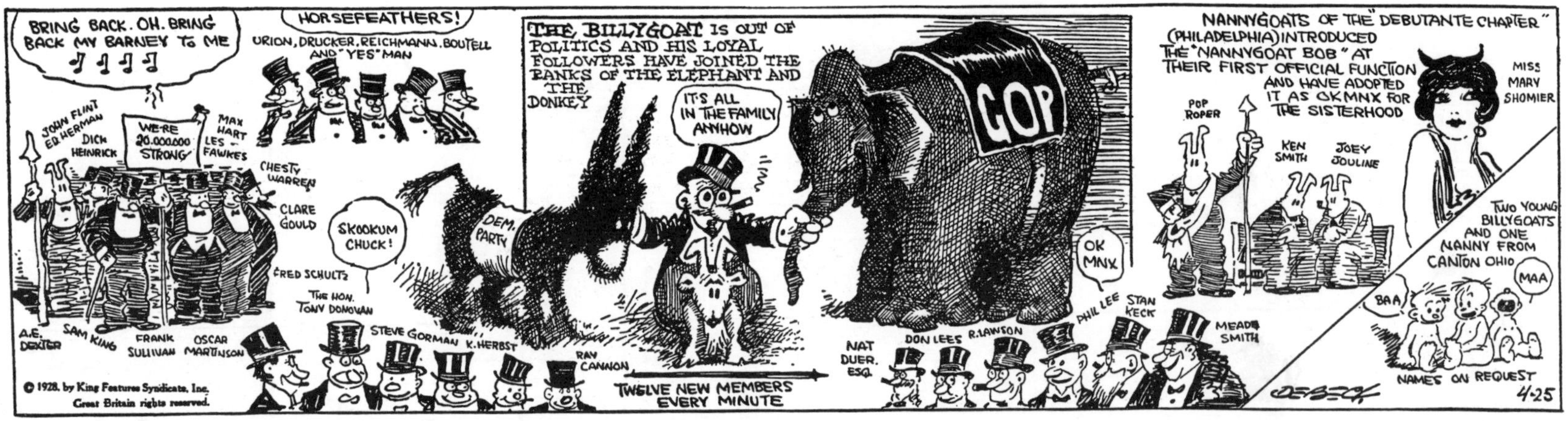
BRING BACK. OH. BRING BACK MY BARNEY TO ME
HORSEFEATHERS!
URION, DRUCKER, REICHMANN, BOUTELL AND "YES" MAN
JOHN FLINT
ED HERMAN
DICK HEINRICK
WE'RE 20.000.000 STRONG
MAX HART
LES FAWKES
CHESTY WARREN
CLARE GOULD
SKOOKUM CHUCK!
FRED SCHULTZ
THE HON. TONY DONOVAN
A.E. DEXTER
SAM KING
FRANK SULLIVAN
OSCAR MARTINSON
STEVE GORMAN
K. HERBST
RAY CANNON
© 1928, by King Features Syndicate, Inc. Great Britain rights reserved.
THE BILLYGOAT IS OUT OF POLITICS AND HIS LOYAL FOLLOWERS HAVE JOINED THE RANKS OF THE ELEPHANT AND THE DONKEY
IT'S ALL IN THE FAMILY ANYHOW
DEM. PARTY
GOP
OK MNX
TWELVE NEW MEMBERS EVERY MINUTE
NAT DUER. ESQ.
DON LEES
R. LAWSON
PHIL LEE
STAN KECK
MEADE SMITH
NANNYGOATS OF THE "DEBUTANTE CHAPTER" (PHILADELPHIA) INTRODUCED THE "NANNYGOAT BOB" AT THEIR FIRST OFFICIAL FUNCTION AND HAVE ADOPTED IT AS OKMNX FOR THE SISTERHOOD
MISS MARY SHOMIER
POP ROPER
KEN SMITH
JOEY JOULINE
TWO YOUNG BILLYGOATS AND ONE NANNY FROM CANTON OHIO
BAA
MAA
NAMES ON REQUEST
DEBECK 4-25

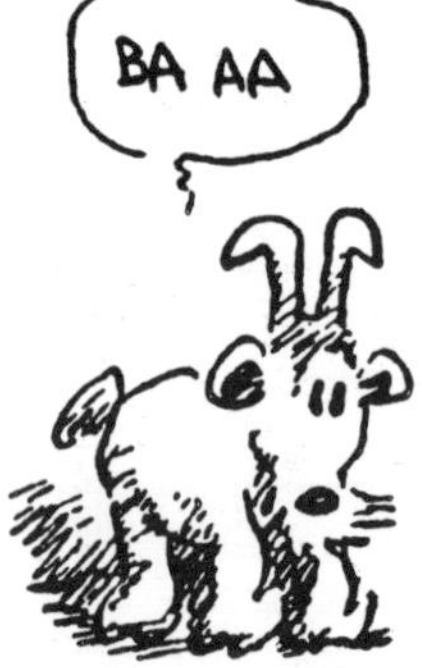
BA AA

Horse-Face Klotz

1928-1929

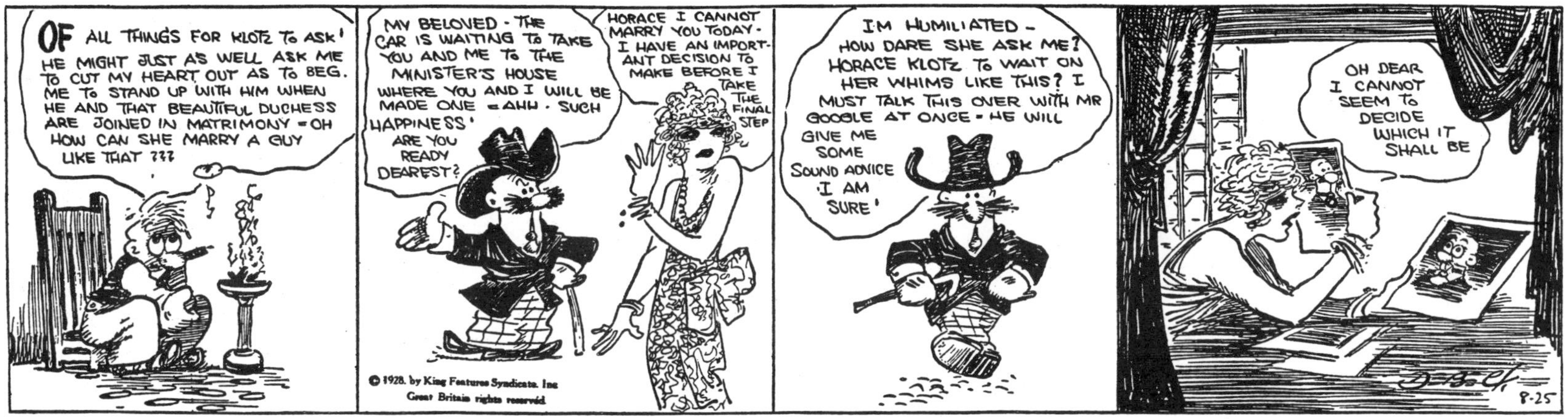
OF ALL THINGS FOR KLOTZ TO ASK! HE MIGHT JUST AS WELL ASK ME TO CUT MY HEART OUT AS TO BEG. ME TO STAND UP WITH HIM WHEN HE AND THAT BEAUTIFUL DUCHESS ARE JOINED IN MATRIMONY = OH HOW CAN SHE MARRY A GUY LIKE THAT ???
MY BELOVED - THE CAR IS WAITING TO TAKE YOU AND ME TO THE MINISTER'S HOUSE WHERE YOU AND I WILL BE MADE ONE = AHH - SUCH HAPPINESS! ARE YOU READY DEAREST?
HORACE I CANNOT MARRY YOU TODAY - I HAVE AN IMPORTANT DECISION TO MAKE BEFORE I TAKE THE FINAL STEP
© 1928, by King Features Syndicate, Inc
Great Britain rights reserved
I'M HUMILIATED - HOW DARE SHE ASK ME? HORACE KLOTZ TO WAIT ON HER WHIMS LIKE THIS? I MUST TALK THIS OVER WITH MR GOOGLE AT ONCE = HE WILL GIVE ME SOME SOUND ADVICE I AM SURE!
OH DEAR I CANNOT SEEM TO DECIDE WHICH IT SHALL BE
DEBECK
8-25

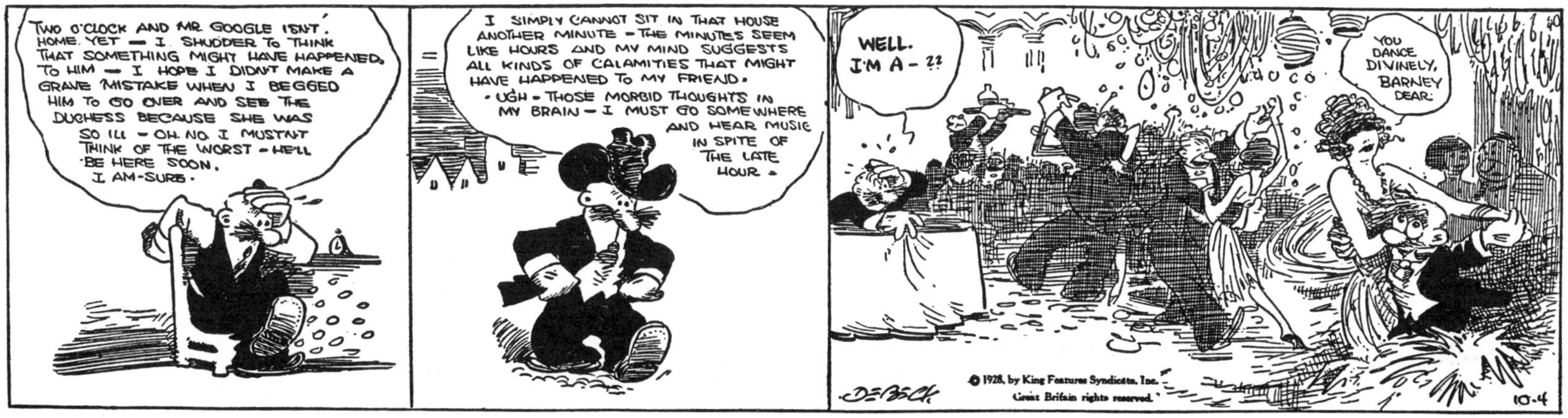
TWO O'CLOCK AND MR GOOGLE ISN'T HOME YET — I SHUDDER TO THINK THAT SOMETHING MIGHT HAVE HAPPENED TO HIM — I HOPE I DIDN'T MAKE A GRAVE MISTAKE WHEN I BEGGED HIM TO GO OVER AND SEE THE DUCHESS BECAUSE SHE WAS SO ILL - OH NO I MUSTN'T THINK OF THE WORST - HE'LL BE HERE SOON, I AM SURE.
I SIMPLY CANNOT SIT IN THAT HOUSE ANOTHER MINUTE - THE MINUTES SEEM LIKE HOURS AND MY MIND SUGGESTS ALL KINDS OF CALAMITIES THAT MIGHT HAVE HAPPENED TO MY FRIEND. - UGH - THOSE MORBID THOUGHTS IN MY BRAIN - I MUST GO SOMEWHERE AND HEAR MUSIC IN SPITE OF THE LATE HOUR -
WELL. I'M A - ??
YOU DANCE DIVINELY, BARNEY DEAR.
DEBECK
© 1928, by King Features Syndicate, Inc.
Great Britain rights reserved.
10-4

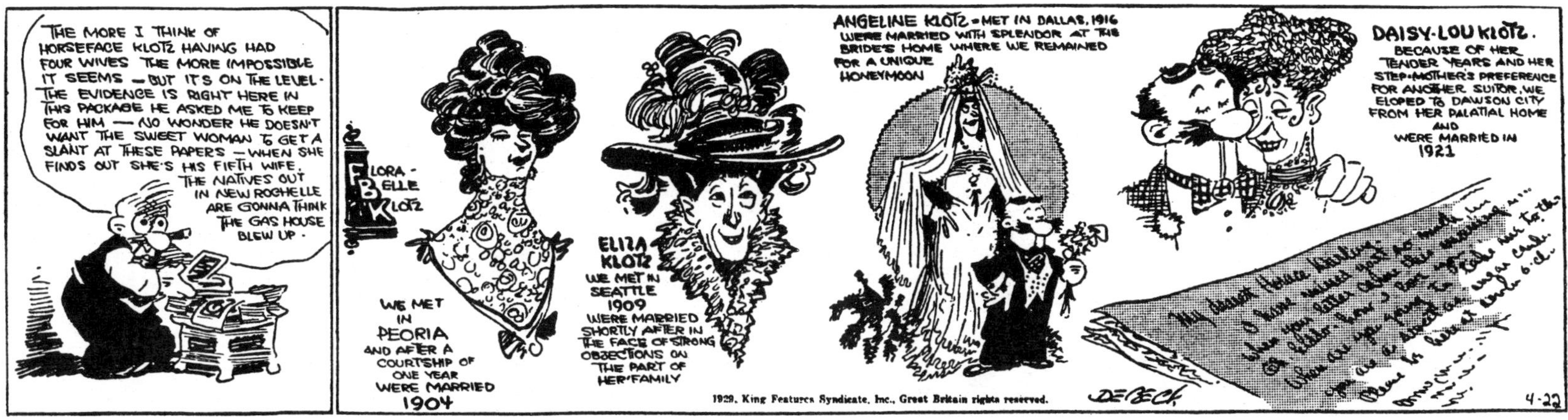
THE MORE I THINK OF HORSEFACE KLOTZ HAVING HAD FOUR WIVES THE MORE IMPOSSIBLE IT SEEMS — BUT IT'S ON THE LEVEL - THE EVIDENCE IS RIGHT HERE IN THIS PACKAGE HE ASKED ME TO KEEP FOR HIM — NO WONDER HE DOESN'T WANT THE SWEET WOMAN TO GET A SLANT AT THESE PAPERS — WHEN SHE FINDS OUT SHE'S HIS FIFTH WIFE, THE NATIVES OUT IN NEW ROCHELLE ARE GONNA THINK THE GAS HOUSE BLEW UP.
FLORA-BELLE KLOTZ
WE MET IN PEORIA AND AFTER A COURTSHIP OF ONE YEAR WERE MARRIED 1904
ELIZA KLOTZ WE MET IN SEATTLE 1909 WERE MARRIED SHORTLY AFTER IN THE FACE OF STRONG OBJECTIONS ON THE PART OF HER FAMILY
ANGELINE KLOTZ = MET IN DALLAS, 1916 WERE MARRIED WITH SPLENDOR AT THE BRIDE'S HOME WHERE WE REMAINED FOR A UNIQUE HONEYMOON
DAISY-LOU KLOTZ. BECAUSE OF HER TENDER YEARS AND HER STEP-MOTHER'S PREFERENCE FOR ANOTHER SUITOR, WE ELOPED TO DAWSON CITY FROM HER PALATIAL HOME AND WERE MARRIED IN 1921
1929, King Features Syndicate, Inc., Great Britain rights reserved.
DEBECK
4-22

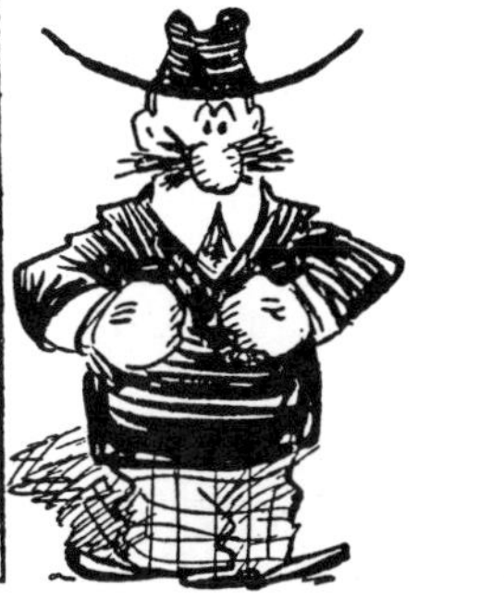

Hello Swifty

1929

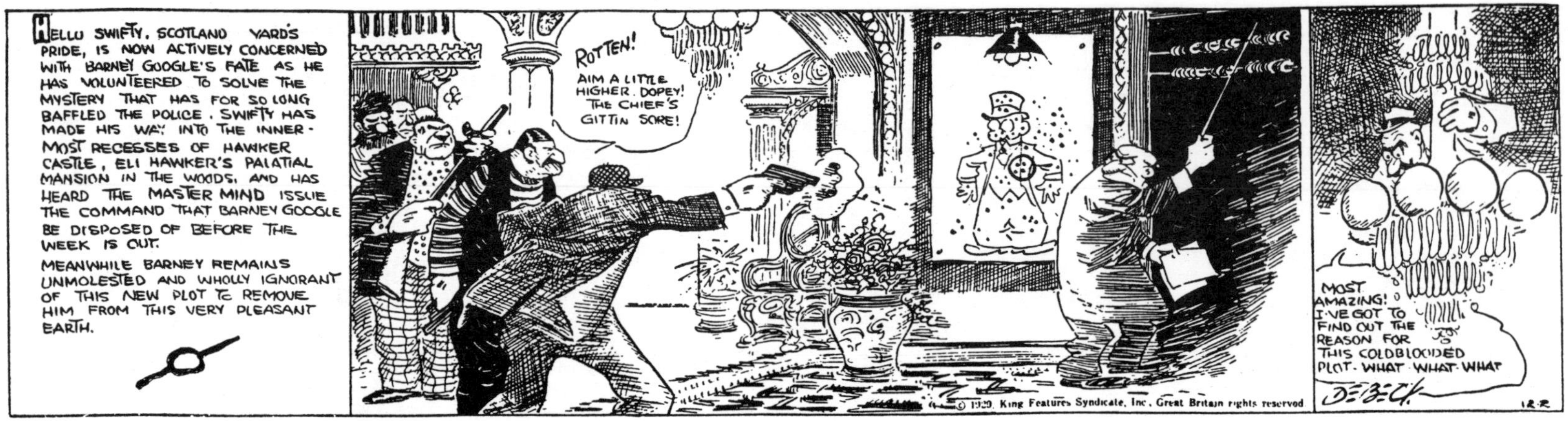
HELLO SWIFTY, SCOTLAND YARD'S PRIDE, IS NOW ACTIVELY CONCERNED WITH BARNEY GOOGLE'S FATE AS HE HAS VOLUNTEERED TO SOLVE THE MYSTERY THAT HAS FOR SO LONG BAFFLED THE POLICE. SWIFTY HAS MADE HIS WAY INTO THE INNER-MOST RECESSES OF HAWKER CASTLE, ELI HAWKER'S PALATIAL MANSION IN THE WOODS, AND HAS HEARD THE MASTER MIND ISSUE THE COMMAND THAT BARNEY GOOGLE BE DISPOSED OF BEFORE THE WEEK IS OUT.
MEANWHILE BARNEY REMAINS UNMOLESTED AND WHOLLY IGNORANT OF THIS NEW PLOT TO REMOVE HIM FROM THIS VERY PLEASANT EARTH.
ROTTEN!
AIM A LITTLE HIGHER. DOPEY! THE CHIEF'S GITTIN SORE!
MOST AMAZING! I'VE GOT TO FIND OUT THE REASON FOR THIS COLDBLOODED PLOT - WHAT - WHAT - WHAT
© 1929, King Features Syndicate, Inc., Great Britain rights reserved
DE BECK
12-2

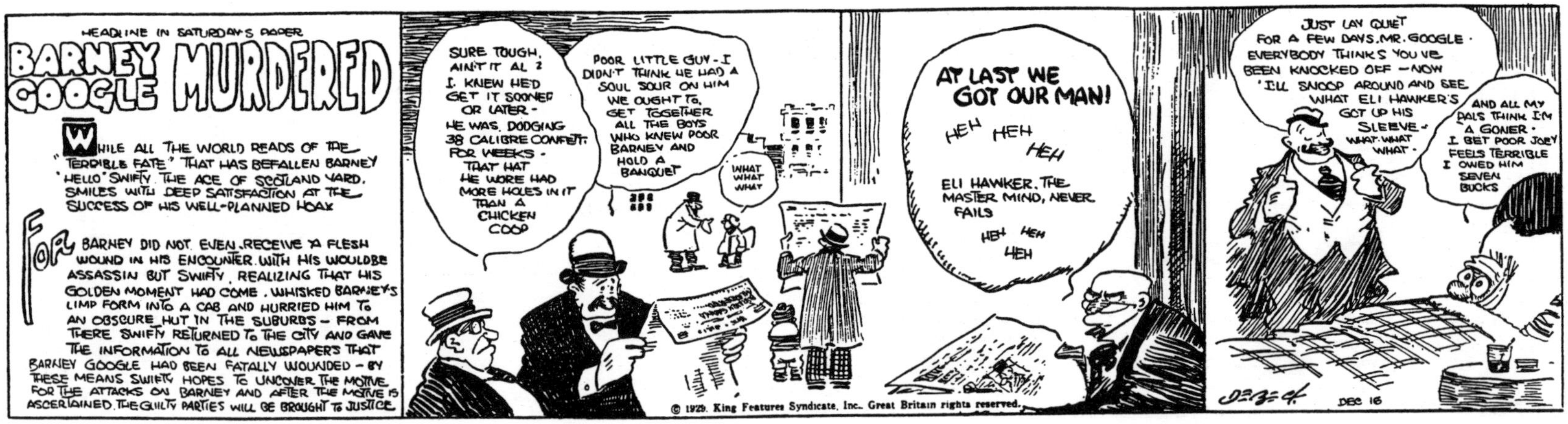
HEADLINE IN SATURDAY'S PAPER
BARNEY GOOGLE MURDERED
WHILE ALL THE WORLD READS OF THE "TERRIBLE FATE" THAT HAS BEFALLEN BARNEY "HELLO" SWIFTY, THE ACE OF SCOTLAND YARD, SMILES WITH DEEP SATISFACTION AT THE SUCCESS OF HIS WELL-PLANNED HOAX
FOR BARNEY DID NOT EVEN RECEIVE A FLESH WOUND IN HIS ENCOUNTER WITH HIS WOULDBE ASSASSIN BUT SWIFTY, REALIZING THAT HIS GOLDEN MOMENT HAD COME, WHISKED BARNEY'S LIMP FORM INTO A CAB AND HURRIED HIM TO AN OBSCURE HUT IN THE SUBURBS - FROM THERE SWIFTY RETURNED TO THE CITY AND GAVE THE INFORMATION TO ALL NEWSPAPERS THAT BARNEY GOOGLE HAD BEEN FATALLY WOUNDED - BY THESE MEANS SWIFTY HOPES TO UNCOVER THE MOTIVE FOR THE ATTACKS ON BARNEY AND AFTER THE MOTIVE IS ASCERTAINED THE GUILTY PARTIES WILL BE BROUGHT TO JUSTICE
SURE TOUGH, AIN'T IT AL? I KNEW HE'D GET IT SOONER OR LATER - HE WAS DODGING 38 CALIBRE CONFETTI FOR WEEKS - THAT HAT HE WORE HAD MORE HOLES IN IT THAN A CHICKEN COOP
POOR LITTLE GUY - I DIDN'T THINK HE HAD A SOUL SOUR ON HIM WE OUGHT TO GET TOGETHER ALL THE BOYS WHO KNEW POOR BARNEY AND HOLD A BANQUET
WHAT WHAT WHAT
AT LAST WE GOT OUR MAN!
HEH HEH HEH
ELI HAWKER, THE MASTER MIND, NEVER FAILS
HEH HEH HEH
JUST LAY QUIET FOR A FEW DAYS, MR. GOOGLE - EVERYBODY THINKS YOU'VE BEEN KNOCKED OFF - NOW I'LL SNOOP AROUND AND SEE WHAT ELI HAWKER'S GOT UP HIS SLEEVE - WHAT-WHAT WHAT -
AND ALL MY PALS THINK I'M A GONER - I BET POOR JOEY FEELS TERRIBLE I OWED HIM SEVEN BUCKS
© 1929, King Features Syndicate, Inc., Great Britain rights reserved.
DE BECK
DEC 18

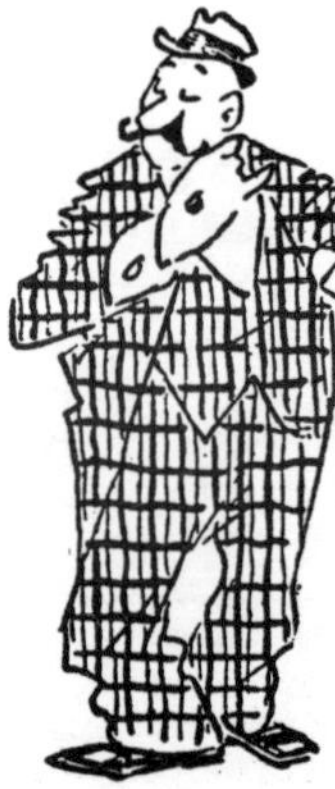

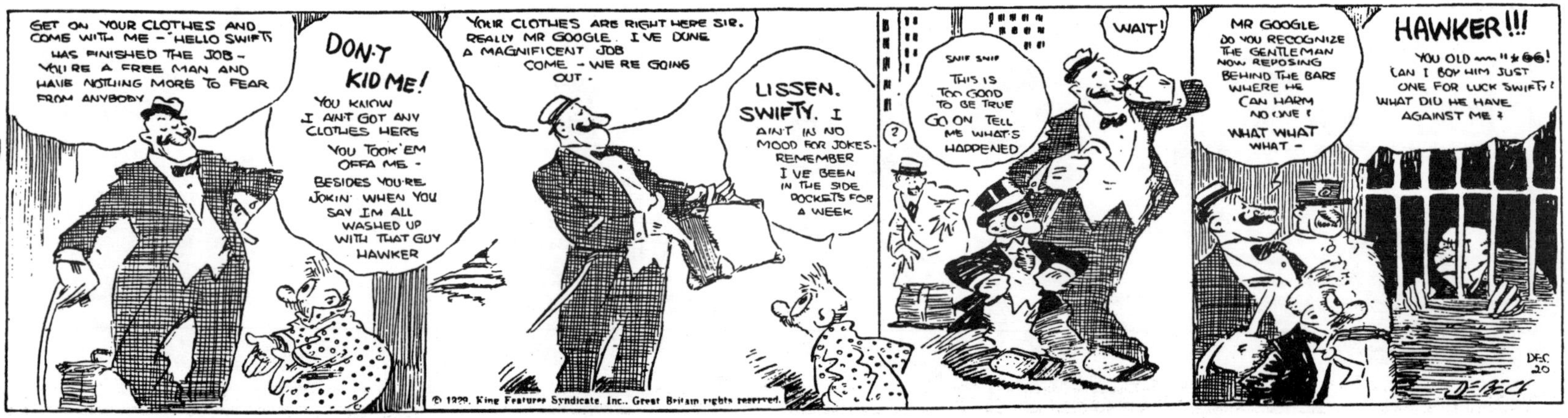
GET ON YOUR CLOTHES AND COME WITH ME - "HELLO SWIFTY" HAS FINISHED THE JOB - YOU'RE A FREE MAN AND HAVE NOTHING MORE TO FEAR FROM ANYBODY
DON'T KID ME! YOU KNOW I AIN'T GOT ANY CLOTHES HERE YOU TOOK 'EM OFFA ME - BESIDES YOU'RE JOKIN' WHEN YOU SAY I'M ALL WASHED UP WITH THAT GUY HAWKER
YOUR CLOTHES ARE RIGHT HERE SIR. REALLY MR GOOGLE. I'VE DONE A MAGNIFICENT JOB COME - WE'RE GOING OUT -
LISSEN, SWIFTY, I AIN'T IN NO MOOD FOR JOKES - REMEMBER I'VE BEEN IN THE SIDE POCKETS FOR A WEEK
WAIT!
SNIF SNIF
THIS IS TOO GOOD TO BE TRUE GO ON TELL ME WHAT'S HAPPENED
?
MR GOOGLE DO YOU RECOGNIZE THE GENTLEMAN NOW REPOSING BEHIND THE BARS WHERE HE CAN HARM NO ONE? WHAT WHAT WHAT -
HAWKER!!!
YOU OLD ---!! ★@@! CAN I BOP HIM JUST ONE FOR LUCK SWIFTY? WHAT DID HE HAVE AGAINST ME?
© 1929, King Features Syndicate, Inc., Great Britain rights reserved.
DEC 20
DE BECK

The Hamburger Stakes

1930

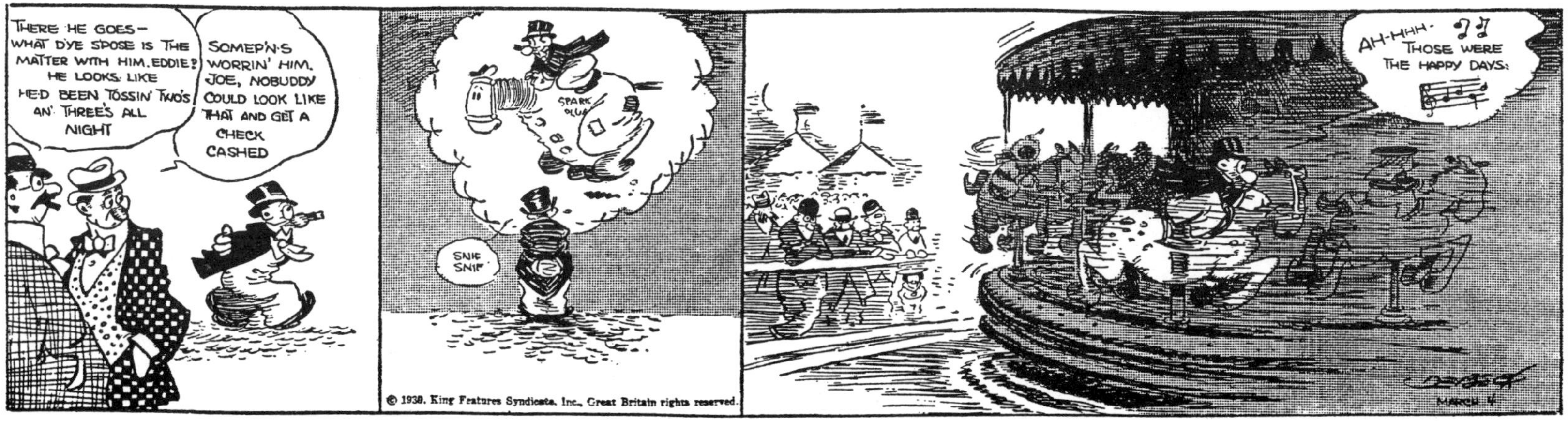

THERE HE GOES — WHAT D'YE S'POSE IS THE MATTER WITH HIM, EDDIE? HE LOOKS LIKE HE'D BEEN TOSSIN' TWO'S AN' THREE'S ALL NIGHT
SOMEP'N'S WORRIN' HIM, JOE, NOBUDDY COULD LOOK LIKE THAT AND GET A CHECK CASHED
SPARK PLUG
SNIF SNIF
AH-HHH- THOSE WERE THE HAPPY DAYS:
© 1930, King Features Syndicate, Inc., Great Britain rights reserved.
DEBECK
MARCH 4

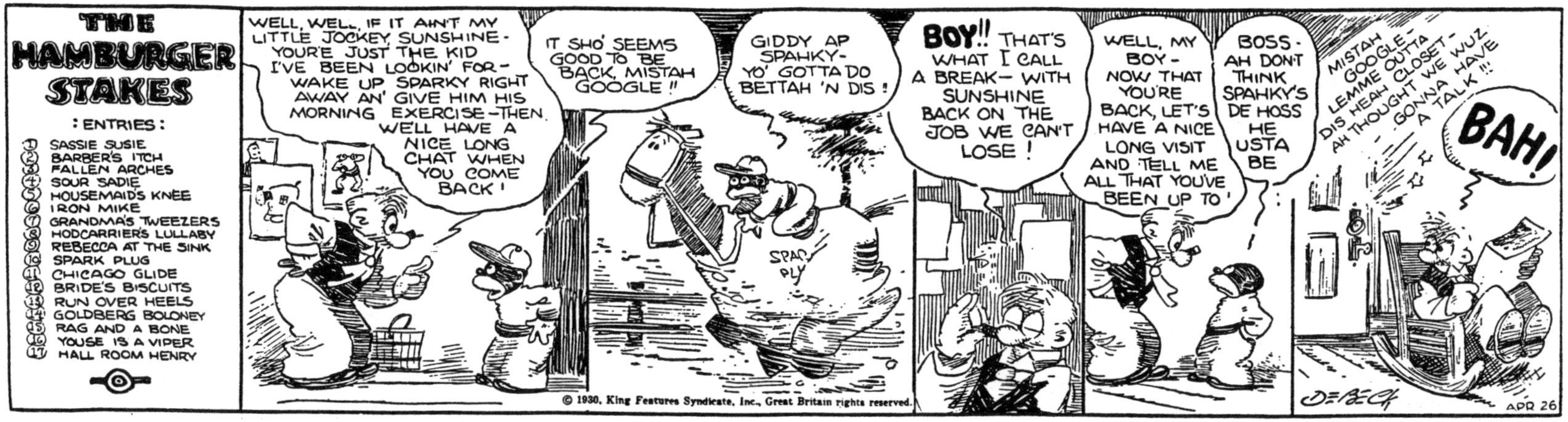

THE HAMBURGER STAKES
: ENTRIES :
1 SASSIE SUSIE
2 BARBER'S ITCH
3 FALLEN ARCHES
4 SOUR SADIE
5 HOUSEMAID'S KNEE
6 IRON MIKE
7 GRANDMA'S TWEEZERS
8 HODCARRIER'S LULLABY
9 REBECCA AT THE SINK
10 SPARK PLUG
11 CHICAGO GLIDE
12 BRIDE'S BISCUITS
13 RUN OVER HEELS
14 GOLDBERG BOLONEY
15 RAG AND A BONE
16 YOUSE IS A VIPER
17 HALL ROOM HENRY
WELL, WELL, IF IT AIN'T MY LITTLE JOCKEY SUNSHINE - YOU'RE JUST THE KID I'VE BEEN LOOKIN' FOR - WAKE UP SPARKY RIGHT AWAY AN' GIVE HIM HIS MORNING EXERCISE - THEN WE'LL HAVE A NICE LONG CHAT WHEN YOU COME BACK!
IT SHO' SEEMS GOOD TO BE BACK, MISTAH GOOGLE!!
GIDDY AP SPAHKY - YO' GOTTA DO BETTAH 'N DIS!
SPARK PLUG
© 1930, King Features Syndicate, Inc., Great Britain rights reserved.
BOY!! THAT'S WHAT I CALL A BREAK — WITH SUNSHINE BACK ON THE JOB WE CAN'T LOSE!
WELL, MY BOY - NOW THAT YOU'RE BACK, LET'S HAVE A NICE LONG VISIT AND TELL ME ALL THAT YOU'VE BEEN UP TO!
BOSS - AH DON'T THINK SPAHKY'S DE HOSS HE USTA BE
MISTAH GOOGLE - LEMME OUTTA DIS HEAH CLOSET - AH THOUGHT WE WUZ GONNA HAVE A TALK!!
BAH!
DEBECK
APR 26

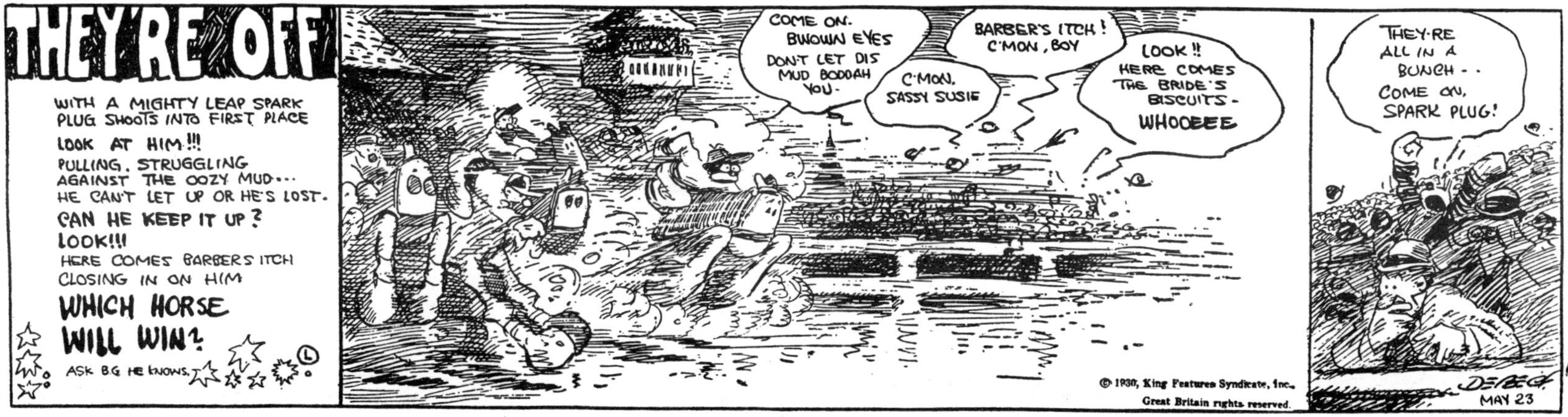

THEY'RE OFF
WITH A MIGHTY LEAP SPARK PLUG SHOOTS INTO FIRST PLACE
LOOK AT HIM!!!
PULLING, STRUGGLING AGAINST THE OOZY MUD... HE CAN'T LET UP OR HE'S LOST.
CAN HE KEEP IT UP?
LOOK!!!
HERE COMES BARBERS ITCH CLOSING IN ON HIM
WHICH HORSE WILL WIN?
ASK B.G. HE KNOWS.
COME ON. BWOWN EYES DON'T LET DIS MUD BODDAH YOU.
C'MON, SASSY SUSIE
BARBER'S ITCH! C'MON, BOY
LOOK!! HERE COMES THE BRIDE'S BISCUITS - WHOOEEE
THEY'RE ALL IN A BUNCH - - COME ON, SPARK PLUG!
© 1930, King Features Syndicate, Inc., Great Britain rights reserved.
DEBECK
MAY 23

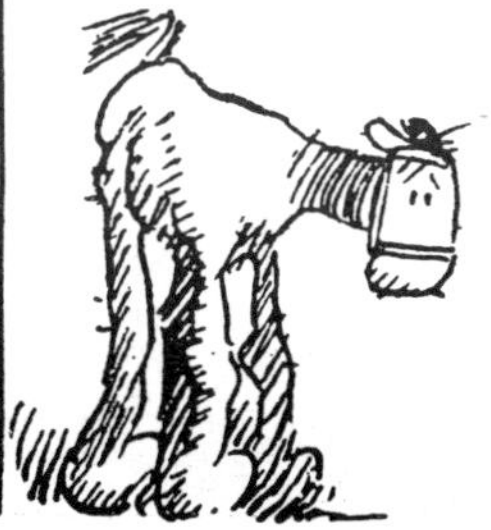

The Comic Strip Derby

1930

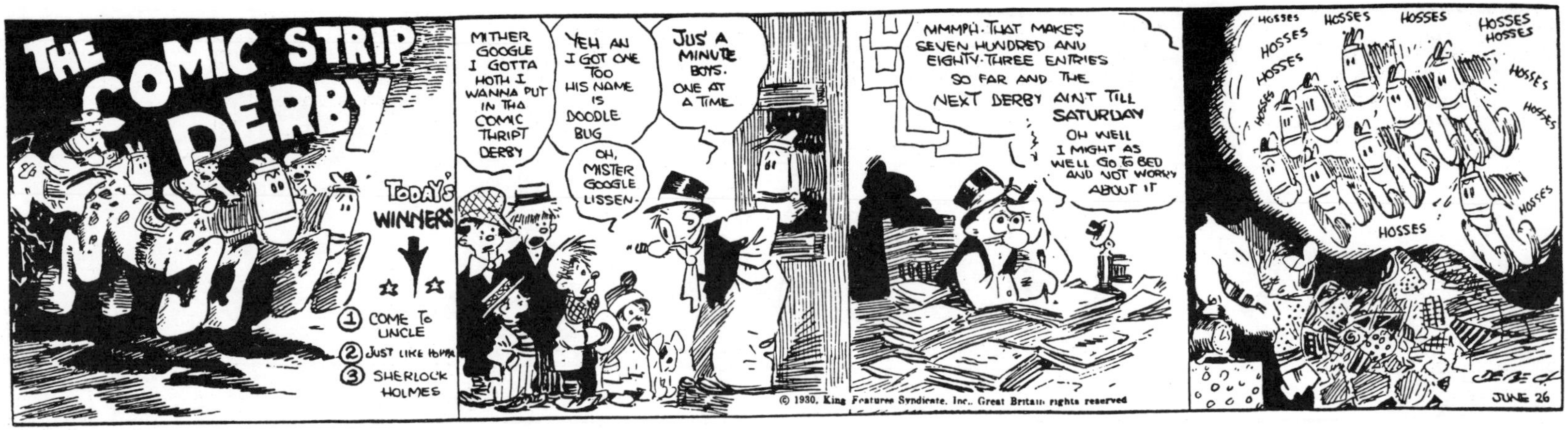

THE COMIC STRIP DERBY
TODAY'S WINNERS
① COME TO UNCLE
② JUST LIKE HOPPA
③ SHERLOCK HOLMES
MITHER GOOGLE I GOTTA HOTH I WANNA PUT IN THA COMIC THRIPT DERBY
YEH AN I GOT ONE TOO HIS NAME IS DOODLE BUG
OH, MISTER GOOGLE LISSEN-
JUS' A MINUTE BOYS. ONE AT A TIME
MMMPH- THAT MAKES SEVEN HUNDRED AND EIGHTY-THREE ENTRIES SO FAR AND THE NEXT DERBY AIN'T TILL SATURDAY
OH WELL I MIGHT AS WELL GO TO BED AND NOT WORRY ABOUT IT
HOSSES HOSSES HOSSES HOSSES HOSSES HOSSES HOSSES HOSSES HOSSES HOSSES HOSSES HOSSES
© 1930, King Features Syndicate, Inc., Great Britain rights reserved
DE BECK
JUNE 26

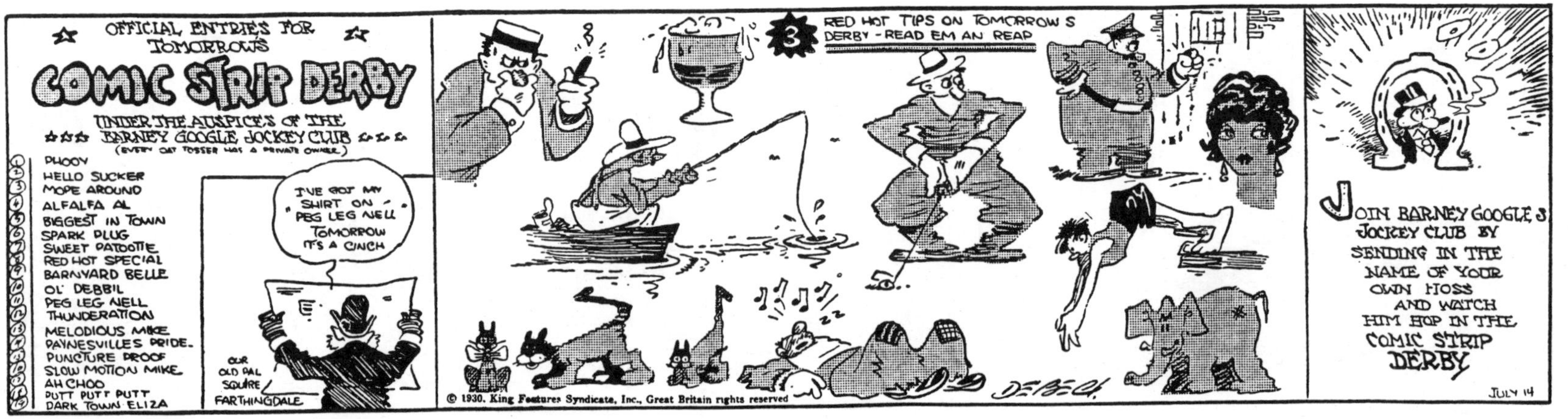

OFFICIAL ENTRIES FOR TOMORROW'S
COMIC STRIP DERBY
UNDER THE AUSPICES OF THE BARNEY GOOGLE JOCKEY CLUB
(EVERY OAT TOSSER HAS A PRIVATE OWNER)
① PHOOY
② HELLO SUCKER
③ MOPE AROUND
④ ALFALFA AL
⑤ BIGGEST IN TOWN
⑥ SPARK PLUG
⑦ SWEET PATOOTIE
⑧ RED HOT SPECIAL
⑨ BARNYARD BELLE
⑩ OL' DEBBIL
⑪ PEG LEG NELL
⑫ THUNDERATION
⑬ MELODIOUS MIKE
⑭ PAYNESVILLES PRIDE.
⑮ PUNCTURE PROOF
⑯ SLOW MOTION MIKE
⑰ AH CHOO
⑱ PUTT PUTT PUTT
⑲ DARK TOWN ELIZA
I'VE GOT MY SHIRT ON "PEG LEG NELL" TOMORROW IT'S A CINCH
OUR OLD PAL SQUIRE FARTHINGDALE
RED HOT TIPS ON TOMORROW'S DERBY - READ EM AN REAP
© 1930, King Features Syndicate, Inc., Great Britain rights reserved
DE BECK
JOIN BARNEY GOOGLE'S JOCKEY CLUB BY SENDING IN THE NAME OF YOUR OWN HOSS AND WATCH HIM HOP IN THE COMIC STRIP DERBY
JULY 14

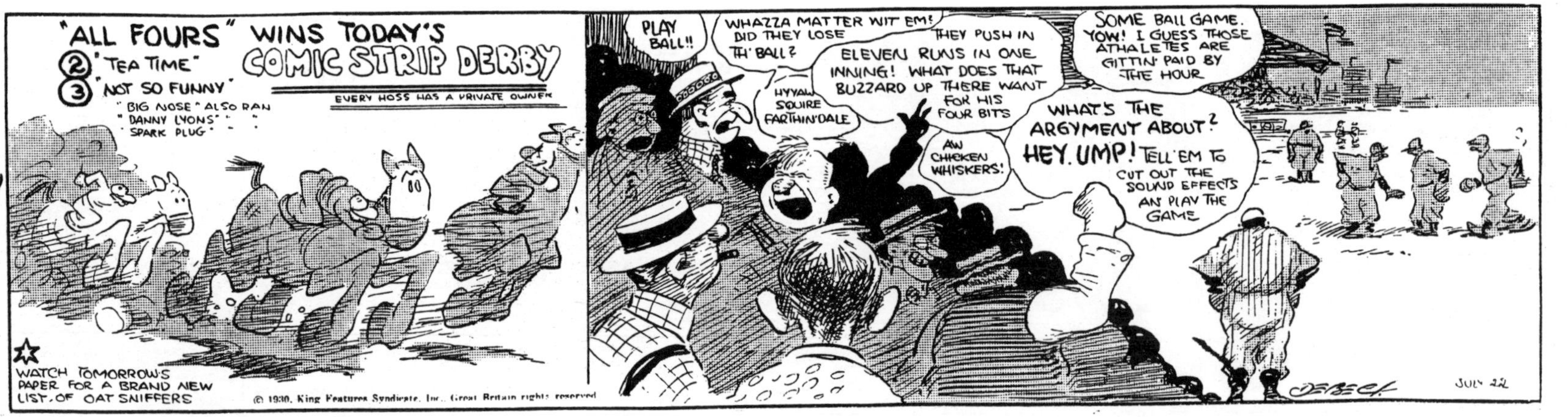

"ALL FOURS" WINS TODAY'S COMIC STRIP DERBY
② "TEA TIME"
③ "NOT SO FUNNY"
"BIG NOSE" ALSO RAN
"DANNY LYONS" " "
"SPARK PLUG" " "
EVERY HOSS HAS A PRIVATE OWNER
WATCH TOMORROW'S PAPER FOR A BRAND NEW LIST OF OAT SNIFFERS
© 1930, King Features Syndicate, Inc., Great Britain rights reserved
PLAY BALL!!
WHAZZA MATTER WIT EM! DID THEY LOSE TH' BALL?
THEY PUSH IN ELEVEN RUNS IN ONE INNING! WHAT DOES THAT BUZZARD UP THERE WANT FOR HIS FOUR BITS
HYYAW SQUIRE FARTHIN'DALE
SOME BALL GAME. YOW! I GUESS THOSE ATHALETES ARE GITTIN' PAID BY THE HOUR
AW CHICKEN WHISKERS!
WHAT'S THE ARGYMENT ABOUT?
HEY. UMP! TELL 'EM TO CUT OUT THE SOUND EFFECTS AN' PLAY THE GAME
DE BECK
JULY 22

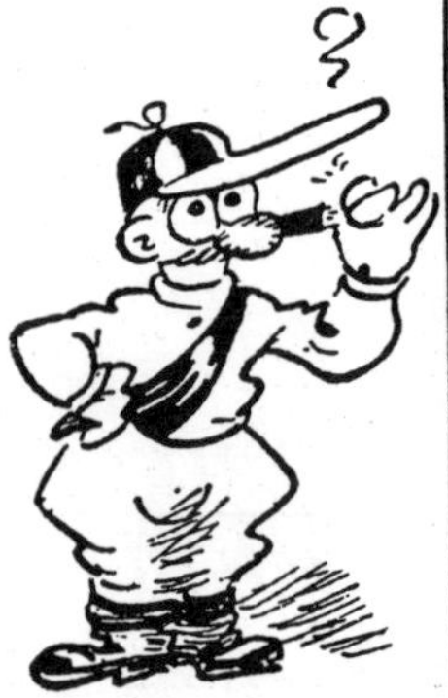

Madame La Mousse

1931

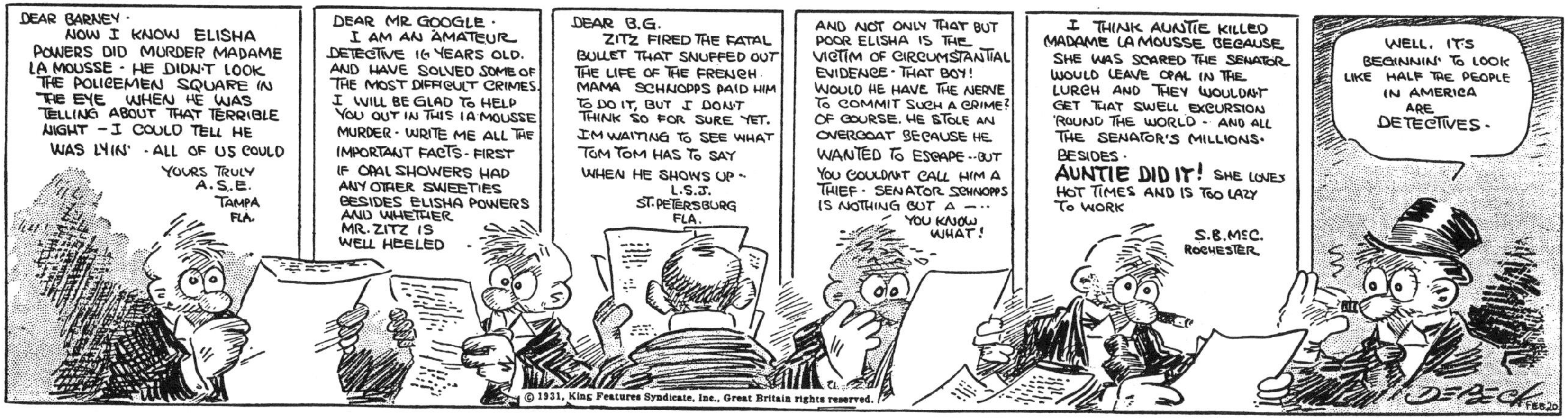
DEAR BARNEY · NOW I KNOW ELISHA POWERS DID MURDER MADAME LA MOUSSE · HE DIDN'T LOOK THE POLICEMEN SQUARE IN THE EYE WHEN HE WAS TELLING ABOUT THAT TERRIBLE NIGHT – I COULD TELL HE WAS LYIN' · ALL OF US COULD
YOURS TRULY A.S.E. TAMPA FLA.
DEAR MR GOOGLE · I AM AN AMATEUR DETECTIVE 16 YEARS OLD. AND HAVE SOLVED SOME OF THE MOST DIFFICULT CRIMES. I WILL BE GLAD TO HELP YOU OUT IN THIS LA MOUSSE MURDER · WRITE ME ALL THE IMPORTANT FACTS · FIRST IF OPAL SHOWERS HAD ANY OTHER SWEETIES BESIDES ELISHA POWERS AND WHETHER MR. ZITZ IS WELL HEELED ·
DEAR B.G. ZITZ FIRED THE FATAL BULLET THAT SNUFFED OUT THE LIFE OF THE FRENCH · MAMA SCHNOPPS PAID HIM TO DO IT, BUT I DON'T THINK SO FOR SURE YET. I'M WAITING TO SEE WHAT TOM TOM HAS TO SAY WHEN HE SHOWS UP --
L.S.J. ST. PETERSBURG FLA.
AND NOT ONLY THAT BUT POOR ELISHA IS THE VICTIM OF CIRCUMSTANTIAL EVIDENCE · THAT BOY! WOULD HE HAVE THE NERVE TO COMMIT SUCH A CRIME? OF COURSE. HE STOLE AN OVERCOAT BECAUSE HE WANTED TO ESCAPE -- BUT YOU COULDN'T CALL HIM A THIEF · SENATOR SCHNOPPS IS NOTHING BUT A --- YOU KNOW WHAT!
I THINK AUNTIE KILLED MADAME LA MOUSSE BECAUSE SHE WAS SCARED THE SENATOR WOULD LEAVE OPAL IN THE LURCH AND THEY WOULDN'T GET THAT SWELL EXCURSION 'ROUND THE WORLD -- AND ALL THE SENATOR'S MILLIONS · BESIDES · AUNTIE DID IT! SHE LOVES HOT TIMES AND IS TOO LAZY TO WORK
S.B.McC. ROCHESTER
WELL, IT'S BEGINNIN' TO LOOK LIKE HALF THE PEOPLE IN AMERICA ARE DETECTIVES ·
© 1931, King Features Syndicate, Inc., Great Britain rights reserved.
DE BECK
FEB 20

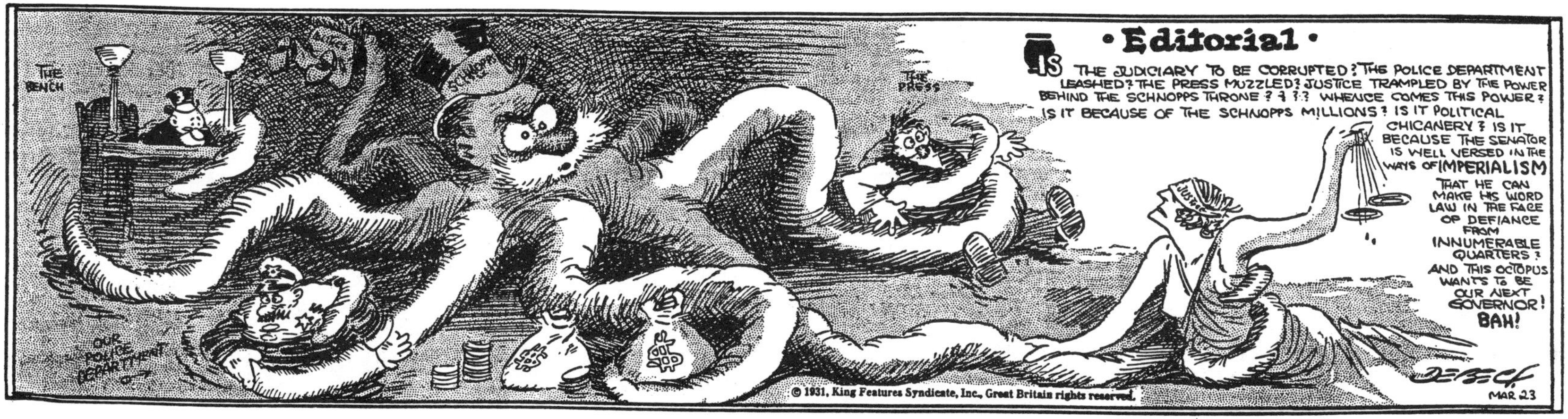
THE BENCH
SCHNOPPS
THE PRESS
OUR POLICE DEPARTMENT
· Editorial ·
IS THE JUDICIARY TO BE CORRUPTED? THE POLICE DEPARTMENT LEASHED? THE PRESS MUZZLED? JUSTICE TRAMPLED BY THE POWER BEHIND THE SCHNOPPS THRONE ? ? ?? WHENCE COMES THIS POWER? IS IT BECAUSE OF THE SCHNOPPS MILLIONS? IS IT POLITICAL CHICANERY? IS IT BECAUSE THE SENATOR IS WELL VERSED IN THE WAYS OF IMPERIALISM THAT HE CAN MAKE HIS WORD LAW IN THE FACE OF DEFIANCE FROM INNUMERABLE QUARTERS? AND THIS OCTOPUS WANTS TO BE OUR NEXT GOVERNOR! BAH!
© 1931, King Features Syndicate, Inc., Great Britain rights reserved.
DE BECK
MAR 23

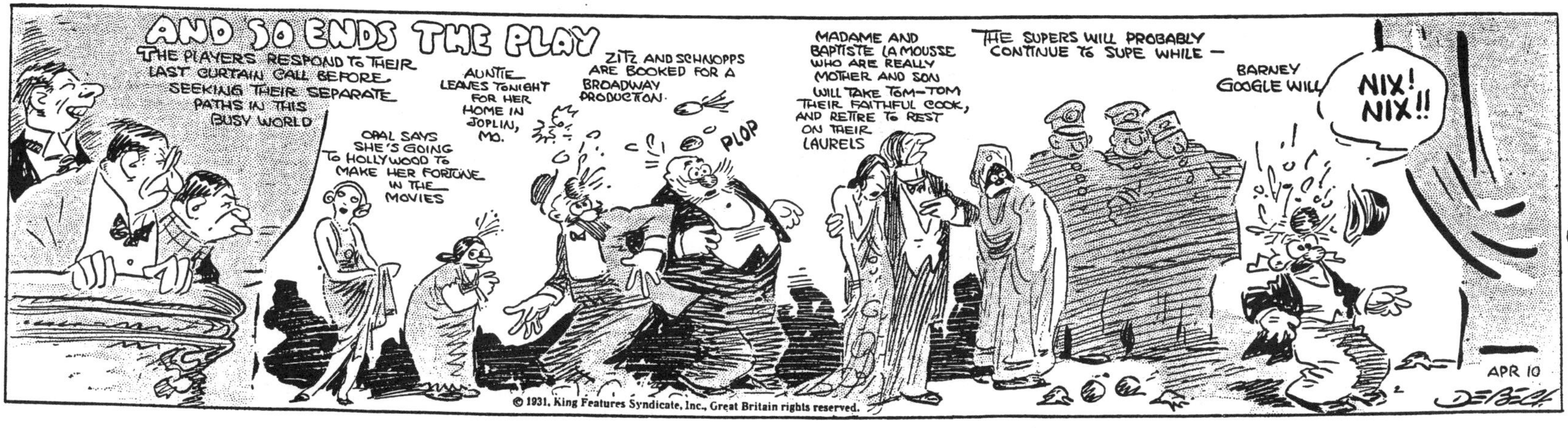
AND SO ENDS THE PLAY
THE PLAYERS RESPOND TO THEIR LAST CURTAIN CALL BEFORE SEEKING THEIR SEPARATE PATHS IN THIS BUSY WORLD
OPAL SAYS SHE'S GOING TO HOLLYWOOD TO MAKE HER FORTUNE IN THE MOVIES
AUNTIE LEAVES TONIGHT FOR HER HOME IN JOPLIN, MO.
ZITZ AND SCHNOPPS ARE BOOKED FOR A BROADWAY PRODUCTION
PLOP
MADAME AND BAPTISTE LA MOUSSE WHO ARE REALLY MOTHER AND SON WILL TAKE TOM-TOM THEIR FAITHFUL COOK, AND RETIRE TO REST ON THEIR LAURELS
THE SUPERS WILL PROBABLY CONTINUE TO SUPE WHILE –
BARNEY GOOGLE WILL
NIX! NIX!!
APR 10
© 1931, King Features Syndicate, Inc., Great Britain rights reserved.
DE BECK

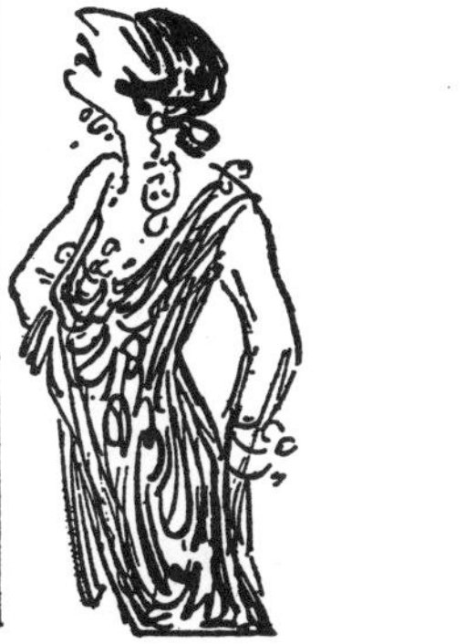

Pony Boy Vs. Sparky

1931

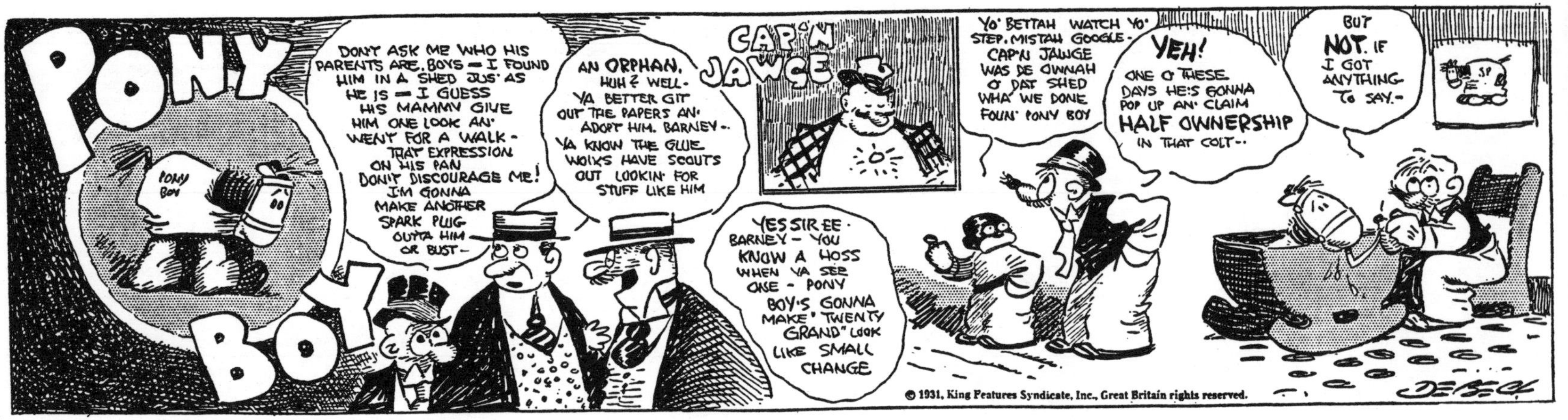

PONY BOY
PONY BOY
DON'T ASK ME WHO HIS PARENTS ARE, BOYS — I FOUND HIM IN A SHED JUS' AS HE IS — I GUESS HIS MAMMY GIVE HIM ONE LOOK AN' WENT FOR A WALK - THAT EXPRESSION ON HIS PAN DON'T DISCOURAGE ME! I'M GONNA MAKE ANOTHER SPARK PLUG OUTTA HIM OR BUST -
AN ORPHAN, HUH? WELL- YA BETTER GIT OUT THE PAPERS AN' ADOPT HIM, BARNEY - YA KNOW THE GLUE WOIKS HAVE SCOUTS OUT LOOKIN' FOR STUFF LIKE HIM
CAP'N JAWGE
YES SIR EE BARNEY - YOU KNOW A HOSS WHEN YA SEE ONE - PONY BOY'S GONNA MAKE "TWENTY GRAND" LOOK LIKE SMALL CHANGE
YO' BETTAH WATCH YO' STEP, MISTAH GOOGLE - CAP'N JAWGE WAS DE OWNAH O' DAT SHED WHA' WE DONE FOUN' PONY BOY
YEH! ONE O' THESE DAYS HE'S GONNA POP UP AN' CLAIM HALF OWNERSHIP IN THAT COLT -
BUT NOT, IF I GOT ANYTHING TO SAY. -
© 1931, King Features Syndicate, Inc., Great Britain rights reserved.
DE BECK

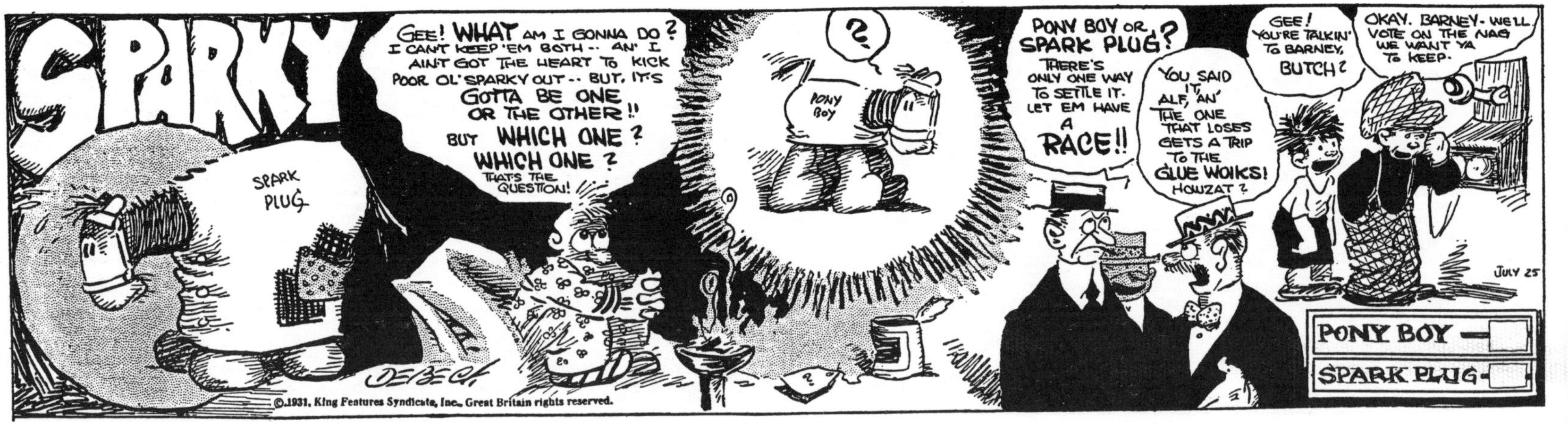

SPARKY
SPARK PLUG
GEE! WHAT AM I GONNA DO? I CAN'T KEEP 'EM BOTH -- AN' I AIN'T GOT THE HEART TO KICK POOR OL' SPARKY OUT -- BUT, IT'S GOTTA BE ONE OR THE OTHER!! BUT WHICH ONE? WHICH ONE? THAT'S THE QUESTION!
?
PONY BOY
PONY BOY OR SPARK PLUG? THERE'S ONLY ONE WAY TO SETTLE IT. LET EM HAVE A RACE!!
YOU SAID IT, ALF, AN' THE ONE THAT LOSES GETS A TRIP TO THE GLUE WOIKS! HOWZAT?
GEE! YOU'RE TALKIN' TO BARNEY, BUTCH?
OKAY, BARNEY - WE'LL VOTE ON THE NAG WE WANT YA TO KEEP.
JULY 25
PONY BOY
SPARK PLUG
DE BECK
©1931, King Features Syndicate, Inc., Great Britain rights reserved.

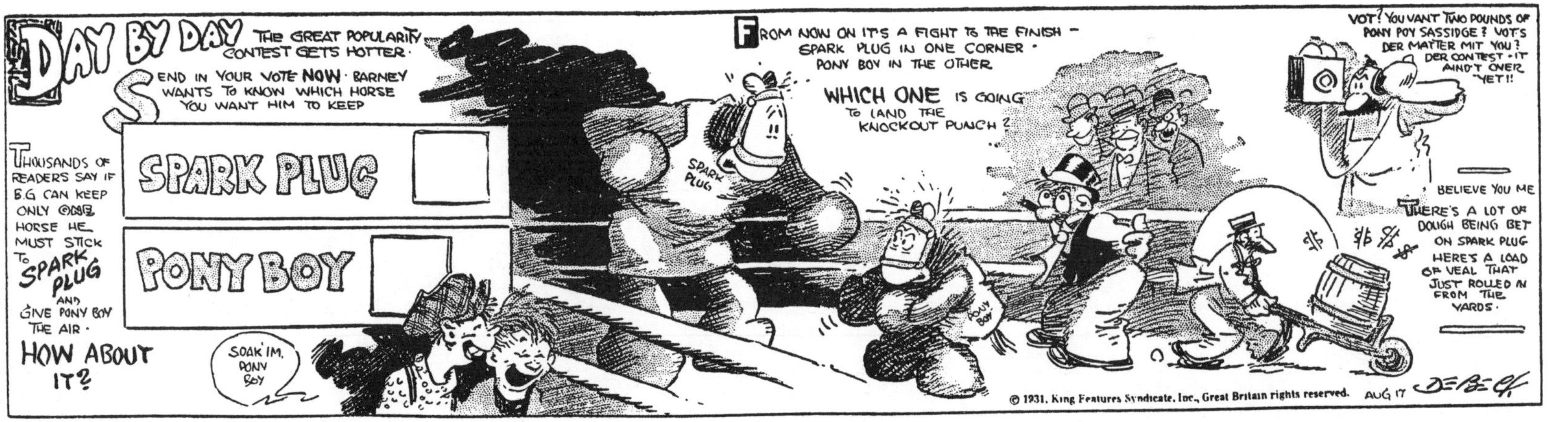

DAY BY DAY THE GREAT POPULARITY CONTEST GETS HOTTER
SEND IN YOUR VOTE NOW - BARNEY WANTS TO KNOW WHICH HORSE YOU WANT HIM TO KEEP
SPARK PLUG
PONY BOY
THOUSANDS OF READERS SAY IF B.G CAN KEEP ONLY ONE HORSE HE MUST STICK TO SPARK PLUG AND GIVE PONY BOY THE AIR - HOW ABOUT IT?
FROM NOW ON IT'S A FIGHT TO THE FINISH - SPARK PLUG IN ONE CORNER - PONY BOY IN THE OTHER
WHICH ONE IS GOING TO LAND THE KNOCKOUT PUNCH?
SPARK PLUG
PONY BOY
VOT! YOU VANT TWO POUNDS OF PONY POY SASSIDGE? VOT'S DER MATTER MIT YOU? DER CONTEST - IT AIN'T OVER YET!!
BELIEVE YOU ME THERE'S A LOT OF DOUGH BEING BET ON SPARK PLUG HERE'S A LOAD OF VEAL THAT JUST ROLLED IN FROM THE YARDS.
SOAK 'IM, PONY BOY
© 1931, King Features Syndicate, Inc., Great Britain rights reserved.
AUG 17
DE BECK

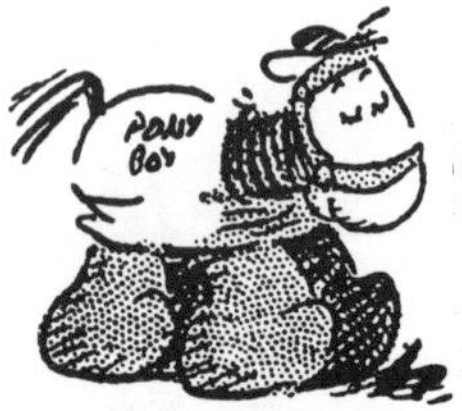

PONY BOY

The Great International Derby

1931

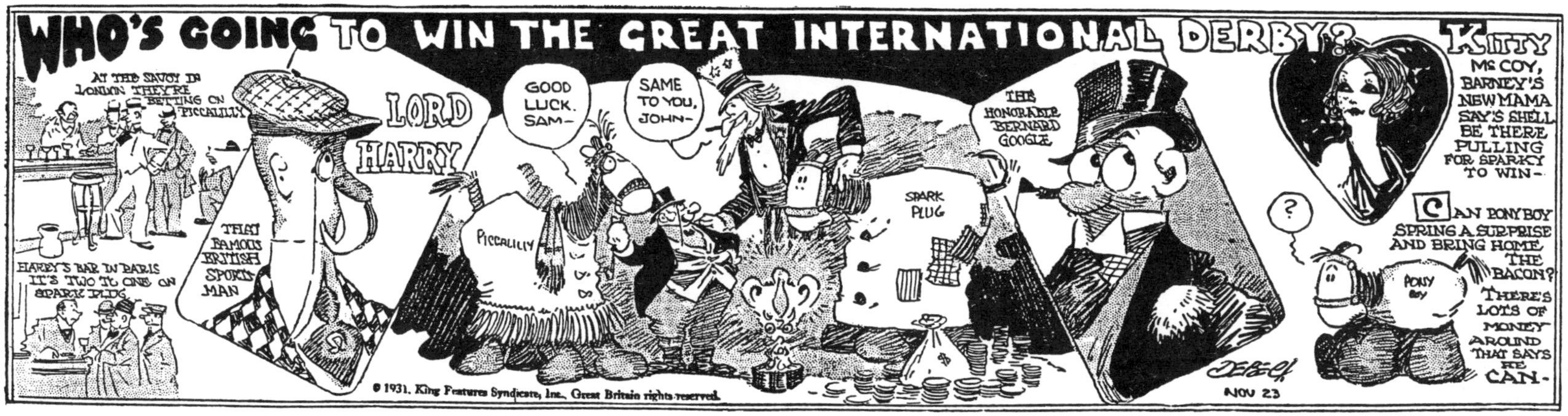

WHO'S GOING TO WIN THE GREAT INTERNATIONAL DERBY?
AT THE SAVOY IN LONDON THEY'RE BETTING ON PICCALILLY
HARRY'S BAR IN PARIS IT'S TWO TO ONE ON SPARK PLUG
LORD HARRY
THAT FAMOUS BRITISH SPORTSMAN
PICCALILLY
GOOD LUCK, SAM—
SAME TO YOU, JOHN—
SPARK PLUG
THE HONORABLE BERNARD GOOGLE
KITTY Mc COY, BARNEY'S NEW MAMA SAY'S SHE'LL BE THERE PULLING FOR SPARKY TO WIN—
?
CAN PONY BOY SPRING A SURPRISE AND BRING HOME THE BACON? THERE'S LOTS OF MONEY AROUND THAT SAYS HE CAN—
PONY BOY
DEBECK
NOV 23
© 1931, King Features Syndicate, Inc., Great Britain rights reserved.

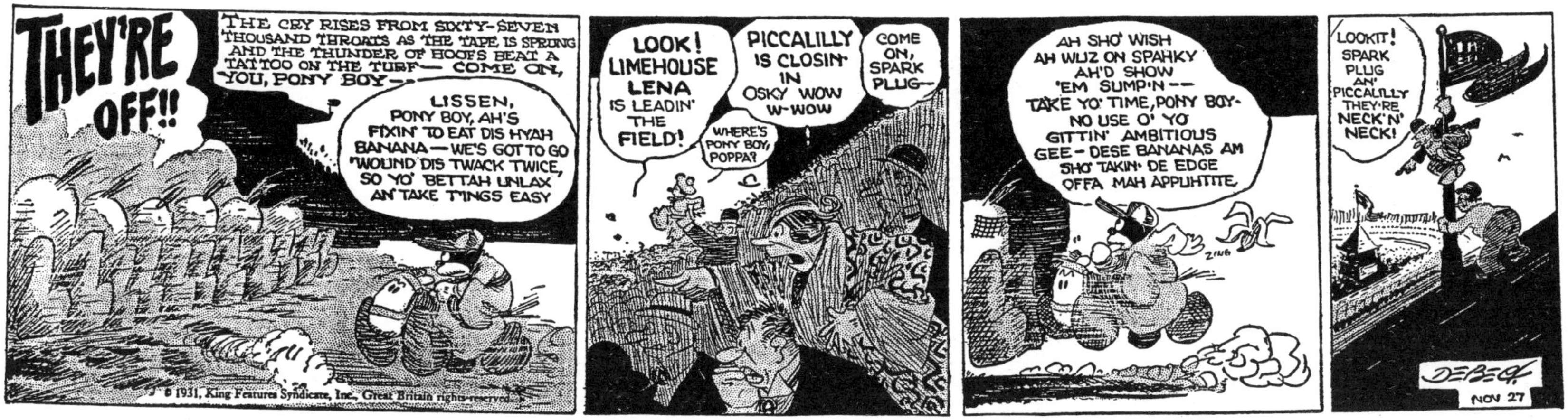

THEY'RE OFF!!
THE CRY RISES FROM SIXTY-SEVEN THOUSAND THROATS AS THE TAPE IS SPRUNG AND THE THUNDER OF HOOFS BEAT A TATTOO ON THE TURF— COME ON, YOU, PONY BOY—
LISSEN, PONY BOY, AH'S FIXIN' TO EAT DIS HYAH BANANA— WE'S GOT TO GO 'WOUND DIS TWACK TWICE, SO YO' BETTAH UNLAX AN' TAKE T'INGS EASY
© 1931, King Features Syndicate, Inc., Great Britain rights reserved.
LOOK! LIMEHOUSE LENA IS LEADIN' THE FIELD!
PICCALILLY IS CLOSIN' IN OSKY WOW W-WOW
COME ON, SPARK PLUG—
WHERE'S PONY BOY, POPPA?
AH SHO' WISH AH WUZ ON SPAHKY AH'D SHOW 'EM SUMP'N— TAKE YO' TIME, PONY BOY— NO USE O' YO' GITTIN' AMBITIOUS GEE— DESE BANANAS AM SHO' TAKIN' DE EDGE OFFA MAH APPUHTITE
ZING
LOOKIT! SPARK PLUG AN' PICCALILLY THEY'RE NECK'N' NECK!
DEBECK
NOV 27

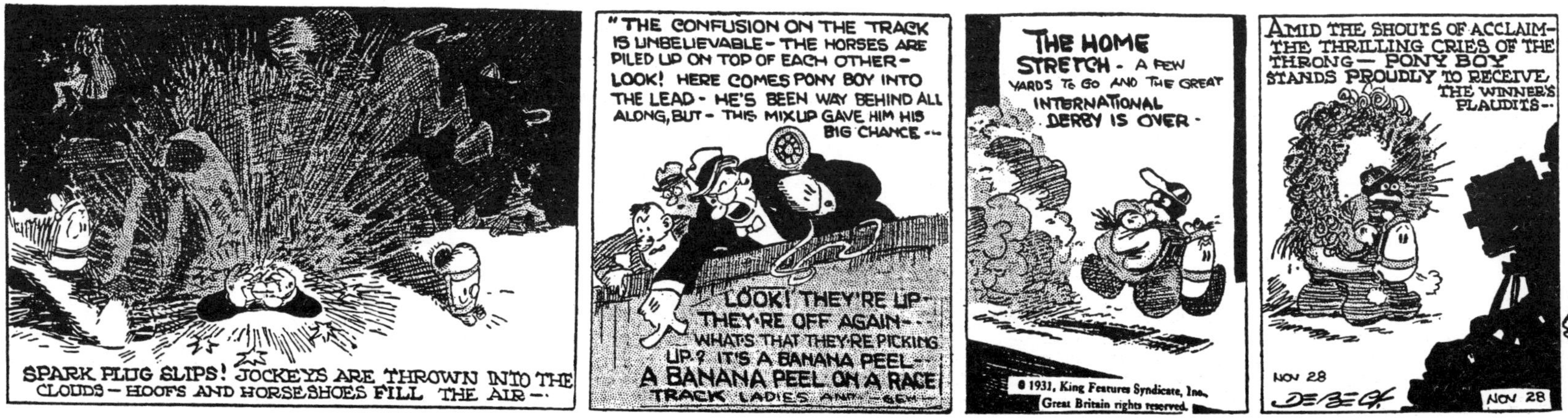

SPARK PLUG SLIPS! JOCKEYS ARE THROWN INTO THE CLOUDS— HOOFS AND HORSESHOES FILL THE AIR—
"THE CONFUSION ON THE TRACK IS UNBELIEVABLE— THE HORSES ARE PILED UP ON TOP OF EACH OTHER— LOOK! HERE COMES PONY BOY INTO THE LEAD— HE'S BEEN WAY BEHIND ALL ALONG, BUT— THIS MIXUP GAVE HIM HIS BIG CHANCE—
LOOK! THEY'RE UP— THEY'RE OFF AGAIN— WHAT'S THAT THEY'RE PICKING UP? IT'S A BANANA PEEL— A BANANA PEEL ON A RACE TRACK LADIES AND GEN—
THE HOME STRETCH— A FEW YARDS TO GO AND THE GREAT INTERNATIONAL DERBY IS OVER—
© 1931, King Features Syndicate, Inc., Great Britain rights reserved.
AMID THE SHOUTS OF ACCLAIM— THE THRILLING CRIES OF THE THRONG— PONY BOY STANDS PROUDLY TO RECEIVE THE WINNER'S PLAUDITS—
NOV 28
DEBECK
NOV 28

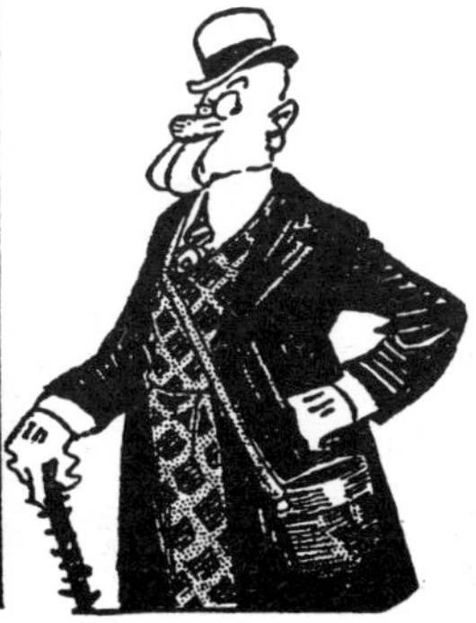

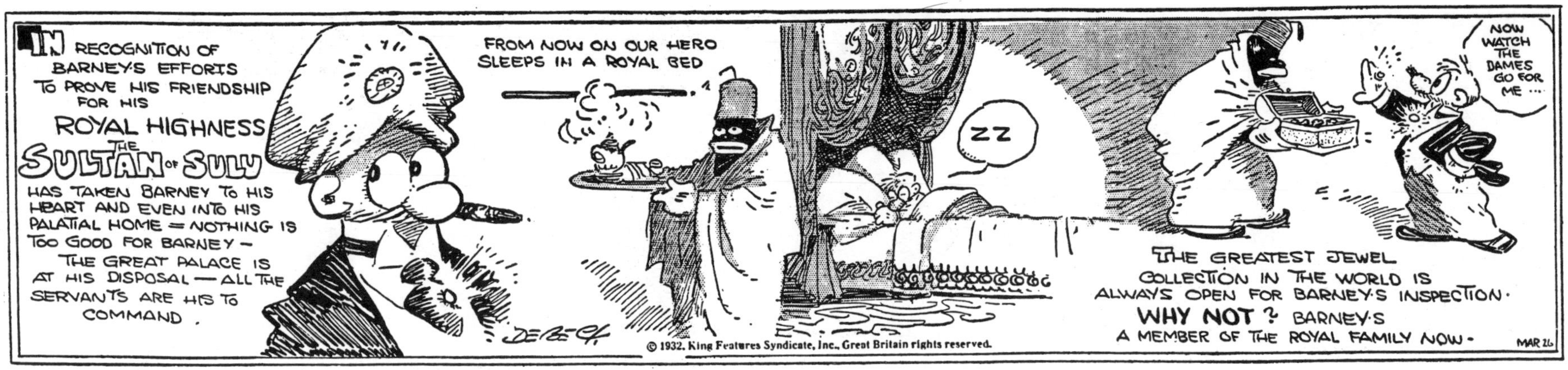
IN RECOGNITION OF BARNEY'S EFFORTS TO PROVE HIS FRIENDSHIP FOR HIS ROYAL HIGHNESS THE SULTAN OF SULU HAS TAKEN BARNEY TO HIS HEART AND EVEN INTO HIS PALATIAL HOME = NOTHING IS TOO GOOD FOR BARNEY - THE GREAT PALACE IS AT HIS DISPOSAL — ALL THE SERVANTS ARE HIS TO COMMAND.
FROM NOW ON OUR HERO SLEEPS IN A ROYAL BED
ZZ
NOW WATCH THE DAMES GO FOR ME ...
THE GREATEST JEWEL COLLECTION IN THE WORLD IS ALWAYS OPEN FOR BARNEY'S INSPECTION. WHY NOT ? BARNEY'S A MEMBER OF THE ROYAL FAMILY NOW -
DE BECK
© 1932, King Features Syndicate, Inc., Great Britain rights reserved.
MAR 26

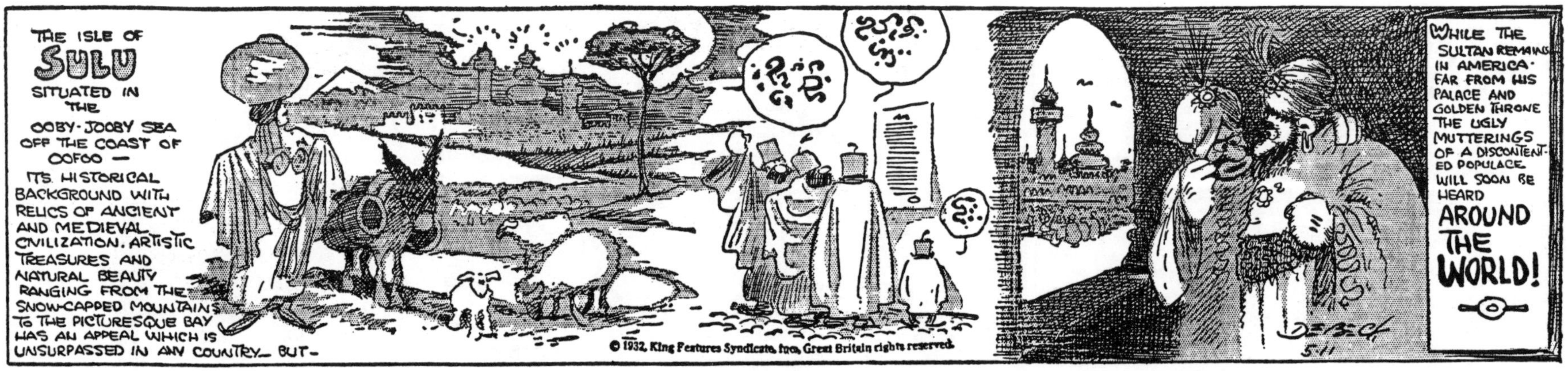
THE ISLE OF SULU SITUATED IN THE OOBY-JOOBY SEA OFF THE COAST OF OOFOO — ITS HISTORICAL BACKGROUND WITH RELICS OF ANCIENT AND MEDIEVAL CIVILIZATION. ARTISTIC TREASURES AND NATURAL BEAUTY RANGING FROM THE SNOW-CAPPED MOUNTAINS TO THE PICTURESQUE BAY HAS AN APPEAL WHICH IS UNSURPASSED IN ANY COUNTRY — BUT -
© 1932, King Features Syndicate, Inc., Great Britain rights reserved.
WHILE THE SULTAN REMAINS IN AMERICA - FAR FROM HIS PALACE AND GOLDEN THRONE THE UGLY MUTTERINGS OF A DISCONTENTED POPULACE WILL SOON BE HEARD AROUND THE WORLD!
DE BECK
5-11

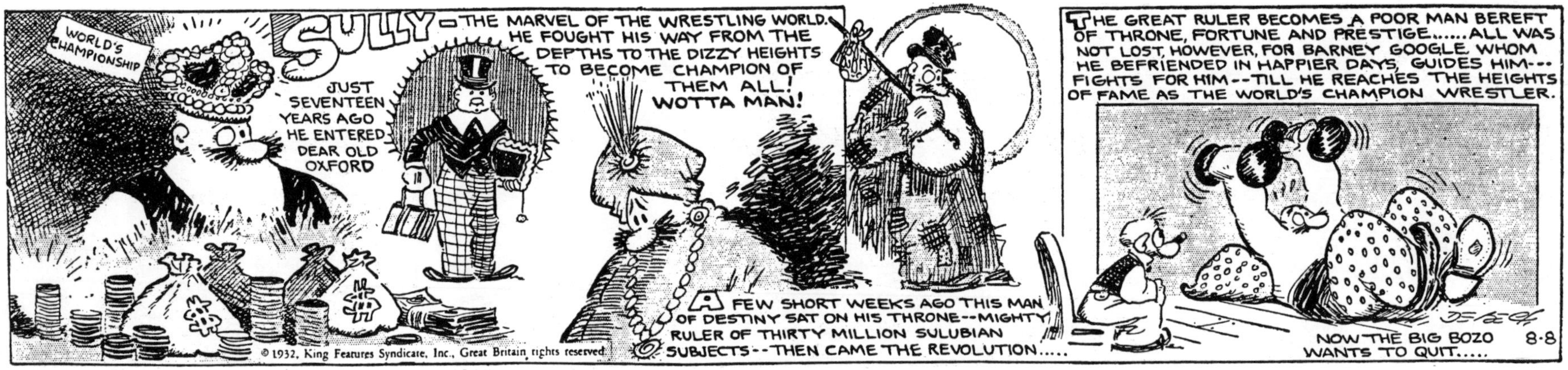
WORLD'S CHAMPIONSHIP
SULLY — THE MARVEL OF THE WRESTLING WORLD. HE FOUGHT HIS WAY FROM THE DEPTHS TO THE DIZZY HEIGHTS TO BECOME CHAMPION OF THEM ALL! WOTTA MAN!
JUST SEVENTEEN YEARS AGO HE ENTERED DEAR OLD OXFORD
A FEW SHORT WEEKS AGO THIS MAN OF DESTINY SAT ON HIS THRONE--MIGHTY RULER OF THIRTY MILLION SULUBIAN SUBJECTS--THEN CAME THE REVOLUTION.....
© 1932, King Features Syndicate, Inc., Great Britain rights reserved.
THE GREAT RULER BECOMES A POOR MAN BEREFT OF THRONE, FORTUNE AND PRESTIGE......ALL WAS NOT LOST, HOWEVER, FOR BARNEY GOOGLE, WHOM HE BEFRIENDED IN HAPPIER DAYS, GUIDES HIM--- FIGHTS FOR HIM--TILL HE REACHES THE HEIGHTS OF FAME AS THE WORLD'S CHAMPION WRESTLER.
NOW THE BIG BOZO WANTS TO QUIT.....
DE BECK
8-8

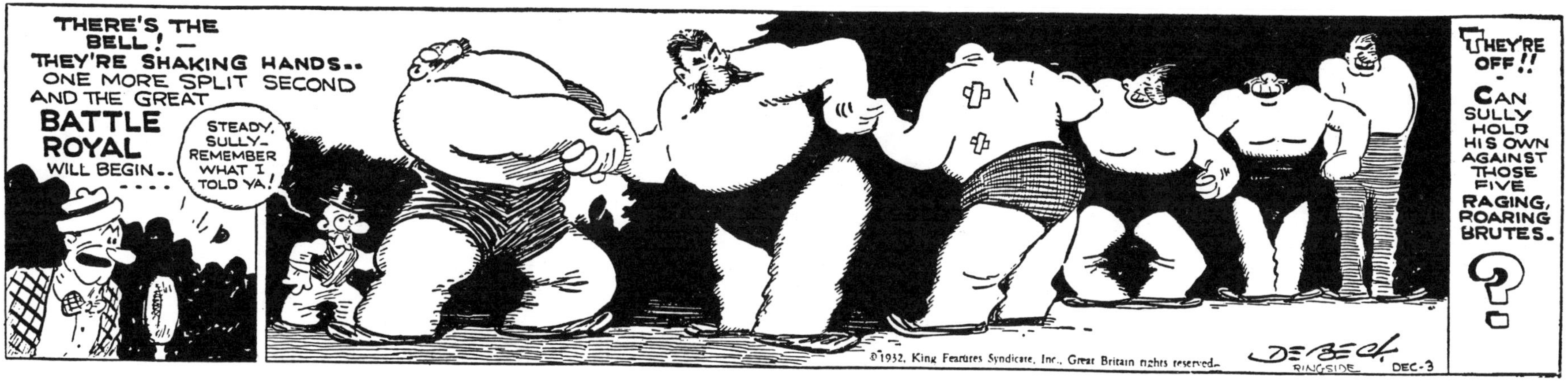
THERE'S THE BELL! — THEY'RE SHAKING HANDS.. ONE MORE SPLIT SECOND AND THE GREAT BATTLE ROYAL WILL BEGIN.. ....
STEADY, SULLY— REMEMBER WHAT I TOLD YA!
THEY'RE OFF!! - CAN SULLY HOLD HIS OWN AGAINST THOSE FIVE RAGING, ROARING BRUTES— ?
©1932, King Features Syndicate, Inc., Great Britain rights reserved—
DE BECK
RINGSIDE
DEC-3

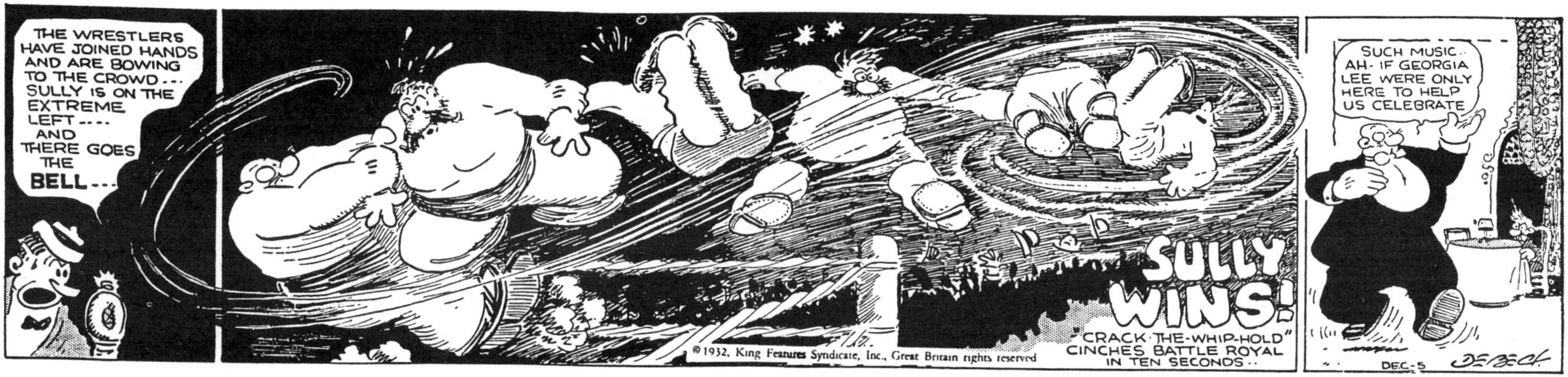
THE WRESTLERS HAVE JOINED HANDS AND ARE BOWING TO THE CROWD--- SULLY IS ON THE EXTREME LEFT---- AND THERE GOES THE BELL---
SULLY WINS!
"CRACK-THE-WHIP-HOLD" CINCHES BATTLE ROYAL IN TEN SECONDS..
©1932, King Features Syndicate, Inc., Great Britain rights reserved
SUCH MUSIC.. AH- IF GEORGIA LEE WERE ONLY HERE TO HELP US CELEBRATE
DEC-5
DE BECK

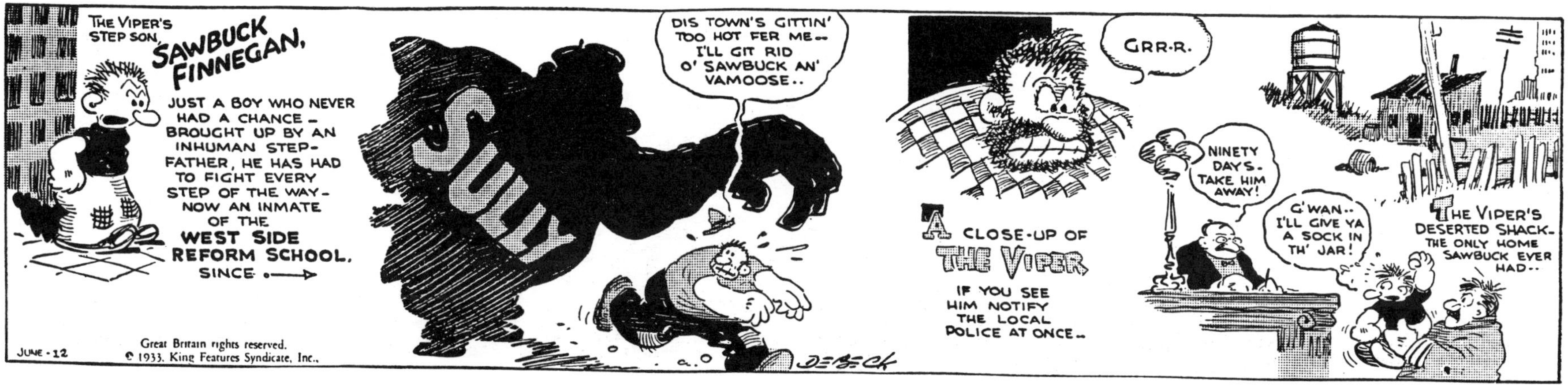
THE VIPER'S STEP SON, SAWBUCK FINNEGAN,
JUST A BOY WHO NEVER HAD A CHANCE — BROUGHT UP BY AN INHUMAN STEP-FATHER, HE HAS HAD TO FIGHT EVERY STEP OF THE WAY - NOW AN INMATE OF THE WEST SIDE REFORM SCHOOL, SINCE →
SULLY
DIS TOWN'S GITTIN' TOO HOT FER ME-- I'LL GIT RID O' SAWBUCK AN' VAMOOSE..
GRR-R.
A CLOSE-UP OF THE VIPER
IF YOU SEE HIM NOTIFY THE LOCAL POLICE AT ONCE—
NINETY DAYS. TAKE HIM AWAY!
G'WAN.. I'LL GIVE YA A SOCK IN TH' JAR!
THE VIPER'S DESERTED SHACK— THE ONLY HOME SAWBUCK EVER HAD--
JUNE-12
Great Britain rights reserved.
© 1933, King Features Syndicate, Inc.,
DE BECK

"As he [Billy DeBeck] waddles toward you he looks like a Dutch comedian and you'd swear that his big checked pants are stuffed with pillows fore and aft; but closer examination shows that it is all DeBeck and a yard wide. He has small, black almond eyes darting out from a brown face, the Oriental effect heightened by two lines which slant up above his eyebrows; and with his straight black hair that comes down in a peak and recedes markedly at each temple, if he put on a Japanese costume he could step right into a part in the Mikado."

Amram Scheinfeld, "Esquire" magazine Nov., 1935

Right: Photograph of Billy DeBeck, late 1920's. Courtesy of The Ohio State University Cartoon, Graphic, and Photographic Research Library.

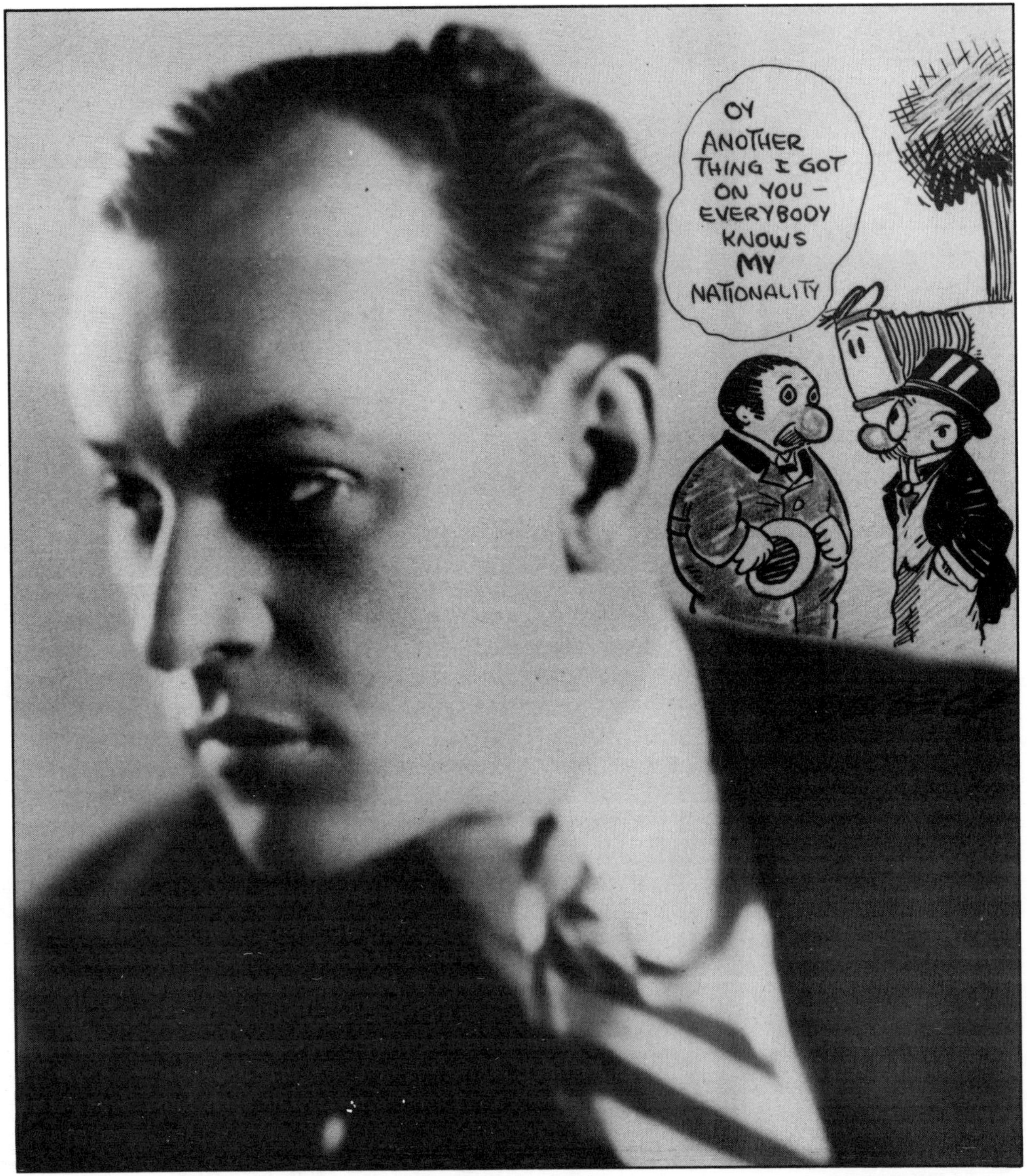
OY ANOTHER THING I GOT ON YOU - EVERYBODY KNOWS MY NATIONALITY

The Life and Times of Billy DeBeck

Billy DeBeck led a public life. Politicians, sports stars, actors, and literary figures were among his friends. He attended banquets and golf tournaments and had his picture taken wherever he went. But very little is known today about his private life.

Although the newspapers recorded his comings and goings, most of the articles were little more than press releases from King Features Syndicate, with the sole purpose of promoting the strip. The few in-depth profiles of DeBeck are filled with tales of his wild drinking and golfing days and are of dubious authenticity.

No diaries and only a handful of personal letters have been discovered. Most of what can be documented about DeBeck's life is taken from marriage licenses, death certificates and obituaries. We know when he was born, when he married, when he died and when his wife Mary died. The DeBecks had no children. The recollections of those who knew him, Fred Lasswell and Ferd Johnson most notably, shed only a little light on his personality.

Thus, the best source for gaining insight into Billy DeBeck's life are the thousands of cartoons he drew during his career, spanning the years from his early days in Ohio in 1910 until his death in 1942. In the panels of his comic strip creations, Billy DeBeck revealed more than he ever did in an interview. Barney Google was Billy's alter ego, and Barney's world was also Billy's world.

It was the world of Jack Dempsey, Babe Ruth and Man O'War. It was filled with the excitement of race tracks, boxing rings and baseball stadiums; with the aromas of smoke-filled rooms, speakeasies and flophouses. It played to the beat of Tin Pan Alley and the Charleston. It flirted with the dangers of bath-tub gin and flag-pole sitting. It was the world of the Roaring Twenties, the Great Depression and World War II, Calvin Coolidge, Warren Harding, Herbert Hoover and Franklin Delano Roosevlet.

DeBeck was a product of his time as well as a cultural barometer of American life in the 1920's and 1930's. His language was the vernacular of the streets. His characters were icons of the era.

Billy's world was also a man's world. Born on the sports pages, "Barney Google" appealed to the lunch pail crowd, the sports fan, the man about town. Barney was the Everyman of the Jazz Age. The audience for newspaper comics in the 1920's was predominately male, and nobody knew this better than Billy DeBeck. Like "Moon Mullins," the brainchild of Billy's lifelong pal Frank Willard, "Barney Google" was a strip that found its humor in the low life. His adventures were the male fantasies of his loyal readers. DeBeck's creation is a reflection of their hopes, dreams and failures. It is a chronicle of Billy's world, a world that is preserved today in the crumbling comic strips of a bygone age.

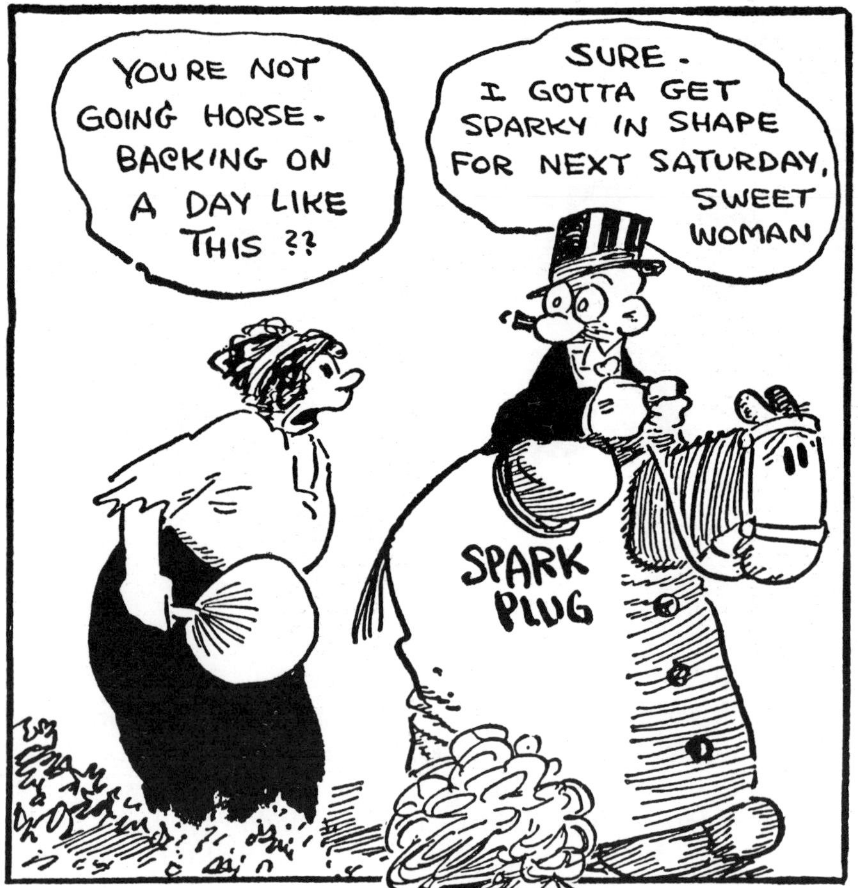
YOU'RE NOT GOING HORSE-BACKING ON A DAY LIKE THIS ??
SURE - I GOTTA GET SPARKY IN SHAPE FOR NEXT SATURDAY, SWEET WOMAN
SPARK PLUG

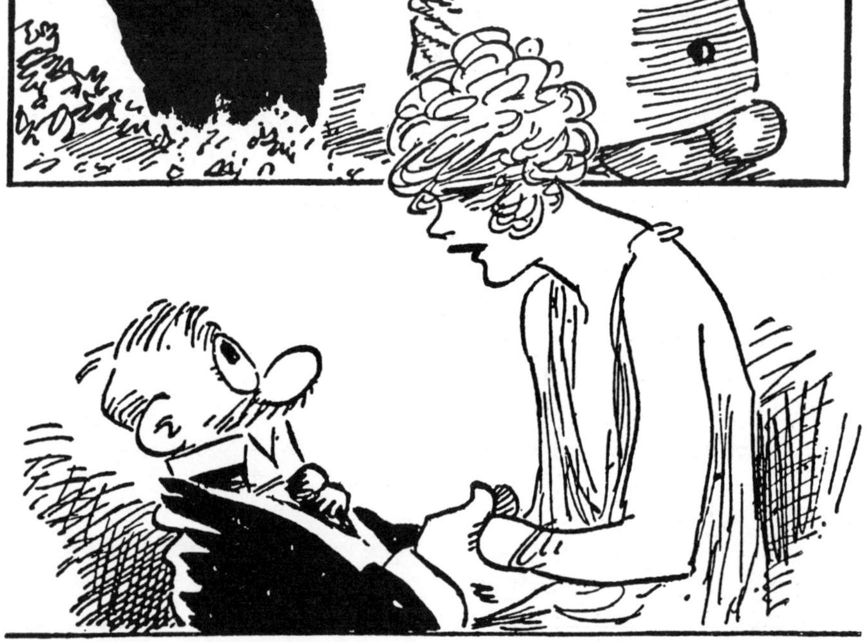

Top: Barney and his "sweet woman," 1924. From the Collection of Bill Janocha.
Above: Barney and a "Sweet Mama,"1928. From the Collection of Ron Goulart.

Gilbert Seldes, author of the landmark study of American popular culture, "The Seven Lively Arts," published in 1924, included "Barney Google" among what he called the "vulgar" comic strips. "Mutt and Jiggs and 'Abie the Agent' and 'Barney Google' and 'Eddie's Friends' have so little respect for law and order, the rights of property, the sanctity of money, the romance of marriage, and all the other foundations of American life," he wrote, "that if they were put into fiction, the Society for the Suppression of Everything would hale them incontinently to court and our morals would be saved again."

Barney Google flaunted the rules most flagrantly when it came to marital infidelity. His wife Lizzie appeared in the first panel of the first strip on June 17, 1919, nagging her husband about hanging around with the prize fighting crowd. Shortly after that episode, on October 20, 1919, Barney was shown sitting on a park bench with a pretty girl saying, "Me married? Why the idea - I'm the most confirmed bachelor you ever saw." From then on, he never thought twice about leaving his wife for long stretches. After Barney joined up with Spark Plug in 1922, months and even years went by without any mention of her whereabouts. In 1928, she returned briefly as the wife of Horseface Klotz, forcing Barney to explain to his friend that he had been married to her long ago. Once again, in 1933, his "sweet woman" reappeared for a brief reunion, but it was not long before Barney resumed his wayward lifestyle. She was never heard from again.

Although Barney was rarely successful in his pursuit of beautiful women, it did not discourage him, or DeBeck for that matter. Billy once described how the "Sweet Mama" theme developed:

"Many years ago, W. R. Hearst wanted a good-looking gal in the 'Barney Google' strip. Several weeks slipped by without any beautiful female. The reason: I'd rather take a beating than draw a fancy dame. Finally I turned out the most voluptuous blonde anybody could ask for. Then the fun began. I didn't know what to call the little lady - Muriel, Jane, Eliza, Annie. None of them seemed to fit the charmer. I was stymied no end.

"Finally I hit on 'Sweet Mama.' Wow! That started something. Letters poured in. The readers wanted to know where her child was. How could a single gal be a mama? Was Barney the father, etc., etc.? We lost several clients. Brisbane phoned. 'Cut out Sweet Mama,' he demanded. 'Go back to Spark Plug.' But in two short weeks the expression 'Sweet Mama' had swept the country. Songs were written about 'Blonde Mamas,' 'Red Mamas,' etc. Brisbane phoned again. 'Put Sweet Mama back in the strip,' he said. 'Don't you know when you've got sump'n?' After that I started to play on certain expressions like 'Heebie Jeebies,' 'So I took the $50,000,' 'Horse Feathers,' 'Puddle Jumper,' etc. Anything for a laugh."

Billy's love life was a little more stable than Barney's. His first wife, Marian Shields, was born on August 24, 1895. She met DeBeck when he was working for the *Youngstown Telegram*, sometime between 1910 and 1912. They married in Youngstown on March 29, 1914, a year and a half after Billy had taken a job on the *Pittsburgh Gazette-Times*. The newspaper described Marian as a "pretty and vivacious girl...popular in Youngstown society."

On August 13, 1916, a curious interview with Mrs. Billy DeBeck appeared in the *Chicago Herald*. Billy's comic strip of domestic discord, "Married Life," had been running in that paper since December 9, 1915. The reporter told Mrs. DeBeck that he was sent to find out, "what you do to DeBeck to make him so sore at the race of wives." "Down at the office he's all right, nothing wrong with his disposition," the reporter continued, "but he's always drawing husbands choking their wives or tying them up in a hog pen or sending them out to sea in a leaky boat or anything to keep 'em from talking and nagging. So they told me to come up to his house while they held him in the office and get a story on how mean you must be to him."

Mrs. DeBeck responded, "So long as we were in Pittsburgh, where we were married, he did political cartoons and nobody felt sorry for me. But when we moved to Chicago and he started that little daily cartoon and the big Sunday comic on 'Married Life' then my troubles began. It's no joke to be a cartoonist's wife, although no home life is happier than ours when he's here. He works all day down there at your paper and then he comes home and draws a sports cartoon and then three nights a week he goes down to the Academy of Fine Arts to teach cartooning! He says sometimes he thinks he'll take a month off and get to really know me again. He says that when we have children he'll start putting them into the cartoons and I hope he will, because then he won't be watching me every meal to see what he can find to work up into a picture quarrel."

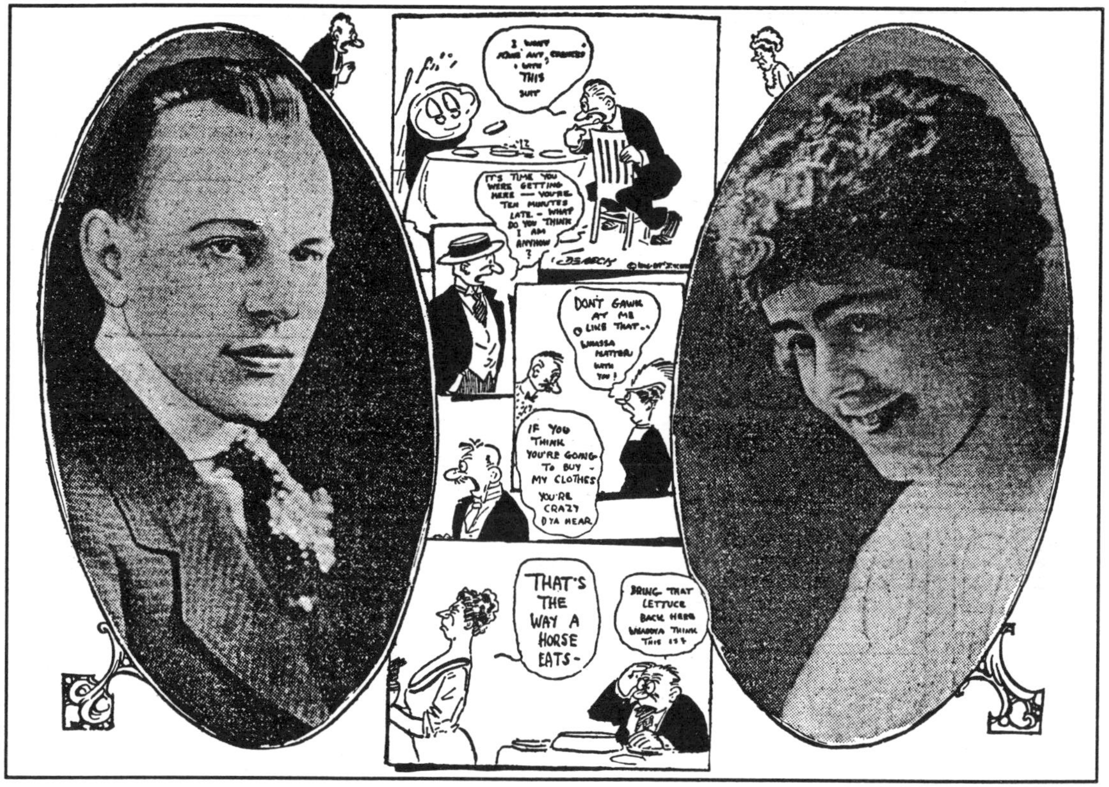
IT'S TIME YOU WERE GETTING HERE — YOU'RE TEN MINUTES LATE - WHAT DO YOU THINK I AM ANYHOW ?
DON'T GAWK AT ME LIKE THAT..
IF YOU THINK YOU'RE GOING TO BUY - MY CLOTHES YOU'RE CRAZY D'YA HEAR
THAT'S THE WAY A HORSE EATS -
BRING THAT LETTUCE BACK HERE

Above: Photos of DeBeck and his first wife, Marian, from the article in the *Chicago Herald*, August 13, 1916. Courtesy of the San Francisco Academy of Comic Art.

This interview was probably meant to be tongue-in-cheek but, there might have been some truth in Mrs. DeBeck's description of her husband's daily routine. At some point in the intervening years, Billy and Marian drifted apart and were divorced. It was rumored that she moved to Hollywood to pursue a career in acting while he went on to fame and fortune as a cartoonist.

An article in the *Chicago Herald and Examiner* on August 23, 1921, reported that DeBeck had remarried Marian Shields in Utica, New York, the previous day. "This is no Bughouse Fable," claimed DeBeck. It is not known why Billy married the same woman twice or when they were divorced again. Marian Shields did end up in Hollywood. Although there is no record of her film career, she eventually married two well-known movie actors: Roland Young and Charlie Ruggles.

The final chapter in the Billy DeBeck - Marian Shields relationship occurred in 1942, just a few months before Billy died of cancer. Ferd Johnson, assistant to Billy's good friend Frank Willard, remembered that, "He [DeBeck] was out here at the Burbank Airport. He knew the end was coming. He came out to see his first wife [Marian Shields]. He made a special trip. Of course, he married this other gal, but I guess he always went for this first gal. He came out to see her, tell her good bye or something. That's the last I saw Billy DeBeck."

Mary Louise Dunne was often credited with sobering up Billy after his years of high living in New York City during the early 1920's. Mary was described as "a pretty, pert Irish girl with blue eyes and a doll-like figure." She was a graduate of the Columbia School of Journalism and worked in the advertising business before she met Billy. Apparently Mary did not like Billy's Broadway crowd and they did not like her. She prevailed.

Mary and Billy were married in 1927, and moved to Paris, where they lived quietly for two years. Billy claimed that during his stay there he never picked up a word of French and was not influenced to change his uniquely American comic strip in the slightest.

Upon returning home, Billy stayed away from the party scene and began a more settled lifestyle with Mary, commuting seasonally between New York and Florida. In the early 1930's, the DeBecks bought a showcase home in the exclusive Snell Island section of St. Petersburg, Florida, called "Villa Florentia." Mary became active in St. Petersburg as a member of the Junior League. She helped set up the first prenatal care unit in the city. She developed plans for the first community blood bank and was the founding president of the Women's Auxiliary of St. Anthony's Hospital. The DeBecks entertained St. Petersburg society as well as colorful characters like Babe Ruth, Dizzy Dean and Damon Runyon in their home.

Mary was by Billy's bedside when he died at Lenox Hill Hospital in New York City at 1:40 AM on November 11, 1942. In her husband's memory, Mary offered to present an award at the annual dinner of the newly formed National Cartoonists Society. The "outstanding cartoonist of the year" received a handsome silver cigarette box with the entire cast of Billy DeBeck's characters etched on the cover. Milton Caniff won the first "Billy DeBeck Award" in 1946, and it was given out every year until 1953, after which it was replaced by the "Reuben Award."

Mary married Fritz Bergman after Billy died and continued to live in Villa Florentia in St. Petersburg. She died in a National Airlines plane crash over the Gulf of Mexico in 1952.

**Photograph of
Mary Louise DeBeck,
late 1920's. From the
Collection of Murray A. Harris**

During his lifetime, Billy DeBeck made friends with some of the most famous people in America. He was an acquaintance of Frank Crowninshield, the sophisticated editor of *Vanity Fair*. He played golf with Dizzy Dean and Babe Ruth. He mugged for the cameras with his pal, Jack Dempsey. He talked sports with Damon Runyon and Grantland Rice. He enjoyed the company of fellow cartoonists Rube Goldberg, Harry Hershfield, George McManus, Robert Ripley and Cliff Sterrett.

Frank Willard, the creator of "Moon Mullins," was probably his best and oldest friend. Willard and DeBeck first met in 1915 when they worked side-by-side at the *Chicago Herald*/Keeley Syndicate. After Willard returned from a tour in the Army during World War I, he returned briefly to Chicago, and then moved in with Billy and his wife Marian in New York City. He assisted Billy on "Barney Google," and, with Billy's recommendation, got a job in the King Features bullpen in 1920 where he created the short-lived feature, "The Outta Luck Club." This experience helped him land a job with the Chicago Tribune-New York News Syndicate, and on June 19, 1923 he launched "Moon Mullins," a "low life" comic strip similar in many ways to"Barney Google."

Frank Willard and his assistant, Ferd Johnson, moved around the country constantly and often visited DeBeck in Florida and New York City. One of the more famous stories about Billy and Frank involved one of these encounters:

"Several years ago he [Billy] and a gang of his friends had gone out of town to a championship fight. At the aftermath there was considerable partying in the DeBeck hotel suite, and it being a hot night, Billy shed his clothes and passed out cold. Some of the boys strewed the ice supply around his head and over his person.

"A while later, Billy's pal, Frank Willard, happened in, mixed a drink and asked for ice. The boys pointed into the next room. Willard peered in at the prostrate Billy at peace under the melting ice cubes.

"'No, I'd better not disturb him,' said Willard, 'he's probably thinking up ideas.'"

In 1942, at the end of his life, Billy flew out to California to see his old friend. Ferd Johnson remembers Billy pulling him aside and saying, "Ferd, I want you to take care of Frank." "I said I would," Ferd says. Willard lived until 1958.

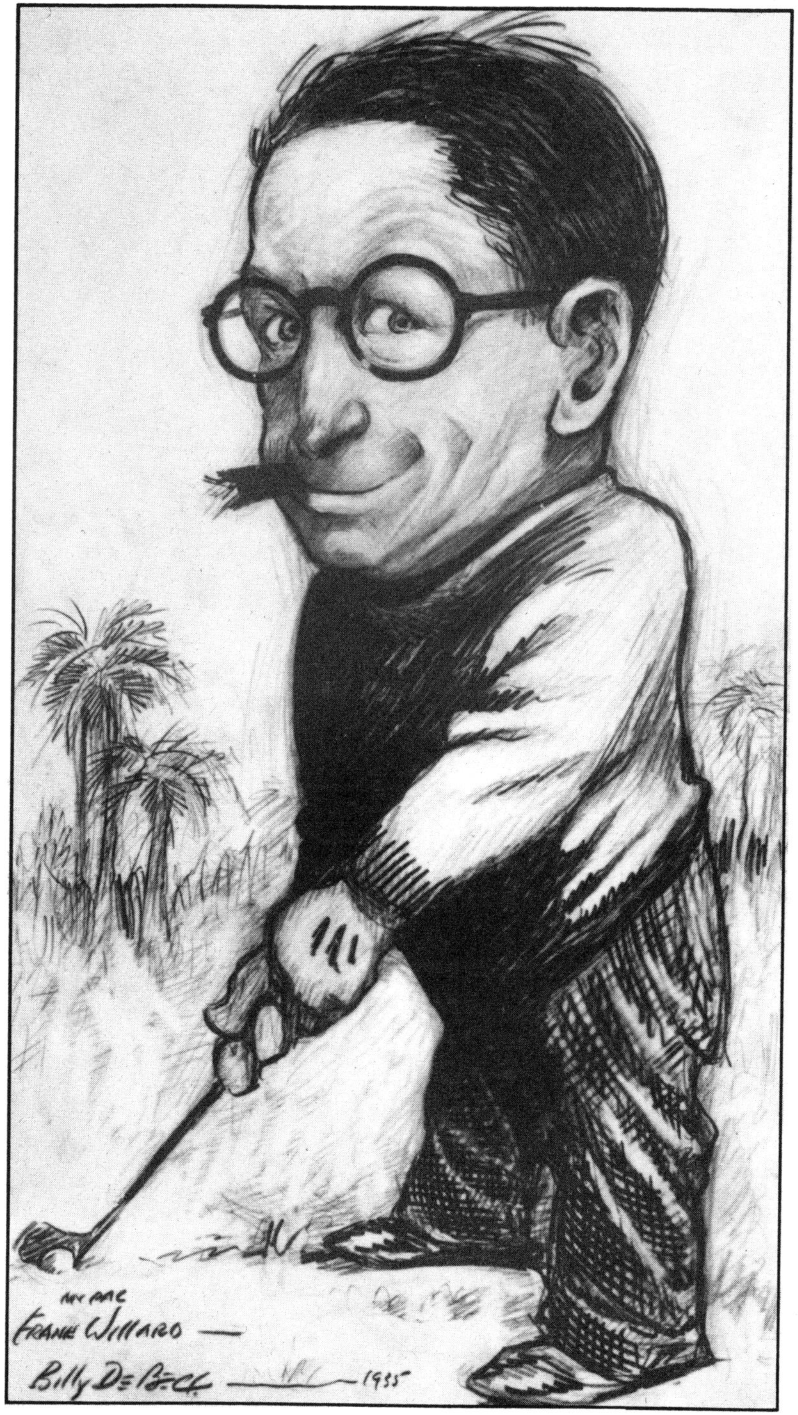
Frank Willard
Billy DeBeck
1935

Right: A caricature of Frank Willard drawn by Billy DeBeck, 1935. Courtesy of Fred Lasswell.

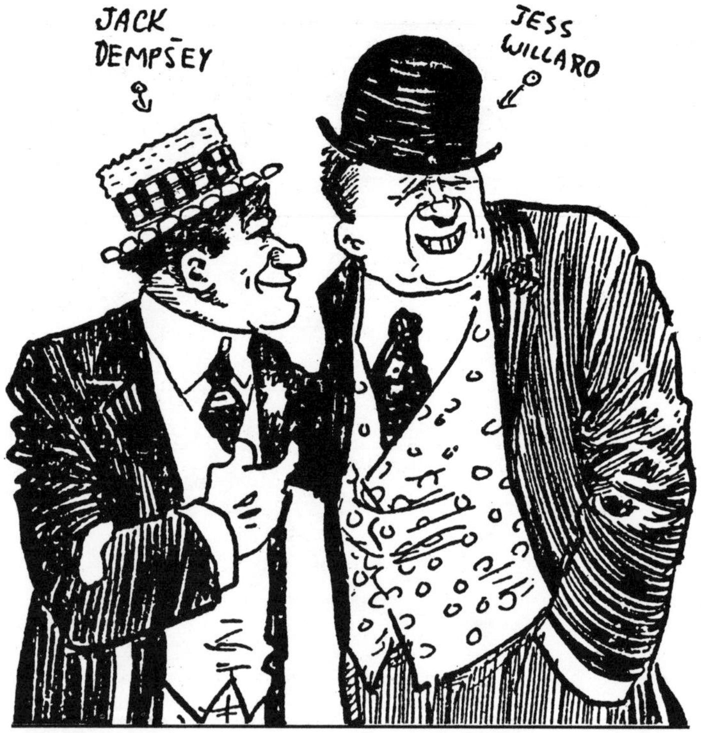
JACK DEMPSEY
JESS WILLARD

The era between 1919 and 1930 is immortalized as the "Golden Age of Sport." Grantland Rice, dean of American sportswriters, stated that these years stand out, "because this postwar period gave the game the greatest collection of stars, involving both skill and color, that sport has ever known." In 1919, the same year that "Take Barney Google, F'rinstance" first appeared in the *Chicago Herald and Examiner*, Babe Ruth started his home run rampage with 29 round-trippers, Jack Dempsey knocked out Jess Willard to become heavyweight champion of the world and the great thoroughbred, Man O'War, began a remarkable string of twenty victories in twenty-one races. The "Golden Age" was also the time of Red Grange and Jim Thorpe in football, Jesse Owens in track, Bobby Jones in golf, Johnny Weismuller in swimming, Bill Tilden in tennis and Damon Runyan, Heywood Broun and Ring Lardner in the pressbox. It also gave us "Barney Google" on the sports pages.

Beginning with the first episodes, set in the Toledo training camps of Jess Willard and Jack Dempsey, "Barney Google" was a sports-related feature. Even when he was not cheering in the stands at a baseball game or risking all his money at the race track, Barney was doing the kinds of things a typical sports fan did in his daily life - sneaking out to play poker with his buddies, flirting with pretty girls or trying to scrape together a little cash to pay the bills. "Barney Google" appeared on the sports pages of most newspapers around the country during the 1920's for a good reason. Sports page readers could identify with this little cigar-smoking, card shuffling, bet-wagering entrepreneur.

Above: Jack Dempsey (left) and Jess Willard (right) by Billy DeBeck, from the *Chicago Herald and Examiner*, 1919. Courtesy of the San Francisco Academy of Comic Art.
Below: Barney makes his prediction for another Dempsey heavyweight bout in the *Chicago Herald and Examiner*, June 16, 1921. From the Collection of Mark Johnson.

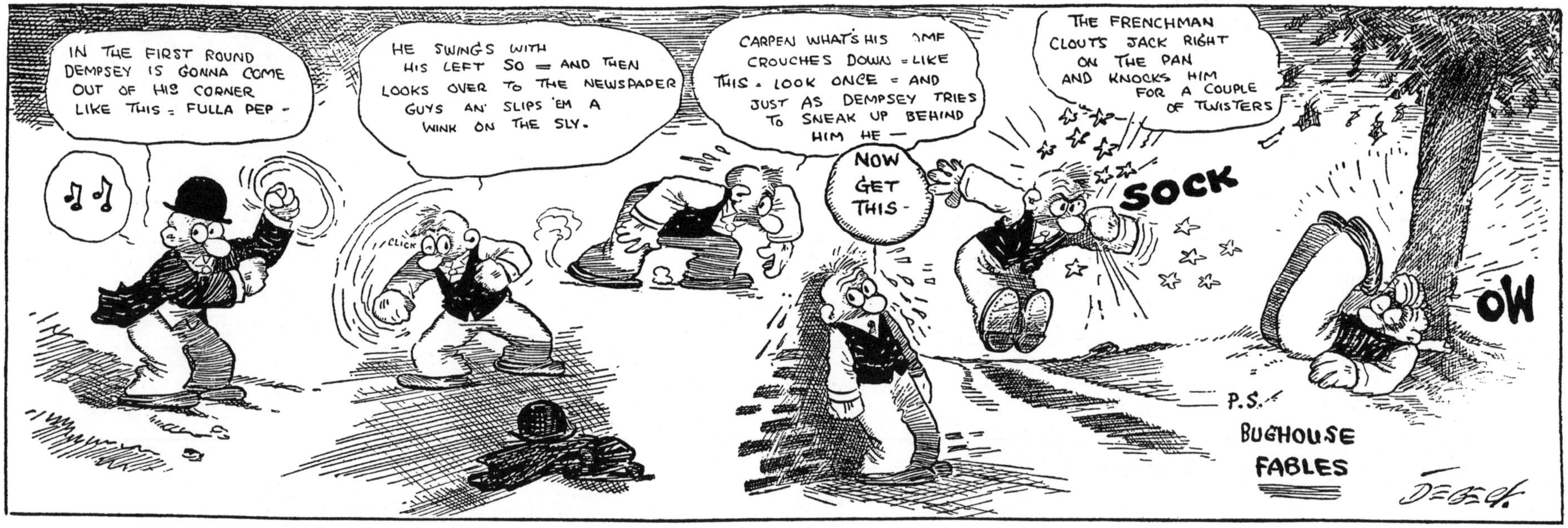
IN THE FIRST ROUND DEMPSEY IS GONNA COME OUT OF HIS CORNER LIKE THIS = FULLA PEP -
HE SWINGS WITH HIS LEFT SO = AND THEN LOOKS OVER TO THE NEWSPAPER GUYS AN' SLIPS 'EM A WINK ON THE SLY.
CLICK
CARPEN WHAT'S HIS
CROUCHES DOWN = LIKE THIS - LOOK ONCE = AND JUST AS DEMPSEY TRIES TO SNEAK UP BEHIND HIM HE —
NOW GET THIS -
THE FRENCHMAN CLOUTS JACK RIGHT ON THE PAN AND KNOCKS HIM FOR A COUPLE OF TWISTERS
SOCK
OW
P.S. BUGHOUSE FABLES
DEBECK

Barney led an idyllic existence, traveling aimlessly from town to town, doing something the average man had very little time for - having fun.

Billy DeBeck was an avid sports fan himself. He attended prize fights, horse races and baseball games regularly. Later in his life, golf and bridge became obsessions. According to Ferd Johnson, Billy was a fairly good golfer, shooting consistently in the high 80's and low 90's. He played at the Palma Ceia Country Club in Tampa, Florida, and the Asheville Country Club in Asheville, North Carolina, with his old cartooning buddy Frank Willard, as well as Babe Ruth and Dizzy Dean.

There were always lots of laughs out on the links. The following is a typical DeBeck golfing story that a reporter recounted in 1935: "It was at an Artists and Writers golf tournament in Florida last winter that short and stocky William Morgan DeBeck drove off into the rough - an' down in them thar parts rough is rough. As little DeBeck and his caddy went to look for the ball, they were promptly swallowed up among the six-foot high palmettos. A long silence - then the caddy's voice, 'Mister DeBeck! I found your ball'. And from somewhere deep in the palmettos issued forth, 'The hell with the ball - come over and find me!"

Billy DeBeck was not known as a joke-telling, wise-cracking kind of a guy. He was usually very quiet in public. But he did know how to have fun. He usually had the most fun out on a golf course or sitting at a card table, and he was always a good sport when it came to losing.

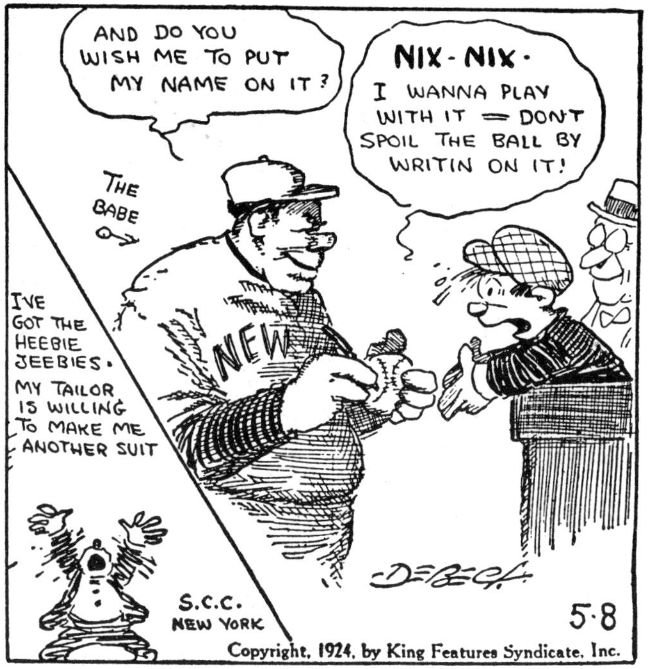
AND DO YOU WISH ME TO PUT MY NAME ON IT?
NIX-NIX. I WANNA PLAY WITH IT = DON'T SPOIL THE BALL BY WRITIN ON IT!
THE BABE
I'VE GOT THE HEEBIE JEEBIES. MY TAILOR IS WILLING TO MAKE ME ANOTHER SUIT
S.C.C. NEW YORK
DEBECK
5-8
Copyright, 1924, by King Features Syndicate, Inc.

Below: Golf humor in "Barney Google", August 6, 1930. Above: Babe Ruth in "Bughouse Fables," May 8, 1924. Both from the Collection of Ron Goulart.

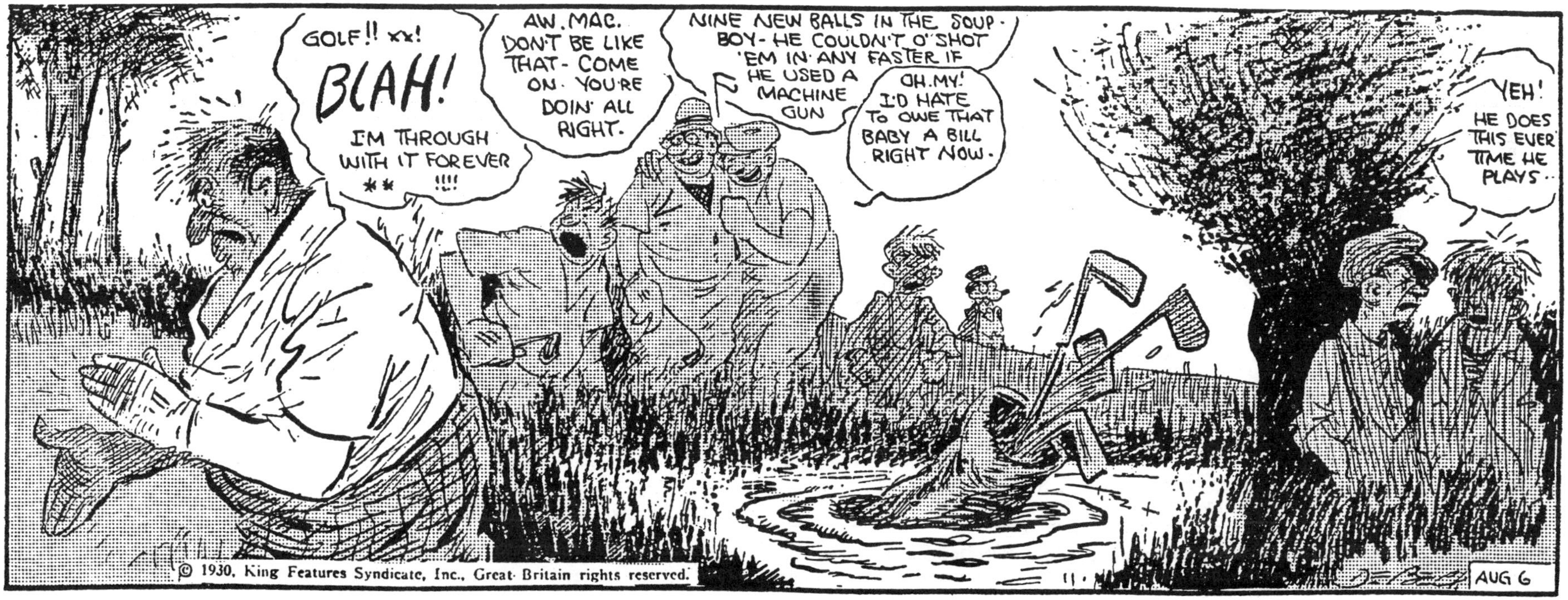
GOLF!! xx! BLAH! I'M THROUGH WITH IT FOREVER ** !!!!
AW, MAC. DON'T BE LIKE THAT - COME ON - YOU'RE DOIN' ALL RIGHT.
NINE NEW BALLS IN THE SOUP - BOY - HE COULDN'T O' SHOT 'EM IN ANY FASTER IF HE USED A MACHINE GUN
OH, MY! I'D HATE TO OWE THAT BABY A BILL RIGHT NOW.
YEH! HE DOES THIS EVER TIME HE PLAYS..
© 1930, King Features Syndicate, Inc., Great Britain rights reserved.
AUG 6

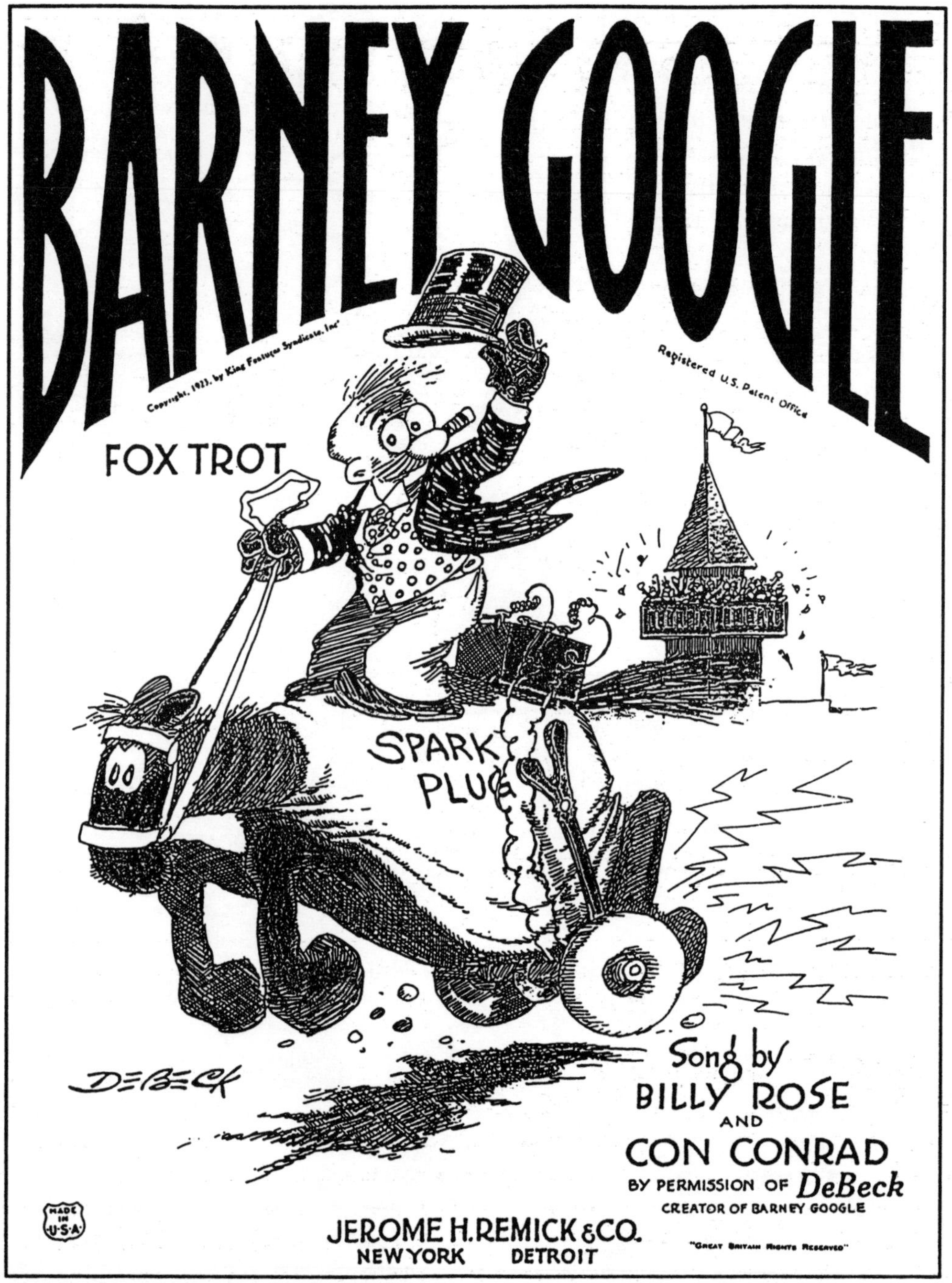
BARNEY GOOGLE
Copyright, 1923, by King Features Syndicate, Inc
Registered U.S. Patent Office
FOX TROT
SPARK PLUG
DEBECK
Song by
BILLY ROSE
AND
CON CONRAD
BY PERMISSION OF DeBeck
CREATOR OF BARNEY GOOGLE
MADE IN U.S.A
JEROME H. REMICK & CO.
NEW YORK DETROIT
"Great Britain Rights Reserved"

Above: Cover artwork for the "Barney Google" sheet music by Billy DeBeck, 1923. Courtesy of the San Francisco Academy of Comic Art. Right: The lyrics to "Barney Google."

Who's the most important man this country ever knew
Who's the man our Presidents tell all their troubles to
No it isn't Mister Bryan and it isn't Mister Hughes
I'm mighty proud that I'm allowed to introduce
Barney Google with his goo-goo googly eyes
Barney Google had a wife three times his size
She sued Barney for divorce
Now he's living with his horse
Barney Google with his goo-goo googly eyes

Who's the greatest lover that this country ever knew
Who's the man that Valentino takes his hat off to
No it isn't Douglas Fairbanks that the ladies rave about
When he arrives who makes the wives chase all their husbands out
Barney Google with his goo-goo googly eyes
Barney Google bet his horse would win the prize
When the horses ran that day
Spark Plug ran the other way
Barney Google with his goo-goo googly eyes

Barney Google with his goo-goo googly eyes
Barney Google bet his horse would win the prize
He got odds of five to eight
Spark Plug came in three days late
Barney Google with his goo-goo googly eyes

Barney Google with his goo-goo googly eyes
Barney Google has a girl that loves the guys
Only friends can get a squeeze
That girl has no enemies
Barney Google with his goo-goo googly eyes

Barney Google with his goo-goo googly eyes
Barney Google is the luckiest of guys
If he fell into the mud
He'd come up with a diamond stud
Barney Google with his goo-goo googly eyes

Barney Google with his goo-goo googly eyes
Barney Google tried to enter paradise
When St. Peter saw his face
He said "Go to the other place"
Barney Google with his goo-goo googly eyes

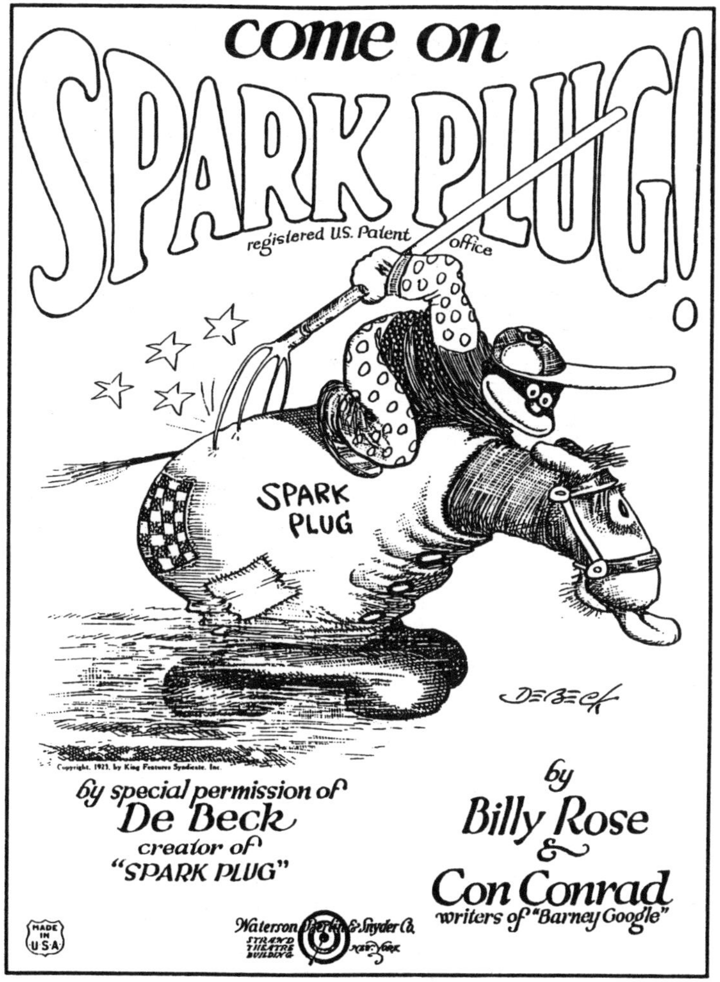
come on
SPARK PLUG!
registered U.S. Patent office
SPARK PLUG
DEBECK
by special permission of
De Beck
creator of
"SPARK PLUG"
by
Billy Rose
&
Con Conrad
writers of "Barney Google"
MADE IN U.S.A.
Waterson & Snyder Co.
New York

Above: Cover artwork for the "Come On Spark Plug" sheet music by DeBeck, 1923. Courtesy of the San Francisco Academy of Comic Art.

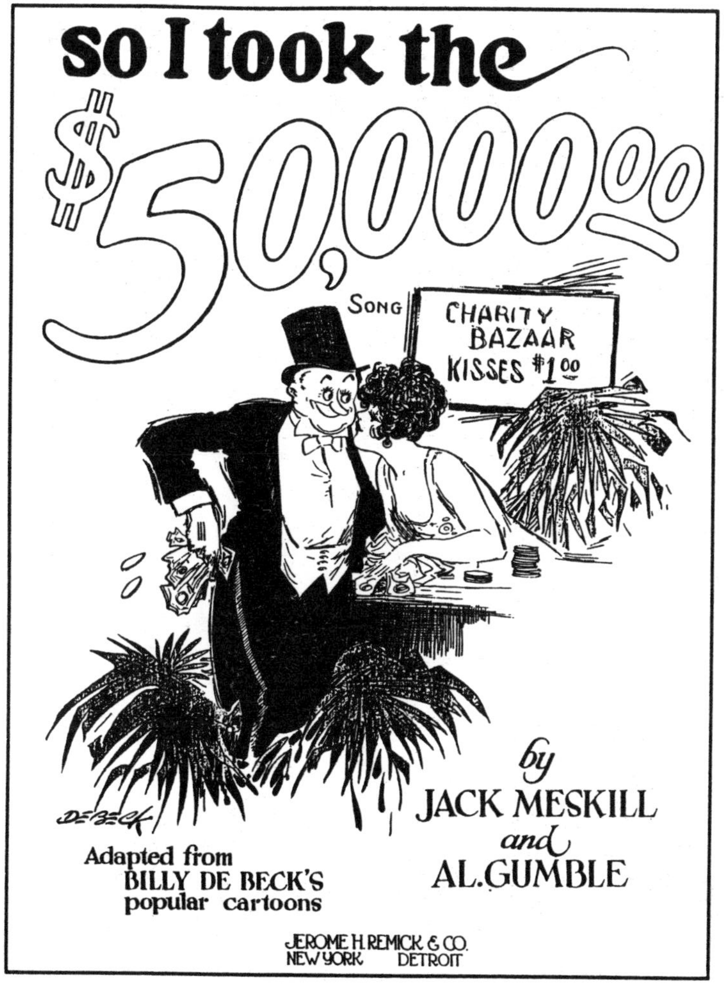
so I took the
$50,000.00
SONG
CHARITY BAZAAR KISSES $1.00
DEBECK
by
JACK MESKILL
and
AL.GUMBLE
Adapted from
BILLY DE BECK'S
popular cartoons
JEROME H. REMICK & CO.
NEW YORK DETROIT

Above: Cover artwork for the "So I Took the $50,000" sheet music by DeBeck, 1923. From the Collection of Richard Marschall.

In 1923, a young songwriter named Billy Rose made an important discovery. After spending three months in the New York Public Library studying the hit songs of the previous thirty years, he determined that they all fit into four categories: 1) love songs, 2) nonsense songs, 3) jingles and 4) songs built around a silly syllable. Rose also concluded from his evidence that the double-o sound - "oo" - was the most successful syllable to build a song around. After reading Billy DeBeck's comic strip in the newspaper, he applied his principles and came up with the unforgettable verse, "Barney Google with the goo-goo googly eyes." "Barney Google" written by Billy Rose and Con Conrad was a smash hit in 1923 and earned Rose $60,000.

Rose and Conrad also wrote a follow-up song, "Come On Spark Plug," in 1923, but it was a flop. In the next eight years, Billy Rose wrote more than 300 songs using the same simple formulas that he discovered in his initial research. Forty were hits including, "Without A Song" (his favorite), "It's Only a Paper Moon," "That Old Gang of Mine" and "I Found a Million Dollar Baby in a Five and Ten Cent Store." Billy DeBeck also tried to strike Tin Pan Alley gold again with other songwriters but never was able to repeat the success of the original "Barney Google" foxtrot.

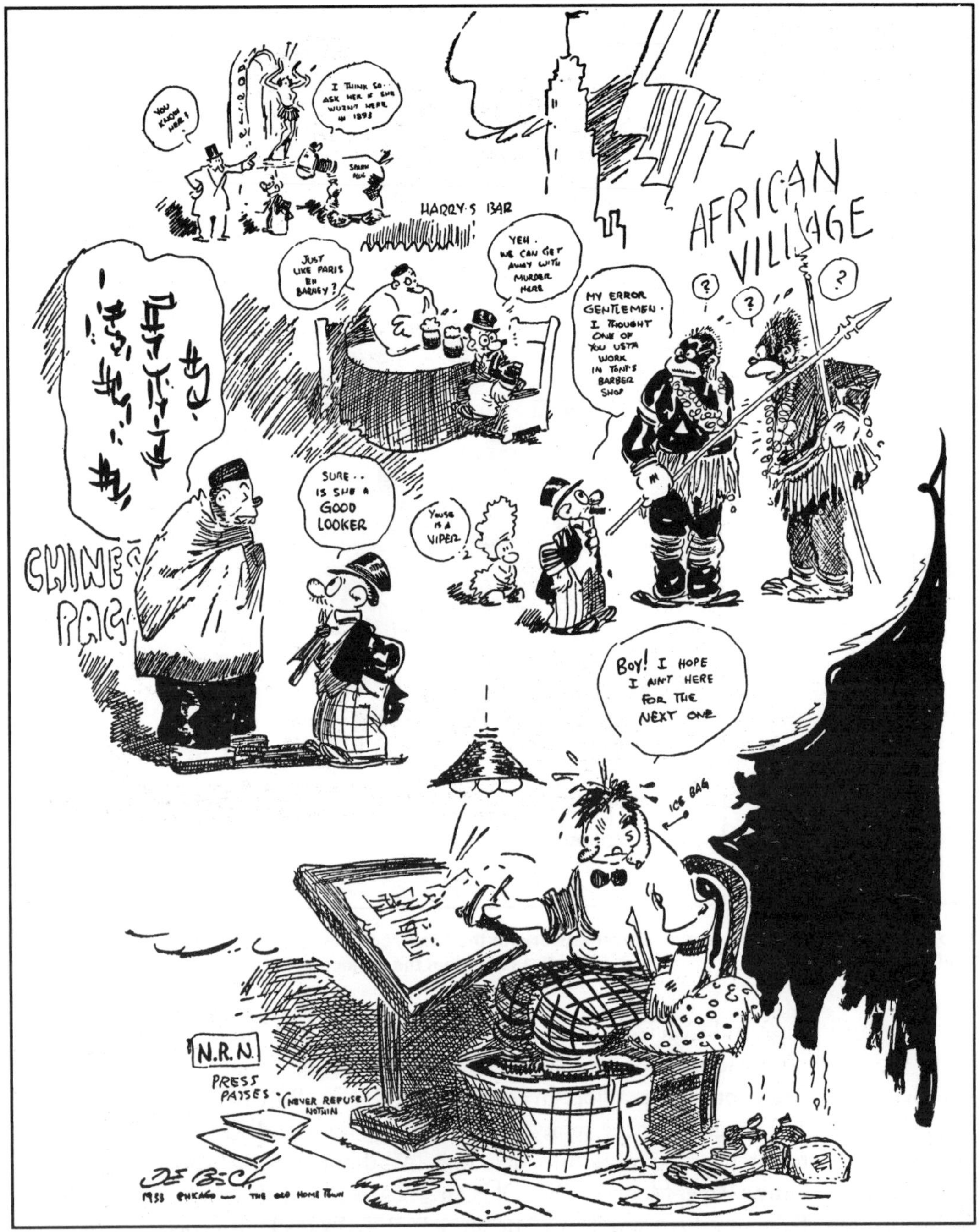
I THINK SO. ASK HER IF SHE WUZN'T HERE IN 1893
HARRY'S BAR
JUST LIKE PARIS EH BARNEY?
YEH. WE CAN GET AWAY WITH MURDER HERE
MY ERROR GENTLEMEN. I THOUGHT ONE OF YOU USTA WORK IN TONY'S BARBER SHOP
AFRICAN VILLAGE
SURE.. IS SHE A GOOD LOOKER
YOUSE IS A VIPER
BOY! I HOPE I AIN'T HERE FOR THE NEXT ONE
ICE BAG
N.R.N.
PRESS PASSES
(NEVER REFUSE NOTHIN)
DE BECK
1933 CHICAGO — THE OLD HOME TOWN

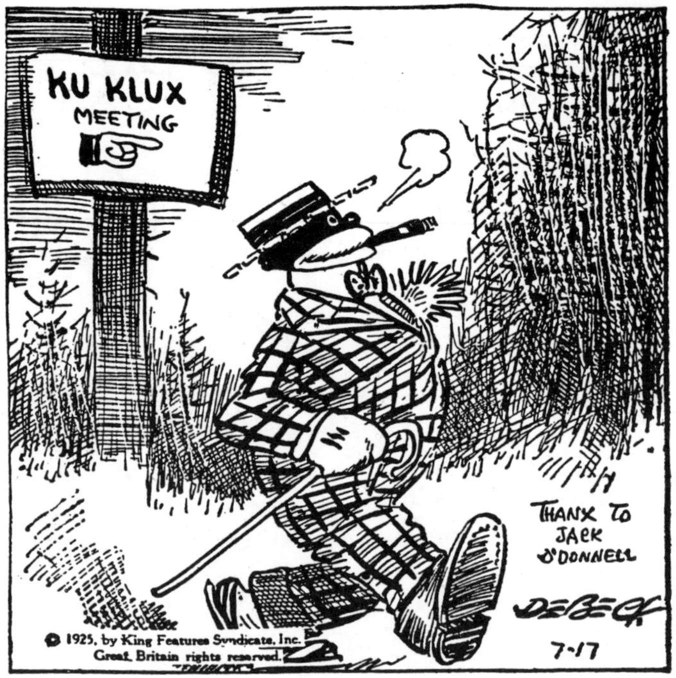
KU KLUX MEETING
THANX TO JACK O'DONNELL
DE BECK
7-17
© 1925, by King Features Syndicate, Inc.
Great Britain rights reserved.

Above: Barney visits the Chicago World's Fair, 1933. Courtesy of the San Francisco Academy of Comic Art.
Upper right: Racial caricature in "Bughouse Fables," July 17, 1925. Collection of Ron Goulart.

Offensive racial and ethnic stereotypes have appeared in American newspaper comics since the slum scenes of "Hogan's Alley" back in 1895. The early strips contained black characters who were almost invariably drawn with round "8-ball" heads, bug-eyes and a large white area around their mouths to suggest oversized lips. Black dialect was used to accentuate their ignorant or foolish behavior.

"How to Draw Funny Pictures" by E. C. Matthews, a cartoon instruction course from 1928, offered the following advice on how to draw African Americans: "The coloured people are good subjects for action pictures; they are natural born humorists and will often assume ridiculous attitudes or say side-splitting things with no apparent intention of being funny. The cartoonist usually plays on the coloured man's love of loud clothes, watermelon, chicken, crap-shooting, fear of ghosts, etc."

Blacks in the comics during the first part of the century were almost always cast in subservient roles like maids, manservants or stableboys. Mushmouth in "Moon

Mullins," Asbestos in "Joe and Asbestos" and Smokey in "Joe Palooka" were typical black characters of the period. The "step n' fetch it" stereotype carried over from the minstrel shows and vaudeville theaters and was popular because it gave white audiences a feeling of superiority.

Billy DeBeck also depicted black characters as domestic servants, train porters and farm workers in these same established traditions of racial stereotyping. On August 2, 1922, in the first Spark Plug sequence, an anonymous black horse trainer appeared as a bit player. Within a year, Sparky's jockey had earned a name, "Sunshine," and a regular place in the cast. He was often heard to exclaim, "Yo sho am a smaht man, mistah Google," expressing loyal subservience to his boss.

Sunshine, along with Spark Plug and Rudy the Ostrich, became part of Barney Google's traveling family in the mid-1920's. Although, he disappeared and reappeared frequently, Sunshine stayed on as Barney's loyal side-kick until the early 1930's. By the time Barney met up with Snuffy Smith in 1934, however, Sunshine had outlived his usefulness and was rarely seen again.

By the 1940's, newspaper syndication had forced many cartoonists to abandon racial and ethnic caricatures, historically an urban tradition. Small town audiences preferred a more homogeneous brand of humor. Although offensive racial stereotyping still exists today, it is no longer regarded as an acceptable form of comedy.

Right: Sunshine is the shorter porter. Below: Sunshine in "Barney Google," February 6, 1926. Both from the Collection of Ron Goulart.

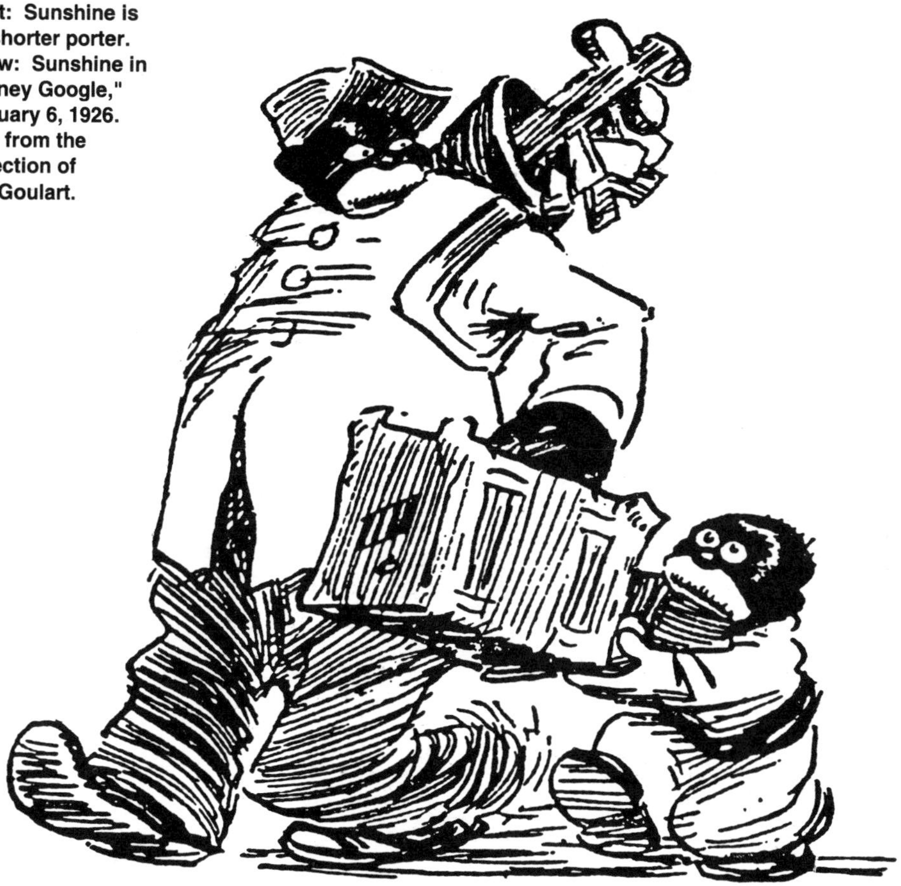

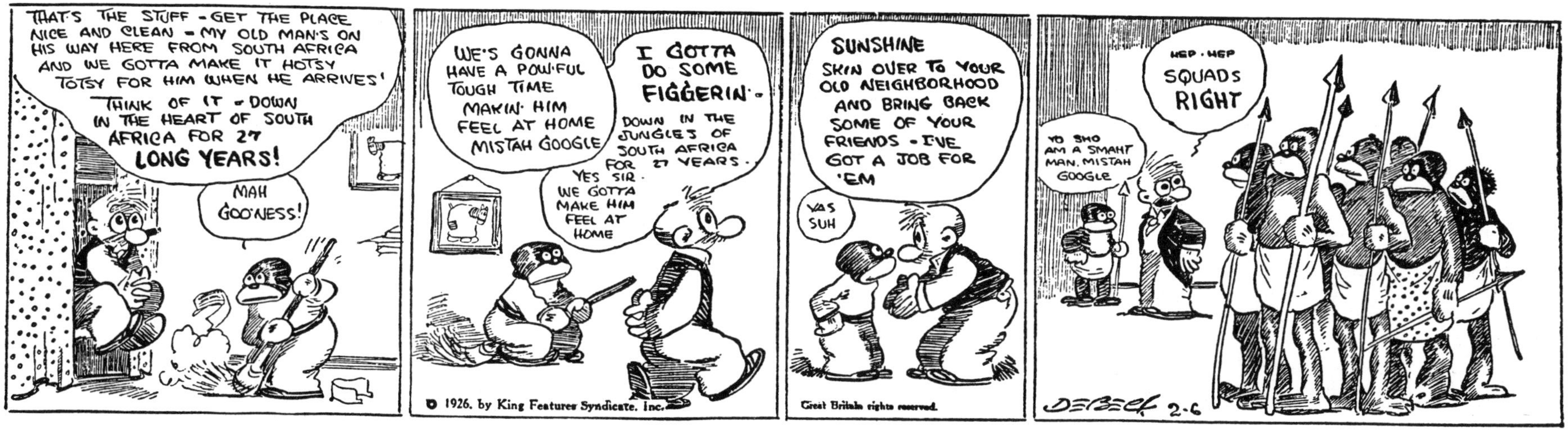
THAT'S THE STUFF - GET THE PLACE NICE AND CLEAN - MY OLD MAN'S ON HIS WAY HERE FROM SOUTH AFRICA AND WE GOTTA MAKE IT HOTSY TOTSY FOR HIM WHEN HE ARRIVES!
THINK OF IT - DOWN IN THE HEART OF SOUTH AFRICA FOR 27 LONG YEARS!
MAH GOO'NESS!
WE'S GONNA HAVE A POW'FUL TOUGH TIME MAKIN' HIM FEEL AT HOME MISTAH GOOGLE
I GOTTA DO SOME FIGGERIN' - DOWN IN THE JUNGLES OF SOUTH AFRICA FOR 27 YEARS.
YES SIR. WE GOTTA MAKE HIM FEEL AT HOME
SUNSHINE SKIN OVER TO YOUR OLD NEIGHBORHOOD AND BRING BACK SOME OF YOUR FRIENDS - I'VE GOT A JOB FOR 'EM
YAS SUH
HEP - HEP SQUADS RIGHT
YO SHO AM A SMAHT MAN, MISTAH GOOGLE
© 1926, by King Features Syndicate, Inc.
Great Britain rights reserved.
DEBECK 2-6

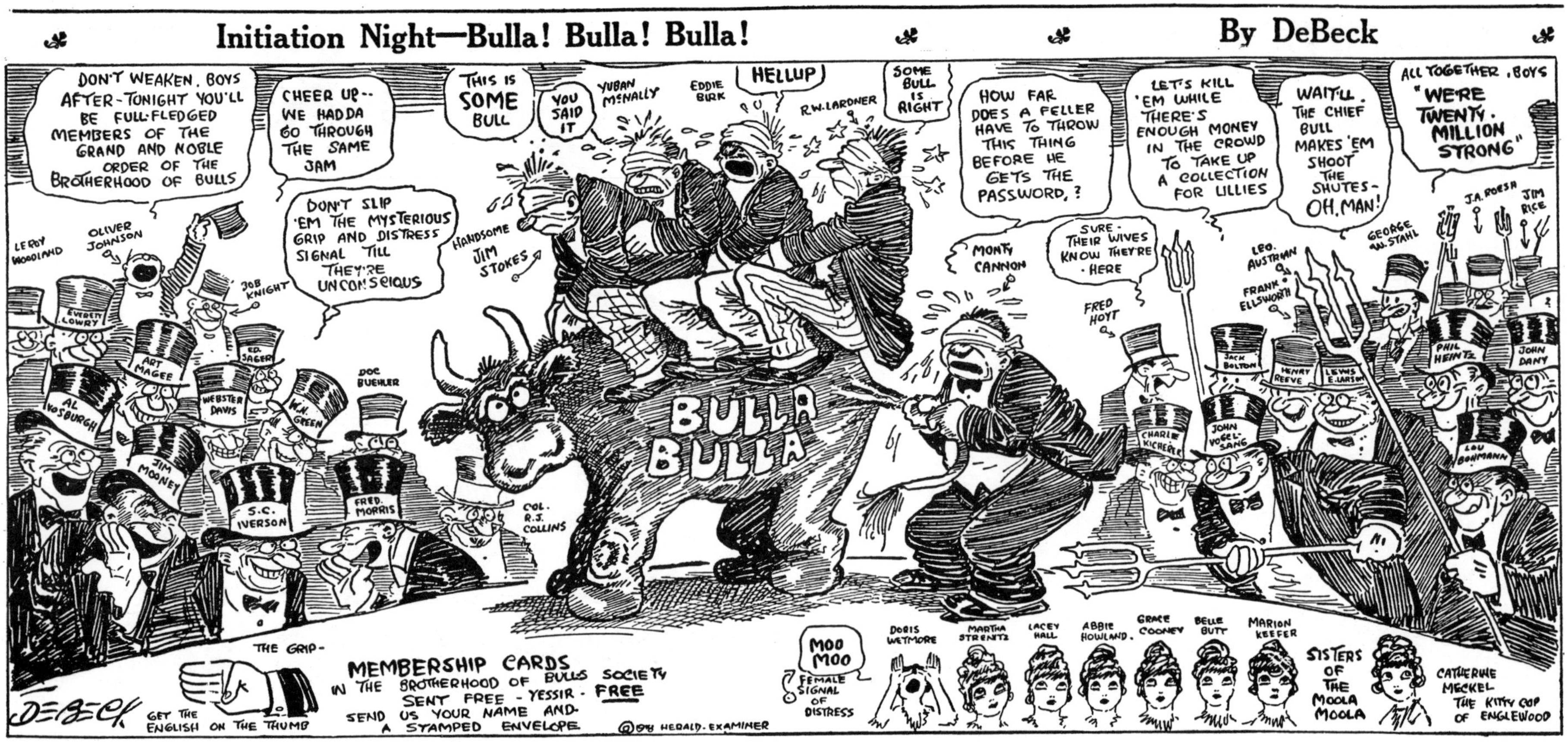
Initiation Night—Bulla! Bulla! Bulla!
By DeBeck
DON'T WEAKEN, BOYS AFTER-TONIGHT YOU'LL BE FULL-FLEDGED MEMBERS OF THE GRAND AND NOBLE ORDER OF THE BROTHERHOOD OF BULLS
CHEER UP-- WE HADDA GO THROUGH THE SAME JAM
THIS IS SOME BULL
YOU SAID IT
YUBAN McNALLY
EDDIE BIRK
HELLUP
R.W. LARDNER
SOME BULL IS RIGHT
HOW FAR DOES A FELLER HAVE TO THROW THIS THING BEFORE HE GETS THE PASSWORD, ?
LET'S KILL 'EM WHILE THERE'S ENOUGH MONEY IN THE CROWD TO TAKE UP A COLLECTION FOR LILLIES
WAIT'LL THE CHIEF BULL MAKES 'EM SHOOT THE SHUTES - OH, MAN!
ALL TOGETHER, BOYS "WE'RE TWENTY MILLION STRONG"
DON'T SLIP 'EM THE MYSTERIOUS GRIP AND DISTRESS SIGNAL TILL THEY'RE UNCONSCIOUS
HANDSOME JIM STOKES
MONTY CANNON
SURE - THEIR WIVES KNOW THEY'RE HERE
FRED HOYT
LEROY WOODLAND
OLIVER JOHNSON
JOB KNIGHT
EVERETT LOWRY
ART MAGEE
ED. SAGER
WEBSTER DAVIS
W.H. GREEN
DOC BUEHLER
AL KOSBURGH
JIM MOONEY
S.C. IVERSON
FRED. MORRIS
COL. R.J. COLLINS
BULLA BULLA
LEO. AUSTRIAN
FRANK ELLSWORTH
GEORGE W. STAHL
J.A. ROESH
JIM RICE
JACK BOLTON
HENRY REEVE
LEWIS E. LARSON
PHIL HEINTZ
JOHN DANY
CHARLIE KICHERER
JOHN VOGEL-SANG
LOU BOHMANN
THE GRIP -
MEMBERSHIP CARDS IN THE BROTHERHOOD OF BULLS SOCIETY SENT FREE - YESSIR - FREE SEND US YOUR NAME AND A STAMPED ENVELOPE
GET THE ENGLISH ON THE THUMB
DEBECK
© 1918 HERALD-EXAMINER
MOO MOO
FEMALE SIGNAL OF DISTRESS
DORIS WETMORE
MARTHA STRENITZ
LACEY HALL
ABBIE HOWLAND
GRACE COONEY
BELLE BUTT
MARION KEEFER
SISTERS OF THE MOOLA MOOLA
CATHERINE MECKEL THE KITTY COP OF ENGLEWOOD

Above: "Brotherhood of Bulls" cartoon from the *Chicago Herald and Examiner*, October 26, 1918. Courtesy of the San Francisco Academy of Comic Art.

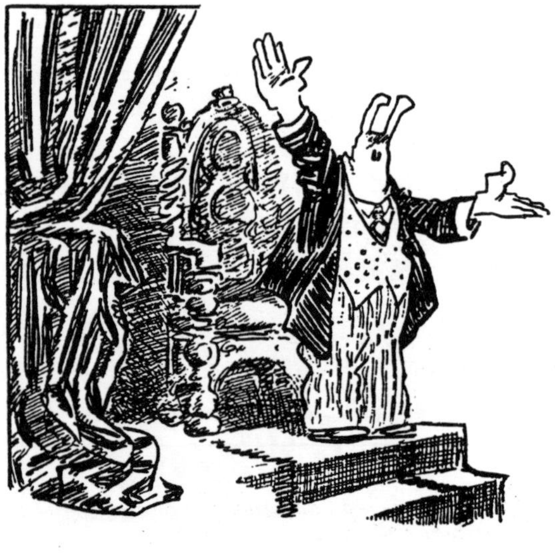

Fraternal orders have been a part of male social life in America since colonial times. In the early years of this century, organizations like the Elks, the Moose, the Red Men, the Knights of Pythias, the Odd Fellows and the Druids met in saloons and clubhouses in cities and towns across the country. Billy DeBeck first began satirizing the signs and rituals of these secret societies in 1918 when he was the sports cartoonist for the *Chicago Herald and Examiner*. "The Brotherhood of Bulls," the first fictitious fraternity DeBeck created, became a local sensation with their "Bulla Bulla" cheer. One Chicago stockyard alone reportedly signed up 15,000 members, and Billy became known as "Chicago's Prince of Wales." He was fixed up with a luxury hotel suite, bands struck up the "Bulla Bulla" song in his honor and gifts were showered on him. Needless to say, all this attention went right to the 28-year-old cartoonist's head.

Almost a decade later, in October, 1927, DeBeck introduced another make-believe organization, "The Mysterious and Secret Order of the Brotherhood of Billy Goats," in his "Barney Google" strip. This time it became a national sensation. An article in the *Tampa Times* on November 28, 1927 , claimed over 100,000 members had already joined and predicted that at least a million "Billy Goats" would sign up by Christmas.

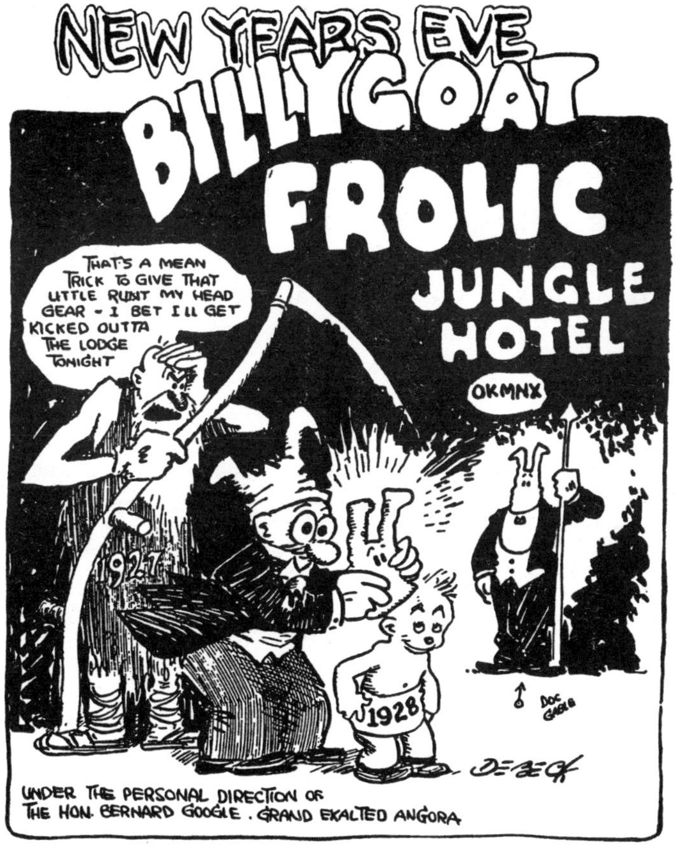
NEW YEARS EVE
BILLYGOAT
FROLIC
JUNGLE HOTEL
THAT'S A MEAN TRICK TO GIVE THAT LITTLE RUNT MY HEAD GEAR - I BET I'LL GET KICKED OUTTA THE LODGE TONIGHT
OKMNX
1927
1928
DEBECK
UNDER THE PERSONAL DIRECTION OF THE HON. BERNARD GOOGLE . GRAND EXALTED ANGORA

Always the promoter, DeBeck milked this story for all it was worth. He designed a membership card, a secret handshake, a password and a mask. He encouraged his readers to organize chapters all over the country as Barney shouted, "We're Twenty Million Strong!" The Brotherhood of Billy Goats was featured in the strip for over nine months, finally fading out in August, 1928. Billy collaborated on a theme song "OKMNX" which was published in 1928 and held a New Year's Eve Billy Goat Frolic in New York.

In all this publicity, there was never any mention of DeBeck actually belonging to any real fraternal organizations, though he was a member of Dutch Treat Club and the Artists and Writers group. Judging by the mail he received, millions of readers got a kick out of the Bulls and the Billy Goats and that must have been a good enough reason for him to persist.

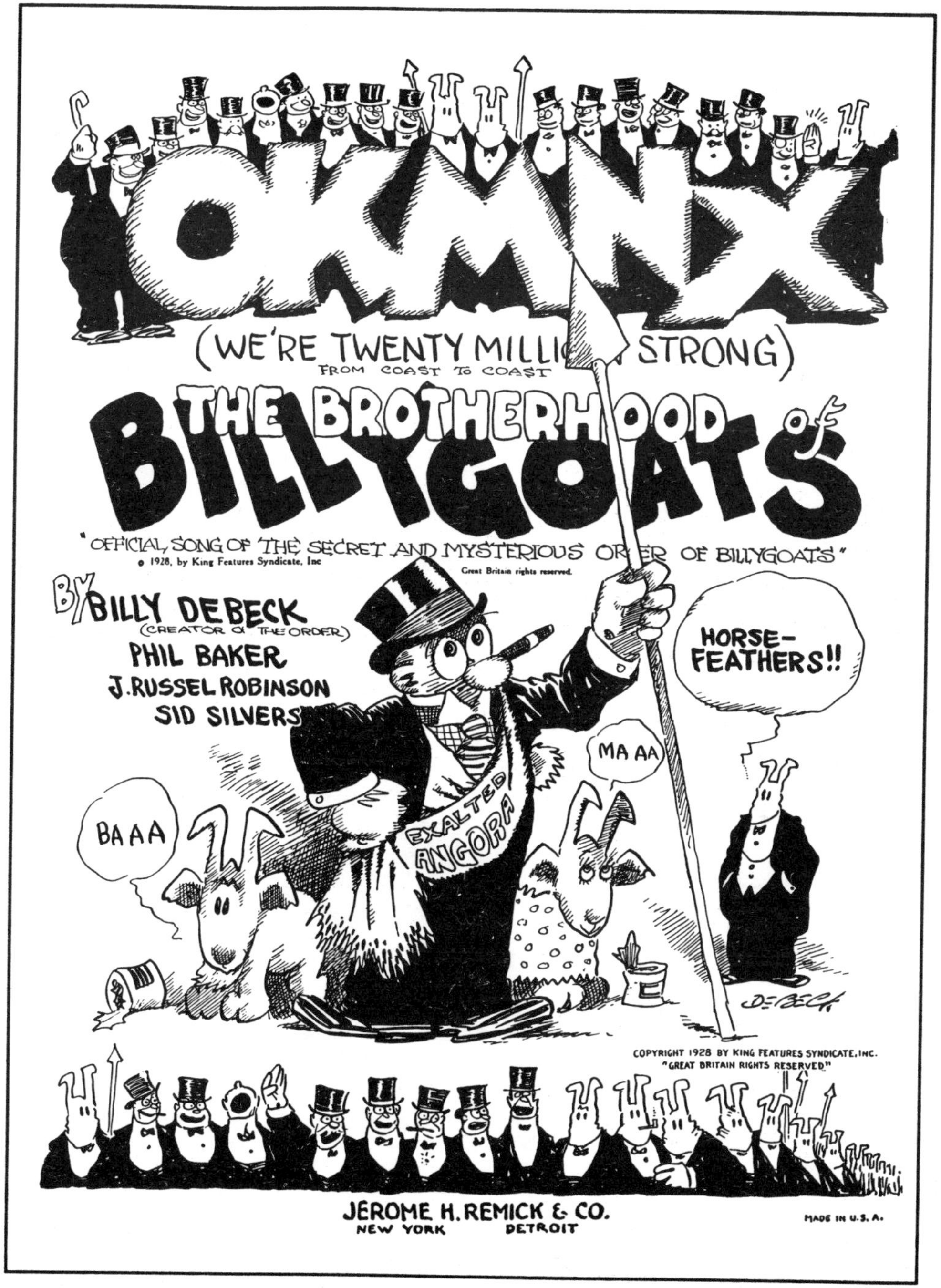
OKMNX
(WE'RE TWENTY MILLI
STRONG)
FROM COAST TO COAST
THE BROTHERHOOD of
BILLYGOATS
"OFFICIAL SONG OF THE SECRET AND MYSTERIOUS OR ER OF BILLYGOATS"
© 1928, by King Features Syndicate, Inc
Great Britain rights reserved.
BY BILLY DEBECK
(CREATOR OF THE ORDER)
PHIL BAKER
J. RUSSEL ROBINSON
SID SILVERS
HORSE-FEATHERS!!
MA AA
BAAA
EXALTED ANGORA
DEBECK
COPYRIGHT 1928 BY KING FEATURES SYNDICATE, INC.
"GREAT BRITAIN RIGHTS RESERVED."
JEROME H. REMICK & CO.
NEW YORK DETROIT
MADE IN U.S.A.

Upper left: Invitation to DeBeck's Billy Goat Frolic, 1927. Above: Cover artwork by Billy DeBeck for the "OKMNX" sheet music, 1928. Both from the Collection of Sy & Sandy Schechter.

The colorful language that Billy DeBeck popularized in his cartoons is another rich legacy he left to American culture. He took the slang of the street, the nightclubs, and the racetracks of his time and spiced his dialogue with it. He invented words that are now common jargon, and he tossed out "bon mots" that are long forgotten.

Among his most famous phrases are: "goo-goo-eyes" (an amorous look), "horsefeathers" (an expression of incredulity), "heebie jeebies" (a nervous feeling), "hotsy totsy" (pretentiousness) and "yardbird" (a rookie soldier in World War II, it now refers to a prison convict).

Hillbilly terms from the Snuffy Smith era which are universally recognized today include: "time's a-wastin," "jughaid," "shifless skonk" and "balls o' fire."

Some of his more outdated sayings include: "Osky Wow Wow" (an exclamation), "Sweet mama" (a pretty girl), "Bughouse Fables" (preposterous fiction) and "I hope you don't feel hurt" (feigned concern).

He also used running gags in his cartoons like: "So I took the $50,000..." (as in "So I took the $50,000 and bought Henry Ford a horse"), "I've got the heebie jeebies..." (as in "I've got the heebie jeebies, my leading man eats garlic.") and "The Guy with the green gloves" (as in "Loan me twenty, Ed." Ed: "Get it from the guy with the green gloves.").

On at least one occasion DeBeck took a popular joke and used it verbatim in his strip. The "OKMNX" Sunday page on the next page is from October 9, 1927. Billy had an ear for this kind of humor.

Below: "Bughouse Fables," July 18, 1924. Collection of Ron Goulart.

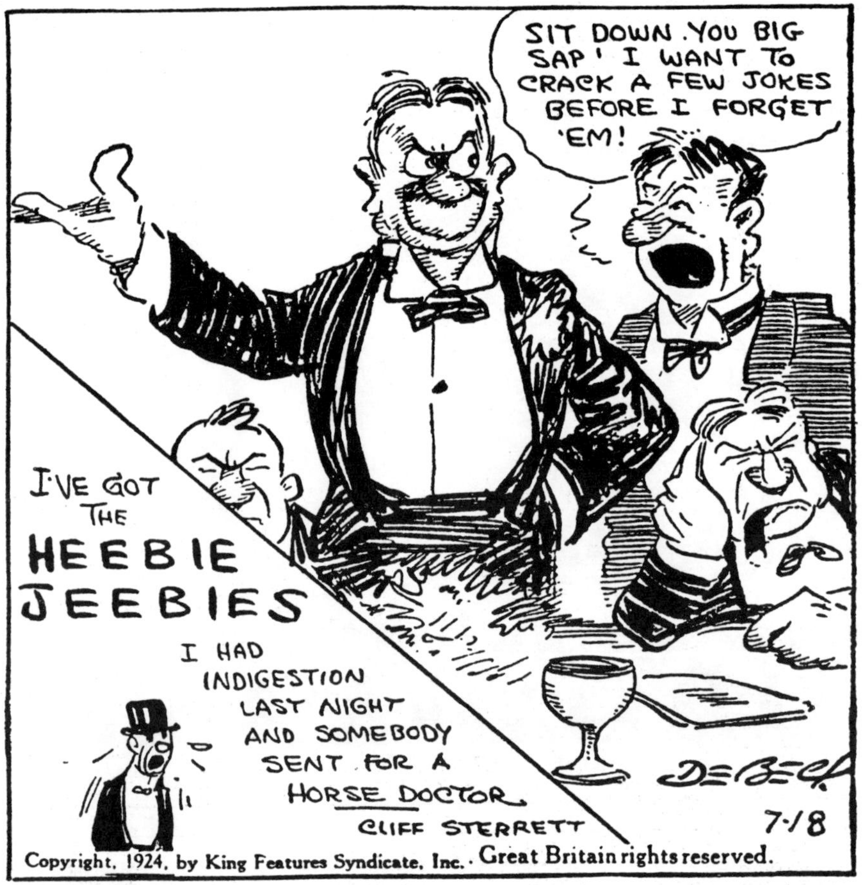
SIT DOWN. YOU BIG SAP! I WANT TO CRACK A FEW JOKES BEFORE I FORGET 'EM!
I'VE GOT THE HEEBIE JEEBIES
I HAD INDIGESTION LAST NIGHT AND SOMEBODY SENT FOR A HORSE DOCTOR
CLIFF STERRETT
DEBECK
7-18
Copyright, 1924, by King Features Syndicate, Inc. Great Britain rights reserved.

Below: "Bughouse Fables," February 25, 1926. Collection of Ron Goulart.

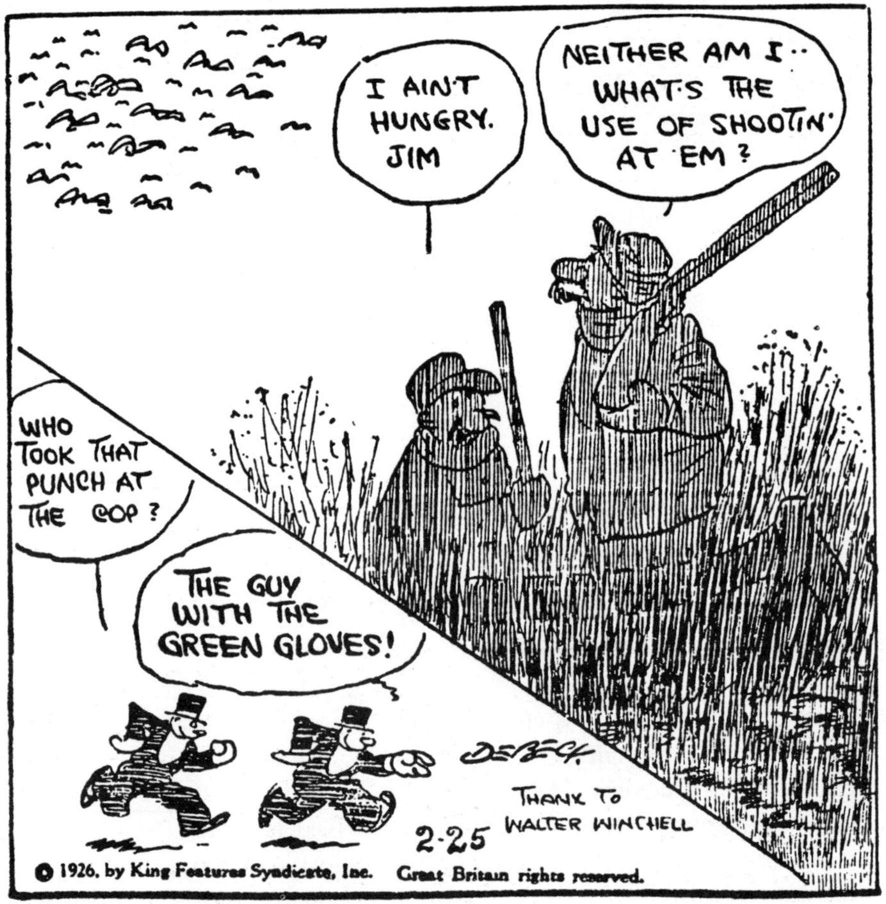
I AIN'T HUNGRY. JIM
NEITHER AM I.. WHAT'S THE USE OF SHOOTIN' AT 'EM?
WHO TOOK THAT PUNCH AT THE COP?
THE GUY WITH THE GREEN GLOVES!
DEBECK
THANK TO WALTER WINCHELL
2-25
© 1926, by King Features Syndicate, Inc. Great Britain rights reserved.

Left: This "Barney Google" Sunday page reveals the joke behind the Brotherhood of Billy Goats' secret password, "OKMNX." October 9, 1927. Courtesy of the San Francisco Academy of Comic Art.

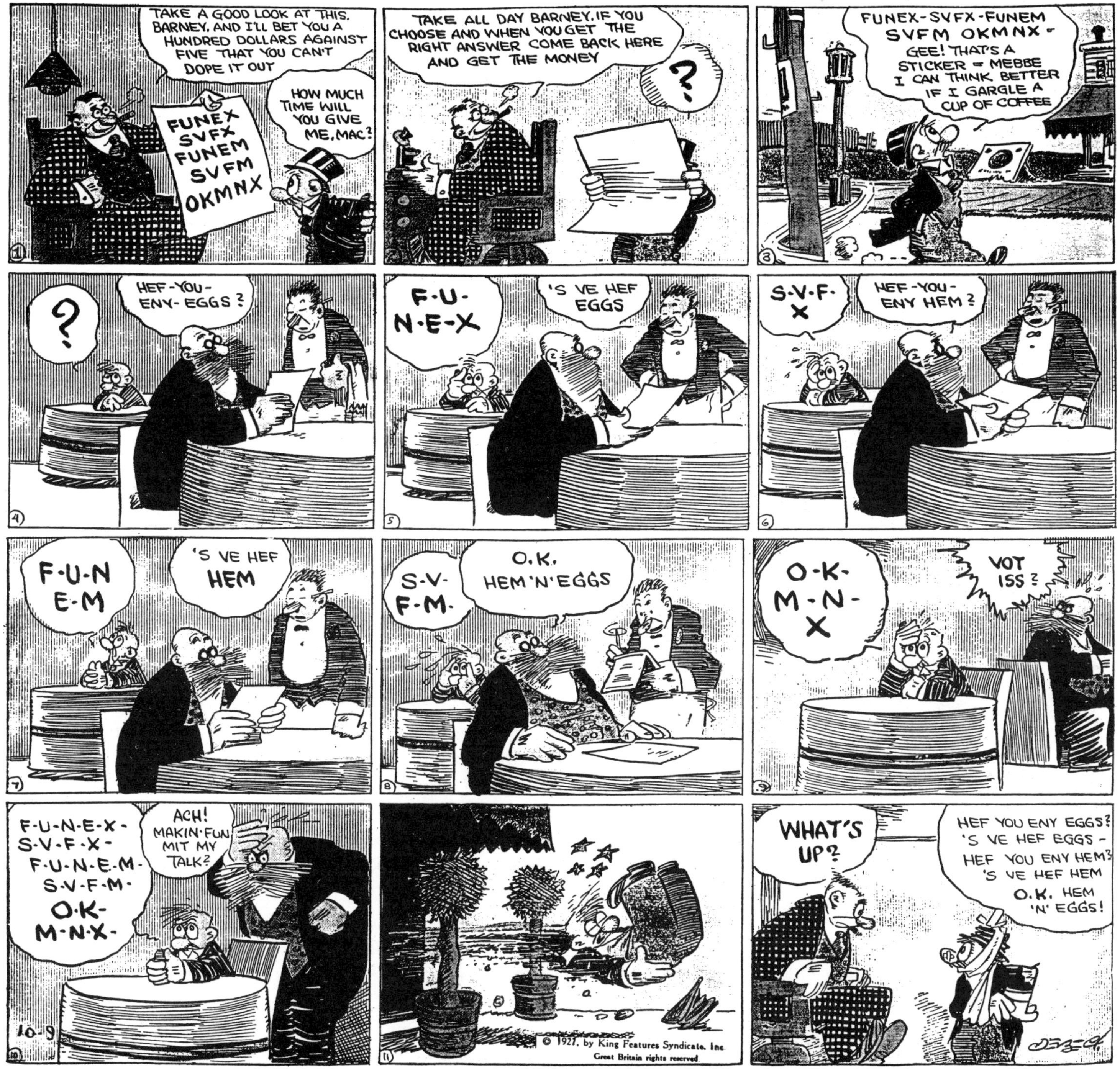
TAKE A GOOD LOOK AT THIS, BARNEY, AND I'LL BET YOU A HUNDRED DOLLARS AGAINST FIVE THAT YOU CAN'T DOPE IT OUT
FUNEX SVFX FUNEM SVFM OKMNX
HOW MUCH TIME WILL YOU GIVE ME, MAC?
TAKE ALL DAY BARNEY. IF YOU CHOOSE AND WHEN YOU GET THE RIGHT ANSWER COME BACK HERE AND GET THE MONEY
?
FUNEX-SVFX-FUNEM SVFM OKMNX - GEE! THAT'S A STICKER - MEBBE I CAN THINK BETTER IF I GARGLE A CUP OF COFFEE
?
HEF-YOU-ENY-EGGS?
F-U-N-E-X
'S VE HEF EGGS
S-V-F-X
HEF-YOU-ENY HEM?
F-U-N E-M
'S VE HEF HEM
S-V-F-M-
O.K. HEM 'N' EGGS
O-K-M-N-X
VOT ISS?
F-U-N-E-X-S-V-F-X-F-U-N-E-M-S-V-F-M-O-K-M-N-X-
ACH! MAKIN' FUN MIT MY TALK?
10-9
© 1927, by King Features Syndicate, Inc.
Great Britain rights reserved
WHAT'S UP?
HEF YOU ENY EGGS? 'S VE HEF EGGS - HEF YOU ENY HEM? 'S VE HEF HEM O.K. HEM 'N' EGGS!

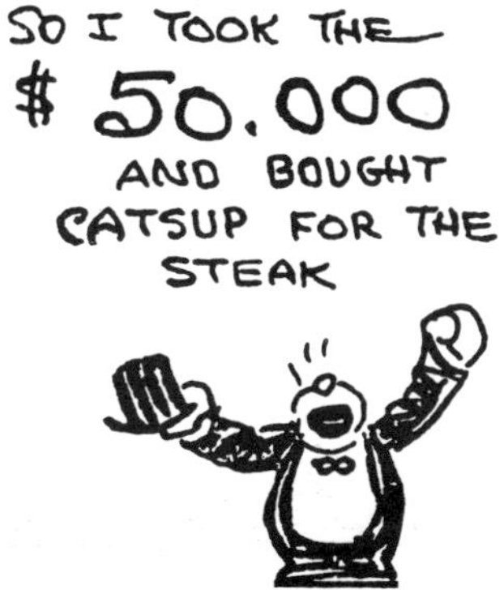
SO I TOOK THE $ 50.000 AND BOUGHT CATSUP FOR THE STEAK

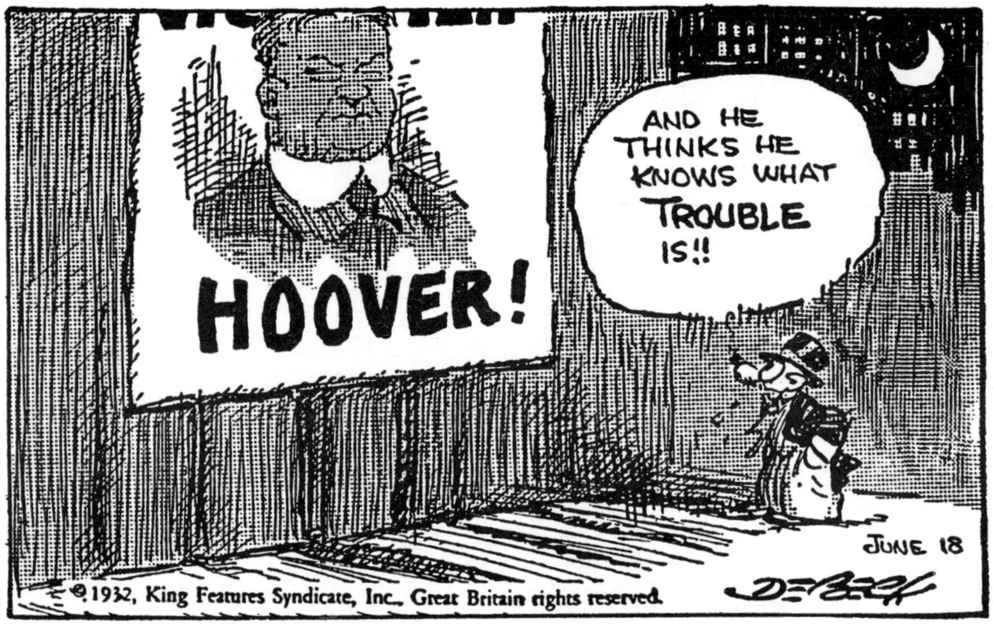
HOOVER!
AND HE THINKS HE KNOWS WHAT TROUBLE IS!!
JUNE 18
©1932, King Features Syndicate, Inc. Great Britain rights reserved.

Above: Political comment in "Barney Google," June 18, 1932. Collection of Ron Goulart.

Next page: Barney runs for President, April 17, 1932. Courtesy of Howard Lowery Gallery.

Below: Barney Google steers the Ship of State, June 12, 1932.
Courtesy of the San Francisco Academy of Comic Art.

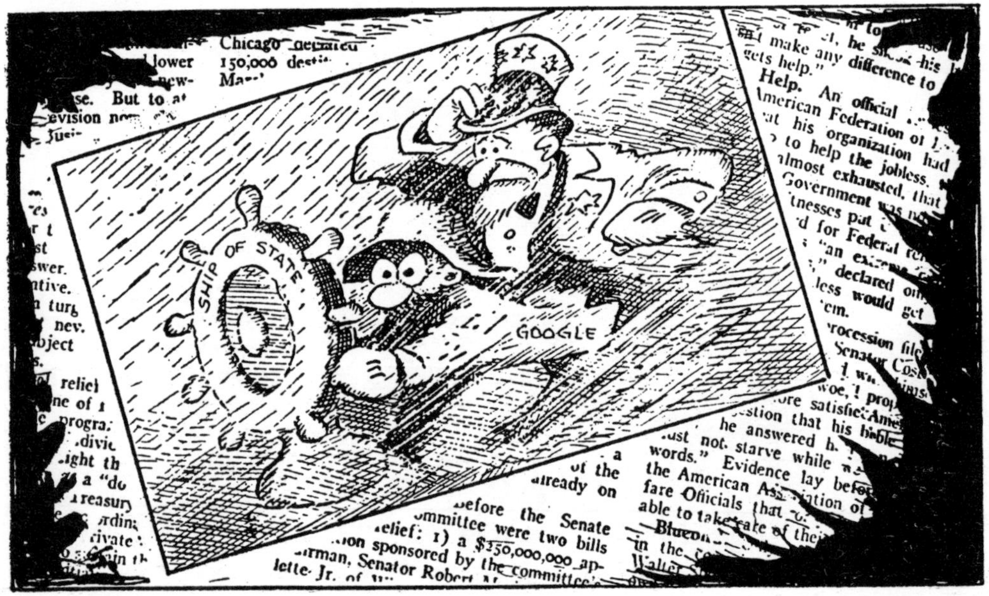
SHIP OF STATE
GOOGLE

Billy DeBeck always claimed he had no interest in world affairs and politics, but on two occasions he featured political satire in "Barney Google" for extended periods of time. In 1928, in the daily continuity, and again in 1932, as a sequence of Sunday pages, Barney ran for President of the United States.

At the close of the annual convention of the "Order of the Brotherhood of Billy Goats" on February 9, 1928, an astounding announcement was made. With a membership of "twenty million strong," the Billy Goats had formed an independent party and nominated Barney Google for President. After some persuasion Barney agreed to run, and the Billy Goats decided to nominate a sister Nanny Goat for Vice President. Barney and his running mate, Fannie Bell Finch, set off on a cross-country goodwill tour, but when Barney tired of her constant nagging, he hopped off the train. He then accepted a $100,000 campaign contribution from a bearded gentleman, who turned out to be the notorious Boss Spider, head of the world's largest smuggling ring. Spider forced Barney to accept him as his Vice President, but Barney secretly helped four Federal agents capture the crook. On April 24, 1928, Barney announced, "I'd rather be Grand Exalted Angora than President. We Billy Goats can better serve our country if we leave politics to the Democrats and Republicans."

Beginning with the Sunday page episode of March 20, 1932, Barney again was pushed into Presidential politics. In his acceptance speech as the candidate of the "Square Deal Party," Barney said, "I ain't no politician but if I'm elected President - buhlieve me - I'll get every guy in this country a swell job. Another thing, I'm for the Full Dinner Pail, free baseball an' no taxes and I'm willin' to take less'n $75,000 a year..I'm for Googlonian Simplicity." During his ill-fated campaign, Barney visited Colorado to view a huge likeness of himself carved out of stone but was crushed in a landslide when the nose fell off. He was electrocuted during an historic radio address. He got a case of the hiccups before an important speech. His run at the Oval Office finally hit the skids when Fanny Annie Boggs was selected as his Vice Presidential running mate. On August 7, 1932, he attempted to back out of the campaign by pretending to go crazy and ended up behind bars in a padded cell.

Barney should have followed the example of his creator. Billy DeBeck always steered clear of politics.

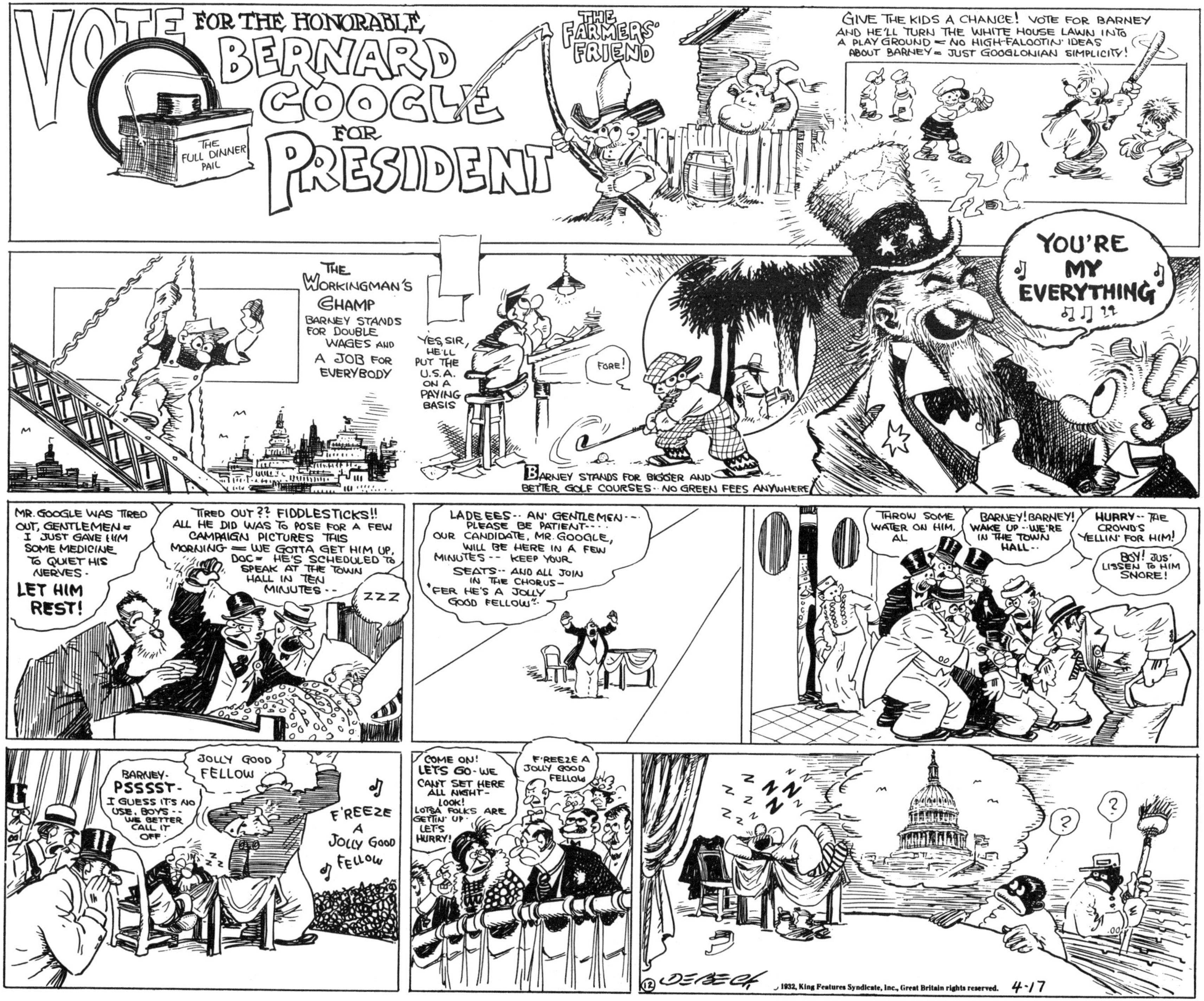
VOTE FOR THE HONORABLE BERNARD GOOGLE FOR PRESIDENT
THE FULL DINNER PAIL
THE FARMERS' FRIEND
GIVE THE KIDS A CHANCE! VOTE FOR BARNEY AND HE'LL TURN THE WHITE HOUSE LAWN INTO A PLAY GROUND = NO HIGH-FALOOTIN' IDEAS ABOUT BARNEY = JUST GOOGLONIAN SIMPLICITY!
THE WORKINGMAN'S CHAMP
BARNEY STANDS FOR DOUBLE WAGES AND A JOB FOR EVERYBODY
YES, SIR, HE'LL PUT THE U.S.A. ON A PAYING BASIS
FORE!
BARNEY STANDS FOR BIGGER AND BETTER GOLF COURSES -- NO GREEN FEES ANYWHERE
YOU'RE MY EVERYTHING
MR. GOOGLE WAS TIRED OUT, GENTLEMEN = I JUST GAVE HIM SOME MEDICINE TO QUIET HIS NERVES - LET HIM REST!
TIRED OUT?? FIDDLESTICKS!! ALL HE DID WAS TO POSE FOR A FEW CAMPAIGN PICTURES THIS MORNING = WE GOTTA GET HIM UP, DOC = HE'S SCHEDULED TO SPEAK AT THE TOWN HALL IN TEN MINUTES --
ZZZ
LADEEES -- AN' GENTLEMEN -- PLEASE BE PATIENT ---- OUR CANDIDATE, MR. GOOGLE, WILL BE HERE IN A FEW MINUTES -- KEEP YOUR SEATS -- AND ALL JOIN IN THE CHORUS - 'FER HE'S A JOLLY GOOD FELLOW'.
THROW SOME WATER ON HIM, AL
BARNEY! BARNEY! WAKE UP -- WE'RE IN THE TOWN HALL --
HURRY -- THE CROWD'S YELLIN' FOR HIM!
BOY! JUS' LISSEN TO HIM SNORE!
BARNEY - PSSSST - I GUESS IT'S NO USE, BOYS -- WE BETTER CALL IT OFF
JOLLY GOOD FELLOW
F'REEZE A JOLLY GOOD FELLOW
COME ON! LET'S GO - WE CAN'T SET HERE ALL NIGHT - LOOK! LOTSA FOLKS ARE GETTIN' UP - LET'S HURRY!
F'REEZE A JOLLY GOOD FELLOW
?
?
DE BECK
12
1932, King Features Syndicate, Inc., Great Britain rights reserved.
4-17

Above: Photo of Billy and Mary Louise DeBeck and their dog, Sparky, upon their return from Europe, December 9, 1929. Courtesy of Ed Black.

Accounts of Billy DeBeck's comings and goings during the mid-1920's give the impression that he was as restless and footloose as his main character. On July 17, 1923, he visited San Francisco. Ten days later on July 27, he greeted President Warren Harding in Seattle. He was in St. Petersburg, Florida, on November 28, 1927, and three months later he was back in Florida riding in a parade in Tampa. Shortly after that trip, he sailed for Paris from New York City with his new bride, Mary Lousie.

Billy was, in fact, one of the first cartoonists to break out of the King Features "bullpen" during the 1920's. Most King artists, including George Herriman and Cliff Sterrett, would report to the syndicate offices in Columbus Circle to work in little cubbyholes producing their daily comic strips. Billy's travels gave him the opporunity to get away from this routine and, when he moved to Paris in 1927, abandon the "bullpen" altogether. Many of the other King cartoonists followed his example.

In the spring of 1929, DeBeck wrote postcards to his friend Ving Fuller from London, Paris and Rome. On December 9, 1929, upon returning from his European holiday of nearly two years, he was greeted at the pier in New York City by Rube Goldberg, Walter Winchell, John Held Jr., Rudy Vallee, Harry Hershfield and other notable cartoonists and columnists.

Barney Google did his share of traveling too. In addition to hopping from one town to another across the continental United States, much like DeBeck, he made two European trips. On October 4, 1926, Barney arrived in London and, after Spark Plug successfully swam the English Channel, visited Paris. He sailed for Europe again in 1929, and in a spectacular sequence of Sunday-page episodes from April 28 to September 22, traveled in the footsteps of his creator. During his European adventure, Barney took in the sidewalk cafes of Paris (June 2), the ruins of Rome (July 28), the gondolas of Venice (August 25) and the fog of London (September 15).

On September 22 , 1929, Barney wrote from Paris: "Dear Pals - I'm coming Home - Europe is okay but gimme the good old U.S.A. where the coffee don't give you any backtalk and there's somp'n to chew on besides VEAL. When I get home I won't be able to look a calf in the face. Will see you all soon. Be sure and meet me. I've got swell presents for everybody. Yours Barney."

Billy DeBeck, who was winding up his own European stay at that time, was probably trying to tell his readers that he had finally gotten homesick, too.

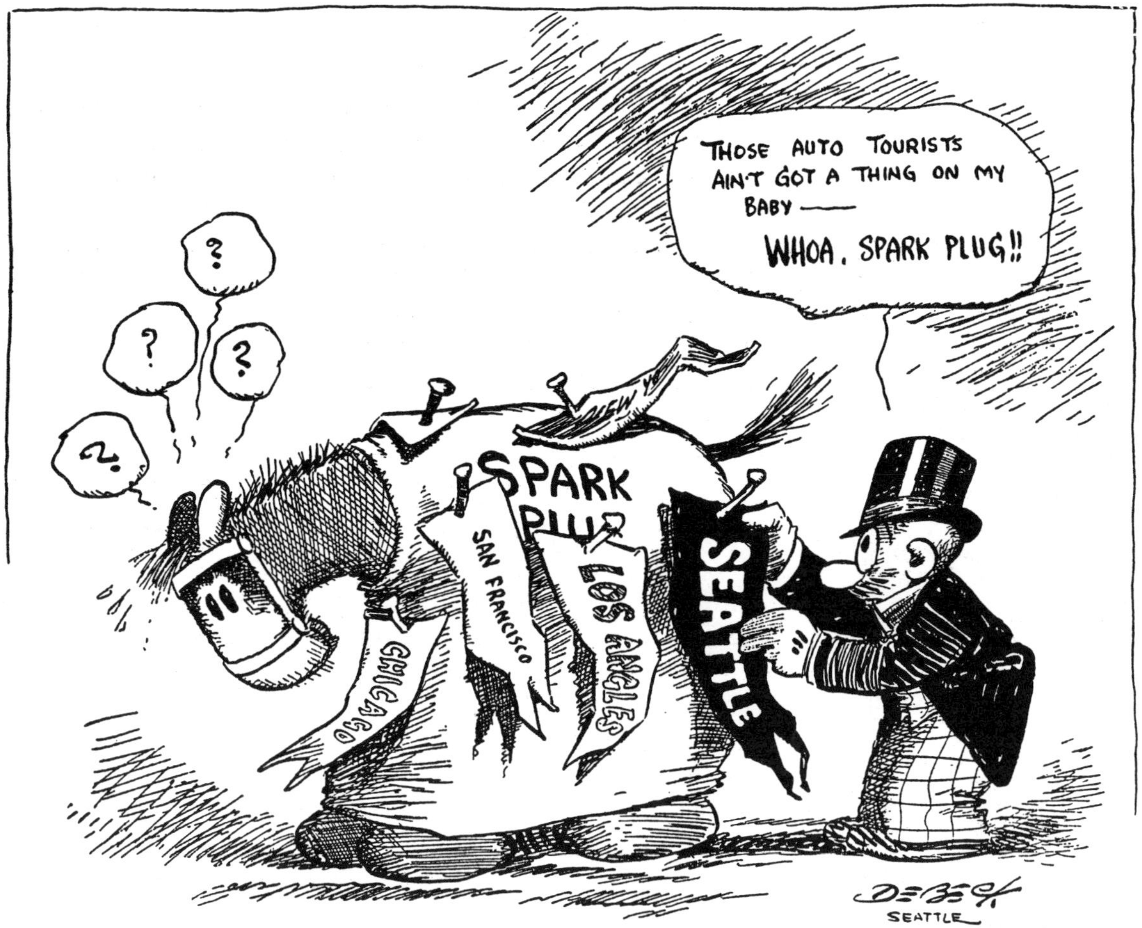
THOSE AUTO TOURISTS AIN'T GOT A THING ON MY BABY ——
WHOA, SPARK PLUG!!
?
?
?
?
SPARK PLUG
SAN FRANCISCO
LOS ANGLES
SEATTLE
CHICAGO
DEBECK SEATTLE

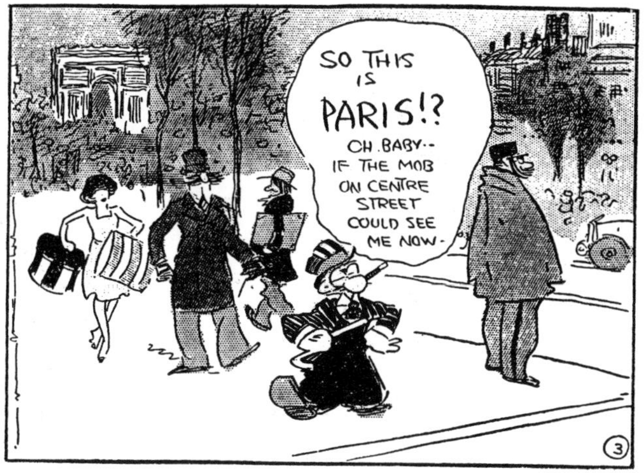
SO THIS IS PARIS!?
OH BABY -- IF THE MOB ON CENTRE STREET COULD SEE ME NOW -

Above: Barney arrives in Paris, May 5, 1929.
Courtesy of the San Francisco Academy of Comic Art.

Left: A cartoon DeBeck drew in his hotel room while visiting Seattle. From the *Seattle Post Intelligencer*, August 13, 1923. Courtesy of the San Francisco Academy of Comic Art.

Below: Barney takes in the sidewalk cafes of Paris, June 2, 1929. Courtesy of the San Francisco Academy of Comic Art.

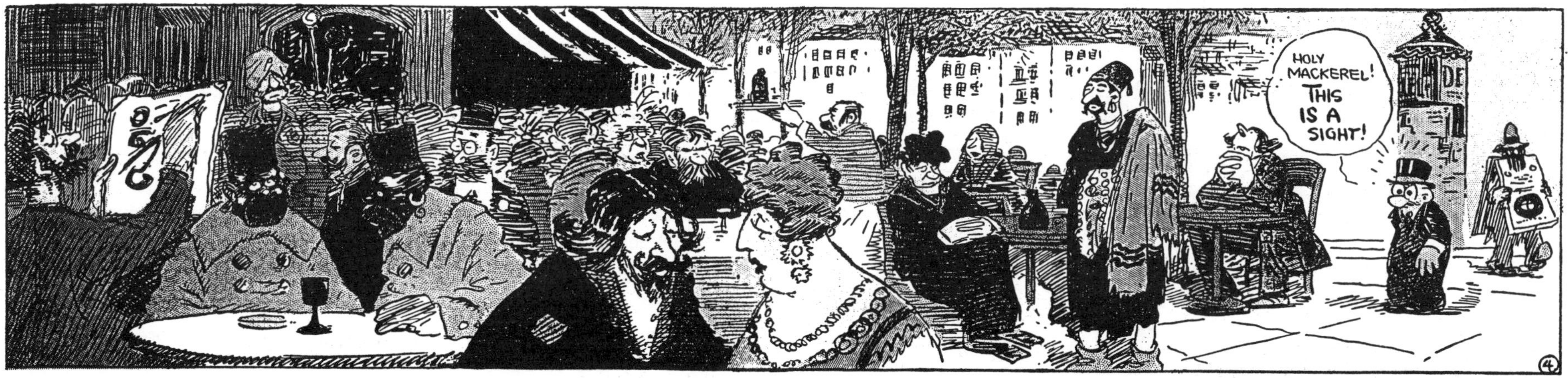
HOLY MACKEREL! THIS IS A SIGHT!

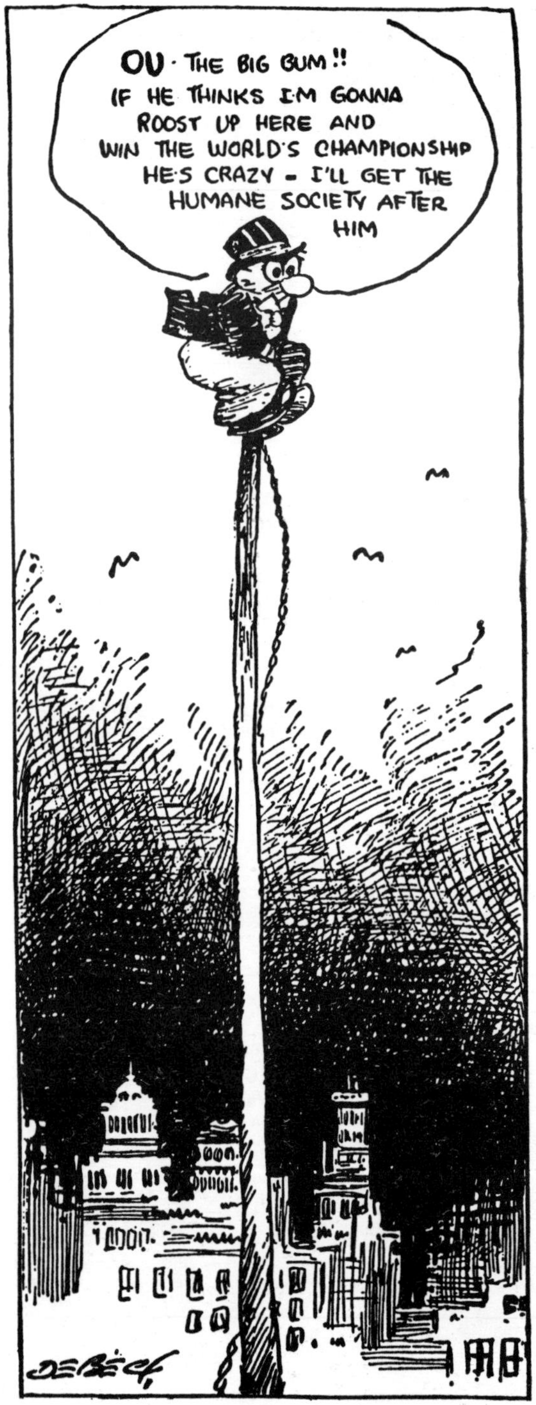
OU · THE BIG BUM!! IF HE THINKS I'M GONNA ROOST UP HERE AND WIN THE WORLD'S CHAMPIONSHIP HE'S CRAZY - I'LL GET THE HUMANE SOCIETY AFTER HIM
DEBECK

Left: Barney flagpole-sitting, June 17, 1927. Courtesy of the San Francisco Adademy of Comic Art.

Right: A Prohibition-era "Bughouse Fable," June 19, 1925. Collection of Ron Goulart.

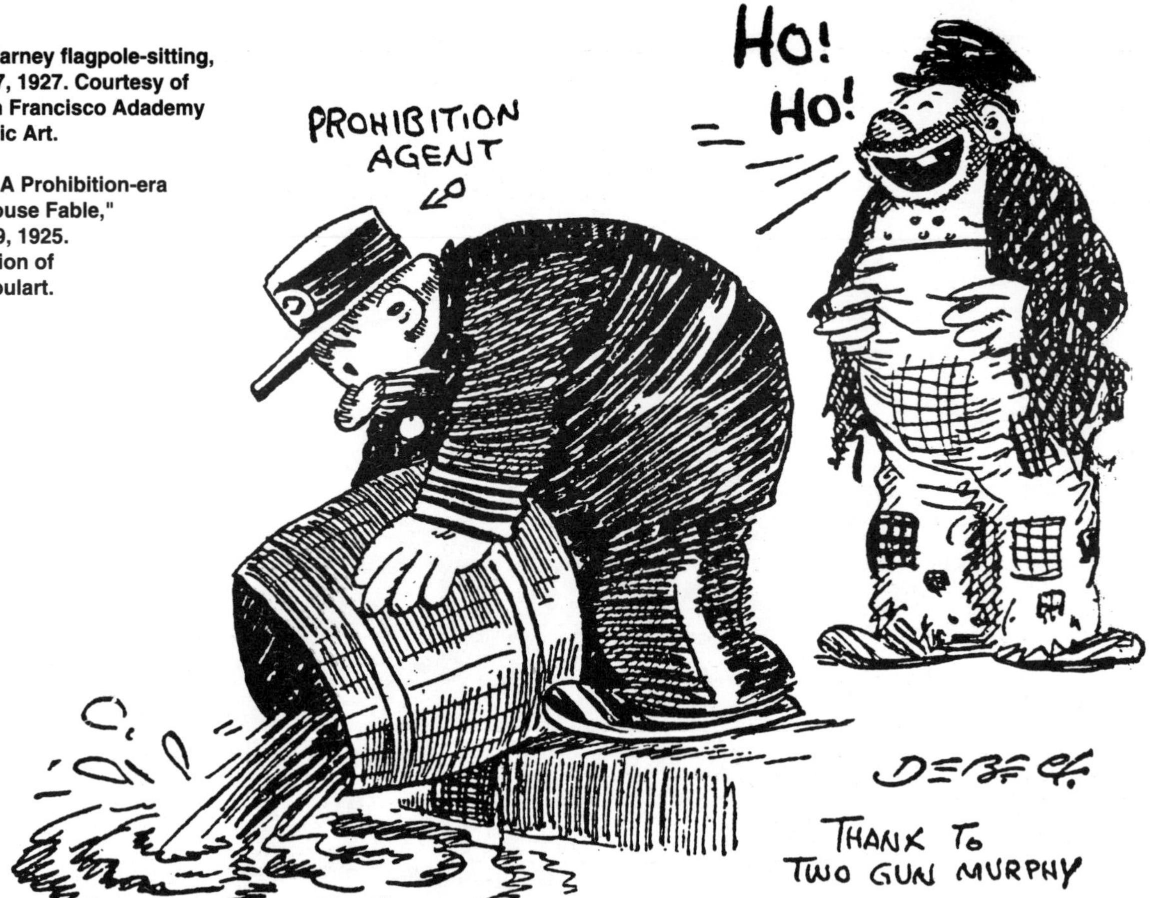
HO! HO!
PROHIBITION AGENT
DEBECK
THANX TO TWO GUN MURPHY

The Roaring Twenties was a decade characterized by wild fads, fantastic athletic stunts and the lawlessness of Prohibition - ideal source material for Billy DeBeck's comic strip. In October, 1919, in the same month the Volstead Act was passed, Barney was already mixing up "Google High Balls" on the kitchen table as his wife Lizzie protested, "You don't catch me trying any of those home-made Prohibition drinks." When Gertrude Ederle swam the English Channel in 1926, Spark Plug followed right in her wake, successfully making the crossing on November 11, 1926.

In September 1927, DeBeck paid his ultimate tribute to the zaniness of the Jazz Age when Barney took a job as a flagpole sitter. Hired to break the world record of 18 days, he hung on through 60 mile-an-hour gale-force winds, pouring rain and vicious slingshot attacks, until he was finally cut down on September 27, breaking the old record by three days! After this feat, Barney waxed poetic: "While I sat there aloft in the good clean air with warm sunshine permeating my entire being, the thought came to me that I must broadcast far and wide to my suffering fellowmen that nature is the greatest healer of all. My slogan is - those who are down must get up in the air." When a newcomer challenged him to a flagpole standing contest, Barney's true nature returned and he left town in the dead of the night.

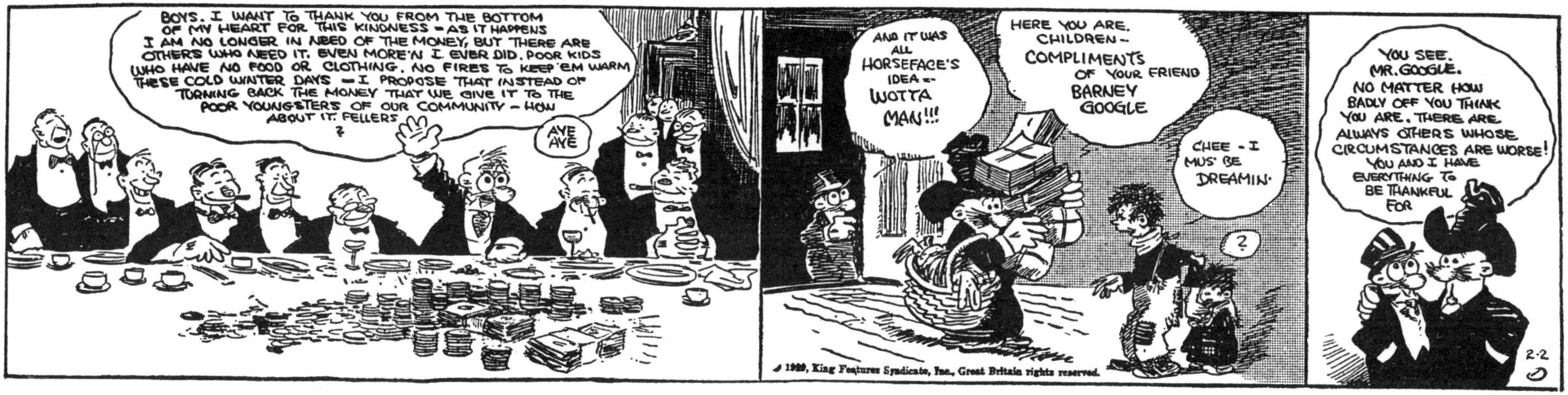
BOYS. I WANT TO THANK YOU FROM THE BOTTOM OF MY HEART FOR THIS KINDNESS - AS IT HAPPENS I AM NO LONGER IN NEED OF THE MONEY, BUT THERE ARE OTHERS WHO NEED IT. EVEN MORE'N I EVER DID. POOR KIDS WHO HAVE NO FOOD OR CLOTHING. NO FIRES TO KEEP 'EM WARM THESE COLD WINTER DAYS - I PROPOSE THAT INSTEAD OF TURNING BACK THE MONEY THAT WE GIVE IT TO THE POOR YOUNGSTERS OF OUR COMMUNITY - HOW ABOUT IT, FELLERS ?
AYE AYE
AND IT WAS ALL HORSEFACE'S IDEA -- WOTTA MAN!!!
HERE YOU ARE. CHILDREN - COMPLIMENTS OF YOUR FRIEND BARNEY GOOGLE
CHEE - I MUS' BE DREAMIN'
?
© 1929, King Features Syndicate, Inc., Great Britain rights reserved.
YOU SEE. MR. GOOGLE. NO MATTER HOW BADLY OFF YOU THINK YOU ARE. THERE ARE ALWAYS OTHERS WHOSE CIRCUMSTANCES ARE WORSE! YOU AND I HAVE EVERYTHING TO BE THANKFUL FOR
2-2

The fun and frivolity of the 1920's came to an abrupt end when the stock market crashed in October 1929. Anticipating the problems the country was heading towards, DeBeck did a story earlier that year about Barney's financial woes. "Some of his friends," the strip from January 21, 1929, read, "realizing that Barney was practically penniless, decided to devise some method of aiding him in his difficulty. Accordingly a benefit has been arranged. A gala dinner and dance will be given. Fifty stars of the stage and screen have consented to appear, and the proceeds will be given to Barney Google, who never refused aid to anyone when he was in a position to give it." When his old pal, Horseface Klotz, came to his rescue, Barney gave an inspirational speech and the proceeds of the benefit were donated to the poor.

The rags-to-riches theme in "Barney Google" was a recurrent one. Barney's fortunes changed from one horse race to the next during the Spark Plug era of 1922 to 1926. The Eric Van Horn episode in 1927 taught Barney the pleasures and pains of living the life of the rich and powerful. The Sawbuck Finnegan story from 1933 was a Depression-era tale in the tradition of Harold Gray's "Little Orphan Annie," complete with lost relatives, an unclaimed inheritance and a kidnapping.

It has been suggested that the Great Depression compromised Billy DeBeck's idealized view of urban America and that he sent Barney Google into the hills of North Carolina in 1934 seeking a rural utopia to replace it. No one knows exactly what his motivations were, but the quaint squalor of the Hootin' Holler mountain shacks and the barefoot innocence of the hillbillies must have seemed less depressing to DeBeck and his readers than the Hoovervilles and homeless street people of our nation's cities during these times of economic hardship.

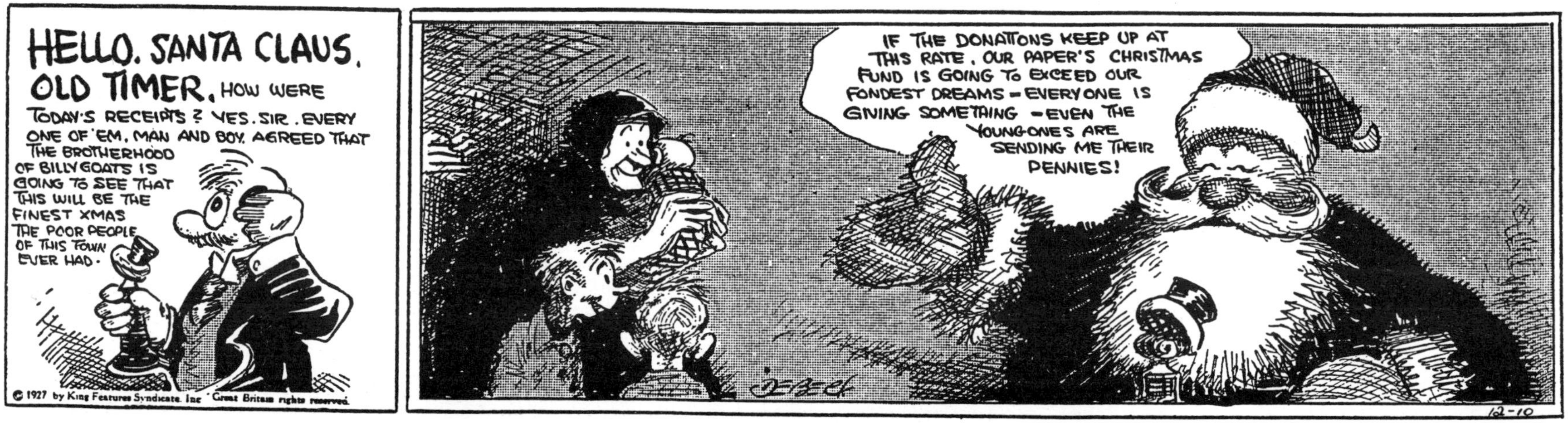
HELLO. SANTA CLAUS. OLD TIMER. HOW WERE TODAY'S RECEIPTS ? YES. SIR. EVERY ONE OF 'EM. MAN AND BOY. AGREED THAT THE BROTHERHOOD OF BILLYGOATS IS GOING TO SEE THAT THIS WILL BE THE FINEST XMAS THE POOR PEOPLE OF THIS TOWN EVER HAD.
© 1927 by King Features Syndicate. Inc. Great Britain rights reserved.
IF THE DONATIONS KEEP UP AT THIS RATE. OUR PAPER'S CHRISTMAS FUND IS GOING TO EXCEED OUR FONDEST DREAMS - EVERYONE IS GIVING SOMETHING - EVEN THE YOUNG ONES ARE SENDING ME THEIR PENNIES!
DEBECK
12-10

Above: "Barney Google" strips, Febraury 2, 1929 (top) and December 10, 1927 (bottom) from the Collection of Ron Goulart.

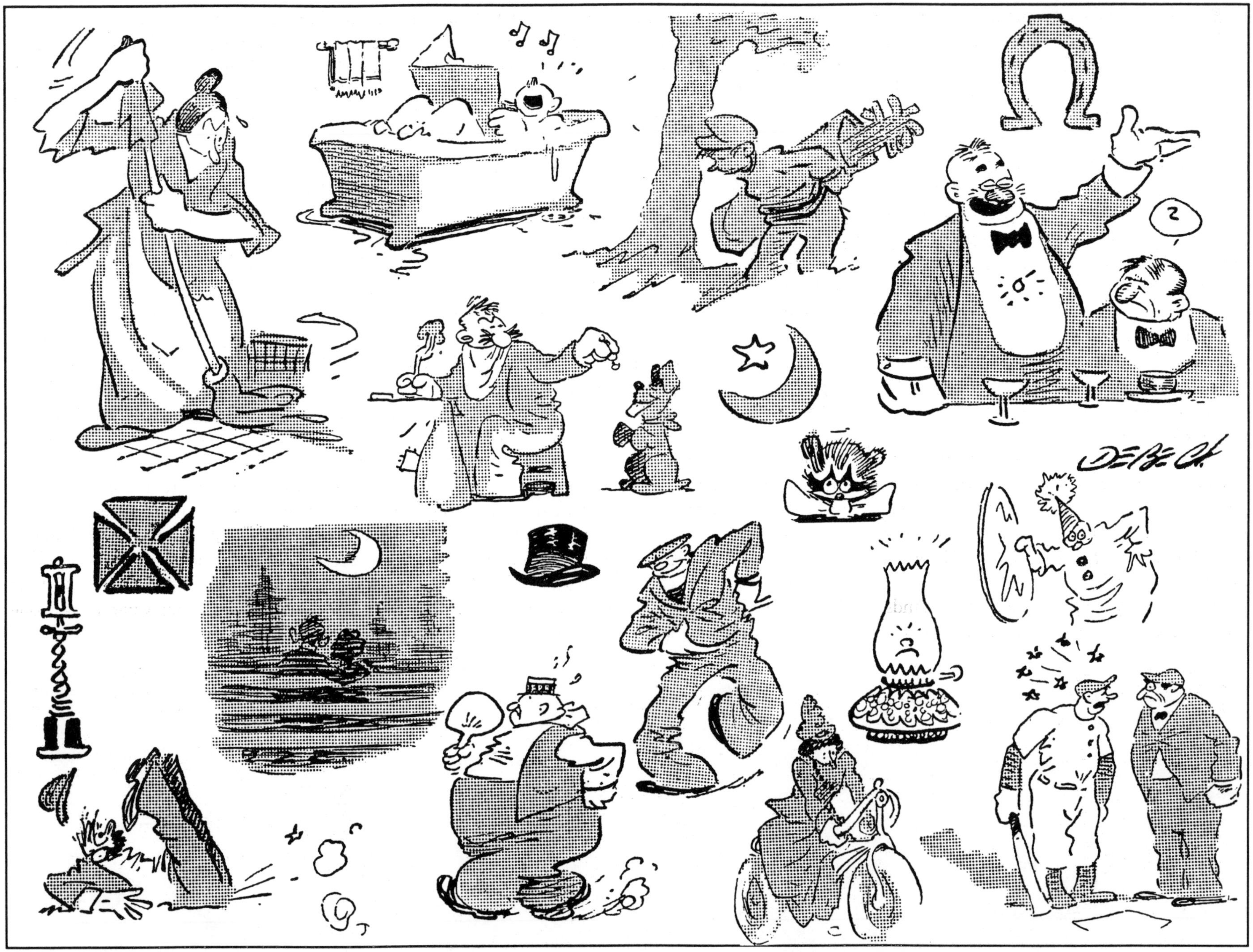
DEBECK

Above: These "spot" drawings by DeBeck appeared in Barney Google's "Comic Strip Derby" sequence, July 16 and 18, 1930. From the Collection of Ron Goulart.

A love for drawing came to Billy DeBeck at an early age. As a boy, he copied the penwork of Charles Dana Gibson and Phil May. He started taking classes at the Chicago Academy of Fine Arts soon after he graduated from high school. He shared what he had learned in his "DeBeck Cartoon Hints" course in 1915 and went back to teach at his old alma mater, the Chicago Academy of Fine Arts, when he became a successful professional. Although he had boyhood dreams of becoming an oil painter, he was a failure as a fine artist. But when it came to cartooning, Billy DeBeck was a natural.

In interviews, he would often describe his working methods for producing the "Barney Google" strips. After penciling the rough outlines of his characters to suggest position and attitude, he would ink the finished strip "straight-ahead." He was extremely adept with a pen, using fluid strokes and varied lines. He experimented constantly with new techniques and employed mechanical shading and scratchboard effects masterfully. Once, he tried drawing with a grease pencil in a style used commonly by the political cartoonists of his day. When doing his finished strips, he claimed he always saved the best for last - the pupils of Barney Google's eyes.

He worked extremely fast. DeBeck said that he once did twelve full weeks, 72 drawings in all, of finished "Bughouse Fables" panels in one eight-hour sitting. He was never able to work on a systematic schedule. He wouldn't draw for days at a time and then he would turn out two weeks of dailies and a couple of Sunday pages of "Barney Google" in a sixteen-hour burst.

"It pays to be a careful observer" he wrote in his cartoon course. DeBeck was always sketching in notebooks and on scraps of paper, napkins, menus, stationary - anything he could get his hands on. He drew people he saw on the streets and in the restaurants to use as incidental characters in the strip. He studied details like the folds in clothing or the design of architecture.

Most cartoonists have strengths and weaknesses, but DeBeck could do it all. He drew gorgeous women and funny-looking men. His characters were distinctive and memorable. He could depict them in violent action or peaceful repose. He was a good letterer and had an excellent sense of design. His famous full-panel "re-cap" strips were filled with decorative calligraphy, vignette portraits and imaginative storytelling. Urban skylines gave his strips an atmosphere of time and place. Mountain landscapes from the hillbilly years evoked a sense of natural beauty. He could be dramatic, poetic, or romantic and still be funny. If Billy DeBeck had a weakness, it was inconsistency. He could never stick with one style or theme for very long and had a hard time finishing his stories.

DeBeck used a number of talented assistants throughout his career. Frank Willard, Paul Fung, Doc Winner and Joe Musial were known to have had a hand in the strip at various points. Fred Lasswell began lettering for him in 1934, and over the next eight years did writing and artwork and even complete continuities until he took over after DeBeck's death in 1942. There was never any doubt, however, that "Barney Google" was Billy DeBeck's creation, and most of what appeared in the strip was his.

As talented artistically as DeBeck was, the real secret to his success was an affinity for the common people. He understood what they wanted and he gave it to them in daily doses - pure entertainment, plain and simple. Through his characters, Barney Google, Spark Plug and Snuffy Smith, he created a sympathetic bond with his readers. There was nothing "high-brow" about Billy DeBeck. He never aspired to be anything other than what he was - one of the greatest cartoonists who ever picked up a pen.

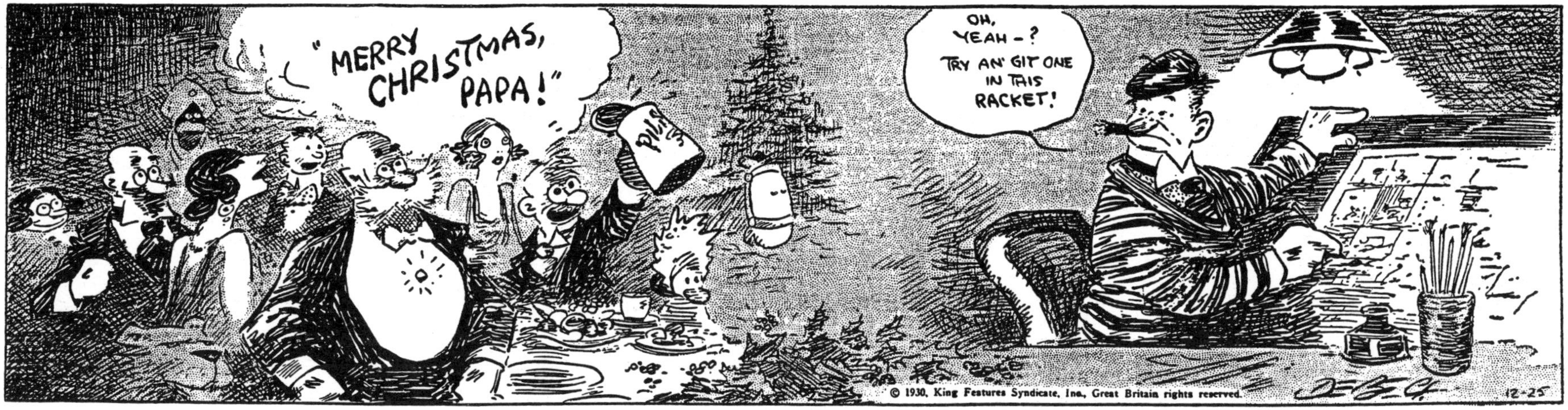
"MERRY CHRISTMAS, PAPA!"
OH, YEAH - ? TRY AN' GIT ONE IN THIS RACKET!
© 1930, King Features Syndicate, Inc., Great Britain rights reserved.
12-25

Above: "Barney Google" strip, December 25, 1930. From the Collection of Ron Goulart.

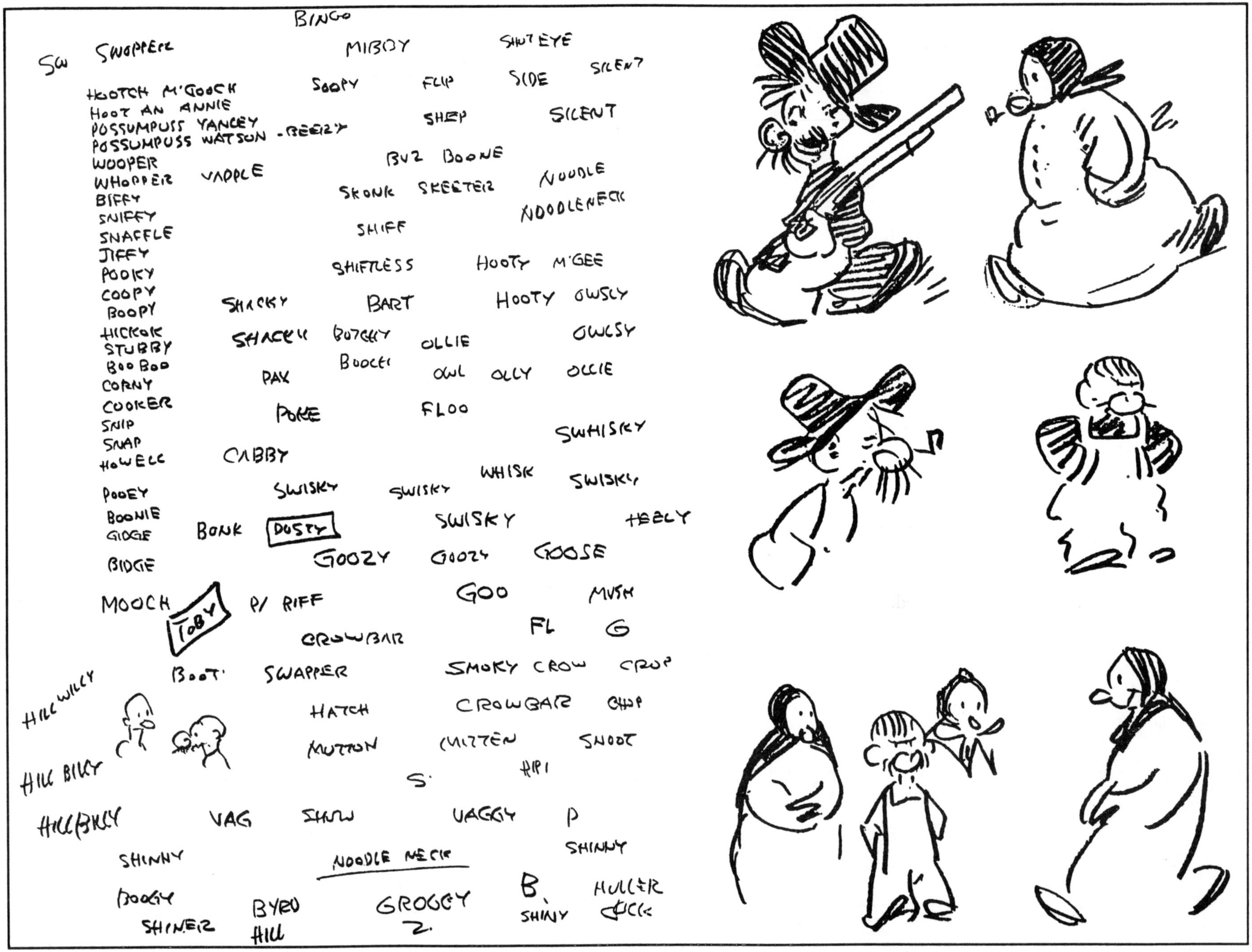
BINGO
SWOPPER
MIBOY
SHUT EYE
HOOTCH M'GOOCH
HOOT AN ANNIE
POSSUMPUSS YANCEY
POSSUMPUSS WATSON
SOOPY
FLIP
SIDE
SHEP
SILENT
WOOPER
WHOPPER
BIFFY
SNIFFY
SNAFFLE
JIFFY
POOKY
COOPY
BOOPY
HICKOK
STUBBY
BOO BOO
CORNY
COOKER
SNIP
SNAP
HOWELL
POOEY
BOONIE
BIDGE
BUZ BOONE
SKONK
SKEETER
NOODLE
NOODLENECK
SHIFF
SHIFTLESS
HOOTY M'GEE
SHACKY
BART
HOOTY OWLSY
OWLSY
OLLIE
OWL
OLLY
PAX
POKE
FLOO
SWHISKY
CABBY
SWISKY
WHISK
BONK
DUSTY
GOOZY
GOOSE
MOOCH
TOBY
RIFF
CROWBAR
GOO
MUSH
SWAPPER
SMOKY CROW
HILLBILLY
HATCH
MUTTON
MITTEN
SNOOT
VAG
VAGGY
SHINNY
NOODLE NECK
BOOGY
SHINER
BYRD
GROGGY
SHINY
HULLER

Above: DeBeck's notes and sketches from the time he was developing his new hillbilly characters , 1934. From the Collection of the International Museum of Cartoon Art.

Sut Lovingood and Snuffy Smith

By M. Thomas Inge

Billy DeBeck's reputation as one of America's most talented and accomplished comic strip artists during the 1920's and 1930's derives from his creation of a bulb-nosed, pop-eyed, dumpy little bummer and sometime racehorse owner named Barney Google. The daily and Sunday comic strip panels he occupied were invaded on November 17, 1934, by an equally dumpy and scruffy little mountaineer named Snuffy Smith, and slowly the hillbilly individualist stole Barney's popularity until the strip's title became "Barney Google and Snuffy Smith," and in many newspapers after DeBeck's death in 1942, just "Snuffy Smith," under the hand of his assistant Fred Lasswell, who today still draws the strip. Anyone familiar with the literature of Appalachia has probably been struck upon encountering Snuffy Smith, Loweezy, and their nephew Jughaid with what seem to be familiar language and situations. This is more than coincidence.

In 1934, Barney Google headed into the Southern hills. This was where he met Snuffy Smith, whose Appalachian world would draw DeBeck more and more deeply into its language, folklore, and customs. This was no accidental excursion for the artist as a brief respite from the city sporting life which Barney loved. It was, instead, the result of a newfound fascination DeBeck had for things having to do with the life and culture of the mountaineer.

What first sparked the cartoonist's interest is not known. We do know, however, that in preparation for the new episodes he traveled through the mountains of Virginia and Kentucky, talked to the natives, made numerous sketches, and read everything he could lay hands on that treated mountaineer life. Just how extensive and thorough the reading was has not been generally known, but it can be documented by an examination of DeBeck's working library, which was donated to the special collections of Virginia Commonwealth University (VCU).

DeBeck did an exhaustive job of familiarizing himself with the literature of Appalachia, both fiction and nonfiction. Without attempting a complete checklist, the VCU collection includes extensive mountaineer fiction by Mary Noailes Murfree, John Trotwood Moore, Lucy Furman, Charles Neville Buck, Rose Butterham, John Fox, Jr., Jean Thomas, Maristan Chapman, Percy Mackaye, and Harry Harrison Kroll. Frontier humorists are represented by George Washington Harris and William Tappan Thompson; the dialect comedians by Artemus Ward, Petroleum V. Nasby, and Henry Hiram Riley; and there are several anthologies of humorous sketches, including Henry Watterson's popular collection of 1883, *Oddities in Southern Life and Character*. There are also selected books of nonfiction describing the folklore and folk customs of Appalachia, including Francis L. Goodrich's *Mountain Homespun*

(1931), Muriel Early Sheppard's *Cabins in the Laurel* (1935), Horace Kephart's *Our Southern Highlands* (1922), and several of Vance Randolph's works including *The Ozarks* (1931), *Ozark Mountain Folk* (1932), and *From an Ozark Holler* (1933).

At least one of these authors, Vance Rudolph, was aware of the influence of his books on Snuffy Smith. Inside the copy of *From an Ozark Holler* are two letters to DeBeck from Randolph. The first is a short and terse note dated January 25, 1939, from Galena, Missouri:

> Dear Mr. DeBeck:
>
> A Texan named Wood writes me that you read some of his Ozark rhymes, and sent him a signed cartoon.
>
> Well by God you can send me a signed cartoon too - a good big one! You certainly have used a lot of my Ozark stuff in "Barney Google."
>
> Cordially,
>
> Vance Rudolph

The second letter, dated February 1, 1939, acknowledges the receipt of the cartoon: "I'm mighty proud to have a DeBeck drawing, and it certainly impresses my fellow villagers. They never heard of my books, but they all know your pictures." Randolph goes on to invite DeBeck to visit him to see his collection of Ozark Humor, some of it "Much better than the items you so flatteringly crib out of my books."

Nearly all of the books in the VCU collection are annotated, some lightly and others extensively, oftentimes with original pencil sketches and cartoons. For example, opposite page 3 of *Mountain Homespun* by Goodrich is a sensitive pencil portrait of a mountain woman dated 1935 (shown here); the cover of Charles Neville Buck's *Hazard of the Hills* contains a characteristic DeBeck comic mountaineer portrait; and page 167 of Murfree's *The Prophet of the Great Smoky Mountains* has a color sketch of Snuffy Smith demonstrating the custom of "tippin' th' jug" (shown on the next page, upper left).

The two authors whose works are most heavily annotated, and obviously most influential on DeBeck's conception of the life and language of the mountaineer, are Mary Noailes Murfree and George Washington Harris. Both authors defined for American literature the character of the Tennessee mountaineer: Harris through his early nineteenth-century humorous sketches about Sut Lovingood and Murfree through her late nineteenth-century local color stories about the quaint customs and superstitions of the hill people. In the latter's books, hundreds of examples of dialogue caught DeBeck's attention, and he marked them heavily - like this passage from page 13 of *Down the Ravine*:

> Ef that thar child don't quit that fool way o' stickin' her head a-twixt the rails ter watch fur her brother, she'll get catched thar some day like a peeg in a pen, an' git her neck brok.

Such passages were likely to appear in a modified form in one of the scenarios acted out by the inhabitants of Snuffy Smith's mountain community.

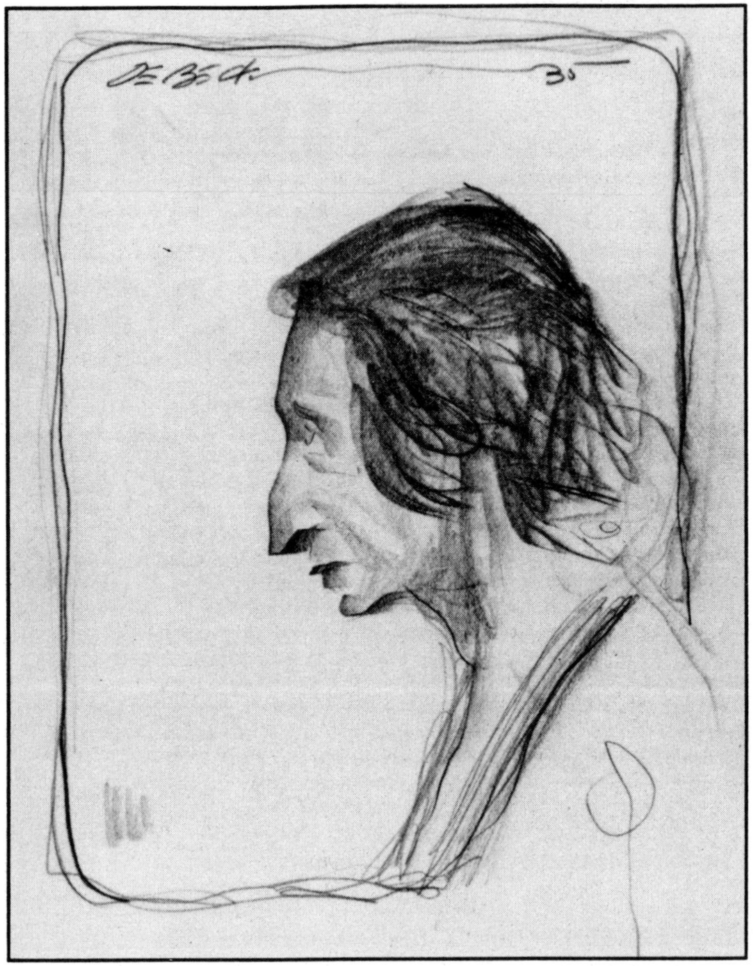
DeBeck 35

Above: Sketch by DeBeck of a mountain woman on page opposite page 3 in Frances L. Goodrich, *Mountain Homespun* (1931), in DeBeck Library. Courtesy of James Branch Cabell Library, Virginia Commonwealth University.

166 THE PROPHET OF THE

the dryadic chorus in the forest without as if the waters that knew but darkness and the cavernous sterilities were already in the liberated joys of the gorge yonder, reflecting the sky, wantoning with the wind, and swirling down the mountain side. The spirits dripped from the worm, the furnace roared, the men's feet grated upon the rocks as they now and then shifted their position.

"Waal," said Amos at last, rising, "I'd better be a-goin'. 'Pears like ez I hev wore out my welcome hyar."

He stood looking at the line of light, remembering desolately Dorinda's buoyant, triumphant mood. Its embellishment of her beauty had smitten him with an afflicted sense of her withdrawal from all the prospects of his future. He had thought that he had given up hope, but he began to appreciate, when he found Rick Tyler in intimate refuge with her kindred, how sturdy an organism was that heart of his, and to realize that to reduce it to despair must needs cost many a throe.

"I hev wore out my welcome, I reckon," he repeated, dismally.

"I dunno what ails ye ter say that. Ye hev jes' got tired o' comin' hyar, I reckon," said old man Cayce. "Wore out yer welcome, — shucks!"

GREAT SMOKY MOUNTAINS. 167

"Mighty nigh wore me out," said Pete, remembering to cough.

"Waal," said Amos, slightly salved by the protestations of his host, "I reckon it air time I war a-puttin' out, ennyhow. Jes' set that thar furnace door on the jar, Pete, so I kin see ter lay a-holt o' the beastis."

The door opened, the red glow flared out, the figures of the moonshiners all reappeared in a semicircle about the still, and as Amos James took the horse's bridle and led him away from the wall the mastodon vanished, with noiseless tread, into the dim distance of the unmeasured past.

The horse's hoofs reverberated down the cavernous depths, echoed, reëchoed, multiplied indefinitely. Even after the animal had been led through the tortuous windings of the passage his tramp resounded through the gloom.

TIPPIN' TH' JUG

DeBeck
1935
166
PAGE 172 ON VERY GOOD
A LITTLE NONSENSE NOW 'N' THEN IS RELISHED BY TH WISEST MEN
#1
HANGIN 267
77
NAMES 21

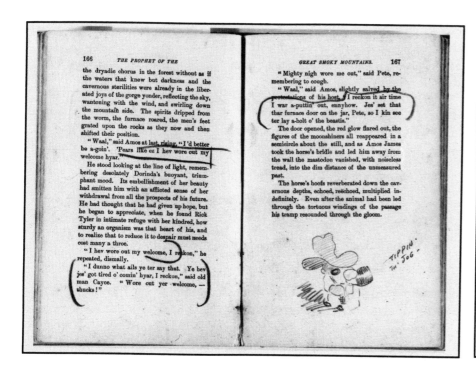

Above: Color sketch by Billy DeBeck of Snuffy "tippin' th' jug" on page 167 of Mary Noailles Murfree, *The Prophet of the Great Smoky Mountains* (1885). DeBeck Library. Courtesy of James Branch Cabell Library, Virginia Commonwealth University.

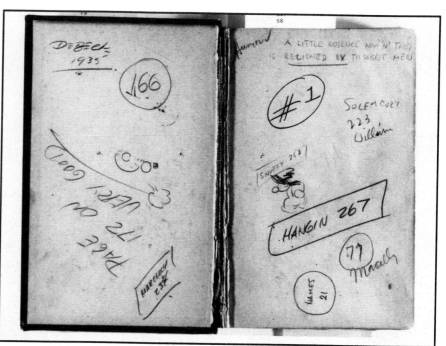

Above: Sketches and notes by Billy DeBeck inside front cover on endpapers of George Washington Harris, *Sut Lovingood Yarns* (1867). DeBeck Library. Courtesy of James Branch Cabell Library, Virginia Commonwealth University.

The single book that most struck DeBeck's imagination and fired his fancy was an 1867 edition of the collected *Sut Lovingood's Yarns*, which he purchased in 1935. Every page of the book is annotated, including the front cover (shown above right), where DeBeck noted "Page 172 on very good" and quoted the book's epigraph, "A little nonsense now and then is relished by the wisest men," amidst many page references and sketches. The book was ranked number one in his library and is so marked on its spine. Above a rough sketch of Snuffy is a reference to page 263, where the following passage is found that inspired the drawing:

> I seed ole Doltin cumin waddlin outen the courthous', wif a paper in his han, an' a big stick onder his arm, lookin to'ards the doggery wif his mouf puss'd up, an' his brows draw'd down.

Inside the back cover, almost as if in tribute to the comic genius of an artist of another century, DeBeck sketched a perfectly detailed and deftly rendered miniature portrait of his contribution to the tradition of Sut Lovingood, Snuffy Smith (shown on the next page).

While neither the full impact nor influence of Harris's Sut Lovingood stories can be explored here due to space limitations, a few observations can be made, especially with regard to the use of dialect. An examination of selected Sunday pages published during the early years of the Snuffy Smith adventures (between 1934 and 1939) indicates that DeBeck borrowed heavily from Harris for his dialect spellings. A selective list of his dialect spellings includes axes (asks), ary (any), atter (after), 'caze (because), daid (dead), ez (as), enuff (enough), fer (for), fust (first), fit (fought), gonter (going to), hit (it), haid (head), hev (have), hyar (here), jes (just), kin (can), kivers (covers), mought (might), orter (ought to), propitty (property), pitcher (picture), rale (real), sich (such), sez (says), sot (set), taters (potatoes), thet (that), ter (to), widder (widow), wun (one), wif (with), and yere (here). Like Harris, DeBeck would mix sound dialect with eye dialect (also called comic misspelling) for no rhyme or reason.

One of Harris's contributions to literary humor was his remarkable facility for some of the most richly metaphoric and figurative language found in

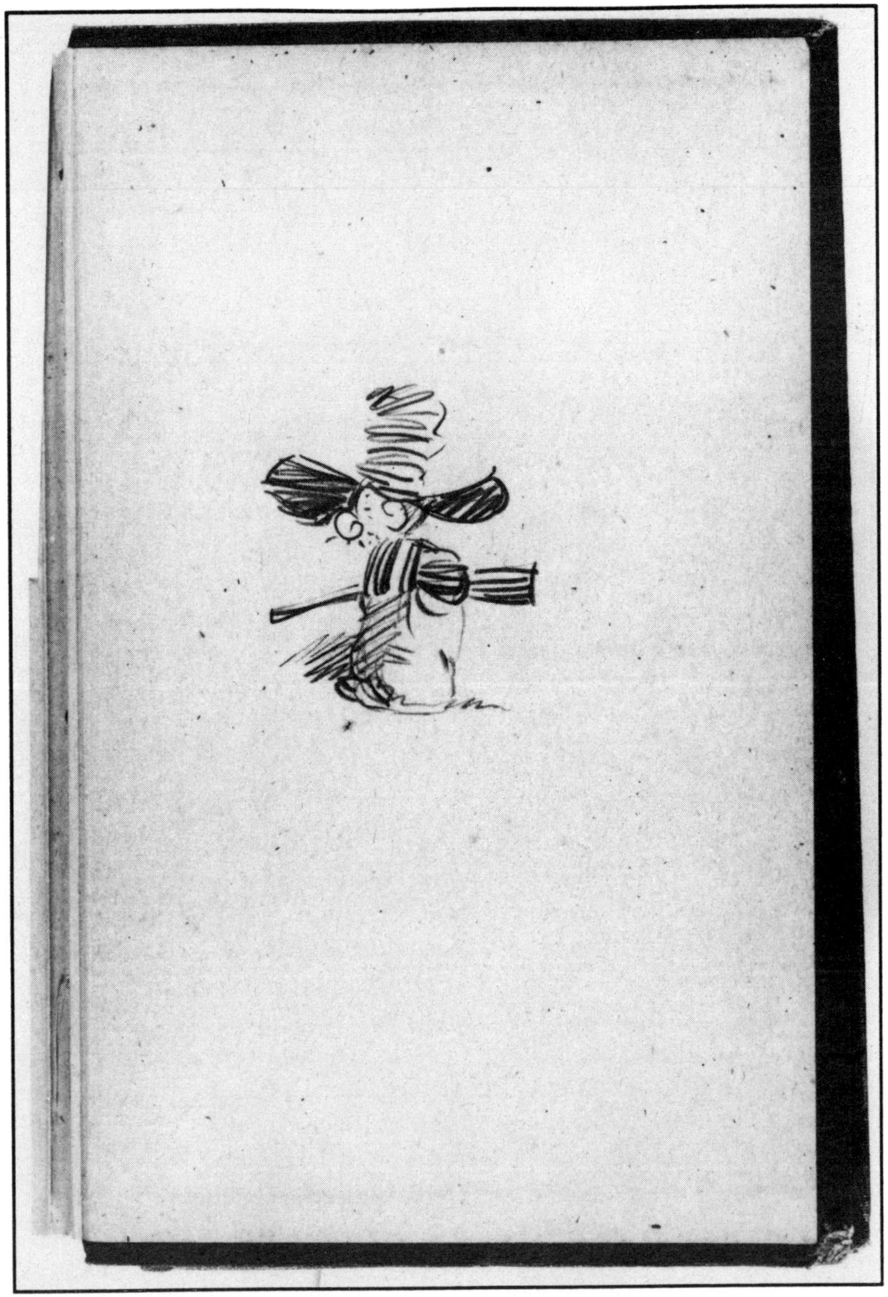

Above: Sketch of Snuffy Smith by Billy DeBeck inside back cover on endpaper of George Washington Harris, *Sut Lovingood Yarns* (1867). DeBeck Library. Courtesy of James Branch Cabell Library, Virginia Commonwealth University.

American prose. A major source of metaphors was the animal life with which the Tennessee mountaineer was intimately familiar. While DeBeck lacked Harris's touch of genius in this regard, he made many interesting efforts as in the following:

> Foolin with him air like makin' faces at a rattlesnake — Hit mought be satisfyin ter the feelin's, but hit ain't safe. (January 13, 1935)

> Her face air th'color o' hawk meat an' she's bellerin' lak some crazy onsettled creature. (October 13, 1935)

> Mah stummick air growlin' wusser'n a houn dorg caught in a b'ar trap. (December 15, 1935)

> A widder man air ez lonesoum ez a b'ar in a holler tree. (January 19, 1936)

Some of those would surely elicit the admiration of Sut Lovingood, under whose influence they were undoubtedly written. It is not at all surprising that on August 4, 1937, a character named Sut Turner turned up in a "Barney Google and Snuffy Smith" Sunday page.

In at least one regard, DeBeck outstripped Harris, and that is in his ability to coin new dialect phrases which had the ring of Appalachian authenticity at the same time that they captured the fancy of the wider American reading public. Among such phrases are "Daider'n a door-knob," "Time's a-wastin'," "A leetle tetched in th'haid," "Shif'less skonk," "Bodacious idjit," and "Ef that don't take the rag off'n th' bush."

DeBeck, of course, drew heavily not only on the Sut Lovingood tales, but on the whole corpus of Appalachian literature for his motifs, stories, themes and anecdotes. For example, ghosts and spirits are frequent sources of humor in the comic strip, although they usually have a natural explanation, as in the Sunday page for September 16, 1934. DeBeck did not hesitate, however, to enter entirely into the realm of the supernatural, as he did in one of the most delightful of Snuffy's adventures. The narrative, which began in June 1939, and ran for two months, concerned the encounters of Barney Google and Snuffy Smith with a whole tribe of devilish dwarfs and mischievous wood goblins called Feather Merchants, familiar figures in the world of folk mythology and folk tales.

DeBeck also employed family feuds of the Hatfield and McCoy variety, usually with the typical star-crossed lovers of both families involved, but his humorous tales more often than not avoid a tragic ending. A rich variety of both literary and oral folk sources appear to have been merged in telling the tale of Hobo Snow and Fanny Parker on January 6, 1935, a prologue to the further adventures of Widder Snow that followed in subsequent weeks.

An interesting coda to DeBeck's self-taught knowledge about mountain folk is that his successor, Fred Lasswell, considers them part of his own heritage. His stories about visiting his grandfather in Kennett, Missouri, could easily be transferred into his comic strip by simply changing some of the character's names. Lasswell also had access to DeBeck's reference library and recalls studying the books there as he began his apprenticeship.

One of the more noticeable changes in "Barney Google and Snuffy Smith" since DeBeck's death has been the decline in the complexity of the dialect used. Lasswell felt that much of the early dialect was too difficult for the general reader to interpret. Another factor has been the decreasing publication size of the comic strip in recent years, which has meant less space for dialogue in speech balloons.

Comic art has often served as a method of preserving and reshaping the concerns of the folk culture into a popular and highly influential mode of expression. It would be revealing to investigate the sources of all the hillbilly comic strips, such as Al Capp's "L'il Abner," Bob Lubbers' "Long Sam" or Ray Gotto's "Ozark Ike," to determine the extent to which they serve as purveyors of the frontier humor tradition. In any case, it is certainly appropriate to consider Snuffy Smith a legitimate addition to the canon of Appalachian-inspired art and literature.

An earlier version of this essay was published in *Comics as Culture* (Jackson: University of Mississippi Press), 69-78.

Right: Sut Turner (with umbrella), 1937. Below: The Feather Merchants, 1939. Both Courtesy of King Features Syndicate.

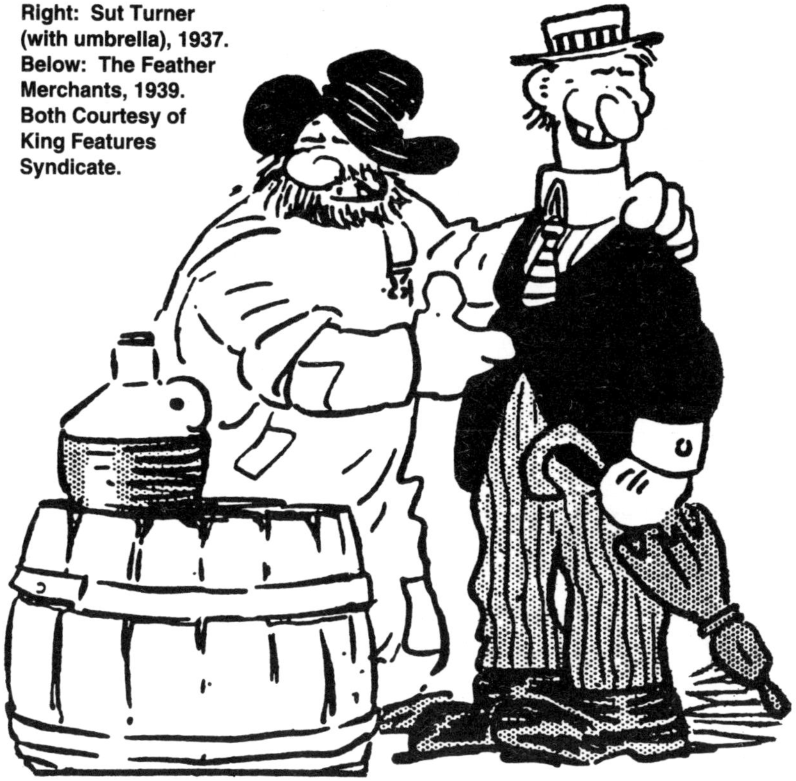

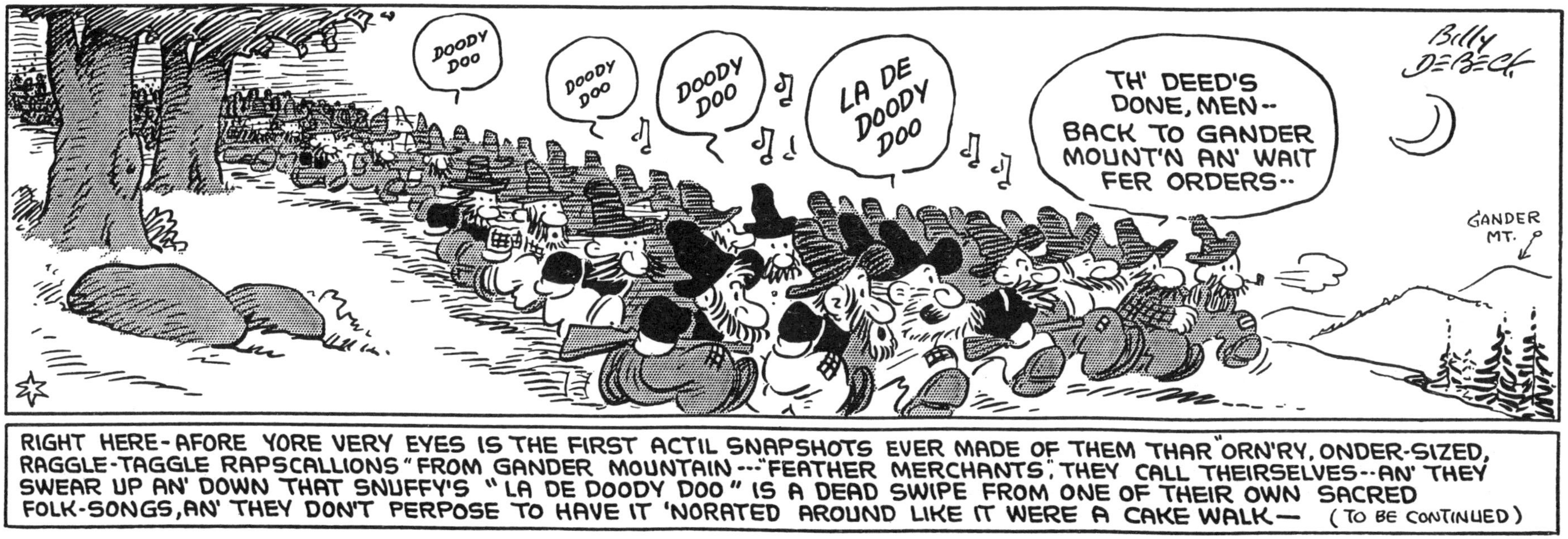
Billy DeBeck
DOODY DOO
DOODY DOO
DOODY DOO
LA DE DOODY DOO
TH' DEED'S DONE, MEN-- BACK TO GANDER MOUNT'N AN' WAIT FER ORDERS--
GANDER MT.
RIGHT HERE-AFORE YORE VERY EYES IS THE FIRST ACTIL SNAPSHOTS EVER MADE OF THEM THAR "ORN'RY, ONDER-SIZED, RAGGLE-TAGGLE RAPSCALLIONS" FROM GANDER MOUNTAIN---"FEATHER MERCHANTS," THEY CALL THEIRSELVES--AN' THEY SWEAR UP AN' DOWN THAT SNUFFY'S "LA DE DOODY DOO" IS A DEAD SWIPE FROM ONE OF THEIR OWN SACRED FOLK-SONGS, AN' THEY DON'T PERPOSE TO HAVE IT 'NORATED AROUND LIKE IT WERE A CAKE WALK— (TO BE CONTINUED)

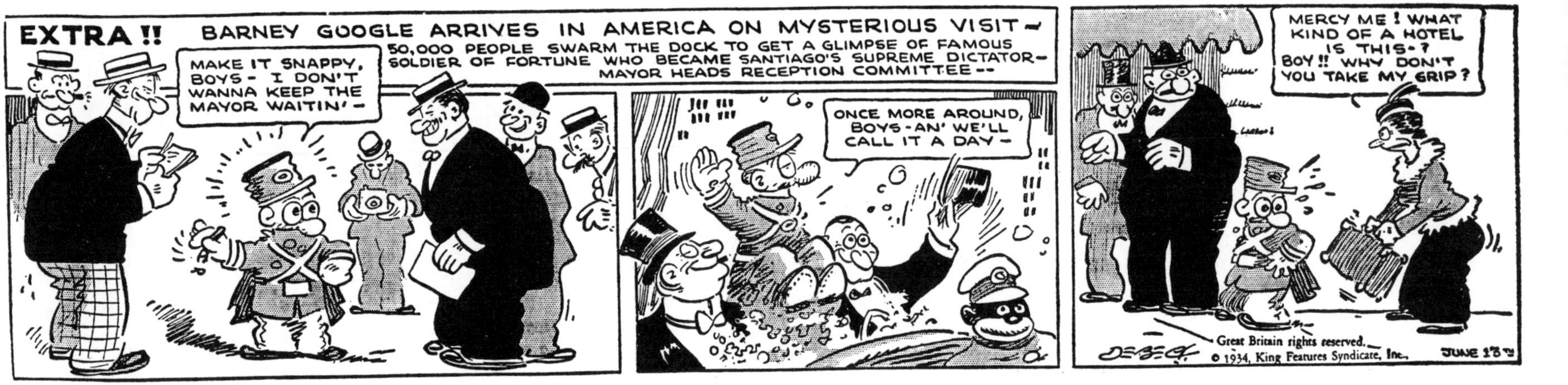
EXTRA !! BARNEY GOOGLE ARRIVES IN AMERICA ON MYSTERIOUS VISIT — 50,000 PEOPLE SWARM THE DOCK TO GET A GLIMPSE OF FAMOUS SOLDIER OF FORTUNE WHO BECAME SANTIAGO'S SUPREME DICTATOR — MAYOR HEADS RECEPTION COMMITTEE --
MAKE IT SNAPPY, BOYS - I DON'T WANNA KEEP THE MAYOR WAITIN' -
ONCE MORE AROUND, BOYS - AN' WE'LL CALL IT A DAY -
MERCY ME ! WHAT KIND OF A HOTEL IS THIS - ? BOY !! WHY DON'T YOU TAKE MY GRIP ?
DE BECK
Great Britain rights reserved.
© 1934, King Features Syndicate, Inc.
JUNE 13TH

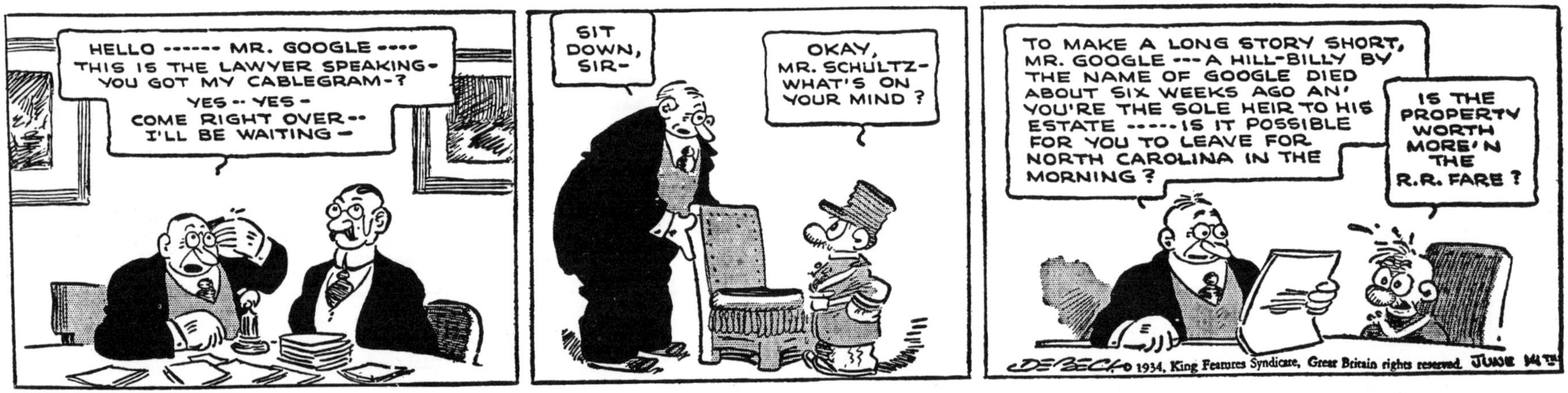
HELLO ------ MR. GOOGLE ---- THIS IS THE LAWYER SPEAKING - YOU GOT MY CABLEGRAM - ? YES -- YES - COME RIGHT OVER -- I'LL BE WAITING -
SIT DOWN, SIR -
OKAY, MR. SCHÜLTZ - WHAT'S ON YOUR MIND ?
TO MAKE A LONG STORY SHORT, MR. GOOGLE --- A HILL-BILLY BY THE NAME OF GOOGLE DIED ABOUT SIX WEEKS AGO AN' YOU'RE THE SOLE HEIR TO HIS ESTATE ----- IS IT POSSIBLE FOR YOU TO LEAVE FOR NORTH CAROLINA IN THE MORNING ?
IS THE PROPERTY WORTH MORE'N THE R.R. FARE ?
DE BECK © 1934, King Features Syndicate, Great Britain rights reserved. JUNE 14TH

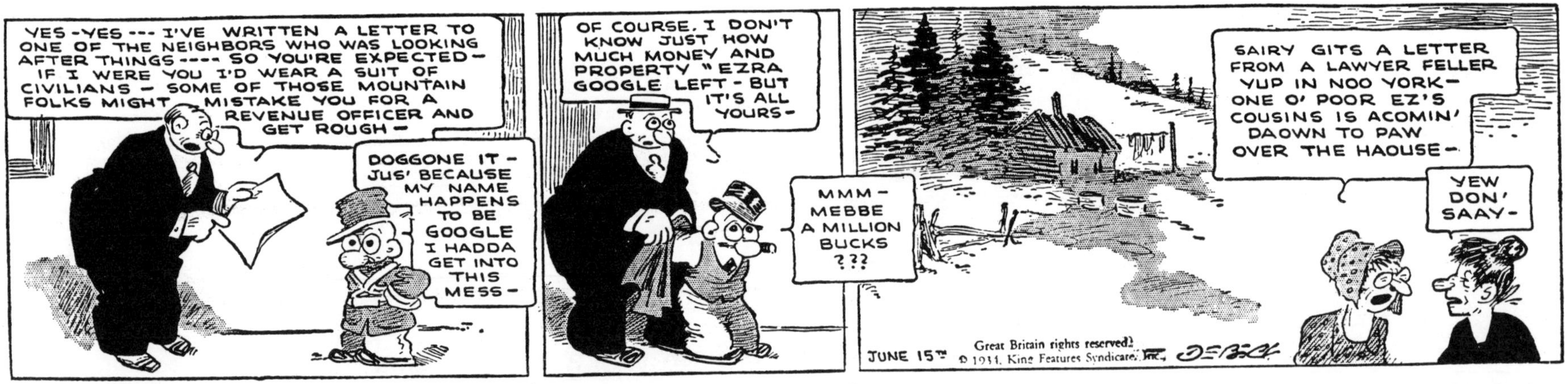
YES - YES --- I'VE WRITTEN A LETTER TO ONE OF THE NEIGHBORS WHO WAS LOOKING AFTER THINGS ---- SO YOU'RE EXPECTED - IF I WERE YOU I'D WEAR A SUIT OF CIVILIANS - SOME OF THOSE MOUNTAIN FOLKS MIGHT MISTAKE YOU FOR A REVENUE OFFICER AND GET ROUGH -
DOGGONE IT - JUS' BECAUSE MY NAME HAPPENS TO BE GOOGLE I HADDA GET INTO THIS MESS -
OF COURSE, I DON'T KNOW JUST HOW MUCH MONEY AND PROPERTY "EZRA GOOGLE LEFT - BUT IT'S ALL YOURS -
MMM - MEBBE A MILLION BUCKS ???
SAIRY GITS A LETTER FROM A LAWYER FELLER YUP IN NOO YORK - ONE O' POOR EZ'S COUSINS IS ACOMIN' DAOWN TO PAW OVER THE HAOUSE -
YEW DON' SAAY -
JUNE 15TH
Great Britain rights reserved.
© 1934, King Features Syndicate, Inc.
DE BECK

The "Barney Google" daily comic strips from 1934 and 1935 are reproduced from newspaper strips. From the Collection of Ron Goulart.

Tetched in th'Haid

1934 — 1945

On April 16, 1934, Barney Google was blissfully unaware of the momentous changes that were about to take place in his life. "Peace has come to Santiago, the jewel of the Caribbean!" that day's strip read. "The beautiful island is ablaze with tropical sunshine, the soft air perfumed by a hundred blooms. At last the people are happy. Senor Google is the man of the hour." Barney returned to America on June 13, and the next day he received news that he had inherited an estate in the mountains of North Carolina from a long-lost relative.

He didn't get a very friendly welcome when he arrived in hillbilly country a few days later. Seems like Google wasn't a very well-liked name in those parts. After dodging the suspicious mountain folk for a few weeks, Barney got tangled up in the romantic adventures of Sairy Hopkins and Dan'l Barlow. On November 10, Barney promised Sairy, "I'm gonna give you an' Dan'l the swellest doggone wedding these hillbillies ever saw, an' I want all your kin-folk to be here, an' I'll pay their travelin' expenses." Only problem was, Dan'l had an ornery uncle named Snuffy Smith.

Judging from the research that he put into developing this story line, Billy DeBeck had obviously made a conscious effort to radically change the direction of his comic strip at this time. No one knows what motivated him to do this. In an interview with the *St. Petersburg Times* in the mid-1930's,

DeBeck said, "People were singing those mountain songs and the whole idea was sweeping the country." During a visit to the Greenbrier resort in White Sulphur Springs, West Virginia, in 1934, DeBeck observed the mountain people working around the hotel. "I studied them and put my ideas into the 'Barney Google' comics strip," he recounted. "At first Lowizie [the spelling was changed to "Loweezy" much later] and Snuffy became foils for Barney, but they stood up so well I reversed the idea and made Barney a stooge for the hillbilly couple."

Fred Lasswell remembers, when he first started working for DeBeck in the summer of 1934, scouring the book shops in lower Manhattan looking for volumes on mountain lore. Fred, a self-described "hayseed," denies he had any influence on the development of Billy's new hillbilly theme.

DeBeck must have known he was on the verge of something historic. Snuffy and Lowizie Smith first appeared as a "teaser" in the last panel of the strip on Saturday, November 17th. Readers had to wait until Monday to find out who these two odd-looking new characters were.

Once he arrived on the scene, it took Snuffy a few weeks to calm down and stop shooting at Barney. Finally, on November 30, 1934, the two shook hands and became eternal friends. It was the beginning of a remarkable relationship.

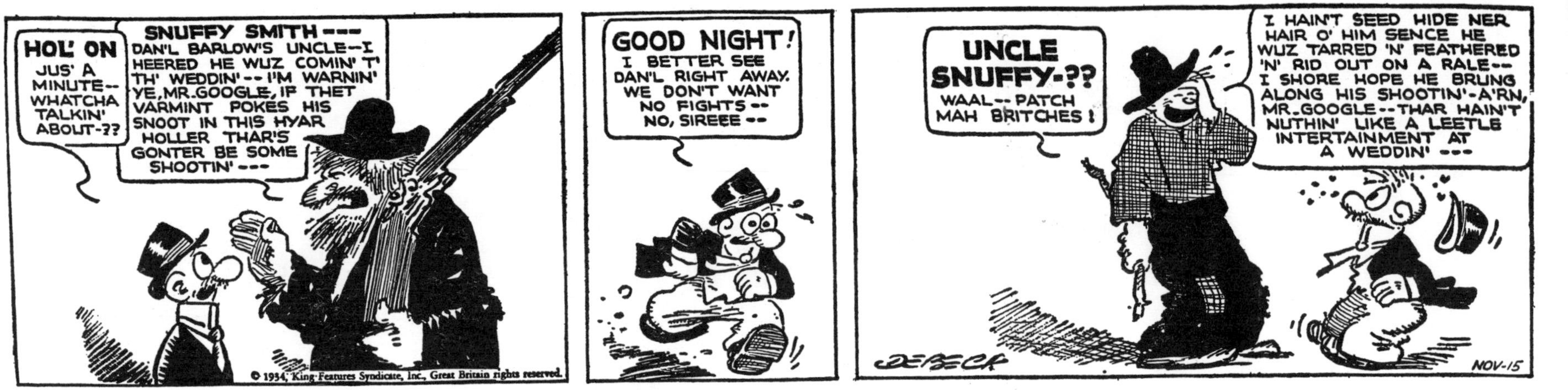
HOL' ON JUS' A MINUTE-- WHATCHA TALKIN' ABOUT-??
SNUFFY SMITH--- DAN'L BARLOW'S UNCLE--I HEERED HE WUZ COMIN' T' TH' WEDDIN'--I'M WARNIN' YE, MR.GOOGLE, IF THET VARMINT POKES HIS SNOOT IN THIS HYAR HOLLER THAR'S GONTER BE SOME SHOOTIN'---
© 1934, King Features Syndicate, Inc., Great Britain rights reserved.
GOOD NIGHT! I BETTER SEE DAN'L RIGHT AWAY. WE DON'T WANT NO FIGHTS-- NO, SIREEE--
UNCLE SNUFFY-?? WAAL--PATCH MAH BRITCHES!
I HAIN'T SEED HIDE NER HAIR O' HIM SENCE HE WUZ TARRED 'N' FEATHERED 'N' RID OUT ON A RALE-- I SHORE HOPE HE BRUNG ALONG HIS SHOOTIN'-A'RN, MR.GOOGLE--THAR HAIN'T NUTHIN' LIKE A LEETLE INTERTAINMENT AT A WEDDIN'---
DEBECK
NOV-15

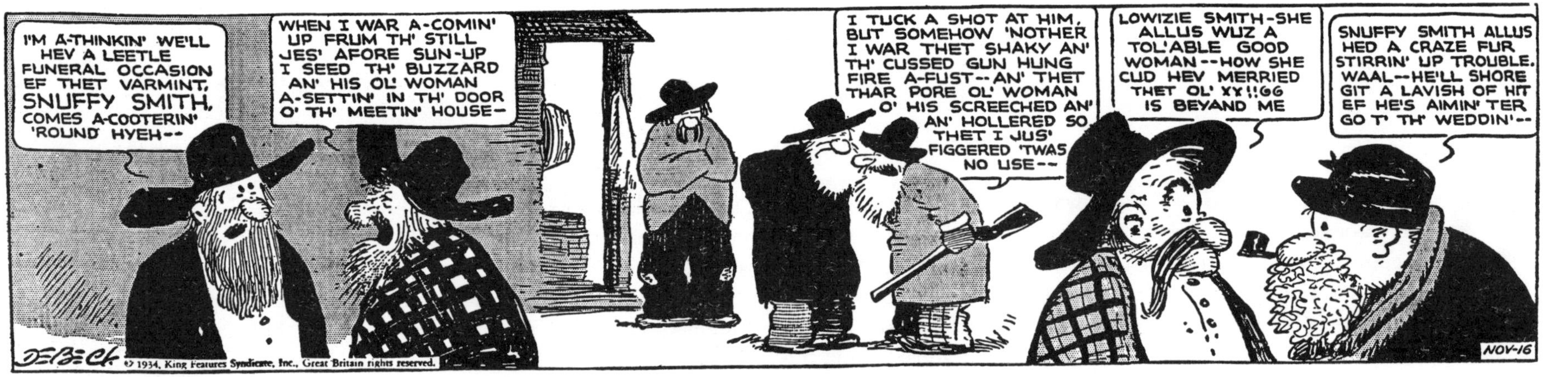
I'M A-THINKIN' WE'LL HEV A LEETLE FUNERAL OCCASION EF THET VARMINT, SNUFFY SMITH, COMES A-COOTERIN' 'ROUND HYEH--
WHEN I WAR A-COMIN' UP FRUM TH' STILL JES' AFORE SUN-UP I SEED TH' BUZZARD AN' HIS OL' WOMAN A-SETTIN' IN TH' DOOR O' TH' MEETIN' HOUSE-
I TUCK A SHOT AT HIM, BUT SOMEHOW 'NOTHER I WAR THET SHAKY AN' TH' CUSSED GUN HUNG FIRE A-FUST--AN' THET THAR PORE OL' WOMAN O' HIS SCREECHED AN' HOLLERED SO THET I JUS' FIGGERED 'TWAS NO USE--
LOWIZIE SMITH-SHE ALLUS WUZ A TOL'ABLE GOOD WOMAN--HOW SHE CUD HEV MERRIED THET OL' XY!!GG IS BEYAND ME
SNUFFY SMITH ALLUS HED A CRAZE FUR STIRRIN' UP TROUBLE. WAAL--HE'LL SHORE GIT A LAVISH OF HIT EF HE'S AIMIN' TER GO T' TH' WEDDIN'--
DEBECK
© 1934, King Features Syndicate, Inc., Great Britain rights reserved.
NOV-16

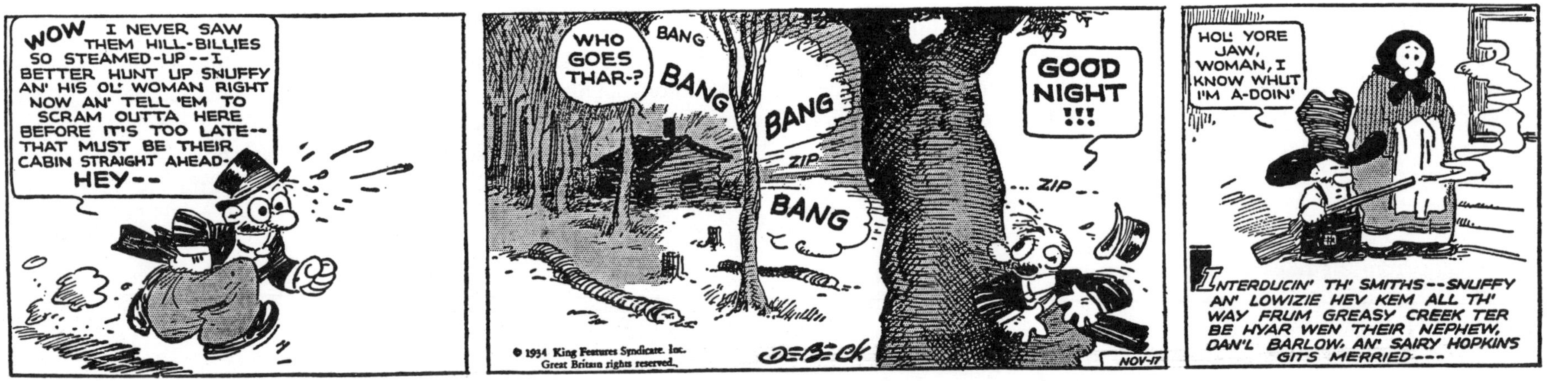
WOW I NEVER SAW THEM HILL-BILLIES SO STEAMED-UP--I BETTER HUNT UP SNUFFY AN' HIS OL' WOMAN RIGHT NOW AN' TELL 'EM TO SCRAM OUTTA HERE BEFORE IT'S TOO LATE-- THAT MUST BE THEIR CABIN STRAIGHT AHEAD- HEY--
WHO GOES THAR-?
BANG
BANG
BANG
ZIP
BANG
GOOD NIGHT !!!
...ZIP..
© 1934 King Features Syndicate. Inc. Great Britain rights reserved.
DEBECK
NOV-17
HOL' YORE JAW, WOMAN, I KNOW WHUT I'M A-DOIN'
INTERDUCIN' TH' SMITHS--SNUFFY AN' LOWIZIE HEV KEM ALL TH' WAY FRUM GREASY CREEK TER BE HYAR WEN THEIR NEPHEW, DAN'L BARLOW. AN' SAIRY HOPKINS GITS MERRIED---

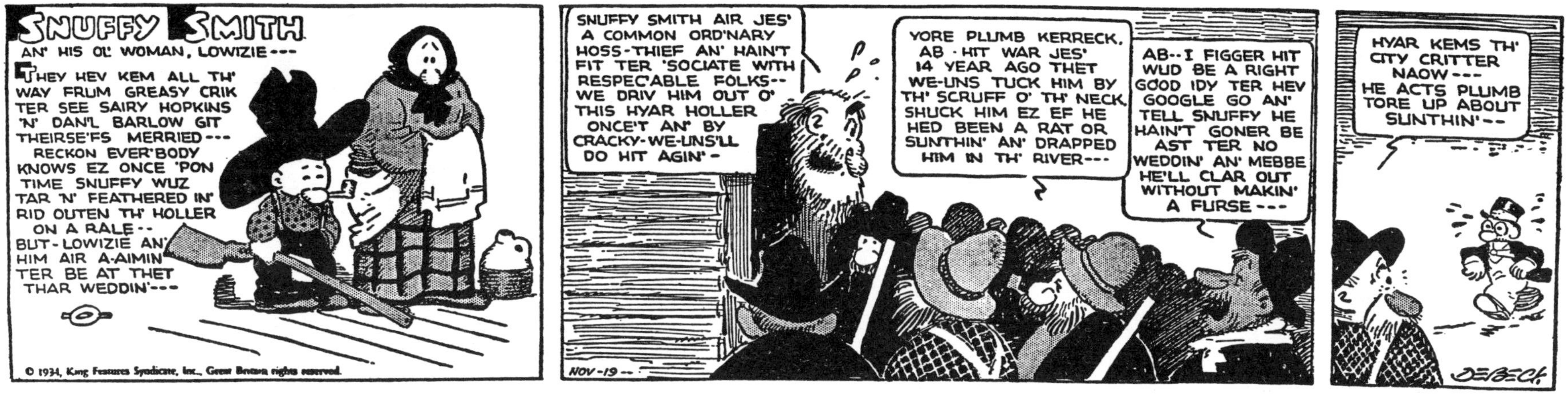
SNUFFY SMITH
AN' HIS OL' WOMAN, LOWIZIE---
THEY HEV KEM ALL TH' WAY FRUM GREASY CRIK TER SEE SAIRY HOPKINS 'N' DAN'L BARLOW GIT THEIRSE'FS MERRIED--- RECKON EVER'BODY KNOWS EZ ONCE 'PON TIME SNUFFY WUZ TAR 'N' FEATHERED IN' RID OUTEN TH' HOLLER ON A RALE-- BUT-LOWIZIE AN' HIM AIR A-AIMIN' TER BE AT THET THAR WEDDIN'---
© 1934, King Features Syndicate, Inc., Great Britain rights reserved.
SNUFFY SMITH AIR JES' A COMMON ORD'NARY HOSS-THIEF AN' HAIN'T FIT TER 'SOCIATE WITH RESPEC'ABLE FOLKS-- WE DRIV HIM OUT O' THIS HYAR HOLLER ONCE'T AN' BY CRACKY-WE-UNS'LL DO HIT AGIN'-
YORE PLUMB KERRECK, AB - HIT WAR JES' 14 YEAR AGO THET WE-UNS TUCK HIM BY TH' SCRUFF O' TH' NECK, SHUCK HIM EZ EF HE HED BEEN A RAT OR SUNTHIN' AN' DRAPPED HIM IN TH' RIVER---
AB--I FIGGER HIT WUD BE A RIGHT GOOD IDY TER HEV GOOGLE GO AN' TELL SNUFFY HE HAIN'T GONER BE AST TER NO WEDDIN' AN' MEBBE HE'LL CLAR OUT WITHOUT MAKIN' A FURSE---
NOV-19--
HYAR KEMS TH' CITY CRITTER NAOW--- HE ACTS PLUMB TORE UP ABOUT SUNTHIN'--
DEBECK

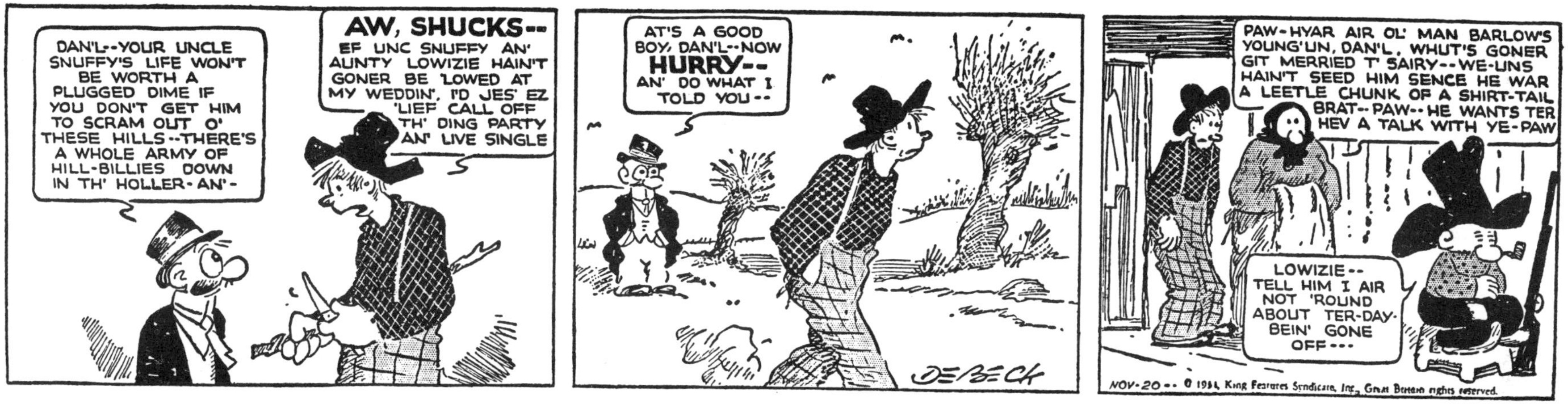
DAN'L--YOUR UNCLE SNUFFY'S LIFE WON'T BE WORTH A PLUGGED DIME IF YOU DON'T GET HIM TO SCRAM OUT O' THESE HILLS--THERE'S A WHOLE ARMY OF HILL-BILLIES DOWN IN TH' HOLLER-AN'-
AW, SHUCKS-- EF UNC SNUFFY AN' AUNTY LOWIZIE HAIN'T GONER BE 'LOWED AT MY WEDDIN', I'D JES' EZ 'LIEF CALL OFF TH' DING PARTY AN' LIVE SINGLE
AT'S A GOOD BOY, DAN'L--NOW HURRY-- AN' DO WHAT I TOLD YOU--
DEBECK
PAW-HYAR AIR OL' MAN BARLOW'S YOUNG'UN, DAN'L, WHUT'S GONER GIT MERRIED T' SAIRY--WE-UNS HAIN'T SEED HIM SENCE HE WAR A LEETLE CHUNK OF A SHIRT-TAIL BRAT--PAW--HE WANTS TER HEV A TALK WITH YE-PAW
LOWIZIE-- TELL HIM I AIR NOT 'ROUND ABOUT TER-DAY-BEIN' GONE OFF---
NOV-20-- © 1934, King Features Syndicate, Inc., Great Britain rights reserved.

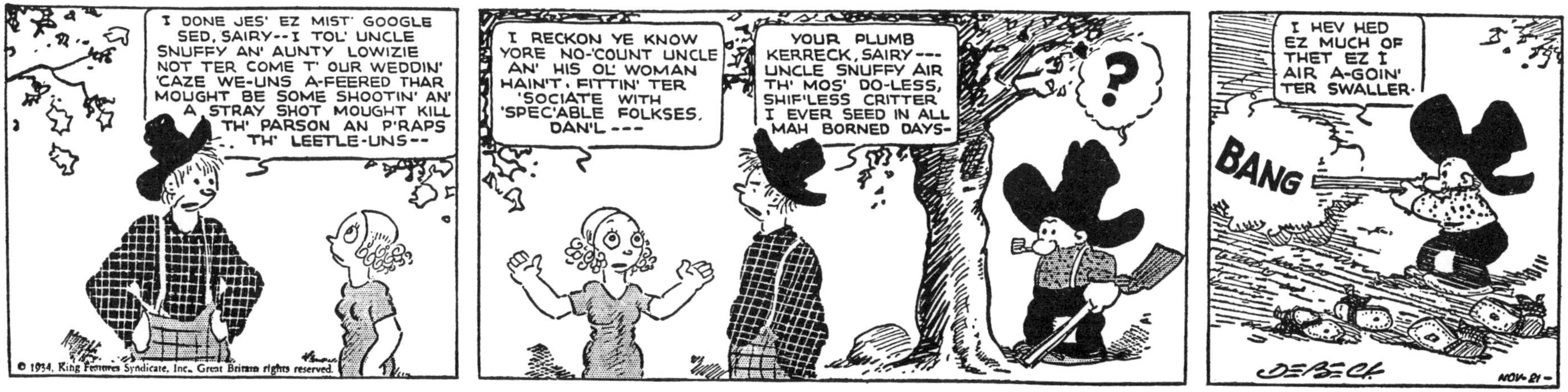
I DONE JES' EZ MIST' GOOGLE SED, SAIRY--I TOL' UNCLE SNUFFY AN' AUNTY LOWIZIE NOT TER COME T' OUR WEDDIN' 'CAZE WE-UNS A-FEERED THAR MOUGHT BE SOME SHOOTIN' AN' A STRAY SHOT MOUGHT KILL TH' PARSON AN P'RAPS TH' LEETLE-UNS--
© 1934, King Features Syndicate, Inc., Great Britain rights reserved.
I RECKON YE KNOW YORE NO-'COUNT UNCLE AN' HIS OL' WOMAN HAIN'T FITTIN' TER 'SOCIATE WITH 'SPEC'ABLE FOLKSES, DAN'L---
YOUR PLUMB KERRECK, SAIRY--- UNCLE SNUFFY AIR TH' MOS' DO-LESS, SHIF'LESS CRITTER I EVER SEED IN ALL MAH BORNED DAYS-
?
I HEV HED EZ MUCH OF THET EZ I AIR A-GOIN' TER SWALLER-
BANG
DEBECK
NOV-21-

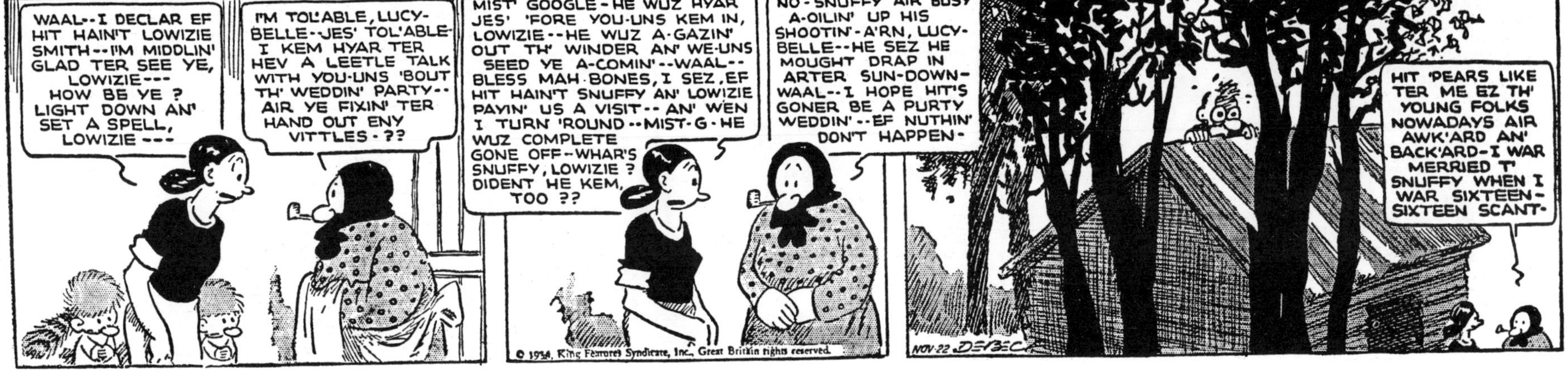
WAAL--I DECLAR EF HIT HAIN'T LOWIZIE SMITH--I'M MIDDLIN' GLAD TER SEE YE, LOWIZIE--- HOW BE YE? LIGHT DOWN AN' SET A SPELL, LOWIZIE---
I'M TOL'ABLE, LUCY-BELLE--JES' TOL'ABLE-I KEM HYAR TER HEV A LEETLE TALK WITH YOU-UNS 'BOUT TH' WEDDIN' PARTY--AIR YE FIXIN' TER HAND OUT ENY VITTLES-??
MIST' GOOGLE-HE WUZ HYAR JES' 'FORE YOU-UNS KEM IN, LOWIZIE--HE WUZ A-GAZIN' OUT TH' WINDER AN' WE-UNS SEED YE A-COMIN'--WAAL--BLESS MAH BONES, I SEZ, EF HIT HAIN'T SNUFFY AN' LOWIZIE PAYIN' US A VISIT--AN' WEN I TURN 'ROUND--MIST-G-HE WUZ COMPLETE GONE OFF--WHAR'S SNUFFY, LOWIZIE? DIDENT HE KEM, TOO??
© 1934, King Features Syndicate, Inc., Great Britain rights reserved.
NO-SNUFFY AIR BUSY A-OILIN' UP HIS SHOOTIN'-A'RN, LUCY-BELLE--HE SEZ HE MOUGHT DRAP IN ARTER SUN-DOWN-WAAL--I HOPE HIT'S GONER BE A PURTY WEDDIN'--EF NUTHIN' DON'T HAPPEN-
HIT 'PEARS LIKE TER ME EZ TH' YOUNG FOLKS NOWADAYS AIR AWK'ARD AN' BACK'ARD-I WAR MERRIED T' SNUFFY WHEN I WAR SIXTEEN-SIXTEEN SCANT-
NOV-22 DEBECK

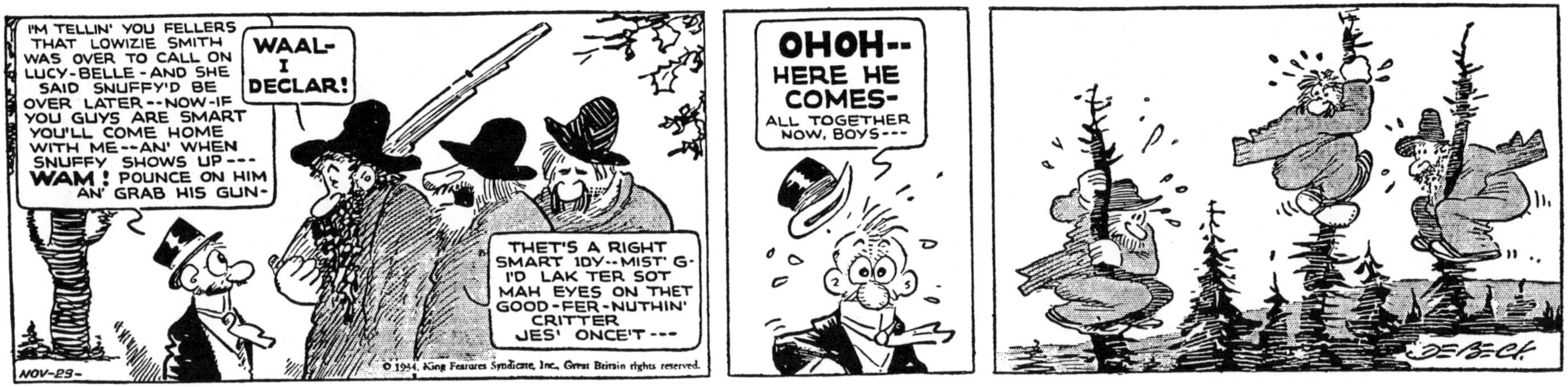
I'M TELLIN' YOU FELLERS THAT LOWIZIE SMITH WAS OVER TO CALL ON LUCY-BELLE-AND SHE SAID SNUFFY'D BE OVER LATER--NOW-IF YOU GUYS ARE SMART YOU'LL COME HOME WITH ME--AN' WHEN SNUFFY SHOWS UP--- WAM! POUNCE ON HIM AN' GRAB HIS GUN-
WAAL-I DECLAR!
THET'S A RIGHT SMART IDY--MIST' G-I'D LAK TER SOT MAH EYES ON THET GOOD-FER-NUTHIN' CRITTER JES' ONCE'T---
NOV-23-
© 1934, King Features Syndicate, Inc., Great Britain rights reserved.
OHOH--HERE HE COMES-ALL TOGETHER NOW, BOYS---
DEBECK

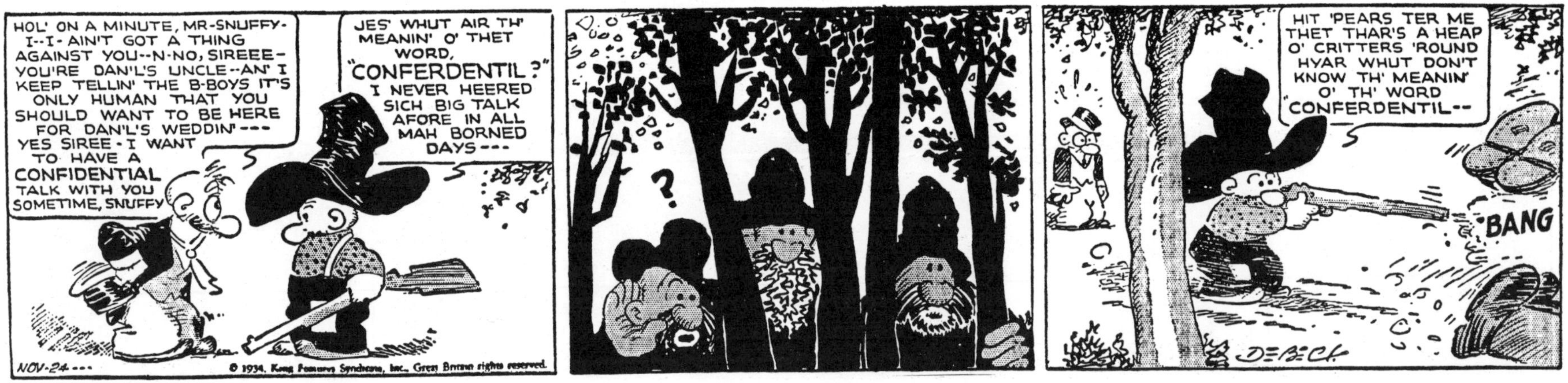
HOL' ON A MINUTE, MR-SNUFFY-I--I-AIN'T GOT A THING AGAINST YOU--N-NO, SIREEE-YOU'RE DAN'L'S UNCLE--AN' I KEEP TELLIN' THE B-BOYS IT'S ONLY HUMAN THAT YOU SHOULD WANT TO BE HERE FOR DAN'L'S WEDDIN'--- YES SIREE-I WANT TO HAVE A CONFIDENTIAL TALK WITH YOU SOMETIME, SNUFFY
JES' WHUT AIR TH' MEANIN' O' THET WORD, "CONFERDENTIL?" I NEVER HEERED SICH BIG TALK AFORE IN ALL MAH BORNED DAYS---
NOV-24---
© 1934, King Features Syndicate, Inc., Great Britain rights reserved.
?
HIT 'PEARS TER ME THET THAR'S A HEAP O' CRITTERS 'ROUND HYAR WHUT DON'T KNOW TH' MEANIN' O' TH' WORD "CONFERDENTIL--
BANG
DEBECK

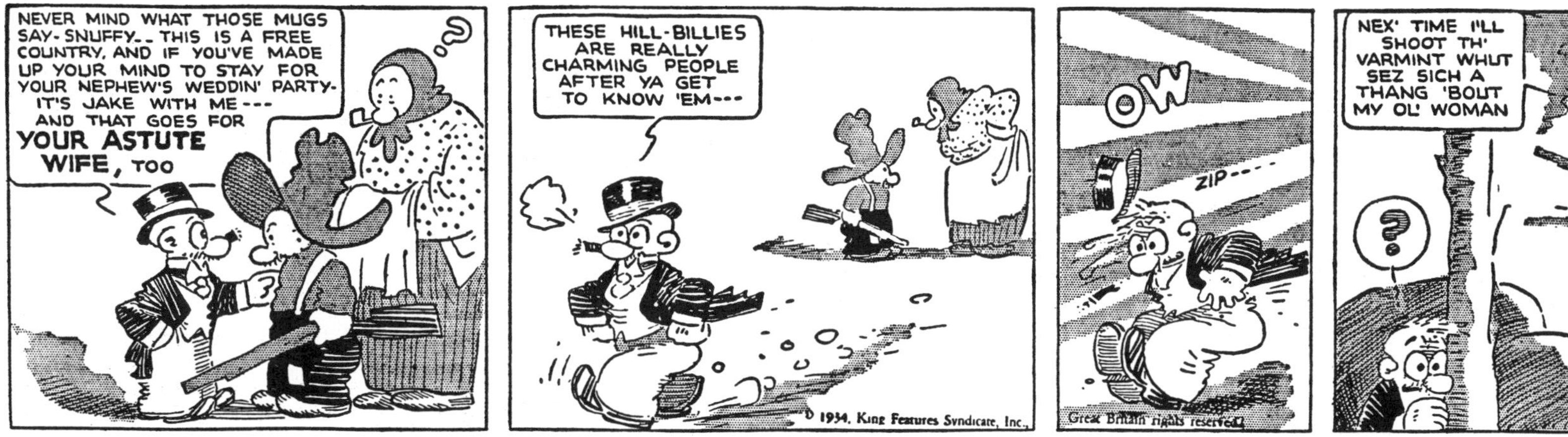
NEVER MIND WHAT THOSE MUGS SAY-SNUFFY-- THIS IS A FREE COUNTRY, AND IF YOU'VE MADE UP YOUR MIND TO STAY FOR YOUR NEPHEW'S WEDDIN' PARTY- IT'S JAKE WITH ME--- AND THAT GOES FOR YOUR ASTUTE WIFE, TOO
?
THESE HILL-BILLIES ARE REALLY CHARMING PEOPLE AFTER YA GET TO KNOW 'EM---
OW
ZIP----
NEX' TIME I'LL SHOOT TH' VARMINT WHUT SEZ SICH A THANG 'BOUT MY OL' WOMAN
?
DE BECK
11-26
© 1934, King Features Syndicate, Inc.,
Great Britain rights reserved.

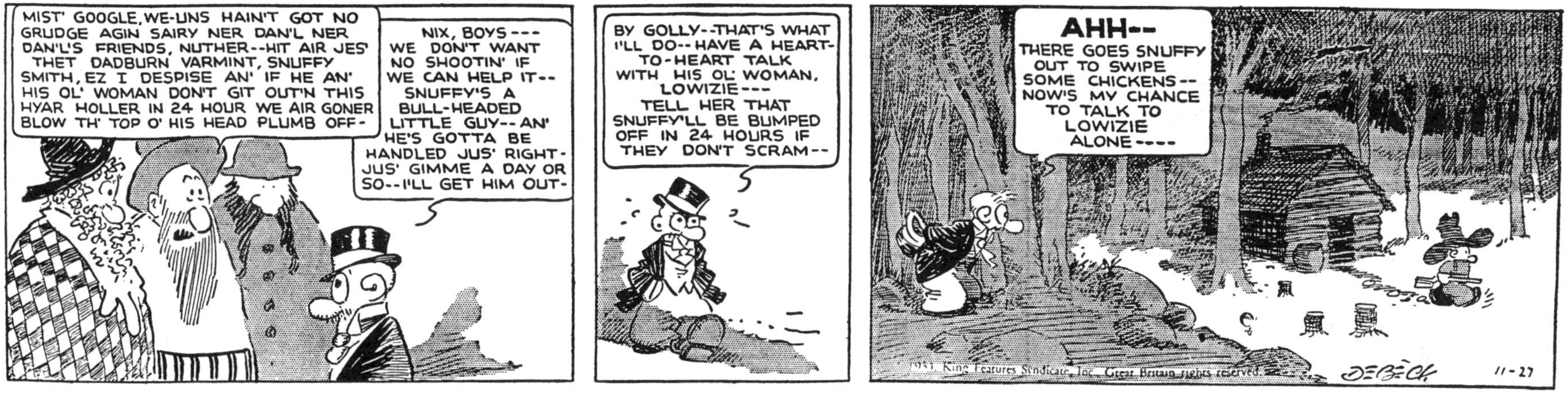
MIST' GOOGLE, WE-UNS HAIN'T GOT NO GRUDGE AGIN SAIRY NER DAN'L NER DAN'L'S FRIENDS, NUTHER--HIT AIR JES' THET DADBURN VARMINT, SNUFFY SMITH, EZ I DESPISE AN' IF HE AN' HIS OL' WOMAN DON'T GIT OUT'N THIS HYAR HOLLER IN 24 HOUR WE AIR GONER BLOW TH' TOP O' HIS HEAD PLUMB OFF-
NIX, BOYS--- WE DON'T WANT NO SHOOTIN' IF WE CAN HELP IT-- SNUFFY'S A BULL-HEADED LITTLE GUY--AN' HE'S GOTTA BE HANDLED JUS' RIGHT- JUS' GIMME A DAY OR SO--I'LL GET HIM OUT-
BY GOLLY--THAT'S WHAT I'LL DO--HAVE A HEART-TO-HEART TALK WITH HIS OL' WOMAN, LOWIZIE--- TELL HER THAT SNUFFY'LL BE BUMPED OFF IN 24 HOURS IF THEY DON'T SCRAM--
AHH-- THERE GOES SNUFFY OUT TO SWIPE SOME CHICKENS-- NOW'S MY CHANCE TO TALK TO LOWIZIE ALONE----
DE BECK
11-27
1934, King Features Syndicate, Inc. Great Britain rights reserved.

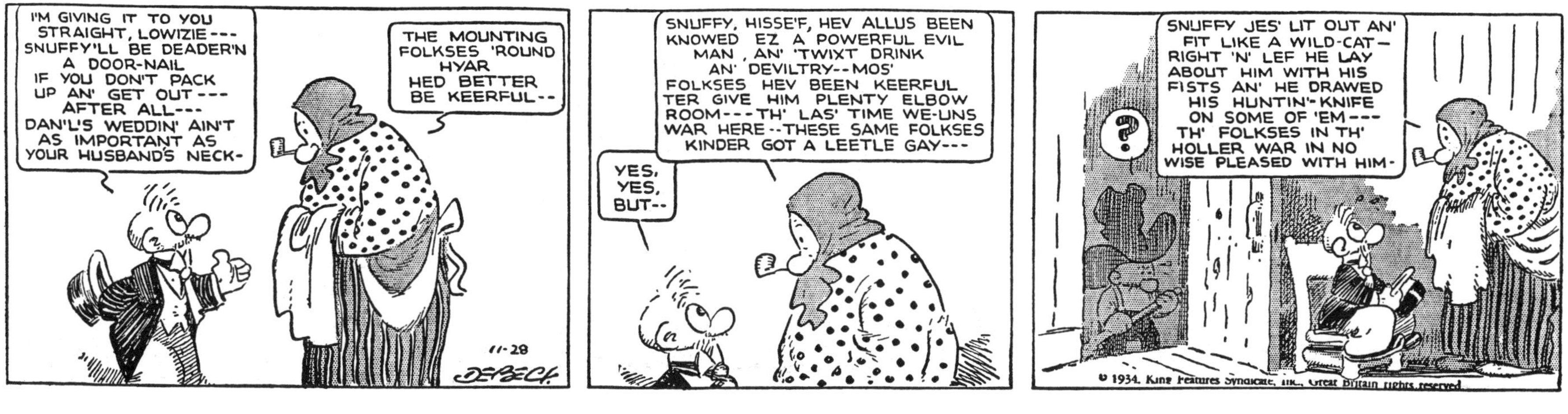
I'M GIVING IT TO YOU STRAIGHT, LOWIZIE--- SNUFFY'LL BE DEADER'N A DOOR-NAIL IF YOU DON'T PACK UP AN' GET OUT--- AFTER ALL--- DAN'L'S WEDDIN' AIN'T AS IMPORTANT AS YOUR HUSBAND'S NECK-
THE MOUNTING FOLKSES 'ROUND HYAR HED BETTER BE KEERFUL--
11-28
DE BECK
SNUFFY, HISSE'F, HEV ALLUS BEEN KNOWED EZ A POWERFUL EVIL MAN, AN' 'TWIXT DRINK AN' DEVILTRY--MOS' FOLKSES HEV BEEN KEERFUL TER GIVE HIM PLENTY ELBOW ROOM---TH' LAS' TIME WE-UNS WAR HERE--THESE SAME FOLKSES KINDER GOT A LEETLE GAY---
YES, YES, BUT--
?
SNUFFY JES' LIT OUT AN' FIT LIKE A WILD-CAT- RIGHT 'N' LEF HE LAY ABOUT HIM WITH HIS FISTS AN' HE DRAWED HIS HUNTIN'-KNIFE ON SOME OF 'EM--- TH' FOLKSES IN TH' HOLLER WAR IN NO WISE PLEASED WITH HIM-
© 1934, King Features Syndicate, Inc., Great Britain rights reserved.

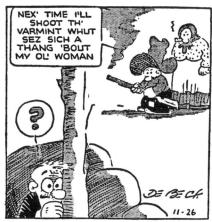

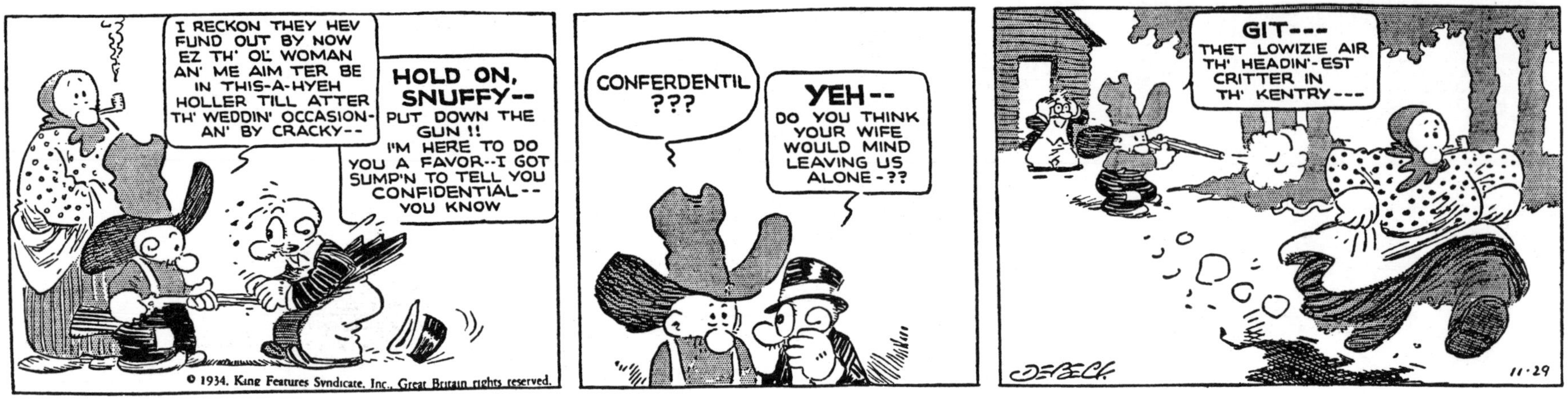
I RECKON THEY HEV FUND OUT BY NOW EZ TH' OL' WOMAN AN' ME AIM TER BE IN THIS-A-HYEH HOLLER TILL ATTER TH' WEDDIN' OCCASION--AN' BY CRACKY--
HOLD ON, SNUFFY-- PUT DOWN THE GUN !! I'M HERE TO DO YOU A FAVOR--I GOT SUMP'N TO TELL YOU CONFIDENTIAL-- YOU KNOW
© 1934, King Features Syndicate, Inc., Great Britain rights reserved.
CONFERDENTIL ???
YEH-- DO YOU THINK YOUR WIFE WOULD MIND LEAVING US ALONE-??
GIT--- THET LOWIZIE AIR TH' HEADIN'-EST CRITTER IN TH' KENTRY---
DEBECK
11-29

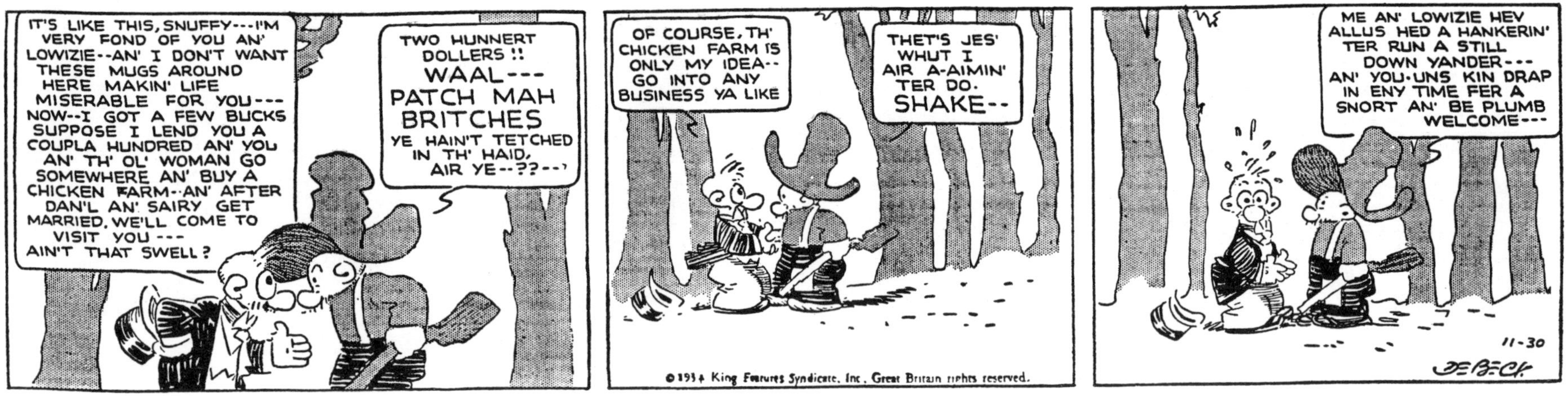
IT'S LIKE THIS, SNUFFY---I'M VERY FOND OF YOU AN' LOWIZIE--AN' I DON'T WANT THESE MUGS AROUND HERE MAKIN' LIFE MISERABLE FOR YOU--- NOW--I GOT A FEW BUCKS SUPPOSE I LEND YOU A COUPLA HUNDRED AN' YOU AN' TH' OL' WOMAN GO SOMEWHERE AN' BUY A CHICKEN FARM--AN' AFTER DAN'L AN' SAIRY GET MARRIED, WE'LL COME TO VISIT YOU--- AIN'T THAT SWELL?
TWO HUNNERT DOLLERS !! WAAL--- PATCH MAH BRITCHES YE HAIN'T TETCHED IN TH' HAID, AIR YE--??--
OF COURSE, TH' CHICKEN FARM IS ONLY MY IDEA-- GO INTO ANY BUSINESS YA LIKE
THET'S JES' WHUT I AIR A-AIMIN' TER DO. SHAKE--
© 1934 King Features Syndicate, Inc., Great Britain rights reserved.
ME AN' LOWIZIE HEV ALLUS HED A HANKERIN' TER RUN A STILL DOWN YANDER--- AN' YOU-UNS KIN DRAP IN ENY TIME FER A SNORT AN' BE PLUMB WELCOME---
11-30
DEBECK

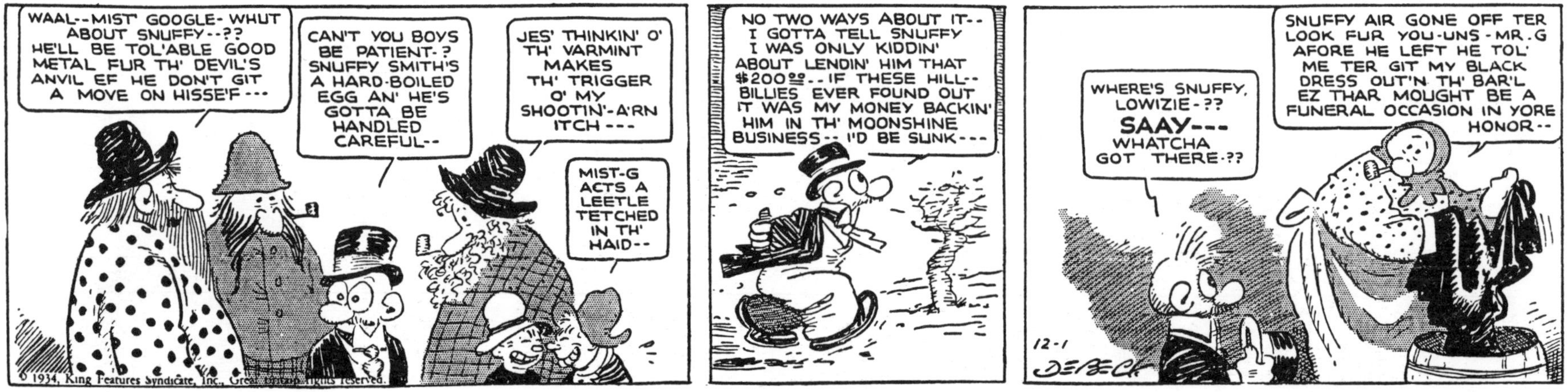
WAAL--MIST' GOOGLE- WHUT ABOUT SNUFFY--?? HE'LL BE TOL'ABLE GOOD METAL FUR TH' DEVIL'S ANVIL EF HE DON'T GIT A MOVE ON HISSE'F---
CAN'T YOU BOYS BE PATIENT-? SNUFFY SMITH'S A HARD-BOILED EGG AN' HE'S GOTTA BE HANDLED CAREFUL--
JES' THINKIN' O' TH' VARMINT MAKES TH' TRIGGER O' MY SHOOTIN'-A'RN ITCH---
MIST-G ACTS A LEETLE TETCHED IN TH' HAID--
© 1934, King Features Syndicate, Inc., Great Britain rights reserved.
NO TWO WAYS ABOUT IT-- I GOTTA TELL SNUFFY I WAS ONLY KIDDIN' ABOUT LENDIN' HIM THAT $200.00--IF THESE HILL--BILLIES EVER FOUND OUT IT WAS MY MONEY BACKIN' HIM IN TH' MOONSHINE BUSINESS-- I'D BE SUNK---
WHERE'S SNUFFY, LOWIZIE-?? SAAY--- WHATCHA GOT THERE-??
SNUFFY AIR GONE OFF TER LOOK FUR YOU-UNS-MR. G AFORE HE LEFT HE TOL' ME TER GIT MY BLACK DRESS OUT'N TH' BAR'L EZ THAR MOUGHT BE A FUNERAL OCCASION IN YORE HONOR--
12-1
DEBECK

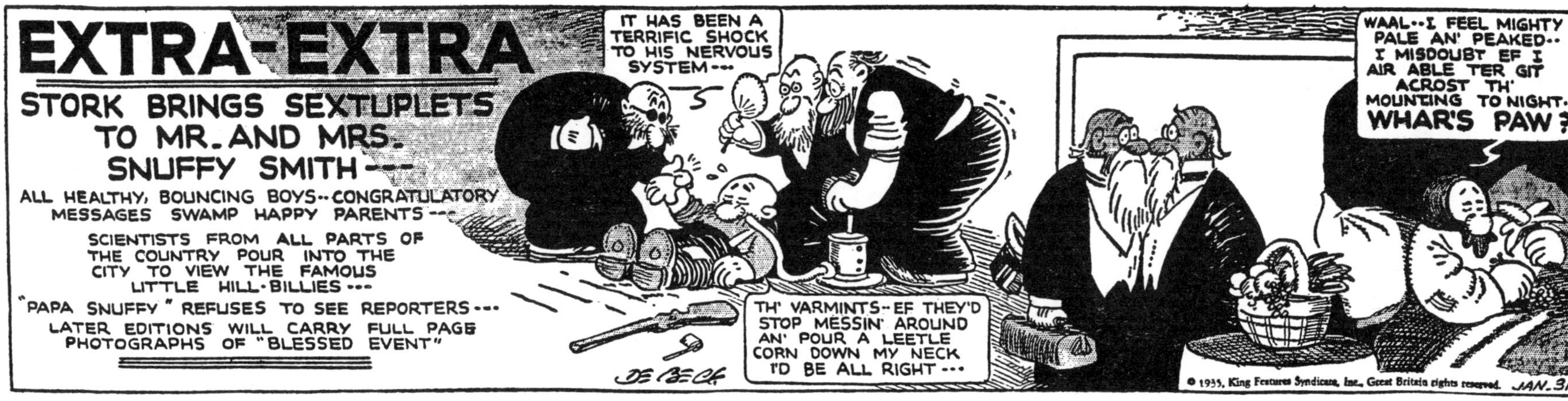
EXTRA-EXTRA
STORK BRINGS SEXTUPLETS TO MR. AND MRS. SNUFFY SMITH ---
ALL HEALTHY, BOUNCING BOYS -- CONGRATULATORY MESSAGES SWAMP HAPPY PARENTS ---
SCIENTISTS FROM ALL PARTS OF THE COUNTRY POUR INTO THE CITY TO VIEW THE FAMOUS LITTLE HILL-BILLIES ---
"PAPA SNUFFY" REFUSES TO SEE REPORTERS ---
LATER EDITIONS WILL CARRY FULL PAGE PHOTOGRAPHS OF "BLESSED EVENT"
DE BECK
IT HAS BEEN A TERRIFIC SHOCK TO HIS NERVOUS SYSTEM ---
TH' VARMINTS -- EF THEY'D STOP MESSIN' AROUND AN' POUR A LEETLE CORN DOWN MY NECK I'D BE ALL RIGHT ---
WAAL -- I FEEL MIGHTY PALE AN' PEAKED -- I MISDOUBT EF I AIR ABLE TER GIT ACROST TH' MOUNTING TO NIGHT. WHAR'S PAW?
© 1935, King Features Syndicate, Inc., Great Britain rights reserved.
JAN. 31.

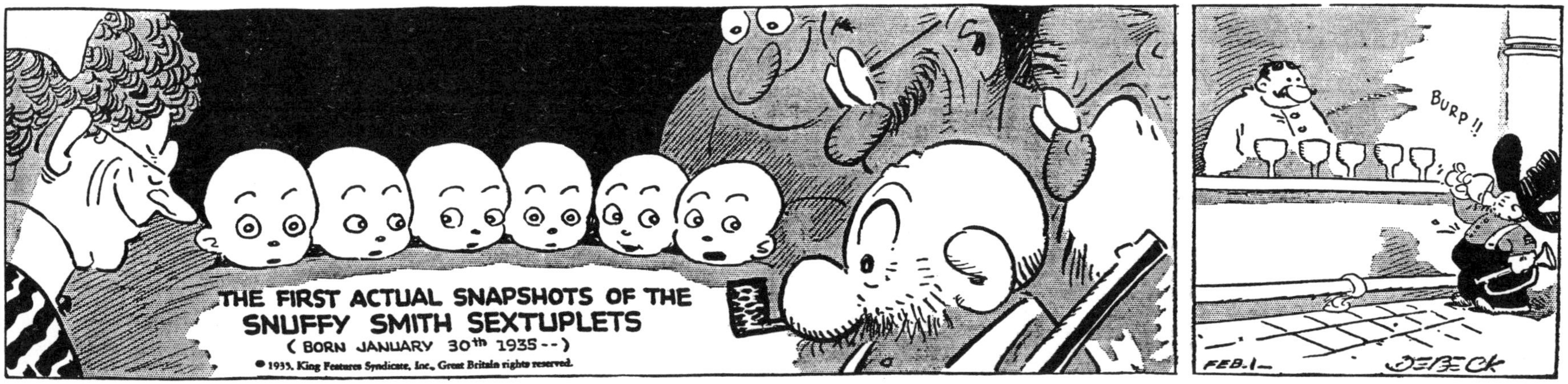
THE FIRST ACTUAL SNAPSHOTS OF THE SNUFFY SMITH SEXTUPLETS
(BORN JANUARY 30th 1935 --)
© 1935, King Features Syndicate, Inc., Great Britain rights reserved.
BURP !!
FEB. 1
DE BECK

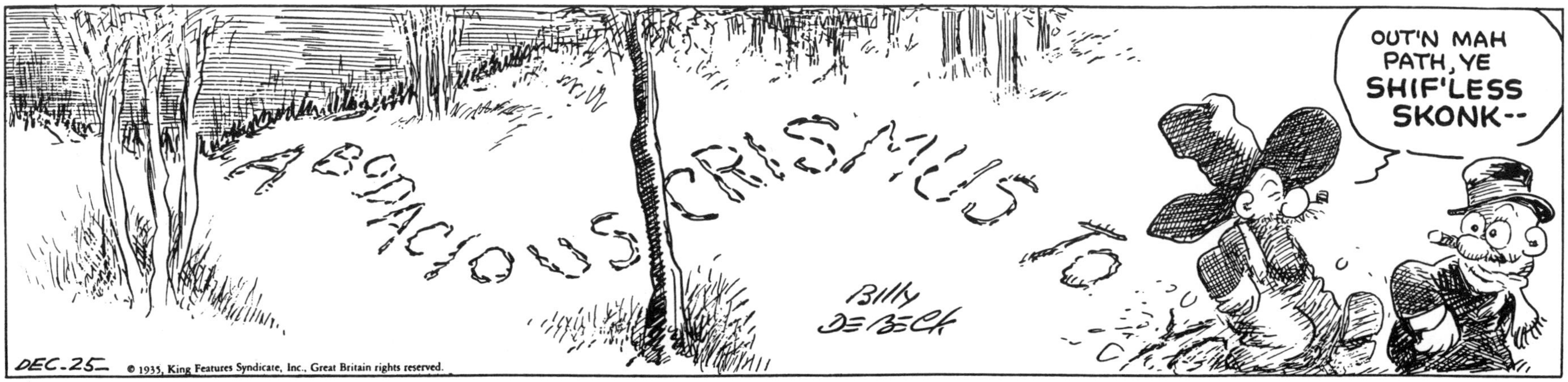
A BODACIOUS CRISMUS TO
OUT'N MAH PATH, YE SHIF'LESS SKONK --
Billy DE BECK
DEC. 25
© 1935, King Features Syndicate, Inc., Great Britain rights reserved.

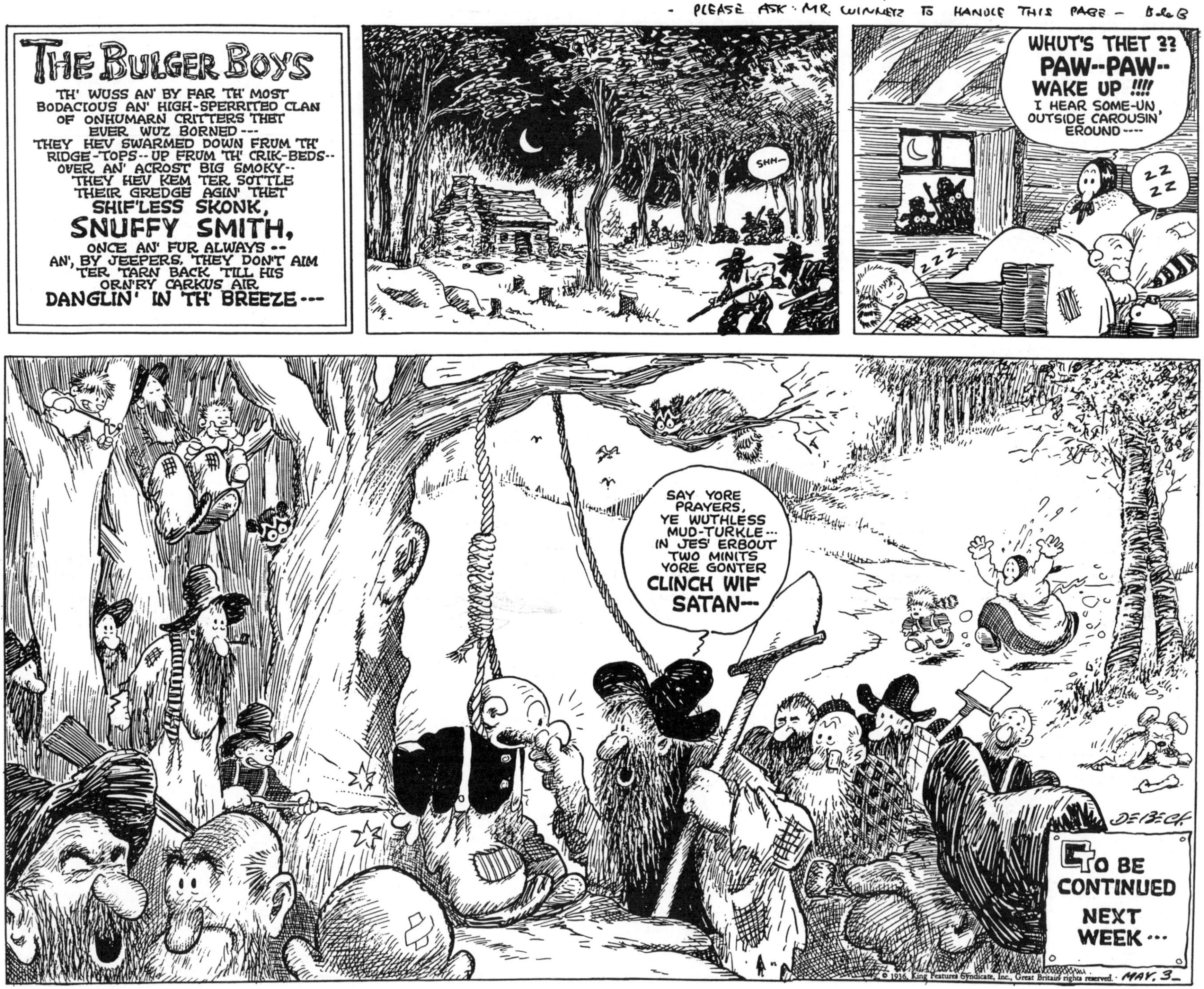

PLEASE ASK MR. WINNEYZ TO HANDLE THIS PAGE
THE BULGER BOYS
TH' WUSS AN' BY FAR TH' MOST BODACIOUS AN' HIGH-SPERRITED CLAN OF ONHUMARN CRITTERS THET EVER WUZ BORNED --- THEY HEV SWARMED DOWN FRUM TH' RIDGE-TOPS -- UP FRUM TH' CRIK-BEDS -- OVER AN' ACROST BIG SMOKY -- THEY HEV KEM TER SOTTLE THEIR GREDGE AGIN' THET SHIF'LESS SKONK, SNUFFY SMITH, ONCE AN' FUR ALWAYS -- AN', BY JEEPERS, THEY DON'T AIM TER TARN BACK TILL HIS ORN'RY CARKUS AIR DANGLIN' IN TH' BREEZE ---
SHH--
WHUT'S THET ?? PAW--PAW-- WAKE UP !!!! I HEAR SOME-UN OUTSIDE CAROUSIN' EROUND ----
Z Z Z Z
Z Z Z
SAY YORE PRAYERS, YE WUTHLESS MUD-TURKLE... IN JES' ERBOUT TWO MINITS YORE GONTER CLINCH WIF SATAN--
DE BECK
TO BE CONTINUED NEXT WEEK...
© 1936, King Features Syndicate, Inc., Great Britain rights reserved.
MAY. 3

Above: "Barney Google and Snuffy Smith" Sunday page, May 3, 1936. From the Collection of Bruce Bergstrom.

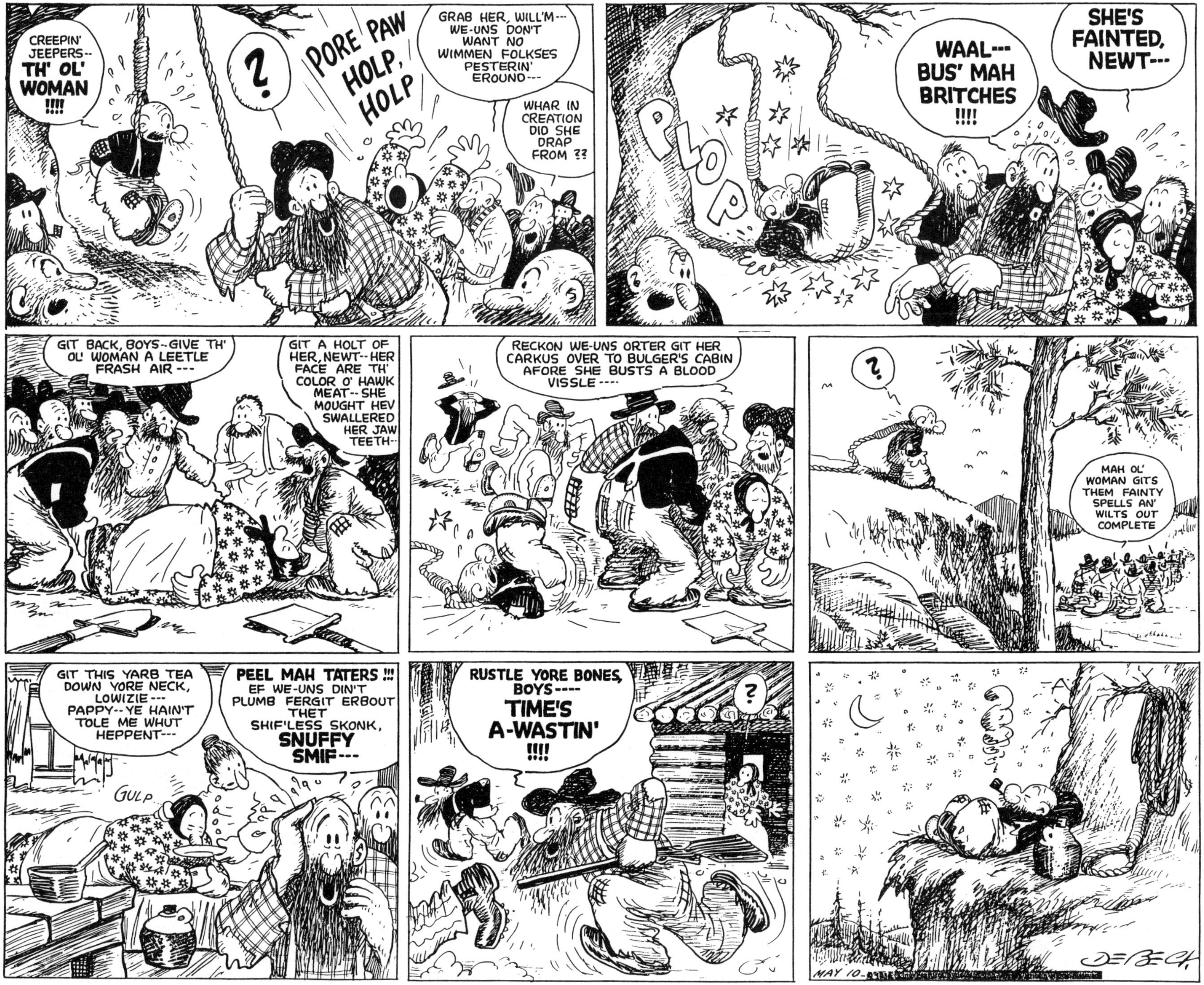

CREEPIN' JEEPERS-- TH' OL' WOMAN !!!!
?
PORE PAW HOLP, HOLP
GRAB HER, WILL'M--- WE-UNS DON'T WANT NO WIMMEN FOLKSES PESTERIN' EROUND---
WHAR IN CREATION DID SHE DRAP FROM ??
PLOP
WAAL--- BUS' MAH BRITCHES !!!!
SHE'S FAINTED, NEWT---
GIT BACK, BOYS--GIVE TH' OL' WOMAN A LEETLE FRASH AIR ---
GIT A HOLT OF HER, NEWT--HER FACE ARE TH' COLOR O' HAWK MEAT--SHE MOUGHT HEV SWALLERED HER JAW TEETH--
RECKON WE-UNS ORTER GIT HER CARKUS OVER TO BULGER'S CABIN AFORE SHE BUSTS A BLOOD VISSLE----
?
MAH OL' WOMAN GITS THEM FAINTY SPELLS AN' WILTS OUT COMPLETE
GIT THIS YARB TEA DOWN YORE NECK, LOWIZIE--- PAPPY--YE HAIN'T TOLE ME WHUT HEPPENT---
GULP
PEEL MAH TATERS !!! EF WE-UNS DIN'T PLUMB FERGIT ERBOUT THET SHIF'LESS SKONK, SNUFFY SMIF---
RUSTLE YORE BONES, BOYS---- TIME'S A-WASTIN' !!!!
?
MAY 10

Above: "Barney Google and Snuffy Smith" Sunday page, May 10, 1936. From the Collection of Morris Weiss.

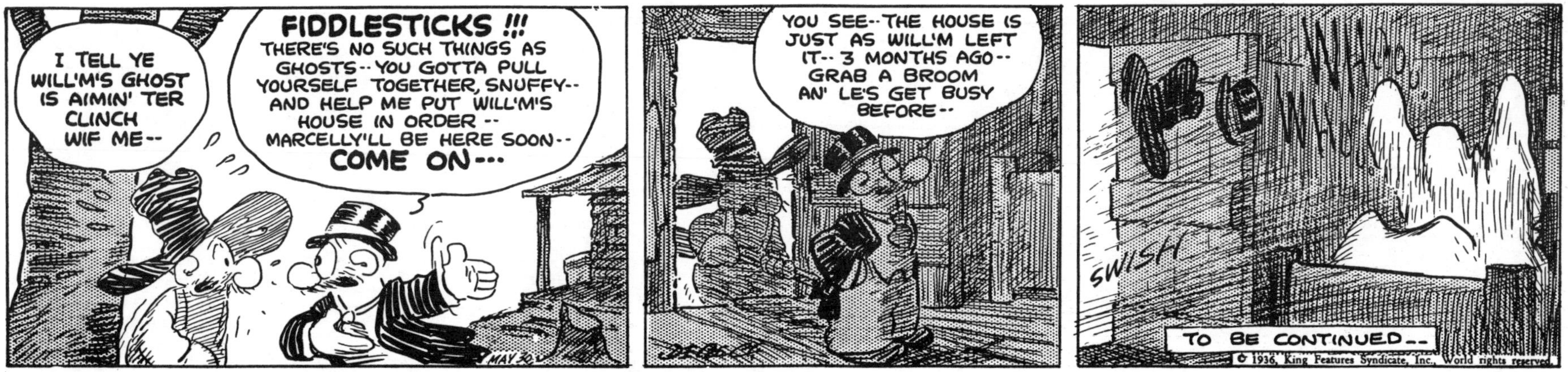
I TELL YE WILL'M'S GHOST IS AIMIN' TER CLINCH WIF ME--
FIDDLESTICKS !!! THERE'S NO SUCH THINGS AS GHOSTS--YOU GOTTA PULL YOURSELF TOGETHER, SNUFFY--AND HELP ME PUT WILL'M'S HOUSE IN ORDER--MARCELLY'LL BE HERE SOON--COME ON---
MAY 30
YOU SEE--THE HOUSE IS JUST AS WILL'M LEFT IT--3 MONTHS AGO--GRAB A BROOM AN' LE'S GET BUSY BEFORE--
DEBECK
SWISH
TO BE CONTINUED--
© 1936, King Features Syndicate, Inc., World rights reserved.

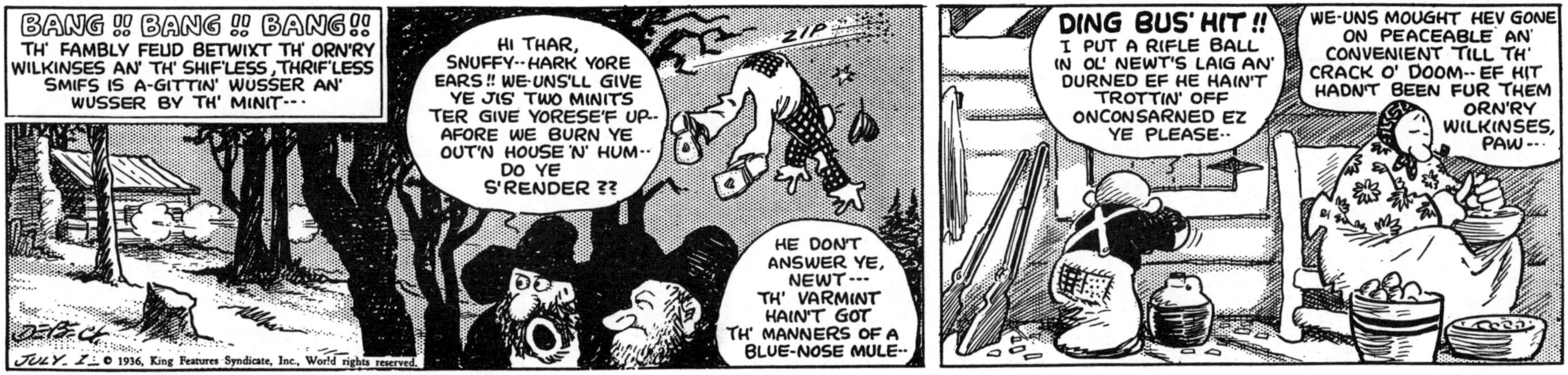
BANG !! BANG !! BANG !!
TH' FAMBLY FEUD BETWIXT TH' ORN'RY WILKINSES AN' TH' SHIF'LESS, THRIF'LESS SMIFS IS A-GITTIN' WUSSER AN' WUSSER BY TH' MINIT---
HI THAR, SNUFFY--HARK YORE EARS!! WE-UNS'LL GIVE YE JIS' TWO MINITS TER GIVE YORESE'F UP--AFORE WE BURN YE OUT'N HOUSE 'N' HUM--DO YE S'RENDER ??
ZIP
HE DON'T ANSWER YE, NEWT---TH' VARMINT HAIN'T GOT TH' MANNERS OF A BLUE-NOSE MULE--
DEBECK
JULY 1 © 1936, King Features Syndicate, Inc., World rights reserved.
DING BUS' HIT !! I PUT A RIFLE BALL IN OL' NEWT'S LAIG AN' DURNED EF HE HAIN'T TROTTIN' OFF ONCONSARNED EZ YE PLEASE--
WE-UNS MOUGHT HEV GONE ON PEACEABLE AN' CONVENIENT TILL TH' CRACK O' DOOM--EF HIT HADN'T BEEN FUR THEM ORN'RY WILKINSES, PAW---

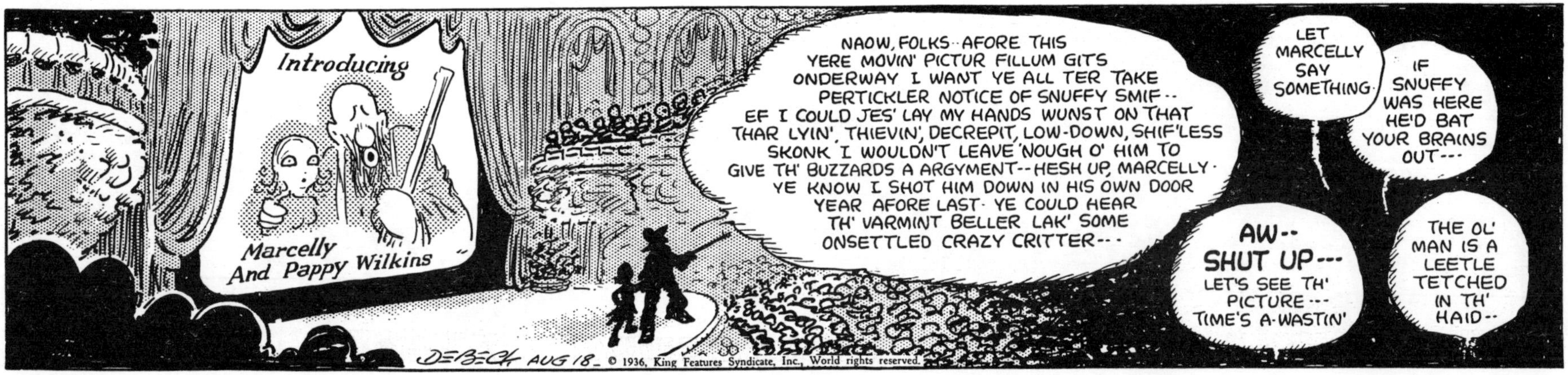
Introducing
Marcelly And Pappy Wilkins
NAOW, FOLKS--AFORE THIS YERE MOVIN' PICTUR FILLUM GITS ONDERWAY I WANT YE ALL TER TAKE PERTICKLER NOTICE OF SNUFFY SMIF--EF I COULD JES' LAY MY HANDS WUNST ON THAT THAR LYIN', THIEVIN', DECREPIT, LOW-DOWN, SHIF'LESS SKONK I WOULDN'T LEAVE 'NOUGH O' HIM TO GIVE TH' BUZZARDS A ARGYMENT--HESH UP, MARCELLY--YE KNOW I SHOT HIM DOWN IN HIS OWN DOOR YEAR AFORE LAST--YE COULD HEAR TH' VARMINT BELLER LAK' SOME ONSETTLED CRAZY CRITTER---
LET MARCELLY SAY SOMETHING
IF SNUFFY WAS HERE HE'D BAT YOUR BRAINS OUT---
AW--SHUT UP--- LET'S SEE TH' PICTURE---TIME'S A-WASTIN'
THE OL' MAN IS A LEETLE TETCHED IN TH' HAID--
DEBECK AUG 18 © 1936, King Features Syndicate, Inc., World rights reserved.

The "Barney Google and Snuffy Smith" daily comic strips from 1936 to 1945 are reproduced from syndicate proofs. Courtesy of King Features Syndicate.

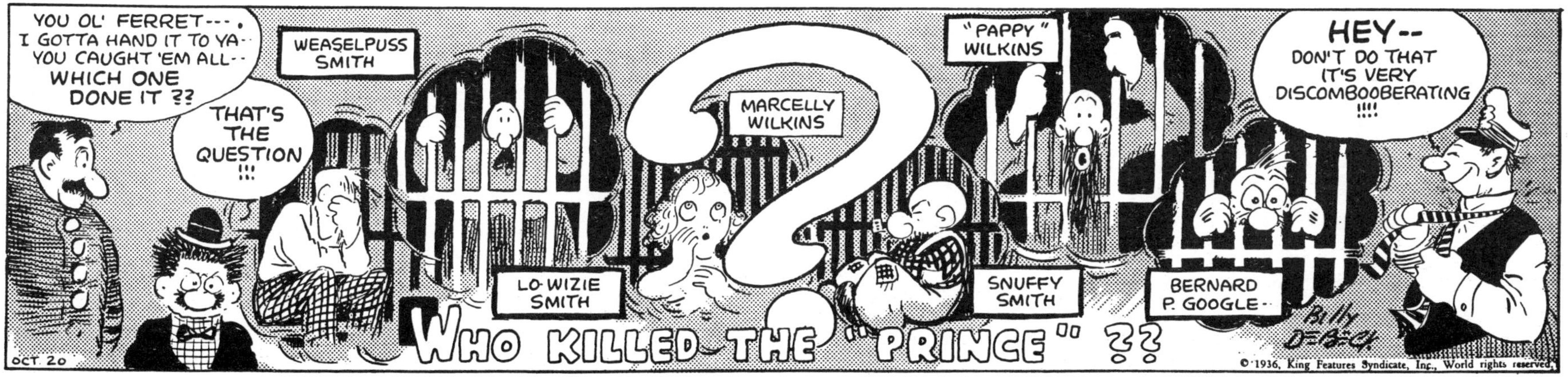
YOU OL' FERRET--- I GOTTA HAND IT TO YA-- YOU CAUGHT 'EM ALL-- WHICH ONE DONE IT ??
THAT'S THE QUESTION !!!
WEASELPUSS SMITH
MARCELLY WILKINS
"PAPPY" WILKINS
HEY-- DON'T DO THAT IT'S VERY DISCOMBOOBERATING !!!!
LO-WIZIE SMITH
SNUFFY SMITH
BERNARD P. GOOGLE--
WHO KILLED THE "PRINCE" ??
BILLY DEBECK
OCT. 20
© 1936, King Features Syndicate, Inc., World rights reserved.

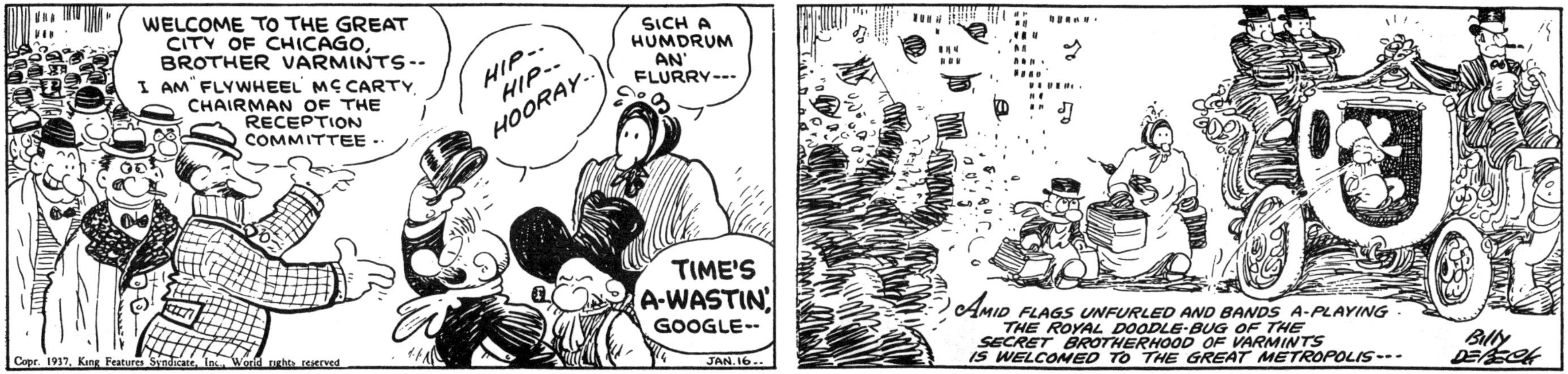
WELCOME TO THE GREAT CITY OF CHICAGO, BROTHER VARMINTS-- I AM "FLYWHEEL" McCARTY, CHAIRMAN OF THE RECEPTION COMMITTEE--
HIP-- HIP-- HOORAY--
SICH A HUMDRUM AN' FLURRY---
TIME'S A-WASTIN', GOOGLE--
Copr. 1937, King Features Syndicate, Inc., World rights reserved
JAN. 16--
AMID FLAGS UNFURLED AND BANDS A-PLAYING THE ROYAL DOODLE-BUG OF THE SECRET BROTHERHOOD OF VARMINTS IS WELCOMED TO THE GREAT METROPOLIS---
BILLY DEBECK

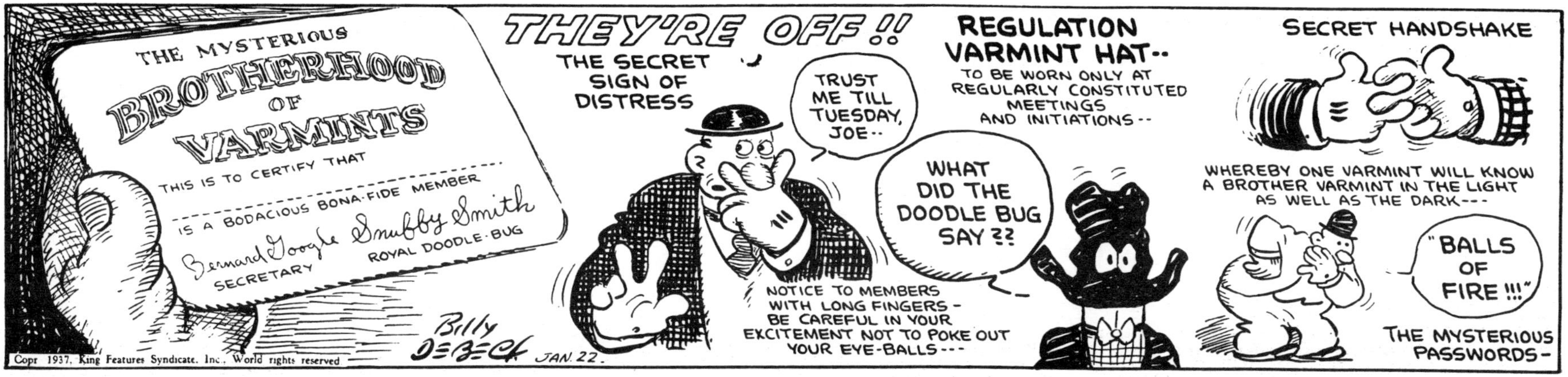
THE MYSTERIOUS BROTHERHOOD OF VARMINTS
THIS IS TO CERTIFY THAT
IS A BODACIOUS BONA-FIDE MEMBER
Bernard Google SECRETARY
Snuffy Smith ROYAL DOODLE-BUG
THEY'RE OFF !!
THE SECRET SIGN OF DISTRESS
TRUST ME TILL TUESDAY, JOE--
NOTICE TO MEMBERS WITH LONG FINGERS - BE CAREFUL IN YOUR EXCITEMENT NOT TO POKE OUT YOUR EYE-BALLS---
REGULATION VARMINT HAT-- TO BE WORN ONLY AT REGULARLY CONSTITUTED MEETINGS AND INITIATIONS--
WHAT DID THE DOODLE BUG SAY ??
SECRET HANDSHAKE
WHEREBY ONE VARMINT WILL KNOW A BROTHER VARMINT IN THE LIGHT AS WELL AS THE DARK---
"BALLS OF FIRE !!!"
THE MYSTERIOUS PASSWORDS-
BILLY DEBECK JAN. 22.
Copr. 1937, King Features Syndicate, Inc., World rights reserved

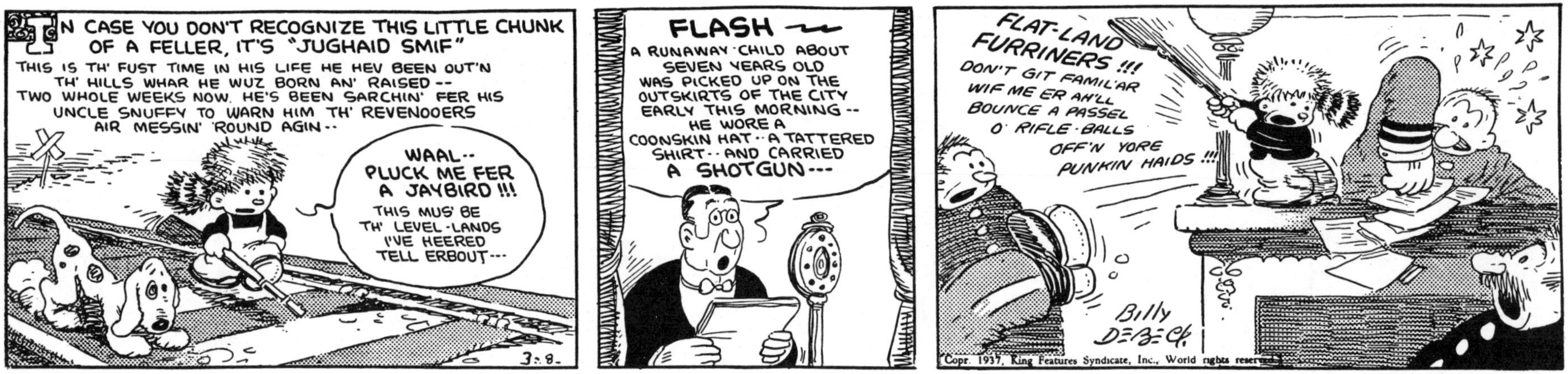
IN CASE YOU DON'T RECOGNIZE THIS LITTLE CHUNK OF A FELLER, IT'S "JUGHAID SMIF"
THIS IS TH' FUST TIME IN HIS LIFE HE HEV BEEN OUT'N TH' HILLS WHAR HE WUZ BORN AN' RAISED -- TWO WHOLE WEEKS NOW. HE'S BEEN SARCHIN' FER HIS UNCLE SNUFFY TO WARN HIM TH' REVENOOERS AIR MESSIN' 'ROUND AGIN --
WAAL -- PLUCK ME FER A JAYBIRD !!! THIS MUS' BE TH' LEVEL-LANDS I'VE HEERED TELL ERBOUT ---
3-8-
FLASH
A RUNAWAY CHILD ABOUT SEVEN YEARS OLD WAS PICKED UP ON THE OUTSKIRTS OF THE CITY EARLY THIS MORNING -- HE WORE A COONSKIN HAT -- A TATTERED SHIRT -- AND CARRIED A SHOTGUN ---
FLAT-LAND FURRINERS !!! DON'T GIT FAMIL'AR WIF ME ER AH'LL BOUNCE A PASSEL O' RIFLE-BALLS OFF'N YORE PUNKIN HAIDS !!!
Billy DeBeck
Copr. 1937, King Features Syndicate, Inc., World rights reserved

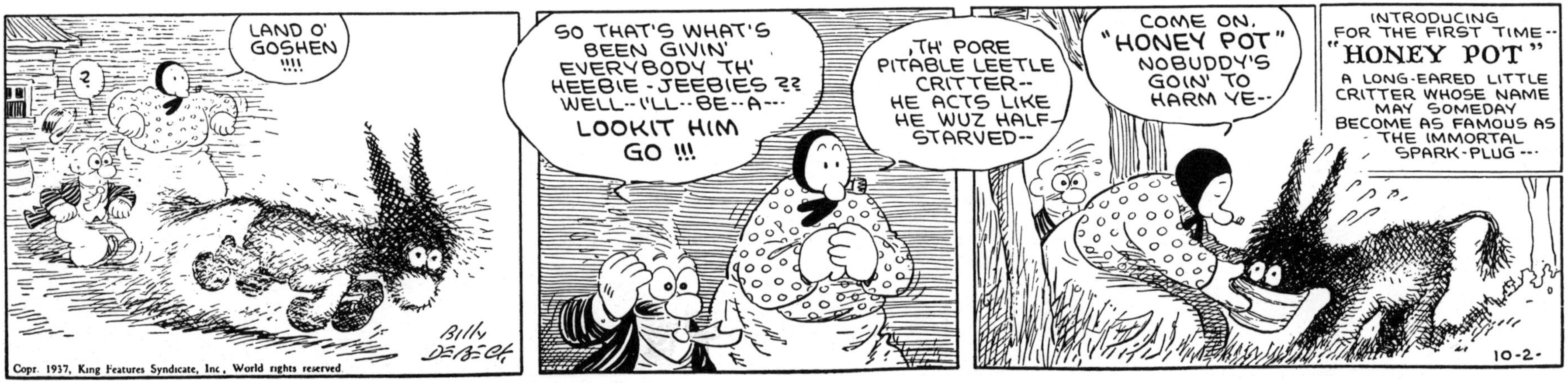
LAND O' GOSHEN !!!!
?
Billy DeBeck
Copr. 1937, King Features Syndicate, Inc., World rights reserved
SO THAT'S WHAT'S BEEN GIVIN' EVERYBODY TH' HEEBIE-JEEBIES ??? WELL -- I'LL -- BE -- A --- LOOKIT HIM GO !!!
TH' PORE PITABLE LEETLE CRITTER -- HE ACTS LIKE HE WUZ HALF-STARVED --
COME ON, "HONEY POT" NOBUDDY'S GOIN' TO HARM YE --
INTRODUCING FOR THE FIRST TIME -- "HONEY POT" A LONG-EARED LITTLE CRITTER WHOSE NAME MAY SOMEDAY BECOME AS FAMOUS AS THE IMMORTAL SPARK-PLUG ---
10-2-

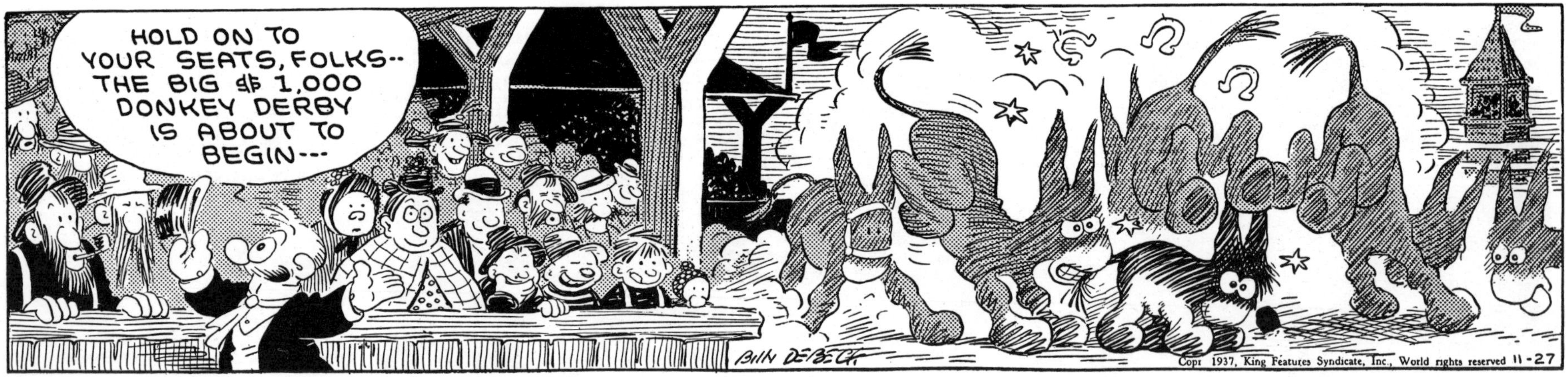
HOLD ON TO YOUR SEATS, FOLKS -- THE BIG $ 1,000 DONKEY DERBY IS ABOUT TO BEGIN ---
BILLY DEBECK
Copr. 1937, King Features Syndicate, Inc., World rights reserved 11-27

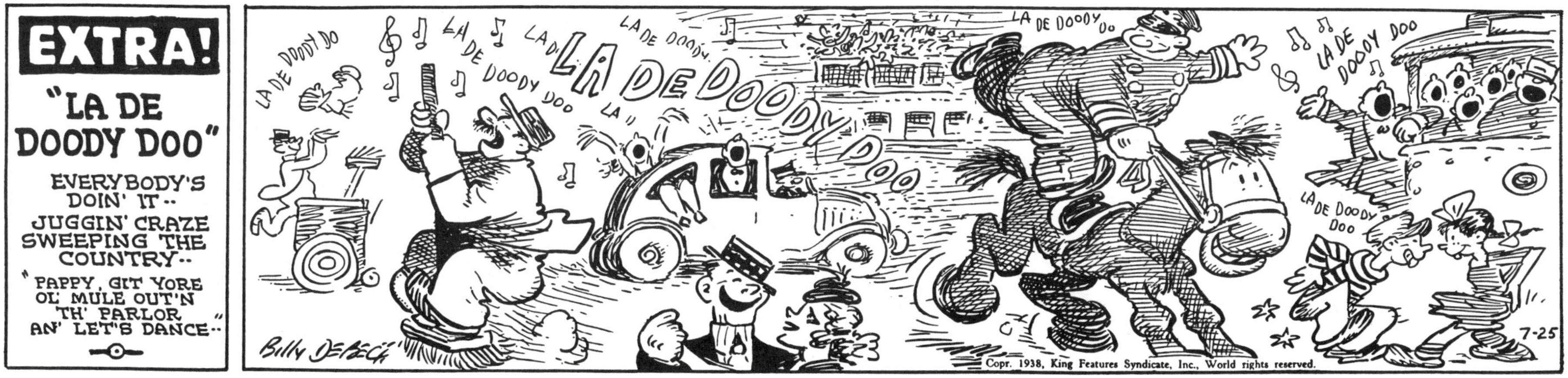
EXTRA!
"LA DE DOODY DOO"
EVERYBODY'S DOIN' IT -- JUGGIN' CRAZE SWEEPING THE COUNTRY --
"PAPPY, GIT YORE OL' MULE OUT'N TH' PARLOR AN' LET'S DANCE" --
LA DE DOODY DO
LA DE DOODY DOO LA
LA DE DOODY
LA DE DOODY DOO
LA DE DOODY DOO
LA DE DOODY DOO
LA DE DOODY DOO
BILLY DEBECK
7-25
Copr. 1938, King Features Syndicate, Inc., World rights reserved.

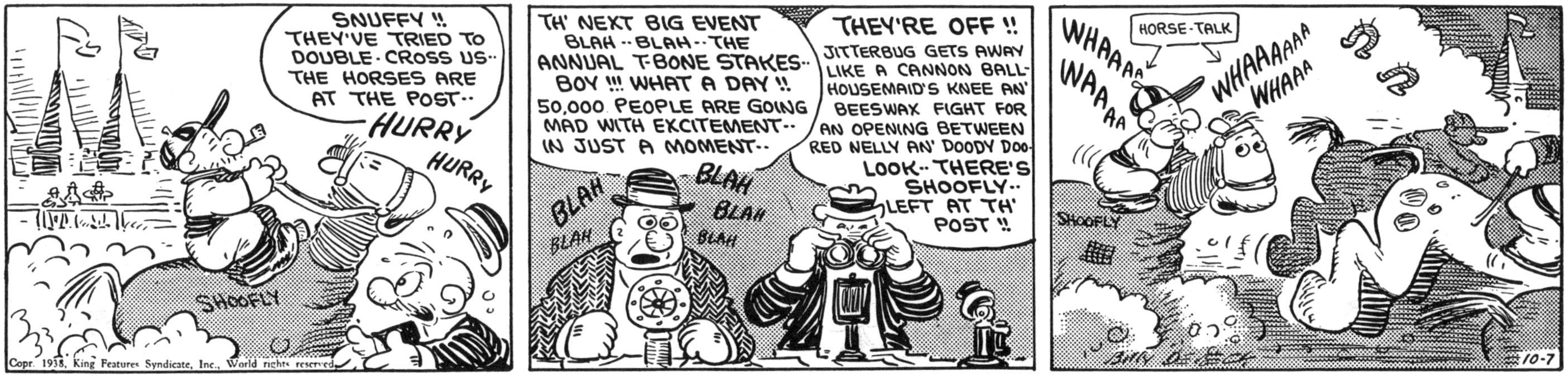
SNUFFY !! THEY'VE TRIED TO DOUBLE-CROSS US -- THE HORSES ARE AT THE POST --
HURRY
HURRY
SHOOFLY
Copr. 1938, King Features Syndicate, Inc., World rights reserved
TH' NEXT BIG EVENT BLAH -- BLAH -- THE ANNUAL T-BONE STAKES -- BOY !!! WHAT A DAY !! 50,000 PEOPLE ARE GOING MAD WITH EXCITEMENT -- IN JUST A MOMENT --
BLAH BLAH BLAH BLAH BLAH BLAH
THEY'RE OFF !! JITTERBUG GETS AWAY LIKE A CANNON BALL -- HOUSEMAID'S KNEE AN' BEESWAX FIGHT FOR AN OPENING BETWEEN RED NELLY AN' DOODY DOO -- LOOK -- THERE'S SHOOFLY -- LEFT AT TH' POST !!
HORSE-TALK
WHAAAAA WAAAAA
WHAAAAAAA WHAAA
SHOOFLY
BILLY DEBECK
10-7

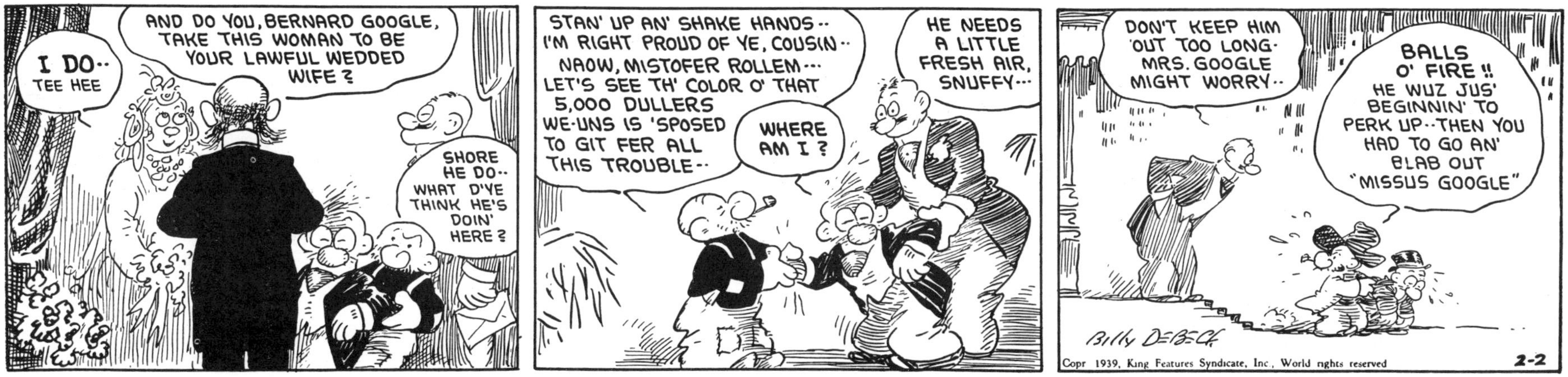
I DO -- TEE HEE
AND DO YOU, BERNARD GOOGLE, TAKE THIS WOMAN TO BE YOUR LAWFUL WEDDED WIFE ?
SHORE HE DO -- WHAT D'YE THINK HE'S DOIN' HERE ?
STAN' UP AN' SHAKE HANDS -- I'M RIGHT PROUD OF YE, COUSIN -- NAOW, MISTOFER ROLLEM --- LET'S SEE TH' COLOR O' THAT 5,000 DULLERS WE-UNS IS 'SPOSED TO GIT FER ALL THIS TROUBLE --
WHERE AM I ?
HE NEEDS A LITTLE FRESH AIR, SNUFFY ---
DON'T KEEP HIM OUT TOO LONG -- MRS. GOOGLE MIGHT WORRY --
BALLS O' FIRE !! HE WUZ JUS' BEGINNIN' TO PERK UP -- THEN YOU HAD TO GO AN' BLAB OUT "MISSUS GOOGLE"
BILLY DEBECK
Copr 1939, King Features Syndicate, Inc., World rights reserved
2-2

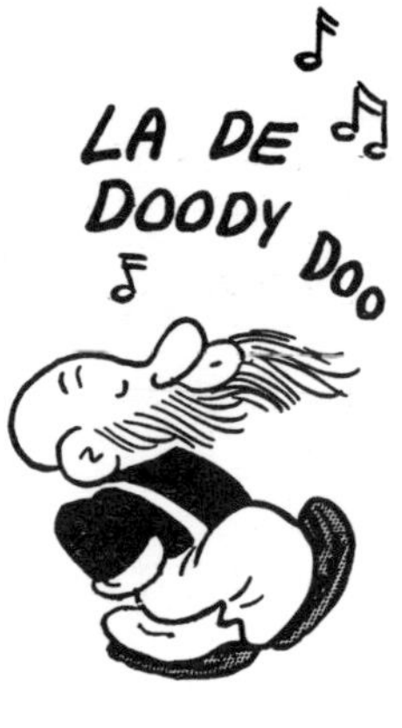
LA DE DOODY DOO

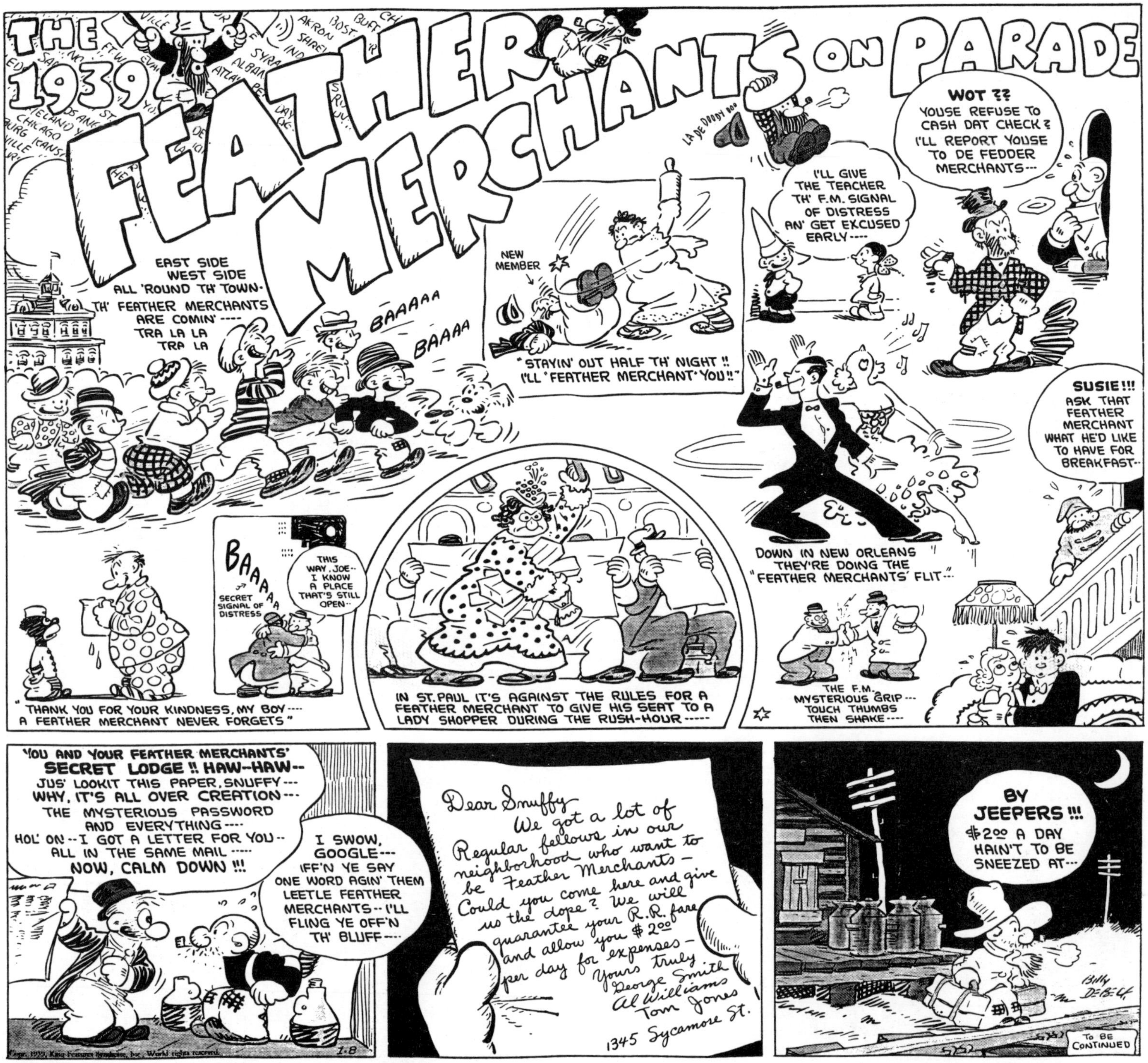
THE 1939 FEATHER MERCHANTS ON PARADE
EAST SIDE WEST SIDE ALL 'ROUND TH' TOWN. TH' FEATHER MERCHANTS ARE COMIN'---- TRA LA LA TRA LA
BAAAAA
BAAAA
NEW MEMBER
"STAYIN' OUT HALF TH' NIGHT !! I'LL 'FEATHER MERCHANT' YOU !!"
LA DE DOODY DOO
I'LL GIVE THE TEACHER TH' F.M. SIGNAL OF DISTRESS AN' GET EXCUSED EARLY----
WOT ?? YOUSE REFUSE TO CASH DAT CHECK ? I'LL REPORT YOUSE TO DE FEDDER MERCHANTS---
DOWN IN NEW ORLEANS THEY'RE DOING THE "FEATHER MERCHANTS' FLIT".
SUSIE!!! ASK THAT FEATHER MERCHANT WHAT HE'D LIKE TO HAVE FOR BREAKFAST-
BAAAAAA
SECRET SIGNAL OF DISTRESS
THIS WAY, JOE- I KNOW A PLACE THAT'S STILL OPEN-
"THANK YOU FOR YOUR KINDNESS, MY BOY---- A FEATHER MERCHANT NEVER FORGETS"
IN ST. PAUL IT'S AGAINST THE RULES FOR A FEATHER MERCHANT TO GIVE HIS SEAT TO A LADY SHOPPER DURING THE RUSH-HOUR-----
THE F.M. MYSTERIOUS GRIP--- TOUCH THUMBS THEN SHAKE----
YOU AND YOUR FEATHER MERCHANTS' SECRET LODGE !! HAW--HAW-- JUS' LOOKIT THIS PAPER, SNUFFY--- WHY, IT'S ALL OVER CREATION--- THE MYSTERIOUS PASSWORD AND EVERYTHING---- HOL' ON--I GOT A LETTER FOR YOU-- ALL IN THE SAME MAIL ----- NOW, CALM DOWN !!!
I SWOW, GOOGLE--- IFF'N YE SAY ONE WORD AGIN' THEM LEETLE FEATHER MERCHANTS--I'LL FLING YE OFF'N TH' BLUFF----
1-8
Dear Snuffy
We got a lot of Regular fellows in our neighborhood who want to be Feather Merchants - Could you come here and give us the dope? We will guarantee your R.R. fare and allow you $2.00 per day for expenses -
Yours truly
George Smith
Al Williams
Tom Jones
1345 Sycamore St.
BY JEEPERS !!! $2.00 A DAY HAIN'T TO BE SNEEZED AT---
Billy DeBeck
TO BE CONTINUED

Right: "Barney Google and Snuffy Smith" Sunday page, January 8, 1939. Courtesy of King Features Syndicate.

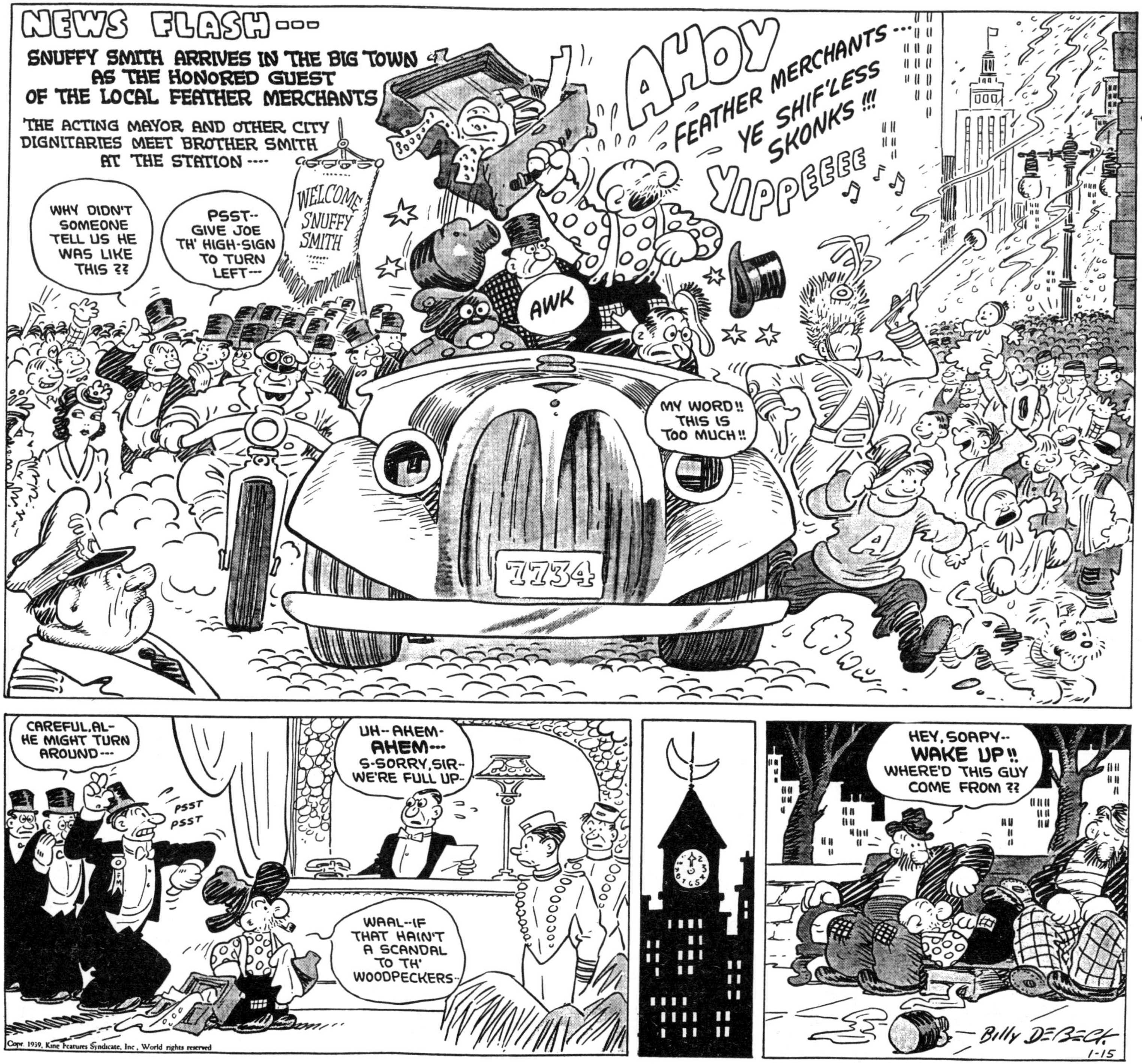
NEWS FLASH---
SNUFFY SMITH ARRIVES IN THE BIG TOWN AS THE HONORED GUEST OF THE LOCAL FEATHER MERCHANTS
THE ACTING MAYOR AND OTHER CITY DIGNITARIES MEET BROTHER SMITH AT THE STATION ----
WELCOME SNUFFY SMITH
WHY DIDN'T SOMEONE TELL US HE WAS LIKE THIS ??
PSST-- GIVE JOE TH' HIGH-SIGN TO TURN LEFT---
AHOY FEATHER MERCHANTS--- YE SHIF'LESS SKONKS !!!
YIPPEEEE
AWK
MY WORD!! THIS IS TOO MUCH!!
7734
CAREFUL, AL- HE MIGHT TURN AROUND---
PSST PSST
UH--AHEM- AHEM--- S-SORRY, SIR- WE'RE FULL UP-
WAAL--IF THAT HAIN'T A SCANDAL TO TH' WOODPECKERS-
HEY, SOAPY-- WAKE UP!! WHERE'D THIS GUY COME FROM ??
Copr. 1939, Kine Features Syndicate, Inc , World rights reserved
BILLY DEBECK
1-15

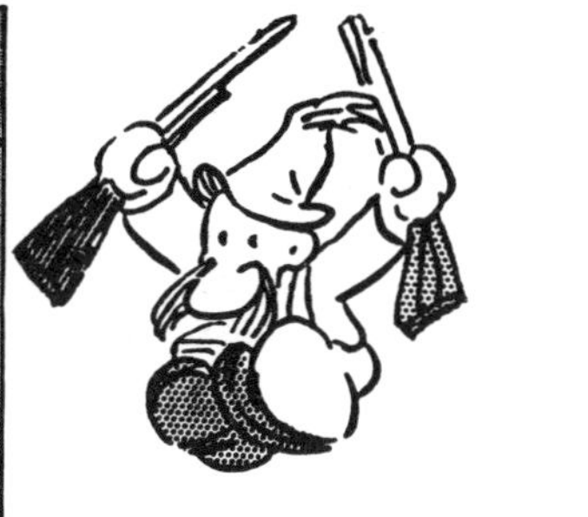

Left: "Barney Google and Snuffy Smith" Sunday page, January 15, 1939. Courtesy of King Features Syndicate.

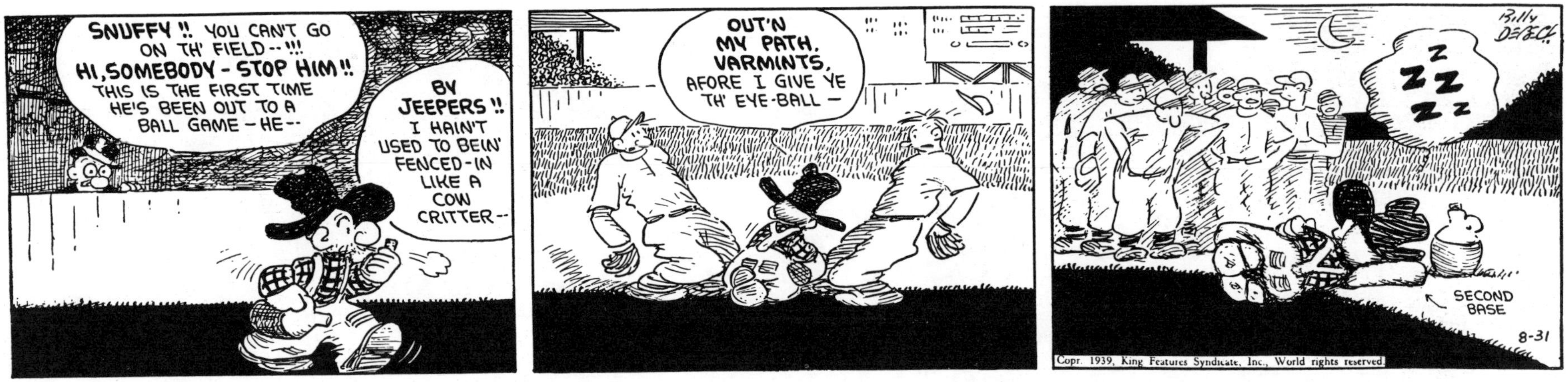
SNUFFY !! YOU CAN'T GO ON TH' FIELD--!!! HI, SOMEBODY - STOP HIM !! THIS IS THE FIRST TIME HE'S BEEN OUT TO A BALL GAME - HE--
BY JEEPERS !! I HAIN'T USED TO BEIN' FENCED-IN LIKE A COW CRITTER--
OUT'N MY PATH, VARMINTS, AFORE I GIVE YE TH' EYE-BALL -
Billy DeBeck
Z Z Z Z Z
SECOND BASE
8-31
Copr. 1939, King Features Syndicate, Inc., World rights reserved.

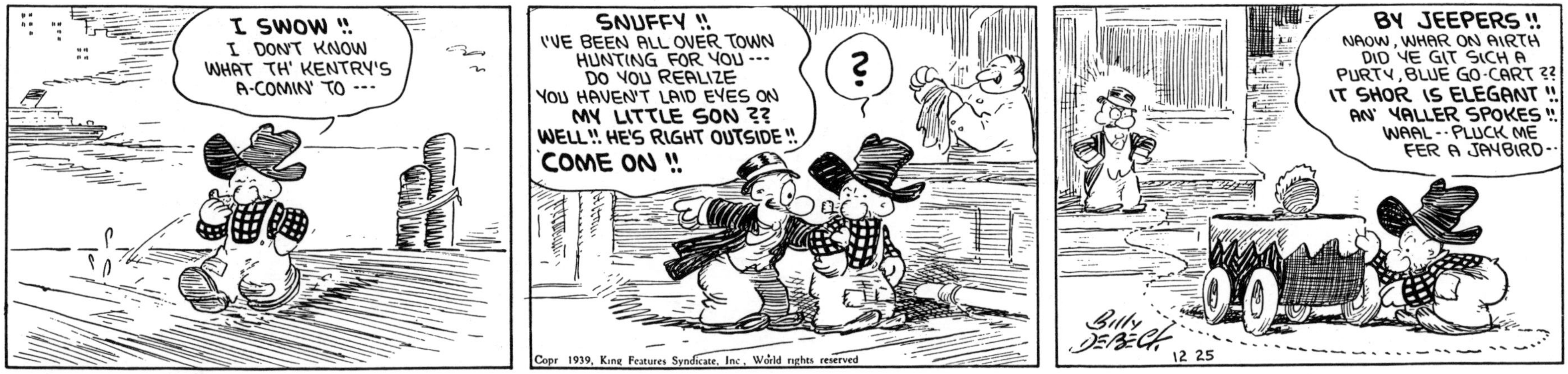
I SWOW !! I DON'T KNOW WHAT TH' KENTRY'S A-COMIN' TO ---
SNUFFY !! I'VE BEEN ALL OVER TOWN HUNTING FOR YOU --- DO YOU REALIZE YOU HAVEN'T LAID EYES ON MY LITTLE SON ?? WELL !! HE'S RIGHT OUTSIDE !! COME ON !!
?
Copr 1939, King Features Syndicate, Inc., World rights reserved
BY JEEPERS !! NAOW, WHAR ON AIRTH DID YE GIT SICH A PURTY, BLUE GO-CART ?? IT SHOR IS ELEGANT !! AN' YALLER SPOKES !! WAAL -- PLUCK ME FER A JAYBIRD--
Billy DeBeck
12 25

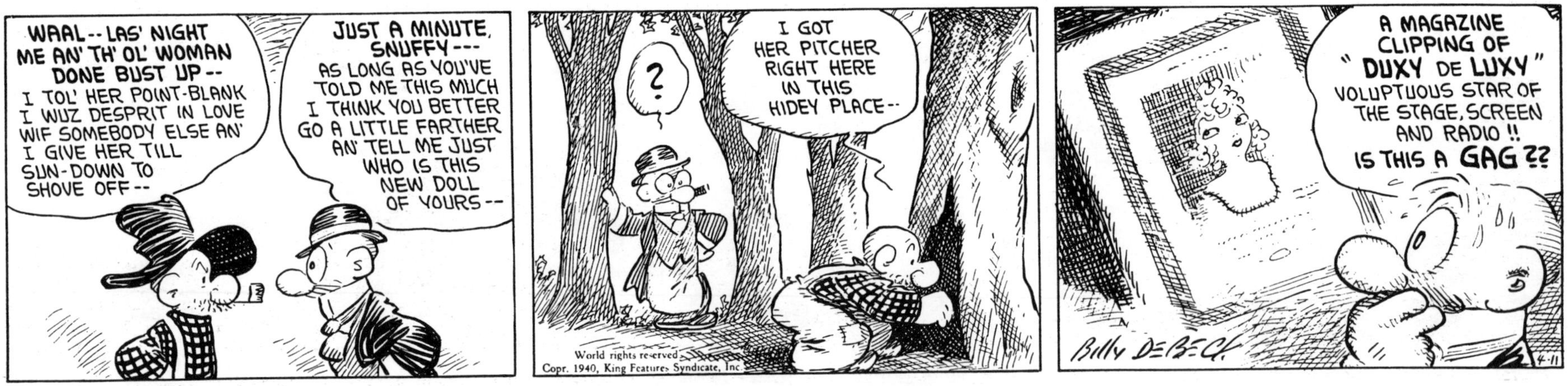
WAAL -- LAS' NIGHT ME AN' TH' OL' WOMAN DONE BUST UP -- I TOL' HER POINT-BLANK I WUZ DESPRIT IN LOVE WIF SOMEBODY ELSE AN' I GIVE HER TILL SUN-DOWN TO SHOVE OFF --
JUST A MINUTE, SNUFFY --- AS LONG AS YOU'VE TOLD ME THIS MUCH I THINK YOU BETTER GO A LITTLE FARTHER AN' TELL ME JUST WHO IS THIS NEW DOLL OF YOURS --
?
I GOT HER PITCHER RIGHT HERE IN THIS HIDEY PLACE--
World rights reserved
Copr. 1940, King Features Syndicate, Inc.
A MAGAZINE CLIPPING OF "DUXY DE LUXY" VOLUPTUOUS STAR OF THE STAGE, SCREEN AND RADIO !! IS THIS A GAG ??
Billy DeBeck
4-11

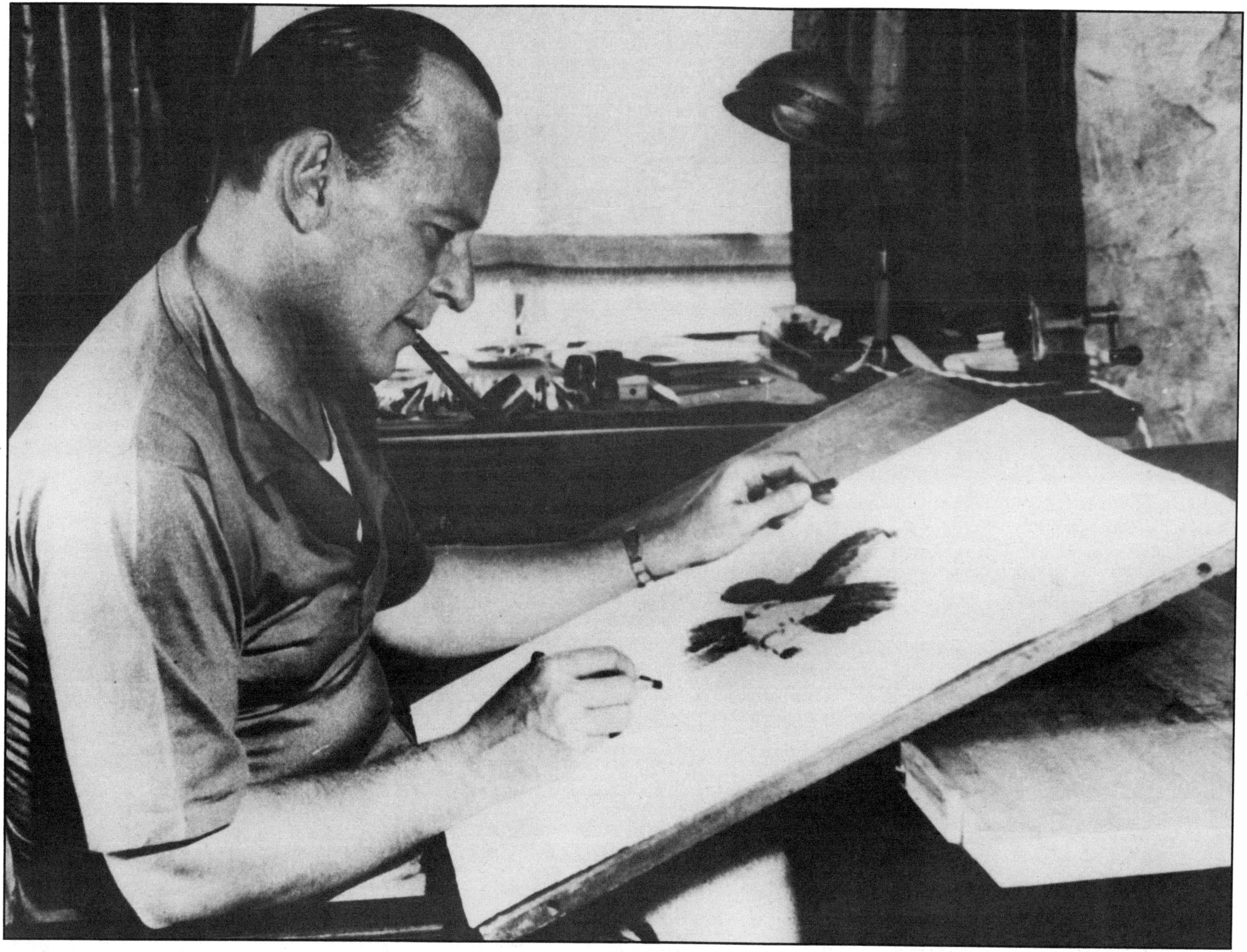

Above: This King Features Syndicate promotion photograph of Billy DeBeck from 1940 appeared in many of his obituaries in November, 1942. Courtesy of Ed Black.

Snuffy Smith and the United States of America were both preparing for war in 1940, over a year before the Japanese surprise attack on Pearl Harbor. Snuffy first tried to register on October 16, 1940, but was turned away because he was "too short in statter" as well as toothless and flat-footed. Intent on doing his patriotic duty and "countin' on that thutty dulers a month," Snuffy went back to the recruitment office day after day for almost a month. Finally, on November 13, he was inducted into the U.S. Army after saving the life of a portly, moustached General.

In the middle of this sequence, beginning on October 28, DeBeck started drawing the strip with a crayon pencil similar to the type used by many editorial cartoonists of that era. Fred Lasswell, DeBeck's assistant at the time, remembers this brief period as another example of his boss's experimenting. By December 15, DeBeck had returned to the traditional pen-and-ink method that he had used for decades.

On February 20, 1941, thirty thousand troops descended on Snuffy's home turf of Hootin' Holler for practice maneuvers. The local hillbillies, thinking the soldiers were "revenooers," commenced shooting and an all-out battle ensued. Finally, on March 29, Snuffy parachuted in to make peace with his neighbors. This six-week episode was written and drawn entirely by Fred Lasswell - his first "solo" assignment. In 1942, Monogram Pictures produced a live-action Snuffy Smith movie, "Snuffy Smith, Yardbird," based on Lasswell's sequence.

Snuffy continued his military adventures, mostly in boot camp, throughout the rest of the year, and in September 1941, Barney Google joined the war effort by signing up with the Navy. DeBeck tried to improve morale with his wartime anthem, "Times A Wastin'," but this tune unfortunately did not repeat the success of the original Billy Rose "Barney Google" song.

By the summer of 1942, Billy DeBeck was dying of cancer. The last time his signature appeared in the daily strip was on July 4, 1942, and in the Sunday page on August 2, 1942. DeBeck had already become too ill at this point to continue drawing and these transition episodes were done by King Features "bullpen" artists. Billy died at Lenox Hill Hospital on November 11, 1942. He had been a professional cartoonist for thirty-two of his fifty-two years.

Fred Lasswell had sailed for Africa in August 1942 to work as a radio operator for Pan American Airways, so "Barney Google and Snuffy Smith" was drawn by Joe Musial (who signed his work "JM") for a brief time after DeBeck's death. Fred returned at the end of 1942 to take over responsibilities on the strip and, after a brief visit home to Florida, enlisted in the Marines. He moved to an apartment in Washington, D.C., where he produced the daily "Barney Google and Snuffy Smith" strips and also worked on *Leatherneck* magazine. The first strip bearing Lasswell's signature appeared on March 8, 1943. Snuffy's subsequent travels from Bermuda to Africa during 1943 and 1944 closely paralleled Lasswell's own international tour with Pan Am in 1942. Joe Musial continued to draw most of the Sunday pages until the war ended in 1945 and also occasionally filled in on the dailies as well. When Fred was discharged on October 15, 1945, he took over the full responsibilities for producing both the dailies and the Sundays. "Barney Google and Snuffy Smith" was now Fred Lasswell's comic strip.

Below: Snuffy finally gets inducted into the U.S. Army, November 13, 1940. This is one of the strips DeBeck drew with a crayon pencil. Courtesy of King Features Syndicate.

WE CAN'T OKAY SNUFFY SMITH FOR THE ARMY — LOOKIT THIS REPORT ON HIM !! FLAT FEET — NO TEETH — OVER-AGE
I TOLD YOU TO TEAR IT UP. IT'S THE GENERAL'S ORDERS !!
OKAY, SMITH - GO RIGHT IN !!
AYE, AYE, SIR
TWO HOURS LATER
HI YAH, GEN'RIL !! YE OL' MUSHRAT — WOT'S ON YORE MIND ??
Billy DeBeck
Copr. 1940, King Features Syndicate, Inc., World rights reserved.
11-13

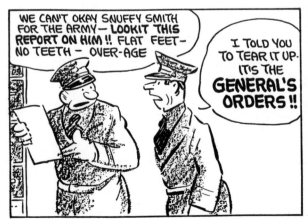

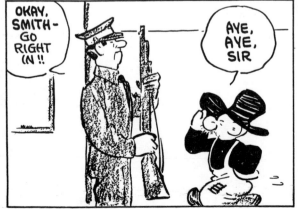

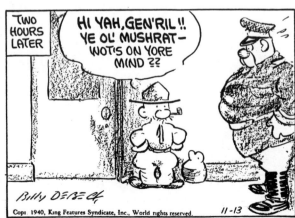

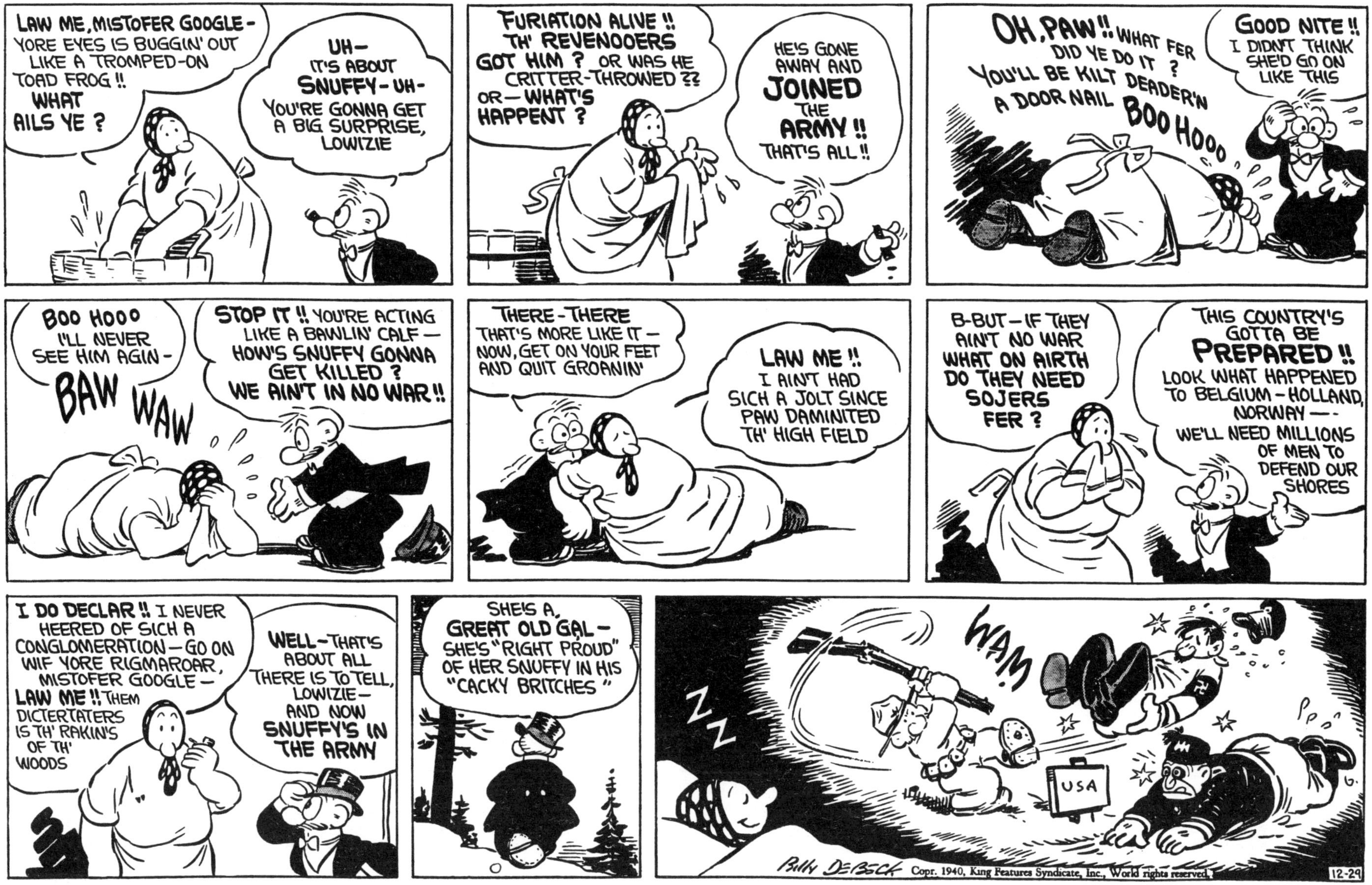
LAW ME, MISTOFER GOOGLE - YORE EYES IS BUGGIN' OUT LIKE A TROMPED-ON TOAD FROG !! WHAT AILS YE ?
UH- IT'S ABOUT SNUFFY - UH - YOU'RE GONNA GET A BIG SURPRISE, LOWIZIE
FURIATION ALIVE !! TH' REVENOOERS GOT HIM ? OR WAS HE CRITTER-THROWED ?? OR - WHAT'S HAPPENT ?
HE'S GONE AWAY AND JOINED THE ARMY !! THAT'S ALL !!
OH, PAW !! WHAT FER DID YE DO IT ? YOU'LL BE KILT DEADER'N A DOOR NAIL BOO HOOO
GOOD NITE !! I DIDN'T THINK SHE'D GO ON LIKE THIS
BOO HOOO I'LL NEVER SEE HIM AGIN -
BAW WAW
STOP IT !! YOU'RE ACTING LIKE A BAWLIN' CALF - HOW'S SNUFFY GONNA GET KILLED ? WE AIN'T IN NO WAR !!
THERE - THERE THAT'S MORE LIKE IT - NOW, GET ON YOUR FEET AND QUIT GROANIN'
LAW ME !! I AIN'T HAD SICH A JOLT SINCE PAW DAMINITED TH' HIGH FIELD
B-BUT - IF THEY AIN'T NO WAR WHAT ON AIRTH DO THEY NEED SOJERS FER ?
THIS COUNTRY'S GOTTA BE PREPARED !! LOOK WHAT HAPPENED TO BELGIUM - HOLLAND, NORWAY - - WE'LL NEED MILLIONS OF MEN TO DEFEND OUR SHORES
I DO DECLAR !! I NEVER HEERED OF SICH A CONGLOMERATION - GO ON WIF YORE RIGMAROAR, MISTOFER GOOGLE - LAW ME !! THEM DICTERTATERS IS TH' RAKIN'S OF TH' WOODS
WELL - THAT'S ABOUT ALL THERE IS TO TELL, LOWIZIE - AND NOW SNUFFY'S IN THE ARMY
SHE'S A GREAT OLD GAL - SHE'S "RIGHT PROUD" OF HER SNUFFY IN HIS "CACKY BRITCHES"
ZZ
WAM
USA
BILLY DE BECK
Copr. 1940, King Features Syndicate, Inc., World rights reserved.
12-29

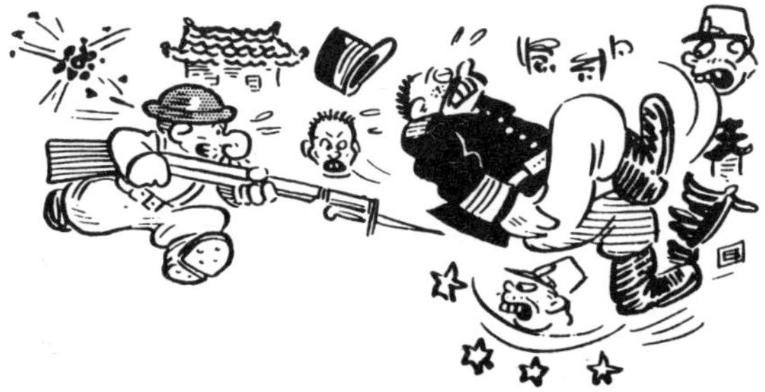

Above: Barney breaks the news to Lowizie about Snuffy's enlistment, "Barney Google and Snuffy Smith" Sunday page, December 29, 1940. Courtesy of King Features Syndicate.

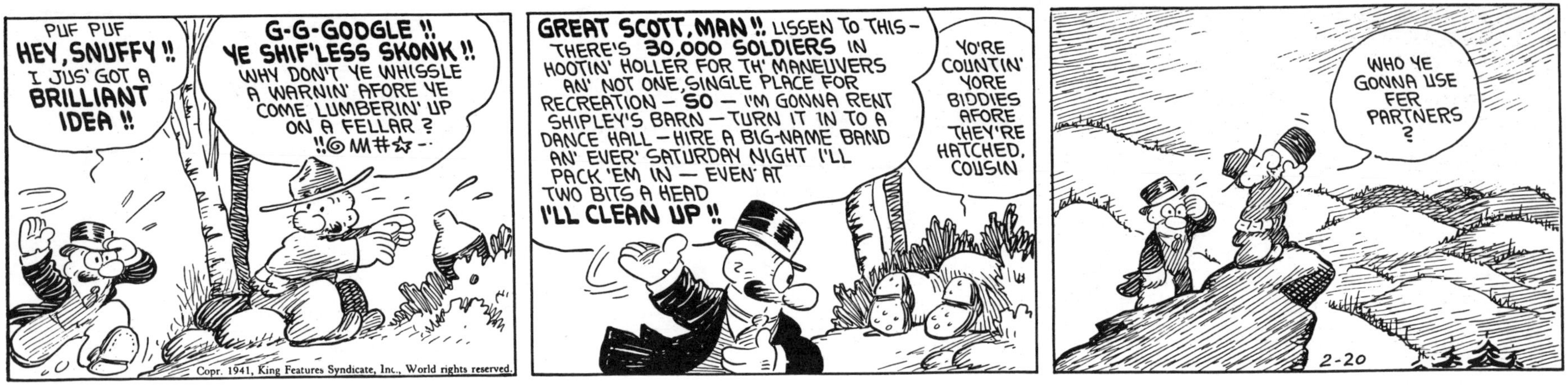
PUF PUF
HEY, SNUFFY !! I JUS' GOT A BRILLIANT IDEA !!
G-G-GOOGLE !! YE SHIF'LESS SKONK !! WHY DON'T YE WHISSLE A WARNIN' AFORE YE COME LUMBERIN' UP ON A FELLAR ? !!GM#☆ - -
Copr. 1941, King Features Syndicate, Inc., World rights reserved.
GREAT SCOTT, MAN !! LISSEN TO THIS— THERE'S 30,000 SOLDIERS IN HOOTIN' HOLLER FOR TH' MANEUVERS AN' NOT ONE, SINGLE PLACE FOR RECREATION — SO — I'M GONNA RENT SHIPLEY'S BARN — TURN IT IN TO A DANCE HALL — HIRE A BIG-NAME BAND AN' EVER' SATURDAY NIGHT I'LL PACK 'EM IN — EVEN AT TWO BITS A HEAD I'LL CLEAN UP !!
YO'RE COUNTIN' YORE BIDDIES AFORE THEY'RE HATCHED, COUSIN
WHO YE GONNA USE FER PARTNERS ?
2-20

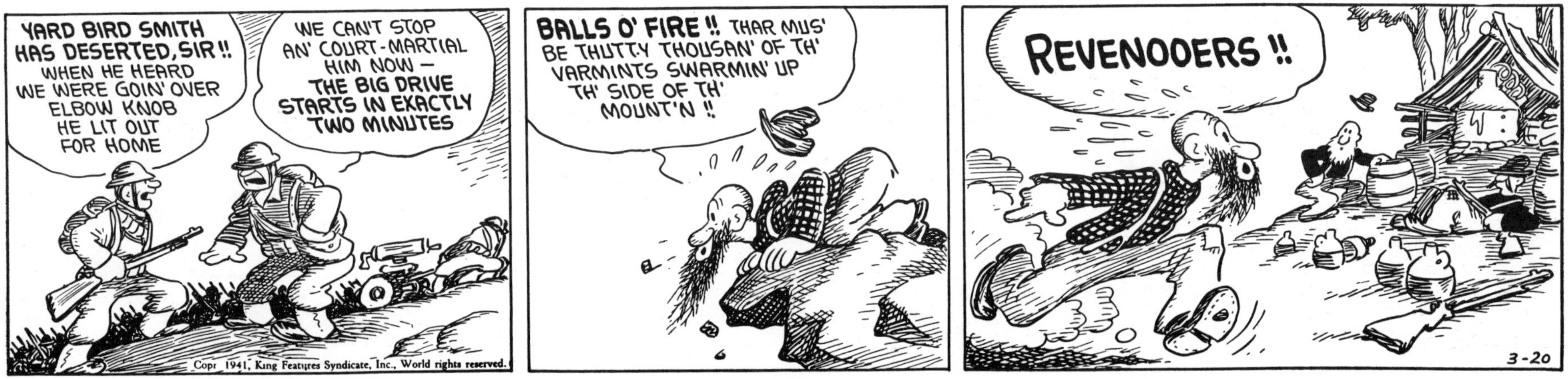
YARD BIRD SMITH HAS DESERTED, SIR !! WHEN HE HEARD WE WERE GOIN' OVER ELBOW KNOB HE LIT OUT FOR HOME
WE CAN'T STOP AN' COURT-MARTIAL HIM NOW — THE BIG DRIVE STARTS IN EXACTLY TWO MINUTES
Copr. 1941, King Features Syndicate, Inc., World rights reserved.
BALLS O' FIRE !! THAR MUS' BE THUTTY THOUSAN' OF TH' VARMINTS SWARMIN' UP TH' SIDE OF TH' MOUNT'N !!
REVENOOERS !!
3-20

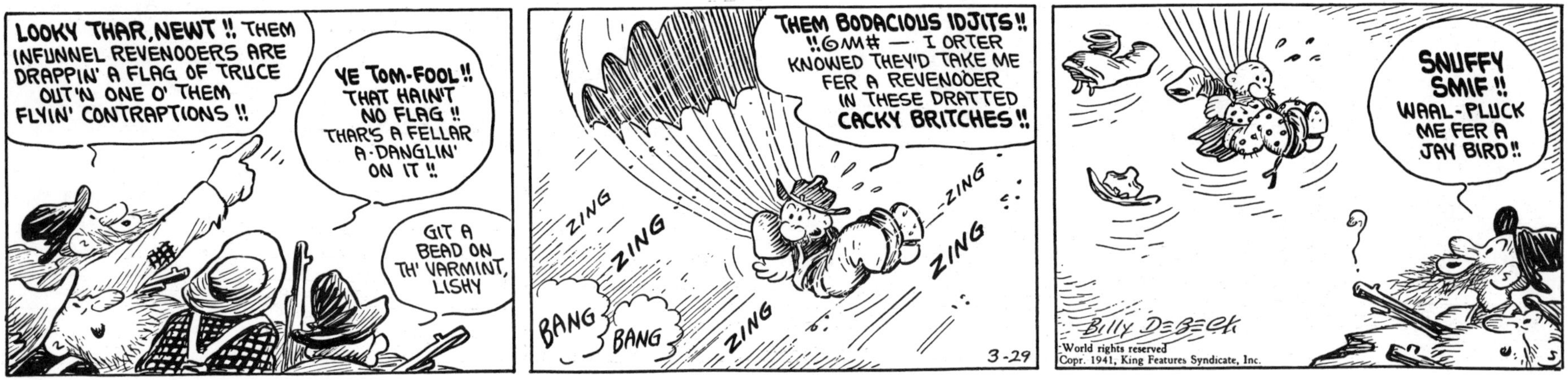
LOOKY THAR, NEWT !! THEM INFUNNEL REVENOOERS ARE DRAPPIN' A FLAG OF TRUCE OUT'N ONE O' THEM FLYIN' CONTRAPTIONS !!
YE TOM-FOOL !! THAT HAIN'T NO FLAG !! THAR'S A FELLAR A-DANGLIN' ON IT !!
GIT A BEAD ON TH' VARMINT, LISHY
THEM BODACIOUS IDJITS !! !!GM# — I ORTER KNOWED THEY'D TAKE ME FER A REVENOOER IN THESE DRATTED CACKY BRITCHES !!
ZING
ZING
ZING
ZING
ZING
BANG
BANG
3-29
SNUFFY SMIF !! WAAL-PLUCK ME FER A JAY BIRD !!
BILLY DEBECK
World rights reserved
Copr. 1941, King Features Syndicate, Inc.

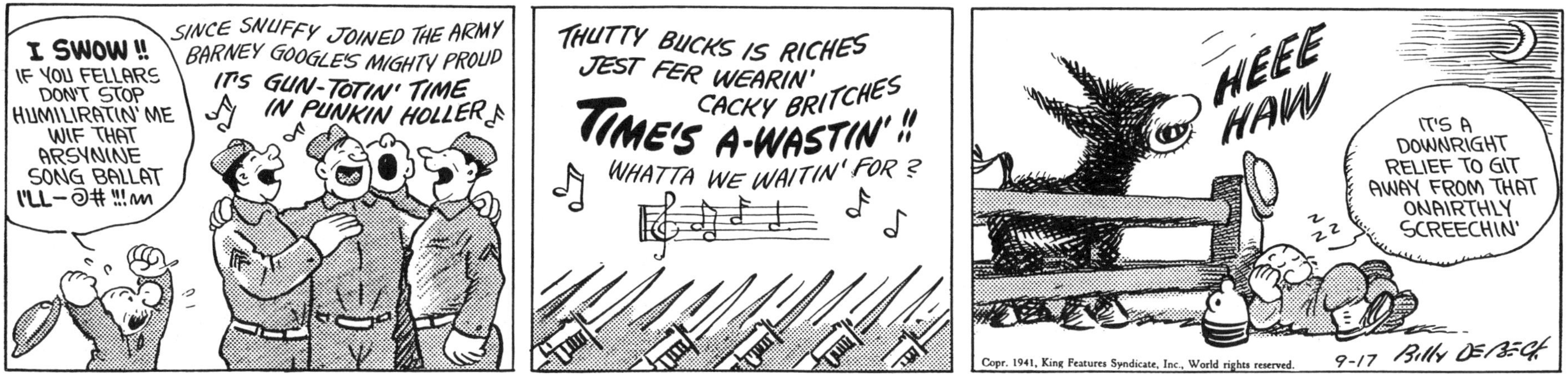
I SWOW !! IF YOU FELLARS DON'T STOP HUMILIRATIN' ME WIF THAT ARSYNINE SONG BALLAT I'LL—@# !!
SINCE SNUFFY JOINED THE ARMY BARNEY GOOGLE'S MIGHTY PROUD
IT'S GUN-TOTIN' TIME IN PUNKIN HOLLER
THUTTY BUCKS IS RICHES JEST FER WEARIN' CACKY BRITCHES
TIME'S A-WASTIN' !!
WHATTA WE WAITIN' FOR ?
HEEE HAW
IT'S A DOWNRIGHT RELIEF TO GIT AWAY FROM THAT ONAIRTHLY SCREECHIN'
Z Z Z
Copr. 1941, King Features Syndicate, Inc., World rights reserved.
9-17
BILLY DE BECK

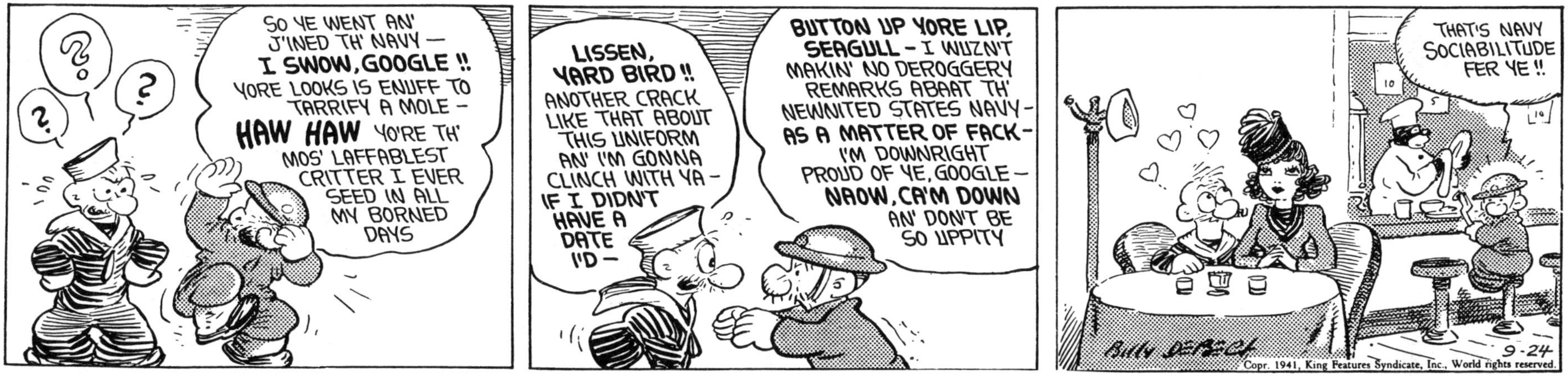
SO YE WENT AN' J'INED TH' NAVY — I SWOW, GOOGLE !! YORE LOOKS IS ENUFF TO TARRIFY A MOLE — HAW HAW YO'RE TH' MOS' LAFFABLEST CRITTER I EVER SEED IN ALL MY BORNED DAYS
LISSEN, YARD BIRD !! ANOTHER CRACK LIKE THAT ABOUT THIS UNIFORM AN' I'M GONNA CLINCH WITH YA — IF I DIDN'T HAVE A DATE I'D —
BUTTON UP YORE LIP, SEAGULL — I WUZN'T MAKIN' NO DEROGGERY REMARKS ABAAT TH' NEWNITED STATES NAVY — AS A MATTER OF FACK — I'M DOWNRIGHT PROUD OF YE, GOOGLE — NAOW, CA'M DOWN AN' DON'T BE SO UPPITY
THAT'S NAVY SOCIABILITUDE FER YE !!
BILLY DE BECK
9-24
Copr. 1941, King Features Syndicate, Inc., World rights reserved.

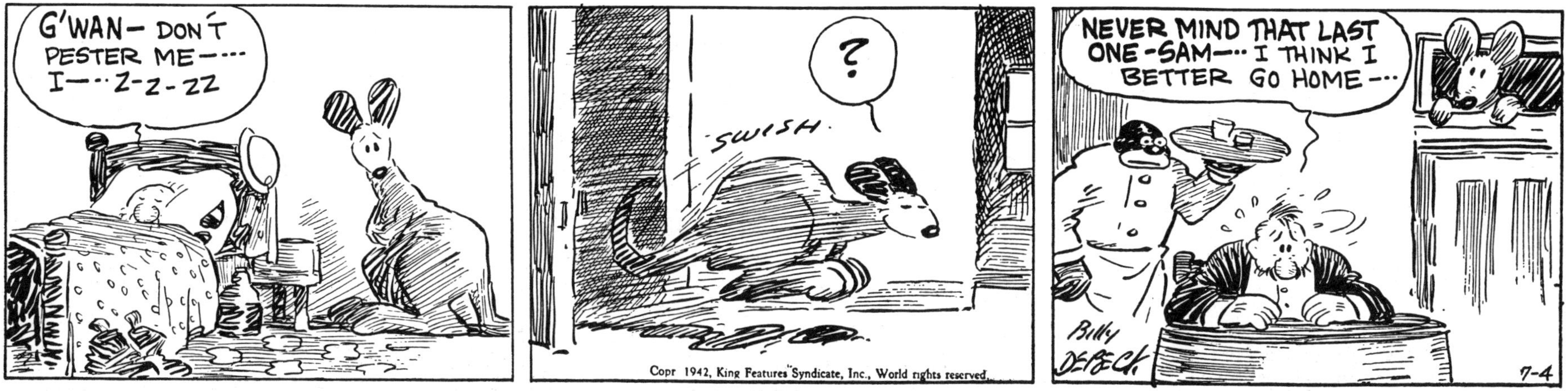
G'WAN — DON'T PESTER ME —··· I—·· Z-Z-ZZ
?
SWISH
Copr 1942, King Features Syndicate, Inc., World rights reserved.
NEVER MIND THAT LAST ONE-SAM—··· I THINK I BETTER GO HOME —···
BILLY DE BECK
7-4

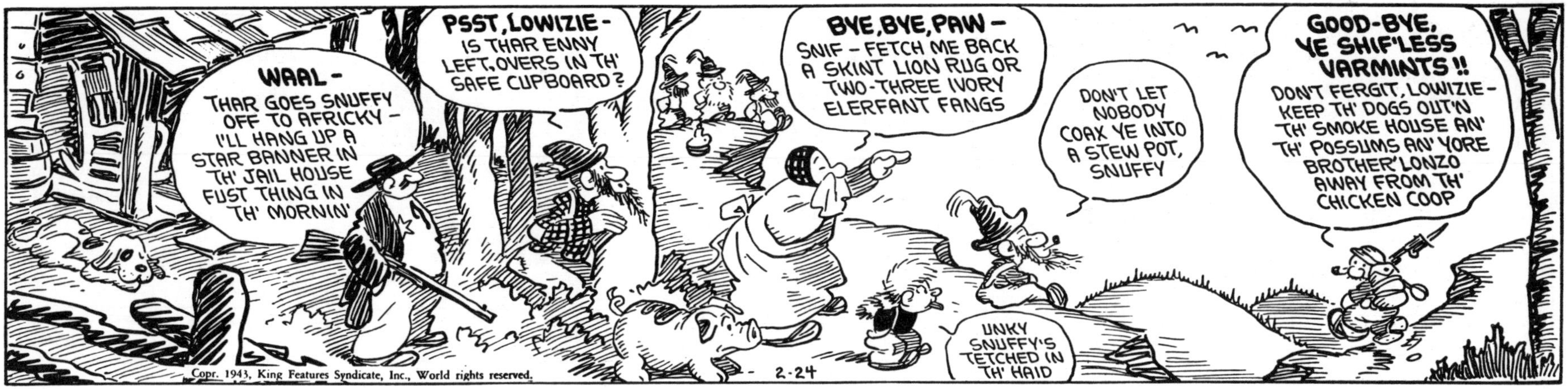
WAAL - THAR GOES SNUFFY OFF TO AFRICKY - I'LL HANG UP A STAR BANNER IN TH' JAIL HOUSE FUST THING IN TH' MORNIN'
PSST, LOWIZIE - IS THAR ENNY LEFT-OVERS IN TH' SAFE CUPBOARD?
BYE, BYE, PAW - SNIF - FETCH ME BACK A SKINT LION RUG OR TWO-THREE IVORY ELERFANT FANGS
UNKY SNUFFY'S TETCHED IN TH' HAID
DON'T LET NOBODY COAX YE INTO A STEW POT, SNUFFY
GOOD-BYE, YE SHIF'LESS VARMINTS!! DON'T FERGIT, LOWIZIE - KEEP TH' DOGS OUT'N TH' SMOKE HOUSE AN' TH' POSSUMS AN' YORE BROTHER 'LONZO AWAY FROM TH' CHICKEN COOP
Copr. 1943, King Features Syndicate, Inc., World rights reserved.
2-24

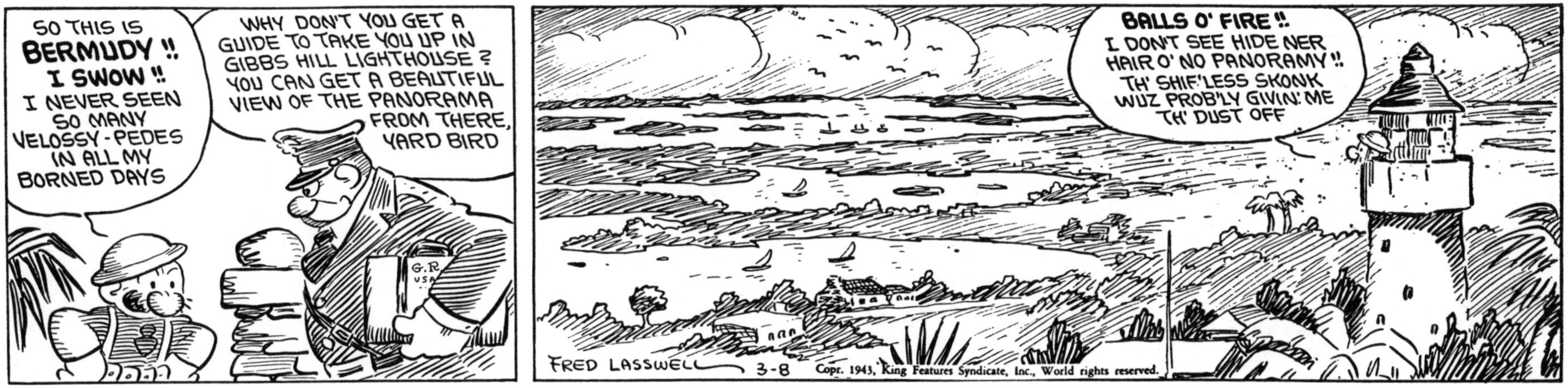
SO THIS IS BERMUDY!! I SWOW!! I NEVER SEEN SO MANY VELOSSY-PEDES IN ALL MY BORNED DAYS
WHY DON'T YOU GET A GUIDE TO TAKE YOU UP IN GIBBS HILL LIGHTHOUSE? YOU CAN GET A BEAUTIFUL VIEW OF THE PANORAMA FROM THERE, YARD BIRD
G.R. USA
BALLS O' FIRE!! I DON'T SEE HIDE NER HAIR O' NO PANORAMY!! TH' SHIF'LESS SKONK WUZ PROB'LY GIVIN' ME TH' DUST OFF
FRED LASSWELL 3-8
Copr. 1943, King Features Syndicate, Inc., World rights reserved.

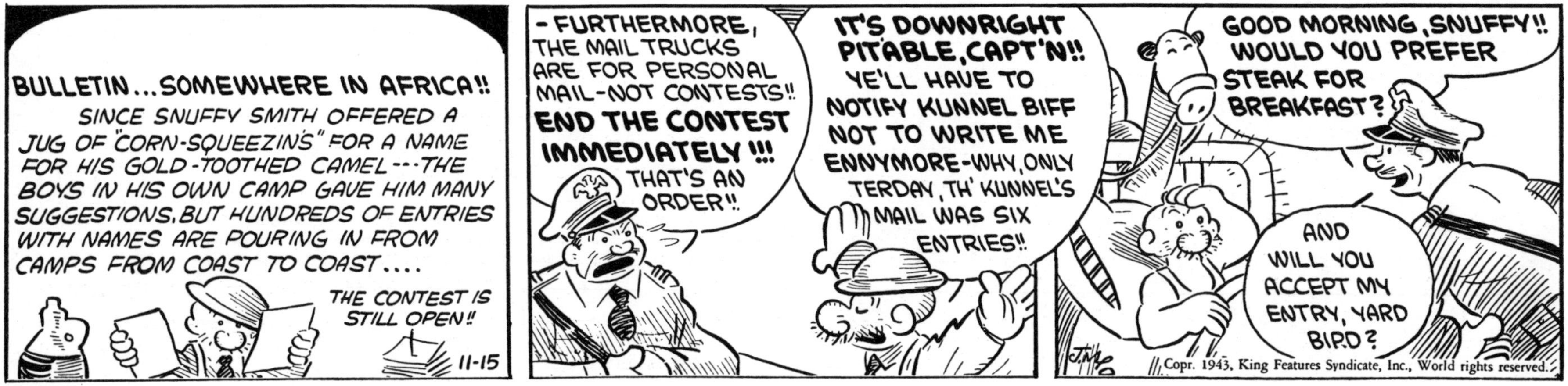
BULLETIN... SOMEWHERE IN AFRICA!! SINCE SNUFFY SMITH OFFERED A JUG OF "CORN-SQUEEZIN'S" FOR A NAME FOR HIS GOLD-TOOTHED CAMEL --- THE BOYS IN HIS OWN CAMP GAVE HIM MANY SUGGESTIONS, BUT HUNDREDS OF ENTRIES WITH NAMES ARE POURING IN FROM CAMPS FROM COAST TO COAST....
THE CONTEST IS STILL OPEN!!
11-15
- FURTHERMORE, THE MAIL TRUCKS ARE FOR PERSONAL MAIL - NOT CONTESTS!! END THE CONTEST IMMEDIATELY!!! THAT'S AN ORDER!!
IT'S DOWNRIGHT PITABLE, CAPT'N!! YE'LL HAVE TO NOTIFY KUNNEL BIFF NOT TO WRITE ME ENNYMORE - WHY, ONLY TERDAY, TH' KUNNEL'S MAIL WAS SIX ENTRIES!!
GOOD MORNING, SNUFFY!! WOULD YOU PREFER STEAK FOR BREAKFAST?
AND WILL YOU ACCEPT MY ENTRY, YARD BIRD?
Copr. 1943, King Features Syndicate, Inc., World rights reserved.

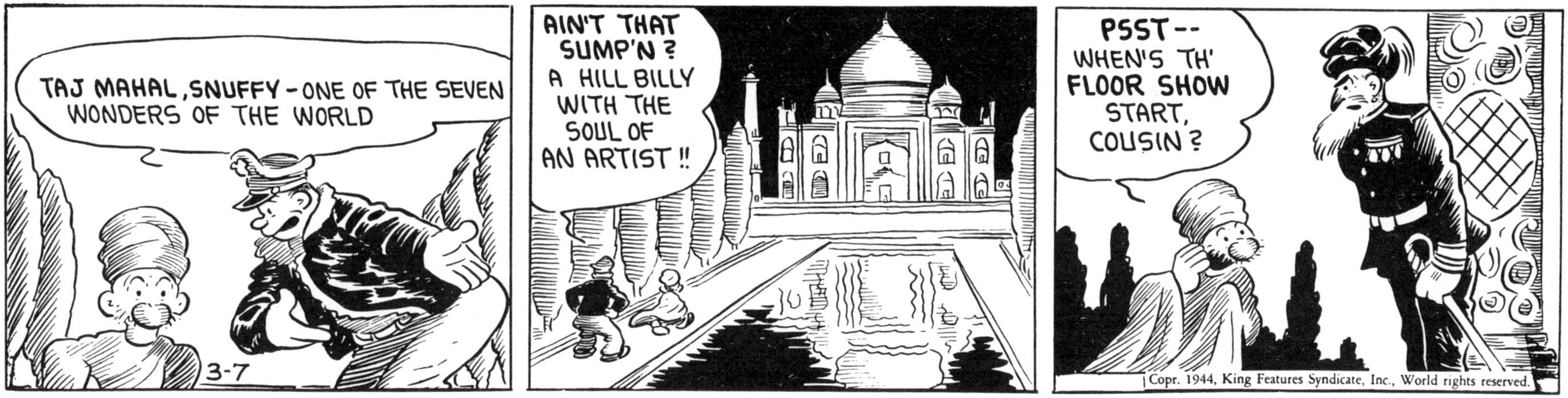
TAJ MAHAL, SNUFFY - ONE OF THE SEVEN WONDERS OF THE WORLD
3-7
AIN'T THAT SUMP'N ? A HILL BILLY WITH THE SOUL OF AN ARTIST !!
PSST-- WHEN'S TH' FLOOR SHOW START, COUSIN ?
Copr. 1944, King Features Syndicate, Inc., World rights reserved.

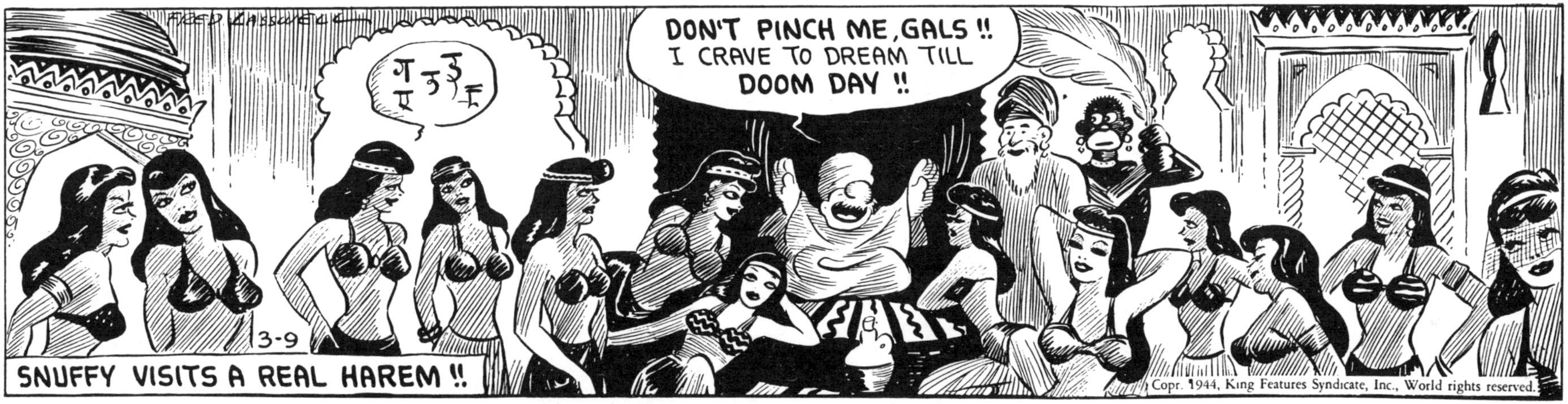
FRED LASSWELL
DON'T PINCH ME, GALS !! I CRAVE TO DREAM TILL DOOM DAY !!
3-9
SNUFFY VISITS A REAL HAREM !!
Copr. 1944, King Features Syndicate, Inc., World rights reserved.

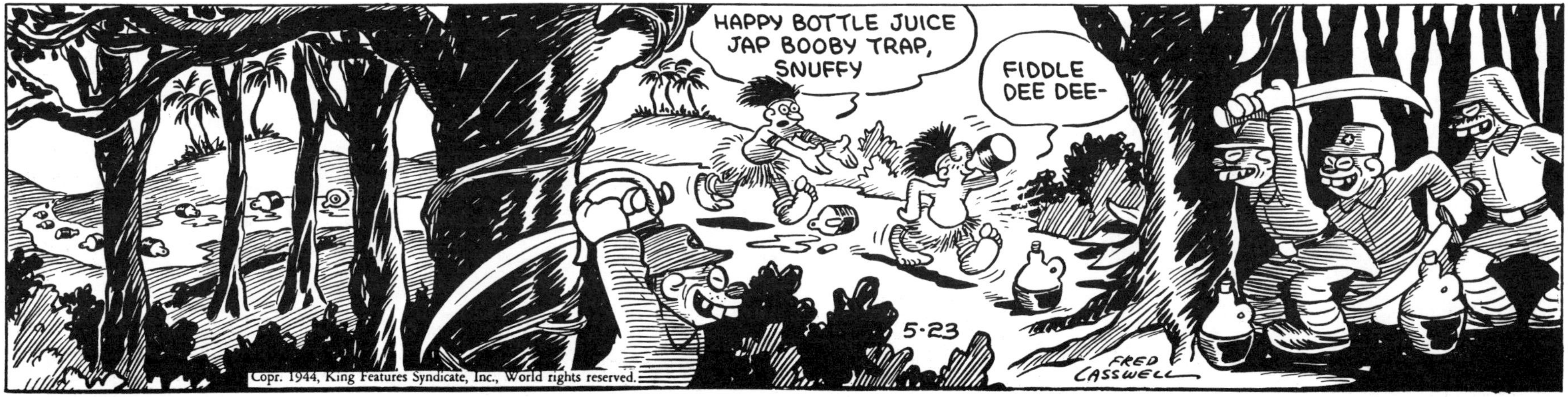
HAPPY BOTTLE JUICE JAP BOOBY TRAP, SNUFFY
FIDDLE DEE DEE-
5-23
FRED LASSWELL
Copr. 1944, King Features Syndicate, Inc., World rights reserved.

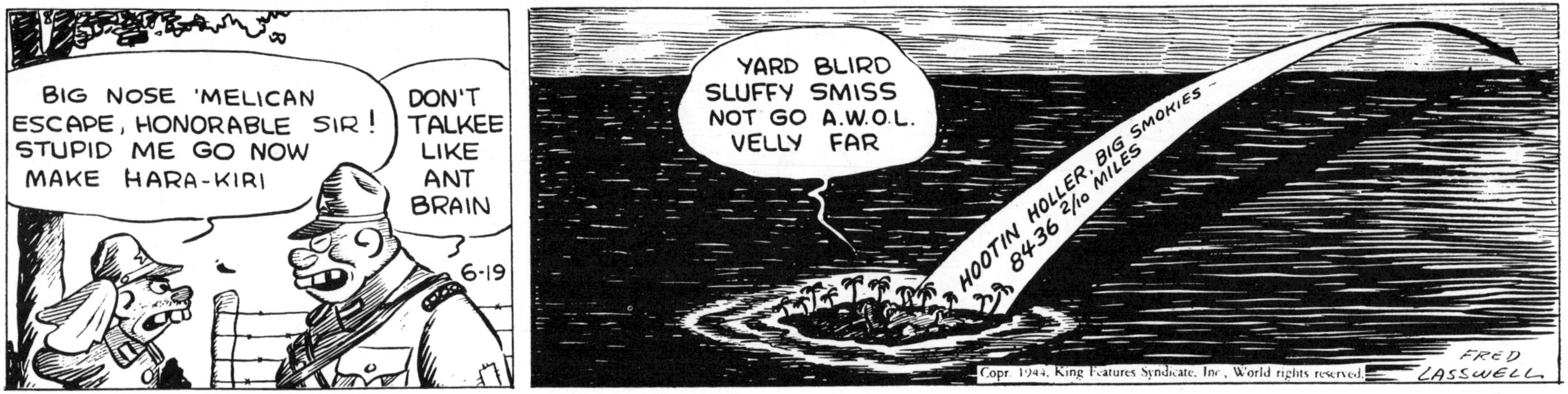
BIG NOSE 'MELICAN ESCAPE, HONORABLE SIR! STUPID ME GO NOW MAKE HARA-KIRI
DON'T TALKEE LIKE ANT BRAIN
6-19
YARD BLIRD SLUFFY SMISS NOT GO A.W.O.L. VELLY FAR
HOOTIN HOLLER, BIG SMOKIES — 8436 2/10 MILES
Copr. 1944, King Features Syndicate, Inc., World rights reserved.
FRED LASSWELL

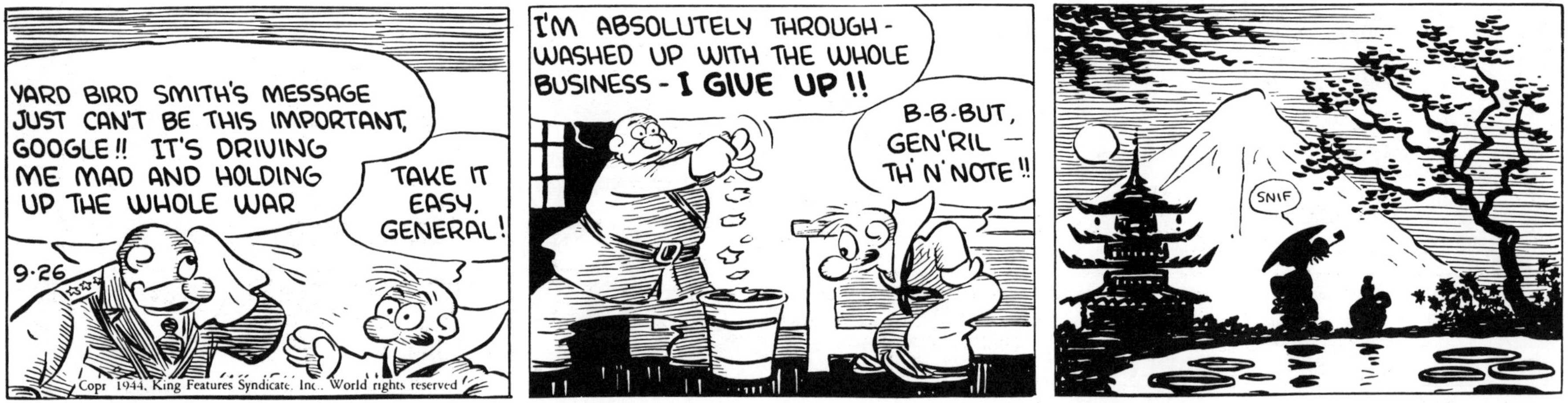
YARD BIRD SMITH'S MESSAGE JUST CAN'T BE THIS IMPORTANT, GOOGLE!! IT'S DRIVING ME MAD AND HOLDING UP THE WHOLE WAR
TAKE IT EASY, GENERAL!
9-26
Copr. 1944, King Features Syndicate, Inc., World rights reserved
I'M ABSOLUTELY THROUGH - WASHED UP WITH THE WHOLE BUSINESS - I GIVE UP!!
B-B-BUT, GEN'RIL — TH' N' NOTE!!
SNIF

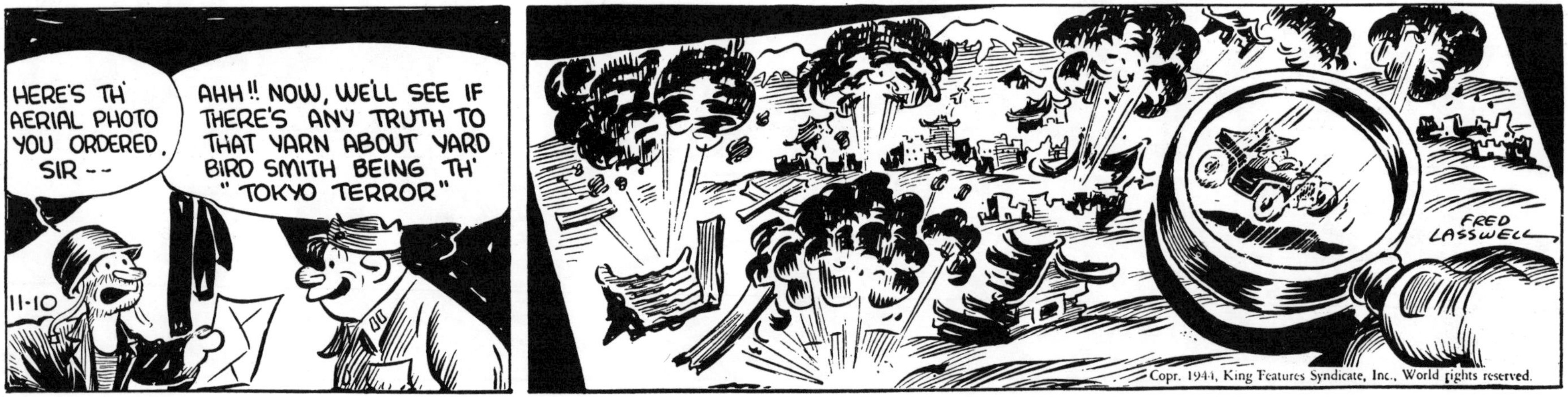
HERE'S TH' AERIAL PHOTO YOU ORDERED, SIR --
AHH!! NOW, WE'LL SEE IF THERE'S ANY TRUTH TO THAT YARN ABOUT YARD BIRD SMITH BEING TH' "TOKYO TERROR"
11-10
FRED LASSWELL
Copr. 1944, King Features Syndicate, Inc., World rights reserved.

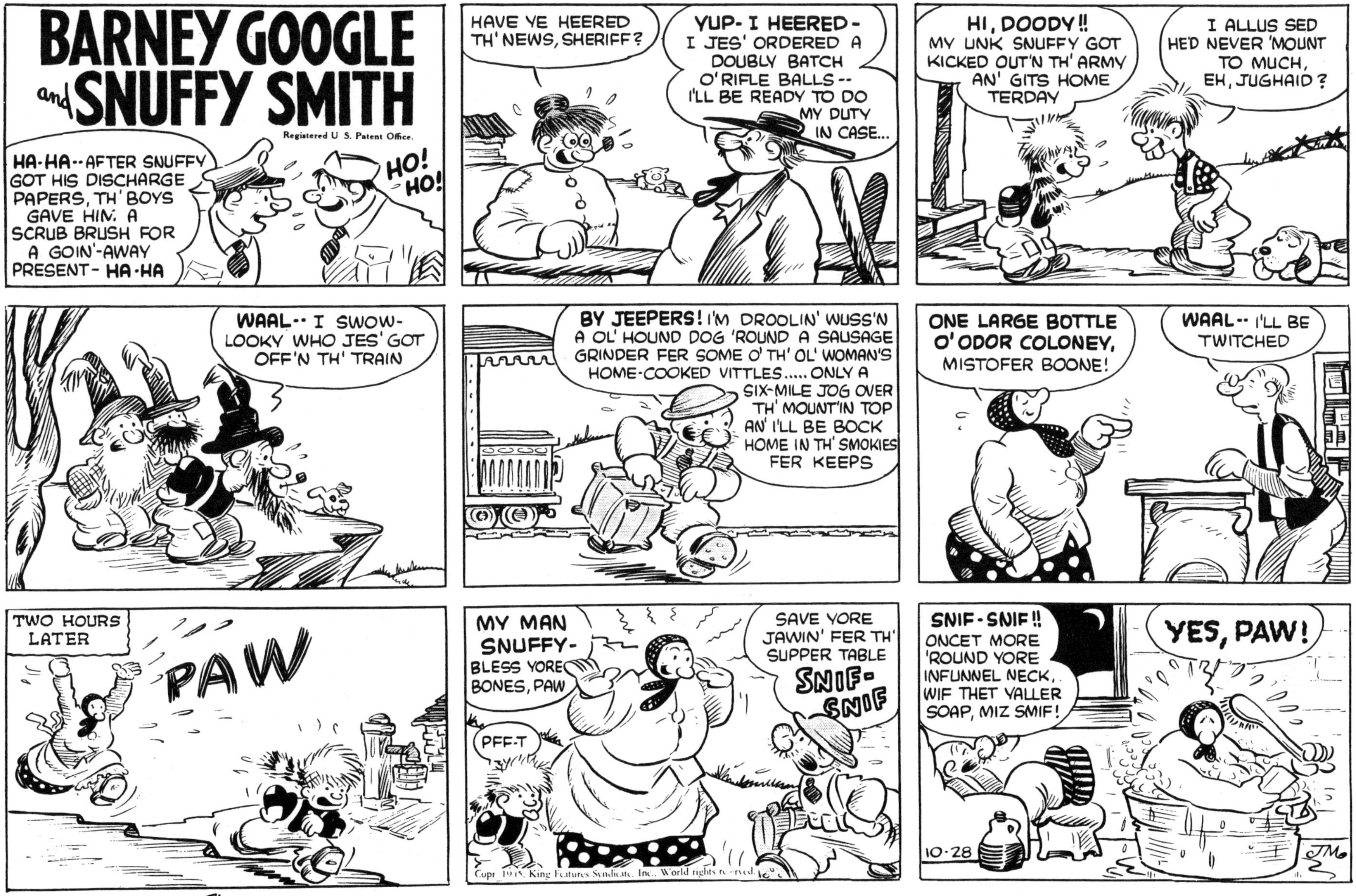
BARNEY GOOGLE and SNUFFY SMITH
Registered U. S. Patent Office.
HA-HA-- AFTER SNUFFY GOT HIS DISCHARGE PAPERS, TH' BOYS GAVE HIM A SCRUB BRUSH FOR A GOIN'-AWAY PRESENT- HA-HA
HO! HO!
HAVE YE HEERED TH' NEWS, SHERIFF?
YUP- I HEERED- I JES' ORDERED A DOUBLY BATCH O'RIFLE BALLS-- I'LL BE READY TO DO MY DUTY IN CASE...
HI, DOODY!! MY UNK SNUFFY GOT KICKED OUT'N TH' ARMY AN' GITS HOME TERDAY
I ALLUS SED HE'D NEVER 'MOUNT TO MUCH, EH, JUGHAID?
WAAL-- I SWOW- LOOKY WHO JES' GOT OFF'N TH' TRAIN
BY JEEPERS! I'M DROOLIN' WUSS'N A OL' HOUND DOG 'ROUND A SAUSAGE GRINDER FER SOME O' TH' OL' WOMAN'S HOME-COOKED VITTLES..... ONLY A SIX-MILE JOG OVER TH' MOUNT'IN TOP AN' I'LL BE BOCK HOME IN TH' SMOKIES FER KEEPS
ONE LARGE BOTTLE O' ODOR COLONEY, MISTOFER BOONE!
WAAL-- I'LL BE TWITCHED
TWO HOURS LATER
PAW
MY MAN SNUFFY- BLESS YORE BONES, PAW
PFF-T
SAVE YORE JAWIN' FER TH' SUPPER TABLE
SNIF- SNIF
SNIF-SNIF!! ONCET MORE 'ROUND YORE INFUNNEL NECK, WIF THET YALLER SOAP, MIZ SMIF!
YES, PAW!
10-28
JM

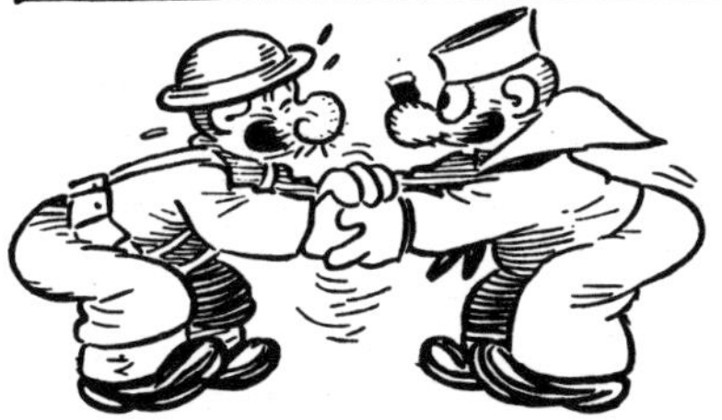

Above: Snuffy returns home after the war, "Barney Google and Snuffy Smith" Sunday page, by Joe Musial, October 28, 1945 Courtesy of King Features Syndicate.

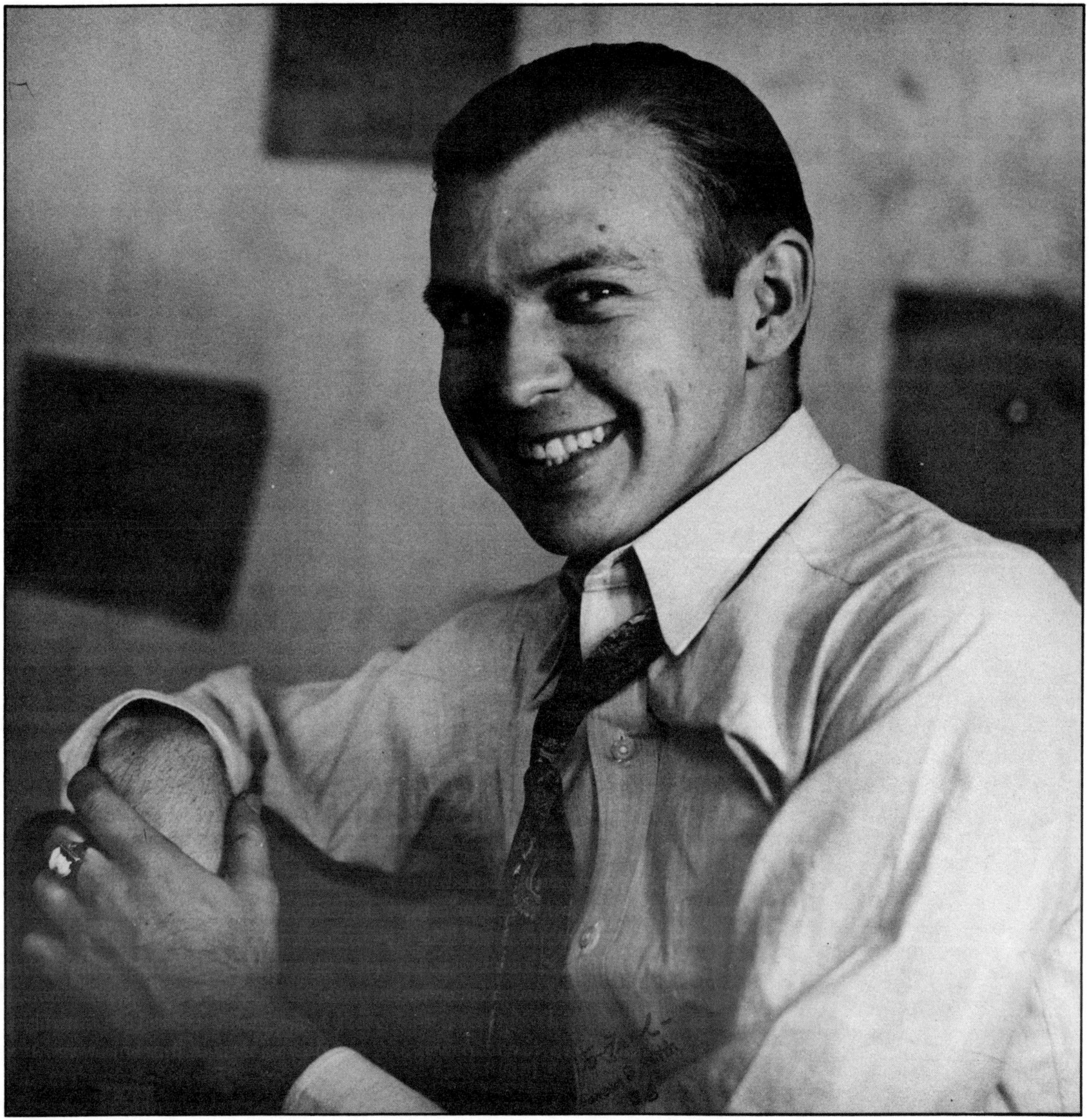

Right: A photograph of
Fred Lasswell from 1936.
Courtesy of Fred Lasswell.

Billy, Barney, Snuffy and Me
By Fred Lasswell

Folks called me a live wire because I was born on Electric Street. That was back on July 25, 1916, in Kennett, Dunklin County, southeastern Missouri, down in the boot heel. My father, Fred, Sr., one of six brothers and a baby sister, was born in Campbell, Missouri, and my mother, Nellie Florence Waldridge, was born in East Prairie, Missouri. My kinfolks all came from Missouri, Kentucky, Tennessee and Virginia. They were a duke's mixture of English, Scottish, Irish, Dutch, German, French, and I don't know what all. Both grandpas were railroad men. W. D. Lasswell built the first railroad in southeastern Missouri and my other grandpa, John Waldridge, was a railroad construction man born in Culpepper, Virginia.

Around 1910, Kennett had a big scare. Somebody forecast that the world was coming to an end at sunrise. On the predicted Sunday, everybody in Kennett, men, women and children, gathered around the church to pray and wait for this terrible disaster to happen. Little did they know that my father had snuck up in the bell tower of the church late the night before. At the first crack of daylight, Daddy cut loose on his bugle. Somebody yelled it was Gabriel blowing his horn. Pandemonium broke loose, with people screaming and hollering and running in all directions. I possibly inherited my sense of humor from Daddy.

Daddy built the first movie house, Fred's Theater, in Campbell, Missouri,

in 1913. My mother, Nellie, adorned the box office. When World War I was declared, Daddy got up on the stage, made the announcement, sold the theater and joined the Navy.

Mama told me about the time Daddy's ship, the SS Augusta, docked in Boston. We went down to see Daddy come in. Mama had dressed me all up in a cute little sailor suit and taught me how to salute. When the first batch of sailors came down the gangplank, I saluted briskly and sung out, "Hello, Daddy!" The sailors all had a big laugh over their newfound young 'un. Needless to say, Mama was in nowise pleased. They all looked like Daddy to me.

After the war, we moved to Gainesville, Florida, and bought a ten-acre farm. On this farm, we had a horse and a wagon and a plow, a cow, a dog, a cat, and 2,000 white leghorns - and we even had a guest room—a hatchery for baby chicks. There was no electricity, telephone, radio, hot or cold running water. We had an outhouse with a croker sack hanging where the door ought to be. In some parts of the country, a croker sack is called a gunny sack.

One time, when my cousin Lonzo came to visit, I got him out in the outhouse to teach him how to smoke rabbit tobacco. We rolled up two whoppers in some paper from our Sears and Roebuck mail order catalog and lit up. Somehow, the croker sack caught on fire. After it burned out, my Aunt Sybil, Lonzo's mother, said, "Thank Goodness!! Now you can put a real wooden door on your outhouse, Nellie." And Mama says, "No, we'll just hang up another croker sack." Privacy wasn't a prime consideration since our nearest neighbor lived about two hoots and a holler down the road.

While he was still farming our little ten-acre patch, Daddy was going to the University of Florida, located there in Gainesville, to study horticulture. He wanted to learn all about raising grapes in Florida. He had already learned how to raise home brew.

My school was a couple of miles from the farm and I walked it every day. I had to go over the Hog Town Creek bridge, and sometimes I would stop by the creek on the way home from school and do some fishing with a bent pin and a little string.

My only playmates on the farm were three little black boys. They lived in a bunkhouse on the next farm. We would shoot marbles by lantern light under our kitchen window. Mama threw her dishwater out that window and it had made the ground smooth and hard, just perfect for shootin' marbles. Sometimes, they would invite me over to their place to eat peanuts. They would pull green peanuts out of the field, shake off the dirt, throw them in a pot of boiling water, and add some salt. When they were done, they would scoop out a bucketful and we would take them in the bunkhouse and eat greenboiled peanuts, shells and all, until they came out of our ears.

Years later, I wrote a four-liner that went like this:

I'm a nutter
For peanut butter.
I like it butter by far
Than caviar.

I remember sitting on our front porch at twilight time in a squeaky old rocking chair. Way off in the distance, you could hear hound dawgs howlin' and yappin' like they had just treed a big ol' fat 'coon. And I'll never forget the mournful cry of the whippoorwills. And you could smell a pine stump smouldering 'way off somewhere. Once in a while, if you listened very carefully, you could hear the chatter of crickets and the frogs croaking in the creek. The world shore was a purty place in them days.

Our next move was to Tampa, Florida, around 1926. Daddy had been there before with my grandpa in 1908. Grandpa chartered two ships, and they sailed across the Gulf of Mexico to Guatemala to buy railroad ties for resale in the United States. Grandpa told me, "Fred, Jr., I came to Tampa from southeastern Missouri, chartered ships, sailed over to Guatemala, loaded up with railroad ties, shipped them up the Mississippi, and sold them at a profit. A better profit than I could make chopping my own timber, hauling it on my

own railroad and cutting the ties in my own sawmill." He told me there is to this day a fortune in veneer in those ties. They came from one of the world's finest hardwood, Guatemalan mahogany.

Grandpa sold his railroad, the K&SE, to the Frisco for cash. This was several months before the disasterous stock market crash of 1929. It was no wonder that Grandpa sometimes sported a diamond tie pin when he took me fishing.

I started the third grade at the Seminole Heights Elementary School in Tampa. I produced my first comic strip in 1928, the year after Charles A. Lindburgh flew solo across the Atlantic. The strip was called "Baseball Hits," by Fred Lasswell, and it ran in our school newspaper, the *Seminole Searchlight*. The paper was mimeographed, but more importantly, I had my first byline. When I was eleven years old, I went back to Kennett to visit Grandma and Grandpa and my cousins. I went down to Grandpa's railroad station, and he asked me if I'd like to ride up in the cab with the engineer to Piggott, Arkansas, and back. That ol' wood-burner was all fired up and ready to go. Grandpa told the engineer that he had a new assistant to help him run the train. When I got up in the cab, the engineer told me to give that cord up there a good pull and we'd get underway. I reached up, pulled down that cord and WHOEEE! I never heard such a beautiful sound as that old steam engine whistle made. I remember people standing all along the tracks and waving. When we got back, Grandpa asked the engineer how his helper made out. He said, "Mr. Lasswell, that young 'un blew the whistle all the way to Piggott and back."

My grandma Lasswell was a driving force in that neck of the woods for the WCTU, the Women's Christian Temperance Union. She would march into the local saloon with her army of raiders, armed with hatchets, and destroy every bottle of demon rum, or any other bottled goods they deemed a threat to sobriety. The barkeep would stand aside until they had sacked the joint and left. Then he would call my Grandpa and give him the bad news. Grandpa always paid up.

One day, sitting in Grandma's kitchen, I pointed out to her that her ice box was leaking. She lifted up the flap, pulled out the drip pan, and there sat six bottles of home brew, cooling off for Grandpa. She took three bottles in each hand and, with the dexterity of a seasoned barmaid, she walked those six bottles out to the back porch and — wham, wham, wham. Suds spewed all over creation. I lit out for the railroad as fast as my two legs would carry me and went barging into Grandpa's office with the bad news. He put both hands over his bald head, looked up at the ceiling, and all he said was "Oh, my God."

Back in Tampa after my exciting holiday, I continued to draw cartoons all through junior high and high school. My folks got me an International

Correspondence course in art, which I never finished. I don't know why. It probably had something to do with money.

I had an art teacher in Tampa who taught fine art, drawing, perspective and stuff like that. He had studied in Germany and said he had to draw with charcoal for two years before they would let him use a paint brush. He was a dandy dresser, and they found him shot out in the woods. So far as I know, they never found out who done it.

During the Great Depression, they were paying some of the teachers in scrip. I quit high school two weeks before graduation because I figured if they weren't paying the teachers, there wasn't much use in getting an education.

I had a paper route with the *Tampa Daily Times*. It was in a Spanish-speaking neighborhood and the paper, delivered on your front porch, in the flower bed or through the window, was fifteen cents a week. The first week I went around to collect, I pecked on the door and said very politely, "I am your paper boy and I've come to collect 15 cents." The lady giggled, "No speakee English," and shut the door in my face. One of my Spanish speaking friends coached me on how to collect my paper money. The next week, I went to the same house, pecked on the door, and when the lady appeared, I sang out, "Yo quiero cobrar quince centavos," which translated means, "I want to collect fifteen cents." I said it twice because she owed me for two weeks.

At the same time, I was hawking papers for the rival *Tampa Morning Tribune*. Newspaper hawkers are a dying breed. They have been replaced by the big coin-operated tin boxes. As soon as the papers came off the press, I would grab an armload and light out, screaming at the top of my lungs like the world had ended, "Hey, get your morning papo' (paper)."

I hawked *Tampa Tribunes* barefooted as a yard dog out in Ybor City (EE-bo) the Latin quarter of Tampa, from eleven at night until about three in the morning. Ybor City, in those days, was a vast recreational area. In a thirty-square-block area, there were a whole lot of small houses side by side, where young ladies lived. And, since it was hard times, four or five of them would share the same house. They had more parties out there than any place I ever saw. It seemed like every night they all were holding open house. It was a great place for a sixteen-year-old to hawk papers.

On the other side of Seventh Avenue, the dividing line of Ybor City, there was a different kind of recreation area. There were more gambling houses than you could shake a stick at. They were mostly run by Spanish, Cuban and Italian entrepreneurs. They were lucrative enterprises. Competition was keen and ownership changed hands frequently.

Everybody played Bolita. It was played with little balls, numbered from one to one hundred. The balls would be put in a bag, sewn up and tossed around the room. Someone would select one of the balls and the houseman would tie it up and cut it out. The number on the ball was the Bolita winner for that day. You could win $7 or $8 for a ten-cent ticket.

They also sold Cuba, a numbers game based on the closing bank balances in Havana, and Celo, played with three dice in a cage. They had lively card games and shot craps. And one another.

During the nine-month period that I hawked papers in this area, about twenty-seven of these entrepreneurs were killed. It was a great place to hawk papers. Every time they shot somebody, I would sell out completely.

Sometimes, on a quiet night, about three o'clock in the morning, I might have some papers left. Then I'd go over in the residential area where everyone was sound asleep. Under the street light, I'd check the obits. I would pick out a name - say, Fernandez. I happened to know for a fact that everybody in Ybor City knew somebody named Fernandez. So, with a voice that would wake the dead, I'd holler, "Fernandez is dead! Fernandez is dead!" Lights would go on all over the place. "Hey, paper boy, paper boy!" They all thought their friend Fernandez had been knocked off. Having sold all my papers, I moved briskly out of the neighborhood. I consoled myself with the thought that my customers would be overjoyed to learn that Senor Fernandez wasn't shot in a gang war but had passed away quietly in his sleep at the age of ninety-seven.

I still wanted to be a cartoonist. So I applied for a job in the art and engraving unit of the *Tampa Daily Times*. They said they didn't have a job for a cartoonist - especially one who had never gotten out of high school. I told them I would work for nothing, just give me a corner to set up a drawing board and I would do anything that came along. I was assigned to a junk heap in the corner. So I got the broom and the mop and made my little corner as pretty as a picture. I ran errands, drew sports cartoons (the Babe Ruth drawing here is an example), retouched photographs and designed cigar box labels. I adopted "Inky" as my byline and slowly started picking up some freelance money. In the afternoons, I worked at an advertising agency, doing cartoons and illustrating newspaper and magazine ads. Space was at a premium at the agency so I wound up working in the men's room. I sat there on the toilet seat, with the lid down

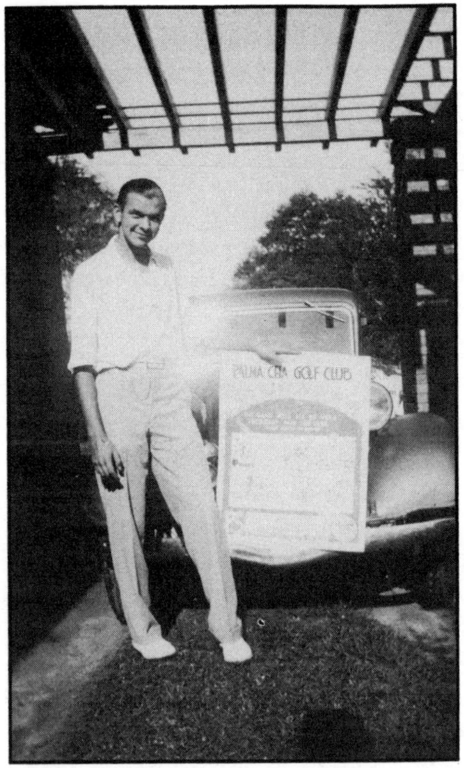
PALMA CEIA GOLF CLUB

and a drawing board on my lap. That's where I was perched when I got a call from Billy DeBeck, the famous cartoonist who drew "Barney Google."

DeBeck had been playing golf in Tampa at the Palma Ceia Golf and Country Club with his pals, Frank Willard, creator of "Moon Mullins," Paul and Dizzy Dean, the baseball greats, and Grantland Rice, dean of America's sportswriters. He had seen a poster that I made for the Chamber of Commerce Jamboree (that's me holding it in the photo) and somehow or other ran me down. He said he was looking for an assistant and would like to see some more of my work. I borrowed $5, got a haircut and a new hat and the next day I was at his studio on Snell Isle in St. Petersburg with an armload of cartoons. My Grandpa drove me over in his new maroon LaSalle with the white sidewall tires and waited for me outside.

Billy liked my cartoons but said he was primarily interested in seeing my lettering. He said he was leaving the next morning for New York and would be in touch when he got back - in about six months.

I told him I had a lot of lettering at home and I could bring it over early tomorrow morning if that would be okay with him. He said, "Sure." I went home and lettered comic strip lettering all night long. Grandpa kept me awake with black coffee and his Havana cigars. When Billy saw all that lettering, he asked, "Why didn't you bring this over yesterday?" and I confessed, "I didn't have it yesterday." So he offered me the job. He asked if I could drive a car and I said, "Sure. I've been driving since I was ten." I drove his Cadillac up to Jacksonville, put it on the Clyde Mallory Line, and drove it off the boat three days later in New York. I dropped it off at Billy's Park Avenue apartment and moved into the Westside YMCA at 5 W. 63rd Street. The room was $6 a week, and the place was packed with doctors and lawyers. These were hard times in New York.

There I was in New York, Billy DeBeck's assistant on the comic strip, "Barney Google," in 1934, and seventeen years old. Billy was a city slicker from Chicago and I was a hayseed from the flatlands of Missouri. I had suddenly become a city slicker myself.

I moved in with Billy and his wife Mary when they rented a home in Great Neck, Long Island. Wherever they moved, I lived with them. At Kings Point, Port Chester, Lake Placid and St. Petersburg, Florida. My starting salary was $25 a week and out of that, Billy took $15 a week for my room and board. That left me $10 whoop-de-do money for Saturday night. I lettered strips, and wrote and submitted daily and Sunday page ideas every week from the beginning, whether Billy used them or not.

Billy would go over my work with me, carefully point out the do's and don'ts and offer suggestions. He was a great teacher and very patient. For my pen work, he put me on a program of copying Charles Dana Gibson, Phil May, the great English black-and-white artist, and his own strips, line for line.

He also started me on a reading program. He would give me a book to read and when I got to a word I didn't know, I had to look it up in the dictionary, write it down, learn how to pronounce it and what it meant. This new-fangled culture became a little embarrassing for me. When I would try out one of my fancy words around my Florida cracker friends, they would hee-haw, slap their legs and roll around on the ground like a bunch of laughing hyenas. I also walked the dog, drove the car and did any other houseboy chores that needed doing. Those were happy days.

I worked long hours, attended the Art Students' League and the Phoenix Art Institute, and was privileged to meet many of Billy's celebrity friends - Jack Dempsey, Gene Tunney, Babe Ruth, Gene Sarazen, Rube Goldberg, Frank Willard, Lowell Thomas and many, many others. I played golf with The Babe and took his daughter dancing, and he even invited me to sit in his box at Yankee Stadium during the World Series. We had hot dogs and pop and laughed and hollered. But best of all, I sat right next to the Babe in the House that he built.

One time, Billy and I were driving from New York to Florida and we stopped at a roadside eating place 'way up in the hills. Billy drew a beautiful cartoon of Barney Google on the clear plastic menu. When the waitress came over, he presented it to her with a flourish. She gawked at it, turned her head one way and another, and gawked at it some more. Billy finally said he hoped he hadn't ruined her menu and she said, "Oh, no, it'll rub right off!"

Billy was fascinated with the people of the Southern Appalachians and collected over 125 books on the subject. When Billy was reading them, he would blue pencil certain words and passages and I would enter them in a log book. I still have it buried away somewhere. They included folk sayings, remedies and superstitions. Some of these were later incorporated into the strip. In one sequence, Billy had Barney 'way back in the hills and introduced Snuffy and Lowizie (Loweezy) from Greasy Creek. They had come to attend the wedding of their nephew, Dan'l Barlow and Sairy Hopkins.

That was when Billy's hillbilly era started.The date was November 17, 1934, and I had been with him for about seven months. The strips in those days were heavy with authentic mountain dialect that Billy had gleaned from his library and were rather difficult for the average flatlander to read and understand.

Through the years, Snuffy became Barney's sidekick, more or less, and they romped through a variety of comic situations. During World War II, Snuffy was inducted into the Army as a "yardbird," one rank below a buck private. Barney joined the Navy and I can't remember what his rank was - if any.

I was working as Billy's assistant and living in New York when a friend of mine that I had been carousing with the night before woke me up and told me that the Japanese had bombed Pearl Harbor. I didn't even know where Pearl Harbor was.

The following day, on Monday, the two of us went down to join the Navy. When they asked me to read the eye test, I was doing great until they told me to take off my glasses. Then I walked all the way up and bumped into the sign. He told me to get the hell out; I was wasting the Navy's time. As I was leaving, my friend was coming out, too. They turned him down because he had flat feet, but he eventually wound up in Italy as a paratrooper. My next thought was to try to join the Merchant Marine as a radio operator. I had fooled around with radios and the Morse code when I was a Boy Scout. The German U-boats were sinking our cargo ships right and left, all over the Atlantic, and I figured there might be some job openings for radio operators.

While these thoughts were running through my mind, I was still working with Billy. I had just delivered a set of strips to King Features and was walking along 45th Street when I noticed a freshly painted sign, "Melville Aeronautical Radio School." I went in, walked up a flight of stairs and asked the fellow if I could get a second-class license at this school. He said, "Absolutely." They could get me a second-class radio license and a job in about six weeks, and it would only cost me $200. I screamed, "Two hundred dollars?" In 1941, that was a pile of money.

He said, "If you think that's too much, come look in here," and he opened the door to a large room. There were all these guys sitting with headphones on, clacking away on typewriters. He said, "Those people over there are from such and such an airline. And there's a group from another airline. And those

twenty over there are from Pan American Airways. They think so much of our program that they send their people over here for training. I said, "That sounds great. I'll be back tomorrow."

So I went downstairs and called the personnel director at Pan American Airways. I asked, "Are you hiring radio operators to go to school?" He says, "Yes, we certainly are. For Pan American Airways African Limited." And he continued: "How many words can you take a minute?" I said, "How many do you have to take?" He said, "Twenty." Then he asked me if I could use a mill. I said, "Sure," not knowing what a mill was. He said, "Great, come on over."

I went over to Pan Am headquarters and filled out the application. He gave me a ticket and said, "I want you to go to the Melville Aeronautical School on 45th Street for a test. Do you think you can find it?" I said, "Oh, yes, I think I can find it."

Bright and early the next morning, I was at the school and the fellow there greeted me with a great big smile. He said, "Well, I see you've made a wise decision." I handed him my ticket for the test and he says, "You son of a bitch. Pan Am doesn't pay us anywhere near $200 a head." I said, "You talk too much."

I went in for the test and there was a tall fellow in charge, so I sidled up to him and whispered low, out of the corner of my mouth, "I bet ten bucks I flunk the test," and he whispered back, out of the corner of his mouth, "You got a bet!" So I folded my $10 neatly, stuck it under my typewriter and put on my earphones. The Morse code started rattling away and I started making like a piano player on the typewriter. After a little while, the tall fellow reached over, pulled the paper out of my typewriter, pocketed my ten spot, looked my paper over, gave the receptionist the OK sign, wadded up my paper and threw it in the trash can.

Six weeks later, I went to the Federal Communications Commission in downtown New York for my license. As we approached a Catholic church nearby, a friend that was with me said, "Let's go in and light a couple of candles before the test." Coming out of the church, I said, "Are you sure those candles are going to work?" And he said, "If they don't, I've got the answers right here under my belt!"

In November of '42, I was a flight radio operator with Pan Am African Limited in Khartoum in the Anglo-Egyptian Sudan. I received a radiogram from King Features that Billy had died. They wanted to know if I could possibly continue the strip. I flew back to Accra in the Gold Coast, now called Ghana. I went into the office of a Mr. Smith who headed up the Pan American operation in Africa. I told him I would like to resign so I could go back to the states and draw a comic strip.

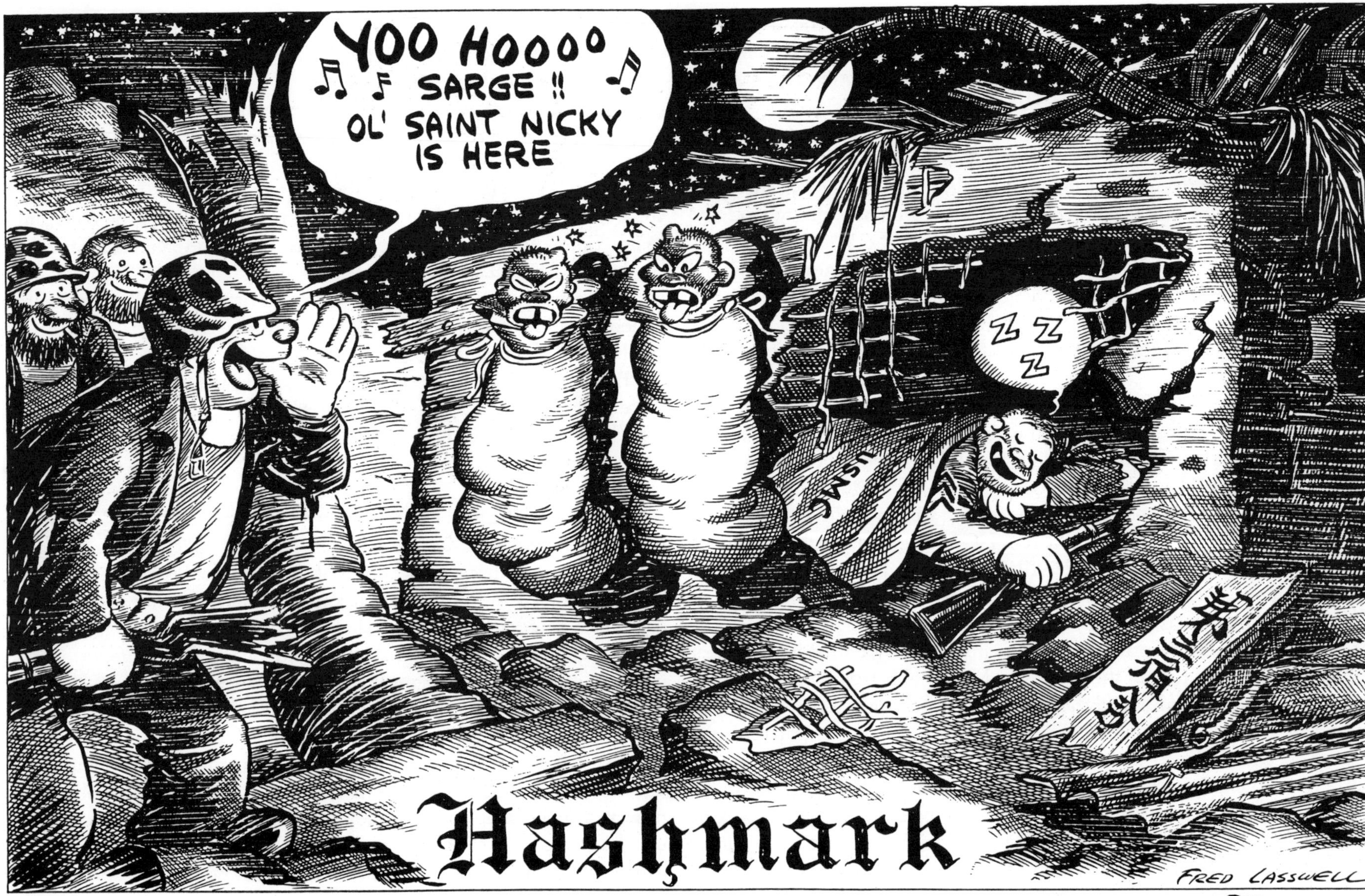
YOO HOOOO SARGE !! OL' SAINT NICKY IS HERE
Z Z Z
USMC
Hashmark
FRED LASSWELL

Above: A "Hashmark" Christmas page from December, 1945. The Japanese caricatures were typical of the propaganda cartoons during World War II. Courtesy of Fred Lasswell.

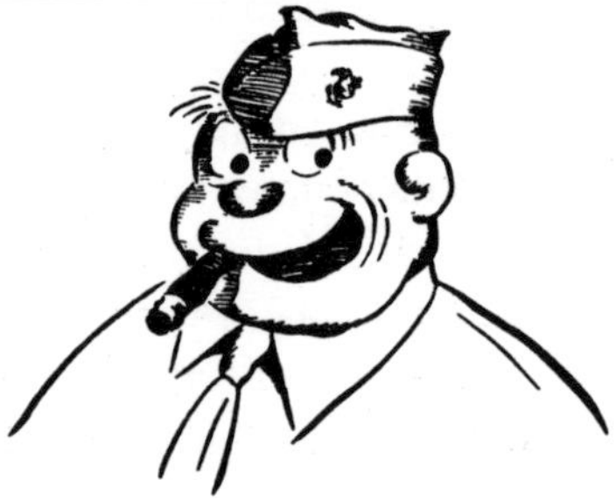

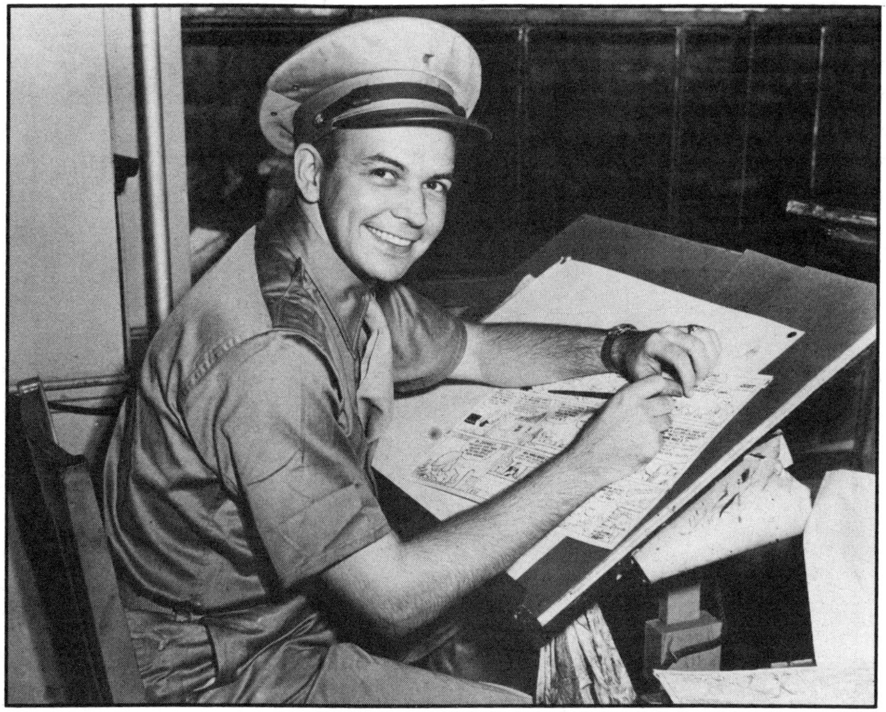

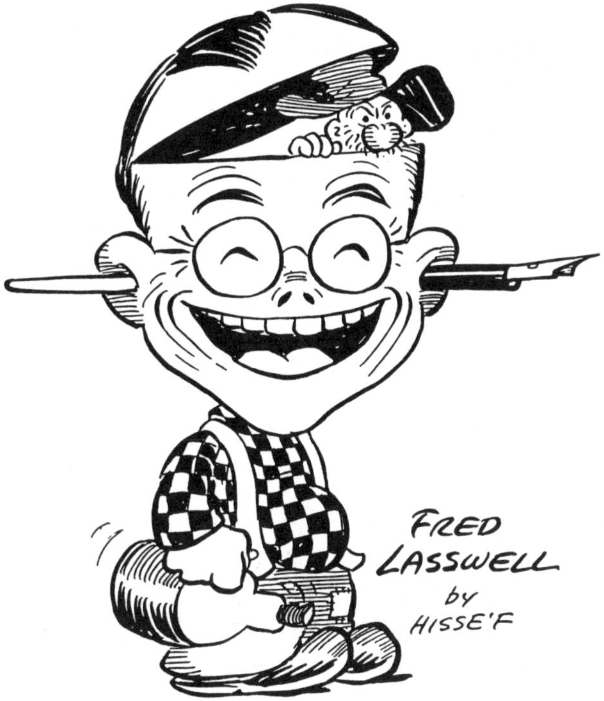
FRED
LASSWELL
by
HISSE'F

Far left: Photo of Fred in his Pan Am uniform working on a "Barney Google and Snuffy Smith" Sunday page, 1943. Collection of Fred Lasswell.

Left: Self-caricature by Fred Lasswell. Late 1940's. Collection of Mark Cohen.

He said there was absolutely no way that I could quit because I was essential to the war effort. I told him that didn't make a lot of sense to me because it was common knowledge that the Army was about to take over the Pan Am operation in Africa at any time. He said be that as it may, the only way I could get out of my contract was by an act of insubordination, such as using profanity to a superior. I said, "Why you old son of a bitch!" And he fired me on the spot. Mr. Smith explained that, by being fired, I could pick up my severance pay in Miami and get a free ride home.

After I returned home, I began producing the "Barney Google" strips and later wound up in the Marine Corps on the staff of the *Leatherneck* magazine in Washington, D.C.. While there, I created the comic strip, "Hashmark," wrote articles and did spot drawings for the magazines. We published three magazines a month: one stateside and two overseas editions. I had an apartment in Washington and was able to continue the strips, do my guard duty, White House and burial details at Arlington, and after hours entertain the troops in The Sandbar with my impressions of Hirohito and General MacArthur.

In the forties, I signed my first contract with King Features Syndicate. I shall never forget that meeting with Joe Connolly. Joe was the head of the Syndicate at that time. I had met Joe Connolly back in the mid-thirties when Barney Google began losing client papers. I remember Billy received all sorts of suggestions from King Features on how to turn the strip around. One suggestion even came from the office boy.

As a result of this pressure, Billy created a new strip which he called "Mr. and Mrs. DeB." We flew down to Miami Beach and met Joe Connolly at Damon Runyon's place on one of those fancy islands. All the furnishings in Runyon's living room were white. I sat on a white satin footstool and they sat on the white satin sofa while Billy showed Joe his strip. Joe turned the strip down, with some kind words, and Billy and I flew back to St. Petersburg.

There are two outstanding highlights in my cartooning career. The first was the opportunity Billy DeBeck afforded me in being his assistant, and the other was my second meeting with Joe Connolly.

We sat alone in his office at 235 East 45th St. in New York City and he got right to the point. He said, "Fred, as you know, Billy lost a lot of client papers and if the trend continues, we'll have to drop it. If you would like to take over the strip, here's what you do: Keep the same general look and flavor of the strip for a brief transition period and then gradually inject your own ideas and your own characters into the strip. I will give you a weekly guarantee. As an added incentive, I'll include a 50-50 clause in the contract. So go to it and lots of luck." I walked out of Connolly's office on air.

Apparently, Joe Connolly's inspiration began to bear fruit. We stopped losing client papers and slowly, month by month, we began a steady climb in papers and income. I have abandoned the authentic mountain dialect in order to reach a broader audience. I just try to keep it folksy, with a country twang. It's gratifying to know that now, in the year 1994, the strip Billy started seventy-five years ago and that was intrusted to my care fifty years ago is still going strong.

Over the years, I have introduced a host of new characters: Little Tater, Loweezy's change of life baby; Elviney, her gossipy neighbor; Lukey, Elviney's henpecked husband; ol' Bullet, Snuffy's hound dog, his pride and joy; Parson Tuttle, always available for vittles; ol' Doc Pritchard, the health care guru of Hootin' Holler; Sheriff Tate; Aunt Sukey, Loweezy's plow mule; Lucifer, Jughaid's frog; Jamey, Jughaid's sidekick; and their school ma'rm, Miss Prunelly; Uriah, the mailman; Silas, the general storekeeper; Samanthy and Mary Beth, Jughaid's little sweet patootie, and many others. I have a great empathy for these folks and critters. I really don't know beans about the racetrack world of Barney Google and Spark Plug, and that is why I have changed it to a Snuffy strip exclusively. I do slip Barney and Sparky back in, from time to time, for the old folks.

I'd like to close this little piece by offering my heartfelt thanks to all of those wonderful people who have made possible any success I may have achieved: my folks; Billy DeBeck; Joe Connolly; Joe D'Angelo; Ted Hannah and all the gang at King Features; and my many assistants through the years, especially Bob Donovan and Bobby Swain. I also offer my deepest appreciation to Lucy Caswell, of Ohio State University, and, last but foremost, my lovely bride, Shirley Ann.

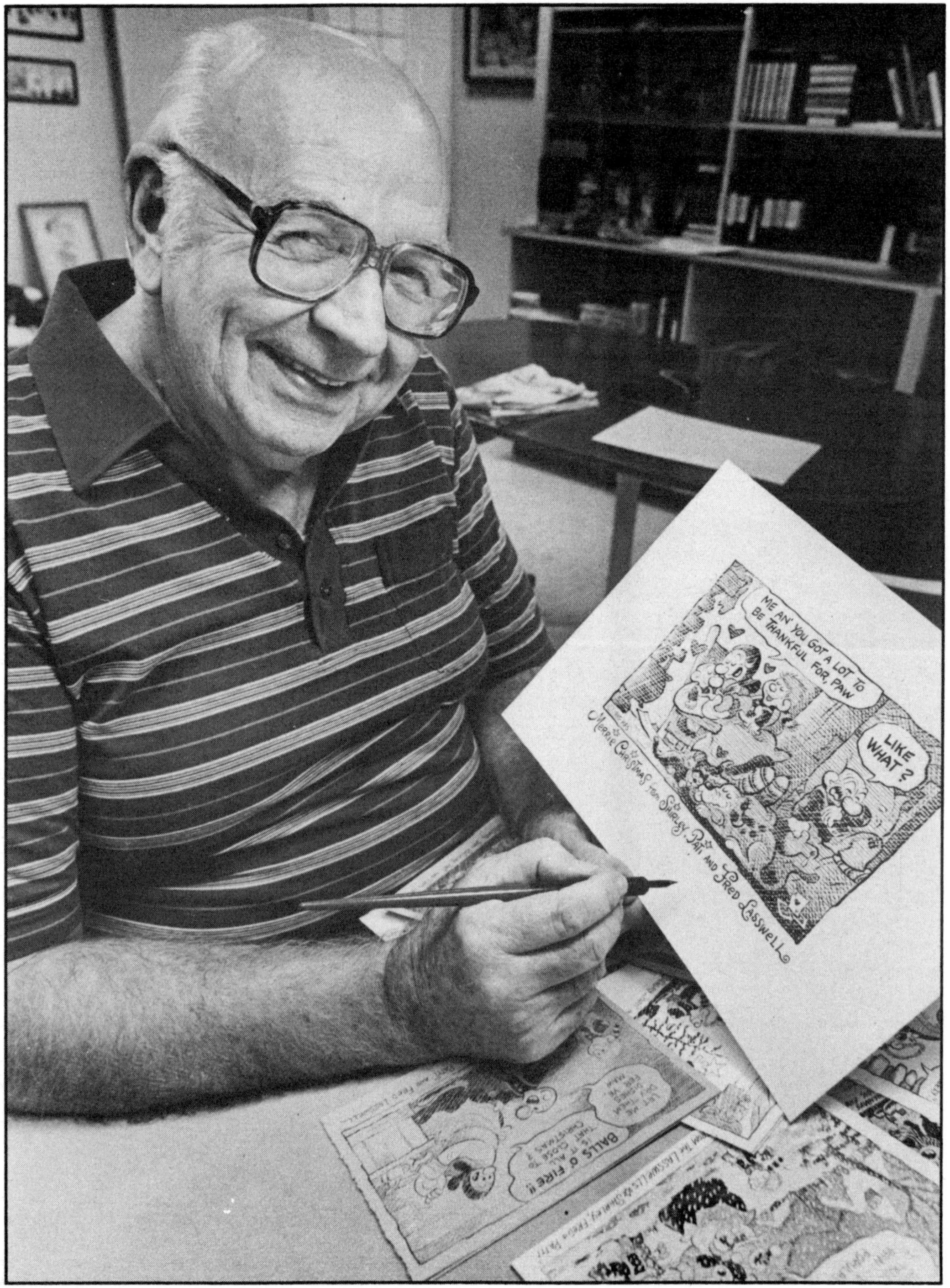

ME AN' YOU GOT A LOT TO BE THANKFUL FOR, PAW
LIKE WHAT?

Right: Fred Lasswell in his studio working on one of his annual Christmas cards, December 10, 1985, Photo by Britt Laughlin. Courtesy of Fred Lasswell.

Next page: Christmas card artwork, 1948 Courtesy of Fred Lasswell.

MERRIE CHRISTMAS

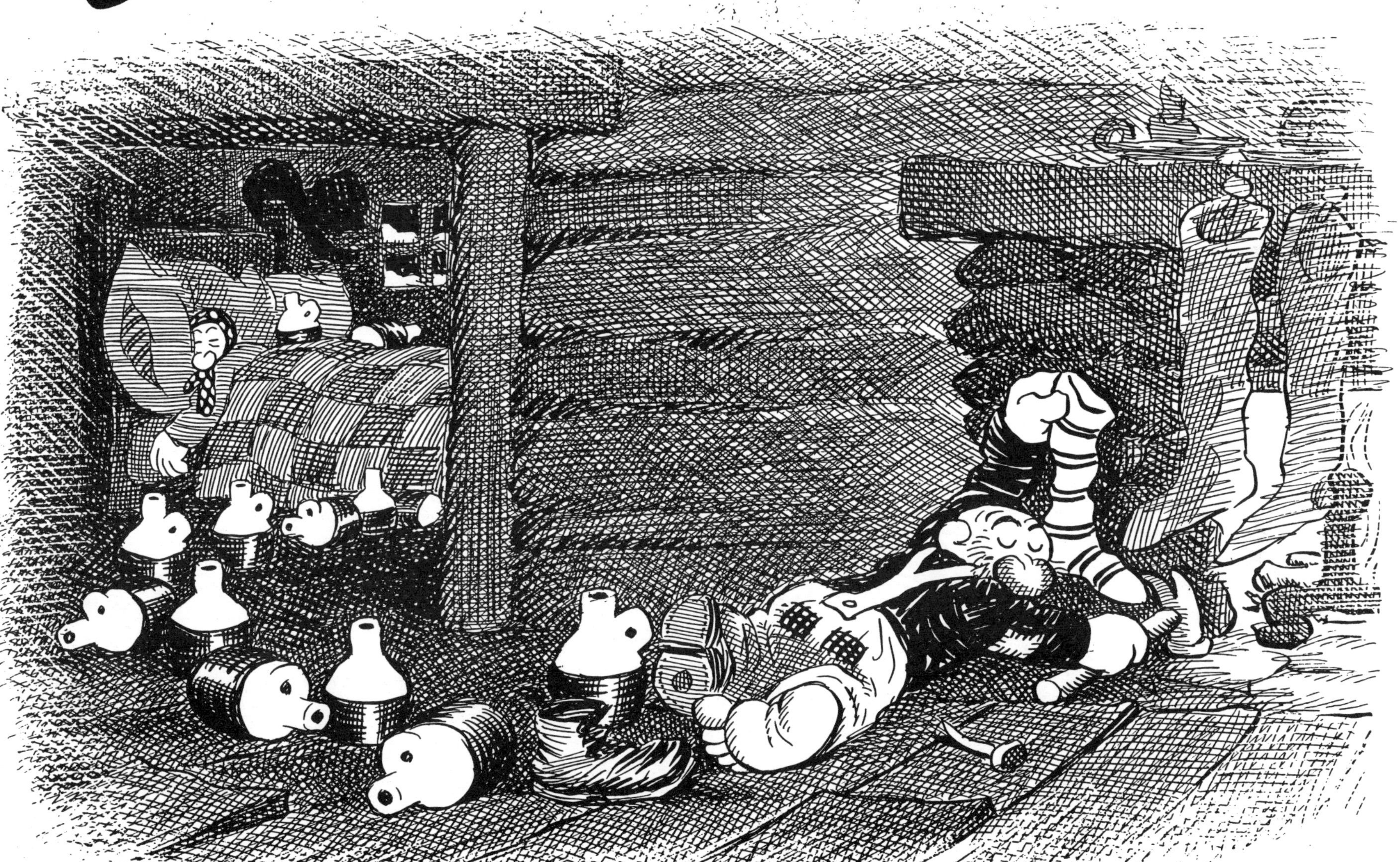

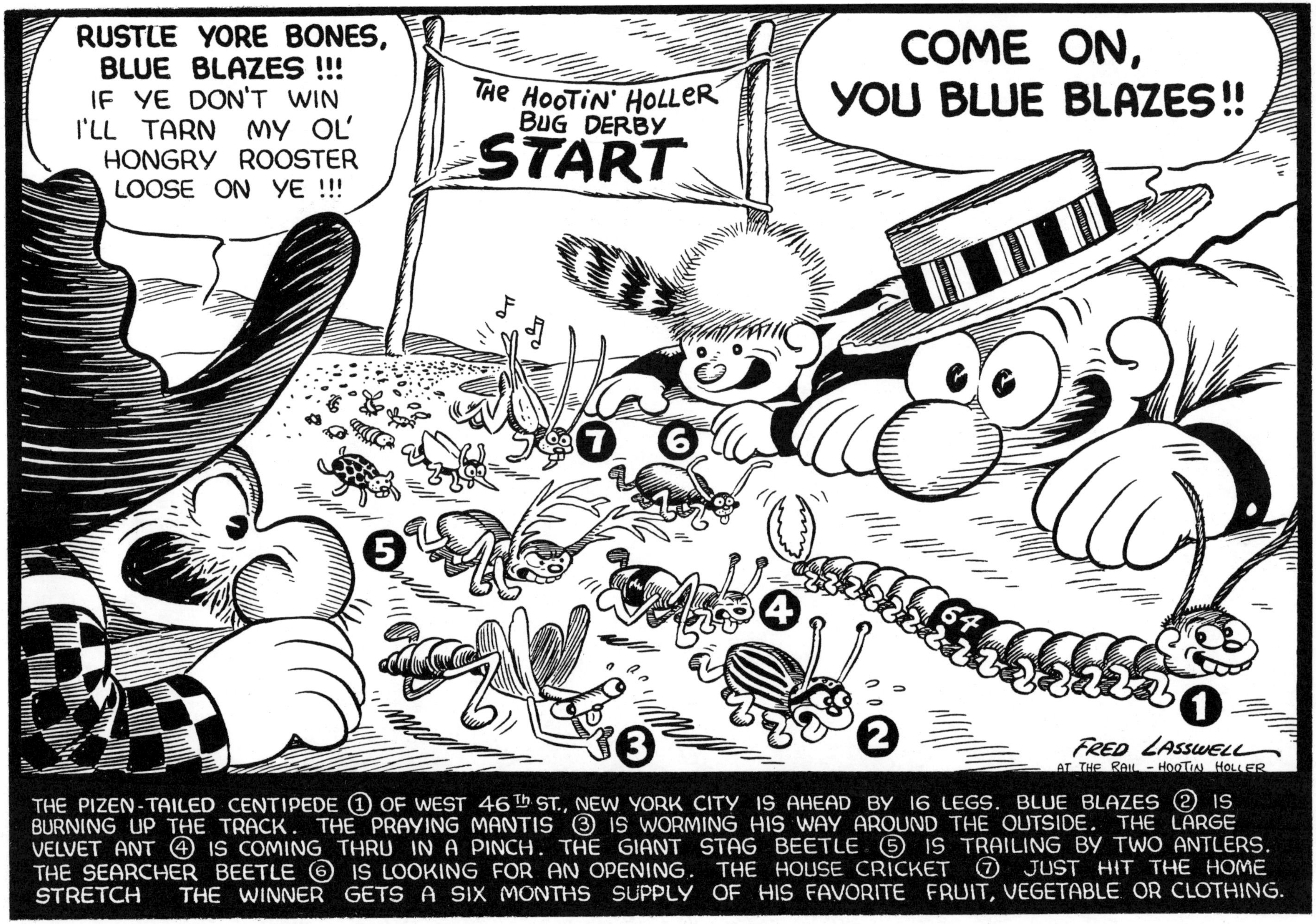
RUSTLE YORE BONES, BLUE BLAZES !!! IF YE DON'T WIN I'LL TARN MY OL' HONGRY ROOSTER LOOSE ON YE !!!
THE HOOTIN' HOLLER BUG DERBY
START
COME ON, YOU BLUE BLAZES!!
7
6
5
4
64
3
2
1
FRED LASSWELL
AT THE RAIL - HOOTIN HOLLER
THE PIZEN-TAILED CENTIPEDE ① OF WEST 46TH ST., NEW YORK CITY IS AHEAD BY 16 LEGS. BLUE BLAZES ② IS BURNING UP THE TRACK. THE PRAYING MANTIS ③ IS WORMING HIS WAY AROUND THE OUTSIDE. THE LARGE VELVET ANT ④ IS COMING THRU IN A PINCH. THE GIANT STAG BEETLE ⑤ IS TRAILING BY TWO ANTLERS. THE SEARCHER BEETLE ⑥ IS LOOKING FOR AN OPENING. THE HOUSE CRICKET ⑦ JUST HIT THE HOME STRETCH THE WINNER GETS A SIX MONTHS SUPPLY OF HIS FAVORITE FRUIT, VEGETABLE OR CLOTHING.

Above: Illustration by Fred Lasswell for a magazine article about the "All American Bug Race," 1946. Courtesy of Fred Lasswell.

The Lasswell Legacy

1946 —

When World War II ended in 1945, Fred Lasswell took over full control of "Barney Google and Snuffy Smith." Barney and Snuffy returned home, and when they were reunited, one of their first co-ventures was organizing the "All American Bug Race." Thousands of readers sent in letters to Fred trying to enter their own insects in the race and some even mailed actual bugs!

During the next eight years, a progression of outrageous characters paraded through the strip. Tiger L'il, a sexy nightclub dancer; Sadie the Bearded Lady, a side-show freak; Mr. Plaster from Paris, a sculptor; and Tieless Ty Tyler - The Tie Tycoon, were among the most memorable. Lasswell also introduced new hillbilly folks from Hootin' Holler in his stories. Blunderbuss Smith, Snuffy's cousin; Miz Meddlin Smif, Snuffy's maw; and Snuffy's long-lost Pappy were poor relations who returned for a visit. Riddles Barlow married Cricket Smif and Inventin' Winton hitched up with Granny Creeps and Snuffy and Loweezy even got re-married. Barney Google continued to come and go, but he gradually took a back seat to the local color.

In 1954, Barney and Snuffy traveled to Washington, DC. This was to be their last long adventure together. When Barney rode out of the strip on September 7, 1954, he ceased to be a regular character in the strip. He continues to make occasional appearances, but never sticks around for long.

In the mid-1950's, Lasswell began to abandon continuing story-lines for a gag-a-day format. Supporting characters like Sheriff Tait, Parson Tuttle, Doc Pritchart, Elviney, Uriah, Samanthy and Miss Prunelly, as well as the Smith clan, Snuffy, Loweezy and Jughaid, were now carrying the strip.

Fred has always claimed that he drew on his own background when he took over "Barney Google and Snuffy Smith." "My folks had come out of a country atmosphere, so I was very comfortable with country people," he says. "I just fell into the spirit of the type of people Snuffy and Loweezy were. So I started concentrating during the transition period on slowly working Barney out of there and trying to get a little more down-home feeling in the strip."

This sensibility is what makes Fred Lasswell's contribution to the legacy of "Barney Google and Snuffy Smith" uniquely his own. The beautifully rendered backgrounds of Fred's Hootin' Holler evoke a rural ambience that is distinct from Billy and Barney's urban milieu. Fred has also established a loving relationship between Snuffy and Loweezy that gives the strip a feeling of warmth and tenderness.

Billy DeBeck created and nurtured "Barney Google and Snuffy Smith" during his 23-year tenure. Fred Lasswell has collaborated on the strip for 60 years and has guided its destiny for over half a century. He took a comic strip that had earned a place in history and developed it into an enduring classic.

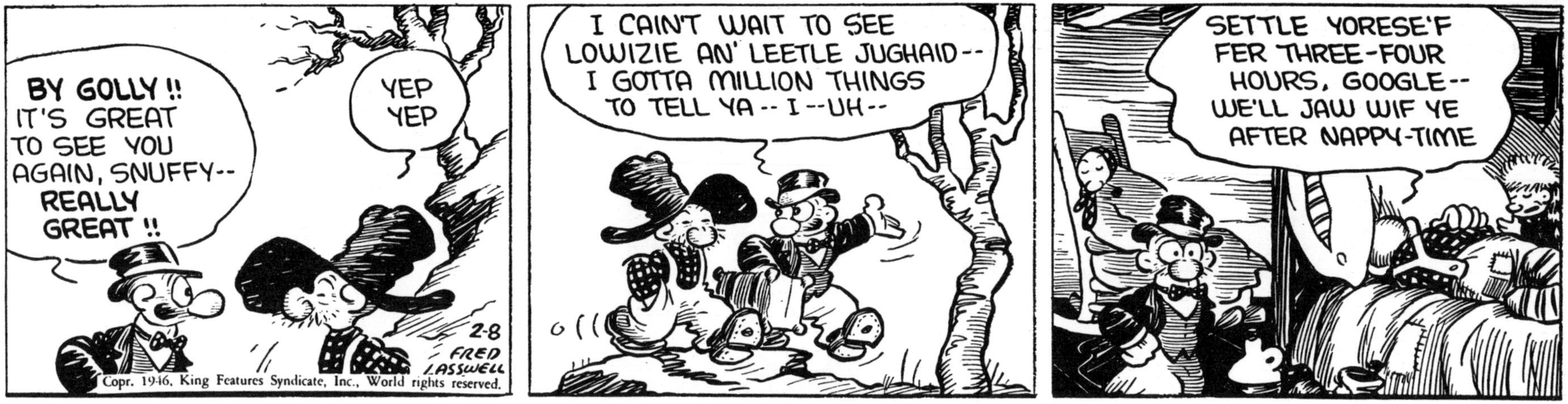
BY GOLLY!! IT'S GREAT TO SEE YOU AGAIN, SNUFFY-- REALLY GREAT!!
YEP YEP
I CAIN'T WAIT TO SEE LOWIZIE AN' LEETLE JUGHAID-- I GOTTA MILLION THINGS TO TELL YA -- I --UH--
SETTLE YORESE'F FER THREE-FOUR HOURS, GOOGLE-- WE'LL JAW WIF YE AFTER NAPPY-TIME
2-8
FRED LASSWELL
Copr. 1946, King Features Syndicate, Inc., World rights reserved.

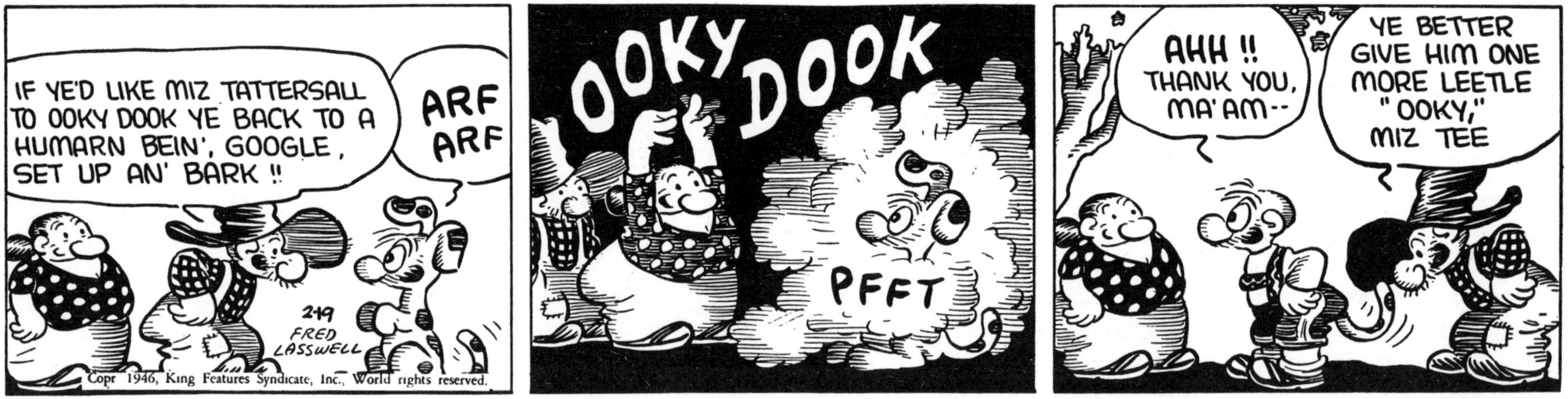
IF YE'D LIKE MIZ TATTERSALL TO OOKY DOOK YE BACK TO A HUMARN BEIN', GOOGLE, SET UP AN' BARK!!
ARF ARF
2-19
FRED LASSWELL
Copr 1946, King Features Syndicate, Inc., World rights reserved.
OOKY DOOK
PFFT
AHH!! THANK YOU, MA'AM--
YE BETTER GIVE HIM ONE MORE LEETLE "OOKY," MIZ TEE

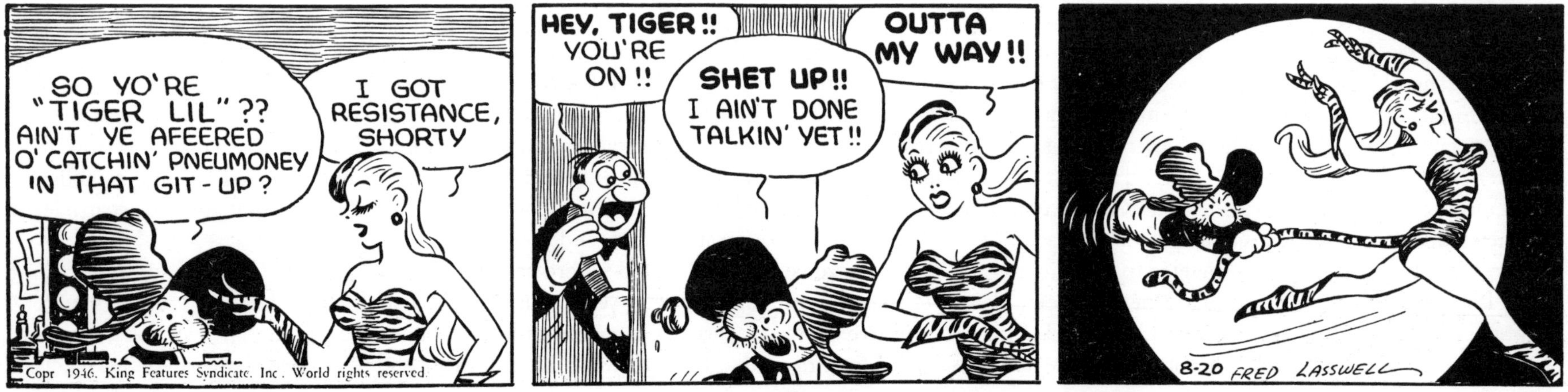
SO YO'RE "TIGER LIL"?? AIN'T YE AFEERED O' CATCHIN' PNEUMONEY IN THAT GIT-UP?
I GOT RESISTANCE, SHORTY
Copr 1946, King Features Syndicate, Inc. World rights reserved.
HEY, TIGER!! YOU'RE ON!!
SHET UP!! I AIN'T DONE TALKIN' YET!!
OUTTA MY WAY!!
8-20 FRED LASSWELL

The "Barney Google and Snuffy Smith" daily comic strips from 1946 to 1994 are reproduced from syndicate proofs. Courtesy of King Features Syndicate.

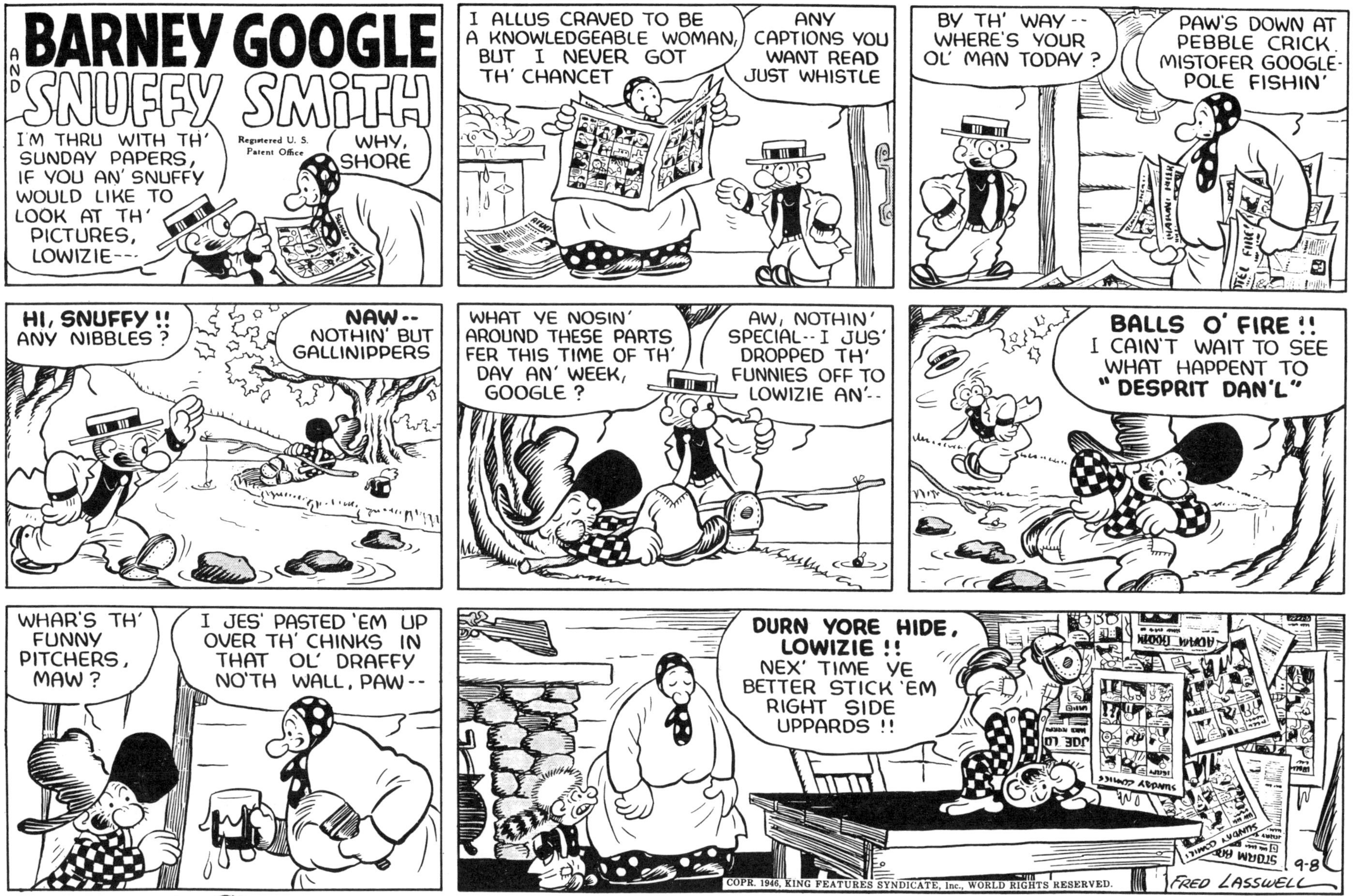
AND
BARNEY GOOGLE
SNUFFY SMITH
Registered U. S. Patent Office
I'M THRU WITH TH' SUNDAY PAPERS, IF YOU AN' SNUFFY WOULD LIKE TO LOOK AT TH' PICTURES, LOWIZIE---
WHY, SHORE
I ALLUS CRAVED TO BE A KNOWLEDGEABLE WOMAN, BUT I NEVER GOT TH' CHANCET
ANY CAPTIONS YOU WANT READ JUST WHISTLE
BY TH' WAY-- WHERE'S YOUR OL' MAN TODAY ?
PAW'S DOWN AT PEBBLE CRICK, MISTOFER GOOGLE-POLE FISHIN'
HI, SNUFFY !! ANY NIBBLES ?
NAW-- NOTHIN' BUT GALLINIPPERS
WHAT YE NOSIN' AROUND THESE PARTS FER THIS TIME OF TH' DAY AN' WEEK, GOOGLE ?
AW, NOTHIN' SPECIAL-- I JUS' DROPPED TH' FUNNIES OFF TO LOWIZIE AN'--
BALLS O' FIRE !! I CAIN'T WAIT TO SEE WHAT HAPPENT TO "DESPRIT DAN'L"
WHAR'S TH' FUNNY PITCHERS, MAW ?
I JES' PASTED 'EM UP OVER TH' CHINKS IN THAT OL' DRAFFY NO'TH WALL, PAW--
DURN YORE HIDE, LOWIZIE !! NEX' TIME YE BETTER STICK 'EM RIGHT SIDE UPPARDS !!
9-8
COPR. 1946, KING FEATURES SYNDICATE, Inc., WORLD RIGHTS RESERVED.
FRED LASSWELL

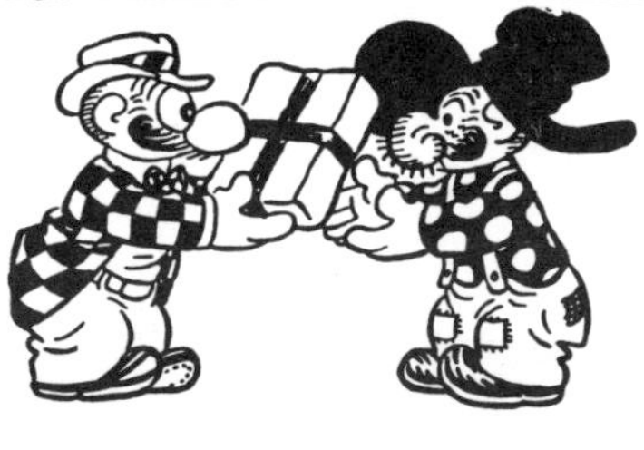

Above: Barney Google brings the Sunday Funnies to Hootin' Holler.
"Barney Google and Snuffy Smith" Sunday page, September 8, 1946.
Courtesy of King Features Syndicate.

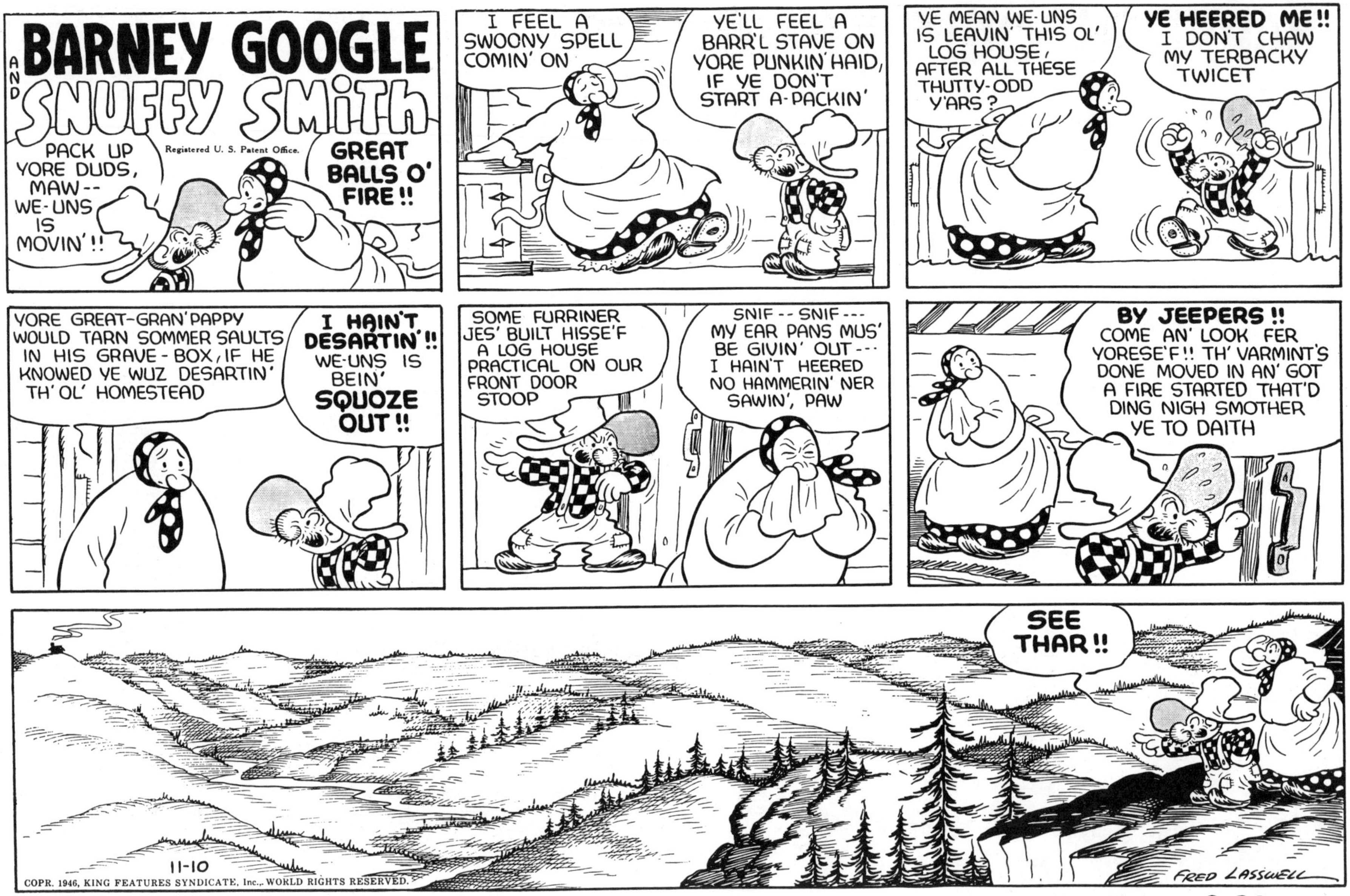
AND
BARNEY GOOGLE
SNUFFY SMITH
Registered U. S. Patent Office.
PACK UP YORE DUDS, MAW -- WE-UNS IS MOVIN' !!
GREAT BALLS O' FIRE !!
I FEEL A SWOONY SPELL COMIN' ON
YE'LL FEEL A BARR'L STAVE ON YORE PUNKIN' HAID, IF YE DON'T START A-PACKIN'
YE MEAN WE-UNS IS LEAVIN' THIS OL' LOG HOUSE, AFTER ALL THESE THUTTY-ODD Y'ARS ?
YE HEERED ME !! I DON'T CHAW MY TERBACKY TWICET
YORE GREAT-GRAN'PAPPY WOULD TARN SOMMER SAULTS IN HIS GRAVE-BOX, IF HE KNOWED YE WUZ DESARTIN' TH' OL' HOMESTEAD
I HAIN'T DESARTIN' !! WE-UNS IS BEIN' SQUOZE OUT !!
SOME FURRINER JES' BUILT HISSE'F A LOG HOUSE PRACTICAL ON OUR FRONT DOOR STOOP
SNIF -- SNIF --- MY EAR PANS MUS' BE GIVIN' OUT --- I HAIN'T HEERED NO HAMMERIN' NER SAWIN', PAW
BY JEEPERS !! COME AN' LOOK FER YORESE'F !! TH' VARMINT'S DONE MOVED IN AN' GOT A FIRE STARTED THAT'D DING NIGH SMOTHER YE TO DAITH
SEE THAR !!
11-10
COPR. 1946, KING FEATURES SYNDICATE, Inc., WORLD RIGHTS RESERVED.
FRED LASSWELL

Above: Snuffy threatens to move because of overcrowding in the hills. "Barney Google and Snuffy Smith" Sunday page, November 10, 1946. Courtesy of King Features Syndicate.

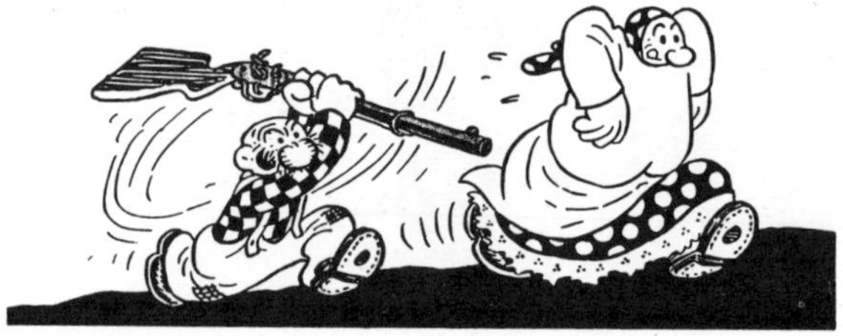

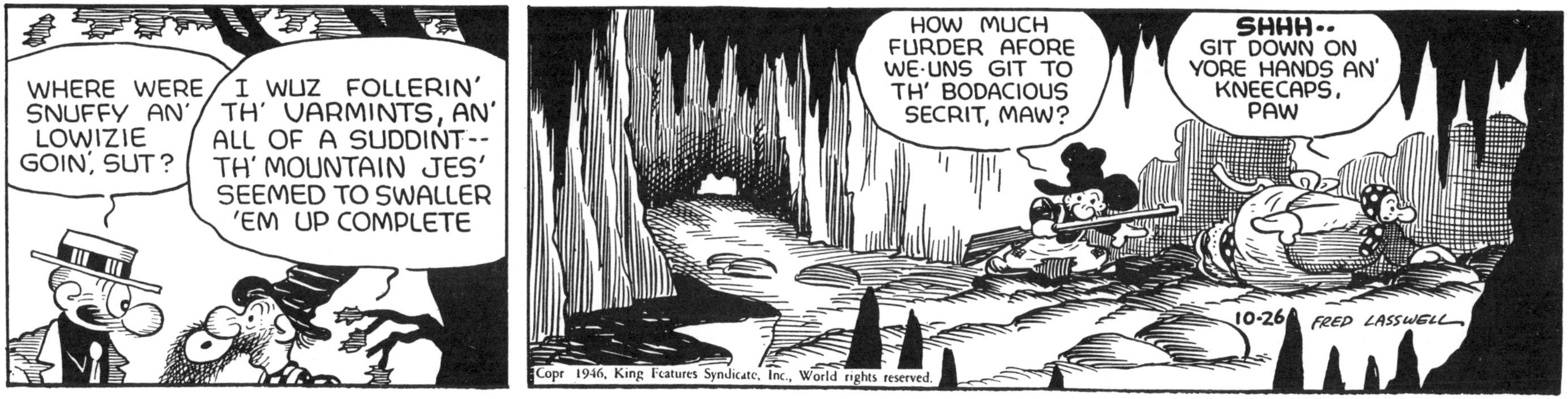
WHERE WERE SNUFFY AN' LOWIZIE GOIN', SUT?
I WUZ FOLLERIN' TH' VARMINTS, AN' ALL OF A SUDDINT-- TH' MOUNTAIN JES' SEEMED TO SWALLER 'EM UP COMPLETE
HOW MUCH FURDER AFORE WE-UNS GIT TO TH' BODACIOUS SECRIT, MAW?
SHHH.. GIT DOWN ON YORE HANDS AN' KNEECAPS, PAW
10-26 FRED LASSWELL
Copr 1946, King Features Syndicate, Inc., World rights reserved.

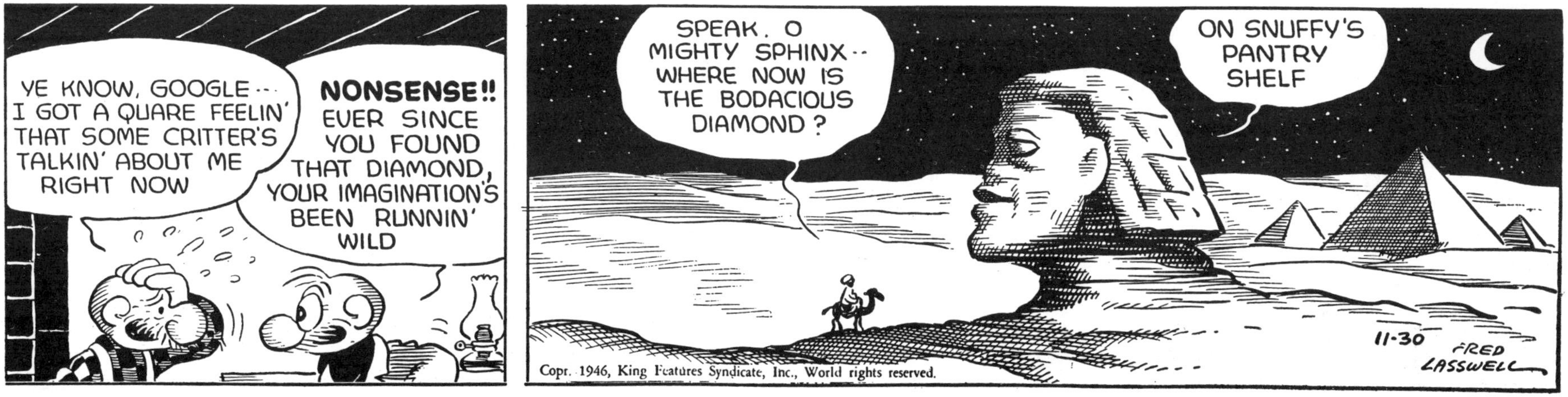
YE KNOW, GOOGLE-- I GOT A QUARE FEELIN' THAT SOME CRITTER'S TALKIN' ABOUT ME RIGHT NOW
NONSENSE!! EVER SINCE YOU FOUND THAT DIAMOND, YOUR IMAGINATION'S BEEN RUNNIN' WILD
SPEAK, O MIGHTY SPHINX-- WHERE NOW IS THE BODACIOUS DIAMOND?
ON SNUFFY'S PANTRY SHELF
11-30 FRED LASSWELL
Copr. 1946, King Features Syndicate, Inc., World rights reserved.

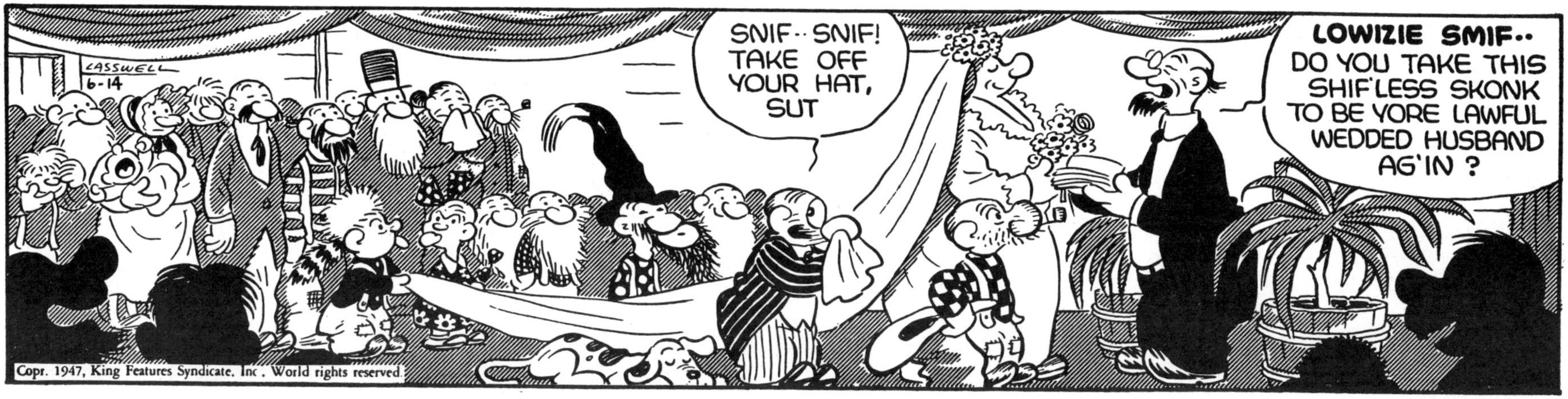
LASSWELL 6-14
SNIF-- SNIF! TAKE OFF YOUR HAT, SUT
LOWIZIE SMIF.. DO YOU TAKE THIS SHIF'LESS SKONK TO BE YORE LAWFUL WEDDED HUSBAND AG'IN?
Copr. 1947, King Features Syndicate, Inc., World rights reserved.

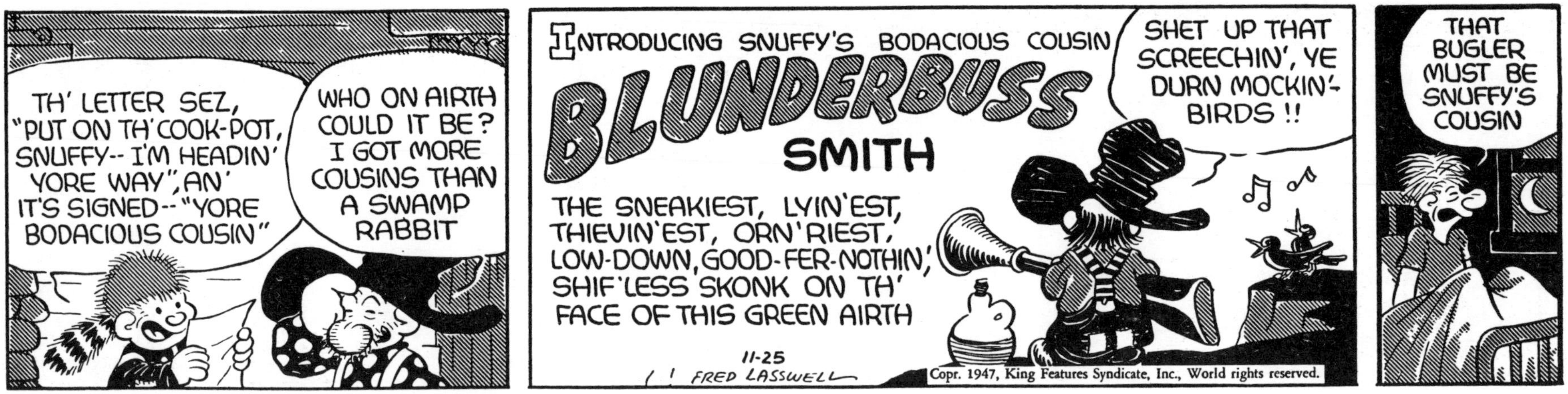
TH' LETTER SEZ, "PUT ON TH' COOK-POT, SNUFFY-- I'M HEADIN' YORE WAY", AN' IT'S SIGNED--"YORE BODACIOUS COUSIN"
WHO ON AIRTH COULD IT BE? I GOT MORE COUSINS THAN A SWAMP RABBIT
INTRODUCING SNUFFY'S BODACIOUS COUSIN
BLUNDERBUSS SMITH
THE SNEAKIEST, LYIN'EST, THIEVIN'EST, ORN'RIEST, LOW-DOWN, GOOD-FER-NOTHIN', SHIF'LESS SKONK ON TH' FACE OF THIS GREEN AIRTH
SHET UP THAT SCREECHIN', YE DURN MOCKIN'-BIRDS !!
11-25
FRED LASSWELL
Copr. 1947, King Features Syndicate, Inc., World rights reserved.
THAT BUGLER MUST BE SNUFFY'S COUSIN

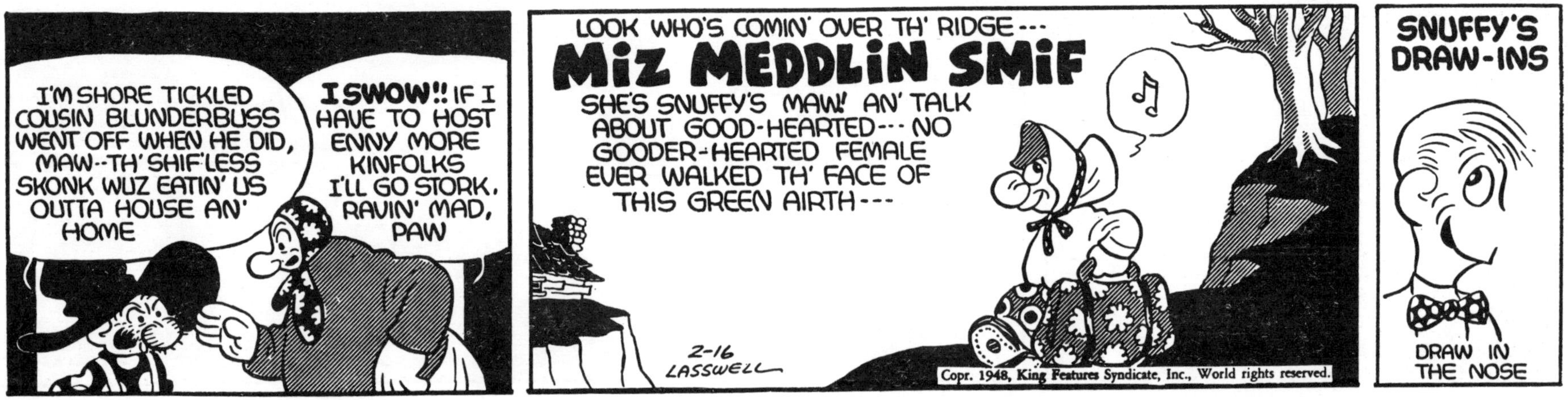
I'M SHORE TICKLED COUSIN BLUNDERBUSS WENT OFF WHEN HE DID, MAW--TH' SHIF'LESS SKONK WUZ EATIN' US OUTTA HOUSE AN' HOME
I SWOW!! IF I HAVE TO HOST ENNY MORE KINFOLKS I'LL GO STORK-RAVIN' MAD, PAW
LOOK WHO'S COMIN' OVER TH' RIDGE---
MIZ MEDDLIN SMIF
SHE'S SNUFFY'S MAW! AN' TALK ABOUT GOOD-HEARTED--- NO GOODER-HEARTED FEMALE EVER WALKED TH' FACE OF THIS GREEN AIRTH---
2-16
LASSWELL
Copr. 1948, King Features Syndicate, Inc., World rights reserved.
SNUFFY'S DRAW-INS
DRAW IN THE NOSE

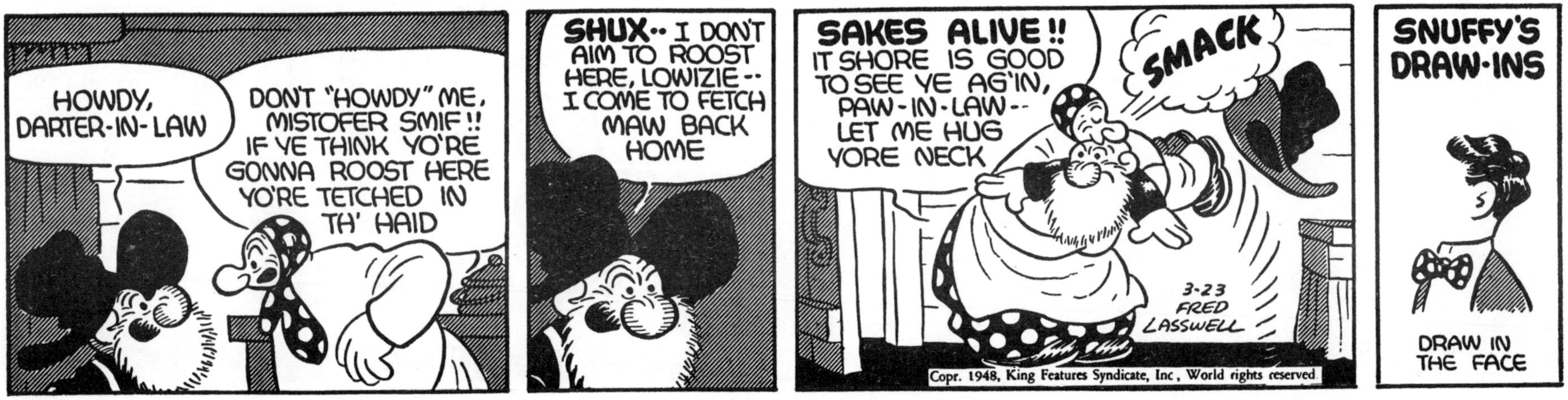
HOWDY, DARTER-IN-LAW
DON'T "HOWDY" ME, MISTOFER SMIF!! IF YE THINK YO'RE GONNA ROOST HERE YO'RE TETCHED IN TH' HAID
SHUX-- I DON'T AIM TO ROOST HERE, LOWIZIE-- I COME TO FETCH MAW BACK HOME
SAKES ALIVE!! IT SHORE IS GOOD TO SEE YE AG'IN, PAW-IN-LAW-- LET ME HUG YORE NECK
SMACK
3-23
FRED LASSWELL
Copr. 1948, King Features Syndicate, Inc, World rights reserved
SNUFFY'S DRAW-INS
DRAW IN THE FACE

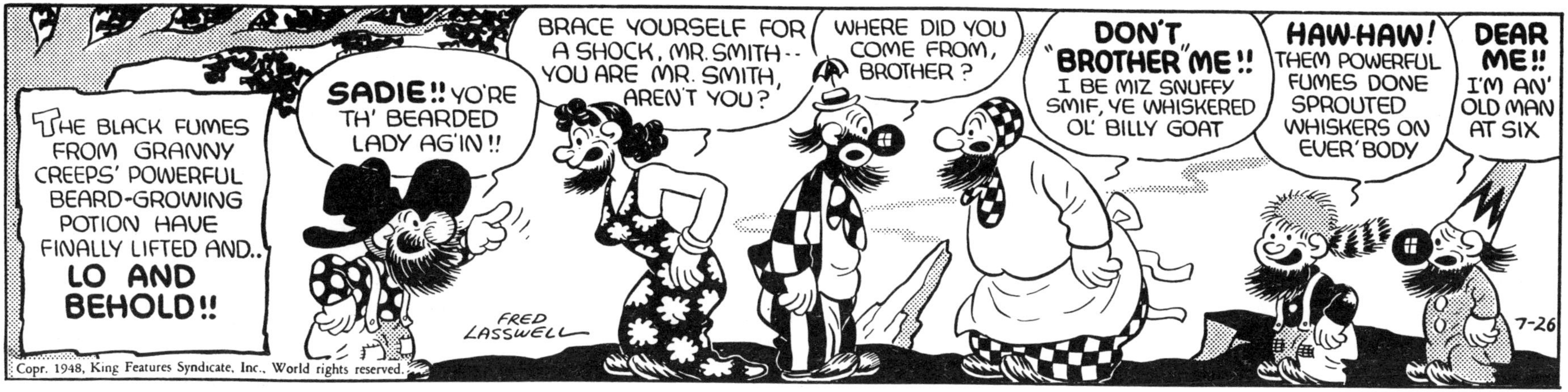
THE BLACK FUMES FROM GRANNY CREEPS' POWERFUL BEARD-GROWING POTION HAVE FINALLY LIFTED AND.. LO AND BEHOLD!!
SADIE!! YO'RE TH' BEARDED LADY AG'IN!!
BRACE YOURSELF FOR A SHOCK, MR. SMITH-- YOU ARE MR. SMITH, AREN'T YOU?
WHERE DID YOU COME FROM, BROTHER?
DON'T "BROTHER" ME!! I BE MIZ SNUFFY SMIF, YE WHISKERED OL' BILLY GOAT
HAW-HAW! THEM POWERFUL FUMES DONE SPROUTED WHISKERS ON EVER'BODY
DEAR ME!! I'M AN' OLD MAN AT SIX
FRED LASSWELL
7-26
Copr. 1948, King Features Syndicate, Inc., World rights reserved.

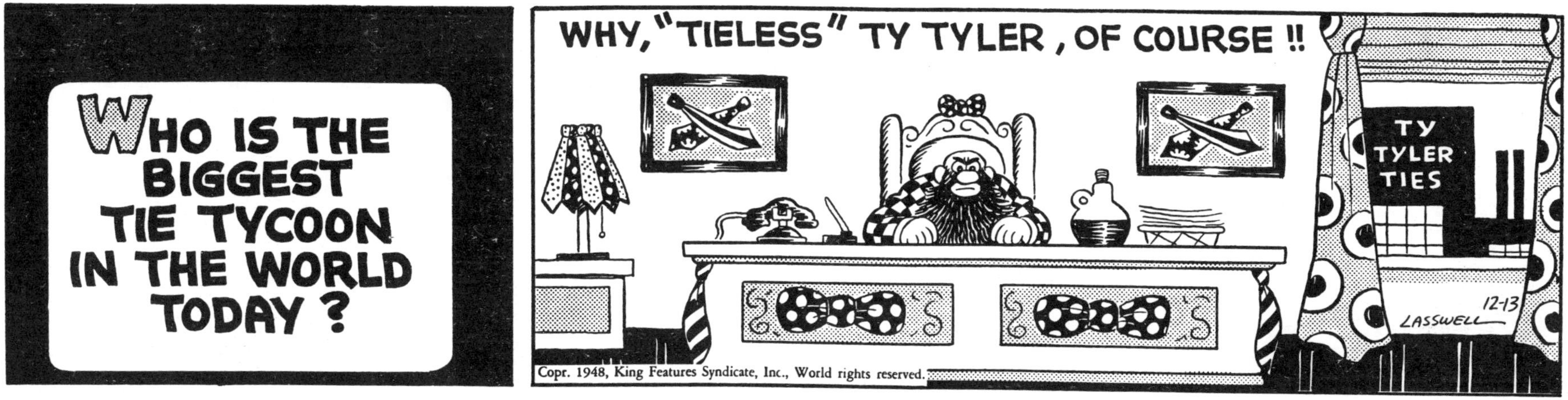
WHO IS THE BIGGEST TIE TYCOON IN THE WORLD TODAY?
WHY, "TIELESS" TY TYLER, OF COURSE!!
TY TYLER TIES
LASSWELL
12-13
Copr. 1948, King Features Syndicate, Inc., World rights reserved.

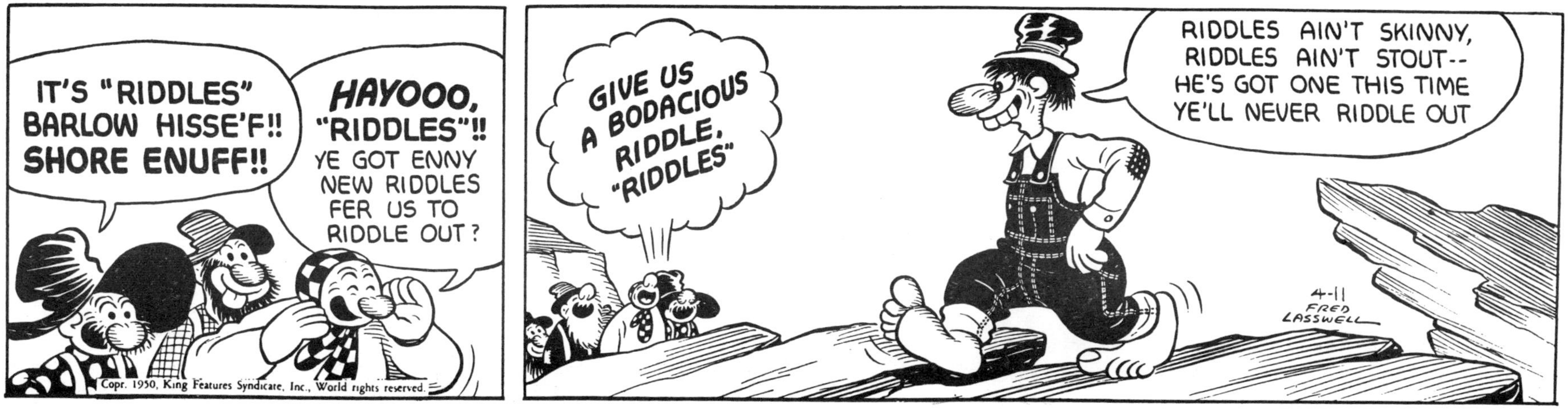
IT'S "RIDDLES" BARLOW HISSE'F!! SHORE ENUFF!!
HAYOOO, "RIDDLES"!! YE GOT ENNY NEW RIDDLES FER US TO RIDDLE OUT?
GIVE US A BODACIOUS RIDDLE, "RIDDLES"
RIDDLES AIN'T SKINNY, RIDDLES AIN'T STOUT-- HE'S GOT ONE THIS TIME YE'LL NEVER RIDDLE OUT
4-11
FRED LASSWELL
Copr. 1950, King Features Syndicate, Inc., World rights reserved.

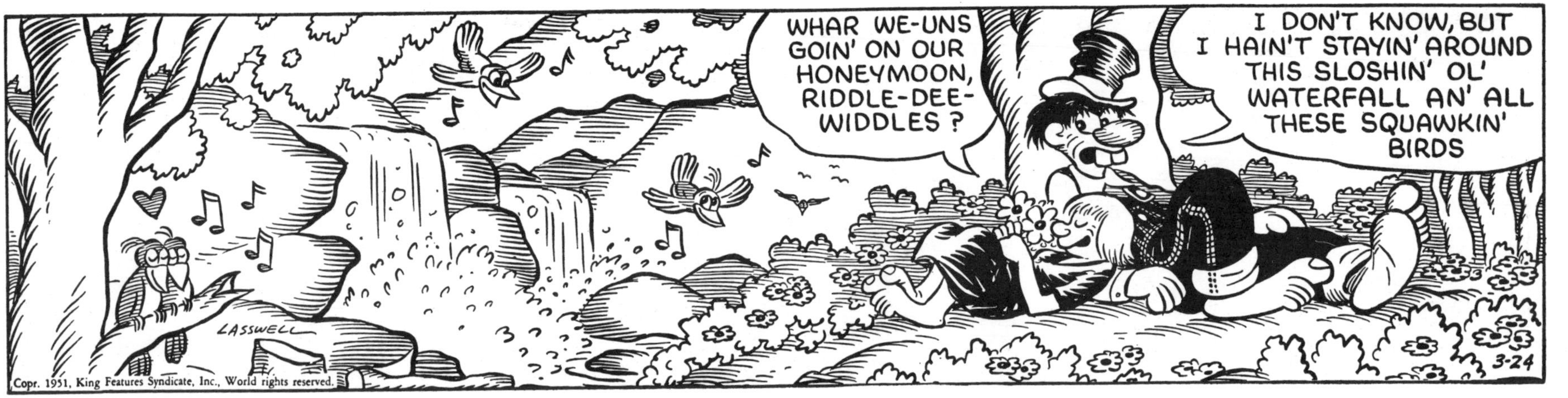
WHAR WE-UNS GOIN' ON OUR HONEYMOON, RIDDLE-DEE-WIDDLES ?
I DON'T KNOW, BUT I HAIN'T STAYIN' AROUND THIS SLOSHIN' OL' WATERFALL AN' ALL THESE SQUAWKIN' BIRDS
LASSWELL
3-24
Copr. 1951, King Features Syndicate, Inc., World rights reserved.

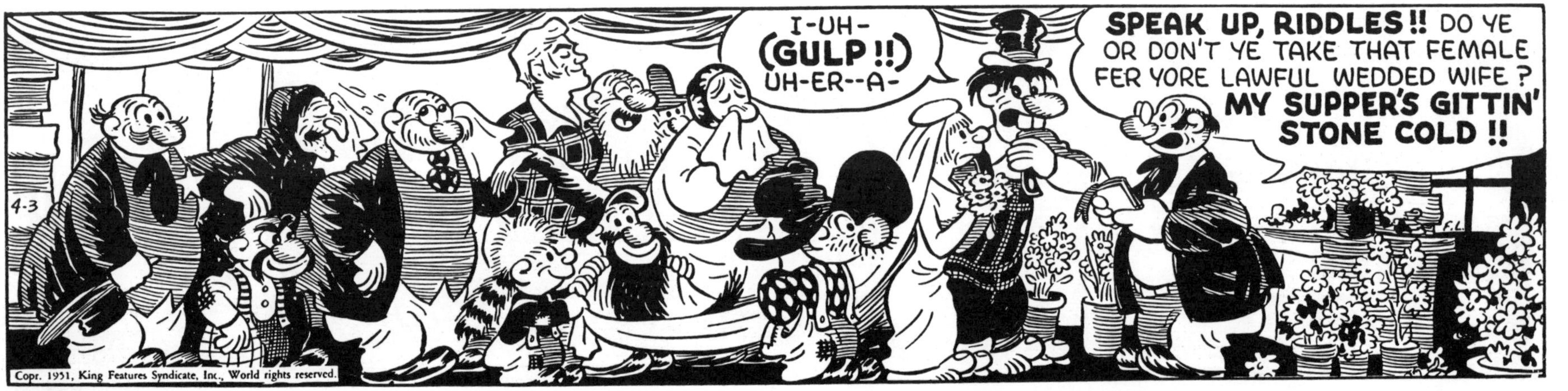
I-UH- (GULP !!) UH-ER--A-
SPEAK UP, RIDDLES !! DO YE OR DON'T YE TAKE THAT FEMALE FER YORE LAWFUL WEDDED WIFE ? MY SUPPER'S GITTIN' STONE COLD !!
4-3
F.L.
Copr. 1951, King Features Syndicate, Inc., World rights reserved.

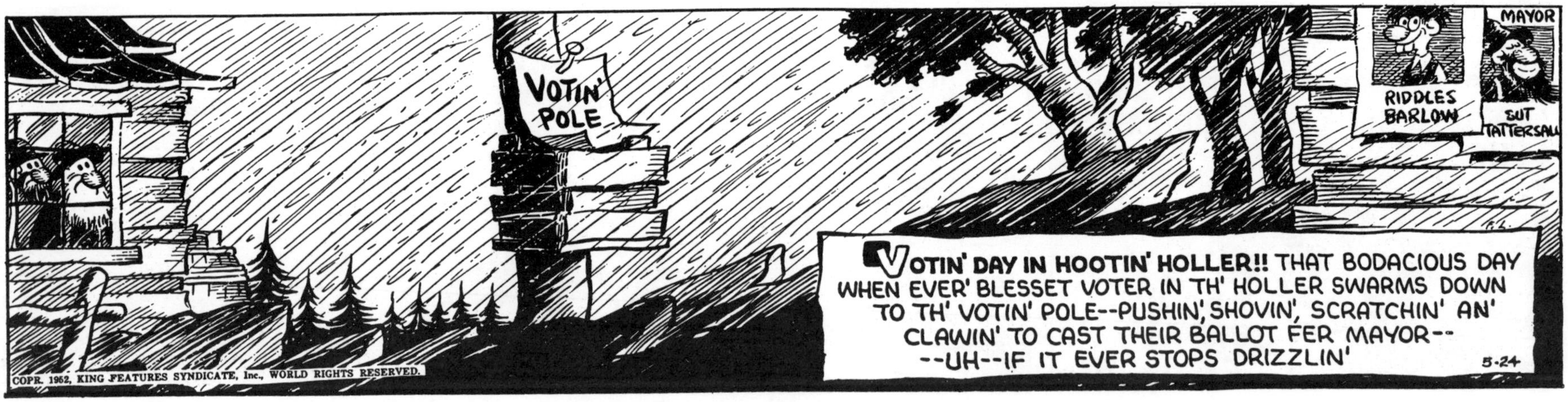
VOTIN' POLE
MAYOR
RIDDLES BARLOW
SUT TATTERSALL
VOTIN' DAY IN HOOTIN' HOLLER!! THAT BODACIOUS DAY WHEN EVER' BLESSET VOTER IN TH' HOLLER SWARMS DOWN TO TH' VOTIN' POLE--PUSHIN', SHOVIN', SCRATCHIN' AN' CLAWIN' TO CAST THEIR BALLOT FER MAYOR-- --UH--IF IT EVER STOPS DRIZZLIN'
5-24
COPR. 1952, KING FEATURES SYNDICATE, Inc., WORLD RIGHTS RESERVED.

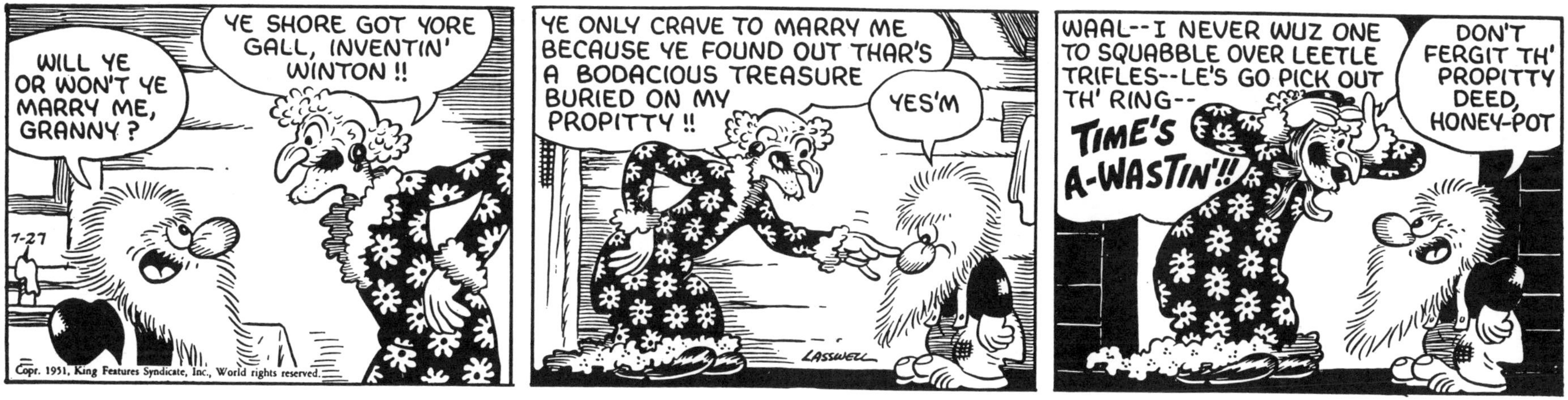
WILL YE OR WON'T YE MARRY ME, GRANNY ?
YE SHORE GOT YORE GALL, INVENTIN' WINTON !!
7-27
Copr. 1951, King Features Syndicate, Inc., World rights reserved.
YE ONLY CRAVE TO MARRY ME BECAUSE YE FOUND OUT THAR'S A BODACIOUS TREASURE BURIED ON MY PROPITTY !!
YES'M
LASSWELL
WAAL--I NEVER WUZ ONE TO SQUABBLE OVER LEETLE TRIFLES--LE'S GO PICK OUT TH' RING--
TIME'S A-WASTIN'!!
DON'T FERGIT TH' PROPITTY DEED, HONEY-POT

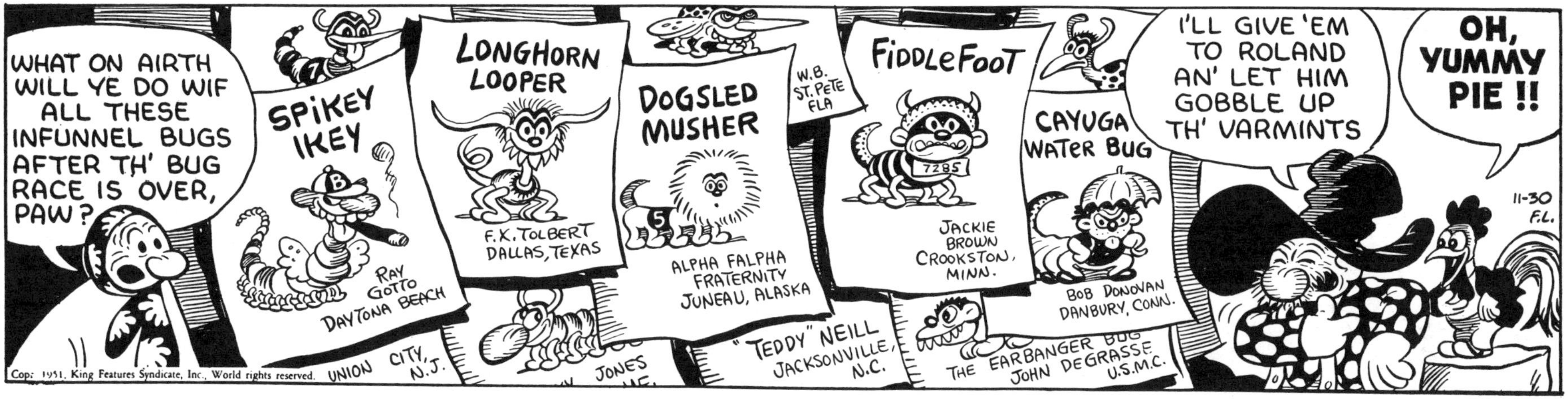
WHAT ON AIRTH WILL YE DO WIF ALL THESE INFUNNEL BUGS AFTER TH' BUG RACE IS OVER, PAW ?
SPIKEY IKEY
RAY GOTTO DAYTONA BEACH
LONGHORN LOOPER
F.K. TOLBERT DALLAS, TEXAS
DOGSLED MUSHER
ALPHA FALPHA FRATERNITY JUNEAU, ALASKA
W.B. ST. PETE FLA
FIDDLEFOOT
7285
JACKIE BROWN CROOKSTON, MINN.
CAYUGA WATER BUG
BOB DONOVAN DANBURY, CONN.
UNION CITY, N.J.
"TEDDY" NEILL JACKSONVILLE, N.C.
THE EARBANGER BUG JOHN DEGRASSE U.S.M.C.
Copr. 1951, King Features Syndicate, Inc., World rights reserved.
I'LL GIVE 'EM TO ROLAND AN' LET HIM GOBBLE UP TH' VARMINTS
OH, YUMMY PIE !!
11-30 F.L.

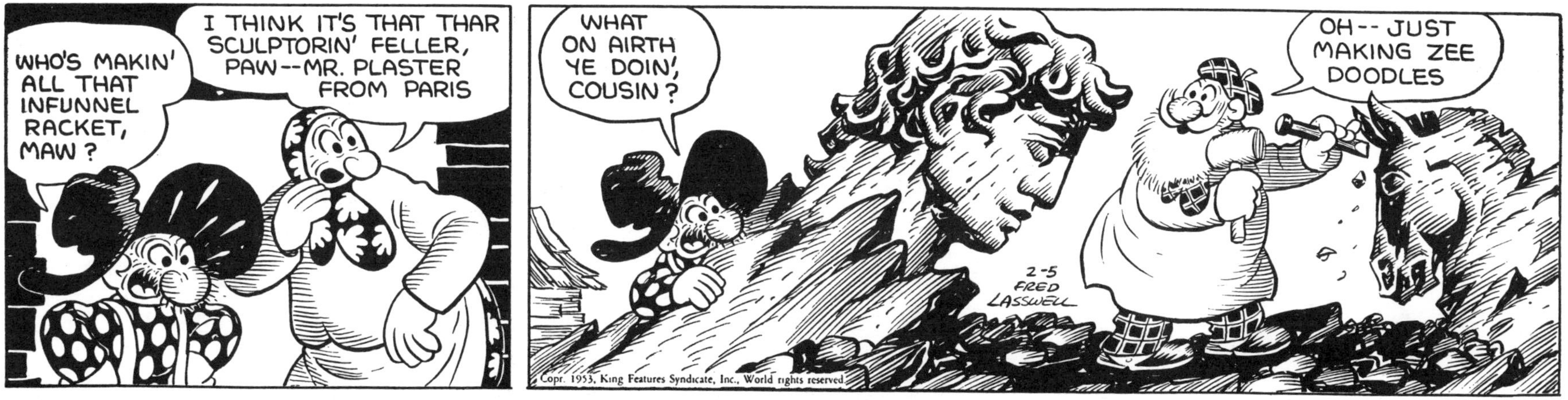
WHO'S MAKIN' ALL THAT INFUNNEL RACKET, MAW ?
I THINK IT'S THAT THAR SCULPTORIN' FELLER, PAW--MR. PLASTER FROM PARIS
WHAT ON AIRTH YE DOIN', COUSIN ?
OH-- JUST MAKING ZEE DOODLES
2-5 FRED LASSWELL
Copr. 1953, King Features Syndicate, Inc., World rights reserved.

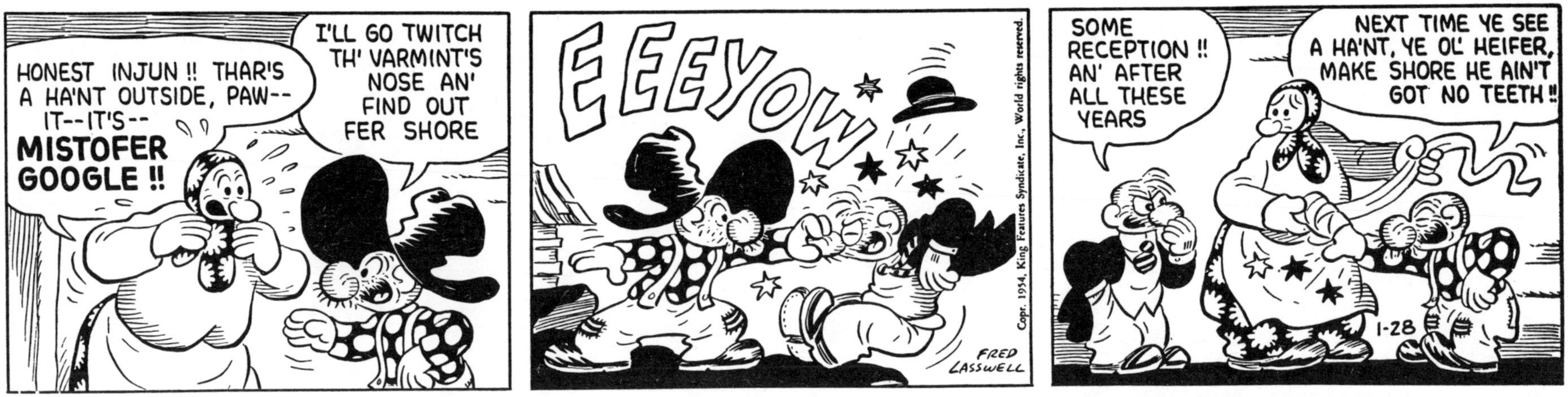
HONEST INJUN !! THAR'S A HA'NT OUTSIDE, PAW-- IT--IT'S-- MISTOFER GOOGLE !!
I'LL GO TWITCH TH' VARMINT'S NOSE AN' FIND OUT FER SHORE
EEEYOW
Copr. 1954, King Features Syndicate, Inc., World rights reserved.
FRED LASSWELL
SOME RECEPTION !! AN' AFTER ALL THESE YEARS
NEXT TIME YE SEE A HA'NT, YE OL' HEIFER, MAKE SHORE HE AIN'T GOT NO TEETH !!
1-28

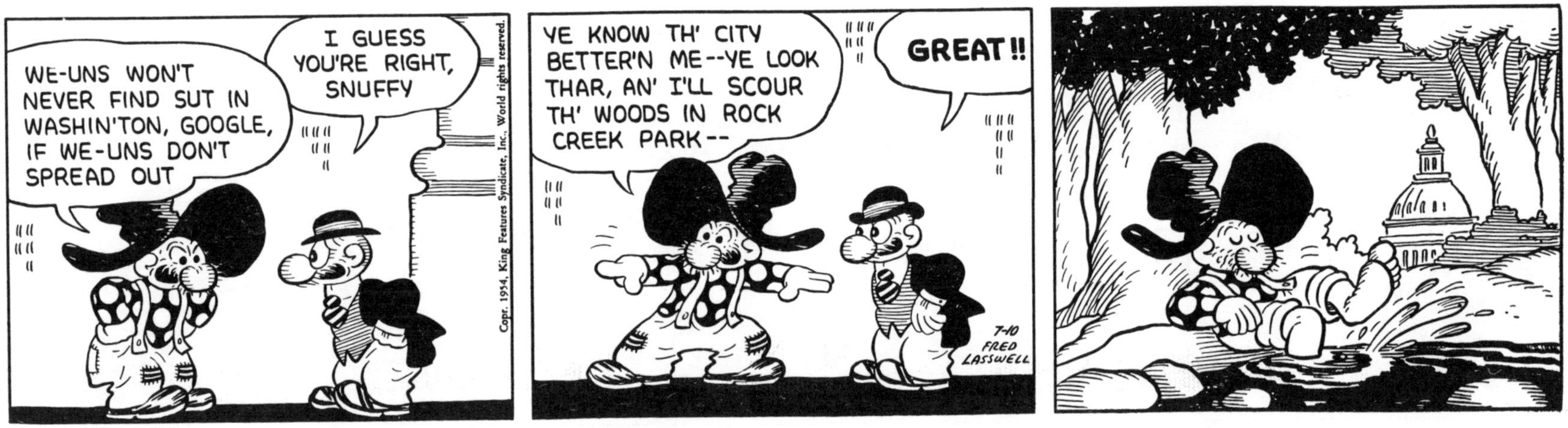
WE-UNS WON'T NEVER FIND SUT IN WASHIN'TON, GOOGLE, IF WE-UNS DON'T SPREAD OUT
I GUESS YOU'RE RIGHT, SNUFFY
Copr. 1954, King Features Syndicate, Inc. World rights reserved.
YE KNOW TH' CITY BETTER'N ME--YE LOOK THAR, AN' I'LL SCOUR TH' WOODS IN ROCK CREEK PARK--
GREAT !!
7-10
FRED LASSWELL

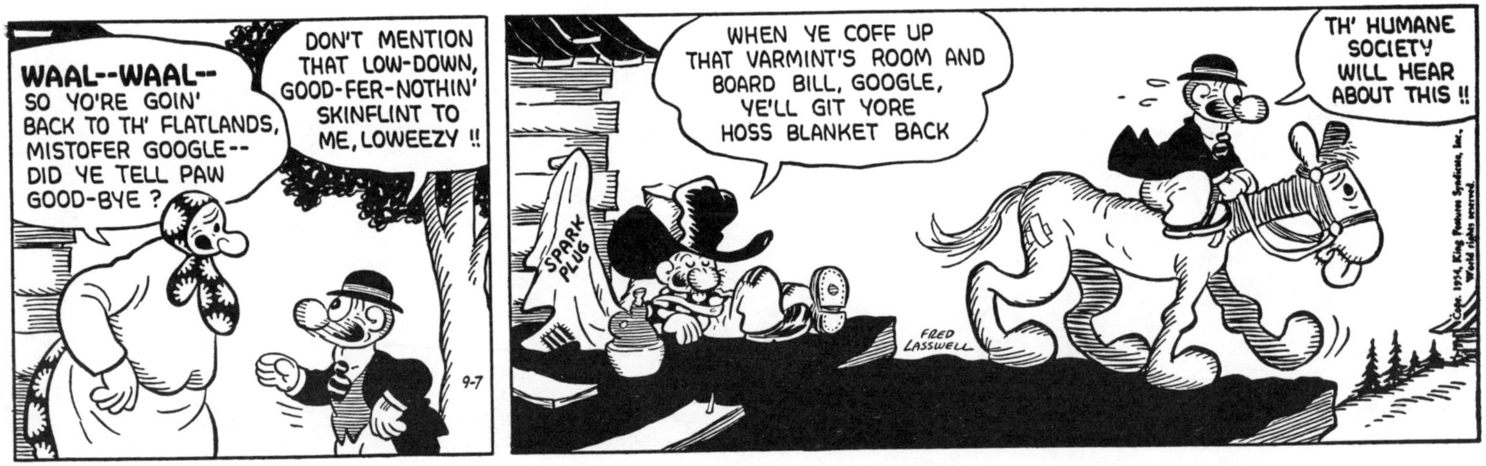
WAAL--WAAL-- SO YO'RE GOIN' BACK TO TH' FLATLANDS, MISTOFER GOOGLE-- DID YE TELL PAW GOOD-BYE ?
DON'T MENTION THAT LOW-DOWN, GOOD-FER-NOTHIN' SKINFLINT TO ME, LOWEEZY !!
9-7
WHEN YE COFF UP THAT VARMINT'S ROOM AND BOARD BILL, GOOGLE, YE'LL GIT YORE HOSS BLANKET BACK
SPARK PLUG
FRED LASSWELL
TH' HUMANE SOCIETY WILL HEAR ABOUT THIS !!

Barney Google

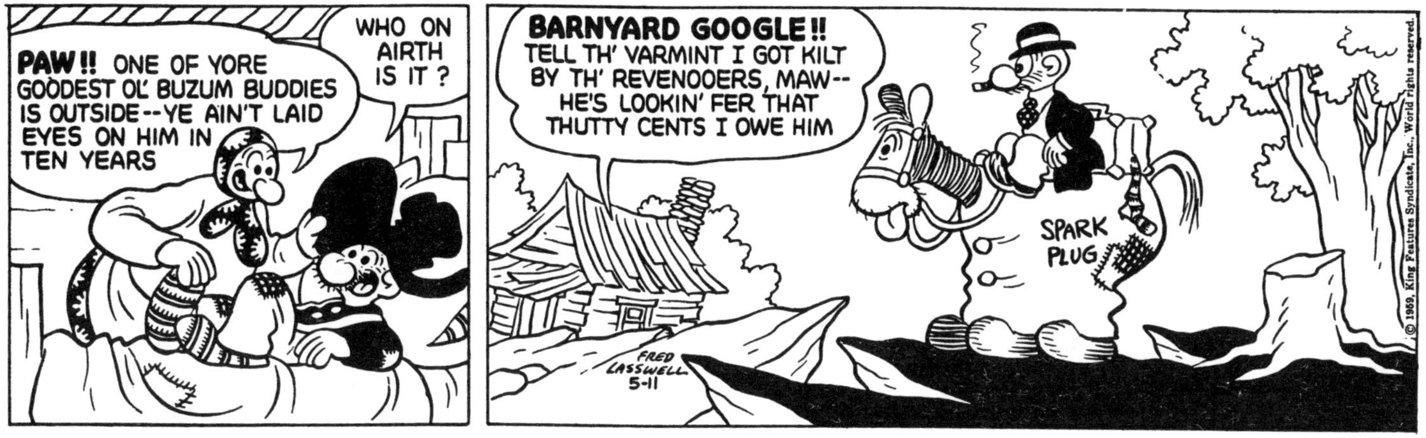

PAW!! ONE OF YORE GOODEST OL' BUZUM BUDDIES IS OUTSIDE--YE AIN'T LAID EYES ON HIM IN TEN YEARS
WHO ON AIRTH IS IT ?
BARNYARD GOOGLE!! TELL TH' VARMINT I GOT KILT BY TH' REVENOOERS, MAW-- HE'S LOOKIN' FER THAT THUTTY CENTS I OWE HIM
SPARK PLUG
FRED LASSWELL 5-11
© 1969, King Features Syndicate, Inc., World rights reserved.

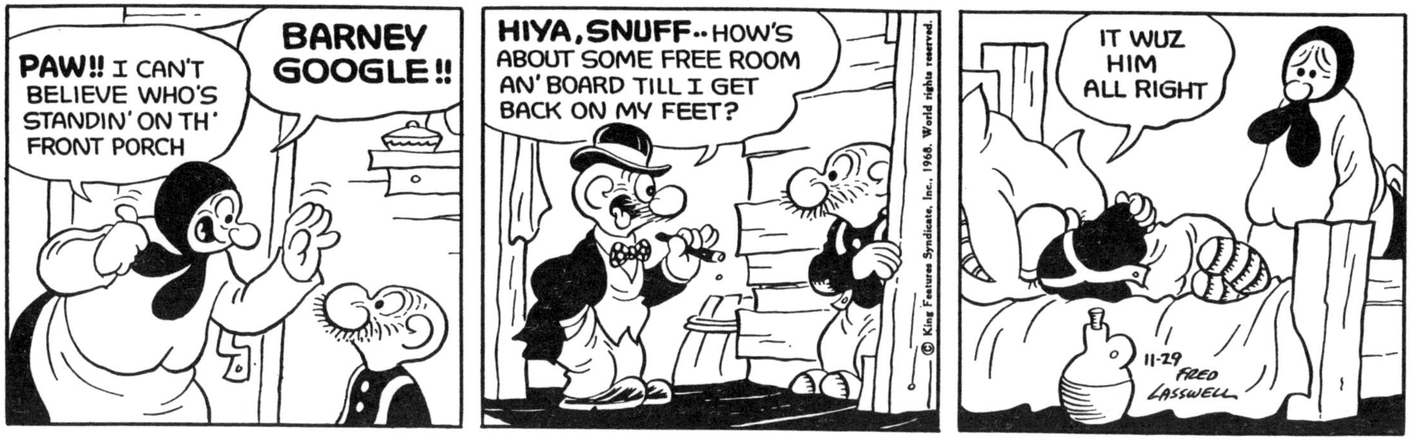

PAW!! I CAN'T BELIEVE WHO'S STANDIN' ON TH' FRONT PORCH
BARNEY GOOGLE!!
HIYA, SNUFF.. HOW'S ABOUT SOME FREE ROOM AN' BOARD TILL I GET BACK ON MY FEET?
© King Features Syndicate, Inc., 1968. World rights reserved.
IT WUZ HIM ALL RIGHT
11-29 FRED LASSWELL

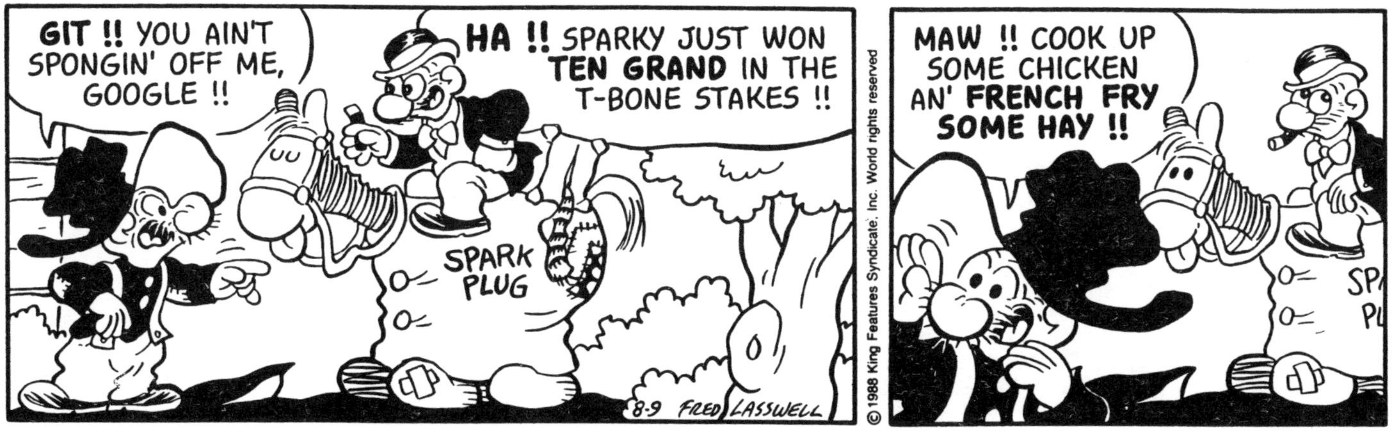

GIT !! YOU AIN'T SPONGIN' OFF ME, GOOGLE !!
HA !! SPARKY JUST WON TEN GRAND IN THE T-BONE STAKES !!
SPARK PLUG
8-9 FRED LASSWELL
© 1988 King Features Syndicate, Inc. World rights reserved
MAW !! COOK UP SOME CHICKEN AN' FRENCH FRY SOME HAY !!

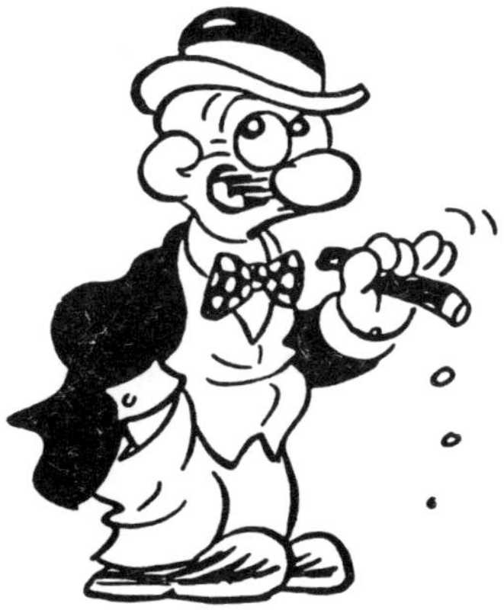

Little Tater

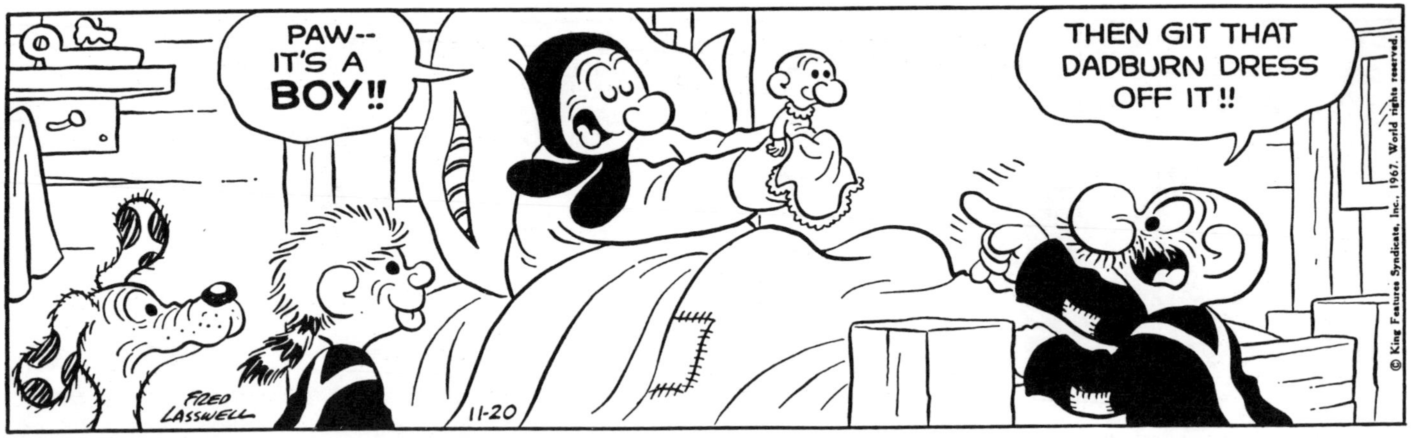
PAW-- IT'S A BOY!!
THEN GIT THAT DADBURN DRESS OFF IT!!
FRED LASSWELL
11-20
© King Features Syndicate, Inc., 1967. World rights reserved.

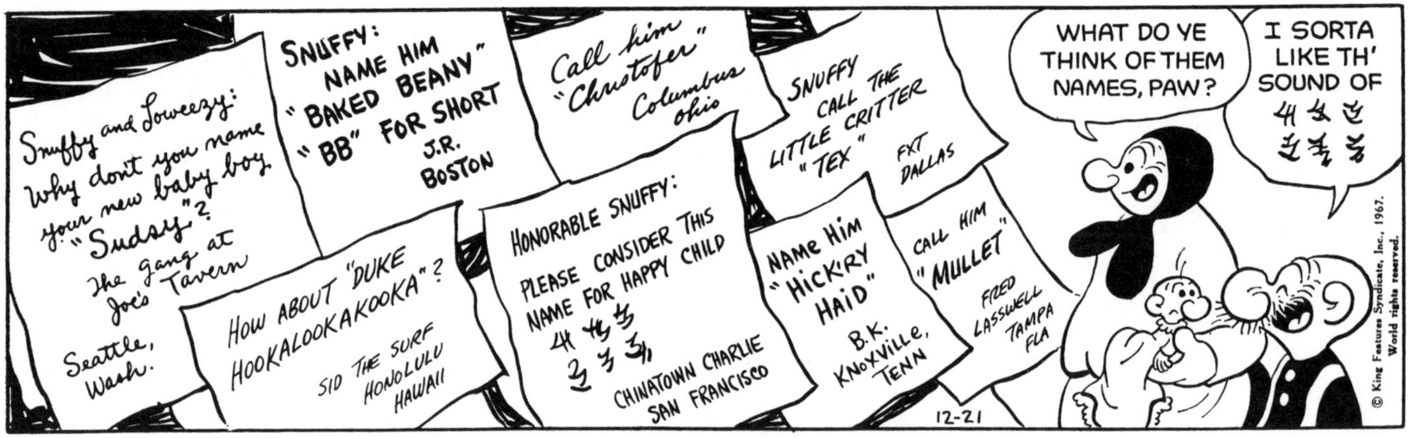
Snuffy and Loweezy: Why don't you name your new baby boy "Sudsy"? The Gang at Joe's Tavern Seattle, Wash.
SNUFFY: NAME HIM "BAKED BEANY" "BB" FOR SHORT J.R. BOSTON
Call him "Christofer" Columbus ohio
SNUFFY CALL THE LITTLE CRITTER "TEX" FXT DALLAS
HOW ABOUT "DUKE HOOKALOOKAKOOKA"? SID THE SURF HONOLULU HAWAII
HONORABLE SNUFFY: PLEASE CONSIDER THIS NAME FOR HAPPY CHILD
CHINATOWN CHARLIE SAN FRANCISCO
NAME HIM "HICK'RY HAID" B.K. KNOXVILLE, TENN
CALL HIM "MULLET" FRED LASSWELL TAMPA FLA
WHAT DO YE THINK OF THEM NAMES, PAW?
I SORTA LIKE TH' SOUND OF
12-21
© King Features Syndicate, Inc., 1967. World rights reserved.

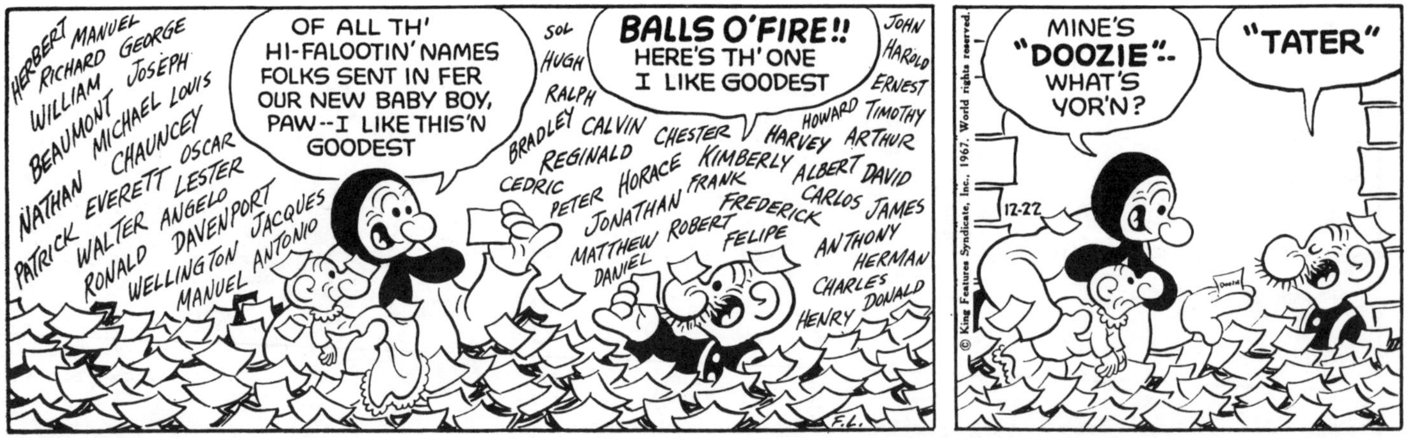
HERBERT MANUEL RICHARD GEORGE WILLIAM JOSEPH BEAUMONT MICHAEL LOUIS NATHAN CHAUNCEY PATRICK EVERETT OSCAR WALTER LESTER RONALD ANGELO DAVENPORT WELLINGTON JACQUES MANUEL ANTONIO
OF ALL TH' HI-FALOOTIN' NAMES FOLKS SENT IN FER OUR NEW BABY BOY, PAW--I LIKE THIS'N GOODEST
SOL HUGH RALPH BRADLEY CALVIN CHESTER REGINALD CEDRIC PETER HORACE KIMBERLY JONATHAN FRANK FREDERICK MATTHEW ROBERT FELIPE DANIEL
BALLS O'FIRE!! HERE'S TH' ONE I LIKE GOODEST
JOHN HAROLD ERNEST HOWARD TIMOTHY HARVEY ARTHUR ALBERT DAVID CARLOS JAMES ANTHONY HERMAN CHARLES DONALD HENRY
F.L.
© King Features Syndicate, Inc., 1967. World rights reserved.
MINE'S "DOOZIE"-- WHAT'S YOR'N?
"TATER"
12-22

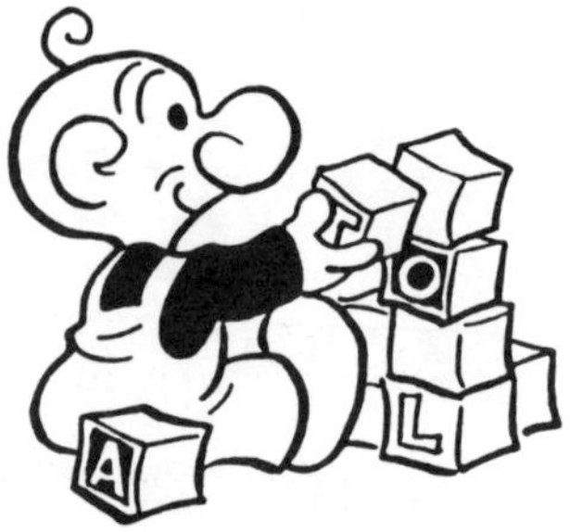
A
L

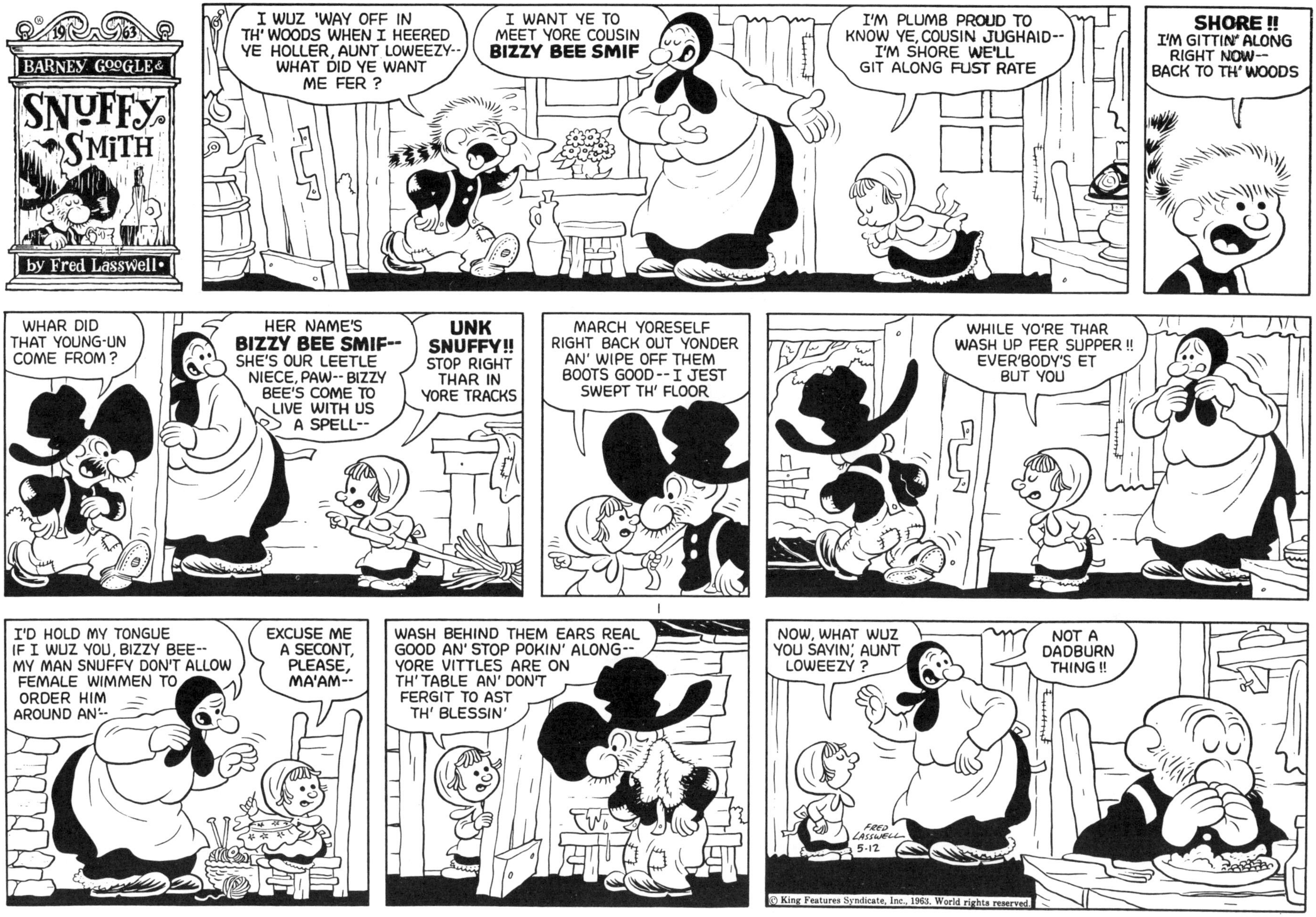

19 63
BARNEY GOOGLE &
SNUFFY SMITH
by Fred Lasswell
I WUZ 'WAY OFF IN TH' WOODS WHEN I HEERED YE HOLLER, AUNT LOWEEZY-- WHAT DID YE WANT ME FER ?
I WANT YE TO MEET YORE COUSIN **BIZZY BEE SMIF**
I'M PLUMB PROUD TO KNOW YE, COUSIN JUGHAID-- I'M SHORE WE'LL GIT ALONG FUST RATE
SHORE !! I'M GITTIN' ALONG RIGHT NOW-- BACK TO TH' WOODS
WHAR DID THAT YOUNG-UN COME FROM ?
HER NAME'S **BIZZY BEE SMIF--** SHE'S OUR LEETLE NIECE, PAW-- BIZZY BEE'S COME TO LIVE WITH US A SPELL--
UNK SNUFFY!! STOP RIGHT THAR IN YORE TRACKS
MARCH YORESELF RIGHT BACK OUT YONDER AN' WIPE OFF THEM BOOTS GOOD-- I JEST SWEPT TH' FLOOR
WHILE YO'RE THAR WASH UP FER SUPPER !! EVER'BODY'S ET BUT YOU
I'D HOLD MY TONGUE IF I WUZ YOU, BIZZY BEE-- MY MAN SNUFFY DON'T ALLOW FEMALE WIMMEN TO ORDER HIM AROUND AN'--
EXCUSE ME A SECONT, PLEASE, MA'AM--
WASH BEHIND THEM EARS REAL GOOD AN' STOP POKIN' ALONG-- YORE VITTLES ARE ON TH' TABLE AN' DON'T FERGIT TO AST TH' BLESSIN'
NOW, WHAT WUZ YOU SAYIN', AUNT LOWEEZY ?
NOT A DADBURN THING !!
FRED LASSWELL 5-12
© King Features Syndicate, Inc., 1963. World rights reserved.

Above: "Bizzy Bee Smif," known as "Bizzy Buzz Buzz" in the series of animated cartoons produced at this time, makes her debut in the strip. "Barney Google and Snuffy Smith" Sunday page, May 12, 1963. Courtesy of King Features Syndicate.

Samanthy

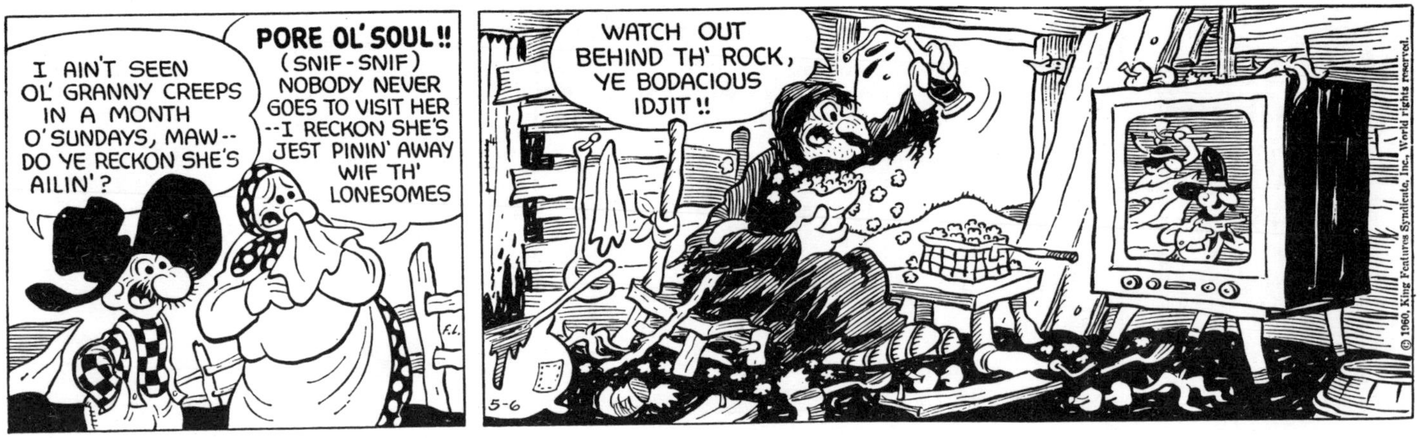
I AIN'T SEEN OL' GRANNY CREEPS IN A MONTH O'SUNDAYS, MAW-- DO YE RECKON SHE'S AILIN'?
PORE OL' SOUL!! (SNIF-SNIF) NOBODY NEVER GOES TO VISIT HER --I RECKON SHE'S JEST PININ' AWAY WIF TH' LONESOMES
F.L.
WATCH OUT BEHIND TH' ROCK, YE BODACIOUS IDJIT!!
5-6
© 1960, King Features Syndicate, Inc., World rights reserved.

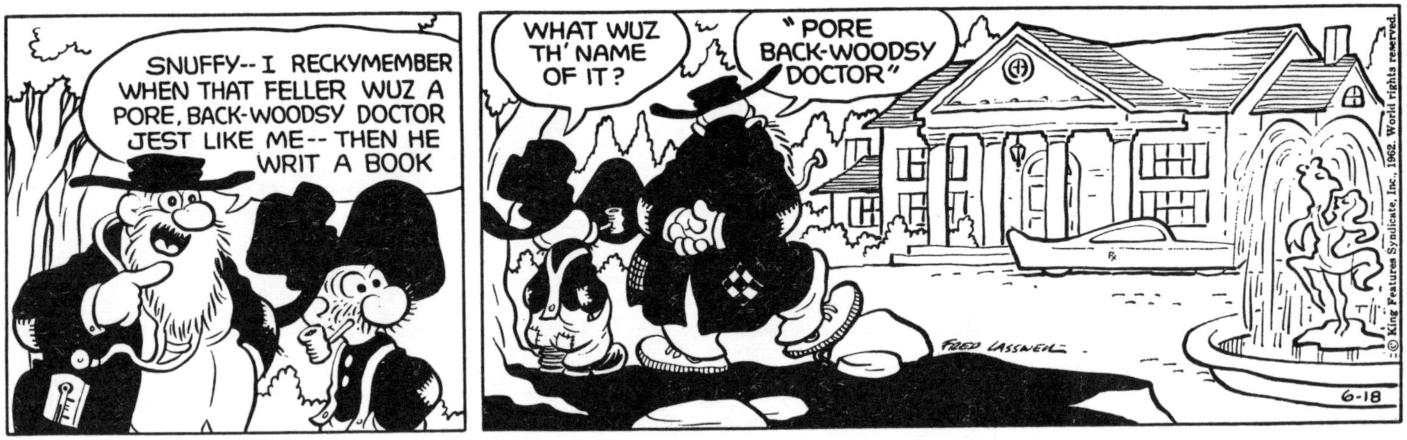
SNUFFY-- I RECKYMEMBER WHEN THAT FELLER WUZ A PORE, BACK-WOODSY DOCTOR JEST LIKE ME-- THEN HE WRIT A BOOK
WHAT WUZ TH' NAME OF IT?
"PORE BACK-WOODSY DOCTOR"
FRED LASSWELL
6-18
© King Features Syndicate, Inc., 1962. World rights reserved.

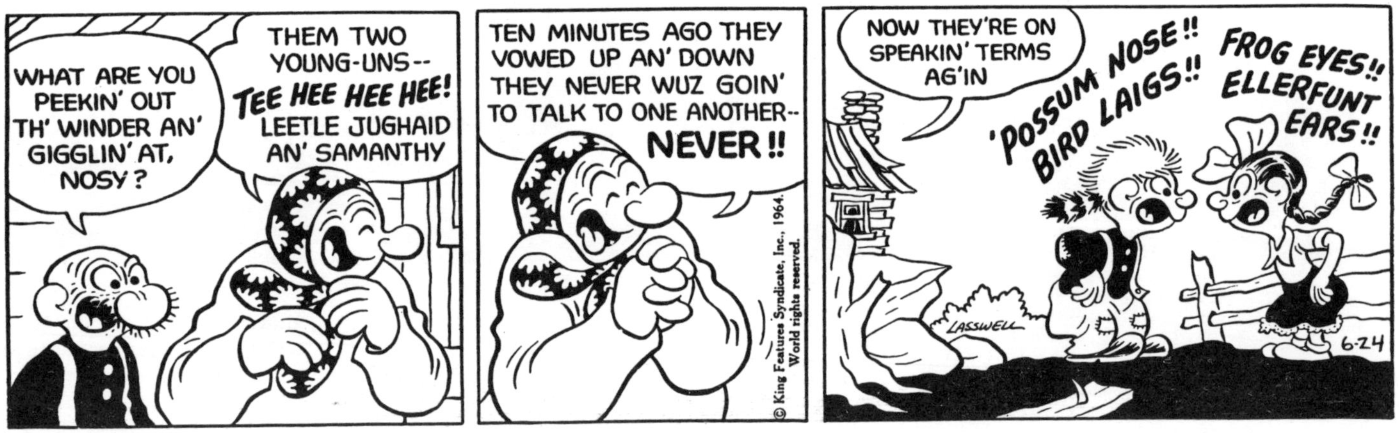
WHAT ARE YOU PEEKIN' OUT TH' WINDER AN' GIGGLIN' AT, NOSY?
THEM TWO YOUNG-UNS-- TEE HEE HEE HEE! LEETLE JUGHAID AN' SAMANTHY
TEN MINUTES AGO THEY VOWED UP AN' DOWN THEY NEVER WUZ GOIN' TO TALK TO ONE ANOTHER-- NEVER!!
© King Features Syndicate, Inc., 1964. World rights reserved.
NOW THEY'RE ON SPEAKIN' TERMS AG'IN
'POSSUM NOSE!! BIRD LAIGS!!
FROG EYES!! ELLERFUNT EARS!!
LASSWELL
6-24

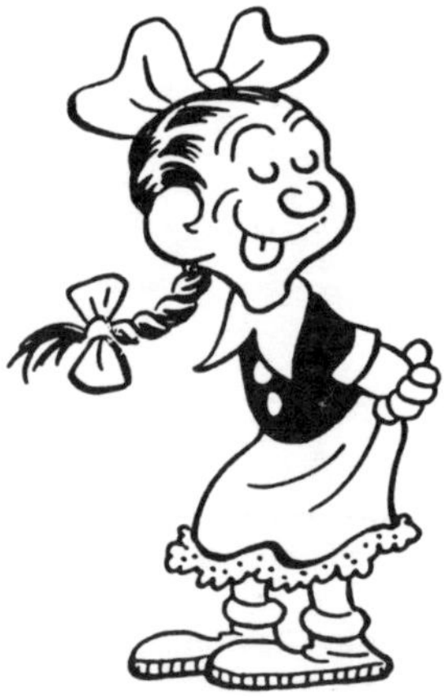

Sheriff Tate

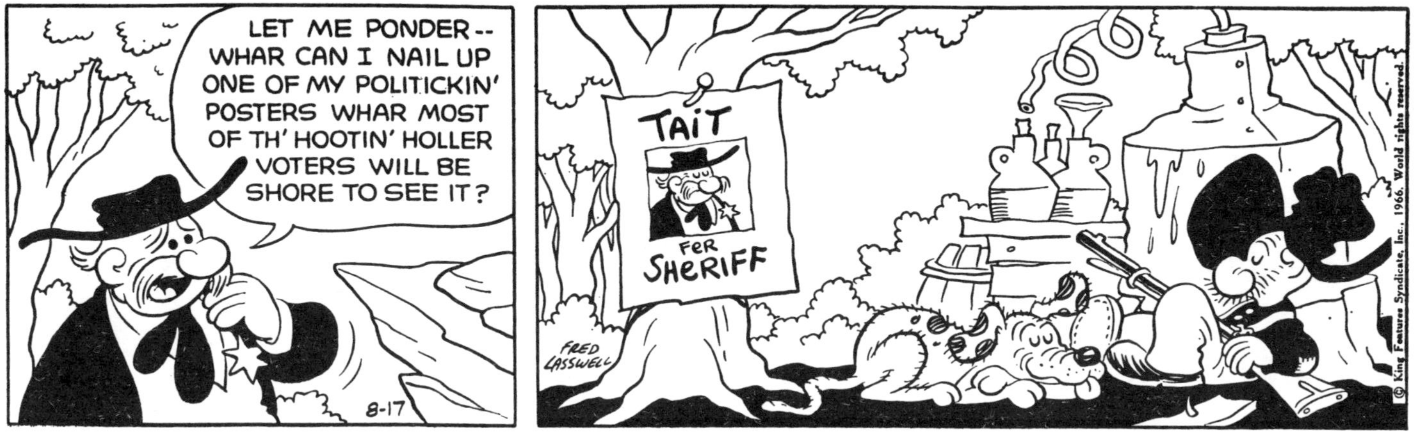

LET ME PONDER -- WHAR CAN I NAIL UP ONE OF MY POLITICKIN' POSTERS WHAR MOST OF TH' HOOTIN' HOLLER VOTERS WILL BE SHORE TO SEE IT?
8-17
TAIT
FER SHERIFF
FRED LASSWELL
© King Features Syndicate, Inc., 1966. World rights reserved.

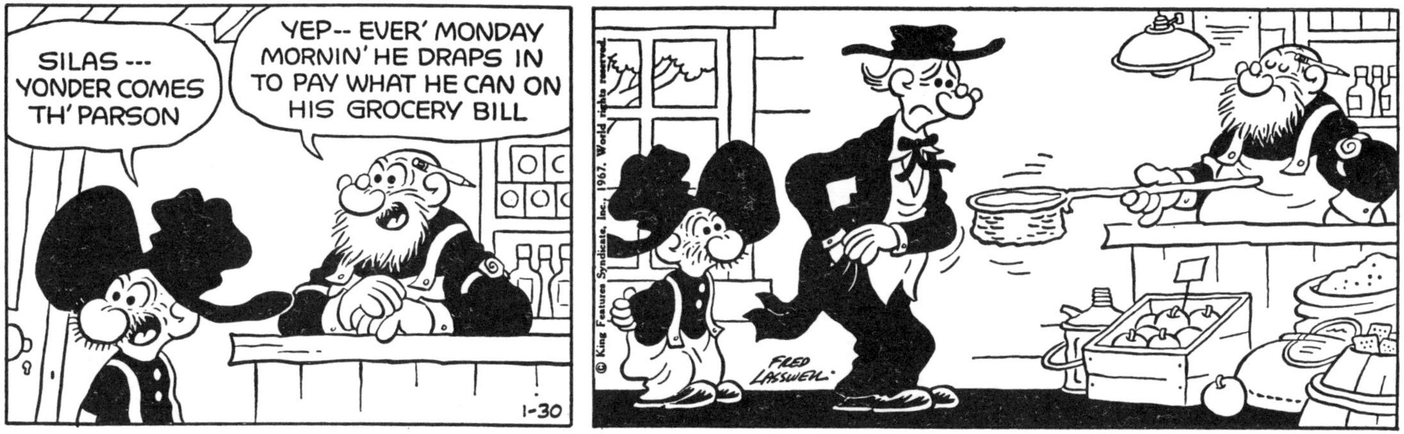

SILAS --- YONDER COMES TH' PARSON
YEP-- EVER' MONDAY MORNIN' HE DRAPS IN TO PAY WHAT HE CAN ON HIS GROCERY BILL
1-30
© King Features Syndicate, Inc., 1967. World rights reserved.
FRED LASSWELL

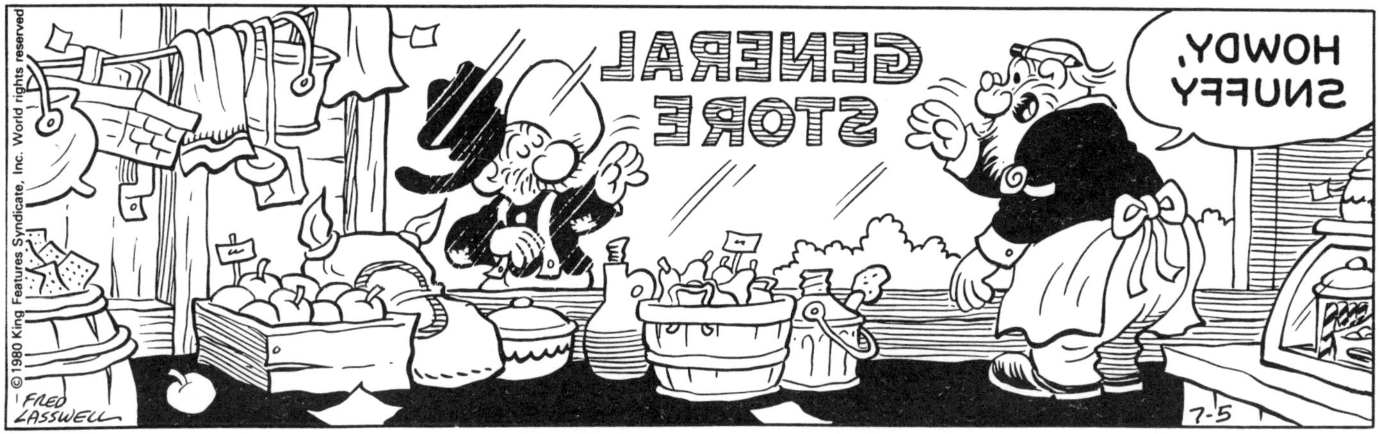

© 1980 King Features Syndicate, Inc. World rights reserved
GENERAL STORE
HOWDY, SNUFFY
FRED LASSWELL
7-5

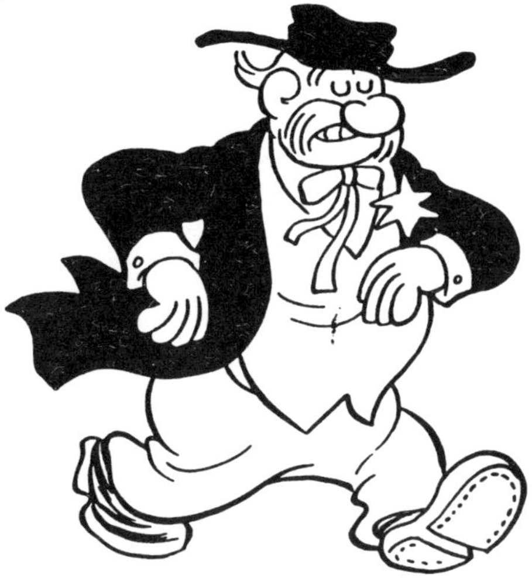

Elviney

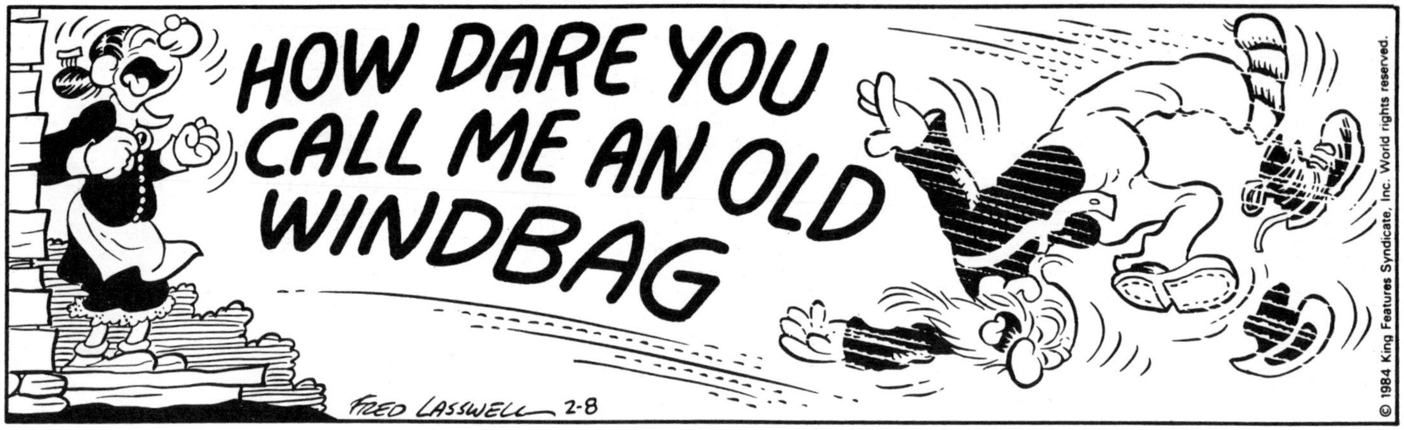
HOW DARE YOU CALL ME AN OLD WINDBAG
FRED LASSWELL 2-8
© 1984 King Features Syndicate, Inc. World rights reserved.

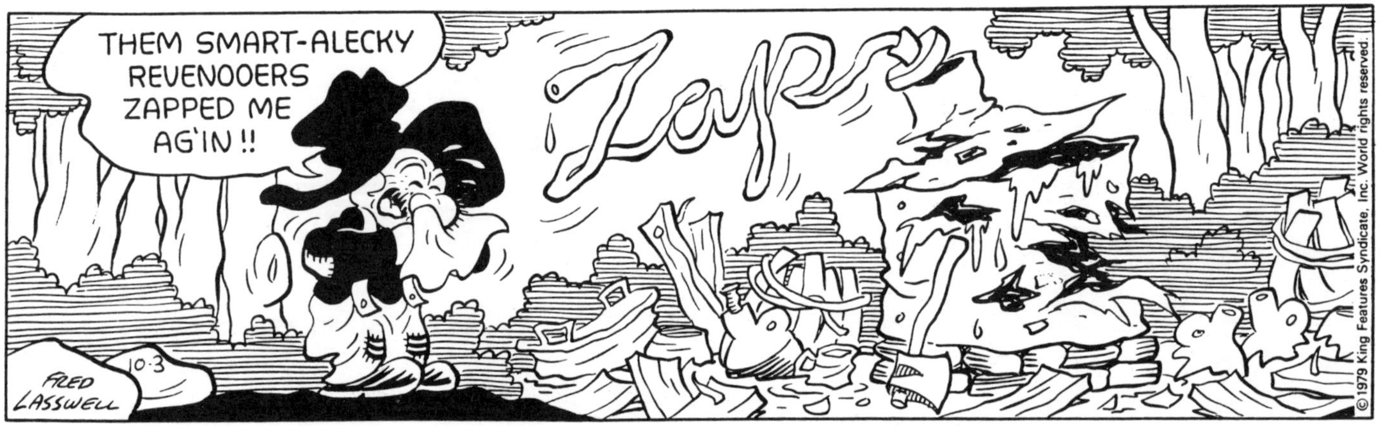
THEM SMART-ALECKY REVENOOERS ZAPPED ME AG'IN !!
FRED LASSWELL 10-3
© 1979 King Features Syndicate, Inc. World rights reserved.

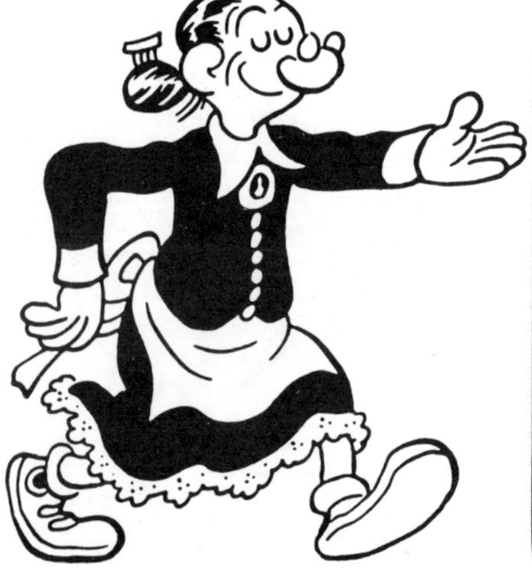

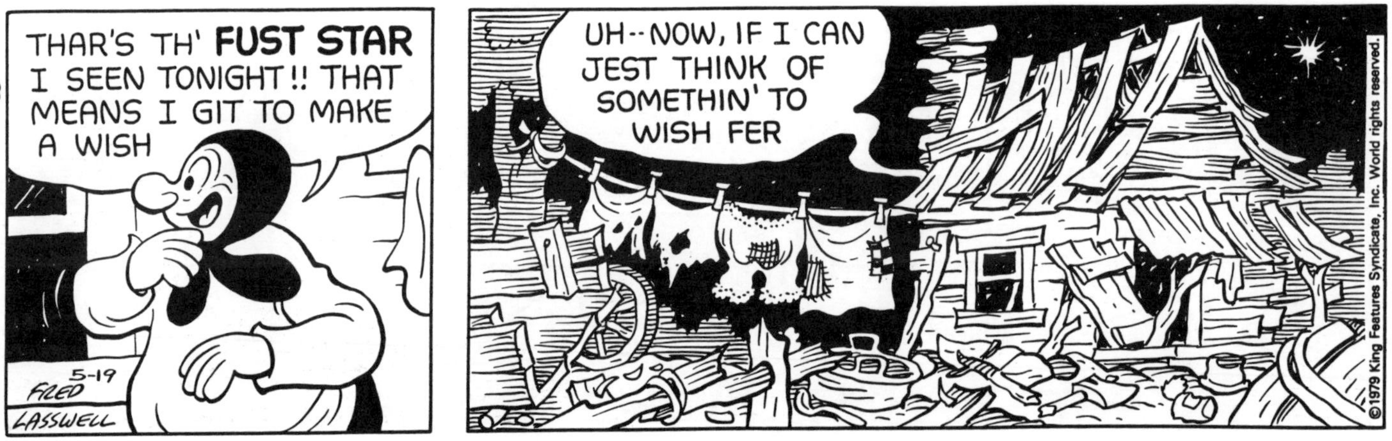
THAR'S TH' FUST STAR I SEEN TONIGHT !! THAT MEANS I GIT TO MAKE A WISH
5-19 FRED LASSWELL
UH--NOW, IF I CAN JEST THINK OF SOMETHIN' TO WISH FER
© 1979 King Features Syndicate, Inc. World rights reserved.

Lukey

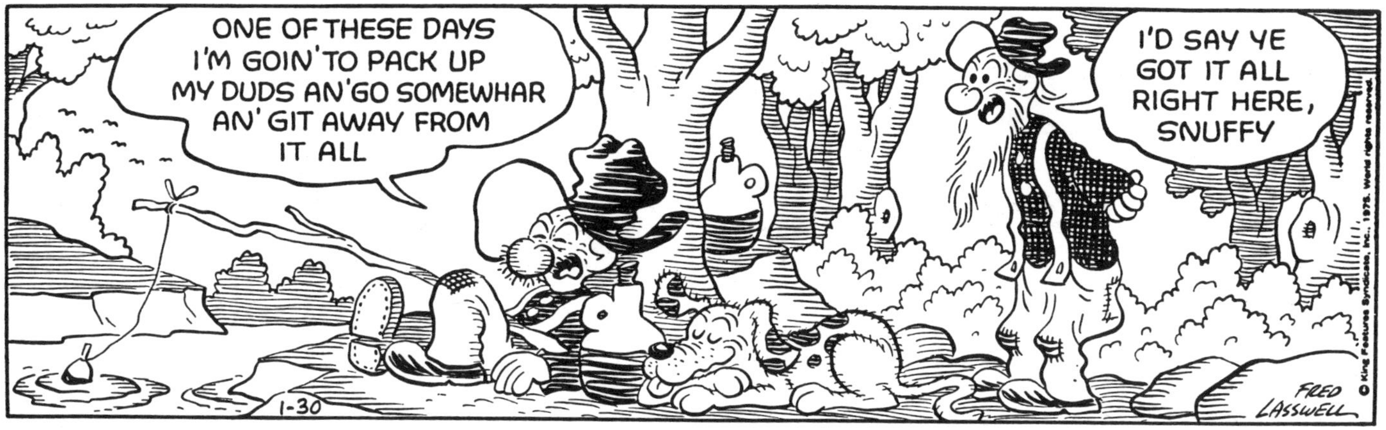

ONE OF THESE DAYS I'M GOIN' TO PACK UP MY DUDS AN'GO SOMEWHAR AN' GIT AWAY FROM IT ALL
I'D SAY YE GOT IT ALL RIGHT HERE, SNUFFY
1-30
FRED LASSWELL
© King Features Syndicate, Inc., 1975. World rights reserved.

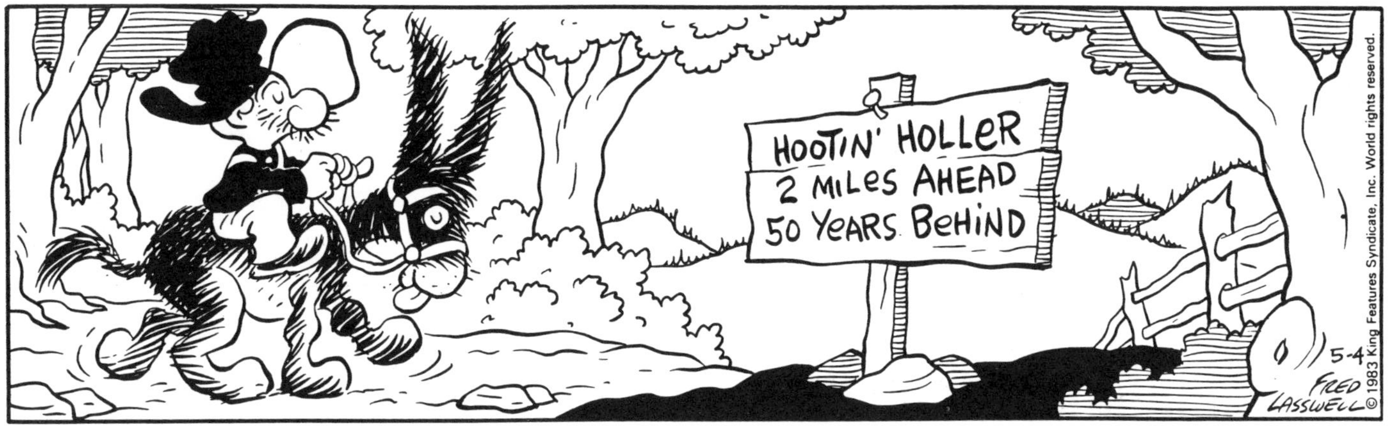

HOOTIN' HOLLER
2 MILES AHEAD
50 YEARS BEHIND
5-4
FRED LASSWELL
© 1983 King Features Syndicate, Inc. World rights reserved.

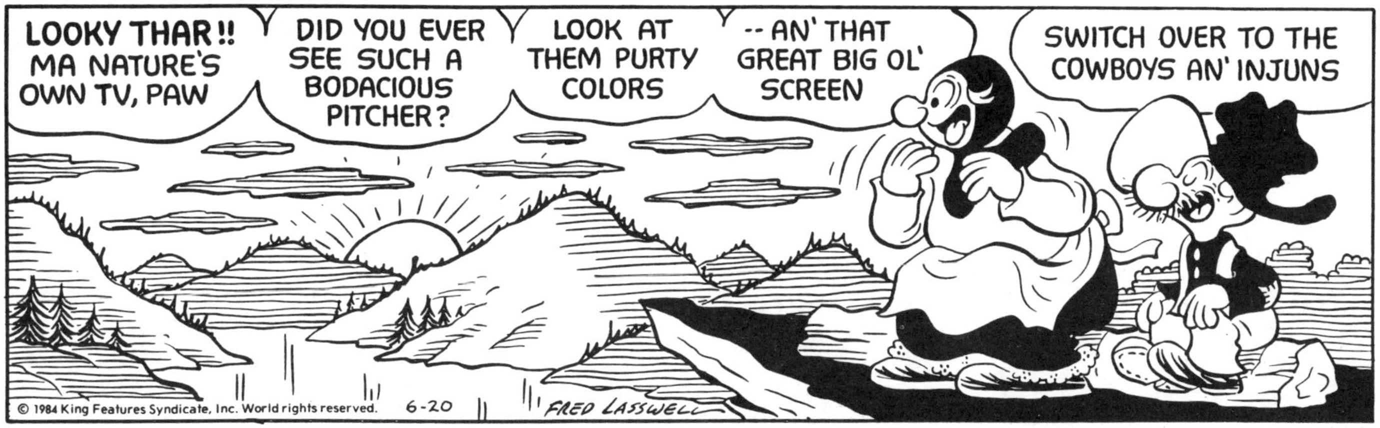

LOOKY THAR!! MA NATURE'S OWN TV, PAW
DID YOU EVER SEE SUCH A BODACIOUS PITCHER?
LOOK AT THEM PURTY COLORS
-- AN' THAT GREAT BIG OL' SCREEN
SWITCH OVER TO THE COWBOYS AN' INJUNS
© 1984 King Features Syndicate, Inc. World rights reserved.
6-20
FRED LASSWELL

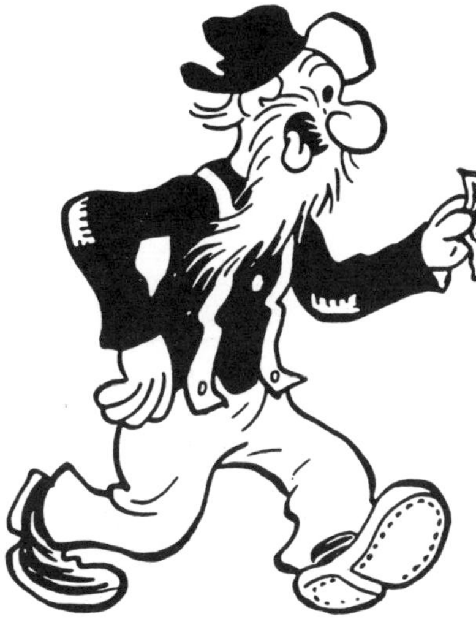

Snuffy

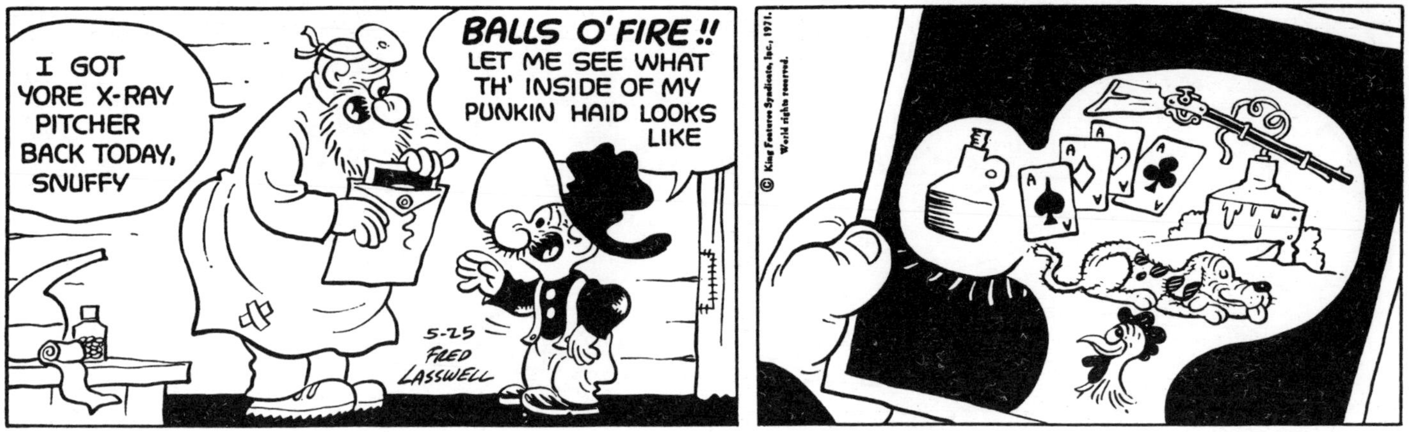

I GOT YORE X-RAY PITCHER BACK TODAY, SNUFFY
BALLS O'FIRE!! LET ME SEE WHAT TH' INSIDE OF MY PUNKIN HAID LOOKS LIKE
5-25
FRED LASSWELL
© King Features Syndicate, Inc., 1971. World rights reserved.

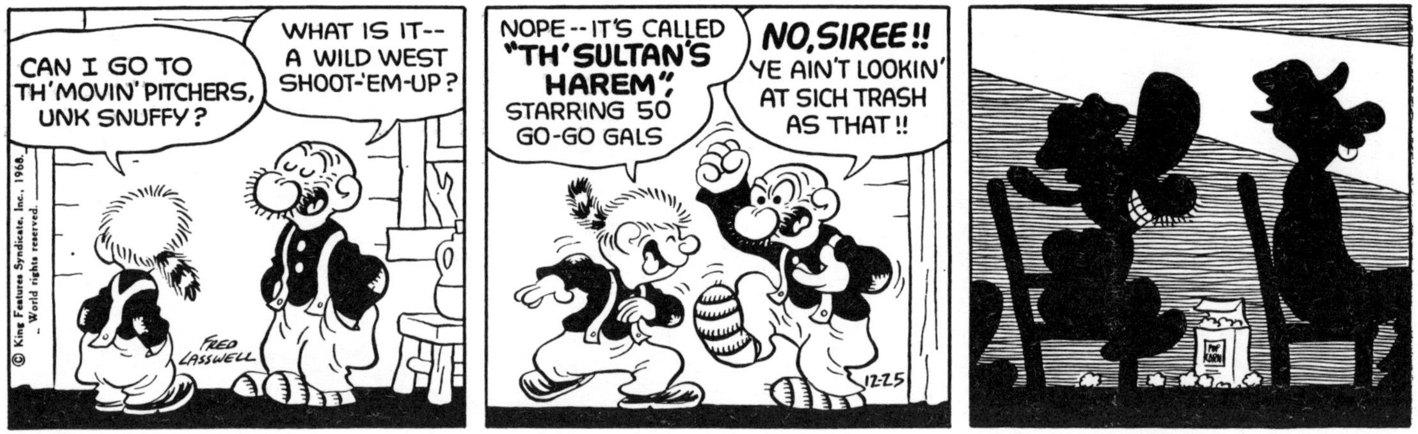

CAN I GO TO TH' MOVIN' PITCHERS, UNK SNUFFY?
WHAT IS IT-- A WILD WEST SHOOT-'EM-UP?
© King Features Syndicate, Inc., 1968. World rights reserved.
FRED LASSWELL
NOPE--IT'S CALLED "TH' SULTAN'S HAREM", STARRING 50 GO-GO GALS
NO, SIREE!! YE AIN'T LOOKIN' AT SICH TRASH AS THAT!!
12-25

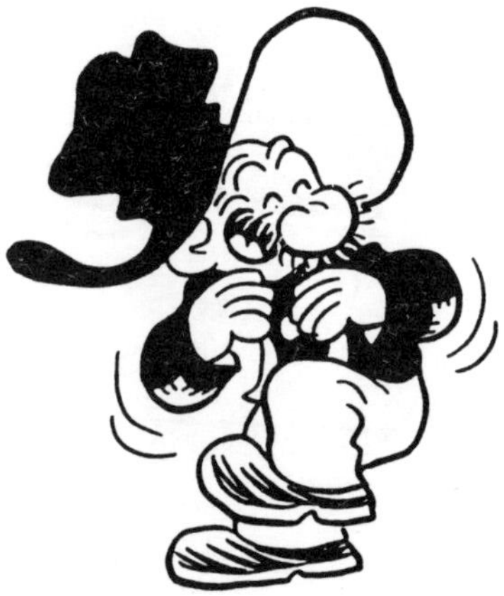

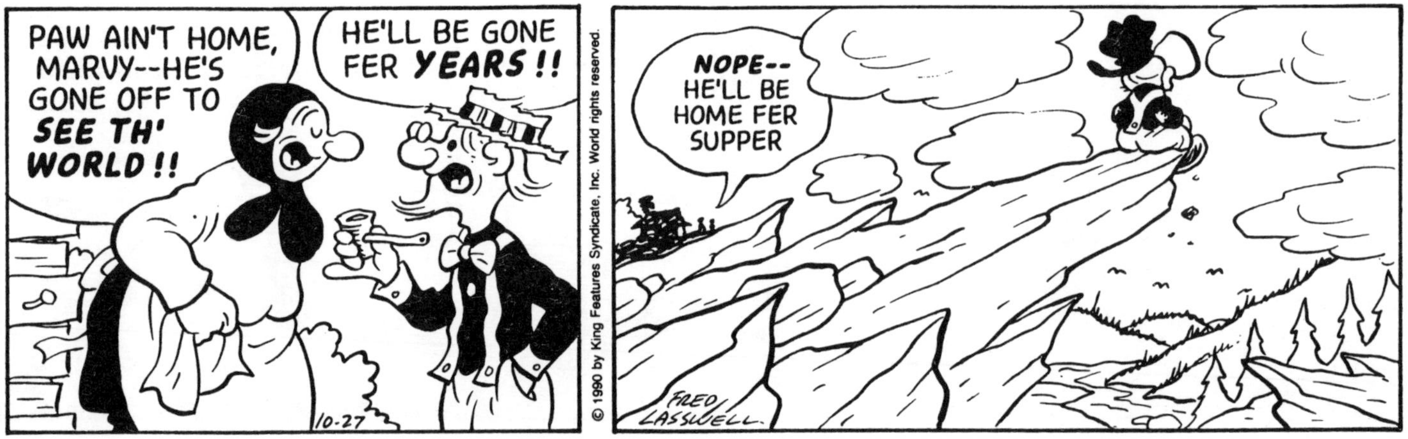

PAW AIN'T HOME, MARVY--HE'S GONE OFF TO SEE TH' WORLD!!
HE'LL BE GONE FER YEARS!!
10-27
© 1990 by King Features Syndicate, Inc. World rights reserved.
NOPE-- HE'LL BE HOME FER SUPPER
FRED LASSWELL

Loweezy

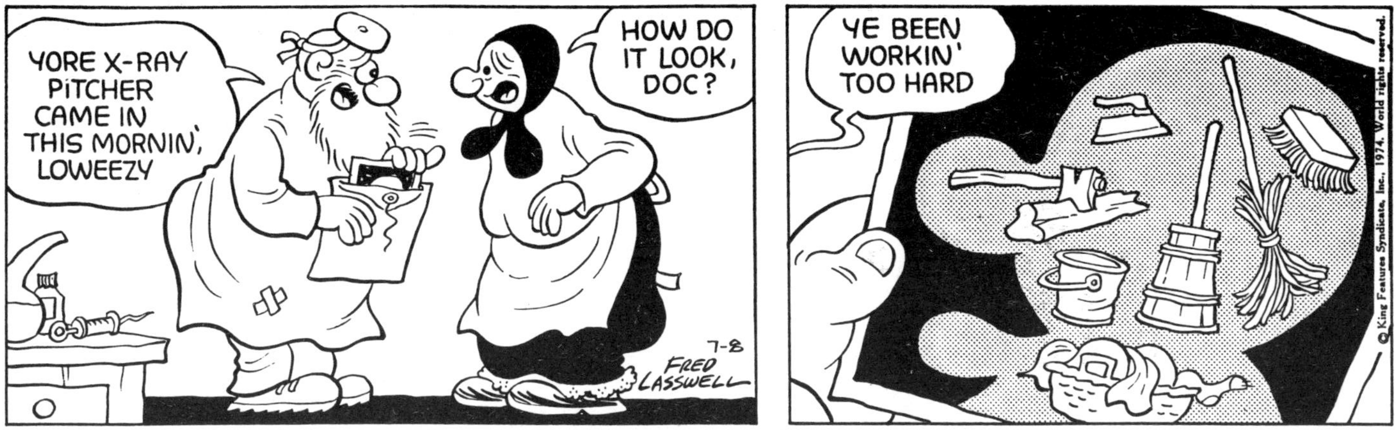
YORE X-RAY PITCHER CAME IN THIS MORNIN', LOWEEZY
HOW DO IT LOOK, DOC?
7-8
FRED LASSWELL
YE BEEN WORKIN' TOO HARD
© King Features Syndicate, Inc., 1974. World rights reserved.

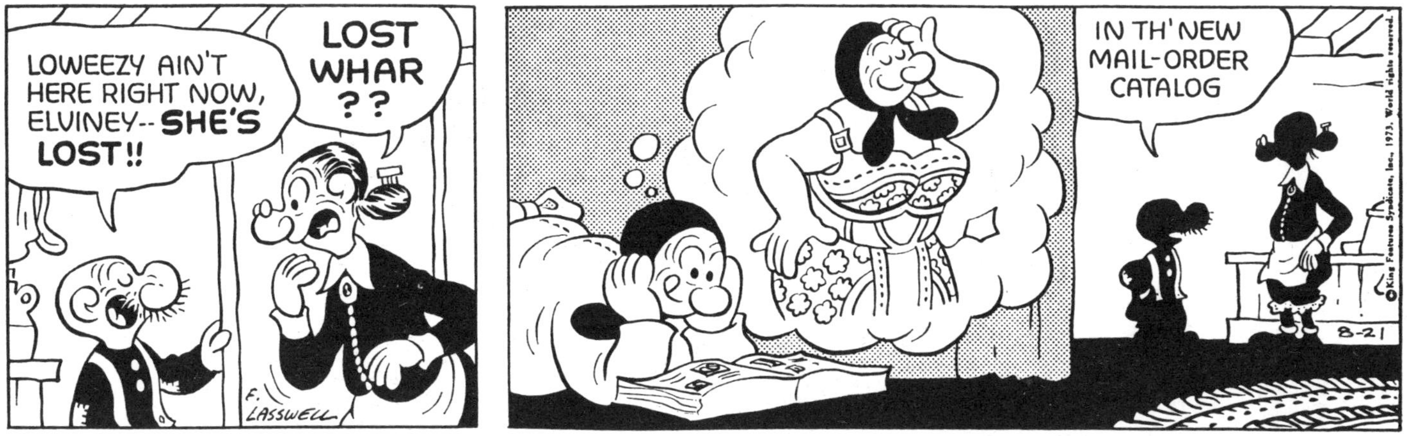
LOWEEZY AIN'T HERE RIGHT NOW, ELVINEY-- SHE'S LOST!!
LOST WHAR ??
F. LASSWELL
IN TH' NEW MAIL-ORDER CATALOG
8-21
© King Features Syndicate, Inc., 1973. World rights reserved.

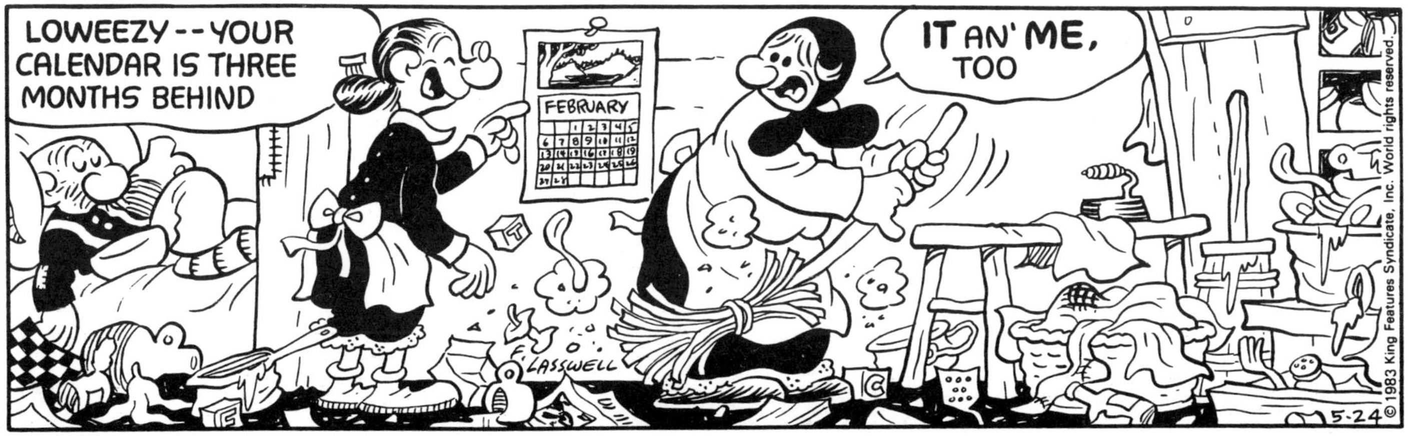
LOWEEZY--YOUR CALENDAR IS THREE MONTHS BEHIND
FEBRUARY
IT AN' ME, TOO
F. LASSWELL
5-24
© 1983 King Features Syndicate, Inc. World rights reserved.

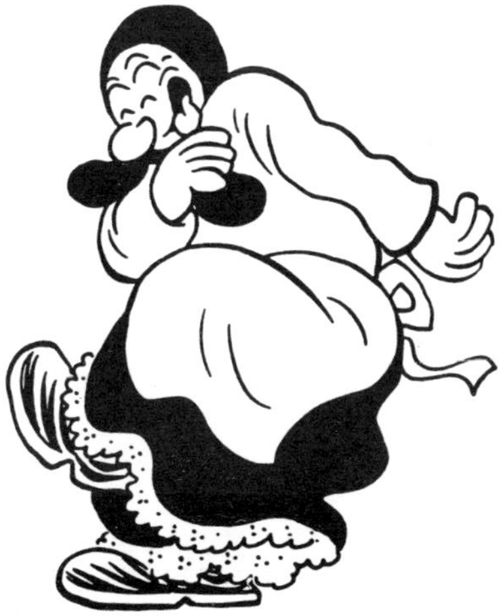

Ol' Bullet

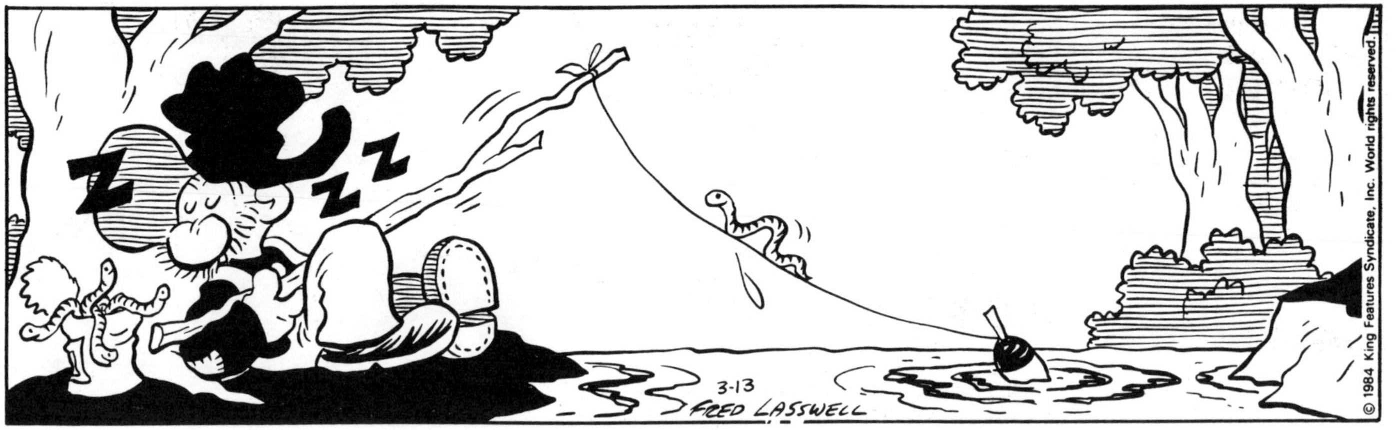

Z
Z Z
3-13
FRED LASSWELL
© 1984 King Features Syndicate, Inc. World rights reserved.

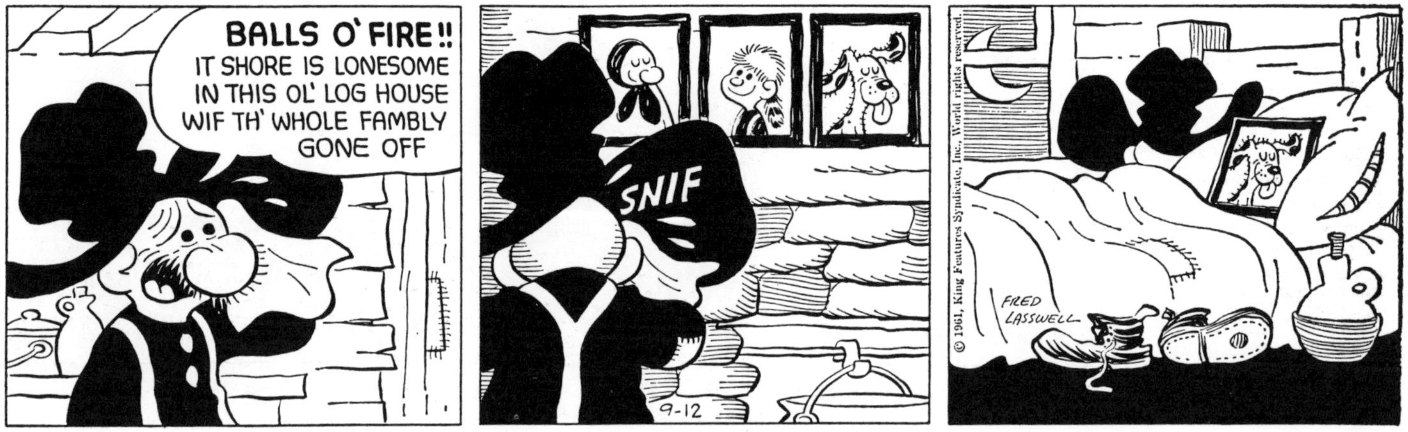

BALLS O' FIRE!! IT SHORE IS LONESOME IN THIS OL' LOG HOUSE WIF TH' WHOLE FAMBLY GONE OFF
SNIF
9-12
© 1961, King Features Syndicate, Inc., World rights reserved.
FRED LASSWELL

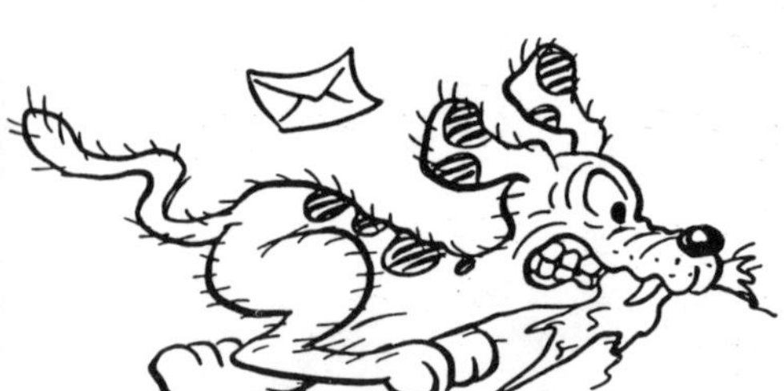

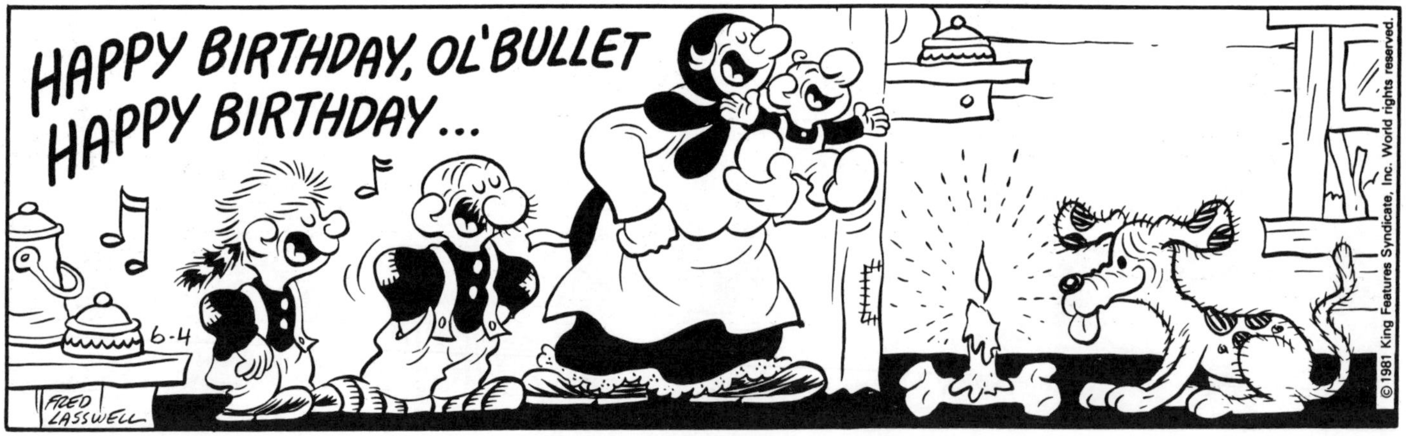

HAPPY BIRTHDAY, OL' BULLET
HAPPY BIRTHDAY...
6-4
FRED LASSWELL
© 1981 King Features Syndicate, Inc. World rights reserved.

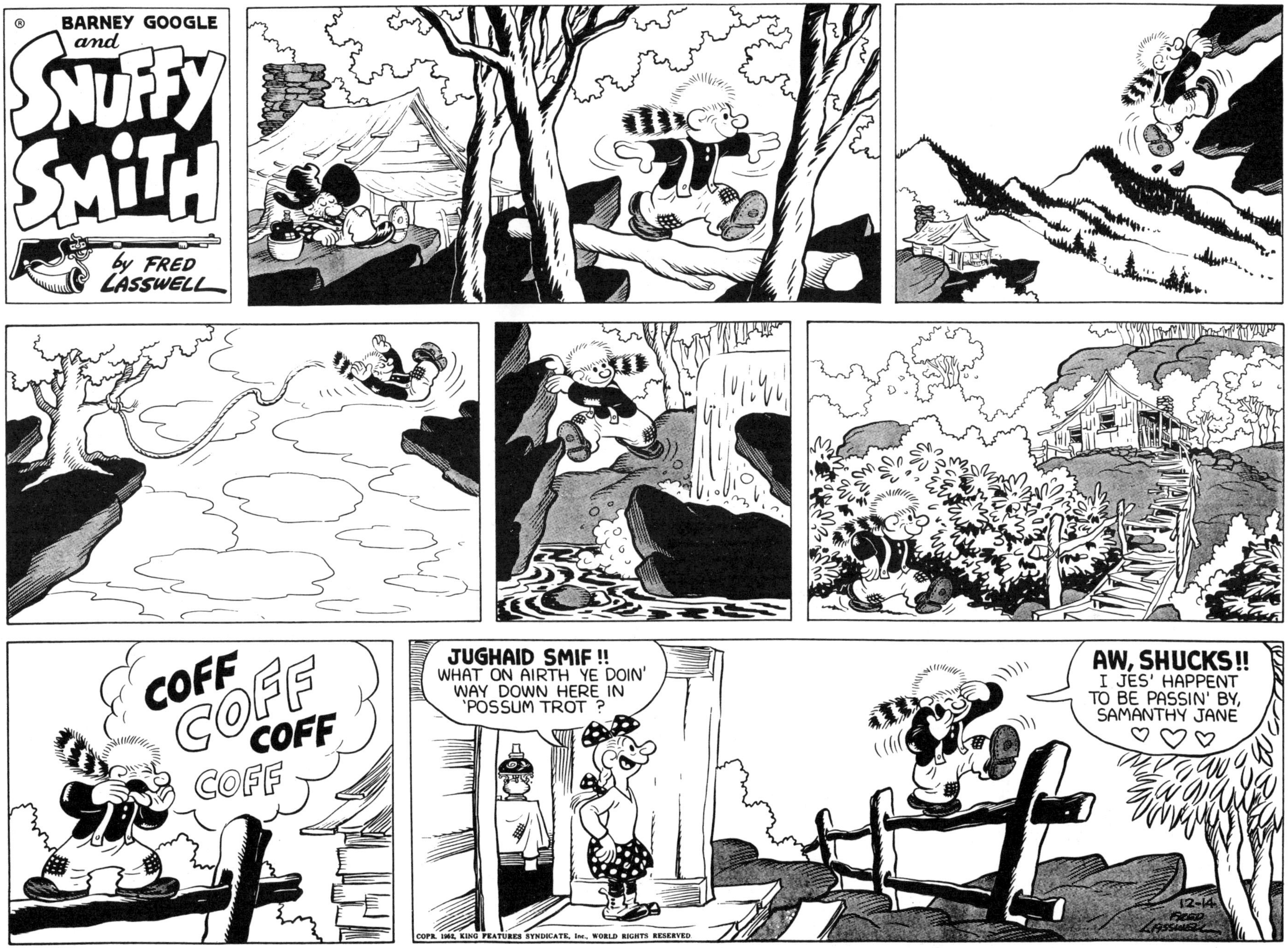
BARNEY GOOGLE
and
SNUFFY SMITH
by FRED LASSWELL
COFF
COFF
COFF
COFF
JUGHAID SMIF !! WHAT ON AIRTH YE DOIN' WAY DOWN HERE IN 'POSSUM TROT ?
AW, SHUCKS !! I JES' HAPPENT TO BE PASSIN' BY, SAMANTHY JANE
12-14
FRED LASSWELL
COPR. 1962, KING FEATURES SYNDICATE, Inc., WORLD RIGHTS RESERVED

Above: A day in the country with Jughaid Smif. "Barney Google and Snuffy Smith" Sunday page, December 14, 1962. Courtesy of King Features Syndicate.

Snuffy & Loweezy

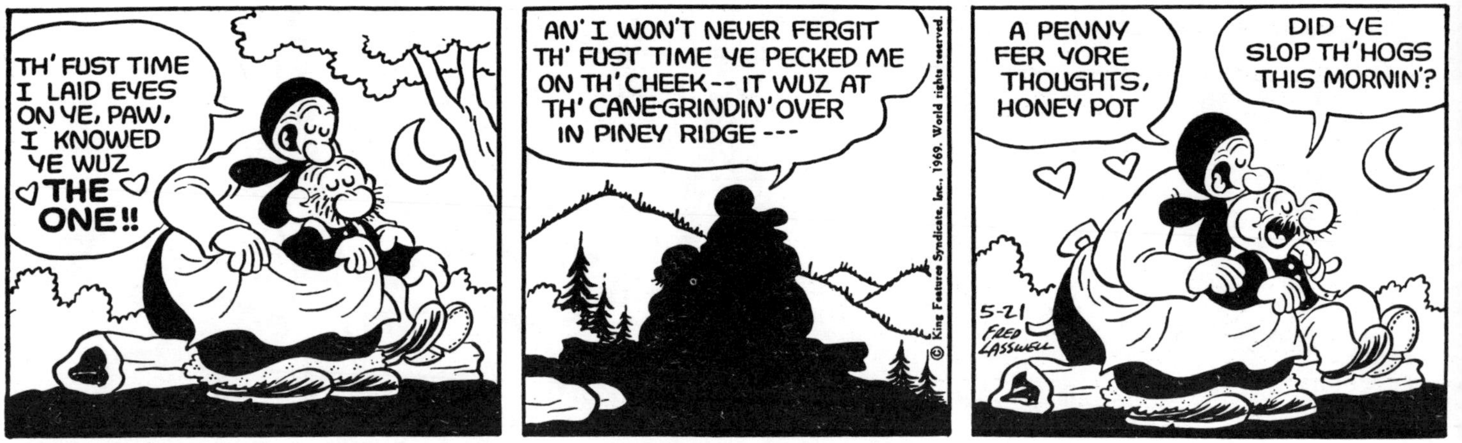
TH' FUST TIME I LAID EYES ON YE, PAW, I KNOWED YE WUZ THE ONE!!
AN' I WON'T NEVER FERGIT TH' FUST TIME YE PECKED ME ON TH' CHEEK -- IT WUZ AT TH' CANE-GRINDIN' OVER IN PINEY RIDGE ---
© King Features Syndicate, Inc., 1969. World rights reserved.
A PENNY FER YORE THOUGHTS, HONEY POT
DID YE SLOP TH' HOGS THIS MORNIN'?
5-21
FRED LASSWELL

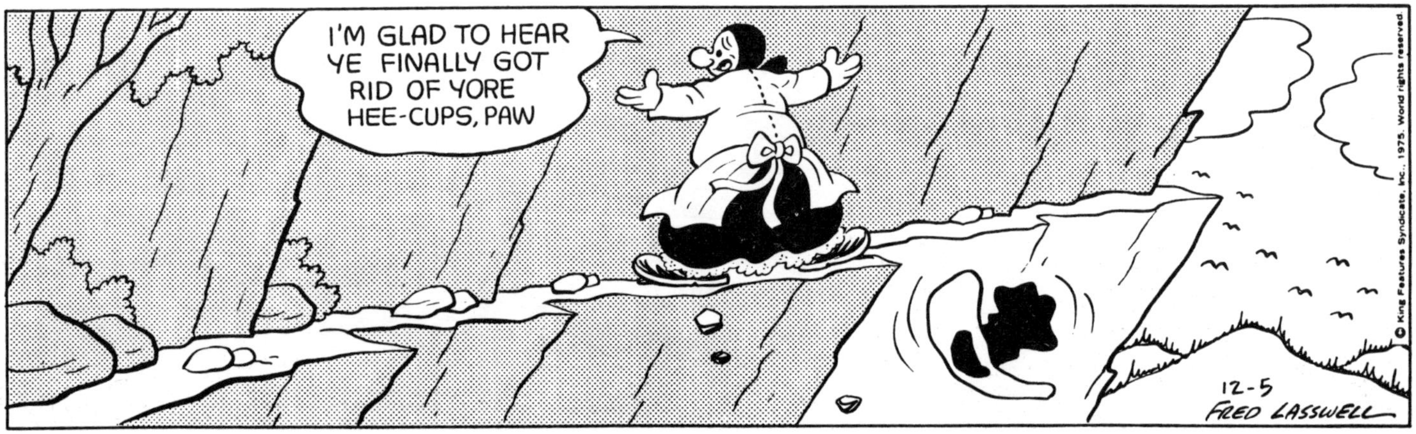
I'M GLAD TO HEAR YE FINALLY GOT RID OF YORE HEE-CUPS, PAW
© King Features Syndicate, Inc., 1975. World rights reserved.
12-5
FRED LASSWELL

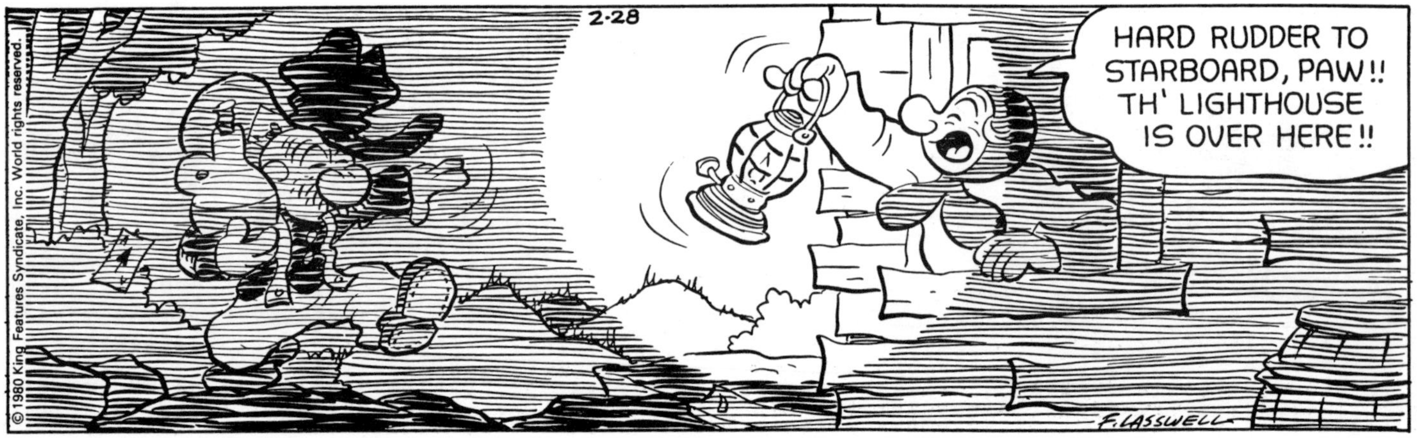
2-28
HARD RUDDER TO STARBOARD, PAW!! TH' LIGHTHOUSE IS OVER HERE!!
© 1980 King Features Syndicate, Inc. World rights reserved.
F. LASSWELL

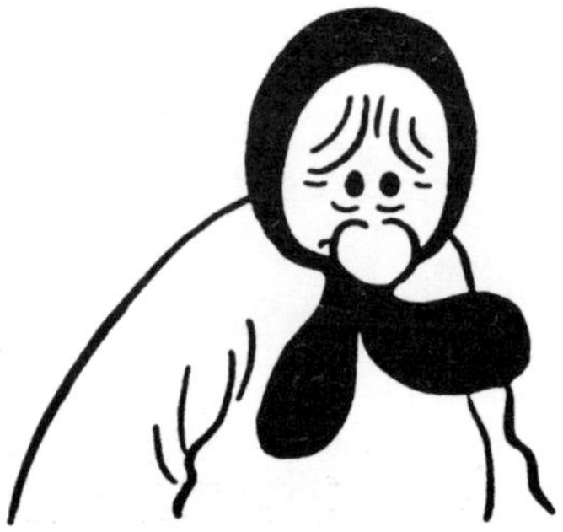

The Smith Family

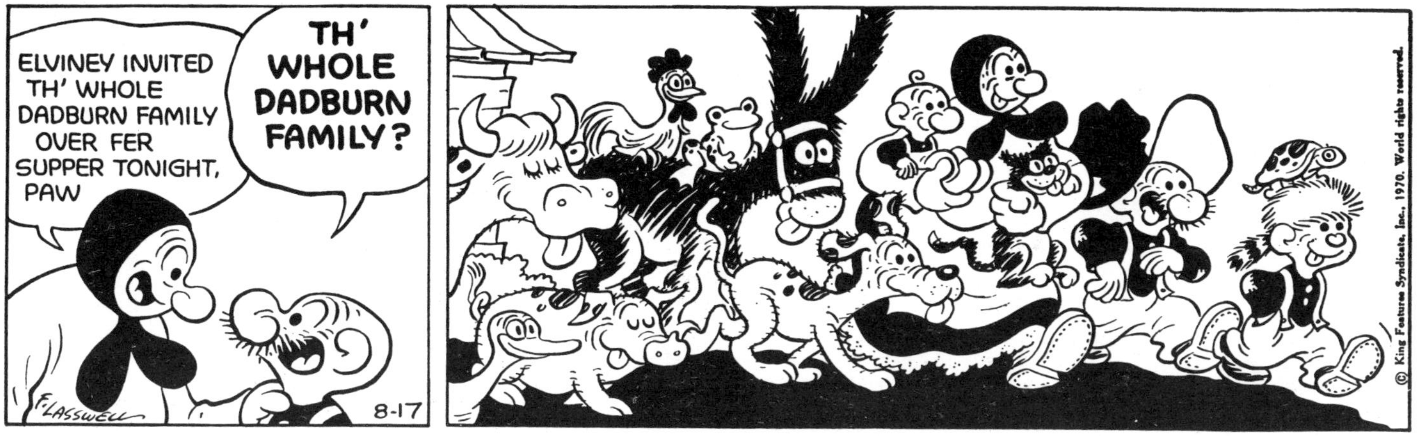
ELVINEY INVITED TH' WHOLE DADBURN FAMILY OVER FER SUPPER TONIGHT, PAW
TH' WHOLE DADBURN FAMILY?
F. LASSWELL
8-17
© King Features Syndicate, Inc., 1970. World rights reserved.

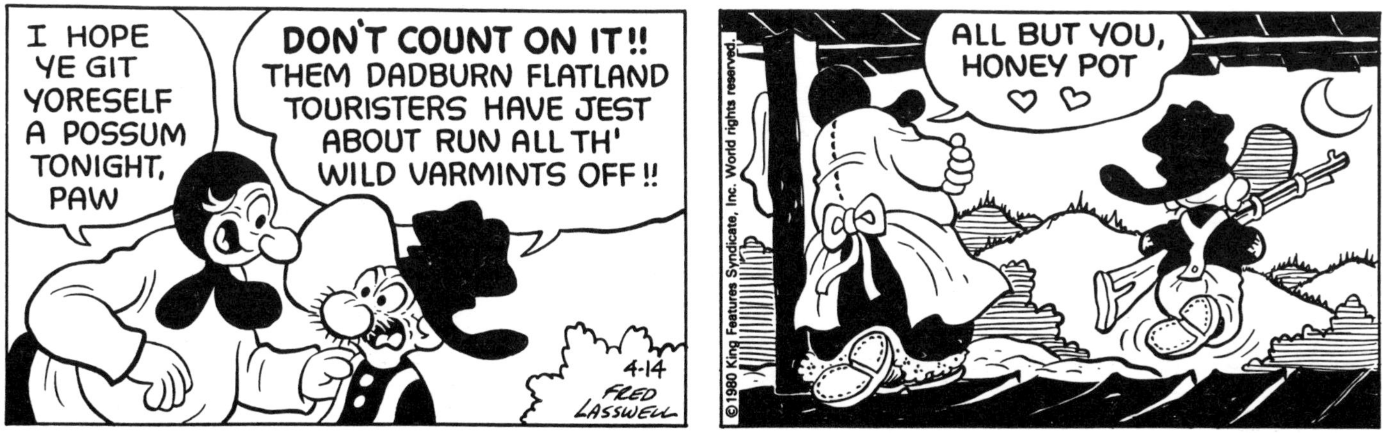
I HOPE YE GIT YORESELF A POSSUM TONIGHT, PAW
DON'T COUNT ON IT!! THEM DADBURN FLATLAND TOURISTERS HAVE JEST ABOUT RUN ALL TH' WILD VARMINTS OFF!!
4-14
FRED LASSWELL
ALL BUT YOU, HONEY POT
© 1980 King Features Syndicate, Inc. World rights reserved.

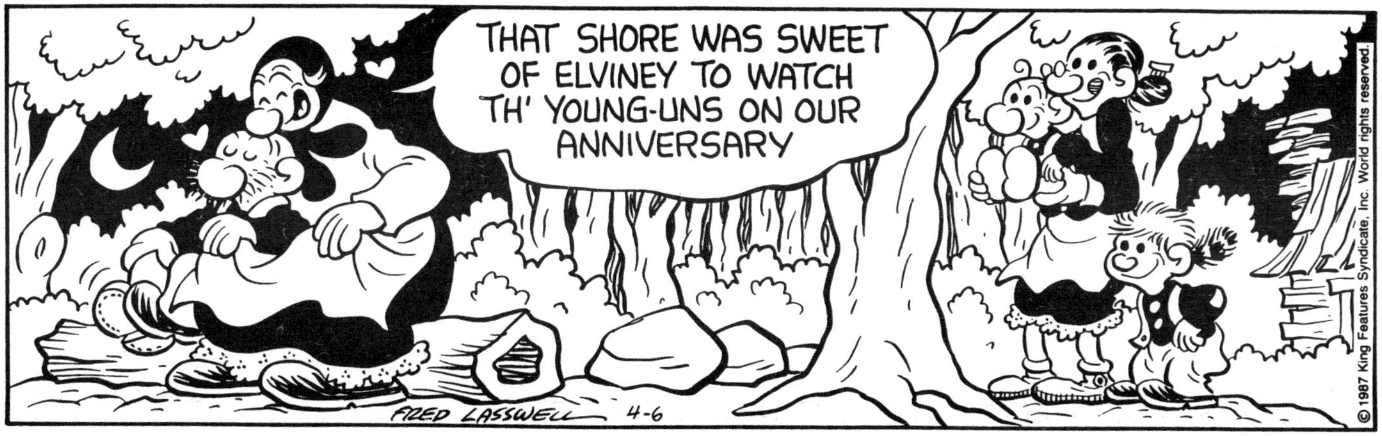
THAT SHORE WAS SWEET OF ELVINEY TO WATCH TH' YOUNG-UNS ON OUR ANNIVERSARY
FRED LASSWELL 4-6
© 1987 King Features Syndicate, Inc. World rights reserved.

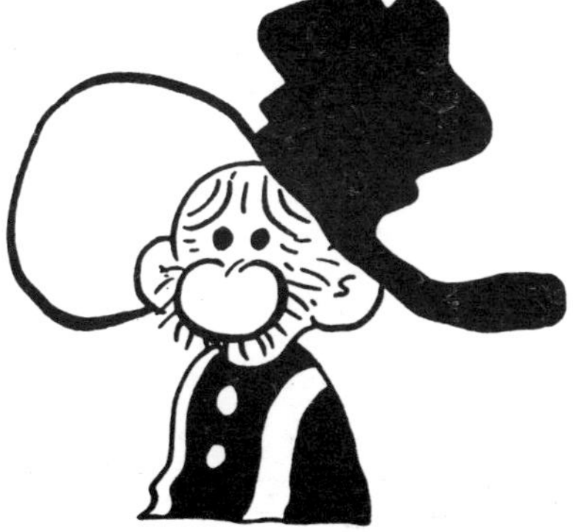

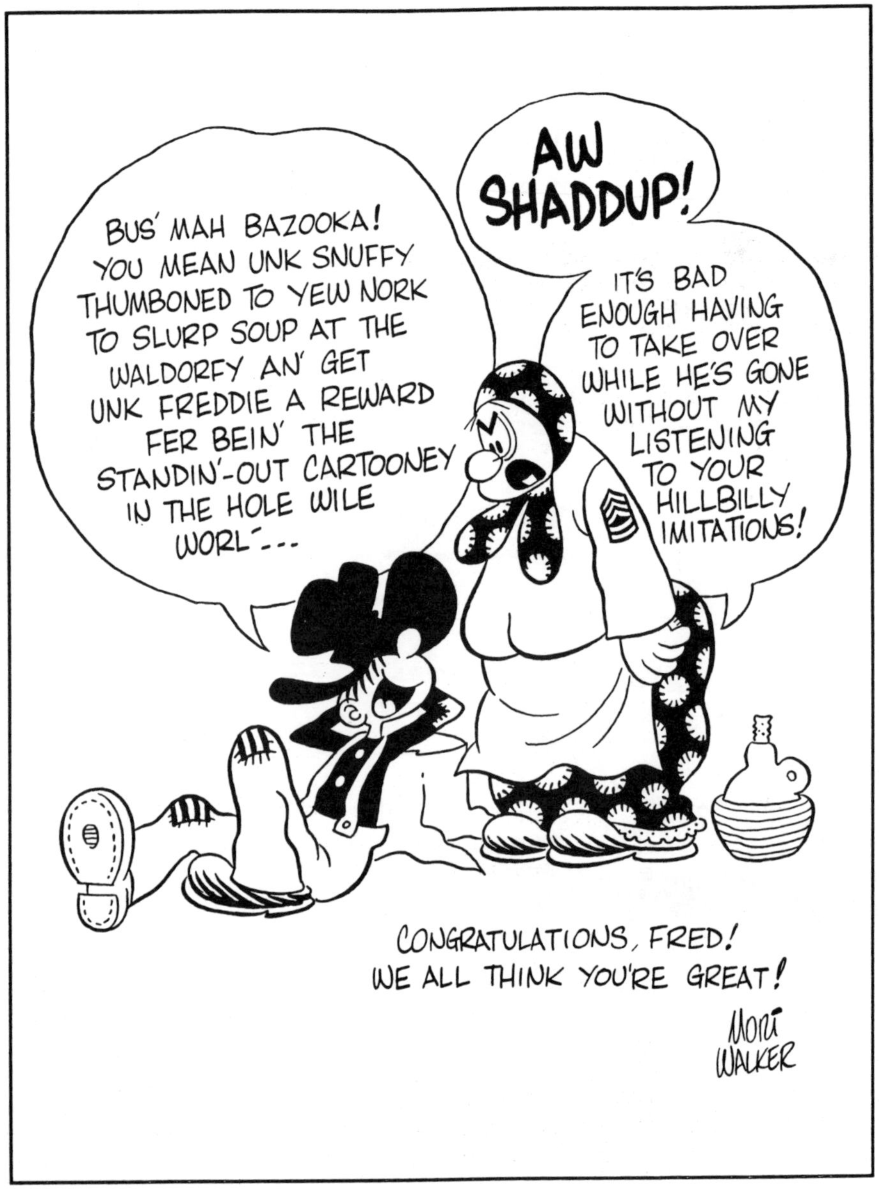
BUS' MAH BAZOOKA! YOU MEAN UNK SNUFFY THUMBONED TO YEW NORK TO SLURP SOUP AT THE WALDORFY AN' GET UNK FREDDIE A REWARD FER BEIN' THE STANDIN'-OUT CARTOONEY IN THE HOLE WILE WORL'...
AW SHADDUP!
IT'S BAD ENOUGH HAVING TO TAKE OVER WHILE HE'S GONE WITHOUT MY LISTENING TO YOUR HILLBILLY IMITATIONS!
CONGRATULATIONS, FRED! WE ALL THINK YOU'RE GREAT!
MORT WALKER

Above: Congratulatory drawing by Mort Walker, from book presented to Fred Lasswell by the Banshees Society on November 1, 1962. Courtesy of Fred Lasswell.

RUBE GOLDBERG

169 East 69th.St.
New York 21 N.Y.
Sept.30,1962

Fred Lasswell
King Features Syndicate
235 East 45th.St.
New York 17
N.Y.

Dear Fred:

When I heard you were selected to receive the Banshees Silver Lady Award I immediately thought of the days when our great and dear friend,Billy De Beck,adopted you as his protege.

Since then I have seen you grow both physically and artistically until you are now a great cartoonist in your own right. Your rare talents for a special type of hillbilly humor have gone into Snuffy Smith until now it is comepletely your own.You are one of the pure comic artists left in our profession and I know you will flourish for many years to come.

Fred,I consider it a privilege to have watched you develop into the fine person and cartoonist you are today.Congratulations from one whose family had always had a personal interest in your ever-growing career.

Bless you and again congratulations

as ever

Rube Goldberg

Above: Congratulatory letter from Rube Goldberg, from book presented to Fred Lasswell by the Banshees Society on November 1, 1962. Courtesy of Fred Lasswell.

75 Years Later
Barney Google & Snuffy Smith Today

Fred Lasswell continues "Barney Google and Snuffy Smith" today, over fifty years and more than 15,000 episodes since he took over after Billy DeBeck's death in 1942. In 1946, the strip had 206 newspaper subscribers. By 1964, the list had climbed to 542 papers, and on its 70th anniversary in 1989, "Barney Google and Snuffy Smith" was being published in nearly 900 newspapers in 21 countries.

On November 1, 1962, Fred Lasswell was presented with the prestigious "Silver Lady Award" from the Banshees Society in New York City, a group of prominent newspaper, magazine, book, radio and television professionals. A large book was given to Lasswell, filled with congratulatory letters from friends and celebrities.

In 1963, Lasswell became the first man in the history of the National Cartoonists Society to win two of its awards in the same year - the "Reuben" as "outstanding cartoonist of the year" and "Best Humor Strip Cartoonist." The NCS also presented Fred with the "Elzie Segar Award" for his "unique and outstanding contributions to the profession of cartooning" in 1984.

Fred Lasswell has also distinguished himself in many other ways. In the 1940's, he created a comic book for the blind, using a system based on Braille. In 1958, he designed a citrus harvesting machine, obtained a patent for it in 1962, and licensed the idea to International Harvester. In 1984, he launched a series of instructional videos for kids, which continue to win rave reviews in parents' magazines.

He has also applied his technical skills to aid with the production of "Barney Google and Snuffy Smith." In the late-1980's, he designed a computer font based on the lettering style he has used for decades. This system not only saves him time, it also allows him to achieve a better balance between the artwork and the dialogue in the strip.

After all these years, Fred is still challenged by the job of creating a daily comic strip. In a recent interview, he had the following words of wisdom: "The gut of a comic is in the characters themselves. If you don't have a bang-clang gag or something that's all polished and beautiful, then just emphasize the character because that way people get to know them. The thing that drives you crazy in this business is that you should acquire two skills - both contradictory. One is having an excellent memory, so you can remember what you did in the past and not do the same thing today. The other is an ability to forget, so you can clear your head and think of something fresh."

The rich comic legacy that Billy DeBeck and Fred Lasswell have left behind will never be forgotten. "Barney Google and Snuffy Smith" is one of the longest running strips in comics history. It might become the first comic strip to celebrate its 100th anniversary. It could last forever.

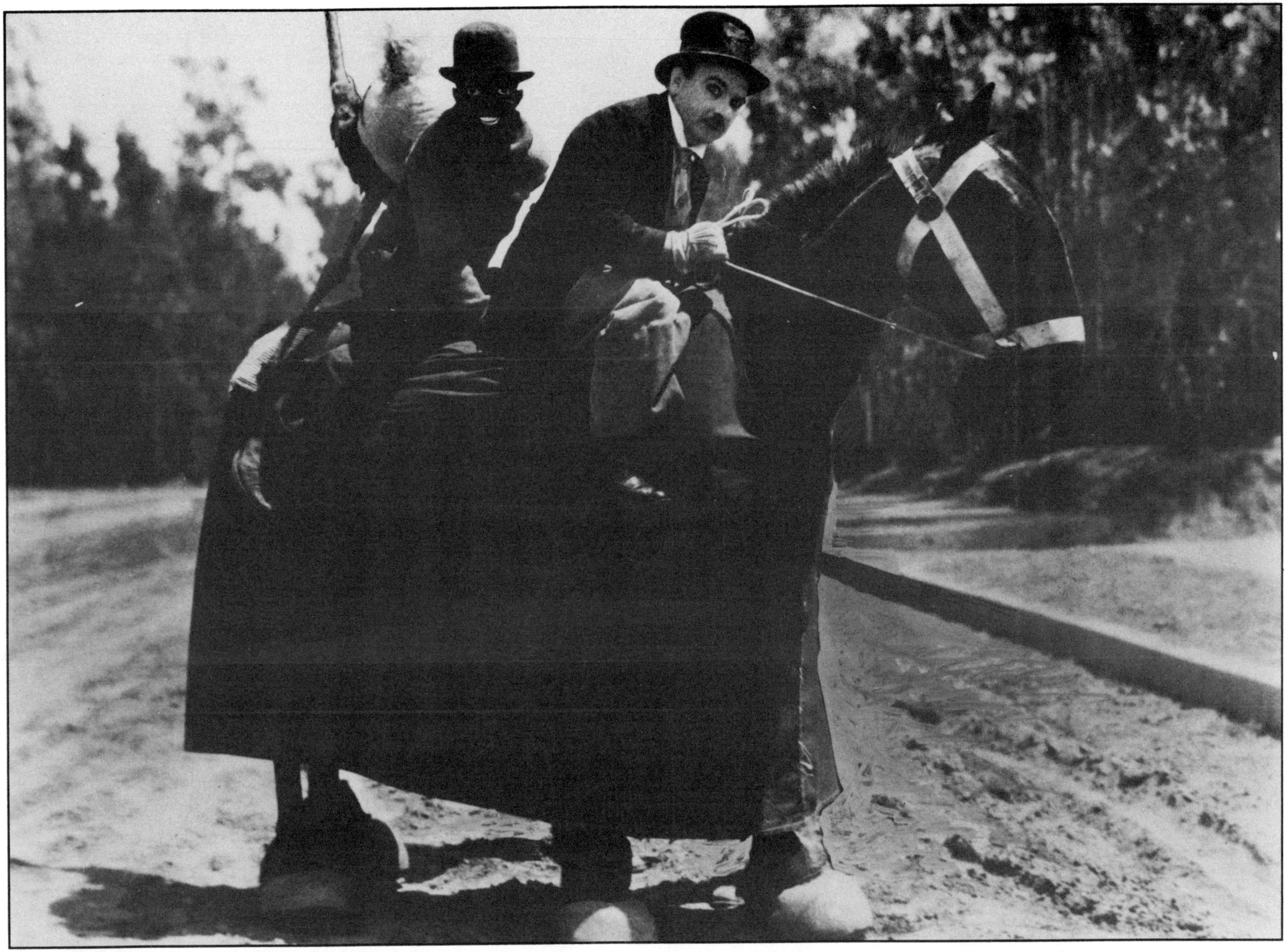

Above: Photograph of Barney Hellum from the "Barney Google and Spark Plug" film shorts produced by F.B.O. Pictures Corp., 1928 and 1929. Courtesy of The New York Public Library for the Performing Arts.

Beyond Newsprint
By Bill Janocha

When Barney Google teamed up with Spark Plug in 1922, the ramifications of that event went far beyond their newspaper appearances. Within a year, songwriters Billy Rose and Con Conrad had the nation singing their "Barney Google" hit tune, and a wave of toys, dolls, and other merchandise, based on DeBeck's characters, filled the toy and department stores. In 1924, a cartoon musical comedy, "Barney Google and Spark Plug," opened at Philadelphia's Chestnut Street Theatre, boasting "an old time thrilling race track scene."

In the late 1920's, F.B.O. Pictures produced a series of silent comedy shorts featuring Barney Hellum as Google and a nag fitted with false feet and a horsecloth as Spark Plug. F.B.O. also produced a similar series based on Jimmy Murphy's "Toots and Casper" comic strip, but lackluster reviews and the advent of sound films terminated both series.

The next screen adaptation of "Barney Google" was a series of four animated color cartoons produced by Charles Mintz's unit at Columbia Pictures in 1935 and 1936. Unfortunately, only silent, edited versions of these cartoons are known to exist today. They reveal unique depictions of DeBeck's complete cast, featuring early appearances of Snuffy and Lowizie, Bunky, and characters already gone from the newspaper strip, including Sully, Sunshine and a very energetic Rudy the Ostrich. The Max Fleischer studio,

famous for the Betty Boop and Popeye animated cartoons, proposed a series featuring King Features properties, including "The Katzenjammer Kids," "Toots and Casper," "Polly and Her Pals" and "Barney Google," for the 1936-37 season, but sadly, it was never produced.

In 1942, Monogram Pictures released two live-action feature films starring Albert "Bud" Duncan, formerly of the Kalem Film Studio's "Ham" comedies of the 1910's. Both "Snuffy Smith, Yardbird" and "Hillbilly Blitzkrieg" dealt with Snuffy's army service in World War II, and co-starred veteran comic actor Edgar Kennedy as a former "revenoor" turned army sergeant. Both films also featured similar plots, involving spies attempting to steal U.S. Government War secrets. Bad reviews of "Blitzkrieg" halted any further sequels.

Snuffy's return from active duty was the subject of "Spree For All," a 1946 Noveltoon from Famous Studios. In 1962, Paramount produced fifty cartoons for its "King Features Trilogy" TV show starring Barney and Snuffy, Beetle Bailey and Krazy Kat. Snuffy's Germanic niece, Bizzy Buzz Buzz, a child with a compulsion for constantly cleaning the Smith's shack, and Barney Google, who at this time was virtually absent from the newspaper strip, also played significant roles. These films resembled the other Paramount films of the period more closely than Lasswell's strip, but managed to stimulate merchandising business with a Bizzy doll, hand puppets and coloring books.

The most authentic "Barney Google and Snuffy Smith" products were the various book and comic magazine reprints of DeBeck's and Lasswell's work, highlighted by a series from Cupples & Leon in the 1920's and two Dell comic books from 1942 and 1944, which reprinted extensively DeBeck's later Sunday pages. Lasswell's work was also reprinted in comic books, starting in 1951.

In 1926, King Features Syndicate issued a color storybook entitled "All the Funny Folks," which featured its entire cartoon stable, gathered together to witness a race between Barney and Spark Plug and Jiggs, from "Bringing Up Father," atop Frederick Opper's "Maude the Mule." This unique publication was illustrated by Louis Biedermann.

DeBeck's characters were also portrayed in several of the sordid and unauthorized "Tijuana Bibles" during the 1930's, which contained eight-page adult escapades drawn by anonymous artists.

In 1967, a New York nightclub, named "Barney Google's," opened with "Stan Rubin and his Tigertown Five" as the house band. Although short-lived, "Barney Google's" was a nostalgic reminder of the simpler, yet hedonistic climate that launched the strip forty-five years earlier.

Barney and Snuffy still visit us daily in close to nine hundred newspapers, proving that, regardless of current fashions or politics, classic works endure.

The following is the most complete list to date of items derived from the comic strip.

LIVE-ACTION FILMS

F.B.O. Pictures Corp. / RKO: "Barney Google and Spark Plug" series of silent two-reel comedies, starring Barney Hellum as Barney Google, produced by Larry Darmour and directed by Ralph Cedar. Eight titles: "Beefsteaks" (December, 1928), "OKMNX" (January, 1929), "Horsefeathers" (February, 1929), "Money Balks" (March, 1929), "T-Bone Handicap" (April, 1929), "Neigh, Neigh Spark Plug" (May, 1929), "Runnin' Thru the Rye" (June, 1929) and "A Horse on Barney" (1929).
Monogram Features: Two titles: "Snuffy Smith, Yardbird" starring Albert "Bud" Duncan as Snuffy Smith, Edgar Kennedy as Sergeant Cooper and Sarah Padden as Lowizie. Produced by Edward Gross and directed by Edward Cline. 67 minutes. (January, 1942). "Hillbilly Blitzkrieg" starring Albert "Bud" Duncan as Snuffy Smith, Cliff Nazarro as Barney Google and Edgar Kennedy as Sergeant Gatling. Produced by Edward Gross and directed by Roy Mack. 63 minutes. (August, 1942).

ANIMATED CARTOONS

Charles Mintz/Columbia Pictures, "Color Rhapsodies" theatrical cartoons. Stories by Sid Marcus, animation by Art Davis. Four titles: "Tetched in the Head" (October, 1935), "Patch Mah Britches" (December, 1935), "Spark Plug" (April, 1936) and "Major Google" (May, 1936).
Famous Studios, "Noveltoon" theatrical cartoon. One title: "Spree for All" (October, 1946).
Paramount, "Comic King" theatrical cartoons. Directed by Seymour Kneitel. Four titles: "Snuffy's Song" (June, 1962), "The Hat" (July, 1962), "The Method and Maw" (August, 1962) and "Take Me to Your Gen'rul" (September, 1962).
Paramount, "Comic King" television cartoons. Directed by Seymour Kneitel. Forty-six titles (1962-1963): "Snuffy's Turf Luck," "Pie in the Sky," "The Berkley Squares," "The Shipwreckers," "The Master," "Barney Deals the Cars," "Snuffy Runs the Gamut," "The Tourist Trap," "Rip Van Snuffy," "Snuffy Goes to College," "Snuffy's Brush with Fame," "Give Me a Jailbreak," "Glove Thy Neighbor," "Snuffy's Fair Lady," "Just Plain Kinfolk," "Off Their Rockers," "Snuffy Hits the Road," "My Kingdom for a Horse," "The Country Club Smiths," "Jughaid's Jumpin' Frog," "Turkey Shoot," "The Work Pill," "Jughaid for President," "Loweezy Makes a Match," "Fishin' Fools," "Little Red Jughaid," "Jughaid the Magician," "A Hoss Kin Dream," "It's Better to Give," "Spring Time and Spark Plug," "There's No Feud like an Old Feud," "A Hauntin' fer a House," "Feudin' and A-Fussin'," "Barney's Blarney," "Do Do That Judo," "Farm of the Future," "Getting Snuffy's Goat," "Barney's Winter Carnival," "Keeping Up with the Joneses," "The Big Bear Hunt," "Ain't it the Tooth," "Bizzy Nappers," "The Buzz in Snuffy's Bonnet," "Settin' and A-Frettin'," "Beauty and the Beast" and "Smoke Screams."

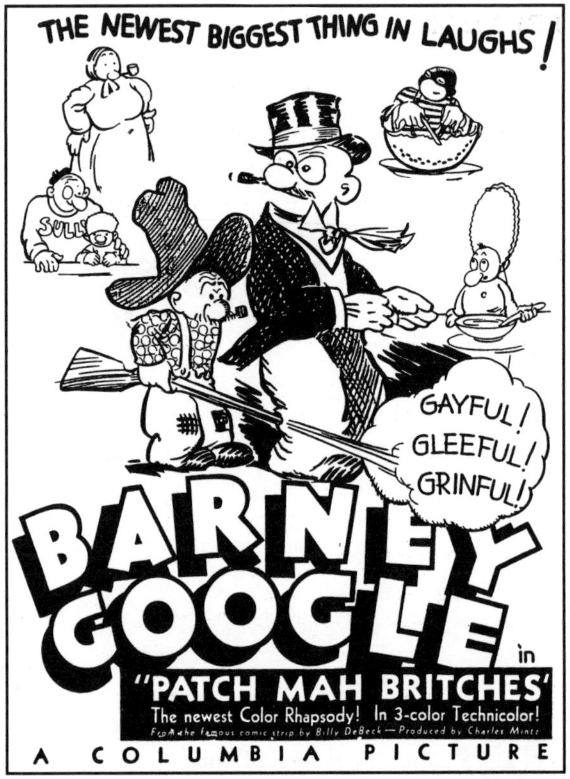
THE NEWEST BIGGEST THING IN LAUGHS!
GAYFUL! GLEEFUL! GRINFUL!
BARNEY GOOGLE in
"PATCH MAH BRITCHES"
The newest Color Rhapsody! In 3-color Technicolor!
A COLUMBIA PICTURE

Above: Magazine announcement for Columbia cartoon, "Patch Mah Britches," (1935). Collection of Bill Janocha.

TOYS & FIGURINES

Barney Google, jointed doll, cloth and wood. First model: 7 3/4" high. Second model: 7 1/4" high, A. Schoenhut & Co. (1922-1930).
Barney Google on pedestal, candy container, painted glass (1923).
Barney Google aside barrel candy container, painted glass (1923).
Barney Google wind-up, tin (ca. 1923).
Barney Google seated minature figure, painted white metal 1 1/4" high. German. (1923-1924).
Barney Google jointed doll, wood with composition head, 9" high. (1920's).
Barney Google figure, plaster, 9" high. (1920's).
Barney Google figure, china, 4" high, German.(1920's).
Barney Google doll, stuffed cloth 12" high. (1920's-1930's).
Barney "G" figure, compostion wood, 4" high. (1944).
Barney Google and Snuffy Smith salt and pepper shaker set, painted plaster, 3" high. (ca. 1943).
Barney Google hand puppet with a voice, cloth with vinyl head, 10" high, Gund Co. (1960's).
Barney Google and Spark Plug figure, bisque, 3" high, German. (1922-1924).
Barney Google, Spark Plug and Sunshine scooter race pull toy, tin, 6" high, Nifty Toy Co., German. (1924).
Barney Google and Spark Plug wind-up, tin, 7" high, Nifty Toy Co., (1920's).
Barney Google and Spark Plug in stable pull toy, tin. (1920's).
Barney Google riding Spark Plug paperweight, painted lead, 3" high. (1930's).
Barney Google riding Spark Plug figure, plaster, 9" high. (1930's).
Bizzy Buzz Buzz rag doll, stuffed cloth with vinyl face, 18" high, Gund Co. (1960's).
Rudy the Ostrich toy, tin, German, Nifty Toy Co. (1924).
Rudy the Ostrich doll, stuffed cloth (1920's).
Snuffy Smith doll, stuffed cloth, 17" high, unauthorized. (1930's).
Snuffy Smith hand puppet with a voice, cloth with vinyl head, 10" high, Gund Co. (1960's).
Snuffy Smith soldier figure, metal with brass finish, 4 3/4" high. (1940's).
Snuffy Smith, Lowizie Smith, Jughaid Smith and Sut Tattersall set of figures, hard plastic, German models painted, American models unpainted, 2-2 1/2" high. Marx Co. (1950's - 1960's).
Spark Plug pull toy on wheels, wood, 5" high. (1922-1923 and 1928).
Spark Plug squeaker toy, rubber, 3" high. (1923).
Spark Plug candy container, clear and painted glass models, 6"high. (1922-1923).
Spark Plug jointed doll figure, cloth and wood, 7 7/8" high, A. Schoenhut & Co. (1922-1930).
Spark Plug and Sunshine racer pull toy, tin. (1924).
Spark Plug doll, stuffed cloth, 7" high. (1920's).
Spark Plug figure, green glass, 2" high. (1920's).
Spark Plug hinged pull toy on wheels, wood, 8" high. (1920's-1930's).
Spark Plug carnival statue, plaster, 10"high. (1930's).
Sunshine pull toy on wheels, painted wood. (1926).

SONG SHEETS

"Barney Google" Fox Trot by Billy Rose and Con Conrad. New York & Detroit: Jerome H. Remick & Co., 1923.
"Bug House Fables" Novelty Fox Trot Song, words and music by Clarence Gaskill. New York: M. Witmark & Sons, 1923.
"So I Took the $50,000," lyrics by Jack Meskill, music by Albert Gumble. New York & Detroit: Jerome H. Remick & Co., 1923.

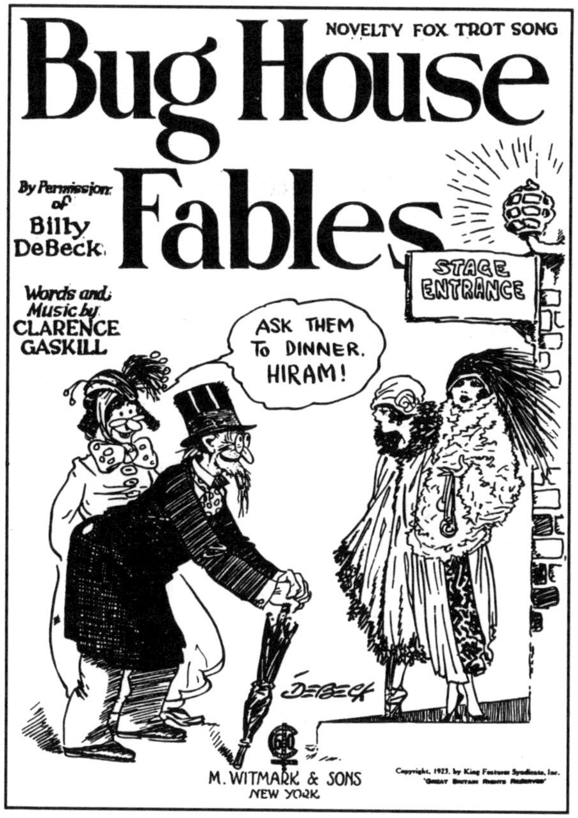
NOVELTY FOX TROT SONG
Bug House Fables
By Permission of Billy DeBeck
Words and Music by CLARENCE GASKILL
STAGE ENTRANCE
ASK THEM To DINNER. HIRAM!
DEBECK
M. WITMARK & SONS NEW YORK

Above: Artwork for "Bug House Fables" song sheet, 1923. From the Collection of Richard Marschall.

"Come On Spark Plug!" by Billy Rose and Con Conrad. New York: Waterson, Berlin & Snyder Co., 1923.
"Barney Google Musical Album" Song Folio by William K. Wells and Dan Doty. New York: Rossiter Music Co., 1923.
"OKMNX, We're Twenty Million Strong, The Brotherhood of Billy Goats," lyrics by Billy DeBeck and Sid Silvers, music by Phil Baker and J. Russel Robinson. New York & Detroit: Jerome H. Remick & Co., 1928.
"La De Doody Doo, The Latest Song Craze," words and music by Duke Ellington, Edward J. Lambert and Stephen Richards. N. Y.: Exclusive, 1938.

PROMOTIONAL BUTTONS

Snuffy Smith "Class of June '36", 1 1/4", West Philadelphia High School, unauthorized. (1936).

Barney Google, 1 1/8", The Atlanta Georgians Silver Anniversary. (1937).

Barney Google #31, 1", *Detroit Times* newspaper contest. (1930's).

Barney Google, *New York Sunday American* newspaper contest. (1930's).

Spark-Plug, *New York Sunday American* newspaper contest. (1930's).

31 Comics in Color, 1 1/8", *Sunday Detroit Times* featuring Barney Google, and others. (1930's).

30 Comics - Barney Google, 1 1/8", *Sunday Chicago Herald and Examiner.* (1930's).

Barney Google, *New York Evening Journal* newspaper contest. (1930's).

Snuffy Smith, *Philadelphia Evening Ledger* Comics. (1930's).

30 Comics - Barney Google, *Detroit Sunday Times.* (1930's).

Barney Google, Kellogg's Pep cereal. (1946).

Snuffy Smith, Kellogg's Pep cereal. (1946).

Snuffy Smith, Sut Tattersall, Riddles Barlow and Cricket Barlow, King Features set. (1950's - 60's).

COLLECTIBLE BOOKS

See bibliography for list of reprint books

All the Funny Folks. by Louis Biedermann and Jack Lait. New York: The World Today, 1926. Rhyme-story featuring King Features characters.

Barney Google. Little Big Book. Akron, Ohio: Saalfield Publishing Co., 1935.

Famous Comics Book Set. Racine, Wis.: Whitman, 1934. Three books in slip case, featuring "Barney Google," "Polly and her Pals," "Little Jimmy," "The Katzenjammer Kids" and "Little Annie Rooney."

Top-Line Comics Book Set. Racine, Wis.: Whitman, 1935. Three books in slipcase featuring "Bunky," "Nicodemus O'Malley," "Alexander Smart, Esq."

Snuffy Smith an' Barney Google TV Cartoon Coloring Book. Kenosha, Wis.: Samuel Lowe Co., 1963.

Four Television Favorites Coloring Book. Kenosha, Wis.: Samuel Lowe Co., 1964. Featuring Snuffy Smith, Barney Google, Beetle Bailey, Krazy Kat and Popeye.

GAMES

Barney Google and Spark Plug Game, Milton Bradley Co. (1923).

Snuffy's Hootin' Holler Bug Derby Exciting Bug Race Game, Jaymar. (late 1940's-1950's).

Barney Google and Snuffy Smith Time's A Wastin' Game, Milton Bradley Co. (1963).

MISCELLANEOUS

"Runnin' Thru the Rye" theater poster for silent, film comedy. F.B.O. Pictures Corp. (1929).

"Barney Google" and "I Love Me," 78 RPM record by Billy Jones and Ernest Hare, Brunswick Recording #2435. (1923).

King Features Comic Strip Calender. Weekly pages of daily strips featuring "Barney Google and Spark Plug," and others. (1925).

"Brotherhood of Billy Goats" and "Sisterhood of Nanny Goats" member cards with facsimile signatures of "Bernard Google," club premiums from *Chicago Herald and Examiner.* (1927-28).

King Features Comic Club stamps. Set of 19 stamps, including Barney Google. (1930's).

Barney Google and Snuffy Smith Christmas bulb shades. Lot of six shades, plastic, GE Mazda. (1930's-1940's).

Snuffy Smith Post Toasties Corn Flakes premium ring. Tin litho, 2 1/2" long. (1949).

Puck-The Comic Weekly Club premium kit. Activity and pencil booklet, membership card, playing pieces and fan picture featuring Snuffy Smith and others. (1949-1950's).

Snuffy Smith comic strip ring. Figural character, plastic, 1/2" long. (1953).

Snuffy Smith whisky jug bank with corncob stopper. Ceramic, 6" high. (1950's).

Snuffy Smith figural mug. Ceramic, 8" high, Puck. (1950's-1960's).

Barney Google and Snuffy Smith Good Humor giveaway. Brush and packet of 1963 daily strips to watercolor. (1960's).

Snuffy Smith , Krazy Kat and Beetle Bailey jigsaw puzzles. Milton Bradley Co. (1964).

King Features Comic Character Christmas tree ornaments. Set of twelve bell-shaped ornaments featuring Snuffy Smith and others 2 1/2" high each. (1960's).

Snuffy Smith limited edition lithograph, hand-signed by Fred Lasswell for The Newspaper Comics Council, Harry N. Abrams. (1978).

"Down Home in Hootin' Holler" videotape of Paramount cartoons. Best Film & Video. (1991).

"Hillbillies 'R' Us" videotape of Paramount cartoons. Best Film & Video. (1991)

"Hootin' and Hollerin'" videotape of Paramount cartoons. Best Film & Video. (1991).

Above: Model sheet drawings of Barney and Spark Plug, Paramount Studios, 1962. Collection of Mark Johnson.

Bibliography

The following is a list of sources used to research this book. The page numbers in each listing refer to entries relating directly to Billy DeBeck, Fred Lasswell, "Barney Google" and/or "Barney Google and Snuffy Smith."

BOOKS

Becker, Stephen. *Comic Art in America*. New York: Simon and Schuster, 1959. pgs. 49, 86, 90-94, 236.

Benton, Mike. *The Comic Book in America: An Illustrated History*. Dallas, Texas: Taylor Publishing Company, 1989. pgs. 14, 167.

Blackbeard, Bill, ed. *Classic American Comic Strips*. Billy DeBeck, *Barney Google: A Complete Compilation, 1919-1920*. Westport, Ct.: Hyperion Press, 1977.

　　The Smithsonian Collection of Newspaper Comics. Washington, D.C.: Smithsonian Institution Press, 1977. pgs. 149-150, 278-319.

Couperie, Pierre and Maurice Horn. *A History of the Comic Strip*. New York: Crown Publishers, 1968. pgs. 48, 49, 53, 159, 166.

DeBeck, Billy. *DeBeck's Cartoon Hints - Book One*. Pittsburgh, Pa.: DeBeck & Carter Feature Service, 1915. (DeBeck advertised a *Book Two*, but no copy could be located).

Gifford, Denis. *The International Book of Comics*. New York: Crescent Books, 1984. pgs. 44, 106.

Goulart, Ron. *The Encyclopedia of American Comics*. New York: Facts On File, Inc., 1990. pgs. 6, 20-22, 26, 58-59, 93, 143, 166, 211, 238, 245, 264-265, 269-270, 367, 386.

　　Over 50 Years of American Comic Books. Lincolnwood, Ill.: Mallard Press, 1991. pg. 14.

Hake, Ted. *Hakes's Guide to Comic Character Collectibles*. Radnor, Pa.: Wallace-Homestead Book Company, 1993. pgs. 10-11, 146.

Inge, M. Thomas. *Comics as Culture*. Jackson, Mississippi: University Press of Mississippi, 1990. pgs. 8, 21, 68-77, 85, 143.

Horn, Maurice, ed. *75 Years of the Comics*. Boston: Boston Book and Art, Publisher, 1971. pg. 36.

　　The World Encyclopedia of Comics. New York: Chelsea House Publishers, revised edition, 1976. pgs. 20, 88, 99-100, 143, 198, 199, 446, 702.

　　Women in the Comics. New York: Chelsea House Publishers, 1977. pgs. 34, 70.

　　Sex in the Comics. New York: Chelsea House Publishers, 1985. pgs. 19-20, 155.

King Features Syndicate. *Famous Artists & Writers of King Features Syndicate.* New York: King Features Syndicate, Inc., 1949. (Profile of Fred Lasswell).

Koenigsberg, M. *King News: An Autobiography.* Philadelphia and New York: F. A. Stokes Company, 1941. Billy DeBeck describes how he created "sweet mama." pg. 452.

Lenburg, Jeff. *The Encyclopedia of Animated Cartoons.* New York: Facts on File, 1991. pgs. 50, 356-357.

Lesser, Robert. *A Celebration of Comic Art and Memorabilia.* New York: Hawthorn Books, 1975. pgs. 82, 117.

Maltin, Leonard. *Of Mice and Magic: A History of Animated Cartoons.* New York: New American Library, revised edition, 1987. pgs. 215, 414, 449, 457.

Marschall, Richard. *The Sunday Funnies: 1896-1950.* New York: Chelsea House Publishers, 1978. Facsimile comic section, "The Sunday Twenties," pg. 2.

   America's Great Comic-Strip Artists. New York: Abbeville Press, 1989. pgs. 16, 123, 124, 276.

Matthews, E. C. *How to Draw Funny Pictures* (illustrated by Eugene Zimmerman). Chicago: Drake, 1928, revised editions, 1935, 1936.

O'Sullivan, Judith. *The Great American Comic Strip.* Boston: Little, Brown and Company, 1990. pgs. 110, 159, 175.

Perry, George and Alan Aldridge. *The Penguin Book of Comics.* London: Penguin Books, revised edition, 1971. pgs. 110, 128.

Robinson, Jerry. *The Comics: An Illustrated History of Comic Strip Art.* New York: G.P. Putnam's Sons, 1974. pgs. 27, 68, 72, 73, 160.

Seldes, Gilbert. *The Seven Lively Arts.* New York: Harper and Brothers, 1924, revised edition, 1957. "The 'Vulgar' Comic Strip," pgs. 193-205.

Sheridan, Martin. *Comics and Their Creators.* Boston: Hale, Cushman & Flint, 1942. pgs. 36-39.

Thorndike, Chuck. *The Business of Cartooning.* New York: The House of Little Books, 1939. Billy DeBeck profile, pg. 12.

Walker, Mort and Bill Janocha, ed. *The National Cartoonists Society Album.* Greenwich, Ct. revised editon, 1988. Fred Lasswell biography, pg. 106.

Waugh, Coulton. *The Comics.* New York: Macmillan, 1947. pgs. 50-56.

ARTICLES

Appel, John J. "Ethnicity in Cartoon Art." *Cartoons and Ethnicity.* Columbus, Ohio: Ohio State University Libraries, 1992. pgs. 13-48.

Berchtold, William E. "Men of Comics." *New Outlook.* May, 1935. pg. 46.

Black, Ed. "The First Step to Fame." DeBeck's early career in Youngstown, Ohio and Pittsburgh, Pa. Unpublished.

Cartoonist PROfiles. "Fred Lasswell." December, 1979. pgs. 76-79.

Cartoons. Chicago: H.H. Windsor Publisher. "A Reactionary Idol - DeBeck in the *Youngstown Telegram.*" May, 1912. pg. 30.

Cartoons Magazine. Chicago: H.H. Windsor Publisher. "The New Hope of Surgery - DeBeck in the *Pittsburgh Gazette-Times.*" April, 1914. pg. 420.

   "What the Cartoonists are Doing." News item about DeBeck's departure from the *Pittsburgh Gazette-Times.* May, 1915. pg. 799.

   Advertisement for "DeBeck Cartoon Hints." June, 1915. pg. 23.

   "What the Cartoonists are Doing: DeBeck's New Comics." Article about DeBeck's return to Chicago and new "Finn an' Haddie" strip. January, 1916. pg. 159.

   Advertisement for DeBeck's Cartoon Course at the Chicago Academy of Fine Arts. June, 1916. pg. 11.

   Advertisement for DeBeck's Cartoon Course at the Chicago Academy of Fine Arts. January, 1917. pg. 16.

   "The Cartoonists' Confessional by DeBeck." June, 1917. pg. 334.

   "What the Cartoonists are Doing: Your First Week as A Cartoonist, It Is Not So Easy as It Looks, According to DeBeck." November, 1917. pg. 719.

   "With the Cartoonists: Changes in Chicago." News article about the merger of the *Chicago Herald* and the *Chicago Examiner.* July, 1918. pg. 135.

Circulation. New York: King Features Syndicate, Inc. "Barney Google's Spark Plug will win for you too in Circulation Sweepstakes." Advertisement. July, 1923. pg. 7.

   "Spark Plug Tip Lucky at Derby." July, 1923. pg. 32.

   "Broadcasting Fun: The Comics on the Air." March, 1926. pg. 16.

   "DeBeck's Comedy of Errors." Promotion for Eric Van Horn story. April, 1927. pg. 14.

Editor and Publisher. "Barney Google Artist to Get Banshees Award." September 22, 1962.

Film Fun. "Mr. Smith Goes to Hollywood." April, 1942.

Goulart, Ron. "The Life and Times of Bunker Hill, Jr." *Nemo: The Classic Comics Library #3.* Stamford, Ct.: Fantagraphics Books, Inc., October, 1983. pgs. 46-58.

   "Barney Google: Meet the man who gave us Spark Plug, Snuffy Smith and lots of laughs." *Comics Scene #4.* New York: Starlog Communications International, Inc., 1988. pgs. 20-22.

"To Be Continued: The Rise and Spread of Humorous Continuity Strips." *What's So Funny? The Humor Comic Strip in America.* Salina, Kansas: Salina Art Center, 1988. pgs. 25-31.

Hardy, Charles. "A Brief History of Ethnicity in the Comics." *Ethnic Images in the Comics.* Philadelphia, PA.: The Balch Institute for Ethnic Studies, 1986. pgs. 7-10.

Harvey, Robert C., "Bud Fisher and the Daily Comic Strip." *INKS: Cartoon and Comic Art Studies, Volume 1, No. 1.* Columbus Ohio: Ohio State University Press, February, 1994. pgs, 14-25.

Johnson, Mark. "DeBeck Before Google." *Strip Scene #10.* Calgary, Alberta: Winter, 1979. pgs. 24-27.

Jones, Steven Loring. "From 'Under Cork' to Overcoming: Black Images in the Comics." *Ethnic Images in the Comics.* Philadelphia, PA.: The Balch Institute for Ethnic Studies, 1986. pgs. 21-30.

Literary Digest. "Comics—and Their Creators." February 17, 1934.

Monchak, Stephen J. "Billy DeBeck Marks 20th Year With King." *Editor and Publisher.* October 7, 1939.

Nelson, Pamela B. "From Subhuman to Superhuman: Ethnic Characters in the Comics." *Ethnic Images in the Comics.* Philadelphia, PA.: The Balch Institute for Ethnic Studies, 1986. pgs. 11-14.

Newsweek. "Barney Google's Birthday: He's 21 Now but Sadly Eclipsed by the Toughie Snuffy Smith." October, 14, 1940. pgs. 59-60.

"Barney Google Man." November 23, 1942. (Billy DeBeck's obituary).

Scheinfeld, Amram. "A Portrait in Zowie." *Esquire.* November, 1935. pgs. 78, 140-144.

Southern Living. "Snuffy Smith's Pappy." July, 1987. pg. 106.

Time Magazine. "DeBeck Dies." November 23, 1942. pgs. 51-52.

Who Was Who in America 2. (1943-50). pg. 149.

INTERVIEWS

"Good Moon Rising: An Interview with Ferd Johnson." by Rick Marschall and Gary Groth. *Nemo Magazine #29.* Westlake Village, Ca.: Fantagraphics Books, Inc., February, 1989. pgs. 18-43.

"Ferd Johnson." interview by Shel Dorf. *Comics Interview.* New York: Fictioneer Books, 1993. pgs. 4-14.

"Ferd Johnson on Billy DeBeck" interview by Ed Black, October 15, 1985. Unpublished.

"Fred Lasswell's Recollections of Billy DeBeck." interview by Ed Black, October 9, 1985. Unpublished.

"A Conversation with Fred Lasswell." interview by Brian Walker, February, 20, 1994. Videotaped interview for this book.

REPRINT BOOKS

The following is a list of books and comic books reprinting "Barney Google" and "Barney Google and Snuffy Smith" strips by Billy DeBeck and Fred Lasswell, in chronological order.

Barney Google - Comic Monthly #4. New York: Embee Distributing Inc., March, 1922. Reprints of 1921 strips.

Barney Google and Spark Plug in the Abadaba Handicap - Comic Monthly #11. November, 1922. Reprint of 1922 strips featuring the debut of Spark Plug.

Barney Google and His Faithful Nag Spark Plug. New York: Cupples & Leon Company, 1923. Reprints of 1923 strips.

Barney Google and Spark Plug #2. New York: Cupples & Leon Company, 1924. Reprints of 1923 strips.

Barney Google and Spark Plug #3. New York: Cupples & Leon Company, 1925. Reprints of 1924 strips.

Barney Google and Spark Plug #4. New York: Cupples & Leon Company, 1926. Reprints of 1925-1926 strips.

Barney Google and Spark Plug #5 and *Barney Google and Spark Plug #6* are believed to have been published by Cupples & Leon Company, but no copies were located.

Barney Google and Snuffy Smith - Four Color #19. New York: Dell, 1942. Reprints of 1936-1937 Sunday pages.

Barney Google and Snuffy Smith - Large Feature Comic #11. New York: Dell, 1943. Reprints of 1941 strips.

Barney Google and Snuffy Smith - Four Color #40. New York: Dell, 1944. Reprints of 1937-1942 Sunday pages.

Barney Google and Snuffy Smith #1 - #4. New York: Toby Press, June, 1951 - February, 1952. Reprints of Lasswell strips.

Barney Google and Snuffy Smith #1. Poughkeepsie, N.Y.: Gold Key, April, 1964. Reprints of Lasswell strips.

Barney Google and Snuffy Smith #1 - #6. Derby Ct.: Charlton, March, 1970 - January, 1971. Original Lasswell material.

Snøfe Smith - Ingen Jul Uten #1 - #24. Oslo, Norway: A/S Hjemmet-Serieforlaget, 1970-1993. Reprints of Lasswell Sunday pages. Christmas specials.

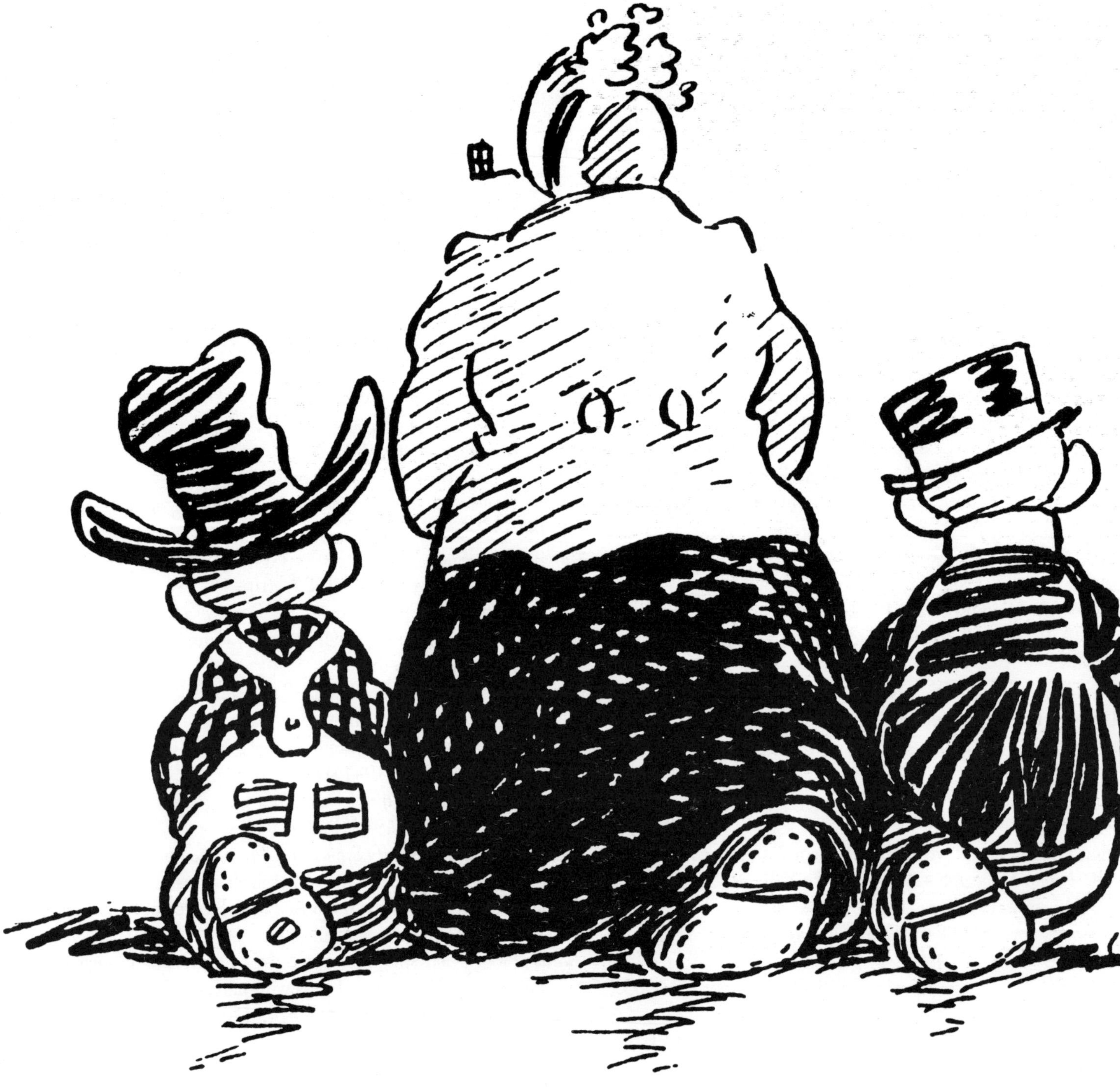